Humanistic and
Transpersonal Psychology

David—front view, by Michelangelo Buonarroti (Photo courtesy of Art Resource, New York).

Humanistic and Transpersonal Psychology

A Historical and Biographical Sourcebook

Edited by DONALD MOSS

Foreword by STANLEY KRIPPNER

Schools of Psychological Thought

Greenwood Press
Westport, Connecticut • London

Library of Congress Cataloging-in-Publication Data

Humanistic and transpersonal psychology : a historical and
  biographical sourcebook / edited by Donald Moss ; foreword by
  Stanley Krippner.
      p.   cm.—(Schools of psychological thought)
    Includes bibliographical references and index.
    ISBN 0–313–29158–6 (alk. paper)
    1. Humanistic psychology.   2. Transpersonal psychology.   I. Moss,
  Donald, 1949–   . II. Series.
  BF204.H865   1999
  150.19'8—dc21   97–32965

British Library Cataloguing in Publication Data is available.

Library of Congress Catalog Card Number: 97–32965
ISBN: 0–313–29158–6

First published in 1999

Greenwood Press, 88 Post Road West, Westport, CT 06881
An imprint of Greenwood Publishing Group, Inc.

Printed in the United States of America

The paper used in this book complies with the
Permanent Paper Standard issued by the National
Information Standards Organization (Z39.48–1984).

P

Contents

Foreword

STANLEY KRIPPNER

Psychological perspectives have reflected external and internal events in various ways. Classical psychoanalysis was influenced by "energy" models predominant at the time, and Freud's model of the psyche resembled a hydraulic pump supplying (or denying) human activities with a supply of libido. The model of Watsonian behaviorism resembled nothing so much as a slot machine; an external stimulus produced an output, and the inner workings of the machine were disregarded. Cognitive psychology elevated this metaphor to a telephone switchboard and later to a computer, but humanistic psychology considers each of these images an inaccurate reflection of human nature.

It is not easy to present a single model of humanistic psychology because each major description reflects the background and interests of its author. As a result, it is more appropriate to refer to the "humanistic psychologies" and to acknowledge that they have made unique contributions with their emphases on the importance of values, creativity, human potentials, and intentionality. Indeed, Charlotte Bühler once defined humanistic psychology as "the scientific study of behavior, experience, and intentionality."

The models of human nature discussed in this book seem to have been informed by Bühler's definition. Humanistic as well as transpersonal psychologists have opposed using natural science prototypes to describe human beings, preferring to study individuals and their differences from a "human science" point of view, a position that marks the point at which they part company with the behavioral and cognitive psychologies. Furthermore, humanistic and transpersonal psychologies have focused on the "well" or "healthy" (and even the "exceptional") human as prototype, diverging from classical psychoanalysis's emphasis on pathology and dysfunction in modeling the human person. These psychologies have incorporated insights and information from psychoanalysis, behaviorism, cognitive science, and the other schools of psychology but have added something of their own to the brew: a recognition that human beings must be appreciated on their own terms.

The paradigms of natural science, the data from the animal laboratories, and the dogmas inherent in hidebound religious, economic, and political theories can be of limited value in fathoming human behavior, experience, and intention. The humanistic and transpersonal psychologies have embraced feminist, cross-cultural, spiritual, and mind-body contributions to human knowledge, noting that a disregard for what postmodernists call "other" severely limits the wholeness required by a dependable and veracious science of persons.

However, there are differences as well as similarities. Some humanistic and transpersonal psychologies hold that humanity possesses an intrinsic tendency toward harmony and self-actualization, while others present a model of the person beset by anxiety, a vulnerable entity torn between his or her expectations and social realities, between the infinite and the finite, between being and nonbeing. For some humanistic psychologists, the "self" is socially constructed; for others, it is an important milestone on life's path but eventually must be transcended. Some humanistic psychologists emphasize the embeddedness of the individual in society, others see human relationships as paramount, and others address the necessity to interact with something greater than both person and community. Some scholars consider transpersonal concerns to be of such gravity that a separate psychology needs to be built around them, while others see them as merely one part of the total human panorama and (in the case of secular humanists) as a potential distraction.

Transpersonal psychologists define their field as one that studies experiences in which one's sense of identity extends beyond the personal to encompass wider aspects of humankind, life, and the cosmos. Humanistic psychologists, as a group, would agree that these experiences are worthy of study and have been ignored by most mainstream psychologists over the years (who have forgotten about William James's interest in the "varieties of religious experience" and related human capacities). But can an entire school of psychology be built around these reports? Are they alone able to provide the building blocks for a well-articulated model of the complete person and his or her social environment? This is the unresolved question that engages adherents on various points of the spectrum. This book will help its readers to come to their own conclusions after weighing the rationales given by various authors.

There is another issue that elevates this book to a level of burning relevance. In the past, most of the dominant psychological schools of thought have tended to trivialize myths, ethics, and issues of personal responsibility, discussing them in terms of social conditioning. But James Bugental has observed that when person and society clash, social change often results, bringing a renewed meaning to suffering, conflict, and grief, as well as to love, joy, and mutuality of relationships.

Mainstream psychology was especially adamant in dismissing these concerns from the pristine atmosphere of the scientific laboratory and the controlled experiment. In an age of research participants' rights, research review boards, and subjects as coinvestigators, such naïveté can no longer be condoned by psychological science or by any other disciplined inquiry. In what Charlotte Buhler referred to as "the torn culture of our time," individuals and groups need to consider adopting ethical stances that emphasize personal and communal responsibility for one's actions.

It has been my great fortune to have met or to have known most of the pioneers discussed in this book: the irrepressible Moshe Feldenkrais, the resolute Erich Fromm, the chivalrous Jack Gibb, the sagacious Amedeo Giorgi, the jovial Sidney Jourard, the tortured Ronald Laing, the astute Alexander Lowen, the genial Abraham Maslow, the elegant Rollo May, the indomitable Ida Rolf, the irascible Fritz Perls, the cagey William Schutz, the magnificent Laura Perls, the endearing Carl Rogers, the erudite Erwin Straus, the magisterial Ken Wilber. It is disturbing that few psychology students, either at the undergraduate or graduate level, have even come into contact with the writings of most of these innovators; this omission is a loss for the students' personal as well as professional development.

Michel Foucault reminds us that the aphorism "knowledge is power" should be stood on its head: The people and institutions in power determine what passes for "truth" and "knowledge," and nowhere is this so apparent as on the university campus. As a result, the humanistic and transpersonal psychologies have been marginalized, despite their potential contributions to human well-being. However, such books as *Humanistic and Transpersonal Psychology* may redress this imbalance, and the demands of the times will quicken the rate at which the humanistic and transpersonal psychologies begin to play a greater role in academic as well as social discourse.

Acknowledgments

The humanistic psychology movement is a network of friendships and shared ideals as much as it is a formal academic school. This project has been an exercise in getting by with a little help from one's friends. I wish to express my gratitude to many individuals who have been helpful in the long process of assembling this book, including all of the contributors. My wife Nancy Anne Moss provided an abundance of encouragement and editorial assistance for this project as it grew beyond the original concept of a "little overview of humanistic psychology."

I am grateful to Fred Wertz of Fordham University, who invited me to consider this project, and to Greenwood Press series editor Donald Dewsbury of the University of Florida at Gainesville. I thank Debra Serna of Holland, Michigan, for her creative pursuit of texts, Les Beach, formerly of Hope College, Holland, Michigan, for early suggestions on the project, and Paul Shane of Fairview, Ohio, for his diligent research assistance. Finally, my special thanks go to Constance T. Fischer, William F. Fischer, Amedeo Giorgi, and the late Rolf von Eckartsberg, who guided my original explorations of existential, phenomenological, and humanistic psychology at Duquesne University in the 1970s.

Introduction

The frontispiece in this volume shows Michelangelo's sculpture of David. The David was chosen, first, because Michelangelo represents the highest achievements of European Renaissance humanism, with its celebration of the beauty and grandeur of the human being, and second, because the David symbolizes the objective of twentieth-century humanism in psychology: a recovery of this appreciation of the human being with its full sensuality, strength, and spirituality. The David is also a potent symbol for the audacity of 1950s-era humanistic psychology in taking on the Goliath of mainstream psychology.

Humanistic psychology began as a bold movement of creative individuals who set out deliberately to remake American psychology in the image of a fully alive and aware human being. Commencing in the United States in the mid-1950s, humanistic psychologists have revitalized the discipline of psychology with a broader understanding of the human being, a broader vision of psychological practice, and a broader approach to a human science. Humanistic psychologists criticize the emphasis of scientific psychology on the measurement, prediction, and control of behavior and protest the exclusion from psychological investigation of such basic aspects of humanness as consciousness, values, creativity, freedom, will, love, and spirit.

Humanistic psychologists draw on the rich perspectives of existential philosophy, literature, and the arts to develop an understanding of human nature more adequate and comprehensive than that found in psychology textbooks and journals. Humanistic psychologists insist that psychological research must develop methodologies that can address the full scope of human experience, and must not limit itself to observable behavior in a laboratory. Humanistic psychology does not reject science, but demands that the science of psychology be a fully "human science," with an approach and method suitable to its subject (Maslow, 1971; Giorgi, 1970).

As humanistic psychology has developed, its followers have increasingly emphasized truths that can be lived and experienced, not merely conceptualized or verbalized. Humanistic psychology began as a protest against rigid methodologies in scientific psychology, but became as well a protest against narrow forms of living. Humanistic psychology is also a psychology of liberation, seeking freedom from gender and racial prejudices, freedom from narrow social and religious expectations, and freedom from limiting conceptions of human nature. Humanistic psychology and its spiritual cousin, transpersonal psychology, have inspired a variety of experiments with alternative lifestyles, alternative forms of community, and the pursuit of alternate forms of consciousness and spiritual awareness. Most of all, humanistic psychology involves a crusade to explore, both scientifically and personally, the highest reaches of human potential. The full cosmos of human potential includes the capacity to make free, positive personal choices, the ability to express human emotion and sexuality in a fully alive and self-regulated body, and the capacity to discover spiritual awareness and meaning in each individual human life.

This volume consists of two parts, the first presenting a historical and conceptual overview of humanistic psychology, and the second presenting biocritical essays on several of the key figures in humanistic psychology. The first part begins by examining the historical place of humanistic psychology. Chapter 1 introduces the historical, social, and cultural context that gave birth to humanistic psychology. The lifestyle and cultural atmosphere of the mid-1950s was one of dynamic economic expansion, technological progress, political conformity, and bland wholesomeness, punctuated by occasional voices of protest. Social critics saw the America of the 1950s as a society pursuing material abundance at the expense of its soul. Humanistic psychology sought to reintroduce questions of human potential, alternative modes of experiencing, and the higher meanings of life.

Chapter 2 turns to the scientific and academic background in psychology against which humanistic psychology developed. The psychology of the 1950s was dominated by what Abraham Maslow called the First Force of psychoanalysis and the Second Force of behaviorism. Each of these schools in psychology accomplished breakthroughs in understanding human behavior and in ameliorating human suffering. Each of these schools also displayed major blind spots, refusing to acknowledge or explore critical dimensions of human life. Human psychology emerged to address these essential deficits in understanding the human being.

Chapter 3 examines the emergence and early development of humanistic psychology, especially the work of Abraham Maslow. The new "Third Force" of humanistic psychology sought to address the reductionism and narrowness of psychoanalysis and behaviorism. At the same time, humanistic psychology sought to rediscover pathways beyond conformity and social adjustment toward self-actualization, personal fulfillment, and the higher reaches of human nature. Chapter 3 also outlines the institutional history of humanistic psychology—its professional associations, journals, key books, schools, and supportive institutions.

Chapters 4 through 10 summarize the major theorists and schools within the diversity of humanistic psychology. Chapter 4 describes the specific contributions of Carl Rogers and client-centered therapy; chapter 5 profiles Fritz Perls and Gestalt therapy; chapter 6 highlights Sidney Jourard, William Schutz, and Jack Gibb and the psychologies of self-disclosure, openness, and community; and chapter 7 introduces Wilhelm Reich, Alexander Lowen, and the body therapies.

Chapter 8 examines the existential and phenomenological approach that began in philosophy and theology and had such a profound effect on psychiatry and psychology in Europe and the Americas. Existentialism is the theoretical inspiration for many humanistic psychologies and stimulated several schools of existential psychotherapy.

Chapter 9 turns to feminist psychology and its place in the human-potential movement. The feminist movement has played a critical role for humanistic psychology. First, feminism has altered women's concept of themselves and their place in society and life and has encouraged individual women to pursue their potential beyond the traditional roles of mother and homemaker. Second, feminism has empowered women psychologists to cultivate their own distinct vision of psychology and human existence. The result has been a challenge to methodologies based on male-dominant modes of perception and cognition, as well as to biased theories of personality, gender identity, and personal growth.

Chapter 10 summarizes the biofeedback movement, which served as the arena where "high tech" could meet the higher states of consciousness. The concept of biofeedback was introduced at a conference in Santa Monica in 1969, and the image of electronic equipment guiding human beings to a greater awareness and control over their own physiology and consciousness appealed to both white-coated experimental scientists and the white-robed gurus of the higher-consciousness movement.

Chapters 11 and 12 follow the development of humanistic psychology beyond the scope of the individual personality and individual consciousness into spiritual territory. Carl Jung speculated that it is a basic trait of human nature to seek the spirit and discover symbolic meaning. Abraham Maslow concluded that the highest levels of self-actualization involve transcendence of self.

Chapter 11 highlights dimensions of humanism in Christian spiritual traditions, evident since the earliest days of the Christian era. The chapter authors cite the fourth-century church father Irenaeus, who believed that the glory of God is a fully alive human being. Today's humanistically oriented Christian authors insist that the pursuit of deeper self-acceptance, relatedness, and a capacity for loving are worthy goals within Christian life. Today's Christian psychologists utilize a new reading of biblical texts and a recasting of many familiar psychological concepts to advance a new Christian humanism.

Chapter 12 moves beyond Christian circles to narrate the development of transpersonal psychology as a Fourth Force in American psychology. Transpersonal

psychology has roots in American transcendentalism and in the psychologies of
William James and Carl Jung. Transpersonal psychology includes efforts to explore Eastern and other world religions, to discover the unrecognized kinship
among the spiritual traditions of mankind, to disclose those substantial contributions that other spiritual traditions might have to make to Western religions,
and to identify the psychological insights and understanding implicit in such
religious systems. Transpersonal psychology pursues the scientific investigation of
such phenomena as the spontaneous yearnings for the spirit, the topography of
meditative consciousness, and the spontaneous, often unchurched human experiences of spiritual realities.

The final chapters in part I overview the heritage and the future of humanistic
and transpersonal psychology. Chapter 13 argues for the continuing need for a
humanistic psychology as we approach a new century. The humanistic critique
has led to many changes in academic psychology, which is now more open to the
study of states of consciousness, cognitions, values, and spiritual experience. Nevertheless, many of the original challenges that led to the birth of humanistic
psychology remain. Psychology is still fragmented, with continuing tensions between psychology and religion and between psychology and the arts. This chapter
revisits the continuing need for a humanization of psychology and for a humanization of the society and culture within which psychology evolves. Our culture
remains challenged, with a breakdown in family life, moral values, and community
safety. In 1994 Frank Farley, at that time president of the American Psychological
Association, criticized psychology for failing to understand and reduce the horror
of existence and for remaining preoccupied with superficial problems. He called
for "a psychology of meaning in the broadest sense . . . showing the road to generosity and love" (Farley, 1996, p. 776; Martin, 1994).

Chapter 14 examines the mission and the promise of revitalized humanistic
and transpersonal psychologies. Humanistic and transpersonal psychologies have
produced an abundant twofold heritage, including both powerful technologies for
personal change and ethical perspectives for personal integrity. This chapter examines the challenge of placing humanistic psychology on a solid research footing.
Research in humanistic psychology must draw on creative methodologies appropriate to the subject matter of humanistic psychology, which is the fully alive
human being. This chapter also faces critiques of the excesses in humanistic psychology and highlights pathways that humanistic psychologists are already mark-
ing out for future exploration.

Part II of this volume includes biographical and critical chapters on key figures
in the development of humanistic psychology, arranged alphabetically. Each chapter provides a brief sketch of the individual's life and professional career and
overviews his or her key contributions to humanistic and/or transpersonal psychology. The humanistic movement is too broad to include all major figures. The
seventeen chosen represent a cross section of the richness and diversity of humanistic and transpersonal psychology. Chronologically, William James (1842–
1910) is the earliest figure selected for inclusion here; many humanistic psychol-

ogists continue to find inspiration in his life and work. Several of the figures described—James Bugental, Amedeo Giorgi, and Ken Wilber—remain active today, continuing to contribute to psychology and contemporary life.

REFERENCES

Farley, F. (1996). From the heart: APA presidential address. *American Psychologist, 51*(8), 772–776.

Giorgi, A. (1970). *Psychology as a human science*. New York: Harper & Row.

Martin, S. (1994). Farley sums up his '93–'94 presidential year. *APA Monitor, 25* (10), 12.

Maslow, A. H. (1971). *The farther reaches of human nature*. New York: Viking.

Part I

Humanistic and Transpersonal Psychology: An Overview

The Historical and Scientific Background of Humanistic Psychology

Humanistic psychology was as much a cultural as a scientific event. Both in its strengths and in its deficiencies, humanistic psychology was a product of the same 1950s era in the United States that produced the Mickey Mouse Club, the beatniks, and Joseph McCarthy's anti-Communist crusade. Humanistic psychology sought to bring existential and spiritual renewal to an era of material affluence. At the same time, humanistic psychology represents a chapter in the history of psychological science. Humanistic psychology developed as the response of a number of influential psychologists to perceived deficiencies in the psychological theory and research of this same time period.

Chapters 1 and 2 set the stage for humanistic psychology. Chapter 1 conveys the dynamic economic and technological strength of post–World War II America and highlights as well the apparent cultural blandness and spiritual atrophy of this period. Chapter 2 reviews the positive contributions of psychoanalysis and behaviorism, but also highlights the blind spots in each of these psychological schools. Just as 1950s-era America seemed at times to emphasize material affluence over existential issues, the psychologies of Freud and Skinner emphasized a biological and deterministic understanding of the human being at the expense of such vital human phenomena as freedom, consciousness, or love.

Chapter 3 describes the emergence of humanistic psychology. The author identifies the roots of humanistic psychology in the previous holistic psychologies of the 1930s and 1940s and describes the central role of Abraham Maslow in translating the widespread yearning for a new kind of psychology into the formal movement of humanistic psychology, which Maslow labeled the "Third Force." Chapter 3 also narrates the institutional history of humanistic psychology, especially its move toward acceptance within mainstream psychology.

1

The Historical and Cultural Context of Humanistic Psychology: Ike, Annette, and Elvis

DONALD MOSS

In 1953 Rollo May published *Man's Search for Himself*; in 1954 Abraham Maslow published *Motivation and Personality*; in 1958 Rollo May published a collection of translations from European existentialists entitled *Existence*; and in 1962 the American Association for Humanistic Psychology was established (later to be known simply as the Association for Humanistic Psychology). We may take these dates, approximately 1953 through 1962, as bracketing the time period in which humanistic psychology came into existence as a self-conscious movement and established itself on the American scene. In this chapter we will explore the historical, sociological, and cultural atmosphere of this era.

AMERICA IN THE AGE OF EISENHOWER AND OZZIE AND HARRIET

What was the America of this era like? What conditions existed to create such a favorable reception for this new intellectual and social movement? I will paint a word picture of this era by highlighting both the great events and the small milestones that created the atmosphere and spirit of the times.

The GI Bill and the Baby Boomers

This was the era in which America's postwar baby boomers grew up. The GIs of World War II came home in 1945 and 1946. Many attended college on the GI Bill; most married and began to raise children between 1946 and 1955. From

1954 through 1964 U.S. births remained above four million, creating the biggest blip ever seen on demographic charts.

In 1952 Dwight D. Eisenhower, the most popular general in America's World War II effort, resigned as supreme allied commander in Europe and was elected president of the United States. Many of the young onetime GIs enthusiastically adopted his probusiness and prosperity message and called themselves "Eisencrats." In 1953 Joseph Stalin died and Nikita Khrushchev was appointed first secretary of the Soviet Union. In 1953 the Korean armistice was signed, and another wave of soldiers returned home in a hurry to resume their domestic lives (Grun, 1991, and Trager, 1992, provide much valuable historical information used in this section).

A Newly Emergent Popular Culture

The Cold War between communism and America was still around, but America was at peace. For the most part Americans were busily absorbed in an optimistic postwar economic expansion and in a newfound consumer lifestyle. Suburban "cocktail parties" caught on, with conversation flitting from remodeling one's home to the fully electric kitchen to one's new Danish modern furniture. Many families were able to buy a new automobile every year, and each year the Detroit auto makers announced new models with innovations distinctive enough to distinguish them from last year's models. The rear tail fins grew more prominent each year, the car bodies grew longer, and Chevrolet introduced its first V-8 engine in 1955. Cartoons of the era showed garages too short for the family auto and began to show two cars in one garage. By 1954 twenty-nine million American homes had televisions. The "Mickey Mouse Club" aired in October 1955, and an entire generation of children grew up with Annette Funicello, Jimmie Dodd, and the Mouseketeers. "I Love Lucy" premiered in 1951, "Ozzie and Harriet" and "American Bandstand" in 1952, "Father Knows Best" in 1954, and "Lassie" in 1955. The new medium of television replaced more traditional family interaction, recreation, and conversation; families drew together each evening, but to sit in silence before a flickering image.

The new television medium portrayed a comfortable and wholesome way of life in America's families that now seems innocent and naïve, but then seemed quite attainable. Further, as Marshall McLuhan was soon to point out (1967), Americans were beginning to learn that the content or message portrayed on television might vary little from previous radio and written stories, but the medium affected the lives of Americans very differently. The medium *is* the message.

The Culture of Business and Material Affluence

In 1955 Sloan Wilson published his novel *The Man in the Gray Flannel Suit*. In 1956 W. H. Whyte published his sociological treatise *The Organization Man*. In 1958 R. S. Peters published *The Concept of Motivation*. The emphasis in both the popular media and academia at this time was on business, success, and afflu-ence. Productivity and efficiency were virtues, and the rewards of a virtuous life were everywhere in evidence. The world of American business created a new second culture in which many Americans spent their daytime hours.

John K. Galbraith's *The Affluent Society* (1958) speculated on the possibility of a permanently expanding prosperity and discussed the sociological implications of individuals not needing to work to enjoy the fruits of industry's ever-growing efficiency and society's material affluence. He observed that the ideas by which modern human beings interpreted their existence were ideas carried over from a passing era of scarcity and want; he asserted further that "the total alteration in underlying circumstances has not been squarely faced" (1958, p. 2). The affluent conditions of which Galbraith spoke were unprecedented. In 1954 the United States had 6% of the world's population, but 60% of all automobiles, 58% of all telephones, 45% of all radios, and 34% of all railroads.

What was good for General Motors really did appear to be good for the United States. Young executives and professionals with a modicum of intelligence and a good work ethic could purchase a new home for the family and provide a degree of material comfort unknown to their parents or grandparents. The homes were often cookie-cutter replicas of each other as large-scale developers produced "Levittowns," entire planned communities in the suburbs, built at once to meet the needs of a rapidly growing population of young marrieds with children. In 1954 the Detroit-area super–shopping mall Northland opened with 100 stores. By 1955 the number of shopping centers in the United States reached 1,800, reflecting the new consumption-oriented and suburban lifestyle. McDonalds was acquired by Ray Krok in 1954 and began its rapid expansion (Trager, 1992, pp. 948–949). Colonel Harland Sanders began to franchise his Kentucky Fried Chicken restaurants in 1955, the same year Coca-Cola became "Coke." The key elements were falling into place for a consumer lifestyle and popular culture that would become the mass culture for much of the world's population by the end of the century. Americans were getting in step, working their way up the ladder, and accepting a large degree of conformity whose material rewards were considerable.

Political Conformity

Dissenting voices were not welcome in this era, and the tone of political debate was muted. Between 1950 and 1954 Senator Joseph McCarthy convened Senate hearings to investigate the alleged presence of Communists and traitors in gov-ernment agencies, the State Department, and eventually the army. McCarthy waved his briefcase at the television cameras, shouted that he had names and evidence in his bag, and denounced individuals as prominent as President Eisen-hower for alleged treasons. The ensuing anti-Communist hysteria spread beyond McCarthy's own activities and blackened the reputations of a generation of Amer-ican politicians, actors, artists, and others for past association with Communist or other socialist political groups. Political dissent, even after McCarthy was censured by the Senate in 1954, remained more cautious. Galbraith observed that "these are the days when men of all social disciplines and all political faiths seek the comfortable and the accepted; when the man of controversy is looked upon as a disturbing influence; when originality is taken to be a mark of instability; and when . . . the bland lead the bland" (1958, p. 5).

Scientific and Technological Progress

The 1950s were years of progress in science and technology, with great impact on American lifestyle and culture. In 1954 Jonas Salk began inoculating Pittsburgh schoolchildren with his antipolio vaccine, the tranquilizer Miltown was introduced, and an oral contraceptive pill was developed by Gregory Pincus, Hudson Hoagland, and Min-Cheh Chang. Linus Pauling won a Nobel Prize in 1954 for his study of molecular forces. The first atomic power plant was opened in Schenectady, New York, in 1955, and the Los Alamos Laboratory produced a "neutrino"—an atomic particle with no electrical charge and essentially no mass— in 1956.

In 1957 the Soviet Union launched Sputnik I and II, the first artificial earth satellites, and in 1958 the United States launched Explorer I. The American/ Russian space race and the race for first place in math, science, and education began. The "new math" was born, replete with Venn diagrams and set theory, and children discovered that their new science books included many new facts and concepts unknown to their parents. In 1900 there were 84 known chemical elements, by 1954 there were 100, and by 1957 2 more. The identification of further atomic and subatomic particles seemed unending. The early stages of the information explosion began to challenge old assumptions about schools providing an education good for a lifetime and about the older generation passing on its skills and knowledge to the young. The acquired knowledge and skills of the old were for the first time obsolete.

VOICES OF DISSENT AND PROTEST

Restless Voices in the Arts

In the 1950s other voices and other less conforming and optimistic messages began to emerge. In 1951 J. D. Salinger's *Catcher in the Rye* introduced a sense of the absurd and a critical questioning of adult hypocrisies that kept echoing through the decade as youth continued to read the work. In 1957 Jack Kerouac wrote his novel *On the Road*, which was to become the classic text of the dropout or beat generation, a movement of men and women who did not want to get in step with the rest of America, with General Motors, or any other large, regimented institution. By 1958 "beatniks" were identified and discussed as a social phenomenon spreading from California and from New York's Greenwich Village to the rest of the country.

In 1955 Bill Haley and the Comets produced their hit record "Rock around the Clock." In 1956 a young Southern boy with a background in hillbilly and gospel music swayed his pelvis as he sang "Hound Dog" and "Don't Be Cruel" on television, and several million teenage girls swooned. Rock-and-roll music had arrived, and Elvis was the King. Parents across the country worried about the impact on their teens of such uncontrolled rhythm and musical protest.

Cultural Critique

Older voices of dissent, left over from a previous era, continued to speak. Perhaps the most far-seeing voice of dissent in this prevailingly optimistic era was a 1954 book, *La technique: ou L'enjeu du siècle* (literally Technique, or the stake of the century, later published in English as *The Technological Society*) by Jacques Ellul, a former fighter in the French resistance to Hitler. Ellul highlighted an entirely new mode of life emerging in Western technological societies and critiqued this emerging life from a sociological as well as a moral-spiritual point of view. He asserted that in technological societies the original goals of human pursuits are lost along the way, and technique as a means to an end becomes the end in itself. The refining of technique and the increase in productivity and efficiency become the criteria for success. The result is that "Humanity seems to have forgotten the wherefore of all its travails. . . . Everything today seems to happen as though ends disappear, as a result of the magnitude of the very means at our disposal" (1954/1964, p. 430). He argued that once the dynamism of a technological society was created, with its tremendous powers for commercializing, industrializing, and especially organizing human action and bringing new areas of life within the scope of the mass culture, few real elements of tradition or autonomous life would long survive.

Like Galbraith, Ellul believed that modern technology could provide human beings with a material golden age of abundance. He defined "technique" to include a continuous refinement of behavioral knowledge, and interventions to render human activity more efficient and productive. Ellul could see that "technique" would eventually be applied not just to factories, but to human beings themselves to refine the efficiency of human actions and to perfect and standardize human nature as well (1954/1964, pp. 344–427, 434). He claimed that education and industry were already showing the marks of a mass organization and standardization. He feared that eventually every field of human activity—even leisure activities and spiritual expression—would show a movement toward greater standardization and efficiency. In a kind of "total integration," even acts designed to get away from civilization would bear the imprint of mass culture and mass regimentation:

The lone city dweller on a camping trip escapes his technical fate momentarily. But suppose that the solitary camper swells to a throng, overflows the countryside, sets the woods on fire. . . . Obligatory campsites are established, complete with regulations. The camper is forced to carry a license, and the erstwhile act of free individual decision becomes a purely technical matter. (p. 419).

Ellul predicted that even acts of political dissent would be accepted, channeled, and reorganized within a technological culture, in some fashion co-opting their energy and trivializing their impact. The best contemporary example might be the fascinating process by which the mass media now grab hold of the latest political protest and channel it onto talk shows, journalistic interviews, and news programs until the would-be rebel has become an MTV performer profitably collecting book royalties and searching for the next profitable cause about which to protest. (For example, former national villains such as Yasser Arafat and Saddam Hussein can become the subject of interviews by CNN or *People* magazine). Ellul expressed concern that in the process of integration, humankind would lose access to meaning and spiritual fulfillment, and that any remaining happiness would be a superficial equivalent to tranquilization.

Other voices were also raised against the new technological society. In 1952 the Swiss psychoanalyst Carl Jung published *Answer to Job*, his most explicitly religious book, because he felt driven by events to deal with the problem of suffering and the "religious problems of modern man" (Jung, 1952/1969). In 1953 Karl Jaspers, one of the great existential psychiatrists of Germany, published his *Tragedy Is Not Enough*, addressing the spiritual needs of modern man. In 1956 Fred Hoyle published his critique of the materialism of current culture, *Man and Materialism*. The old problems of seeking a deeper meaning in life, exploring human suffering, and finding an answer beyond tragedy were still being voiced.

Humanistic Psychology Seeks Meaning beyond Affluence

The stage appeared to be set for the movement of humanistic psychology, which would challenge authority and conformity, reject superficial optimism and materialism, and promise to move beyond mere achievement and affluence toward a deeper meaning in human existence. The extraordinary success of what Galbraith called "the affluent society" made possible a new pursuit of human growth and spiritual fulfillment. No longer was the average citizen chained to an exhausting struggle for physical survival. These same conditions of material abundance made the renewed pursuit of existential and spiritual renewal necessary.

REFERENCES

Because of the historical emphasis of this book, many books are cited in the text with two dates of publication: first, the date of publication in the original language or first edition, and second, the date of the edition cited and listed in the references section.

Ellul, J. (1964). *The technological society* (J. Wilkinson, Trans.). New York: Alfred A. Knopf. (Original French publication 1954)

Galbraith, J. K. (1958). *The affluent society*. Boston: Houghton Mifflin.

Goble, F. (1970). *The third force: The psychology of Abraham Maslow*. New York: Grossman.

Grun, B. (1991). *The timetables of history: A horizontal linkage of people and events* (3rd rev. ed.). New York: Simon & Schuster. (Based on W. Stein, *Kulturfahrplan*. Original German publication date 1946)

Hoyle, F. (1956). *Man and materialism*. New York: Harper.

Jaspers, K. (1953). *Tragedy is not enough*. London: V. Gollancz.

Jung, C. G. (1969). Answer to Job. In *The collected works of C. G. Jung* (Vol. 11, pp. 355–470). Princeton: Princeton University Press. (Original German publication date 1952)

Kerouac, J. (1957). *On the road*. New York: Viking.

Maslow, A. H. (1954). *Motivation and personality*. New York: Harper.

May, R. (1953). *Man's search for himself*. New York: W. W. Norton.

May, R., Angel, E., & Ellenberger, H. F. (Eds.). *Existence: A new dimension in psychiatry and psychology*. New York: Basic Books.

McLuhan, M. (1967). *The medium is the message: An inventory of effects*. New York: Bantam.

Peters, R. S. (1958). *The concept of motivation*. New York: Humanities Press.

Salinger, J. D. (1951). *The catcher in the rye*. Boston: Little, Brown.

Trager, J. (1992). *The people's chronology* (rev. ed.). New York: Henry Holt & Company.

Whyte, W. H. (1956). *The organization man*. New York: Simon & Schuster.

Wilson, S. (1955). *The man in the gray flannel suit*. New York: Simon & Schuster.

2

The Scientific and Philosophical Context of Humanistic Psychology

DONALD MOSS

PSYCHOANALYSIS AND BEHAVIORISM: THE FIRST FORCE AND THE SECOND FORCE

The major influences in psychology in the 1950s were psychoanalysis and behaviorism. We will overview each of these movements in turn, highlighting both their strengths and those limitations that called forth the humanistic critique.

Of course there were many other voices within psychology, presenting creative and more holistic alternatives to the Freudian and behavioristic determinisms. In Europe existential and phenomenological psychiatry and Gestalt psychology had been active since the 1920s. Abraham Maslow gave much credit to the presence in the 1940s in New York City of the very best and most progressive of Europe's intellectuals, including such figures as Alfred Adler, Erich Fromm, Karen Horney, Ruth Benedict, and Max Wertheimer:

I think it's fair to say that I have had the best teachers, both formal and informal, of any person who ever lived, just because of the historical accident of being in New York City when the very cream of European intellect was migrating away from Hitler. New York City in those days was simply fantastic. There has been nothing like it since Athens. (Maslow, personal letter, cited by Goble, 1970, p. 11)

Nevertheless, the establishment of psychology in the 1950s was influenced extensively either by Freud and his psychoanalytic model for research and clinical treatment or by the behavioristic tradition of experimental research conducted largely in animal laboratories. The humanistic critique of psychological theory and research focused largely on the deficiencies of psychoanalysis and behaviorism.

THE FIRST FORCE: PSYCHOANALYSIS

Sigmund Freud (1856–1939) was a Jewish citizen of the Austro-Hungarian Empire who spent almost the entirety of his adult life in the imperial capital of Vienna. After flirting with philosophy and attending lectures by Franz Brentano, the forerunner of phenomenological psychology, Freud devoted himself to the study of medicine, physiology, and neurology. He came strongly under the influence of Ernst Brucke, a famous physiologist and rigorous natural scientist who was dedicated to discovering the fundamental physical-chemical forces underlying biological phenomena. Freud sought an academic career in the scientific faculty at Vienna, but because of his Jewish origins and his desire to marry and support a family, he was forced into the private practice of medicine, specifically treating nervous diseases.

Psychoanalysis: The Talking Cure

Freud studied hypnosis in France with Jean-Martin Charcot, then collaborated with Joseph Breuer on applying hypnosis and a new form of "talking cure" for the treatment of hysteria. Freud's joint publication with Breuer of *Studies on Hysteria* (Freud, *Standard Edition*, vol. 2, 1893–1895/1955) marks a preliminary formulation of psychoanalysis, as both a new psychological understanding of human behavior and an approach to the clinical treatment of nervous and mental disorders. Freud developed the concepts and techniques of his psychoanalytic approach more extensively over the next five years, and his new science was essentially in place when Freud published his classic *The Interpretation of Dreams* in late 1899 (Freud, *SE*, vol. 4, 1900/1953). "The interpretation of dreams," Freud insisted, "is the royal road to the unconscious in mental life" (Freud, cited by Gay, 1988, p. 104).

The human psyche, according to Freud, is made up of a vast amount of unconscious mental processes that are actively repressed from conscious awareness. Long-forgotten infantile experiences contribute to many of the images in the dream and contribute as driving forces to our waking actions. Our mind operates through both a primary process and a secondary process. The primary and more powerful mental processes give little heed to the logic of everyday reality and waking life and are dominated by the pleasure principle. The wish or the desire is the driving force in mental life. The secondary process involves the mind's practical efforts to compromise with and accommodate to the needs of everyday reality.

Metapsychology: A Psychic Apparatus and a Topography of Mind

Through the remainder of his career Freud continually refined his understanding of the internal "psychic apparatus" of the human being. He defined a number of mental schemata to portray a topography of the mind. He created the now-familiar schema of id, ego, and superego to describe the contributions of the instinctual drives in the id, the mind's recognition and accommodation to external reality in the ego, and the mind's internalization of parental disciplines and morality in the superego. Freud's original German terms *das Es, das Ich,* and *das Überich* translate literally as the "It" for the impersonal biological forces, the "I" for the largely conscious personal sense of agency, and the "Over-I" for the moral censor (Freud, *SE*, vol. 19, 1923/1961). Many of the crippling neurotic disorders Freud treated were the result of unconscious and unrecognized conflicts among these forces within the personality. Freud's therapeutic recipe was straightforward. The unconscious must become conscious, that is, the anonymous and unconscious forces of instinct must be brought into the daylight of personal consciousness and language.

Freud developed other overlapping models: (1) the energetic/hydraulic model of instinctual energies that were channeled into partial fulfillment or kept in check by repression and suppression, but that could break through in psychic disorders; (2) the psychosexual-stages model that accents the primacy of certain bodily zones and functions in each of the phases of human development—the oral stage, the anal stage, the phallic stage, and the genital stage—and (3) the later dualistic model showing psychic life as a tension between Eros and Thanatos, the life and the death instincts.

Seeking a Biology of Mind

Freud was a prolific writer and published articles and monographs filling twenty-four volumes in the *Standard Edition* of his works. His case histories of patients in psychoanalytical treatment read like literature, and he won the coveted Goethe Prize for his literary style. Many serious scholars have closely read Freud to discover an implicit existential and humanistic understanding of human nature and behavior (Fromm, 1959; Rieff, 1959; Ricoeur, 1970; Bettelheim, 1983). Yet Freud's explicit goal remained to explain the human mind by a reduction to biological and instinctual causes. Freud asserted that all human behavior is determined by the instinctual drives, especially the sexual drives, which contribute to the foundations of the personality (Sulloway, 1979). The personality is formed primarily by the impact of the first three years of life and the identifications and relationship complexes the child develops in infancy.

Psychoanalytic Reductionism

Freud took pleasure in seeing the narcissism of too-proud humankind humbled. He highlighted the three great indignities that human beings have had to accept in the face of science: First, there is the Copernican revolution, the recognition that the sun and the solar system do not revolve around the earth. Second, there is the Darwinian revolution, the discovery that man is descended from lower forms of life and continues to share many features in common with lower forms of life. Finally, there is the Freudian revolution, the insight that the human being is not the lord and master of his or her own thought processes (Freud, *SE*, vol. 14, 1914/ 1957, p. 91). According to Freud, human actions are caused by unconscious forces beyond individual awareness and are not the mere choices or decisions of the conscious ego. The human being is not the lord of the cosmos, of the animal kingdom, or of his or her own mind.

The influence of Freud's psychoanalysis came into America especially through clinical psychiatry, but also through academic psychology. Freud's first and only visit to the United States was for his 1909 address at Clark University, at the invitation of Clark University psychologist G. Stanley Hall. The visit included a meeting with William James, probably America's foremost psychologist of the time. The American reception was mixed, with a curiosity both in academic and lay circles for this novel viewpoint. Freud's insistence on the importance of sexual instincts in early childhood development provoked some resistance, as did his adamant atheism, as elaborated in his critical monographs on religion, *The Future of an Illusion* (Freud, *SE*, vol. 21, 1927/1961) and *Moses and Monotheism* (Freud, *SE*, vol. 23, 1939/1964).

For Freud, religion, like a neurosis, was just another form of human delusion motivated by the mind's desire to defend itself against primitive anxieties. He believed that the idea of God is simply a psychological defense mechanism by which the immature human being imagines a God figure with the all-powerful qualities that children see in their parents. Freud's *Civilization and Its Discontents* (*SE*, vol. 21, 1930/1961) applied this same kind of reductionism to civilization and culture, explaining that the human being is forced by culture to renounce basic instinctual needs and then engages in artistic and cultural activities as safe substitutes for real biological satisfaction. Freud went beyond the widespread view that some aspects of culture and religion have been used to deceive or to oppress, to the nihilistic view that culture and religion are nothing but deception and oppression.

By 1955, however, psychoanalysis had become a pervasive ideology among educated Americans. Few psychiatrists or psychologists of the time remained Freudians in the original narrow sense. The neo-Freudians of Germany and the American ego psychologists went a long way toward showing the role of language and society in the formation of personality. Several generations of Freud's disciples in Europe and the United States developed divergent forms of psychoanalysis, including Alfred Adler's emphasis on styles of life and social interest; Carl Jung's exploration of spirituality and of self and symbols as integrative functions; Wilhelm Reich's exploration of the body's defensive character armor against impulses; and Harry Stack Sullivan's emphasis on the role of interpersonal relationships in personality formation. American academic psychology also assimilated Freud's work with a great deal of critical reworking. David Rapaport's ego psychology, for example, borrowed many psychoanalytical concepts, but integrated them with the empirical findings and cognitive concepts of American scientific psychology.

Nevertheless, the prevailing psychoanalytic concept of human nature in 1955, especially in lay circles, remained a natural scientific and deterministic model, explaining current actions by reference to instinctual drives, early experiences, and unconscious conflicts. The great achievements of artists and creative minds were merely the products of instinctual drives sublimated into substitute channels. In his *New Introductory Lectures on Psychoanalysis* (*SE*, vol. 22, 1933/1964) and in *Civilization and Its Discontents* (*SE*, vol. 21, 1930/1961), Freud wrote that most of the apparently altruistic and admirable actions of individuals can be explained psychoanalytically as self-serving and self-deceptive forms of instinctual gratification. Further, he interpreted religious principles such as loving one's neighbor as mere cultural defenses against man's biological instinct toward aggression. He interpreted the highest precepts of Christianity and Judaism as further evidence for the depravity of human nature (see also Goble, 1970, p. 6).

Freud's was a downward-looking view of human nature that used the concepts developed from psychopathology and the disturbed population to explain the best in humankind. It was not Freud the humanist or Freud the winner of the Goethe Prize for literature that humanistic psychology would attack, but rather, Freud the reductionist, the mechanist, the atheist, and the cynic.

THE SECOND FORCE: BEHAVIORISM

Those readers familiar with the often eclectic and open-minded behaviorism of the 1990s may fail to understand the strident opposition of humanistic psychologists to behaviorism in the 1950s and 1960s. A look at the work of John B. Watson and Burrhus F. Skinner will remind one of the basis for this critical reaction of humanistic psychology. In particular, Watson's volume *Behaviorism* (1924; revised edition, 1930) and Skinner's work *Beyond Freedom and Dignity* (1971) are ideological masterpieces that serve well to remind one of the original power and determination of behaviorism in destroying the previous psychologies of consciousness and holism.

John B. Watson: Behaviorism as an Ideology of Science

John B. Watson (1878–1958) formulated the theory and broad assumptions of American behaviorism early in the twentieth century. Watson, a professor of psychology at Johns Hopkins, sought to make the study of human behavior as objective and scientific as possible. A later influence on Watson was the work of the Russian physiologist and psychologist Ivan Pavlov. Pavlov's original animal research led to his concept of the conditioned reflex and the understanding of what we now call classical conditioning. If an unconditioned reflex, such as a dog's salivating when meat is presented, is evoked while a neutral stimulus such as a bell is present, the bell will eventually also evoke the salivation response.

Watson's behaviorism emphasized the environmental conditions outside the organism that evoke and condition behavior. While Freud's theory emphasized the instincts and the internal psychic apparatus of the human being, the behaviorists asserted that all human behavior could be controlled or altered by modifying external conditions.

Methodological Reductionism

Watson played a role in systematically and deliberately eliminating from psychological discourse any reference to internal events within the person, which are not subject to objective observation and measurement: "The Behaviorist dropped from his scientific vocabulary all subjective terms such as sensation, perception, image, desire, purpose, and even thinking and emotion as they were subjectively defined" (Watson, 1930, p. 6). Watson also excluded from consideration any reference to consciousness or mental state: "I believe we can write a psychology . . . and never go back upon our definition; never use the term consciousness, mental states, mind, . . . and the like" (Watson, 1913, p. 166). Watson preferred to disregard exactly those qualities that humanistic psychologists regard as the uniquely human qualities of human beings; his clear objective was to advance the progress of a methodologically precise science of animal and human behavior: "The behaviorist, in his efforts to get a unitary scheme of animal response, recognizes no dividing line between man and brute" (Watson, 1913, p. 158). Watson dismissed as "timid souls" those psychologists who were unwilling to follow him all the way in this methodological revolution: "The raw fact that you as a psychologist, if you are to remain scientific, must describe the behavior of a man in no other terms than those you would use in describing the behavior of the ox you slaughter, drove and still drives many timid souls away from behaviorism" (1930, p. v).

Like Freud, Watson interpreted all concepts of soul, spirit, and religion as vestiges of a primitive mentality of superstition and magic. Watson, however, categorized consciousness along with soul as a magical concept (1930, pp. 2–3) and predicted that Freudian psychoanalysts would in two decades be regarded on a plane with phrenologists studying the lumps on a head (1930, p. 297). He took pride in disposing of all such "mediaeval conceptions" (1930, p. 5).

The Costs of Behaviorism

Most historians of psychology, including many advocates of cognitive psychology, would agree with Watson that there were elements of superstition, metaphysical assumptions, and uncritical mentalistic conceptions in the psychology of the early 1900s. Nevertheless, Watson's behaviorism threw out the best as well as the worst of the previous psychologies. He dismissed William James, E. B. Titchener, and Wilhelm Wundt entirely for their introspective methodology and their interest in the phenomena of consciousness (Watson, 1930, pp. 1–3). James's influence survived in the area of personality theory, and his reputation has recently undergone a broader renaissance, leading to an August 1990 "Principles of Psychology Congress," held in Amsterdam, celebrating the centennial of James's best-known work. Unfortunately, many students of psychology still know Wundt and Titchener only in light of the behavioristic criticisms and understand nothing of the positive contributions made by these giants to early psychological science.

The damage to clinical psychology and psychiatry has been even greater. It took psychology and psychiatry until the 1980s to catch up with the phenomenological understanding of normal and disturbed consciousness that the French physicians Jean-Martin Charcot and Pierre Janet and the American Morton Prince were approaching. The clinical understanding and treatment of dissociative disorders, hypnotic states, and other phenomena of altered consciousness still have much to learn from the theories and case reports of these pioneers (see Janet, 1901; Putnam, 1989; and Hilgard, 1991).

Watson's Social Blueprint

The early successes of behaviorism produced a boundless enthusiasm and optimism over the possibilities of this new science. Watson made an extravagant claim in the first edition of his *Behaviorism* volume: "Give me a dozen healthy infants, well-formed, and my own specified world to bring them up in and I'll guarantee to take one at random and train him to become any kind of specialist I might select . . . regardless of his talents, penchants, tendencies, abilities, and race of his ancestors" (Watson, 1924, p. 82). Floyd Matson cites similar boasting by Watson and highlights Watson's belief that the possibilities for shaping human behavior in any direction are almost endless (Matson, 1964). Watson projected a vision of a world made better through raising children by behavioral principles: "Will not these children in turn, with their better ways of living and thinking, replace us as society, and in turn bring up their children in a still more scientific way, until the world finally becomes a place fit for human habitation"? (Watson, 1930, pp. 303–304).

Edward L. Thorndike and Clark Hull

A number of other early psychologists contributed to the foundations of American behaviorism. Edward L. Thorndike made many early contributions, including formulating the "law of effect" and the "law of exercise" for learning theory. According to the law of effect, any action followed by satisfaction to the animal will be more firmly connected to the situation and will be more likely to recur, whereas any action followed by discomfort will have its connections with that situation weakened and will be less likely to recur. Thorndike defined a satisfying state of affairs in an entirely behavioral fashion as one that the individual does not avoid and that he often tries to preserve or attain, and conversely defined a discomforting state of affairs as one that the individual avoids or attempts to change (Thorndike, 1911, pp. 244–245). The law of exercise states that any response to a situation will be more strongly connected to the situation in proportion to the number of times it has been connected to that situation, and to the average vigor and duration of the connections (1911, p. 244).

Clark Hull also exerted a major influence on American learning theory and behavioristic psychology. Hull attempted to mathematically formulate the principles of learning and explored the neurophysiological foundations of learning. Further, Hull attempted to extend the influences of behaviorism into the fields of psychiatry, sociology, and anthropology as well. Nevertheless, as late as 1953, Kenneth Spence observed that the basic postulates of John B. Watson's behavioristic formulations continued to form the basic working assumptions of the "great majority of present-day American psychologists" (Spence, cited by Matson, 1964, p. 47).

B. F. Skinner: Radical Behaviorism Moves beyond Freedom and Dignity

The second enduring force in American behaviorism is Burrhus Frederic Skinner. Skinner's operant conditioning model, or stimulus-response psychology, completed the behavioristic revolution begun by Watson. B. F. Skinner dedicated his efforts from his earliest days as a graduate student at Harvard University to creating an objective and empirical analysis of the behavior of organisms. He was influenced by the philosophers of science Ernst Mach and P. W. Bridgman, who advocated an objective natural science approach, as well as by Pavlov and Watson, whose behaviorism he wished to further develop (Iversen, 1992). Skinner's guiding principles were simple:

We undertake to predict and control the behavior of the individual organism. (1953, p. 35)

The object has been to discover the functional relations which prevail between measurable aspects of behavior and various conditions and events in the life of the organism. The success of such a venture is gauged by the extent to which behavior can, as a result of the relationships discovered, actually be predicted and controlled. (1972, pp. 257–258)

A *scientific psychology*, according to this view, seeks to measure, predict, and control behavior, and a *radical behaviorism* sets aside from the focus of its research any element that is not subject to measurement, prediction, and control.

Skinner contributed a solid body of research studies on animal learning, with an emphasis on what he called "operant conditioning" or instrumental learning (1938, 1953). He showed that any behavior that brings about a positive consequence ("positive reinforcement") is likely to recur. Any behavior that brings about a negative consequence, no consequence, or an end to a positive reinforcement, will become less frequent. Skinner's operant reinforcement schema presents a refinement of Thorndike's law of effect. Skinner showed that operant learning is a distinct learning process, a form of learning not explained by Pavlov's classical conditioning or previous stimulus-response theory.

A Technology for Behavior Change

Skinner and his followers brought a tremendous creativity to the technology of animal research, including the versatile "Skinner box," and an impressive repertoire of behavior-modification techniques and principles, with demonstrated applications in many settings to both animals and humans. Skinner's techniques revolutionized the care for developmentally disabled individuals, autistic children, and many other populations of mentally ill or otherwise mentally impaired persons (Martin & Pear, 1992). These individuals can often be more effectively and more humanely managed in residential settings utilizing "token economies," "shaping," "positive reinforcement," "extinction," and a variety of other behavioral principles. The use of physical restraints, heavy doses of tranquilizing agents, and punishment can be minimized using Skinnerian behavior modification.

Behavioristic Determinism

Upon this basis of laboratory animal research, Skinner formulated a theory of human nature and a social program for moving society toward a utopian balance. Skinner articulated utopian concepts of social engineering first in *Walden Two* (1948) and later in *Beyond Freedom and Dignity* (1971). Skinner proposed a deterministic view of human beings, asserting that all human behavior is caused by reinforcement contingencies and environmental conditions. In spite of four and a half decades of critique, many still see Skinner's ideas as contributing toward a more just society (Rakos, 1992). In Skinner's view, freedom of will is an illusion that may serve to increase self-esteem, but has no place in social planning. The human being does not determine the outcome of his or her life; this is laid out in the conditioning he or she undergoes in the course of life. Social engineering and manipulation can be more humane and more positive for the individual if it relies on positive reinforcement and rewards, rather than older forms of social control relying on punishment or shame.

In summary, Skinner, Watson, and the other behaviorists produced a highly effective practical technology for the prediction and control of human behavior. Both Watson and Skinner envisioned a utopian society based on the external manipulation of human actions to produce a more beneficial cooperation and a reduction in the psychological pain produced by shaming, punishment, and maladjustment. However, by the rules that Watson and Skinner had established, this new behavioristic science of psychology could not account for such phenomena as freedom, will, meaning, and fulfillment.

Berelson and Steiner in 1964 published *Human Behavior: An Inventory of Scientific Findings*, an exhaustive inventory of 1,045 scientific findings about the human being. The authors were forced by their evidence to an acknowledgment:

Indeed, as one reviews this set of findings, he may well be impressed by another omission perhaps more striking still. As one lives life or observes it around him (or within himself) or finds it in a work of art, he sees a richness that somehow has fallen through the present screen of the behavioral sciences. This book, for example, has rather little to say about the central human concerns: nobility, moral courage, ethical torments, the delicate relation of father and son or the marriage state, life's way of corrupting innocence, the rightness and wrongness of acts, evil, happiness, love, hate, even sex. (p. 666)

THE THIRD FORCE: HUMANISTIC PSYCHOLOGY ADDRESSES THE DEFICIENCIES OF THE FIRST AND SECOND FORCES

The uniquely human properties of humans remained beyond the scope of scientific behavioral psychology. Methodologically, behaviorism preferred to focus on the commonalities between human and animal behavior and excluded from scientific discussion any aspects of conscious experiencing. The behavioral technologies for behavior change were rich, but both methodologically and conceptually the borders for scientific discourse in psychology had been drawn too narrowly.

As we have seen, psychoanalysis elected to focus on inferred instinctual and biological bases for behavior in hopes of achieving a biological model of psychic functioning. Psychoanalytic reductionism did not exclude higher human accomplishments from discussion; rather, psychoanalysis explained the highest achievements of art and culture as disguised forms of instinctual striving.

As the decade of the 1950s unfolded, a number of gifted individuals throughout psychology simultaneously began to challenge these prevailing forms of determinism and reductionism, which would not or could not do justice to human experience. Humanistic psychology remained indebted to previous psychological schools, especially psychoanalysis. Many humanistic therapists continue to use an analytic model of verbal psychotherapy, but with new conceptual frameworks for interpreting the human being's actions and experiences. Existential categories and modes of interpretation have replaced instinct theory and deterministic inferences about childhood causes.

Similarly, humanistic psychology took from the empirical research tradition of behavioral psychology a lasting appreciation for methodologically rigorous investigations. However, humanistic psychologists have called for innovative research models that are more adequate for exploring the uniquely human aspects of behavior and experience (Giorgi, 1970, 1992; see also the discussion of research methods in chapters 8 and 14 of this volume).

REFERENCES

Because of the historical emphasis of this book, many books are cited in the text with two dates of publication: first, the date of publication in the original language or first edition, and second, the date of the edition cited and listed in the reference section.

Berelson, B., & Steiner, G. A. (1964). *Human behavior: An inventory of scientific findings.* New York: Harcourt, Brace, & World.

Bettelheim, B. (1983). *Freud and man's soul.* New York: Alfred A. Knopf.

Freud, S. (1953–1974). *The standard edition of the complete psychological works of Sigmund Freud* (24 vols.; J. Strachey, Ed.). New York: Macmillan.

Fromm, E. (1959). *Sigmund Freud's mission.* New York: Harper & Brothers.

Gay, P. (1988). *Freud: A life for our time.* New York: W. W. Norton.

Giorgi, A. (1970). *Psychology as a human science.* New York: Harper & Row.

Giorgi, A. (1992). Whither humanistic psychology? In F. J. Wertz (Ed.), *The humanistic movement in psychology: History, celebration, and prospectus* [Special issue]. *Humanistic Psychologist, 20* (2–3), 422–438.

Goble, F. (1970). *The third force: The psychology of Abraham Maslow.* New York: Grossman.

Hilgard, E. (1991). A neo-dissociation interpretation of hypnosis. In S. J. Lynn & J. Rhue (Eds.), *Theories of hypnosis: Current models and perspectives* (pp. 83–104). New York: Guilford.

Hull, C. L. (1943). *Principles of behavior: An introduction to behavior theory.* New York: Appleton-Century.

Iversen, I. H. (1992). Skinner's early research: From reflexology to operant conditioning. *American Psychologist, 47* (11), 1318–1328.

Janet, P. (1901). *The mental state of hystericals.* New York: Putnam.

Martin, G., & Pear, J. (1992). *Behavior modification: What it is and how to do it* (4th ed.). Englewood Cliffs, NJ: Prentice Hall.

Matson, F. W. (1964). *The broken image: Man, science, and society.* New York: George Braziller.

Misiak, H., & Sexton, V. S. (1973). *Phenomenological, existential, and humanistic psychologies: A historical survey.* New York: Grune & Stratton.

Pavlov, I. (1927). *Conditioned reflexes* (G. V. Anrep, Trans.). London: Oxford University Press.

Putnam, F. W. (1989). Pierre Janet and modern views of dissociation. *Journal of Traumatic Stress, 2,* 413–429.

Rakos, R. F. (1992). Achieving the just society in the 21st century: What can Skinner contribute? *American Psychologist, 47* (11), 1499–1506.

Ricoeur, P. (1970). *Freud and philosophy: An essay on interpretation* (D. Savage, Trans.). New Haven: Yale University Press.

Rieff, P. (1959). *Freud: The mind of the moralist.* New York: Viking.

Skinner, B. F. (1938). *The behavior of organisms: An experimental analysis.* New York: Appleton-Century.

Skinner, B. F. (1948). *Walden Two.* New York: Macmillan.

Skinner, B. F. (1953). *Science and human behavior.* New York: Macmillan.

Skinner, B. F. (1971). *Beyond freedom and dignity* (3rd ed.). New York: Knopf.

Skinner, B. F. (1972). *Cumulative record.* New York: Appleton-Century-Crofts.

Sulloway, F. J. (1979). *Freud: Biologist of the mind.* New York: Basic Books.

Thorndike, E. L. (1911). *Animal intelligence.* New York: Macmillan.

Watson, J. B. (1913). Psychology as the behaviorist views it. *Psychological Review, 20,* 158–177.

Watson, J. B. (1924). *Behaviorism.* New York: People's Institute.

Watson, J. B. (1930). *Behaviorism.* (rev. ed.). Chicago: University of Chicago Press.

3
_____

Abraham Maslow and the Emergence of Humanistic Psychology

DONALD MOSS

ABRAHAM MASLOW AND THE THIRD FORCE

More than any other single person, Abraham Maslow gave birth to humanistic psychology. He labeled it the "Third Force" and conceived it as a reaction against the first force of psychoanalytic psychology and the second force of behaviorism. He did not reject either Freud or behaviorism, but found both models of psychology to be incomplete and inadequate. He spoke of himself as "epi-Freudian" and "epi-behavioristic," signifying that he wanted to build upon and add to the foundations of the previous viewpoints. Already in the 1930s, Maslow said, he began to focus on certain psychological problems that could not be answered within the scope of a "behavioristic," "value-free," and "mechanomorphic" psychology (1971, p. 3). While remaining a scientist, he increasingly challenged the prevailing model of science. Human experience and action are not neutral and value free, and one cannot approach and understand them with a science that ignores personal values, purposes and goals, and intentions and plans (1971, p. 5).

Maslow never claimed to be the sole representative or founder of humanistic psychology or the Third Force. He conceived this movement generously and broadly. He included as part of the Third Force the Adlerians, Rankians, Jungians, neo-Freudians, post-Freudians, Gestalt psychologists, existential and phenomenological psychologists, and self psychologists (1962, p. ix). We will examine the contributions of several of these precursors and then turn to Maslow's vision of humanistic psychology.

ANTECEDENTS IN EUROPEAN AND AMERICAN PSYCHOLOGY

Of immediate importance for their crucial role in influencing Maslow's work and in creating many of the key concepts and images of the humanistic viewpoint are two European imports, Kurt Goldstein (1939) and Andras Angyal (1941), and several American psychologists, especially Henry Murray, Gordon Allport (1955), and Gardner Murphy (1958).

Kurt Goldstein and the Organismic Approach

Kurt Goldstein (1878–1965) was a gifted German medical scientist whose research on neurologically damaged individuals provided major contributions to German neurology, Gestalt psychology, and phenomenological psychology. He immigrated to the United States in 1935, where his work entered a new phase in which he applied his concepts beyond the neurological sphere to personality and human experience. Goldstein provided a holistic or organismic theory of the person as a totality. His major work in English is *The Organism: A Holistic Approach to Biology Derived from Pathological Data in Man* (1939). His emphasis was on the self-actualization of the organism at both a biological and psychological level. The healthy organism is one "in which the tendency towards self-actualization is acting from within, and overcomes the disturbance arising from the clash with the world, not out of anxiety but out of the joy of conquest" (1939, p. 305). When sickness occurs, self-actualization is disrupted, and the organism's responses become rigid and compulsive. When major stress occurs, the organism shows a catastrophic reaction, with agitation, fearfulness, and a reluctance to undertake even the simplest tasks. As health is restored, so are the process of self-actualization and the organism's mastery of the environment.

Andras Angyal: The Personality as a Holistic System

Andras Angyal (1902–1960) born in Hungary and educated in medicine at Vienna and Turin, came to the United States in 1932. His two major works were *Foundations for a Science of Personality* (1941) and a posthumous collection of his papers, *Neurosis and Treatment: A Holistic Theory* (1965). Angyal provided a creative and original view of the human personality as a holistic system, and of health and neurosis as two opposing organized processes, each fighting to organize the same material within the human personality. For Angyal, a human being is either healthy or neurotic, depending on which of these processes dominates in each moment. For him, psychotherapy is a process of demolition and clearing away in which the organizing forces of neurosis are slowly dismantled, leaving a free path for the spontaneous emergence of healthy systems within the personality.

Henry Murray and Personology

Henry Murray (1893–1988) began his career in biochemical and medical research, but found himself drawn inexorably toward psychology by his fascination with the human personality. He later recalled that he completed a "modest study of 25 of my classmates" in medical school and spent a then-improper amount of time as a surgeon inquiring into psychogenic factors in his patients (Murray, 1940, pp. 152–153). Murray was influenced by Carl Jung's book *Psychological Types* and was profoundly affected by several days spent with Jung in Zurich in 1925. Murray joined the psychology faculty at Harvard in 1927, became director of the Harvard Psychological Clinic in 1928, and completed a training analysis under the gifted duo of Franz Alexander and Hanns Sachs by 1935.

Murray evolved his own original science of "personology," an empirical science of the fluid and dynamic structure of the personality and of its key motives, needs, and complexes (Murray, Barrett, Langer, Morgan, Homburger, and other collaborators at the Harvard Psychological Clinic, 1938). Clinically, his major contributions remain in the development of projective psychological testing, especially the Thematic Apperception Test, and his empirical investigations of psychological needs. Murray's sensitive holistic formulations of the personality as a structure always in flux never gave way to the reductionistic oversimplifications of behaviorism or the dogmatism of orthodox psychoanalysis:

A personality is a full Congress of orators and pressure groups, of children, demagogues, communists, isolationists, war-mongers, mugwumps, grafters, log-rollers, lobbyists, Caesars and Christs, Machiavellis and Judases, Tories and Promethean revolutionists. And a psychologist who does not know this, whose mind is locked against the flux of images and feelings, should be encouraged to make friends, by being psychoanalyzed, with the various members of his household. (Murray, 1940, pp. 160–161)

Murray was a precursor of Abraham Maslow in discovering the lines of personality not only in the psychological clinic, but in the examination of strong, healthy individuals and in the pages of literature. He spent World War II directing a project for the Office of Strategic Services (OSS, now known as the Central Intelligence Agency), developing methods for assessing candidates for secret and dangerous missions abroad. This project is summarized in the OSS volume *Assessment of Men* (1948). Murray also dedicated twenty-five years to his sensitive studies of Herman Melville's fictional works.

Gordon Allport: Patterns of the Individual Life

Gordon Allport (1897–1967) devoted his attention throughout his lengthy career to the patterns of the individual life (1937, 1955, 1961, 1965). Rooted in the scientific traditions of American psychology, grounded in the insights of Freud's psychoanalysis, and influenced by the holistic structural orientation of

German psychology, Allport expressed an organismic vision of each individual's unique adjustment to his or her environment. He emphasized a holistic view that was psychophysical, with equal emphasis on the body and the mind, and dynamic, portraying a personality that is always developing and changing. His 1955 book *Becoming* explored some of the foundations for a psychology of growth and self-knowledge, including an analysis of the concept of self and of conscious, "oriented" becoming.

Allport insisted on the value of nomothetic research methodologies, which accent the patterns evident within one person's life. This is evident in his publication of an interesting volume, *Letters from Jenny*, a collection of very expressive letters written by an isolated widow between her fifty-eighth and her seventieth years. Allport intended these letters to present a challenge to students of personality and to current theories of personality: How well do our concepts account for the concrete details of this particular human life?

Gardner Murphy: An Organismic Biosocial View

Gardner Murphy (1895–1979) was a multitalented individual who contributed significantly to research in social, general, and educational psychology and wrote one of the earliest comprehensive examinations of the history of psychology (Murphy, 1929). For Gardner Murphy, the divisions within psychological science were artificial, as was the perceived split between mind and body in the human organism. Murphy's books on personality, *Personality* (1947) and *Human Potentialities* (1958), present an organismic biosocial picture of personality development, proceeding through three key stages: undifferentiated wholeness, differentiation, and integration. He also described the typical individual's regression and progression through these stages.

Murphy's personal influence in promoting humanistic psychology went far beyond his published works. He contributed significantly to encouraging psychical research in American psychology, co-edited *William James on Psychical Research* (Murphy & Ballou, 1960), and guided the experimental research of the American Society for Psychical Research (Taylor, 1991, p. 60). Murphy also figured centrally in the birth of the biofeedback movement. Murphy and two others (Barbara Brown and Kenneth Gaarder) undertook the planning for the initial national conference at the Surfrider Inn in Santa Monica, California, in 1969, where the new technique of biofeedback was defined and named (Moss, 1994). That conference gave birth to the Biofeedback Research Society (now the Association for Applied Psychophysiology and Biofeedback).

ABRAHAM MASLOW AND HUMANISTIC PSYCHOLOGY

Maslow's Theories of the Self and Self-Actualization

Abraham Maslow, more than any other individual, translated the widespread yearning for a different kind of psychological theory and practice into a cohesive viewpoint on humanistic psychology with its own journals, conferences, and formal organization. For example, Maslow articulated a core of common assumptions that, he asserted, serve to unify humanistic psychologists (1962, p. 3). The basic assumptions include the following:

- Human beings have an essential inner nature, which is in part species-wide, and in part unique to each person.
- This inner nature can be studied scientifically.
- This inner nature is either neutral and pre-moral or good. It is not intrinsically evil.
- It is best to encourage and bring out this inner nature, not to suppress or deny it.
- Psychological health and productivity is the result when individuals are encouraged to actualize their inner nature.
- Psychological sickness results when individuals suppress or fight against this nature.
- The human being's inner nature is weak, and easily overcome by cultural pressure and wrong attitudes. Yet this same nature persists and continues to press toward actualization.
- The movement toward self-actualization is a difficult one involving discipline, deprivation, frustration, pain and tragedy. Self-actualization is neither a trivial nor an easy pathway. (Maslow, 1962, p. 3)

Maslow stated clearly that the human individual's "inner nature" was there to be discovered and not invented (Maslow, 1962, p. 3). After four decades of research on the individual and social construction of the self, Maslow's statements about a real inner nature or self, there to be discovered, now seem naïve and simplistic (Markus & Nurius, 1986; Moss, 1989). The postmodernistic and constructivist approach differs radically from Maslow's portrayal of the inner self as a pregiven construct (Gergen & Davis, 1985; Guidano, 1991; Mahoney, 1995).

Nevertheless, Maslow's core of assumptions about a real inner self, persisting through adversity and awaiting its awakening, spurred much of the vibrance and energy of the early movement of humanistic psychology. Carl Rogers's client-centered or person-centered therapy and Sidney Jourard's psychology of self-disclosure are largely an elaboration on the interpersonal conditions most helpful in awakening and actualizing the inner self. Even today therapeutic schools as divergent as Ericksonian hypnotherapy, biofeedback, and eye-movement desensitization and reprocessing (EMDR) rely on the shared expectation that once internal psychological obstacles, neurophysiological tensions, and negative cognitions are cleared away, the human organism will show a yearning toward growth, health, and self-actualization.

Maslow's Humanistic Ethics

Maslow believed that a scientifically based humanistic ethics can be derived from these core assumptions to guide individuals toward the solution of many individual and social problems. Maslow was not content to describe how the average human develops; he spoke of a "normative biology," a science of the human organism that addresses how human beings ideally can and should develop. He conceived the role of the humanistic scientist as keeping in sight a higher vision of what is possible beyond present factual reality.

Maslow envisioned humanistic psychology as a psychology of the whole person, based on the study of healthy, fully functioning, creative individuals. He criticized the psychologists of his time for spending too much time studying mentally ill and maladjusted humans and for seeking to explain higher levels of human experience by means of neurotic mechanisms.

The Higher Limits of Human Nature

Maslow proposed an investigation of "superior specimens" as a pathway to understanding the highest potentials of human nature (1950, 1971). He turned empirically to the study of "self-actualized" persons and the patterns of their lives, selecting both living and dead individuals who had strained their human nature to its highest limits, such as Abraham Lincoln, William James, Jane Addams, Eleanor Roosevelt, Albert Einstein, and Albert Schweitzer (Maslow, 1950). He found that such individuals share a number of idealized characteristics: boldness in living, courage, freedom, spontaneity, integration, and self-acceptance. They are realistic, yet not held back by present realities. They are autonomous, democratic in values, and capable of loving deeply. They show a sense of humor and an ability to identify beyond themselves with the needs and well-being of humankind. They are able to transcend their own narrow personal perspective and needs and able to transcend as well their own culture and life situation. Maslow believed that better psychological understanding of such characteristics of higher self-actualization would help psychologists to show the average person the pathway toward growth. He hoped that such knowledge would lead to the answer to questions such as "What is the good life? . . . How can people be taught to desire and prefer the good life? How ought children be brought up to be sound adults?" (Maslow, 1962, p. 149).

Maslow conceptualized self-actualization, the full utilization of personal capacities, talents, and potential, as a basic need driving much of human behavior. In *Motivation and Personality* (1954), Maslow described basic motivating forces such as the physiological needs for food, sleep, and sex; relational needs for love and acceptance; the need for self-esteem; a need for knowledge; and the higher-level need for aesthetic satisfaction. He differentiated between "deficiency needs" and "growth needs" or "being needs." Deficiency needs and deficiency motivation are oriented simply to filling a current lack. If it is hungry, the human organism, like the animal organism, seeks food. Here animal and human nature converge. Growth needs, on the other hand, concern the uniquely human yearning to fulfill one's own nature or actualize one's own being.

Maslow highlighted the "peak experience," those wonderful moments of sublime, ecstatic awareness when a human being comes to insight, realizes artistic or spiritual fulfillment, or discovers deep intimacy and harmony with another person. He felt that such peak moments, found in the lives of most average individuals, could show us something about the higher reaches of human being. He studied the thinking and awareness of persons in such moments, as well as the values that human beings seem to hold in such experiences.

Maslow accused Freudian and behavioristic psychologists of seeking to explain the human being's higher growth-oriented motivations and actions in terms of the lower deficiency needs. Further, there is an entire range of "Being values" that these previous objectivistic scientific psychologies were not equipped to understand. Maslow elaborated on these values in his 1962 work *Toward a Psychology of Being*, but we will simply list them here: wholeness, perfection, completion, justice, aliveness, richness, simplicity, beauty, goodness, uniqueness, effortlessness, playfulness, truth, honesty, reality, and self-sufficiency. Maslow found these values to be alive intermittently in the peak experiences of the average person and more consistently in the everyday experiences of the superior or more self-actualized person.

Maslow (1968, pp. 152–163) asserted that human needs comprise a hierarchy from the lowest biological deficiency needs to the highest spiritual growth needs. When lower deficiency-oriented needs are not met, the human being will fixate on what is lacking and cannot move toward higher forms of growth. The lower needs begin with hunger, thirst, and shelter and move toward safety and security, then upward toward love and intimacy, beauty and goodness, freedom, self-esteem, self-actualization, and, at the highest reaches of human nature, self-transcendence. "The human being needs a framework of values, a philosophy of life . . . to live by and understand by, in about the same sense that he needs sunlight, calcium or love" (Maslow, 1968, p. 206). Maslow's work, especially on the phenomenon of self-transcendence and the recognitions of dimensions beyond the person, will be discussed further in the chapter on transpersonal psychology.

THE "OFFICIAL" DEVELOPMENT OF HUMANISTIC PSYCHOLOGY

Misiak and Sexton (1973), Bühler and Allen (1972), Welch, Tate, and Richards (1978), and DeCarvalho (1991) provide helpful summaries of the early developments of humanistic psychology as a formal movement in the United States. The following early publications heralded the emergence of the movement: Carl Rogers's 1942 book *Counseling and Psychotherapy*, Maslow's 1950 paper on self-actualizing human beings, his 1954 book *Motivation and Personality*, Rollo May's 1953 *Man's Search for Himself*, Gordon Allport's 1955 *Becoming*, Clark Moustakas's 1956 *The Self*, and Gardner Murphy's 1958 *Human Potentialities*.

Maslow played a central role in organizing the many figures seeking a new kind of psychology into one specific school of humanistic psychology. In 1950, when Maslow and his colleague James Klee formed the psychology department at Brandeis University, they called their vision of a revitalized psychology a "general psychology" because they wished to "acknowledge the whole range of human experience and expression previously recognized and explored by early psychologists such as Wilhelm Wundt and William James" (Klee, cited in Welch, Tate, & Richards, 1978, p. ix). Maslow created a mailing list in 1954, addressing "people who are interested in the scientific study of creativity, love, higher values, growth, self-actualization, basic need gratification" (Misiak & Sexton, 1973, p. 111). In 1955 Hadley Cantril used the term "humanistic psychology" in his article "Toward a Humanistic Psychology." In 1956 Maslow published another article with the same title, "Toward a Humanistic Psychology." In 1958 Maslow coined the name Third Force for humanistic psychology as a response and alternative to the First Force of psychoanalysis and the Second Force of behaviorism. In 1958 Rollo May, Ernest Angel, and Henri Ellenberger brought out their landmark volume *Existence*, a collection of articles and case histories translated from the European existential and phenomenological psychiatrists.

In 1961 Abraham Maslow and Anthony Sutich founded the *Journal of Humanistic Psychology* with Sutich as its first editor. Henry Murray served on the editorial board of the journal. In 1962 the American Association for Humanistic Psychology (later simply the Association for Humanistic Psychology) was founded with James Bugental as its first president. Gordon Allport arranged financial support from the American Psychological Foundation and the Ella Lyman Cabot Trust to assist the new association (Taylor, 1991, p. 65).

In 1962 James Bugental presented a manifesto for the new association and the Third Force movement: "Humanistic Psychology: A New Breakthrough" (published in the *American Psychologist* the following year, Bugental, 1963). Bugental's leadership and vision were critical in directing the new association in a positive direction. A proliferation of books and articles and an increase in enthusiasts followed rapidly after the birth of the journal and the association. The first ten presidents of the Association for Humanistic Psychology were the following (Misiak & Sexton, 1973, p. 128):

1962–1963: James F. T. Bugental

1963–1964: Sidney Jourard

1964–1965: Edward J. Shoben

1965–1966: Charlotte Bühler

1966–1967: S. Stansfeld Sargent

1967–1968: Jack R. Gibb

1968–1969: Gerard V. Haigh

1969–1970: Floyd Matson

1970–1971: Denis O'Donovan

1971–1972: Fred Massarik

Maslow's election in 1968 as president of the American Psychological Association signaled a growing respect for this new humanistic viewpoint within the mainstream of psychology. In 1970 the American Psychological Association approved a Division of Humanistic Psychology, signaling further credibility and acceptance.

A number of professional conferences also played a significant role in the emergence of humanistic psychology. Erwin Straus, a major figure in European phenomenological psychiatry, author of several works in phenomenology psychology, and another émigré from Hitler's Germany, established a seminar in phenomenological psychology at the Veterans' Administration Hospital at Lexington, Kentucky. In the 1960s Straus organized a series of Lexington Conferences on Phenomenology: Pure and Applied. Both Straus's informal teaching and his Lexington conferences had a major impact on the development of existentialism and phenomenology in American psychology and philosophy. Straus's students included William Fischer, Joseph Lyons, Constance Fischer, Richard Griffiths, Erling Eng, and many others, who carried Straus's vision of a phenomenological psychology from Lexington to university centers throughout the country.

In 1964 a conference was held in Old Saybrook, Connecticut. Maslow, Sutich, Bugental, Rollo May, Carl Rogers, and others, leaders of the new movement of humanistic psychology, were joined and encouraged by such already-prominent figures as Henry Murray, Gordon Allport, and Gardner Murphy (Taylor, 1991, 1995; DeCarvalho, 1991). In 1970 the Association for Humanistic Psychology convened the First International Conference on Humanistic Psychology in Amsterdam, with Charlotte Bühler elected as president for the international conference. A second international conference followed in Würzburg, Germany, in 1971.

Other institutional developments paralleled the birth of the professional association and the journal. In 1963 Sonoma State College in California opened a master's program in humanistic psychology. Later humanistic programs also opened at West Georgia College, the Center for Humanistic Studies in Detroit, Michigan, Seattle University, Union Graduate School, and Fielding Institute. In 1970 the American Association for Humanistic Psychology directly founded the Humanistic Psychology Institute, an independent doctoral program, later renamed the Saybrook Institute (Taylor, 1995, p. 15).

Duquesne University in Pittsburgh developed a master's and doctoral program in existential and phenomenological psychology in 1959 and 1962, respectively, and a parallel clergy-education program in 1965. In 1980 the Simon Silverman Phenomenology Center opened, including extensive archives for research on European phenomenology. Duquesne University has become an international center for scholarship and publications in phenomenological philosophy and psychology.

In 1962 the Esalen Institute opened at Big Sur in California, dedicated to the exploration and expansion of Eastern spiritual disciplines and the higher reaches of human nature. Esalen became the experiential training ground for the human-potential movement and the encounter-group movement. Shaffer (1978, p. 1) described the human-potential movement as "a movement that attempts to liberate people from a dehumanizing culture through a series of specific techniques." The techniques of the human-potential movement included the sensitivity-training group or encounter group, Gestalt therapy awareness exercises, body-work and movement therapies, Yoga, Zen Buddhism, and psychodrama. The leaders in the encounter-group movement over the years comprise a who's who of humanistic psychology, including such charismatic individuals as Carl Rogers, Sidney Jourard, William Schutz, Fritz Perls, Charlotte Bühler, and James Bugental. The encounter-group movement will be discussed further in chapter 6.

The encounter group became synonymous with the new humanistic belief that the only psychological truths of real significance were those that could be immediately experienced and realized in the life of the person. Humanistic psychology is not interested in mere research findings or textbook insights. Moving one step farther, humanistic psychology might agree with the theologian Joseph Campbell: "Words are only expressive of our limitations" (cited by Polowniak, 1994, p. xv). Like the Danish existentialist theologian Søren Kierkegaard, the humanistic vision of truth emphasizes a subjective consciousness that challenges each individual to reach his or her higher potential. Bühler and Allen (1972, p. 1) cite a guiding dictum from an early brochure of the Association of Humanistic Psychology:

A centering of attention on the experiencing person, and thus a focus on experience as the primary phenomenon in the study of man. Both theoretical explanations and overt behavior are considered secondary to experience itself and to its meaning to the person.

The impact of the original encounter-group movement continues today through a number of other humanistic organizations whose goal is to cultivate networks of humanistic relationships in an impersonal society. One such organization is TORI, a community of several thousand lay and professional people dedicated to the cultivation of Trust, Opening, Realizing, and Interdepending (see Gibb, 1991). Chapter 6 in the present volume will examine further the humanistic psychological approach to the cultivation of trust, openness, and community.

APPLICATIONS OF HUMANISTIC PRINCIPLES TO SOCIETY

The ultimate goal of humanistic psychology was a radical transformation of society and all human relations, with an emphasis on encouraging human potential. The applications of humanistic principles quickly reached beyond the clinic to embrace the worlds of education and business (Shaffer, 1978). Paul Goodman's *Growing Up Absurd* (1960) portrayed growing up in America as a process encouraging mindless conformism and a stifling of creativity (see chapter 25 on Fritz Perls and Paul Goodman in part II). A. S. Neill (1960) described the educational program at Summerhill; this humanistically oriented private school became a paradigm for humanistic education for a generation of student teachers. Rollo May identified schools and the educational process as the primary sources of anxiety and helpless feelings in the developing child (1967). May criticized the schools' authoritarian imposition of external values and facts and advocated a shift in emphasis to the facilitation of an inner-directed growth and self-actualization. Similarly, Carl Rogers (1969) published his *Freedom to Learn*, advocating greater flexibility in curriculum in order to increase the student's freedom to self-select more personally meaningful learning goals. Rogers introduced a number of educational concepts that later earned a place in American schools: theme-centered small discussion groups, individual learning contracts with students, differential tracking or grouping of students for the most suitable learning modalities, and increased student participation in the grading process. In spite of occasional backlashes against "unstructured classrooms" and "permissive educators," the field of education continues to assimilate the themes of humanistic psychology and the pursuit of self-actualization.

Maslow advocated a reemphasis in business and industry on humanistic principles and B values—being or growth-oriented values. His 1965 volume *Eupsychian Management: A Journal*, asserts the importance of higher needs in all employees, whatever their level in a company. He insisted that authoritarian "top-down" management strategies robbed companies of their workers' intelligence and creativity and robbed the individual worker of an opportunity to experience the fulfillment of true productive work. His emphasis on more democratic boss-worker relationships has been echoed in the later developments of worker self-management, quality circles, and other participative management strategies designed to mobilize the knowledge, creativity, and energy of workers.

HUMANISTIC PSYCHOLOGY AND THE COUNTERCULTURE

Humanistic psychologists dreamed of remaking human society and the human individual. Chapter 1 has provided a glimpse of American society and lifestyle of the 1950s, with its material affluence and vacuum of meaning. Many social critics and many alienated private individuals viewed this American way of life as a wasteland and sought new forms for social interaction and living (Roszak, 1972).

Humanistic psychology from the outset became intertwined with the counterculture that emerged at the same time. Both took on a strong antiestablishment tone and invited adherents who were disenchanted with the mainstream of American society and values. Charles Reich wrote the best-known manifesto for the counterculture, *The Greening of America*. According to him, the counterculture offers a transformation of the person and a revolution of society, but without violence: "It promises a higher reason, a more human community, and a new liberated individual. Its ultimate creation will be a new and enduring wholeness and beauty—a renewed relationship of man to himself, to other men, to society, to nature, and to the land" (Reich, 1970, p. 2). The shared pursuit of human potential, the search for new values, and the exploration of altered states of consciousness linked humanistic psychology and the counterculture. They shared a fascination with Eastern religions, a search for intimacy and community, and a dedication to human liberation. Esalen and the Association for Humanistic Psychology (AHP) became experimental laboratories for new forms of human behavior. A visit to an AHP conference often involved encountering Sufi dance troupes performing in the hallways, individuals engaging in mutual massage and body work, and an unending series of informal encounter groups.

This identification of humanistic psychology with the counterculture was not entirely positive; it contributed to the excesses and extremes of humanistic psychology. Humanistic psychology's investigation of altered states of consciousness served to justify the counterculture's fascination with drugs; humanistic psychology's ideology of personal liberation gave strength to the counterculture's rebellion against social and political authority; and the humanistic emphasis on defining one's own meaning and direction in life gave strength to the counterculture's opposition to the values of the establishment. At the fringes, individuals' lives were damaged, and society blamed its own multiple transitions on hippies, the counterculture, and the narcissism of the "me generation."

REFERENCES

Allport, G. (1937). *Personality: A psychological interpretation.* New York: Henry Holt & Company.

Allport, G. (1955). *Becoming: Basic considerations for a psychology of personality.* New Haven: Yale University Press.

Allport, G. W. (1961). *Pattern and growth in personality.* New York: Holt, Rinehart & Winston.

Allport, G. W. (Ed.) (1965). *Letters from Jenny.* New York: Harcourt, Brace, & World.

Angyal, A. (1941). *Foundations for a science of personality.* New York: Commonwealth Fund.

Angyal, A. (1965). *Neurosis and treatment: A holistic theory.* New York: Wiley.

Bugental, J. F. T. (1963). Humanistic psychology: A new breakthrough. *American Psychologist, 18*(9), 563–567.

Bühler, C., & Allen, M. (1972). *Introduction to humanistic psychology.* Monterey, CA: Brooks/Cole.

Cantril, H. (1955). Toward a humanistic psychology. *Etc.: A Review of General Semantics, 12,* 278–298.

DeCarvalho, R. J. (1991). *The founders of humanistic psychology.* New York: Praeger.

Gergen, K. J., & Davis, K. E. (Eds). (1985). *The social construction of the person.* New York: Springer.

Gibb, J. (1991). *Trust: A new vision of human relationships for business, education, family, and personal living* (2nd ed.). North Hollywood, CA: Newcastle.

Goble, F. (1970). *The third force: The psychology of Abraham Maslow.* New York: Grossman.

Goldstein, K. (1939). *The organism: A holistic approach to biology derived from pathological data in man.* New York: American Book Company.

Goodman, P. (1960). *Growing up absurd: Problems of youth in the organized system.* New York: Random House.

Guidano, V. (1991). *The self in process.* New York: Guilford.

Mahoney, M. J. (Ed.). (1995). *Cognitive and constructive psychotherapies: Theory, research, and practice.* New York: Springer.

Markus, H., & Nurius, P. (1986). Possible selves. *American Psychologist, 41*(9), 954–969.

Maslow, A. H. (1950). Self-actualizing people: A study of psychological health. Reprinted in R. J. Lowry (Ed.) (1973). *Dominance, self-esteem, self-actualization: Germinal papers of A. H. Maslow* (pp. 177–201). Monterey, CA: Brooks/Cole.

Maslow, A. H. (1954). *Motivation and personality.* New York: Harper.

Maslow, A. H. (1956). Toward a humanistic psychology. *Etc.: A Review of General Semantics, 13,* 10–22.

Maslow, A. H. (Ed). (1959). *New knowledge in human values.* New York: Harper.

Maslow, A. H. (1962). *Toward a psychology of being.* New York: Van Nostrand.

Maslow, A. H. (1965). *Eupsychian management: A journal.* Homewood, IL: Richard D. Irwin Publications.

Maslow, A. H. (1966). *The psychology of science.* New York: Harper & Row.

Maslow, A. H. (1968). *Toward a psychology of being* (2nd ed.). Princeton, NJ: D. Van Nostrand.

Maslow, A. H. (1971). *The farther reaches of human nature.* New York: Viking.

May, R. (1953). *Man's search for himself.* New York: W. W. Norton.

May, R. (1967). *Psychology and the human dilemma.* Princeton: Van Nostrand.

May, R., Angel, E., & Ellenberger, H. F. (Eds.). (1958). *Existence: A new dimension in psychiatry and psychology.* New York: Basic Books.

Misiak, H., & Sexton, V. S. (1973). *Phenomenological, existential, and humanistic psychologies: A historical survey.* New York: Grune & Stratton.

Moss, D. (1989). Psychotherapy and human experience. In R. Valle & S. Halling (Eds.), *Existential-phenomenological perspectives in psychology* (pp. 193–213). New York: Plenum.

Moss, D. (Ed.). (1994). *Twenty-fifth anniversary yearbook.* Wheat Ridge, CO: Association for Applied Psychophysiology and Biofeedback.

Moustakas, C. (1956). *The self: Explorations in personal growth.* New York: HarperCollins.

Murphy, G. (1929). *An historical introduction to modern psychology.* New York: Harcourt, Brace, & Co.

Murphy, G. (1947). *Personality: A biosocial approach to origins and structure.* New York: Harper.

Murphy, G. (1958). *Human potentialities.* New York: Basic Books.

Murphy, G., & Ballou, R. (Eds.). (1960). *William James on psychical research.* New York: Viking.

Murray, H. A. (1940). What should psychologists do about psychoanalysis? *Journal of Abnormal and Social Psychology, 35,* 150–175.

Murray, H. A., Barrett, W. G., Langer, W. C., Morgan, C. D., Homburger, E., & others. (1938). *Explorations in personality.* New York: Oxford University Press.

Neill, A. S. (1960). *Summerhill: A radical approach to child rearing*. New York: Hart.

Office of Strategic Services Assessment Staff. (1948). *Assessment of men*. New York: Rinehart.

Polowniak, W. (1994). *On creating a community*. Cardiff-by-the-Sea, CA: Quantum Publications.

Reich, C. A. (1970). *The greening of America*. New York: Random House.

Rogers, C. (1942). *Counseling and psychotherapy*. Boston: Houghton Mifflin.

Rogers, C. R. (1969). *Freedom to learn: A view of what education might become*. Columbus, OH: C. E. Merrill.

Roszak, T. (1972). *Where the wasteland ends*. Garden City, NY: Doubleday.

Shaffer, J. B. P. (1978). *Humanistic psychology*. Englewood Cliffs, NJ: Prentice-Hall.

Taylor, E. (1991). William James and the humanistic tradition. *Journal of Humanistic Psychology, 31*(1), 56–74.

Taylor, E. (1995, Spring). Humanistic psychology: The next phase. *Saybrook Perspective*, pp. 14–21.

Welch, I. D., Tate, G. A., & Richards, F. (1978). *Humanistic psychology: A sourcebook*. Buffalo, NY: Prometheus Books.

Major Schools and Theorists in Humanistic Psychology

Chapters 4 through 10 present the familiar schools and theorists that we recognize as making up humanistic psychology. Chapter 4 introduces Carl Rogers and his client-centered therapy. Rogers's clinical guidelines and his empirical approach to investigating therapeutic process have served as the foundation for much of humanistic psychotherapy. Chapter 5 overviews Gestalt therapy, covering both the familiar contributions of Frederick "Fritz" Perls and the less familiar Gestalt therapeutic approaches of the cofounders of Gestalt therapy, Paul Goodman and Laura Perls. Chapter 6 discusses the humanistic psychologies of self-disclosure, relationship, and community, highlighting the contributions of Martin Buber on the I-thou encounter, Sidney Jourard and James Pennebaker on self-disclosure, William Schutz on the encounter movement, and Jack Gibb and Bill Polowniak on the humanistic psychology of community.

Chapter 7 introduces the humanistic body therapies, commencing with the seminal contributions of Wilhelm Reich and his student Alexander Lowen. The chapter also highlights the independent contributions of three distinct schools of body work: the Alexander technique, the structural integration of Ira Rolf, and the functional integration of Moshe Feldenkrais. Chapter 8 presents the philosophical and psychological traditions of existentialism and phenomenology. Both existentialism, with its emphasis on the individual person, freedom, and responsibility for one's own existence, and phenomenology, with its emphasis on the immediate experiential perspective of each individual, have had a far-reaching influence on psychiatry, psychology, and psychotherapy in Europe and the United States.

Chapter 9 explores the relationships between feminist psychology and humanistic psychology and between the liberation of women and the liberation of human potential. The authors highlight the contributions of feminist psychology in the areas of psychological theory and women, women's lives and experience, women's health, violence against women and children, and the troubled embodiment of women. Chapter 10 introduces biofeedback, which brings together humanistic conceptions of mind and body with sophisticated electronic technology to produce powerful strategies for self-control over consciousness, emotion, and physiology.

4

Carl Rogers, the Person-Centered Approach, and Experiential Therapy

DONALD MOSS

CARL ROGERS AND CLIENT-CENTERED THERAPY

Just as Abraham Maslow offered the central conceptual approach for the humanistic psychology movement, Carl Rogers provided the central clinical framework for the humanistic therapies. Both as a theorist and an educator, Rogers provided leadership for three generations of humanistically inclined clinicians. (See chapter 27 in part II of this book for the chronology of Rogers's life and career and a more detailed discussion of his approach. See also Kirschenbaum, 1979, and Raskin, 1996b.)

Rogers's first major work (Rogers, 1942) already showed the mark of originality, bringing a fresh perspective to clinical practice, which at that time was heavily influenced by psychoanalysis. He later characterized his new approach as releasing the integrative capacities of the individual (1951, p. 8). From the beginning Rogers reconceptualized treatment as the process of freeing the individual to help himself, that is, of "removing obstacles so that he can again move forward" (Rogers, 1942, p. 29).

The Necessary and Sufficient Conditions for Personal Change

Rogers spent his early career researching the ideal conditions or, as he termed them, the "necessary and sufficient conditions" that would enable the individual client to spontaneously grow and seek fulfillment (Rogers, 1957, 1961, 1967). Rogers defined these conditions variously: (1) two persons are in psychological or emotional contact, (2) one of them, here called the client, is displaying anxiety, vulnerability, or incongruence, (3) the other, called the therapist, experiences and displays genuineness or congruence in the relationship, (4) the therapist experiences and displays unconditional positive regard for the client, (5) the therapist accomplishes an empathic understanding for the client's internal, phenomenological viewpoint and expresses this understanding to the client, and (6) the client perceives, at least to a minimal degree, the genuineness, the positive regard, and the sensitive understanding of the therapist. Once these conditions are present, Rogers believed, a process is set in motion involving spontaneous self-directed personal change.

Once Rogers understood the factors facilitating personal healing and growth, he extended his approach to groups, marriages, education, communities, and the world community (Rogers, 1969, 1970, 1972, 1980, 1983). He spent the final decade of his life teaching his life-affirming and person-centered philosophy and exercising an active role in resolving conflicts in divided communities.

Carl Rogers's Influence on the Profession

Rogers brought to clinical practice the American psychologist's interest in pragmatic interventions, operational definitions, and scientific research (1951, p. 4). Rogers introduced the rigorous study of transcripts and videotapes of actual therapy sessions into psychotherapy research. His publications were unique and original in including long verbatim transcripts of therapist-client dialogue, illustrating the actual therapeutic interaction. Rogers's orientation shifted the attention of psychotherapy research away from the internal dynamics of the patient and toward these transactions between therapist and patient. The result is a large body of empirical research on the therapeutic process.

Rogers also contributed in major ways to transforming and establishing the field of clinical psychology as we know it today. Prior to the 1940s psychotherapy was primarily the domain of psychiatry, and both Rogers's book *Counseling and Psychotherapy* and his extensive training program at the University of Chicago Counseling Center played major roles in the movement of psychologists into psychotherapy (Raskin, 1996a). The Veterans Administration also played a central role in the early 1950s in pioneering a treatment role for psychologists, and many VA psychologists completed their therapeutic training at the University of Chicago. Rogers maintained close associations with several leading figures in the VA programs, including Stanley Lipkin and James G. Miller (Raskin, 1996a). Rogers also served as president of the American Psychological Association and earned the abiding respect of his peers in psychology.

Rogers's Understanding of the Person

Rogers cited the strongest conceptual influences on his work as the focus in European existential philosophers and theologians on the individual human life, the emphasis in Gestalt psychology on the wholeness and structure of the personality, and the interest in phenomenological psychology on subjective experience. Other immediate influences included Abraham Maslow's personality theory, the theology of Paul Tillich, and the will psychology of Otto Rank.

Rogers's personality theory parallels and overlaps that of Maslow. His emphasis is primarily on the internal, experiential frame of reference of each individual, through which that person observes the surrounding world. Rogers emphasized that each person is unique, and that there is a spontaneous drive within the individual toward self-actualization. He emphasized the experiential basis of the self, the experience of "me" or "I." Positive, affirming parenting facilitates the formation of a positive and flexible self-concept. It is equally important that the parent encourage and affirm the child's gradual movement toward autonomy. Critical, rejecting, and nonaffirming interactions with parents and others contribute more negative and degrading elements to the self-concept. Once formed, this self-concept shapes later experiences of life.

Rogers pointed out that a later life event can be (a) perceived and organized into some relationship to the self, (b) ignored because it presents no apparent significance to one's self, or (c) actively denied or rejected because the event is inconsistent with the structure of one's self (1951, p. 503). When the individual's self-concept is too narrow, there is an increasing lack of congruence between self-concept and experience, and psychological maladjustment is the result. Meador and Rogers (1979) describe various kinds of incongruence that can occur in maladjusted persons: incongruences between the self-concept and new experiences, between actual self as found in behavior and the internally perceived self, and among thoughts, feelings, and actions. Counseling, in turn, can provide the kind of positively affirming interpersonal experiences that heal such internal divisions.

Client-Centered Therapy: Against Interpretation

Technically, Rogers was critical of the cherished psychoanalytic emphasis on interpretation. Rogers believed that the patient's own internal framework of experience provides the best context to understand the client's symptoms or problems. He opposed therapeutic efforts to interpret unconscious or invisible drives to explain current behavior.

Rogers proclaimed less emphasis overall on technical skills; nevertheless, several key interventions emerged as characteristic of his work. First, Rogers sought to clarify the client's emotional experiencing. He placed questions that led the client to elaborate on his or her immediate perceptions of life problems and his or her immediate feelings toward the situation. Rogers's work as a therapist was directed throughout therapy at achieving a deep, empathic understanding of the client's emotions and experiences. Next, Rogers reflected or mirrored back to the client this empathic understanding of the client's feelings. Finally, he sought to convey his acceptance or unconditional positive regard for the client as a person.

Stages in the Development of the Person-Centered Approach

Rogers's school of therapy was successively known as nondirective therapy, client-centered therapy, experiential therapy, and the person-centered approach (Rogers, 1951; Corey, 1986, pp. 110–111). Rogers's initial formulation emphasized that the therapist is a nondirective mirror, bringing little of his or her own values, beliefs, and feelings to the therapy dialogue and encouraging the entire initiative for change to emerge from within the client's own personality. The therapist in this model is not an authority guiding a dependent client, but a facilitator encouraging the client to discover himself or herself. The therapist's involvement consists largely of paraphrasing or mirroring the client's feelings and experiences. This early restrictive model of the therapist's role evoked many critiques of a passive therapist nodding and repeating ad nauseam, "Mmmhmmm, you seem to be feeling . . ."

Later Rogers emphasized the client-centeredness of his counseling because the counselor concentrates on how "the client seems to himself" (1951, p. 30). Rogers encouraged the therapist to put aside his or her preoccupation with actively diagnosing, evaluating, or guiding the patient. Instead, the therapist must place his or her entire personal energies into understanding the patient at a deep emotional level and into conveying a genuine acceptance for the client.

In the next phase Rogers labeled his approach experiential as he expanded his concept of the therapist's personal contribution to therapy. If the therapist is challenged to be genuine with the client, then, Rogers reasoned, it is artificial to suspend the entire range of his or her personal feelings and experiences from the therapeutic dialogue. Rogers now encouraged the therapist to express personal reactions in a facilitating way and to establish a full reciprocity between client and counselor in the therapeutic dialogue. He emphasized that if the therapist's actions and statements were congruent with what he or she felt and believed, then their impact would be therapeutic for the client.

In the final phase of his life's work Rogers rechristened his approach as person-centered in order to specifically enlarge the relevance of the approach to nonclinical settings, where no one is the client. The guiding principles in Rogers's philosophy of therapy and life were to remain genuine in all interactions, to hold and express unconditional positive regard for the other human being, to accomplish a deep empathic understanding at a feeling level for the other person, and to strive for reciprocity in all relationships. Rogers conceptualized these guidelines as fundamental humanistic values, with as much application in everyday life as in the counseling office. He believed that teaching and actualizing these values in our lives will bring about the growth of healthier relationships in families, schools, communities, and societies. Person-centered principles have been applied to the training of Peace Corps and Vista volunteers; marriage and family therapy; staff relationships within corporations, schools, hospitals, and clinics; management development; and foreign relations (Corey, 1986, p. 111; Rogers, 1980, 1983). In

Rogers's vision of a better society, the growth of all persons and groups will be nurtured as a way of being (Rogers, 1962, 1980).

THE INFLUENCE OF PERSON-CENTERED THERAPY

Developments within Person-Centered Therapy

A number of authors have continued to reexamine and extend both Rogers's work and the person-centered therapy model. The journal *Person-Centered Review* published a special edition in November 1990 honoring the fifty-year life span of the client-centered/person-centered approach. This special issue highlighted Rogers's original contributions and current new applications and investigations. Cain (1990) reviewed the impact of client-centered therapy to date and called for new applications specifically directed toward problems facing people today, such as drug abuse, child abuse, and divorce. Cain challenged researchers to publish more in mainstream journals to have greater impact on the profession at large. Zimring (1990) submitted some of Rogers's therapy transcripts to reanalysis and found a strong therapeutic influence of Rogers's positive beliefs about the person. Tobin (1991) and Kahn (1989) compared Rogers's client-centered theory and therapeutic model to those of Heinz Kohut's psychoanalytic self psychology. Rogers himself had recognized both the close parallels and the distinct divergences between his work and Kohut's and had expressed regrets at not enjoying a face-to-face dialogue before Kohut's death (Rogers & Sanford, 1985).

Usher (1989) critiqued several cultural biases in the person-centered approach, including an overemphasis on independence, a neglect of the client's support system, and an exclusive focus on changing the client and not the interpersonal system surrounding the client. Nevertheless, in spite of these apparent cultural biases, the person-centered approach continues to find acceptance and new applications throughout the world (Rogers & Sanford, 1985; Orlov, 1992).

The Experiential Response, Focusing, and Experiential Psychotherapy

Eugene Gendlin (1973) and Alvin Mahrer (1983) developed a strain of client-centered-therapy research into a distinct therapeutic approach called experiential therapy. Initially Gendlin conducted research on the process of client-centered psychotherapy and identified a critical moment in the therapeutic process that he called the experiential response (Gendlin, 1968). In the experiential response, the client experiences a breakthrough in understanding and abruptly responds at a deeply felt bodily and emotional level. Later Gendlin relabeled this moment as a "felt shift" or as "focusing" and observed that this breakthrough includes a sudden new understanding, a sense of emotional release, and a tangible physical feeling of change. Don (1977/1978) found neurophysiological correlates to this "felt shift." Just before the client experiences the shift, an EEG recording shows a dramatic change in cortical alpha-and theta-range activity. The continued EEG tracings after this moment suggest extensive neural reorganization (Gendlin, 1981). Gendlin concluded that in such moments therapy leaves the verbal plane and has a deep-reaching affective and neurophysiological impact on the person.

Further research demonstrated that many clients show the presence of this focusing already in the first two sessions of therapy. Gendlin claimed to predict later success in therapy from the presence or absence of this response in initial sessions (Gendlin, 1981). Successful patients evidently came into therapy with some ability to focus, or to give a full cognitive, emotional, and physical response to new perspectives in sessions; in the course of later sessions they showed improved focusing and more instances of such focusing. However, few of the patients who lacked the focusing response in early sessions acquired it later. Gendlin concluded that psychotherapy was failing to teach clients this necessary skill for therapeutic success.

Gendlin learned first that he could teach other professionals to recognize this moment in therapy, enhancing each therapist's understanding of the therapeutic process. Then he developed and refined instructions for clients to teach the client to stay concentrated and attentive to the immediate flow of feelings about one's total emotional situation. Gendlin (1973) and Mahrer (1983) designed a number of specific guidelines for therapists to assist the patient in entering into and staying in an "experiential state" in sessions. The result was a new therapeutic approach, experiential therapy. Experiential therapy is distinctive in its emphasis on a shift toward deeper affective experiencing in therapy sessions, a more deeply felt self-encounter, and an earlier move toward closure on emotional issues (Friedman, 1976; Moss, 1989).

Gendlin refined his guidelines on focusing so that individuals could better help themselves to enter this experiential state outside of therapy. He found that the average individual can learn to focus and remain more fully present to emotional experiences and benefit from the use of this skill in a variety of problem situations (Gendlin, 1981).

Rogers's Influence on Other Approaches

Carl Rogers's deepest impact on the profession of psychology and psychotherapy goes beyond specific approaches and schools. The well-trained clinician in all approaches and behavioral disciplines now inherits Rogers's appreciation for the therapist-client relationship, the importance of reaching and communicating empathy, and "staying with" the patient in an experiential fashion throughout the process of any intervention or treatment (Moss, 1989). Aaron Beck has taken this into account in his cognitive-behavioral therapy, calling for the therapist to listen attentively to the patient's perception of the world before any behavioral interventions are attempted (Beck, 1976; Beck, Rush, Shaw, & Emery, 1979).

REFERENCES

Beck, A. T. (1976). *Cognitive therapy and the emotional disorders.* New York: International Universities Press.

Beck, A. T., Rush, A. J., Shaw, B. F., & Emery, G. (1979). *Cognitive therapy of depression.* New York: Guilford.

Cain, D. J. (1990). Celebration, reflection, and renewal: 50 years of client-centered therapy and beyond. Fiftieth anniversary of the person-centered approach [Special issue]. *Person-Centered Review, 5*(4), 357–363.

Corey, G. (1986). *Theory and practice of counseling and psychotherapy* (3rd ed). Pacific Grove, CA-Brooks/Cole Publishing Co.

Don, N. (1977/1978). The transformation of conscious experience and its EEG correlates. *Journal of Altered States of Consciousness, 3*(2), 147–168.

Friedman, N. (1976). From the experiential in therapy to experiential psychotherapy: A history. *Psychotherapy: Theory, Research, and Practice, 13*(3), 236–243.

Gendlin, E. T. (1968). Client-centered: The experiential response. In E. F. Hammer (Ed.), *Use of interpretation in treatment* (pp. 208–237). New York: Grune & Stratton.

Gendlin, E. T. (1973). Experiential psychotherapy. In R. Corsini (Ed.), *Current psychotherapies* (pp. 317–352). Itasca, IL: F. E. Peacock.

Gendlin, E. T. (1981). *Focusing.* New York: Bantam.

Kahn, E. (1989). Heinz Kohut and Carl Rogers: Toward a constructive collaboration. *Psychotherapy, 26*(4), 555–563.

Kirschenbaum, H. (1979). *On becoming Carl Rogers.* New York: Delacorte Press.

Mahrer, A. (1983). *Experiential psychotherapy: Basic practices.* New York: Brunner/Mazel.

Maslow, A. H. (1954). *Motivation and personality.* New York: Harper.

Maslow, A. H. (1962). *Toward a psychology of being.* New York: Van Nostrand.

Meador, B. D., & Rogers, C. R. (1979). Person-centered therapy. In R. J. Corsini (Ed.), *Current psychotherapies* (2nd ed.) (pp. 119–165). Itasca, IL: F. E. Peacock.

Moss, D. (1989). Psychotherapy and human experience. In R. S. Valle & S. Halling (Eds.), *Existential-phenomenological perspectives in psychology* (pp. 193–213). New York: Plenum.

Orlov, A. B. (1992). Carl Rogers and contemporary humanism. *Journal of Russian and East European Psychology, 30*(1), 36–41.

Raskin, N. J. (1996a, August). The life and work of Carl Rogers. In D. Moss (Chair), *Legacies of the founders: Contemporary implications of humanistic psychology.* Symposium at the annual meeting of the American Psychological Association, Toronto.

Raskin, N. J. (1996b). Person-centered psychotherapy: Twenty historical steps. In W. Dryden (Ed.), *Developments in psychotherapy: Historical perspectives* (pp. 1–27). London: Sage.

Rogers, C. R. (1942). *Counseling and psychotherapy: Newer concepts in practice.* Boston: Houghton Mifflin.

Rogers, C. R. (1951). *Client-centered therapy: Its current practice implications, and theory.* Boston: Houghton Mifflin.

Rogers, C. R. (1957). The necessary and sufficient conditions of therapeutic personality change. *Journal of Consulting Psychology, 21*, 95–103.

Rogers, C. R. (1961). *On becoming a person.* Boston: Houghton Mifflin.

Rogers, C. R. (1962). Toward becoming a fully-functioning person. In J. Couch (Ed.), *Readings in human adjustment* (pp. 1–13). New York: Selective Academic Readings Press.

Rogers, C. R. (1967). The conditions of change from a client-centered viewpoint. In B. Berenson & R. Carkhuff (Eds.), *Sources of gain in counseling and psychotherapy.* New York: Holt, Rinehart & Winston.

Rogers, C. R. (1969). *Freedom to learn.* Columbus, OH: Charles E. Merrill.

Rogers, C. R. (1970). *Carl Rogers on encounter groups.* New York: Harper & Row.

Rogers, C. R. (1972). *Becoming partners: Marriage and its alternatives.* New York: Delacorte.

Rogers, C. R. (1980). *A way of being.* Boston: Houghton Mifflin.

Rogers, C. R. (1983). *Freedom to learn for the 80's.* Columbus, OH: Charles E. Merrill.

Rogers, C. R., & Sanford, R. C. (1985). Client-centered psychotherapy. In H. I. Kaplan & B. J. Sadock (Eds.), *Comprehensive textbook of psychiatry* (vol. 4. pp. 1374–1388). Baltimore: Williams & Wilkins.

Tobin, S. A. (1991). A comparison of psychoanalytic self psychology and Carl Rogers's person centered therapy. *Journal of Humanistic Psychology, 31*(1), 9–33.

Usher, C. H. (1989). Recognizing cultural bias in counseling theory and practice: The case of Rogers. *Journal of Multicultural Counseling and Development,* 17(2), 62–71.

Zimring, F. (1990). A characteristic of Rogers's response to clients. Fiftieth anniversary of the person-centered approach [Special issue]. *Person-Centered Review, 5*(4), 433–448.

5

Gestalt Therapy: The Once and Future King

PAUL SHANE

THE IRONIES OF HISTORY

It was commonly believed during the advent of Gestalt therapy that its own success and notoriety as a therapeutic innovation springing from several basic insights of Gestalt psychology would save the latter from becoming little more than a footnote in history. Several decades later one finds, not without some dismay and embarrassment, that Hunt's (1993) massive history of psychology devotes an entire chapter to Gestalt psychology, while Gestalt therapy receives a mere two paragraphs, and these devoted only to Fritz Perls. Hunt (1993) concludes this paltry section by saying that "in filmed episodes of therapy, Perls seems at times almost sadistic, but with some patients he was very effective. Gestalt therapy was popular and deemed important in humanistic circles during the 1960s and 1970s; today it plays only a small part in the world of psychotherapy" (p. 591). Did Gestalt therapy flash across the skyline of contemporary psychotherapy like a meteor of humanistic thought, bright and dazzling, only to fall to earth in darkness? Is it time to say a "requiem for Gestalt," as did one of Fritz and Laura Perls's original students (From, 1984)? If so, what were the causes of its sudden rise in the halcyon days of the humanistic movement of the 1960s and 1970s and now its apparent fall in the postmodern 1980s and 1990s? Does Gestalt therapy have a future, and, if so, by which directions will it arrive there?

Ironies abound in the history and development of Gestalt therapy. The first is that the seeds of the alleged demise of Gestalt therapy were first sown by one of its founders and most active popularizers, Frederick "Fritz" Perls. Perls's application of Gestalt therapy revolved around his own personal style and interpretation of Gestalt therapy, which emphasized his own personal prejudices, technical preferences, and intellectual "hobbyhorses" such as the empty chair, personal confrontation, assumption of individual responsibility, workshop-demonstration format, and the "awareness continuum" of human perception and experience. It was his break from the original New York group of Gestalt therapists in the mid-1950s—from Laura Perls, Paul Goodman, Isadore From, Paul Weiss, Elliott Shapiro, and others—to take his "own show on the road," as it were, that began the popularization of the "Fritz style" of Gestalt therapy. In the mid-1950s Perls had abandoned his wife and colleagues in New York and had gone to California by way of Florida, where, feeling his age and a sense of personal failure and bitterness, as well as bearing a heart condition, he was preparing himself to die. By chance, he landed at the right place at the right time at Esalen Institute, where he found followers and admirers aplenty and, perhaps nurtured by the loving atmosphere and healthy environment, his heart began to heal. Perls made Esalen, then the hotbed of human-potential practices, his own bully pulpit from which he preached his brand of Gestalt therapy. From then on, Gestalt therapy became synonymous with Fritz Perls. As Laura Perls (1992) once observed:

The style that Fritz Perls developed in demonstration workshops for professionals during the last few years of his life has become widely known through films and video tapes and through *Gestalt Therapy Verbatim* . . . the transcripts of these tapes. The dramatization of dreams and fantasies is a beautiful demonstration method, particularly in workshops with professionals who have already had their personal analysis or therapy, and are themselves experienced in working with people. But it is only *one* aspect of the infinite possibilities in the Gestalt approach. (p. 4)

What was the "Fritz style" of Gestalt therapy? Space does not permit a lengthy discussion, but it can be summarized in his own credo, the infamous "Gestalt prayer," the words he lived by:

I do my thing, and you do your thing.
I am not in this world to live up to your expectations
And you are not in this world to live up to mine.
You are you and I am I,
And if by chance we find each other, it's beautiful.
If not, it can't be helped. (F. S. Perls, 1973, p. 4)

Ironically, such a prayer is really a personal ode to anomie or a credo of "egocentric hedonism," and although it does contain some essential truths about human life and relationship, such as the importance of self-responsibility, there is some inherent foolishness within it as well (Crocker, 1983). Another irony, as Yalom (1980) cogently points out, is that Perls's penchant for forcing responsibility back onto the client was self-contradictory:

Though Perls' words leave no doubt that he was highly sensitive to the issue of personal responsibility and cognizant of the fact that the therapist must not accept the burden of the patient's responsibility, he was never able to solve (or for that matter, I believe, to recognize fully) the paradox of his approach to therapy. "Assume responsibility" the patient is told. But what is the rest of the patient's experience? An encounter with an enormously powerful, charismatic, wise old man who pronounces nonverbally: "And I'll tell you precisely how, when and why to do it." Perls' active personal style, his aura of power and omniscience contradicted his words. (p. 250)

More to the point, though, Perls's "prayer" is in some ways antithetical to the actual theory, philosophy, and spirit of Gestalt therapy. What Perls demonstrated was not Gestalt therapy in its purest sense but more a Gestalt therapy refracted through the prism of his own personality.

For example, what further damaged the reputation and popular understanding of Gestalt therapy was that Perls's personal and professional style abjured intellectual exploration; indeed, he savaged any potential development on the part of his followers along these lines by denigrating such things as "mind fucking" or "spinning your computer." Perls, although a courageous man and a brilliant therapist, was not a scholar, as were his wife and Paul Goodman; this was part of the reason he abandoned New York, as he could not compete on that level (Gaines, 1979; Shepard, 1975; Stoehr, 1994). Perls was not a man for extended rumination; he was a man of aphorism and action.

This leads to a fourth irony. Much of Gestalt therapy, through Perls's popularization of it, became associated with an aggressive technique and a hyperindividualism. Time has proven that neither of these qualities are enough to sustain a psychotherapeutic movement because they, when taken alone, neglect too many other ingredients necessary to address the human predicament (Wheeler, 1991). Simply put, Gestalt therapy is not a technique but is closer to an applied philosophy or an aesthetic point of view. As Laura Perls (1992) points out, "The basic concepts of Gestalt therapy are philosophical and aesthetic rather than technical" (p. 4). The philosophical roots of Gestalt therapy rise from a great many sources, including Aristotle, William James, John Dewey, Immanuel Kant, and specialized gleanings from the existential philosophers and theologians such as Søren Kierkegaard, Friedrich Nietzsche, Martin Buber, Paul Tillich, Martin Heidegger, and the phenomenology of Edmund Husserl as well as Zen Buddhism and Taoism (Perls, Hefferline, & Goodman, 1951; Stoehr, 1994; Wheeler, 1991). One researcher, after interviewing twenty-two American Gestalt therapists and examining Perls's collected works, concluded that Gestalt therapy borrowed from twenty-seven theoreticians as well as the various schools of Eastern and Western philosophy just named (Barlow, 1983).

Gestalt therapy is founded on an essential rediscovery made by Gestalt psychology that human beings organize their own reality, a phenomenon previously examined by Kant that is now experiencing a rebirth in the form of constructivism. Human beings perceive and experience in organized wholes called *Gestalten*, which are defined by Laura Perls (1992) as "a holistic concept (*ein Ganzheitsbegriff*). A Gestalt is a structured entity that is more than, or different from, its parts. It is the foreground figure that stands out from its ground, it 'exists' " (p. 5). The fundamental thrust of the Gestalt model concerns how human beings structure and organize their experience and behavior. Given this, the Gestalt model focuses on what experience is about and what behavior is directed toward, that is, the point of contact of consciousness with what is. Put differently, the Gestalt model concerns the intentionality of one's being in the world. The concept of "contact" is the fundamental insight of Fritz and Laura Perls and Paul Goodman; this is what distinguishes Gestalt therapy from all other schools of psychotherapy (From, 1984/1994; Wheeler, 1991; Zinker, 1994). As Gestalt therapy is founded upon an appreciation of the *form* of human contact, which encompasses experience, behavior, and interpersonal relationships, it moves into the realm of aesthetic perception and values. But here we are getting ahead of ourselves, and these points will be taken up again later in the chapter.

EVOLUTION AND DEVELOPMENT

Since the inception of Gestalt therapy, many excellent works have been published describing its theory and methodology. Several may be considered classics in the literature, beginning with the oftentimes unwieldy, yet profound, *Gestalt Therapy* (Perls, Hefferline, & Goodman, 1951) and proceeding to the works of Latner (1973, 1992), Polster and Polster (1973), Wheeler (1991), and Zinker (1977, 1994). Yet the critical examination of the history of its theoretical development (Wheeler, 1991), along with the long-overlooked, yet influential role played by Paul Goodman (Stoehr, 1994), has only recently begun.

The theory of Gestalt therapy, as noted by Latner (1992), springs from Freudian psychoanalysis, existential and Eastern philosophies, and Gestalt psychology. Frederick Perls and Laura Perls were trained as orthodox Freudians. While Frederick Perls undertook analysis with Karen Horney and Wilhelm Reich and worked briefly under Kurt Goldstein at the latter's neurological clinic for brain-damaged World War I veterans, Laura studied under Adhemar Gelb, a protégé of both Max Wertheimer and Kurt Goldstein, as well as with Martin Buber and Paul Tillich (Wysong & Rosenfeld, 1982). The first idea that led to the inspiration and development of Gestalt therapy came from Fritz Perls and Laura Perls reevaluating the Freudian doctrine that resistances are essentially anal in nature. Their experiences and observations of the feeding and weaning of their first baby prompted them to deeper examination of the human oral function—aggression, dentition, digestion, assimilation, and rejection—as a metaphor of mental metabolism and psychological health (Wysong & Rosenfeld, 1982). This, in turn, led Perls to present an ill-received paper, "The Oral Resistances," to a psychoanalytic convention in 1936 and, even though he failed to gain acceptance in Freudian circles, to continue his exploration along these lines. Both he and Laura found that several basic concepts of Gestalt psychology, specifically, organized perception, figure-ground, and the persistence of the memory of incomplete tasks—what later became commonly known as "unfinished business"—could also be applied as psychotherapeutic concepts (Wheeler, 1991).

Perls's Initial Model

Having been rejected by the Freudians and in danger from the Nazis, Fritz and Laura Perls fled Germany and founded a psychoanalytic practice in South Africa, where they resided in comfort and safety throughout World War II. It was during this South African sojourn that the Perlses continued developing their ideas but still worked within a psychoanalytic cast. This work resulted in Frederick Perls's first book, *Ego, Hunger, and Aggression* (1947/1969), to which Laura maintained that she contributed two chapters. The book is an odd little rambling affair that as Wheeler (1991) concludes after a lengthy analysis, fails at achieving its stated revisionist aims but does show Perls's intention of establishing a psychotherapeutic approach based on organismic functioning—an outgrowth of his interest in orality and Reichian character analysis—and the revolutionary change from working with the client's past memories in favor of immediate experience, what he termed at this time the "sense of actuality." Perls's conception of the organism, like Wilhelm Reich's, is exclusively focused on the body rather than on the organism-environment field à la Lewin or Goldstein.

After the war, the Perlses emigrated to New York City, aided by Laura's brother, who was already a resident, as well as by Karen Horney and Erich Fromm. The year was 1949, and Perls, who had developed another rough manuscript of his ideas, was looking for editorial assistance. Perls needed someone who was familiar with both psychoanalysis and Reichian character analysis, and because of the language barrier, he needed an accomplished writer. He found all of this and more in Paul Goodman.

The Perls/Goodman Model

Goodman's participation in reworking the manuscript that was to become *Gestalt Therapy* (1951) quickly grew with his energetic zeal into coauthorship as he eventually wound up penning the entire second half dealing with theory. Perls was the idea man, while Goodman was the writer who organized and fleshed everything out. Goodman, a student of Aristotle, Kant, and Taoism as well as an anarchist-communitarian in the vein of Bakunin and Kropotkin, brought a decidedly social and political view to Perls's ideas. Much of this revolved around the concept of contact and what he called the "autonomous criterion of value"—of the expression and satisfaction of organismic needs in the context of the felt urgency of figure-against-background. This was perhaps an oversimplification of the dynamically organized hierarchy of figures against the field of the ground as found in Lewin and Goldstein, but, nonetheless, it served as the foundation for an entirely new approach to therapy and living (Wheeler, 1991). It also served as a new theory of the self, a self found in the boundary of contact between the organism and its environment, along with a concrete exposition of a core group of "resistances" to contact. The contact model is also the basis for Perls's insightful critique of Freud's theory of repression. Linked with an interpretation of Husserl's phenomenological methodology as well as Otto Rank's view of the artist, the *Gestalt Therapy* text offered a new and novel view of human nature: a positive, radical reevaluation of desire, the self as artist, and the therapist focused on the *process* of the client's immediate experience. It proposed that therapeutic intervention was an "experiment" in the "safe emergency" created during the therapy session. This was all heady stuff for the socially uptight and repressed 1950s and, in Perls's hedonistic hands, perfect for the burgeoning social and sexual revolution of the 1960s and 1970s.

Yet Fritz Perls and Goodman held antithetical stances toward one another in terms of both philosophy and personality. Perls's ideal of mental health and personal growth was a kind of hyperindividualism and independence, while for Goodman mental health and growth revolved around personal expression and satisfaction of the most pressing need and, through this, the creative adjustment of the individual within the context of community. In simplest terms, Perls emphasized the individual and the body, the organism rather than the environment, while Goodman saw organism-environment as a systemic whole. This fundamental difference was to lead them both along different paths later in life and toward mutual antipathy. By the 1960s Perls became the humanistic maverick, while Goodman rose to the forefront of the pressing social and political issues of that time (Stoehr, 1994).

The Cleveland School

Gestalt Therapy (1951) was taken into the larger professional circle around Fritz and Laura Perls and Paul Goodman as a basic treatise for discussion; from this group the New York Institute for Gestalt Therapy formed. The book also attracted the interest of a handful of psychotherapists in Cleveland, Ohio, who, after visiting in New York, soon began importing the two Perlses, Goodman, and From to Cleveland for individual therapy and for group workshops. This particular group was formed among peers, so no single personality or point of view ever became dominant. They instead enjoyed a collegial atmosphere of mutual support and growth. In time, through their interpretation and development of the Gestalt doctrine, the Cleveland school focused on Perls's concept of "mental metabolism" (F. S. Perls, 1947/1969) as elaborated by Goodman into the "contact cycle," a six-stage sequence whereby an organism achieves homeostatic balance. The Cleveland group named this the "cycle of experience." The cycle of experience can be considered as a lens through which to view intrapsychic, interpersonal, or group processes; this lens is also useful in identifying points for therapeutic intervention (see Merry & Brown, 1987; Nevis, 1987; Zinker, 1994). The Cleveland school also focused on the concept of devising therapeutic "experiments"; each experiment provides the client or group a means for exploring new behaviors and/ or of integrating psychological conflicts. The use of the experiment is taken by Zinker (1977) to a dynamic and aesthetic level. Zinker (1996), in reflecting upon those early days of the Gestalt Institute of Cleveland in the late 1950s, states, "What we originally created in Cleveland was humanistic. It was focused on the person and it was about joy."

RECENT TRENDS AND FUTURE DIRECTIONS

The reports of my death have been greatly exaggerated.

—Mark Twain

Today, with the humanities in seeming retreat in the universities, with cognitive behaviorism in the driver's seat as the preferred means of psychotherapy, with managed care dictating the course of therapeutic service, and with an increasingly conservative political climate, it is little wonder that Hunt (1993) may have inferred that Gestalt therapy is a school whose time has come and gone. Even though the existential-humanistic approach may be in a period of retrenchment, Gestalt therapy possesses a rich theory that in the right hands leads to creative new approaches and a continued exploration of new veins of thought and application. This section will identify seven areas in which Gestalt therapy continues its development. Due to space limitations the following section is offered as a representative sampling of recent activity and is by no means a comprehensive literature review.

Wider Applications

While once considered applicable mainly to overly socialized and highly cognitive neurotics—cases of the "worried well," as Torrey (1988) might put it—the Gestalt model lends itself to new ways of working with serious psychological problems such as alcoholism (Carlock, Glaus, & Shaw, 1992; Clemmens, 1997; Roche, 1986), the personality disorders (Melnick & Nevis, 1992), and schizophrenia (Harris, 1992), as well as borderline personality disorder (Greenberg, 1989; Polo, 1993).

The Integration of Systems Theory

Gestalt therapy, because it is founded in Gestalt psychology with a view to the organism-environment as a field of activity (e.g., Koffka, 1935/1963), is in some ways a precursor of modern systems theory. When combined, Gestalt therapy and systems theory seem to dovetail naturally. Related to the field concept is the notion of boundary. Boundary is one fundamental principle of Gestalt therapy, as seen in the contact boundary, and is central in terms of study, theory, and practice. As Skolnik notes, "Gestalt therapy is the only organized therapy whose fundamental model is based on *the relation between*" (1990 p. 60; emphasis in original). In this way Gestalt therapy anticipated many systems of family therapy that emphasize boundary interactions. As such, Gestalt therapy, in its recent elaboration and extension by contemporary practitioners and theorists, finds itself already grounded as a practical model for working with complex systems. Much fruitful work has been done in this regard with couples and families (Andrews, 1989; Espy, 1994; Frew, 1982; Greenbank, 1990; Howard, 1987; Randolph, 1988; Wheeler & Backman, 1994; Yates, 1991; Zinker, 1994) and organizations (Merry & Brown, 1987; Nevis, 1987).

Applied Aesthetics

The original Gestalt psychologists, while being rigorously empirical, were themselves aesthetically oriented because they were concerned with how human beings perceive, experience, and organize perception and experience. As Van Campen (1994) notes, Max Wertheimer's Gestalt theory of perception shares affinities with aesthetic philosophies, and this aesthetic aspect emerged at the same time as experimental psychology. The founders of Gestalt therapy, on the other hand, were artists in their own rights. Fritz Perls was interested in theater and opera, Laura Perls was a dancer and musician, and Paul Goodman was a poet, novelist, and playwright. Hearkening back to Otto Rank's influence upon Goodman (Perls, Hefferline, & Goodman, 1951; Stoehr, 1994) and the idea of the self as being the artist of life, Zinker (1977, 1994) has taken the Gestalt model, delineated its underlying values, and applied it as an aesthetic frame of reference with which to conduct individual, couple, and group therapy. Flying in the face of the empiricist model of psychotherapy as an applied "science," Zinker (1994) boldly asserts that Gestalt therapy is an application of aesthetic principles, and that the therapy situation itself can be conceptually regarded as an artistic event. Paralleling Zinker (1994) in this respect, McClure, Merrill, and Russo (1994) turn to the world of art and the perceptual strategies developed by the artist Betty Edwards; they integrate these strategies with Gestalt therapy techniques. They utilize this combination in training to show how artistic perception and technique can be practically applied to the counseling relationship.

Spirituality and Feminist Theory

It has long been recognized that the perceptual principles of Gestalt psychology can be applied to religious thought and experience (Rutledge, 1949; Wells, 1985). Gestalt therapy springs from both Gestalt psychology and Eastern philosophy and has implications for spiritual experiencing (Walker, 1970; Zamborsky, 1982), spiritually oriented psychotherapy (Keding, 1988; Kent, 1983; Richardson, 1976; Scerbo, 1983), and pastoral care (Hamilton, 1994; Killoran, 1993).

Doelger (1978) and Horne (1973) have explored the spiritual consequences of the basic Gestalt therapy principles of awareness and of the integration of polarities. These are two areas where, perhaps surprisingly, Gestalt therapy blends in a marvelous and profound way. There has been a recent rebirth of interest in the work of Martin Buber, one of the core influences on Gestalt theory (Wilburger, 1989) and one long overlooked. This parallels the renewed interest in the lifelong work of Laura Perls with her special emphasis on the more "feminine" aspects of human relationship, including support and contact. Hycner (1991) and Friedman (1985) have developed Buber's philosophy into a formal psychotherapy in their "dialogical therapy." Hycner and Jacobs (1995) take Buber's dialogal point of view farther by melding it with Gestalt therapy and self psychology into a dynamically coherent approach. Likewise, Filippi (1990) has shown how Buber, Gestalt therapy, feminist theology, and pastoral counseling can be creatively united.

Gestalt therapy had little explicit to say about God. Fritz Perls himself could be considered an atheist or at least an agnostic. Laura, with her ties to Buber and Tillich, seems to have preferred to find the spiritual in experiences of nature and personal encounter. Goodman, a Taoist influenced by both Kierkegaard and Buber, was religious in the sense that he put his faith in a "creator spirit" and in the greater force of nature. Thus it is hard to imagine that a specifically religious dimension can be found in the work of Fritz Perls, with his emphasis on the "impasse" point in therapy where equal energies counter one another in a temporary moment of stasis. Yet Beaumont (1976) has done so; he identifies the impasse as a religious process. Similarly, Au (1991) reports that if we conceive of Gestalt therapy as a process of focused contemplation, this focusing can be used to realize the kind of spiritual transformation sought by St. Ignatius Loyola.

Feminist theory may not at first glance appear as a suitable partner for a psychotherapy. It is still commonly accepted that psychotherapy should remain apolitical (although Paul Goodman would have heartily disagreed). Yet several authors have observed that feminist theory offers an intriguing complement to Gestalt therapy.

Turbiner's (1982) phenomenological examination of the feminine experience of self lends support to the Gestalt model and to the proposition that Gestalt methods can be used to positively affect women's self-esteem (McGrath, 1989). Enns (1987) explores the value of self-responsibility, integrates it with a feminist perspective, and notes that such a combination holds the promise of unifying the feminist understanding of relationship. This parallels Laura Perls's long-held position linking feminism with personal responsibility. This approach not only aids in personal development but draws attention to the environmental constraints and socialization that affect women's choices. In this context, Enns's work brings together two worlds that have long been estranged from one another in Gestalt therapy, both literally and figuratively: those of Fritz and Laura Perls.

Refinement of Physical Process

Fritz Perls was sensitized to the body through his work with Wilhelm Reich. Laura Perls brought the body into her applications of Gestalt therapy through her training in modern dance and eurhythmics. Goodman was influenced by Reich through his therapy with Alexander Lowen. Even though the model of Gestalt therapy in Perls's presentation may be "figure bound" to the body, as observed by Wheeler (1991), it is and remains grounded in the reality of physical experience. Indeed, Gestalt therapy and Reichian therapy are considered to be the first physically oriented psychotherapies (see, e.g., E.W.L. Smith, 1985).

The first person to extend Gestalt therapy's emphasis on working with the body was Barry Stevens (1975); she used a spontaneous form of the client's free physical expression. Stevens's approach never gained popularity, but the study of the body was taken up by other practitioners.

Rubenfeld (1992) combined the Alexander technique, Feldenkrais's functional integration, and Gestalt therapy into a working whole called "Rubenfeld synergy." Kepner (1987), who was trained in both body work and Gestalt therapy, used the "cycle of experience" of the Cleveland school as a model to address the significance of physical process in psychotherapy. This led to a new model for working with emotional and physical trauma (Kepner, 1996). Green (1985) proposed a new form of transpersonal body work by integrating transpersonal psychology, Lomi body work (a synthesis of Gestalt therapy and structural integration), and psychosynthesis. Moss (1981) combined Gestalt therapy, feminist therapy (radical therapy, Reichian therapy, and bioenergetics), and the movement and energy work of Doris Breyer into a "feminist body psychotherapy."

The efficacy of Gestalt therapy in working with the body has been confirmed in a variety of studies. In a recent study of body image Clance, Thompson, Simerly, and Weiss (1994) showed that Gestalt therapy can positively affect body-cathexis/self-cathexis scores. Hill, Beutler, and Daldrup (1989) treated adult females suffering with active rheumatoid arthritis using a focused Gestalt therapy; the results suggest that high levels of patient participation are related to reduced patient distress. Donley (1990) described a physical approach to psychotherapy based on the contact-withdrawal cycle of experiencing. Sheets (1988) found that Gestalt group work and process-oriented body work can help augment the healing process of codependents when used with other therapies. O'Grady (1986) found that a bioenergetic body technique made the Gestalt "two-chair" dialogue more effective. Stein (1984) discovered that Gestalt awareness exercises resulted in a measurable decrease in anxiety. Woods (1983) investigated the relationship of anger expression to chronic arthritis pain utilizing Gestalt expressive techniques; she discovered a relationship between anger and arthritis pain.

On the negative side, however, some researchers have found certain Gestalt techniques ineffective with somatic-psychological complaints. Coffey (1986) found that although short-term Gestalt group therapy proved somewhat helpful to bulimics, it was no more effective than other treatments. K. Z. Smith (1981) found no measurable reduction in self-reported levels of psychic pain and stress in subjects treated with the Gestalt method of "acting out" images of personal pain.

Personality and Developmental Theory and Research

Gestalt therapy has long been criticized as lacking a fully articulated model of personality and development. This is partly attributable to the heirs of Gestalt therapy not following Goodman's exposition of the "self as contact" given in the original *Gestalt Therapy* (Perls, Hefferline, & Goodman, 1951); many of the critics appear unaware of this model. The late Isadore From and his students in New York pursued this direction by attempting to develop a "Gestalt language" with which to frame personality and its disturbances (From, 1984/1994). Likewise, Cahalan (1983) returned to the existential and social aspects of Gestalt therapy theory and sought to elaborate a more complete theory of personality. Norton (1980) presented a model of child development based on a Perlsian understanding of oral aggression—an inherent "hunger" for growth—in which developmental stages are marked by the child's perception of the environment and growing organizational abilities.

Other writers propose augmenting Gestalt therapy with more established theories. For example, Breshgold and Zahm (1992) and Tobin (1990) suggested utilizing Kohut's self-psychology theory to create a Gestalt model of development. Mullen (1990) proposed further attention to constructive developmental theory because of Gestalt therapy's central tenets of contact and contact boundaries.

Relationship to Constructivism: Ground over Figure

To close this section of the discussion and draw together its many threads, we turn to the idea of constructivism. Constructivism, or the idea that human beings tend to create reality, is a very old notion, dating back probably to ancient Greece. More recently we can trace the development of constructivist ideas from Immanuel Kant to the experimental studies of the Gestalt psychologists, Exner, Ehrenfels, Wertheimer, Koffka, and Köhler, and ultimately to Gestalt therapy and the modern schools of constructivist psychology. It can be argued that Gestalt therapy in many ways anticipated modern constructivist theory. Gestalt psychology discovered that humans perceive phenomena in an organized *whole*, a *Gestalt* against a background that, by virtue of its presence and properties, lends form to the perceived whole. Kurt Lewin (1917) articulated this idea from his experience as a soldier in World War I and utilized this concept as the foundation for his field theory. The founders of Gestalt therapy developed this idea into a new psychotherapy by asserting that humans organize their perception and experience—indeed, their personal "worlds"—around things that are of personal interest or concern. Consequently, the Gestalt model is grounded in constructivist thought and offers practitioners of any theoretical persuasion a "lens" through which to see phenomena within the psychotherapeutic context (Wheeler, 1994). The Gestalt model provides access as well to a coherent value system (Zinker, 1994; Zinker & Nevis, 1994). Wheeler (1994), in discussing the Gestalt model and the usefulness of its various "lenses," summarizes by saying:

> The Gestalt model, with its emphasis on field unity, its insistence that the "self" is not prior to the "other," but that both arise phenomenologically in the same experiential act of feeling and constructing the "self boundary," holds out the promise that we may yet unify psychology and psychotherapy in a different direction: the direction of holism, humanism in the communitarian sense, and true ecology of the mind and spirit. (1994, p. 29)

CONCLUSION: T'SHUVAH

Martin Buber had a word for it: *t'shuvah*. It is a Hebrew term meaning both a turning and a renewal, a return to the roots for sustenance. Regardless of how talented and innovative a therapist he indeed was, Fritz Perls did not espouse Gestalt therapy in its purest sense. Often he merely acted out his own personal style within the situation of the moment. Gestalt therapy has had both to share in the success of Perls's popularization and to live down those of his idiosyncrasies that became associated with the Gestalt name. As is written in the Bible, "The fathers have eaten sour grapes and the children's teeth are set upon edge" (Ezekiel 18:2). In spite of this, Gestalt therapy has endured and, in the last two decades or so, has sought to reexamine, redefine, and extend itself into new venues. It will continue to renew itself, for, as I have tried to make clear, the simplicity and richness of its model lends itself to many paths that are only now beginning to be explored. Herein lies the future of Gestalt therapy from which it will draw its strength for renewal. As From (1994) said:

> I am not urging a going back to Gestalt therapy, but a getting on with it and a restoring of Gestalt therapy to its proper place in the mainstream of psychotherapy. Much of what I've said may be a requiem for Gestalt but, hopefully, may also facilitate a resurrection of Gestalt therapy, not from the dead, but from being neglected. (p. 17)

Despite the prevailing political and social winds, I believe that Gestalt therapy will survive and prosper in the years to come. To do so calls for *t'shuvah*—a movement toward self-examination and renewal. Gestalt therapy is in the early stages of this renewal, and, as we continue the task of deconstructing and dismissing the follies and foibles of Fritz Perls as well as cherishing his pioneering genius and creative verve, it will continue to grow and develop. Although Gestalt therapy suffers from a colorful and often contradictory history, its theoretical richness and therapeutic efficacy cannot be denied, but this is not what will carry it through. Gestalt therapy is a part of the humanistic-existential-transpersonal tradition, and this is the realm in which miracles occur in the meeting of human hearts. It is this simple truth that will preserve both Gestalt therapy and the humanistic tradition.

REFERENCES

Andrews, J. (1989). *A Gestalt-based family systems therapy: Toward a model of theory integration.* Unpublished doctoral dissertation, Union Institute, Cincinnati, OH.

Au, W. (1991). Gestalt therapy and the spiritual exercises of St. Ignatius. *Studies in Formative Spirituality, 12*(2), 197–213.

Barlow, A. R. (1983). *The derivation of a psychological theory: Gestalt therapy.* Unpublished doctoral dissertation, University of Wollongong, Australia.

Beaumont, E. H. (1976). *Gestalt therapy impasse as a religious process.* Unpublished doctoral dissertation, School of Theology at Claremont, Claremont, CA.

Breshgold, E., & Zahm, S. (1992). A case for the integration of self psychology developmental theory into the practice of Gestalt therapy. *The Gestalt Journal, 15*(1), 61–93.

Cahalan, W. (1983). An elaboration of the Gestalt personality theory: The experience of self in social relations. *The Gestalt Journal, 6*(1), 39–53.

Carlock, C. J., Glaus, K. O'H., & Shaw, C. A. (1992). The alcoholic: A Gestalt view. In E. C. Nevis (Ed.), *Gestalt therapy: Perspectives and applications* (pp. 191–237). New York: Gardner Press.

Chey, J. (1993). *Perceptual organization in schizophrenia: The employment of Gestalt principles.* Unpublished doctoral dissertation, Harvard University, Cambridge, MA.

Clance, P. R., Thompson, M. B., Simerly, D. E., & Weiss, A. (1994). The effects of the Gestalt approach on body image. *The Gestalt Journal, 17*(1), 95–114.

Clemmens, M. (1997). *Getting beyond sobriety: Clinical approaches to long-term recovery.* San Francisco: Jossey-Bass.

Coffey, J. I. (1986). *A short-term Gestalt therapy group approach to the treatment of bulimia.* Unpublished doctoral dissertation, University of North Carolina, Chapel Hill.

Crocker, S. F. (1983). Truth and foolishness in the "Gestalt prayer." *The Gestalt Journal, 6*(1), 4–15.

Doelger, D. K. (1978). *A systematic comparison of Gestalt therapy as written by Frederick S. Perls and the philosophy of the "Tao Te Ching" by Lao Tzu.* Unpublished doctoral dissertation, St. Louis University, St. Louis, MO.

Donley, J. A. (1990). *A somatic approach to psychotherapy.* Unpublished doctoral dissertation, Union Institute, Cincinnati, OH.

Enns, C. Z. (1987). Gestalt therapy and feminist therapy: A proposed integration. *Journal of Counseling and Development, 66*(2), 93–95.

Espy, J. (1994). The character-disordered family system. *The Gestalt Journal, 17*(2), 93–105.

Filippi, L. J. (1990). *Of sweet grapes, wheat berries, and simple meeting: Feminist theology, Gestalt therapy, pastoral counseling, and the earth.* Unpublished doctoral dissertation, School of Theology at Claremont, Claremont, CA.

Frew, J. E. (1982). *A study of interpersonal contact in Gestalt therapy and its relationship to marital adjustment.* Unpublished doctoral dissertation, Kent State University, Kent, OH.

Friedman, M. (1985). *The healing dialogue in psychotherapy.* Northvale, NJ: Jason Aronson.

From, I. (1994). Reflections on Gestalt therapy after thirty-two years of practice: A requiem for Gestalt. *The Gestalt Journal, 17*(2), 7–17. (Original work published 1984).

Gaines, J. (1979). *Fritz Perls: Here and now.* Millbrae, CA: Celestial Arts.

Gayle, R. (1994). *An interaction between Western psychotherapeutic methodology and Eastern Buddhist spirituality.* Unpublished doctoral dissertation, California Institute of Integral Studies, San Francisco.

Green, T. (1985). *Branches of a tree: A study in transpersonal bodywork.* Unpublished doctoral dissertation, Union for Experimenting Colleges and Universities, Cincinnati.

Greenbank, M. (1990). *Home-based families entering treatment: Gestalt family contact styles, family functioning, and ways of coping, with perceived stress.* Unpublished doctoral dissertation, Kent State University, Kent, OH.

Greenberg, E. (1989). Healing the borderline. *The Gestalt Journal, 12*(2), 11–55.

Hamilton, J. D. (1994). *Applications of Gestalt principles to pastoral caring.* Unpublished doctoral dissertation, United Theological Seminary, Dayton, OH.

Harris, C. O. (1992). Gestalt work with psychotics. In E. C. Nevis (Ed.), *Gestalt therapy: Perspectives and applications* (pp. 239–261). New York: Gardner Press.

Hill, D., Beutler, L. E., & Daldrup, R. (1989). The relationship of process to outcome in brief experiential psychotherapy for chronic pain. *Journal of Clinical Psychology, 45*(6), 951–957.

Horne, R. A. (1973). *A world-view synthesis of Gestalt therapy and J. Krishnamurti.* Unpublished doctoral dissertation, California School of Professional Psychology, Los Angeles.

Howard, S. A. (1987). *Family theory and practice: An interpersonal sequential analysis of Boszormenyi-Nagy and Kempler.* Unpublished doctoral dissertation, Fuller Theological Seminary, Pasadena, CA.

Hunt, M. (1993). *The story of psychology.* New York: Anchor.

Hycner, R. (1991). *Between person and person.* Highland, NY: Center for Gestalt Development.

Hycner, R., & Jacobs, L. (1995). *The healing relationship in Gestalt therapy: A dialogic/self psychology approach.* Highland, NY: The Gestalt Journal Press.

Keding, B. M. (1988). *Gestalt therapy: Limitations and extensions necessary for clients with a theistic worldview.* Unpublished master's thesis, CBN University.

Kent, J. P. (1983). *Psychospiritual process in integral psychotherapy: Gestalt therapeutic methods as applied in integral psychotherapeutic counseling.* Unpublished doctoral dissertation, California Institute of Integral Studies, San Francisco.

Kepner, J. I. (1987). *Body process: A Gestalt approach to working with the body in psychotherapy.* New York: Gardner Press.

Kepner, J. I. (1995). *Healing tasks: Psychotherapy with adult survivors of childhood abuse.* San Francisco: Jossey-Bass.

Killoran, C. A. (1993). *A spiritual dimension of Gestalt therapy.* Unpublished doctoral dissertation, Garrett-Evangelical Theological Seminary, Evanston, IL.

Kinzey, D. A. (1988). *The unification of opposites in Gestalt theory and therapy, Patanjali yoga sutras, and Hegelian dialectics.* Unpublished doctoral dissertation, Saybrook Institute, San Francisco, CA.

Koffka, K. (1935/1963). *Principles of Gestalt psychology.* New York: Harcourt, Brace & World.

Kudirka, N. (1992). A talk with Laura Perls about the therapist and the artist. In E.W.L. Smith (Ed.), *Gestalt voices* (pp. 85–92). Norwood, NJ: Ablex.

Therapy 63

Latner, J. (1973). *The Gestalt therapy book*. New York: Bantam.

Latner, J. (1992). The theory of Gestalt therapy. In E. C. Nevis (Ed.), *Gestalt therapy: Perspectives and applications* (pp. 13–56). New York: Gardner Press.

Lax, W. D. (1983). *An historical and comparative analysis of the concept of awareness in Gestalt therapy and mindfulness in Theravada Buddhism*. Unpublished doctoral dissertation, Fielding Institute, Santa Barbara, CA.

Lewin, K. (1917). *Kriegslandschaft* [War landscape]. *Zeitschrift für angewandte Psychologie, 12*, 440–447.

McClure, B. A., Merrill, E., & Russo, T. R. (1994). Seeing clients with an artist's eye: Perceptual simulation exercises. *Simulation and Gaming, 25*(1), 51–60.

McGrath, E. W. (1989). *The impact of Gestalt awareness training on women's self-esteem*. Unpublished doctoral dissertation, University of California, Santa Barbara.

Melnick, J., & Nevis, S. M. (1992). Diagnosis: The struggle for a meaningful paradigm. In E. C. Nevis (Ed.), *Gestalt therapy: Perspectives and applications* (pp. 57–78). New York: Gardner Press.

Merry, U., & Brown, G. I. (1987). *The neurotic behavior of organizations*. New York: Gardner Press.

Moss, L. E. (1981). *A woman's way: A feminist approach to body psychotherapy*. Unpublished doctoral dissertation, Union for Experimenting Colleges and Universities.

Mullen, P. F. (1990, Spring). Gestalt therapy and constructive developmental psychology. *The Gestalt Journal, 13*(1), 69–90.

Nevis, E. C. (1987). *Organizational consulting: A Gestalt approach*. New York: Gardner Press.

Norton, R. F. (1980). *Toward a Gestalt theory of early child development*. Unpublished doctoral dissertation, California School of Professional Psychology, Fresno.

O'Grady, D. F. (1986). *The effects of adding a somatic intervention to the Gestalt two-chair technique on career decision-making*. Unpublished doctoral dissertation, Loyola University, Chicago.

Perls, F. S. (1969). *Ego, hunger, and aggression: The beginning of Gestalt therapy*. New York: Vintage Books. (Original work published 1947)

Perls, F. S. (1973) *Gestalt therapy verbatim*. Moab, UT: Real People Press.

Perls, F., Hefferline, R., & Goodman, P. (1951). *Gestalt therapy: Excitement and growth in the human personality*. New York: Julian Press.

Perls, L. (1992). Concepts and misconceptions of Gestalt therapy. In E.W.L. Smith (Ed.), *Gestalt Voices* (pp. 3–8). Norwood, NJ: Ablex.

Polo, P. M. (1993). The borderline case: A consideration from the point of view of Gestalt therapy. *Studies in Gestalt Therapy, 2*, 53–61.

Polster, E., & Polster, M. (1973). *Gestalt therapy integrated: Contours of theory and practice*. New York: Vintage.

Randolph, K. (1988). *An investigation of the relationship between Gestalt resistance styles and perceived family environment*. Unpublished doctoral dissertation, Fielding Institute, Santa Barbara, CA.

Richardson, R. W. (1976). *The implications of Gestalt therapy for Christian ministry*. Unpublished doctoral dissertation, Colgate Rochester Divinity School, Bexley Hall, Crozer Theological Seminary, Rochester, NY.

Roche, K. E. (1986). *The character and process of recovery from alcoholism and the influence of psychological variables from Gestalt therapy homeostasis theory*. Unpublished doctoral dissertation, Kent State University, Kent, OH.

Rubenfeld, I. (1992). Gestalt therapy and the bodymind: An overview of the Rubenfeld synergy ® method. In E. C. Nevis (Ed.), *Gestalt therapy: Perspectives and applications* (pp. 147–177). New York: Gardner Press.

Rutledge, A. L. (1949). *The implications of Gestalt psychology for religion.* Unpublished doctoral dissertation, Southern Baptist Theological Seminary, Louisville, KY.

Scerbo, J. M. (1983). *Reconciliation: The purpose of spirit-directed therapy.* Unpublished doctoral dissertation, Graduate Theological Union, Berkeley, CA.

Sheets, C. H. (1988). *Co-dependency and the healing process.* Unpublished doctoral dissertation. The Union for Experimenting Colleges and Universities, Cincinnati.

Shepard, M. (1975). *Fritz.* New York: E. P. Dutton.

Skolnik, T. (1990, Spring). Boundaries, boundaries, boundaries. *The Gestalt Journal, 13*(1), 55–68.

Smith, E.W.L. (1985). *The body in psychotherapy.* Jefferson, NC: McFarland & Company.

Smith, K. Z. (1981). *Comparison of image and image/Gestalt techniques in stress and pain reduction.* Unpublished doctoral dissertation, Wright Institute.

Stein, J. A. (1984). *The therapeutic effects of awareness on anxiety disorders.* Unpublished doctoral dissertation, Pennsylvania State University, University Park, PA.

Stevens, B. (1975). Gestalt body work. In J. O. Stevens (Ed.), *Gestalt is.* Moab, UT: Real People Press.

Stoehr, T. (1994). *Here, now, next: Paul Goodman and the origins of Gestalt therapy.* San Francisco: Jossey-Bass.

Tobin, S. (1990). Self psychology as a bridge between existential-humanistic psychology and psychoanalysis. *Journal of Humanistic Psychology, 30*(1), 14–63.

Torrey, E. F. (1988). *Nowhere to go: The tragic odyssey of the homeless mentally ill.* New York: Harper & Row.

Turbiner, M. R. (1982). *An empirical phenomenological investigation of the experience of self for adult females.* Unpublished doctoral dissertation, University of Pittsburgh, Pittsburgh, PA.

Van Campen, C. (1994). *Gestalt from Goethe to Gibson: Theories on the vision of beauty and order.* Unpublished doctoral dissertation, Utrecht University, Utrecht, Netherlands.

Walker, J. L. (1970). *Body and soul: An essay on Gestalt therapy and religious experience.* Unpublished doctoral dissertation, Graduate Theological Union, Berkeley, CA.

Wells, C. R. (1985). *Perception and faith: The integration of Gestalt psychology and Christian theology in the thought of C. S. Lewis.* Unpublished doctoral dissertation, Baylor University, Waco, TX.

Wheeler, G. (1991). *Gestalt reconsidered.* New York: Gardner Press.

Wheeler, G. (1994). Introduction: Why gestalt? In G. Wheeler & S. Backman (Eds.), *On intimate ground: A Gestalt approach to working with couples* (pp. 1–30). San Francisco: Jossey-Bass.

Wheeler, G., & Backman, S. (Eds.). (1994). *On intimate ground: A Gestalt approach to working with couples.* San Francisco: Jossey-Bass.

Wilburger, A. (1989). *The importance of Martin Buber's anthropology for psychotherapy: Discussed by the "Gestalt therapy" and the analysis of relationships by Thea Bauried.* Unpublished doctoral dissertation, Innsbruck University, Innsbruck, Austria.

Woods, D. E. (1983). *Arthritis and anger: An application of anger therapy as a Gestalt counseling strategy with rheumatoid arthritic women.* Unpublished doctoral dissertation, University of Arizona, Tucson.

Wysong, J., & Rosenfeld, E. (1982). *An oral history of Gestalt therapy*. Highland, NY: Center for Gestalt Development.

Yalom, I. D. (1980). *Existential psychotherapy*. New York: Basic Books.

Yates, J. M. (1991). *A re-vision of Gestalt therapy: Reframing Gestalt therapy theory through systems theory and field theory*. Unpublished doctoral dissertation, Union Institute, Cincinnati, OH.

Zamborsky, L. J. (1982). *The use of Gestalt therapy with clients expressing religious values*. Unpublished doctoral dissertation, Kent State University, Kent, OH.

Zinker, J. (1977). *Creative process in Gestalt therapy*. New York: Vintage.

Zinker, J. (1994). *In search of good form: Gestalt therapy with couples and families*. San Francisco: Jossey-Bass.

Zinker, J. (1996, February 25). Personal communication with the author. Cleveland Heights, OH.

Zinker, J., & Nevis, S. M. (1994). The aesthetics of Gestalt couples therapy. In G. Wheeler & S. Backman (Eds.), *On intimate ground: A Gestalt approach to working with couples* (pp. 356–399). San Francisco: Jossey-Bass.

6

The Humanistic Psychology of Self-Disclosure, Relationship, and Community

DONALD MOSS

Humanistic psychology has been attacked by many social critics and religious spokespersons as a psychology of selfishness and narcissism insensitive to the social responsibilities of mature human beings (Lasch, 1979; Solomon, 1989). The humanistic psychology movement drew these criticisms down on its own head by 1960s-era excesses in the identification between academic humanistic psychology and the counterculture. The pursuit of self-actualization has been associated with the "me generation," a generation of individuals more interested in personal gratification than service to one's fellow man. Further, Fritz Perls's (1973) infamous Gestalt prayer focused on the separateness and autonomy of persons and not their interdependence (see chapter 5).

Nevertheless, none of the core theories of humanistic psychology, including Gestalt psychology, give credence to a view of a self-in-isolation out of relationship to its context. Nor does humanistic psychology advocate the pursuit of one's own needs at the expense of others. Abraham Maslow's examples of exemplary self-actualizers included such altruistic individuals as Albert Schweitzer and Eleanor Roosevelt, who found their highest self-fulfillment in serving the needs of others. This chapter will highlight the relational nature of the self in self-actualization.

THE SELF, SELF-ACTUALIZATION, AND SELF-ESTEEM

The humanistic psychology of Maslow and the client-centered counseling approach of Carl Rogers took as their foundation a phenomenological theory of the self. Rogers viewed the self as something within the person that tends spontaneously toward an unfolding and ripening process, culminating in a full actualization of this person's potentialities. This view stands in sharp contrast to the earlier behavioristic view that "there is nothing within to develop" (Watson, 1928, p. 41). Rogers also acknowledged the role of positive early childhood experiences and current interpersonal relations in forming a positive self-concept that facilitates self-actualization and, inversely, the role of negative life experiences in creating a neurotic and negative self-concept that inhibits the movement toward fulfillment. Once the individual forms a concept of himself or herself, that person will adopt behaviors that are largely consistent with and supportive of this concept.

Maslow spoke of the self in terms similar to those of Rogers. Maslow also contributed the schema of a hierarchy of needs. Human beings will not proceed up the path of self-actualization until their needs are reliably met at lower levels. The individual whose basic physiological needs for food, drink, and shelter are unmet is less likely to spend his or her energies pursuing esteem or actualizing higher potentials. Similarly, the individual who remains lacking in basic trust will not easily set aside his suspicions and fears and enter into a loving relationship.

Hamacher (1971) cited Harry Stack Sullivan's concept of "reflected appraisals" as crucial in understanding the development of the self. The human infant is immersed in a continuous stream of interpersonal situations and takes into himself or herself many of the positive and negative appraisals of others. Through assimilating these "reflected appraisals," the infant develops expectations and attitudes toward himself or herself. In this fashion the infant surrounded by critical and hostile adults typically develops a disparaging and hostile self-image (Hamacher, 1971, p. 49).

Hamacher also cited Karen Horney's theory of neurotic personality formation. According to Horney, a wide range of adverse factors in the child's early environment, ranging from parental indifference to a lack of reliable warmth, can contribute to a child developing a pervasive basic anxiety, accompanied by deep feelings of isolation and a self-concept of helplessness. Such early negative experiences also predispose a child toward ten neurotic or irrational needs, ranging from a neurotic and excessive need for affection and approval to a neurotic need for perfection and unassailability (Hamacher, 1971, pp. 50–52). The self-esteem of such an individual remains fragile, entirely dependent on these neurotic strategies for living. In other words, such an individual is left with the perception and belief that "I am only a worthwhile person if I can somehow win the unadulterated love and approval of everyone I meet, or if I can achieve the most unrealistic ambitions," without regard to any actual abilities or talents.

MARTIN BUBER: PHILOSOPHY OF DIALOGUE

Martin Buber provided a seminal philosophical framework for the humanistic psychology of the self in relationship. Buber, a Jewish theologian and intellectual, published his work *I and Thou* (*Ich und du*) in its original German edition in 1923. Four decades later, this small, poetic, and often obscure text carried Buber's message of a "dialogical philosophy" to the American movement of humanistic psychology.

I and Thou, I and It

Buber described the human world as falling into two dimensions. He defined these two dimensions linguistically as the realm of the I-thou relationship and the realm of the I-it interaction. For Buber there is no I without the second term in a fundamental pairing: "I-Thou" or "I-it." When a human being says "thou" (or "you" in an intimate sense), he is entering an intimate encounter that transforms oneself as well. The "I" that an individual experiences himself or herself to be is shaped by the mode of connection with the second term in the pairing. When a human being addresses a thou, this individual enters the realm of presence and encounter. In the realm of the I and the thou, the I becomes part of a relationship, experiences self as involved with another, and discovers love as the "responsibility of an I for a You" (Buber, 1923/1970, p. 66).

When an individual addresses an "it"—a thing or object—this individual enters a realm of use and objective knowing. This is the "It-world" of practical utility and objective attributes. Objects in the It-world are knowable and open to manipulation. On the other hand, the other human being, as a thou in encounter, is neither knowable nor useful.

When Buber discusses the "It-world," he means more than simply an area of life where a person interacts with a nonhuman thing. Rather, he is also describing a transformed mode of interaction that focuses on objectivity and usefulness. A nonhuman object may also transcend the It-world. Buber points out that a human being may encounter a tree as a thou, a limitless presence that one appreciates in its relatedness to oneself (Buber, 1923/1970, pp. 57–58). At that moment the tree is no longer simply a visual object, an array of organic processes, or a source for lumber; rather, in this encounter I become aware of my relationship with this tree as a living presence of nature.

Inversely, one human being may interact with another human being as an "it," a useful object to be exploited and perceived objectively, outside of any personal relationship. The salesclerk at the supermarket may be merely an anonymous "it," a helpful source of services. Or, if the customer pauses and allows a personal encounter to unfold, the objective dimension may dissolve into a sense of the presence of a thou, another human person without definition or borders.

Buber described all human societies and cultures as tending to enlarge the realm of the "it-world," the realm of knowledge and utility. However, he described the present historical era as one of an especially intense alienation and loss of dialogue:

> In sick ages it happens that the It-world, no longer irrigated and fertilized by the living currents of the You-world, becomes a gigantic swamp phantom and overpowers man. As he accommodates himself to a world of objects that no longer achieve any presence for him, he succumbs to it. (Buber, 1923/1970, p. 102)

In contrast, Buber described healthy ages as times in which confidence and inspiration flow from "men of the spirit" to all the people, intermingling the dimension of personal presence and spiritual encounter with the practical dimensions of life (p. 102). Buber carried this mission into his intensely personal manner of teaching. A meeting with Buber was a challenge to authentic dialogue, an exposure of oneself to Buber in an intensely personal fashion, beyond all differences of age, language, or culture (Kaufmann, in Buber, 1923/1970, p. 22).

Applications of Buber's Philosophy

Buber's message carried a special appeal for humanistic psychology, and many of the humanistic efforts of the 1960s were aimed at restoring the dimension of dialogue and encounter within contemporary life. Buber's description of the I-thou relationship served as a paradigm, first of all, for the deep personal encounter that stands at the core of psychotherapy. The encounter model remains basic for all humanistic psychotherapies and group therapies (Brace, 1992). Both diagnostic knowledge and practical therapeutic objectives are critiqued in humanistic psychology insofar as they detract from this core of authentic encounter between doctor and patient. The first and most fundamental gift that the existential or humanistic therapist brings to the patient is to be with that individual in an immediate affirming presence beyond professional roles and technical interventions (Rogers, 1951; Moss, 1989, 1990).

One apparent divergence between Buber and his disciples in humanistic psychology lies in the critical or adulatory attitude toward "experience." Buber described experiencing as a degraded mode of relating to objects (Buber, 1923/1970, p. 38). Humanistic psychologists, on the other hand, regard immediate, feelingful "experiencing" as the most appropriate way to interact and be present with other persons. This difference may be entirely linguistic, since two distinct German words are frequently translated into the English word "experience." *Erfahren* connotes practical knowledge, learning by doing, and utilizing a thing or object. This is the kind of experiencing that Buber associated with the I-it relationship. *Erleben*, on the other hand, comes from a root word meaning to live and connotes to be with a situation in an emotional fashion and to live through an experience. This is the vital, fully emotional, and lively experiencing that humanistic psychologists advocate.

In a remarkable 1957 dialogue, Martin Buber and Carl Rogers compared their viewpoints on mutuality and healing (Kirschenbaum & Henderson, 1989). Buber and Rogers found common ground in their beliefs that healing takes place through a meeting of two persons and, at least initially, through one individual's acceptance of another. They diverged in Rogers's greater emphasis on the primacy of self-actualization and Buber's on dialogue (see Friedman, 1994, for additional detail). A number of authors have found a basis in Buber's work for the understanding of psychotherapy (Heard, 1993), family therapy (Friedman, 1989; Inger, 1993), and personal relationships (Ticho, 1974).

Beyond therapeutic circles, Buber's distinction between the world of encounter and the alienated "It-world" also served as a paradigm for humanistic social reform and communitarian values. The encounter-group movement sought to recover the trust, openness, and authentic presence in dialogue that Buber had highlighted.

THE PSYCHOLOGY OF SELF-DISCLOSURE

Sidney Jourard, Self-Disclosure, and the Transparent Self

Sidney Jourard began the first serious empirical investigations linking self-discovery with disclosure of oneself to others (1964, 1971b), see chapter 21 in part II for the chronology of Jourard's life and career and a critical examination of his theory). Jourard's research began with a fascination with the dramatic openness of the client in psychotherapy. How is it that a near stranger will so often pour out his or her deepest secrets and then comment that "you are the first person that I have ever become completely honest with" (Jourard, 1971b, p. x)?

Jourard's investigations led him to the hypothesis that human beings can achieve health and fullest personal development only when they take the risk of being themselves with others (1971b, p. ix). Further, he concluded that no human being "can come to know himself except as an outcome of disclosing himself to another person" (1971b, p. 6).

Jourard's research demonstrated the personal value of self-disclosure, but the same research also demonstrated the pervasive presence in human society, and even in the family, of dissembling and concealment. Much of human life is transacted like a poker game, with each participant masking his or her face and masking the cards held at the moment. Children and parents, and husbands and wives, are strangers in many respects to one another (1971b, p. 6).

Jourard acknowledged the necessity for social roles that give shape to the life of society. However, he highlighted the dangers for physical health, self-esteem, and emotional well-being when an individual loses a sense of self independent of the momentary role. He cited the earlier work of Karen Horney, Erich Fromm, and others on the self-alienation that results from excesses in social alienation (Jourard, 1971b).

Jourard observed the particular inhibitions on self-disclosure for American males and the price that this nondisclosure exacts (Jourard, 1971b; Jourard & Landsman, 1960). Males, according to Jourard, selectively ignore both emotional feelings and physical sensations and postpone medical attention to illness beyond the danger point. Similarly, males who frequently avoid recognition of their own feelings are less sensitive to the feelings of their partner in love or marriage.

Jourard identified several concepts conducive to deepening openness and intimacy in relationships (Jourard, 1971a). First, he identified the dyadic effect or dyadic principle. The shortest pathway to inviting self-disclosure is to disclose oneself. Self-disclosure invites disclosure by the other. Expressing warmth or closeness invites expression of closeness by the other, and so on. Second, Jourard described the relationship between the human ability to become transparent and the security of the current environment. If I am assured of the safety and trustworthiness of both the physical surroundings and my current companions, I will more easily take the step to let you get to know me. Therapeutic conversation begins with assuring the client of his or her physical and emotional safety, including privacy, and proceeds only then to openness. Authentic dialogue presumes that both participants make themselves vulnerable and available. When one party remains distant and aloof, openness is inhibited. Finally, Jourard concluded that the ideal pathway to assure optimal mental health lies in maintaining at least one intimate relationship within which one freely discloses the entirety of one's self. This willingness to be fully open and vulnerable with one person assures a unification of identity beyond the fragmentation of modern life.

Continuations of Jourard's Work

Jourard died prematurely, with his research on self-disclosure still in the formative stage. His work has been continued by a number of others (see Derlega & Berg, 1987). I will highlight a handful of the hundreds of studies directly inspired by Jourard's work. In a study of repression and sensitization Friedman (1977) found evidence that self-disclosure facilitates the movement from self-alienation to self-integration; in other words, revealing oneself to others helps one to know, accept, and unify one's own personality. Mahon (1982), studying an undergraduate population, verified that the more individuals self-disclose, the less loneliness they feel; inversely, the more interpersonally dependent they are, the more lonely they are. Interestingly, the magnitude of recent life changes had no measurable impact on the subjects' loneliness. Stokes (1987) also investigated the close linkage between subjective isolation and the failure to self-disclose.

Another team of investigators (LeVine & Franco, 1983; Franco & LeVine, 1985) studied the impact of therapist variables, including gender, ethnicity (Anglo or Mexican American), and verbal style (nondirective, directive, and neutral), on self-disclosure. They found large but complex impacts on self-disclosure as measured by the Jourard Self-Disclosure Questionnaire, as well as by the subjects' willingness to sign up for a private counseling session. For example, Anglo subjects of both genders and Hispanic females were more likely to agree to a private session with a male examiner if he employed a more directive verbal style.

Other studies explored the relationship between the content and length of early recollections and current self-disclosure (Barrett, 1983), the (negligible) impact of attending a marital encounter on measured self-disclosure (Milholland & Avery, 1982), and the impact of muscle relaxation on self-disclosure (Malec, Sipprelle, & Behring, 1978). Finally, two teams critiqued Jourard's Self-Disclosure Questionnaire for (1) not satisfactorily measuring the kind of self-disclosure Jourard's theory refers to (Bayne, 1977) and (2) being confounded by test items that primarily measure poor adjustment (Raphael & Dohrenwend, 1987).

Raphael and Dohrenwend (1987) attribute some of the inconsistent results in the self-disclosure research literature to the internal inconsistency in the questionnaire.

James Pennebaker: The Healing Power of Confiding in Others

James Pennebaker and his colleagues have conducted a broad program of empirical research, demonstrating in abundant detail the experiential and physiological importance of confession and self-disclosure (Pennebaker, 1989, 1990; Pennebaker, Kiecolt-Glaser, & Glaser, 1988; Pennebaker, Barger, & Tiebout, 1989; Pennebaker, Colder, & Sharp, 1990). Like Jourard, Pennebaker was struck by the human need to confess one's deepest and often most shameful secrets in psychotherapy, but also in a variety of other contexts. Pennebaker cited what he called the "polygraph confession effect." In many instances, individuals break down and disclose their crime during a "lie-detection exam" and then show a paradoxical effect. The guilty party, now facing probable conviction, appears to relax and show relief. At least occasionally, such individuals display a grateful friendliness with the polygrapher. Pennebaker (1990, p. 16) cited the case of a bank vice-president who confessed to embezzlement during a polygraphic exam. His heart rate and blood pressure lowered, his hands were no longer sweaty, and his respiration slowed. This same white-collar criminal later sent the polygrapher a Christmas card from the penitentiary. Pennebaker concluded that the process of concealing the truth—the inhibition or withholding of one's story—involves demanding psychological and physiological effort, with serious emotional and physiological consequences. In confession or personal disclosure the individual is liberated from that inhibitory work.

Pennebaker's research led him to a theory of inhibition and confession (1990, p. 21), which I will summarize here:

1. Inhibition is physical work.
2. Inhibition affects short-term biological change and long-term health.
3. Inhibition influences thinking abilities.
4. Confrontation/confession reduces the effects of inhibition.
5. Confrontation/confession forces a rethinking of events.

Pennebaker and his colleagues conducted a series of creative investigations to document the full psychophysiological impact of self-disclosure. In two studies, college students were instructed to write about either traumatic experiences or superficial topics for fifteen to twenty minutes a day for four consecutive days. Those students journaling about traumatic events showed a reduction in the use of medical care in the ensuing four months (Pennebaker & Beall, 1986) and an enhancement in serum immune function for up to eight weeks after the journaling (Pennebaker, Kiecolt-Glaser, & Glaser, 1988). Additional studies found that writing about traumatic experiences produced better performance at school and work (Pennebaker, 1995b, p. 4). Further, not talking about or not acknowledging negative experiences was associated with increased health problems, elevated autonomic nervous system activity, and cognitive rumination (Pennebaker, 1995b, p. 4).

Oral disclosure of traumatic events can also have immediate and lasting physiological effects. In one impressive study, Pennebaker, Barger, and Tiebout (1989) recorded physiological measures while Holocaust survivors described their concentration-camp experiences to an interviewer. Many of these individuals had not discussed their concentration-camp experiences in any detail with a single person in over thirty years, so this disclosure was a personally meaningful and often emotional event. Participants in the study were categorized into three groups. Galvanic skin response (GSR) proved to be the most statistically significant physiological index of response to disclosure. The high disclosers really "let go" during the interview, disclosed deeply traumatic memories, and showed a lessening of GSR as the interview progressed. The low disclosers were more guarded in their personal disclosures, showed visible signs of conflict and inhibition during the interview, and displayed increases in GSR as the interview progressed. An undifferentiated third group fell in between in their response to the interview.

The study showed that both the high-disclosing group and the undifferentiated group utilized less medical care in subsequent months, whereas the low disclosers showed an increased utilization in medical care. For this latter group, self-disclosure of long-suppressed memories seems to have adversely affected their health. The more the individual's GSR decreased during traumatic disclosures, the less likely the subject was to visit a physician for illness. Pennebaker and his colleagues cite these results as evidence that for most human beings the best guideline for coping is the familiar "confession is good for the soul" hypothesis. They also acknowledged, however, that for a minority of low-disclosing subjects, the contrasting "let sleeping dogs lie" hypothesis may be a better guideline for coping with painful memories.

Further research, inspired by the work of Jourard and Pennebaker, reveals the true complexity of self-disclosure. A recent volume edited by Pennebaker (1995a) contains fifteen contributions by researchers in six countries highlighting the culturally variable significance of both self and self-disclosure, the cognitive processes involved in inhibiting and disclosing, the role of emotional expression in psychosomatic health and disease, and the clinical implications of research on self-disclosure. In this volume Georges (1995) discussed the historical development of the positive Western valuation of confession and self-disclosure from the time of the Stoics (first and second centuries A.D.), who saw disclosure as a tool for self-knowledge, through the early Christian church, where confession was seen as healing the spirit, to the work of Freud, who advocated the healing of internal conflicts through the "fundamental rule" of unrestricted disclosure of all associations and reactions to the therapist. Georges also discussed the equally absolute cultural sanction against self-disclosure among the Balinese and the Chinese. She cited Kleinman's investigations of psychiatry in the People's Republic of China, where the patient is typically cautioned to "swallow the seeds of the bitter melon" and to avoid expressing distress (Kleinman, 1988).

THE ENCOUNTER-GROUP MOVEMENT AND THE PSYCHOLOGY OF COMMUNITY

William Schutz and the Interpersonal Underworld

William Schutz was a leader in the encounter-group movement, was active as a facilitator and instructor at Esalen, and was the author of several influential books on humanistic psychology, body therapy, and encounter groups (Schutz, 1966, 1967, 1971). Schutz embodied the humanistic value of complete personal openness, which he firmly believed would facilitate resolution of any difficult personal issue or conflict. He wrote frankly about his LSD trips, his experiences of his own body in nude encounter sessions, and his anxiety over the possible meaning of cryptic comments by Fritz Perls (see Schutz, 1971).

Participants in encounter groups with Schutz were encouraged to "let it all hang out" and to "stop bullshitting," that is, to stop engaging in any kind of self-deception or interpersonal concealment. His method was to bring a painful personal issue to full exposure before the group, encourage other members of the group to respond spontaneously and honestly, and to confront any defensiveness or inhibitions that blocked this full open processing.

Like Jourard, Schutz attacked the devious and hypocritical trends in contemporary life, the social pretending that blocks a realistic awareness of problems. Schutz frequently turned the full attention of an encounter group to the individual's physical posture or muscular tensions, which in many cases serve to block feeling, to inhibit self-expression, or to portray a false message about oneself. The danger for the human being when even one's own body becomes involved in "living a lie" is that one becomes alienated from oneself, loses identity, and becomes progressively more cut off from real vital interactions with others (1971, pp. 38–39).

Schutz's Contributions to Relationship Assessment

Schutz developed a useful, practical understanding of interpersonal relationships that continues to guide many marital and family counselors today. Schutz's approach is based on identifying what he called the Fundamental Interpersonal Relationship Orientation (or FIRO) of each person. Schutz's FIRO-B, FIRO-F, and other relationship inventories are designed to measure this fundamental orientation; these basic questionnaire tools continue in widespread use today.

Schutz identified three dimensions within interpersonal relationships and characterized the individual's behavior and feelings on each of these dimensions: Inclusion, Control, and Affection. There are many possible profiles for each of the three dimensions (see a commentary on the FIRO-B test by Leo Ryan, 1977). There are also many possible ways to utilize these dimensions to characterize interpersonal behavior and an individual's experiences within a relationship (Schutz, 1966).

The Inclusion dimension involves the individual's readiness to reach out and invite involvement and companionship with others and to accept or welcome the overtures of others for such companionship. On the Inclusion dimension, an individual may be what Leo Ryan labels a Loner, a person who neither seeks contact with others nor accepts others' efforts at involvement. Inversely, a People Gatherer both initiates sharing and companionship and welcomes others' invitations to companionship. An Inhibited Individual wants others to initiate companionship, yet is reluctant to reach out himself or herself. An undersocial person, who has little inclusion, tends to be introverted and withdrawn and to experience feelings of unworthiness and expectations of rejection by others. An oversocial person, high in inclusion, tends toward extroversion, seems driven to seek acceptance and companionship, and may experience unacknowledged doubts about being accepted.

The Control dimension involves the individual's readiness to take charge of situations, tasks, and other persons and willingness to accept the influence and control of others. An individual may be control-seeking or excessively submissive. Some persons, whom Ryan (1977) labels Rebels, are neither able to exercise control nor to accept others' control. Their orientation seems to be "You don't tell me what to do, and I won't tell you what to do." Other persons may be Matchers, who will accept moderate responsibility and control as long as other persons involved in the situation do likewise (Ryan, 1977).

The Affection dimension involves the individual's readiness to express and seek warmth and closeness and to accept others' efforts at warmth and closeness. Here too there are many possible profiles: Optimists who both initiate and accept high amounts of affection, Pessimists who neither give nor accept affection, and Cautious Lovers who want affection from others, but hesitate to express warmth themselves (Ryan, 1977).

Schutz's framework, as simple as it may seem, is able to produce a rich understanding of much interpersonal behavior. For instance, a wife who is eager to receive affection from an unaffectionate husband may remind him over and over of her unmet yearnings. The husband, in turn, may perceive the wife's reminders as efforts to control him, since his own interpersonal orientation emphasizes an avoidance of others' control. Yet the wife is acting primarily out of her affection needs and not out of any desire to control. Such distinctions frequently enable partners within a relationship to understand one another's needs, feelings, and statements more effectively and accurately and to better resolve recurrent interpersonal conflicts.

Schutz's framework shows that the seeming focus of many marital and family arguments, whether it be sharing a bathroom, coming home from work late, or selecting a vacation spot, are in most cases significant only because they symbolize basic differences or antagonisms among the parties' interpersonal orientations. The factual problems are more easily solved when the basic interpersonal sources of hurt and resentment are recognized.

Schutz contributed other useful observations about the task of building more satisfying relationships in a society that does not support intimacy. He pointed out, for example, that an individual can work out matters of inclusion or control with an entire family or work group at once, negotiating creative solutions that meet the inclusion and control needs of all concerned. However, to establish affection requires one-on-one contact, and failure to prioritize such intimacy will invariably frustrate affection needs. This principle holds true for parent-child, husband-wife, and friendship relationships.

THE HUMANISTIC PSYCHOLOGY OF COMMUNITY

William Schutz (1971), Fritz Perls (1969), and Carl Rogers (1970) contributed substantially to the understanding of small-group process and its power for unleashing personal change in the individual. Later Gestalt therapists developed a more detailed transactional understanding of the interpersonal process in groups and the strategic use of interactions among members as a therapeutic tool (Polster & Polster, 1973).

Many figures within humanistic psychology have envisioned wider horizons, creating experiments in communal living, undertaking local political activism, and seeking to remake the larger society. Esalen, founded in 1962, was the prototype of humanistic communities and more than three decades later remains a center for humanistic education, the cultivation of self-actualizing lifestyles, and experiments in new modes of community. Each such experiment in "intentional community building" then becomes a kind of experimental laboratory testing once again the viability of living by the humanistic principles elaborated in this chapter. These communities are called intentional communities because they seek to create attachment and involvement among persons who have not been spontaneously linked by family, work, or geographic proximity. The Fellowship for Intentional Community publishes a journal called *Communities: Journal of Cooperative Living*, as well as a directory listing hundreds of cooperative communities (see Polowniak, 1994, pp. 231–234, for a list of organizations supporting communitarian lifestyles).

Jack Gibb, Trust Theory, and TORI

Jack Gibb (1961, 1991) developed a conceptual framework for understanding and building humanistic communities. He also created a network of actual humanistic communities and fellowships called TORI, existing without geographic borders, dedicated to creating the conditions for optimal interpersonal sharing and personal growth. Gibb proposed a "trust theory" and highlighted the four dimensions of trust, openness, realizing, and interdepending, which form the acronym TORI. TORI is now a community of several thousand lay and professional people dedicated to meeting regularly, often in intensive weekend group experiences, in a climate nurturing interpersonal trust and openness.

Gibb emphasizes the role of fear in constraining personal growth and wellness and elaborates a series of "discovering processes" designed to enhance trust and heal fears: (1) trusting involves "being me"—accepting, centering, and creating oneself; (2) opening involves "showing me"—letting others in, disclosing oneself, and spontaneously tuning into others; (3) realizing involves "doing what I want"—discovering and clarifying one's own wants, asserting them, and fulfilling oneself; and (4) interdepending involves "being with others"—participating, cooperating, joining, and sharing with others. According to Gibb's model, development of these four dimensions leads to an optimal sense of fellowship and community with others.

Gibb (1961, 1991) also highlights a number of fear-driven defensive processes that interfere with the establishment of healthy relationships and community: (1) "de-personing" involves abandoning one's spontaneous personal experiencing and expressing, and hiding out in detachment, impersonal actions, and social roles; (2) "masking" involves building a facade, concealing one's actual feelings and intentions, and consciously pursuing a hidden agenda and hidden strategies to obtain what one wants; (3) "oughting" involves abandoning spontaneity and acting out of what one should do or what others expect of one; and (4) "depending" involves controlling oneself and the other, sacrificing one's own fulfillment to the task of making others meet one's needs.

Much of Gibb's work consists of further exploring how to be personal, spontaneous, and transparent or open with others, and identifying practical steps useful in creating communities that allow this kind of interpersonal openness to occur (Bradford, Gibb, & Benne, 1964). Gibb's research involves exploring many practical aspects of community building: environmental and housing design, modes of artistic self-expression, and open-phone systems, community diaries, and other vehicles for facilitating cohesiveness in intentional communities (Gibb, 1991). Gibb and others have also applied TORI theory to business organizations, education, and the counseling process (Gibb, 1972, 1991; Garner, 1970).

William Polowniak and the Creation of Community

William Polowniak (1994) takes as his point of departure the concepts of humanistic psychology, especially the psychology of self-actualization, and the trust theory of Jack Gibb. His work is dedicated to the practical mechanics of community building. Polowniak explores the naturally occurring sense of community that links human beings in ethnic neighborhoods, church communities, the community in the workplace, and the community that emerges among individuals all facing the same crisis (earthquake victims, members of Alcoholics Anonymous, or soldiers in combat). His work is equally theoretical and practical, exploring how such spontaneous communities emerge and cohere, but also how we can make them more cohesive and supportive.

Polowniak identifies four general processes in the development of community: (1) acceptance and membership, which determine who is "in" a community and to what extent each member feels trust and acceptance within the group, (2) decision making, which involves means for sharing information and distributing control over options facing the group, (3) productivity, which involves the ability of a group to mobilize its resources toward common goals, and (4) organization, which describes the functional structure of the group, its internal communication, routines, and emotional atmosphere. A healthy community gives each member a feeling of acceptance, a belief that he or she can influence personally relevant group decisions, and a trust that the group will utilize its resources to accomplish goals of relevance to the person and will establish conditions that allow the individual to pursue his or her own goals. When any community—whether a workplace, a neighborhood, or a city—breaks down and fails to realize members' needs along one or more of these dimensions, a number of negative results ensue: internal conflicts among groups or individuals, departure or noncooperation of members, deteriorating well-being and motivation among members, and/or the death of the community.

Polowniak also highlights intentional communities, those that result from the decision of two or more individuals to cast their lives together in one course. He includes marriage and family life as an intentional community, formed by decision and maintained only by a continued commitment of both parties. Spontaneity, trust, and open expression of feelings are signs of healthy community in a corporation or a marriage. Experiences with high-trust communities such as Esalen, T-groups, and TORI provide lessons for enhancing the health of more mainstream communities. Polowniak highlights the need to maintain (1) a trust-saturated environment, (2) a sense of freedom of space, a comfortable, nonrestrictive physical layout conducive to spontaneity and interaction, (3) a manageable group size conducive to the kind of disclosure and intimacy desired, and several other factors that have proven to enhance intimacy and cohesiveness in high-trust communities (Polowniak, 1994, pp. 81–84).

CRITIQUES OF THE HUMANISTIC APPROACH TO RELATIONSHIP AND COMMUNITY

Neither the theory nor the practice of humanistic psychology advocates a selfish self, a self seeking gratification out of relationship with others. Many of the central figures of humanistic psychology devoted their work to discovering ways to enhance deeper intimacy, disclosure to other persons, and cohesive relationships and communities. Further, Galbreath (1991) subjected the four Christian Gospels to a close content analysis and found strong parallels between the gospel presentation of Jesus and fourteen characteristics associated with Maslow's self-actualization model: acceptance, spontaneity, naturalness, problem centering, need for privacy, autonomy, and so on.

Nevertheless, the criticism of humanistic psychology as a selfish psychology persists, both from moral and theoretical standpoints. One central critique of humanistic psychology is that even its theories of relationship and community remain egocentric. Jourard's work advocates self-disclosure on the basis that it enhances one's own personal growth. Gibb emphasizes individual dimensions of seeking community—individual self-expression, spontaneity, and need satisfaction. Humanistic relationship therapy advocates individual assertion within a marriage because it serves better self-actualization. Even Maslow's transpersonal psychology, which advocates self-transcendence and altruism, seems to do so on the basis that it is the highest tool for personal fulfillment. In other words, the humanistic movement began with a basic self-actualization paradigm and remains caught now within its paradigm, even when it seeks to advocate relationship and community. Humanists may argue back that most of these "selfish" practices are conducive to the well-being of the dyad or the community, but the critique of the paradigm's conceptual limitations remains. The paradigm, for example, limits one's openness for any concept of submission or subordination to the greater well-being of a spouse, family, or community as ends in themselves.

Another pointed criticism is that some of humanistic psychology's theories have been simplistic, missing the complexities of human nature, and for that reason have led to unintended negative consequences. Lasch (1979), for example, critiqued the radical humanistic belief in sexual liberation. Humanistic psychologists, according to Lasch, advocated greater spontaneity and personal expressiveness in sexual encounters to make sex a more normal and healthy part of life. The traditional restrictive and possessive attitude toward sex seemed to inhibit natural sexual expression and feeling. Sexual liberation would allow more intense personal and emotional pleasure in erotic activity. The movement for sexual liberation, however, has backfired for many, serving to emphasize the technique and behavior of sex in detachment from the emotional context of a long-term relationship. The attempt to free sex to be a more "total experience" has produced a series of empty, numbing sexual experiences, lacking the depth of true intimacy or commitment (Lasch, 1979, pp. 338–341). The motion picture *Looking for Mr. Goodbar* conveyed the ultimate alienation of an anonymous sexual quest. Lasch carried his critique farther, viewing the human-potential movement as a continuation of the nineteenth-century American belief in atomizing individualism (Lasch, 1979, pp. 36–37). He expressed concern that the extremes of humanistic rhetoric reinforce an "isolation of the self," self-absorption, and self-indulgence.

Other elements of humanistic relationship theory and practice occasionally misfire. Solomon (1989, p. 12) observes that increased assertiveness is a positive tool for self-development, but that assertive entitlement, the view that "the world and others owe me gratification once I learn to express my needs," is a reversion to a primitive narcissism. She critiques the narcissistic belief that "I am the center of the world," as well as what she calls the myth of autonomy, the myth of romantic love, the myth of positive divorce, and a number of other contemporary myths (Solomon, 1989, pp. 9–21).

Similarly, some of the inconsistent and negative outcomes in research on self-esteem enhancement suggest that overly simplistic views of self-esteem as a mental-verbal self-appraisal are counterproductive (Bednar & Peterson, 1995; Greenier, Kernis, & Waschull, 1995; Kernis, 1995; Epstein & Morling, 1995). Group self-esteem interventions often overemphasize writing and reciting verbal self-affirmations and forming positive mental images of oneself, divorced from accompanying changes in behavior. Such cognitive interventions can facilitate behavioral change and life changes, but they can also produce individuals who speak more positively about themselves but continue to engage in antisocial, self-defeating, or impulsive behaviors. The long-term result of such empty changes is realistic self-doubts, realistic negative self-attributions, and realistic pessimism about the future. The development of autonomy, self-efficacy based on competence, and realistic life skills may provide a more solid long-term basis for self-esteem (Deci & Ryan, 1995; Kernis, 1995).

It is not only conservatives who have critiqued humanistic psychology for its egocentrism and social blind spots. Rollo May (1969) critiqued the post–World War II changes in sexual morality and the dangerous new assumptions about romantic behavior, which have too often separated sexuality from intimacy. May called for a return to a personal communion between lovers. Diana Baumrind, speaking from a dual perspective as psychologist and Marxist humanist, redefines self-actualization in a moral context balancing individual rights and responsibilities with the well-being of others. She argues that justice and compassion are implicit in "true self-interest" (1992, p. 268), and that self-actualization depends on "right relations with others" (1992, p. 258; see chapter 15 in part II of this volume for a discussion of Baumrind's approach of "responsible relatedness" among human beings). Chapter 9 on "Feminist Psychology and Humanistic Psychology" in this volume also provides longer-term political and cultural perspectives on the changes under critique here, which did not begin with but only culminated in the era of humanistic psychology. One might assert, for example, that many of the present-day changes in sexual mores and gender roles began on the day in 1831 that George Sand moved out of her chateau, left her husband, donned trousers, began to take lovers, and created an independent life in Paris. "My profession," wrote Sand, in a sentiment entirely at one with humanistic psychology, "is to be free" (Wernick, 1996, p. 126).

In summary, both conservative and radical social critics and religious spokespersons have decried the overemphasis on the concept of self-actualization in humanistic theory and practice. The contributions of the humanistic movement, however, are undeniable. This chapter has highlighted the rich armamentarium of personal change techniques, intimacy-building techniques, and community-building techniques developed and perfected over the past three decades. Humanistic psychology has also contributed a set of humanistic values that for the most part serve to enhance both individual growth and relationship. The message of the critics seems to be that we must recognize the dark shadows or the blind spots of humanistic values and protect ourselves from their unintended harm.

A number of authors have suggested supplementing humanistic psychological concepts with other conceptual frameworks. Rolf von Eckartsberg (1992) asserted that social psychology must be polyparadigmatic, shifting from model to model to do justice to the complex nature of social phenomena. He proposed a "Way of Life" psychology as an integration of multiple perspectives. Lowenstein (1990) advocated that humanistic psychologists adopt an "eclectic realism," supplementing the self-actualization model with concepts taken from other schools of thought. Lowenstein also recommended a tempering or moderating of the naïve optimism of humanistic psychology and a better recognition of the real limits of human freedom.

Similarly, in Martin Buber's famous dialogue with Carl Rogers, Buber differed from Rogers's optimism in that Buber insisted that human nature is polar, tending toward both good and bad, and not to be trusted fully (Friedman, 1994). We may close with this reservation that both traditional religious values and social philosophies may provide a broader context within which to apply the insights of humanistic psychology. It suggests the arrogance of a science in its infancy to absolutize one's own newfound perspective and to ignore the tempering messages of other viewpoints, including the perennial wisdoms enfolded into traditional religious values.

REFERENCES

Barrett, D. (1983). Early recollections as predictors of self-disclosure and interpersonal style. *Individual Psychology: Journal of Adlerian Theory, Research, and Practice, 39*(1), 92–98.

Baumrind, D. (1992). Leading an examined life: The moral dimension of daily conduct. In W. M. Kurtines, M. Azmitia, & J. L. Gewirtz (Eds.), *The role of values in psychology and human development* (pp. 256–280). New York: John Wiley.

Bayne, R. (1977). The meaning and measurement of self-disclosure. *British Journal of Guidance and Counselling, 5*(2), 159–166.

Bednar, R. L., & Peterson, S. R. (1995). *Self-esteem: Paradoxes and innovations in clinical theory and practice*. Washington, DC: American Psychological Association.

Brace, K. (1992). I and thou in interpersonal psychotherapy. Approaches to selfhood [Special theme issue]. *Humanistic Psychologist, 20*(1), 41–57.

Bradford, L. P., Gibb, J., & Benne, K. (Eds.). (1964). *T-group theory and laboratory method*. New York: Wiley.

Buber, M. (1970). *I and thou*. (W. Kaufmann, Trans.). New York: Charles Scribner's Sons. (Original work *Ich und du* published 1923)

Cissna, K. N., & Anderson, R. (1994). The 1957 Martin Buber–Carl Rogers dialogue, as dialogue. Dialogue [Special issue]. *Journal of Humanistic Psychology, 34*(1), 11–45.

Deci, E. L., & Ryan, R. M. (1995). Human autonomy: The basis for true self-esteem. In M. H. Kernis (Ed.), *Efficacy, agency, and self-esteem* (pp. 31–49). New York: Plenum.

Derlega, V. J., & Berg, J. H. (Eds.). (1987). *Self-disclosure: Theory, research, and therapy: Perspectives in social psychology.* New York: Plenum.

Epstein, S., & Morling, B. (1995). Is the self motivated to do more than enhance and/or verify itself? In M. H. Kernis (Ed.), *Efficacy, agency, and self-esteem* (pp. 9–29). New York: Plenum.

Franco, J. N., & LeVine, E. (1985). Effects of examiner variables on reported self-disclosure: Implications for group personality testing. *Hispanic Journal of Behavioral Sciences, 7*(2), 187–197.

Friedman, M. (1977). Self-alienation and sensitization. *Psychological Reports, 41*(3, Pt.1), 746.

Friedman, M. (1989). Martin Buber and Ivan Boszormenyi-Nagi: The role of dialogue in contextual therapy. *Psychotherapy, 26*(3), 402–409.

Friedman, M. (1994). Reflections on the Buber-Rogers dialogue. Dialogue [Special issue]. *Journal of Humanistic Psychology,* 34 (1), 46–65.

Galbreath, P. (1991). Self-actualization as a contemporary Christological title. *Journal of Psychology and Christianity, 10*(3), 237–248.

Garner, H. G. (1970). *Effects of human relations training on the personal, social, and classroom adjustment of elementary school children with behavior problems.* Unpublished doctoral dissertation, University of Florida.

Georges, E. (1995). A cultural and historical perspective on confession. In J. W. Pennebaker (Ed.), *Emotion, disclosure, and health* (pp. 11–22). Washington, DC: American Psychological Association.

Gibb, J. (1961). Defensive communication. *Journal of Communication, 11*(3), 141–148.

Gibb, J. (1972). TORI theory: Consultantless team building. *Journal of Contemporary Business, 1*(3), 33–42.

Gibb, J. (1991). *Trust: A new vision of human relationships for business, education, family, and personal living* (2nd ed.). North Hollywood, CA: Newcastle.

Greenier, K. D., Kernis, M. H., & Waschull, S. B. (1995). Not all high (or low) self-esteem people are the same: Theory and research on stability of self-esteem. In M. H. Kernis (Ed.), *Efficacy, agency, and self-esteem* (pp. 51–71). New York: Plenum.

Hamacher, D. E. (1971). *Encounters with the self.* New York: Holt, Rinehart & Winston.

Heard, W. G. (1993). *The healing between: A clinical guide to dialogical psychotherapy.* San Francisco: Jossey-Bass.

Inger, I. B. (1993). A dialogic perspective for family therapy: The contributions of Martin Buber and Gregory Bateson. *Journal of Family Therapy, 15*(3), 293–314.

Jourard, S. (1964). *The transparent self.* New York: Litton Educational Publishing.

Jourard, S. (1971a). *Self-disclosure: An experimental analysis of the transparent self.* New York: Wiley.

Jourard, S. (1971b). *The transparent self* (2nd rev. ed.). New York: D. Van Nostrand Company.

Jourard, S., & Landsman, M. J. (1960). Cognition, cathexis, and the "dyadic effect" in men's self-disclosing behavior. *Merrill-Palmer Quarterly of Behavioral Development,* 6, 178–186.

Kernis, M. H. (Ed.). (1995). *Efficacy, agency, and self-esteem.* New York: Plenum.

Kirschenbaum, H., & Henderson, V. L. (Eds.). (1989). *Carl Rogers: Dialogues: Conversations with Martin Buber, Paul Tillich, B. F. Skinner, Gregory Bateson, Michael Polanyi, Rollo May, and others.* Boston: Houghton Mifflin.

Kleinman, A. (1988). *Rethinking psychiatry: From cultural category to personal experience.* New York: Free Press.

Lasch, C. (1979). *The culture of narcissism: American life in an age of diminishing expectations.* New York: Warner Books.

LeVine, E., & Franco, J. N. (1983). Effects of therapist's gender, ethnicity, and verbal style on client's willingness to seek therapy. *Journal of Social Psychology, 121*(1), 51–57.

Lowenstein, L. F. (1990). Humanism as a basis of psychotherapy: Are there any new directions? *New Jersey Journal of Professional Counseling, 53*(1), 6–16.

Mahon, N. E. (1982). The relationship of self-disclosure, interpersonal dependency, and life changes to loneliness in young adults. *Nursing Research, 31*(6), 343–347.

Malec, J. F., Sipprelle, C. N., & Behring, S. (1978). Biofeedback-assisted EMG reduction and subsequent self-disclosure. *Journal of Clinical Psychology, 34*(2), 523–525.

May, R. (1969). *Love and will.* New York: W. W. Norton.

Milholland, T. A., & Avery, A. W. (1982). Effects of marriage encounter on self-disclosure, trust, and marital satisfaction. *Journal of Marital and Family Therapy, 8*(2), 87–89.

Moss, D. (1989). Psychotherapy and human experience. In R. Valle & S. Halling (Eds.), *Existential-phenomenological perspectives in psychology* (pp. 192–213). New York: Plenum.

Moss, D. (1990). [Review of K. E. Bühler and H. Weiss (Eds.), *Kommunikation und Perspektivitat: Beiträge zur Anthropologie aus Medizin und Geisteswissenschaften*]. *Journal of Phenomenological Psychology, 21*(1), 96–101.

Moss, D., & Keen, E. (1981). The nature of consciousness: The existential-phenomenological approach. In R. Valle & R. von Eckartsberg (Eds.), *The metaphors of consciousness* (pp. 107–120). New York: Plenum.

Pennebaker, J. W. (1989). Confession, inhibition, and disease. In L. Berkowitz (Ed.), *Advances in Experimental Social Psychology* (Vol. 22, pp. 211–244). New York: Academic Press.

Pennebaker, J. W. (1990). *Opening up: The healing power of confiding in others.* New York: William Morrow & Company.

Pennebaker, J. W. (Ed.). (1995a). *Emotion, disclosure, and health.* Washington, DC: American Psychological Association.

Pennebaker, J. W. (1995b). Emotion, disclosure, and health: An overview. In J. W. Pennebaker (Ed.), *Emotion, disclosure, and health* (pp. 3–10). Washington, DC: American Psychological Association.

Pennebaker, J. W., Barger, S. D., & Tiebout, J. (1989). Disclosure of traumas and health among Holocaust survivors. *Psychosomatic Medicine, 51*, 577–589.

Pennebaker, J. W., & Beall, S. K. (1986). Confronting a traumatic event: Toward an understanding of inhibition and disease. *Journal of Abnormal Psychology, 95*, 274–281.

Pennebaker, J. W., Colder, M., & Sharp, L. K. (1990). Accelerating the coping process. *Journal of Personality and Social Psychology, 58*, 528–537.

Pennebaker, J. W., Kiecolt-Glaser, J. K.; & Glaser, R. (1988). Disclosure of traumas and immune function: Health implications for psychotherapy. *Journal of Consulting and Clinical Psychology, 56*, 239–245.

Perls, F. (1973). *Gestalt therapy verbatim.* Moab, UT: Real People Press.

Polowniak, W. (1994). *On creating a community.* Cardiff-by-the-Sea, CA: Quantum Publications.

Polster, E., & Polster, M. (1973). *Gestalt therapy integrated: Contours of theory and practice.* New York: Brunner/Mazel.

Raphael, K. G., & Dohrenwend, B. P. (1987). Self-disclosure and mental health: A problem of confounded measurement. *Journal of Abnormal Psychology, 96*(3), 214–217.

Rogers, C. R. (1951). *Client-centered therapy: Its current practice, implications, and theory.* Boston: Houghton Mifflin.

Rogers, C. R. (1970). *Carl Rogers on encounter groups.* New York: Harper & Row.

Ryan, L. (1977). *Clinical interpretation of the FIRO-B* (rev. ed.). Palo Alto, CA: Consulting Psychologists Press.

Schutz, W. (1966). *The interpersonal underworld.* Palo Alto, CA: Science & Behavior Books.

Schutz, W. (1967). *Joy: Expanding human awareness.* New York: Grove Press.

Schutz, W. (1971). *Here comes everybody: Bodymind and encounter culture.* New York: Harrow Books/Harper & Row.

Solomon, M. F. (1989). *Narcissism and intimacy: Love and marriage in an age of confusion.* New York: W. W. Norton.

Stokes, J. A. (1987). The relation of loneliness and self-disclosure. In V. J. Derlega & H. H. Berg (Eds.), *Self-disclosure: Theory, research, and practice: Perspectives in social psychology* (pp. 175–201). New York: Plenum.

Ticho, E. A. (1974). Donald W. Winnicott, Martin Buber, and the theory of personal relationships. *Psychiatry, 37*(3), 240–253.

von Eckartsberg, R. (1992). Plurality in social psychology. *Theoretical and Philosophical Psychology, 12*(2), 79–102.

Watson, J. B. (1928). *Psychological care of infant and child.* New York: W. W. Norton.

Wernick, R. (1996, December). A woman writ large in our history and hearts. *Smithsonian, 27*(9), 122–136.

7

Body Therapies in Humanistic Psychology

DONALD MOSS AND PAUL SHANE

THE BODY IN PSYCHOTHERAPY

> Behold, the body includes
>   and is the meaning,
>   the main concern,
>   and includes and is
>   the soul.
>
> —Walt Whitman, *Leaves of Grass*

Humanistic psychology has criticized the tendency of modern science to split body and mind and deal with each in isolation. Humanistic psychology would agree with Walt Whitman that the body "includes and is the soul." Phenomenological psychology provides a sophisticated conceptual basis for understanding the unity of mind and body (see chapter 8 on existential-phenomenological psychology). Humanistic psychology, however, has been more eager to discover pathways toward an immediate experience of body-mind. Massage, body work, and body therapies have had tremendous appeal within humanistic psychology, with their enhancement of intimacy and sensuality, facilitation of emotional release, and immediate impact on long-embedded inhibitions. This chapter will review several traditions of body work, including Wilhelm Reich and bioenergetics, the Alexander technique, Gestalt body work, the structural integration of Ida Rolf, and the Feldenkrais method.

PSYCHOANALYSIS AND THE BODY

The role of the body in undergirding human personality and in shaping human experiencing has been evident since the beginning of the development of modern psychotherapy. Freud began his psychoanalytic research with patients under hypnosis. After abandoning hypnosis, he continued to invite his patients to recline on a couch, suspend all mental inhibitions and censorship, and speak whatever came to mind (Freud, 1904/1959). Cultivation of some form of low-arousal physiological state has been part of the framework of psychodynamic psychotherapeutic change since the beginning.

Another psychoanalyst, Sandor Ferenczi, wrote a number of early papers on helpful modifications of psychoanalytic techniques. In 1919 Ferenczi commented on the "parallelism," "mutual conditioning," and "demonstrable quantitative reciprocity" between muscular activity and psychic activities of thought and attention (Ferenczi, 1919/1953, p. 232). Ferenczi highlighted the manner in which patients in analysis suddenly suspend a muscular activity at the moment in which they inhibit a new thought or impulse from verbal expression. Several of Ferenczi's therapeutic innovations involved disrupting the muscular activity that supported psychological defensive processes (1919/1953, 1920/1953). In 1925 Ferenczi also commented at the Ninth International Psychoanalytical Congress, "I have since learnt that it is sometimes useful to advise relaxation exercises, and that with this kind of relaxation one can overcome the physical inhibitions and resistances to association" (Ferenczi, 1925/1953, p. 226).

THE RELAXATION THERAPIES AND PSYCHOTHERAPY

Most psychotherapists are familiar with the development of progressive relaxation by Edmund Jacobsen (1938) and autogenic training by J. H. Schultz and W. Luthe (Schultz, 1932; Schultz & Luthe, 1959), approaches that make relaxation a therapy modality in itself. There are many reports that such cultivation of relaxation and low arousal produces an emotional catharsis, spontaneous emergence of buried memories, and other emotional breakthroughs (Jacobsen, 1938; Schultz & Luthe, 1959; Lichtstein, 1988; Wickramasekera, 1988). These relaxation techniques have served widely as an adjunctive tool to enhance the patient's receptivity for psychotherapy.

WILHELM REICH, ALEXANDER LOWEN, AND BIOENERGETICS

Wilhelm Reich took the lead not only in understanding the role of the body in "resistance" to psychotherapy, but in developing imaginative forms of body therapy. Reich was a brilliant psychoanalyst and student of Freud who practiced initially in Austria and Germany and emigrated to the United States in 1938. He became best known in psychoanalytic circles for his important contributions to the field of character analysis. He showed that the patient's resistances to therapeutic insight and his or her typical defense mechanisms reflect the structure and formation of that individual's character.

On the road to a body-oriented therapy, Reich introduced the idea of a "character armor," the characteristic, typical patterns in each individual's psychological defenses by means of which the individual protects himself or herself against perceived threats in the environment and within the inner emotional realm. According to Reich, this defensive armor enables an individual to establish a neurotic balance, but also blocks any deeper-seated change. Anna Freud later paraphrased Reich's words in her classic study *The Ego and the Mechanisms of Defense*: "The defenses meet our eyes in a state of petrification when we analyze the permanent 'armor plating of character' (i.e., rigidities of posture, mannerisms, etc.)" (A. Freud, 1936/1948, p. 36).

Reich added the concept of a "muscular armor"; in other words, the human individual uses recurrent patterns of physical tensing and bracing to block emotional expression. The result is a "frozen history," in which long-resisted affective experiences and impulsive discharges are suspended into a "character rigidity." As long as the body remains rigid, the memory of the original experience and any related emotion are blocked. "The tensions of the body can be viewed as a series of constrictions, the function of which is to limit movement, breathing and feeling" (Boadella, 1973, p. 121).

Reich extensively investigated the variety of neurotic character types that we might now recognize under the heading of personality styles and disorders. Each has its accompanying patterns in musculoskeletal bracing patterns, its own affective inhibitions, and its characteristic orientations toward life. Reich developed a therapeutic approach he called "vegetotherapy" whose goal is to relax this muscular armor through a combination of direct massage and pressure on the muscles, voluntary releasing of tensions by the patient, and verbal interpretation of resistance and blocking.

The desired results of vegetotherapy included a variety of intense physical and emotional discharges and an increase in flexibility in movement and emotional expression. Reich emphasized that through successful vegetotherapy the patient moves toward *self-regulation*, which in Reich's perspective implied a variety of characteristics, including free, spontaneous functioning, self-direction, and flexibility in movement, emotion, and relating.

Reich also described his body work as leading the individual toward a fuller "orgasmic functioning," which for Reich signified both a greater literal freedom for sexual relations and also a broad liberation of personal energies and creativity. One of Reich's major works was *The Function of the Orgasm* (1942). Just as Freud's scheme of psychosexual development culminated in an individual functioning fully at the "genital stage," which included productivity and creativity, Reich's fully orgasmic individual was free to feel, think, care, and create.

Reich generalized many of his concepts of personal sexual liberation into a concern for the sexual liberation of society and advocated many sexual reforms that shocked Austrian circles in the late 1920s. He founded a series of free clinics that provided education, counseling, and sexual advice to anyone, including un-married and adolescent patients. He advocated public sex education, access to contraceptive methods for all, and women's right to choose whether to abort a pregnancy. His advocacy of sexual liberation contributed to Reich's appeal for both humanistic psychology and the counterculture.

Boadella (1973, p. 123) reported that the psychophysiological releases in ve-getotherapy produce immediate episodes of screaming and sobbing, a sense of clearing in the head, and a feeling of unity between the head and the trunk. Ola Raknes, a Norwegian student of Reich, reported the following changes resulting from vegetotherapy:

The body stature is elastically erect; no cramps or jerks. . . .
The skin is warm with a plentiful blood supply. . . .
The muscles can change between tension and relaxation, being, however, neither chroni-cally contracted nor flaccid; peristalsis is easy. . . .
The facial features are lively and mobile, never set or mask like. . . .
There is complete deep expiration with a pause before new inspiration; free and easy movements of the chest.
The pulse is usually regular, calm and strong; normal blood pressure, neither too high nor too low. (Raknes, 1970, p. 125)

On the psychological side, the result was described as improved "psychic contact," the ability to relate to other people. This psychic contact was characterized as including

Capacity for complete concentration . . .
Capacity for and feelings of contact both with oneself and with other people, with nature and art. . . .
Freedom from anxiety when there is no danger, and ability to react rationally even in dangerous situations.
A deep and enduring feeling of well-being and strength. . . . (Raknes, 1970, p. 124)

Reich developed the classical formulation of body-oriented therapies: When we are verbally stuck, we may do something to and through the body, and vice versa:

When a character inhibition would fail to respond to psychic influencing, I would work at the corresponding somatic attitude. Conversely, when a disturbing muscular attitude proved difficult of access, I would work on its characterological expression and thus loosen it up. (Reich, 1942, p. 241)

Alexander Lowen formulated many additional principles for physical intervention in his *bioenergetic approach*, which builds on both the concepts and practical pro-cedures of Reich's vegetotherapy:

Analysis on the somatic level had revealed that patients hold their breath and pull in their belly to suppress anxiety and other sensations. (Lowen, 1958, p. 15)

Movement and expression are the tools of all analytic procedures and these are supplemented where necessary by direct work upon the muscular rigidity. (Lowen, 1958, p. 15)

Lowen was also able to show that not all character types are "armored" in the sense of a tense bracing against feeling. Nevertheless, each has its typical posture shaping its mode of experience (1958/1971). Lowen's works were scholarly and exhaustive in their analysis of the physical and psychological underpinnings of character. In practice, bioenergetics was anything but intellectual; the bioenergetic therapist aggressively pursued the expression of feeling, especially anger, by physical manipulation and emotional confrontation. This vigorous, feelingful approach to liberating human emotions and energies was harmonious with the humanistic energies of the times. Lowen's timing was also perfect, with his major books on bioenergetics becoming available just as humanistic psychology was emerging (1958/1971, 1965).

Further developments in Wilhelm Reich's work are beyond the limits of this chapter. Reich was a product of the ideological tensions of Europe in the 1920s and 1930s and was a fanatical opponent of Nazism. Like Theodor Adorno and Erich Fromm, he applied his psychoanalytic concepts to the social psychological basis for authoritarian dictatorships and fascism. His own preferred political system was a version of Marxist socialism with a wide range of personal freedoms (Reich, 1933/1946), although after his emigration to the United States Reich repudiated his radicalism and embraced a surprising political conservatism. (The reader is referred to chapter 18 on Erich Fromm in part II of this book for a discussion of the socialism of several German psychoanalysts in the 1930s, and to chapter 25 on Fritz Perls and Paul Goodman for additional information on Wilhelm Reich's politics in the United States.)

Reich's research on biological energies moved farther and farther from orthodox science to a fascination with "cosmic orgone energies," which he believed to have impact on the psychophysiology of the human being. Reich died in an American prison in 1957, having been convicted for claiming to cure cancer through cosmic orgone energy collected in orgone boxes.

The remainder of this chapter will overview a variety of other approaches to body work for personal change. The reader is also referred to the chapters on Fritz Perls and Paul Goodman, Laura Perls, Ida Rolf, and Moshe Feldenkrais in part II of this book.

THE ALEXANDER TECHNIQUE

F. M. Alexander developed his approach many years before Reich and the others described in this chapter developed the modern body therapies (Kurtz & Prestera, 1976; Jones, 1976). Alexander was a Shakespearean actor in the late

1800s who began to suffer from chronic loss of voice. He studied his own body in a five-way mirror and discovered a postural pattern producing the constriction in his vocal chords: throwing his head "backward and down," lifting his chest and hollowing his back, taking a shallow gasp of breath, and suppressing his larynx. This postural pattern created a tension around the vocal chords and blocked the normal mechanics of speech. He studied these distortions exhaustively until he could see an interrelationship; together they served to alter the directional axis of the head with the torso. These distortions in alignment produced an increase of muscular tension throughout his upper body. Correcting his postural alignment, Alexander reduced the tensions throughout his body and recovered the power of his voice.

Alexander called the alignment of the head, neck, and torso the "primary control," and this principle became the eventual core of his Alexander technique (Kurtz & Prestera, 1976). He taught individuals to let the neck be free, allow the head to go forward and up, and allow the torso to lengthen and widen out (Alexander, 1955). He taught that few symptoms are under local control; rather, the posture of the body as an organic whole produces local tensions and distress.

Following the Alexander technique, the therapist first assesses the postural sources of distress. Then the individual is encouraged to "do nothing," to let go of all physical and mental efforts, to become increasingly aware of the body's alignment as a totality, and to correct destructive postural habits and inhibitions. Although Alexander formulated his goal as one of "conscious control," at this early stage in the technique the individual sets free his body's own "primary control" by giving up physical and mental strivings.

Alexander sought a healthy and flexible integration of mind and body through a conscious control of postural change. For Alexander and many of his students, this technique became a powerful tool for personal change and a lively physical well-being. Alexander eventually claimed that his approach set free man's highest potentials. In his farthest-reaching book, *Man's Supreme Inheritance* (1910), Alexander wrote, "The great phase in man's advancement is that in which he passes from subconscious to conscious control of his own body and mind" (cited by Jones, 1976, p. 22).

IDA ROLF AND STRUCTURAL INTEGRATION

Ida Rolf developed the technique that she called structural integration and that came to be more widely known as "Rolfing" (Rolf, 1962, 1975, 1977; Kurtz & Prestera, 1976; Schutz, 1971). She believed that poor posture and emotional trauma contributed to blockages in the muscles and surrounding fascia. She used a deep massage of the musculature and sought to restore the body's original alignment. She believed that both mental and physical well-being were enhanced by realignment. Like Reich, she claimed that specific emotional blockages produce specific muscular distortions and cannot be released until the muscle tensions are released. Rolfing is a vigorous physical technique, with heavy and often painful kneading of the muscles, and often produces intense emotional abreactions. The Rolfer uses both hands and elbows to push deeper into the muscles.

GESTALT BODY WORK

> The body never lies.
>
> —Martha Graham

Chapter 5 has already overviewed the contributions to humanistic psychology of Fritz Perls and Gestalt therapy. Laura Perls, who was Fritz's wife and cocreator of Gestalt therapy, discussed the origins of Gestalt therapy body work in a 1977 address in Austria (L. Perls, 1977/1978). She listed her lifelong involvement with modern dance and eurhythmics, her early study of Ludwig Klages's book on expressive movement and creativity, and her long familiarity with the Alexander technique and the Feldenkrais method. She reported that work with breathing, posture, coordination, voice, sensitivity, and mobility was already a part of her therapeutic style in the 1930s, when she and Fritz Perls still called themselves psychoanalysts. Laura Perls also acknowledged the influence on her therapeutic work of Wilhelm Reich and his concept of character armor. For her, the character armor is a "fixed Gestalt" that becomes a block in the ongoing organization of new experiences. In other words, the Gestalt therapist confronts any physical posture, gesture, or tension that interferes with the immediate flow of awareness, or that blocks a lively contact with oneself, one's body, and one's surrounding world.

Fritz Perls shared with Wilhelm Reich an emphasis on liberating the human being through liberating the body from a habitual suppression of impulses. In Gestalt therapy Perls consistently focused on facial expressions and posture and mercilessly confronted muscular blocking and defensiveness. Analytically he viewed areas of bodily tension as made up of the polarized and suspended conflict between two opposing urges to action. The original censored impulse and the contrary self-squeezing and self-throttling action both continue indefinitely in the musculature as actions begun but never completed. In Perls's interventions he sought to amplify the suppressed actions and impulses and free the personal energy that remains locked up in this blocking process.

Fritz Perls developed and popularized a variety of Gestalt body-awareness exercises, encouraging the individual to become aware of polarities or dissociations between specific body organs or physical features and the ego. In such experiential exercises the individual often speaks poignantly of the body as the last reservation of suppressed wishes and impulses. The patient is encouraged to allow himself, for example, to listen attentively to the symptomatic area of the body and to bring to expression whatever feelings, impulses, or desires emerge. In many instances the mere recognition of a denied urge enables the individual to move from a suffering and "sick" state to an awareness of conflicting desires or interpersonal resentments (Perls, Hefferline, & Goodman, 1951, pp. 161–174).

Perls particularly opposed a "premature" relaxation process; he believed that it was essential to express and recognize the interpersonal situation or urge involved in a bodily complaint. Perls believed that both physiological release and emotional/interpersonal change were necessary for lasting effect. To simply relax the forehead musculature may already in itself release a burst of tears, but Perls was concerned that an individual might remain vulnerable, for example, to continuously accepting a self-effacing, victim role with others unless the entire muscular-affective-interpersonal complex was expressed and released (Perls, Hefferline, & Goodman, 1951, p. 163).

MOSHE FELDENKRAIS AND FUNCTIONAL INTEGRATION

Moshe Feldenkrais (1904–1984) was a multitalented Russian-born physicist, educator, engineer, and judo master. Like F. M. Alexander, he faced a personally disabling condition, a crippling injury to both knees, and developed his method of "functional integration" in the process of rehabilitating himself. He studied neurophysiology and psychology and developed a method that emphasizes a series of precise patterned muscular movements, designed to realign the body in movement. Feldenkrais advocated replacing habitual unconscious movement patterns with conscious, flexible patterns better suited to the present situation. Feldenkrais observed that human beings tend to transfer an entire fixed action sequence from an earlier situation to a later situation. His interventions instead enabled the individual to "bring to bear on the present situation only those aspects of the previous experience that he deems consciously necessary" (Feldenkrais, 1949, p. 154). Central to Feldenkrais's approach was his belief that behavioral or emotional change undertaken without realignment of movement patterns will not have lasting effect. Feldenkrais believed that orthodox psychotherapy and psychiatry were misguided in ignoring the need for a change in muscular patterning, because the attitudes and perceptual biases accompanying dysfunctional movement patterns will inevitably produce a relapse into the original emotional state.

In practice, functional integration is applied in two forms: (1) a Feldenkrais movement teacher conducts private sessions and provides individually tailored guidance to redirect the client's dysfunctional movement patterns, or (2) a highly structured form of the Feldenkrais method, "awareness through movement," is taught in group settings, following prescribed sequences of corrective movements (Feldenkrais, 1977). (See chapter 17 on Feldenkrais in part II for more detail.)

The effectiveness of Feldenkrais's method has been documented in the physical rehabilitation of the elderly and the handicapped and in pursuing optimal performance in sports, drama, music, and dance. Feldenkrais's system has also had significant impact on other humanistic schools of body work, including Gestalt therapy (L. Perls, 1977/1978).

THE PSYCHOPHYSIOLOGICAL PRINCIPLE

We will close this chapter with the "psychophysiological principle," a concept introduced into biofeedback theory by Elmer Green and his colleagues.

Every change in the physiological state is accompanied by an appropriate change in the mental emotional state, conscious or unconscious, and conversely, every change in the mental emotional state, conscious or unconscious, is accompanied by an appropriate change in the physiological state. (Green, Green, & Walters, 1970, p. 3)

Biofeedback, which will be addressed in chapter 10, is a research-based empirical approach, with greater emphasis on replication of results and cautious examination of evidence. Yet biofeedback pursues the same goal as other body therapies, that of using individual awareness and control over the body to enhance personal potential, health, and growth.

Each school of body therapy or body work presents a different manifestation of the fundamental psychophysiological principle that we can intervene somatically and produce changes in emotion and relationship, and inversely, that we can intervene psychologically, with somatic consequences. Each of the body-therapy approaches emphasizes a dual psychological and somatic intervention, and each emphasizes breathing, muscular rigidity, and the physical blocking of memories and affective experiencing. In turn, each body therapy seeks to release the individual from physical inhibitions and to restore a full psychophysiological self-regulation.

REFERENCES

Alexander, F. M. (1955). *Use of the self.* New York: Integral Press.

Alexander, F. M. (1974). *The resurrection of the body.* New York: Delta.

Boadella, D. (1973). *Wilhelm Reich: The evolution of his work.* New York; Dell/Laurel Edition.

Brennan, R. (1991). *Alexander technique.* Rockport, MA: Element.

Feldenkrais, M. (1949). *Body and mature behaviour: A Study of anxiety, sex, gravitation, and learning.* New York: International Universities Press.

Feldenkrais, M. (1977). *Awareness through movement: Health exercises for personal growth.* New York: Harper & Row.

Ferenczi, S. (1919). Thinking and muscle innervation. In S. Ferenczi (1953), *Further contributions to the theory and technique of psychoanalysis* (pp. 230–232). New York: Basic Books.

Ferenczi, S. (1920). The further development of an active therapy in psycho-analysis. In S. Ferenczi (1953), *Further contributions to the theory and technique of psychoanalysis* (pp. 198–217). New York: Basic Books.

Ferenczi, S. (1925). Contra-indications to the "active" psycho-analytical technique. In S. Ferenczi (1953), *Further contributions to the theory and technique of psychoanalysis* (pp. 217–230). New York: Basic Books.

Freud, A. (1936/1948). *The ego and the mechanisms of defense*. London: Hogarth Press.

Freud, S. (1959). Freud's psychoanalytic method. In *Collected Papers*, (Vol. 1, pp. 264–271). New York: Basic Books. (Original work published 1904)

Green, E., Green, A. M., & Walters, E. D. (1970). Voluntary control of internal states: Psychological and physiological. *Journal of Transpersonal Psychology, 2*, 1–26.

Jacobsen, E. (1938). *Progressive relaxation*. Chicago: University of Chicago Press.

Jones, F. P. (1976). *Body awareness in action*. New York: Schocken Books.

Kurtz, R., & Prestera, H. (1976). *The body reveals: An Illustrated guide to the psychology of the body*. New York: Harper & Row.

Leibowitz, J., & Connington, B. (1990). *The Alexander technique*. New York: Harper Perennial.

Lichstein, K. L. (1988). *Clinical relaxation strategies*. New York: Wiley.

Lowen, A. (1971). *The language of the body*. New York: Collier (Original work published as A. Lowen (1958), *Physical dynamics of character structure*. New York: Grune and Stratton.).

Lowen, A. (1965). *Love and orgasm*. New York: Macmillan.

Perls, F. S., Hefferline, R. F., & Goodman, P. (1951). *Gestalt therapy: Excitement and growth in the human personality*. New York: Julian Press.

Perls, L. (1978). Concepts and misconceptions of Gestalt therapy. *Voices, 14*(3), 31–35. (Original address to the European Association for Transactional Analysis, Seefeld, Austria, 1977.)

Raknes, O. (1970). *Wilhelm Reich and orgonomy*. New York: St. Martin's Press.

Reich, W. (1942). *The function of the orgasm*. New York: Orgone Institute Press.

Reich, W. (1946). *The mass psychology of fascism*. New York: Orgone Institute Press. (Original work published 1933)

Reich, W. (1949). *Character analysis* (3rd ed.). New York: Orgone Institute Press. (Original work published 1933)

Rolf, I. P. (1962). *Gravity: An unexplored factor in a more human use of human beings*. Boulder, CO: Ida P. Rolf Foundation.

Rolf, I. P. (1975). *Structural integration*. New York: Viking/Esalen.

Rolf, I. P. (1977). *Rolfing: The integration of human structures*. New York: Harper & Row.

Rycroft, C. (1971). *Reich*. London: Fontana-Collins.

Schultz J. H. (1932). *Das autogene Training: Konzentrativ Selbstentspannung*. Stuttgart: Georg Thieme Verlag.

Schultz, J. H., & Luthe, W. (1959). *Autogenic therapy*. New York: Grune & Stratton.

Schutz, W. (1971). *Here comes everybody: Bodymind and encounter culture*. New York: Harrow Books/Harper & Row.

Wickramasekera, I. (1988). *Clinical behavioral medicine*. New York: Plenum Press.

Existential–Phenomenological Psychology

STEEN HALLING AND ALEX CARROLL

In this chapter we provide an overview of the existential-phenomenological (E-P) tradition in psychology, especially as it exists in North America. We begin with a summary of thinkers and ideas within existential and phenomenological philosophy that have been particularly important in creating the foundations of E-P psychology. Second, we discuss the "classic" phenomenological and existential movement within European psychiatry, a movement that continues in its own right while also serving as a rich source of insight for much of contemporary E-P psychology.

Next, we examine the E-P tradition in North America. In this discussion we have kept in mind the French phenomenological philosopher Maurice Merleau-Ponty's (1945/1962) famous assertion that "phenomenology can be practiced and identified as a manner or style of thinking, that it existed as a movement before arriving at complete awareness of itself as a philosophy" (p. viii) or, in this context, a psychology. Accordingly, we look at several scholars and clinicians (e.g., Helen Lynd and Andras Angyal) who, although they are not typically considered part of the E-P movement, nonetheless might be considered "protophenomenologists" because of their ongoing concern with understanding human experience on its own terms. However, we give most attention to those thinkers who explicitly identify themselves with the E-P orientation (e.g., Rollo May and Amedeo Giorgi).

Our discussion would not be complete without considerations of the relationship between humanistic psychology and E-P psychology, both of which are regarded as part of the "Third Force" in psychology. More specifically, we look at phenomenological themes in the work of humanistic psychologists such as Gordon Allport, Carl Rogers, and Abraham Maslow. We conclude the chapter with some suggestions about the value of E-P psychology for humanistic psychology.

THE FOUNDATION: EXISTENTIAL-PHENOMENOLOGICAL PHILOSOPHY

Existentialism and phenomenology, which began as separate movements, have converged to a large extent in this century. For this reason we speak, rather broadly, of the existential-phenomenological movement. Yet while these movements constitute complementary approaches, certain distinctions can be made.

Existential Philosophy: Kierkegaard and Nietzsche

The Danish thinker Søren Kierkegaard (1813–1855) is regarded as the founder of existential philosophy, whereas Edmund Husserl (1859–1938), a German philosopher, is credited as the primary proponent of phenomenology. For Kierkegaard, it was imperative that philosophy address itself to the concrete existence of the individual person and attempt to elucidate the fundamental themes with which human beings invariably struggle (e.g., finding meaning in life, reconciling oneself to one's mortality). Husserl's approach was more "scientific": phenomenology means the methodologically rigorous and unbiased study of things as they appear so that one might come to an essential understanding of human consciousness and its relationship to the objects of experience.

Kierkegaard's writings have had a great impact on philosophers (e.g., Martin Buber, Martin Heidegger, Karl Jaspers) as well as psychiatrists and psychologists (e.g., R. D. Laing, Rollo May, Irvin Yalom) in this century. Yet his formal influence was minimal in his own time, a time largely dominated by the thought of the German philosopher Georg Hegel (1770–1831). Kierkegaard was opposed to this abstract philosophy, of which he wrote, "It is about like reading out of a cookbook to a man who is hungry" (Lowrie, 1970, p. 115). He argued that such speculative thinking disregards the concrete individual living in a specific time and place. Moreover, Kierkegaard vehemently opposed Hegel's efforts to subsume Christianity to philosophy. He attacked Hegel's rationalization of faith, the state church, and comfortable, bourgeois Christianity alike as inimical to authentic living. Critics have often labeled Kierkegaard as antiscientific or irrational, yet many scholars disagree, citing the inner unity of his work and the importance he attached to intersubjective verification of analyses (see, e.g., Malantschuk, 1971; Nordentoft, 1972/1978). His examination of despair, for example, shows that this phenomenon is rooted in the insistence that one be something one is not; thus despair is fundamentally a stance of repudiating oneself and one's actual situation (Kierkegaard, 1849/1941).

A generation later, the German philosopher Friedrich Nietzsche (1844–1900) expressed strikingly similar criticisms of European society. However, Nietzsche saw Christianity itself as a root source of the cultural crisis and conventionality of his day. Nietzsche proposed to make way for the new person—the *Übermensch*, creator of authentic values. This notion of the "overman" has often been misconstrued and seen as a precursor of Nazism. Yet Kaufmann (1967), among others, suggests that the overman is someone "who has organized the chaos of his passions, given style to his character, and become creative. Aware of life's terrors, he affirms life without resentment" (p. 511). Such a person, one might say, lives courageously by overcoming illusions and taking responsibility for his or her own life.

A number of thinkers are indebted to Nietzsche, including Martin Heidegger, Karl Jaspers, Jean-Paul Sartre, Martin Buber, Paul Tillich, and Rollo May. Some commentators assert that Freud's notions of Thanatos, superego, and unconscious motivation correspond markedly to Nietzschean ideas (Hubben, 1962; Jones, 1957). At the very least, Nietzsche's profound psychological insights have "paved the way for modern psychoanalysis" (Hubben, 1962, p. 123). But only after World War I had devastated European optimism did these prophetic existentialist voices gain a widely receptive audience.

Phenomenology: Brentano and Husserl

The early phenomenologists' concern for developing a faithful and rigorous approach to studying human behavior grew out of a critical stance toward the emerging discipline of psychology that under the leadership of Wilhelm Wundt (1832–1920) came to be defined as an experimental science. Notable among these phenomenologists, Franz Brentano (1833–1911) has been called "the forerunner of the phenomenological movement" (Misiak & Sexton, 1966, p. 407). In *Psychologie vom empirischen Standpunkt* (1874) he introduced the term "intentionality" to refer to consciousness's always-existing relationship to some object of consciousness. This term refers to the connection between subject and object and remains a central concept in phenomenology (Spiegelberg, 1982).

It is ironic that Wundt (1902) himself, in contrast to some of his followers, believed that experimental methods were only appropriate for the study of simpler psychical processes. He spent the last two decades of his life developing the idea of a folk psychology, arguing for the use of observational methods in the study of complex human phenomena and thereby coming close to a phenomenological perspective (Giorgi, 1970).

Edmund Husserl's project was far more ambitious than that of his predecessors. After finishing a doctorate in mathematics, Husserl wrote a philosophy of arithmetic, which was criticized for subordinating mathematical concepts to psychological processes, a critique he carefully examined.

In one of Husserl's first phenomenological studies, *The Logical Investigations* (1900/1970b), he insisted on clearing away preconceptions about experience and returning "to the things themselves." This process, the *epoché*, promotes an attitude of wonder and openness toward phenomena. Through a method called the "phenomenological reduction" one sets aside "the natural attitude," or the everyday belief in the existence of realities independent of us. Using a related principle, the "eidetic reduction," one seeks to identify the universal essence of a particular phenomenon. "Free imaginative variation" is the method used to identify this essence.

Husserl's expanded notion of intentionality was critical in overcoming the prevailing notion that the subjective and the objective exist as dichotomous realities. Intentionality implies that persons and the world are always in an interactive relationship, as opposed to being independent entities. Through intentions humans "cocreate" phenomena rather than just passively registering an object's existence.

Lebenswelt (lifeworld) is one of the last notions Husserl (1936/1970a) articulated. This is the realm of immediate human experience existing prior to the abstractly conceived world of natural science. The lifeworld is a realm the sciences tend to ignore or negate through reductionistic explanations (Giorgi, 1970; Spiegelberg, 1982).

The Confluence of Existentialism and Phenomenology: Heidegger, Sartre, and Merleau-Ponty

Martin Heidegger (1889–1976), a German philosopher, united existential concerns and phenomenological method. While he was inspired by his predecessors, especially Kierkegaard and Husserl, his basic project is original. By his own definition he was an ontologist (ontology is that branch of philosophy that concerns itself with the ultimately real), answering questions of the meaning of Being (Spiegelberg, 1982). Yet his work clearly bears an affinity to both existentialism and phenomenology.

In *Being and Time* Heidegger (1927/1962) aimed "to work out the question of the meaning of Being and to do so concretely" (p. 1). This work concerns itself with "the to-be of whatever is" rather than with the nature of specific objects or individual persons. Although Heidegger's writings are obtuse to the uninitiated reader, the subject of his discourse is not an abstract entity. As Kiesel (1979) states, "The question of what it means to be for man, . . . can pose itself in his unique existence as the first and most pressing of all questions" (p. 14). In other words, the question of Being is the question of what one can most fundamentally say about existence. When Heidegger indicated that he would pursue this question "concretely," he meant that he would proceed by looking at specific "existences" in his effort to uncover the basic nature of "Existence."

Although Heidegger acknowledged his debt to Husserl, he spoke of a reawakening of wonder in the face of Being rather than through consciousness. He also found the phenomenological description to be an inadequate method of revealing Being since Being is partly "in darkness" and hidden from view. Further, Heidegger proposed a method of phenomenological hermeneutics: "the interpretive process of existence to allow Being to uncover itself in and through man himself" (Sadler, 1969, p. 71).

Heidegger's analysis of human existence begins with his interpretation of *Dasein*. In English *Dasein* translates roughly as Being-there or There-being. *Da* suggests our inherent relatedness to that which is other than us; that transcendence, or openness to possibility and that which is beyond ourselves, is intrinsic to existence. *Sein* implies that we are not static entities. Though humans may not have an explicit understanding of Being, we "are immersed up to our necks, and indeed over our heads" (Barrett, 1958, p. 213) in Being. Lastly, the term *Dasein* suggests that the human is that being for whom Being is a question. Heidegger also spoke of human existence as "being-in-the-world," meaning that human existence is relational to its very core.

Heidegger viewed existence as radically historical and temporal. Transcendence implies openness to what has not yet occurred, to possibility. Death is one inevitable possibility: a stark reminder of our finitude that we continually evade. In confronting our deaths, we can embrace our individuality and our freedom to live authentically. This freedom exists in relation to "thrownness"; that is, we are born into a world not of our making and live under conditions over which we have little control. Inauthenticity occurs when we get caught up in the "they" (*das Man*) and forget our individuality as we follow the dictates of anonymous "authorities," thereby obscuring Being. We are called back to authentic living as we confront death and face situations requiring us to take a stand.

Being and Time was fervently commended throughout Europe after publication, yet recent reexaminations have called Heidegger's integrity and philosophical works into question due to his affiliation with the Nazi party. Interested readers may consult Sheehan (1988, 1993), Wolin (1991), Rockmore (1992), and Ott (1988/1993). While "we are morally compelled to read his philosophy with a certain suspicion" (Paskow, 1991, p. 524), the majority of philosophers agree that Heidegger remains one of the most innovative philosophers in this century.

For many, Jean-Paul Sartre (1905–1984) is also considered synonymous with existential philosophy. Sartre's basic categories are being for-itself (consciousness) and being in-itself (objects). He conceived of the subject (being for-itself) as pure Nothingness—freedom that is transparent to itself. In *Being and Nothingness* (1943/1965) he described how the other's looking at me threatens to objectify me. In turn, I recover my freedom by objectifying the other. Sartre's (1939/1948a) theory of emotions suggests that emotionality serves as a substitute for genuine action in situations that impose limitations on one's freedom. His theory of hallucinations blends with his understanding of imagination in that he contended that consciousness, which is basically transparent to itself, does not confuse the imagined or the hallucinated with the real (Sartre, 1940/1948b).

Sartre's *Existential Psychoanalysis* (1940/1953), which was originally composed as part of *Being and Nothingness*, offers an alternative to Freud's conceptions of the unconscious, the nature of neurosis, and the therapeutic relationship. Sartre substituted the notion of self-deception for repression. In neurosis we hide from "the original free choice by which the individual relates himself to the world" (Barnes, 1953, pp. 31–32).

Sartre's contemporary, Maurice Merleau-Ponty (1908–1961), worked closely with psychological theories and data as he developed his basic philosophical positions. In fact, his first appointment at the Sorbonne was not in philosophy but in child psychology (Spiegelberg, 1972). In several of his major works, Merleau-Ponty (1942/1963; 1945/1962) drew on Gestalt psychology's research on perception as well as Kurt Goldstein's studies of brain-damaged patients. In articulating a systematic understanding of human existence, he proceeded by showing how careful reflection on descriptions of key human phenomena reveals the inadequacies of both empiricism and idealism. In respect to empiricism he critiqued the stimulus-response conception of the early behaviorists by showing that behavior is always a response to a context as a whole. In regard to idealism he brought into question the subjectivism implicit in Sartre's philosophy (e.g., the notion of the subject as transparent freedom and therefore somehow independent of the world), as well as in some of Husserl's formulations.

Although Merleau-Ponty appeared to view his work, especially his earlier writings, as a continuation and elaboration of Husserl's phenomenological project, his philosophy is distinctive and original in many respects. For example, he put more emphasis on the situated, embodied, historical, and social nature of human life and thought than did Husserl, while also placing greater value on the insights provided by the social sciences. With these emphases, he also distinguished himself from Heidegger. At the same time, in his discussions of topics such as temporality, Merleau-Ponty (1945/1962) showed his appreciation of Heidegger's thought.

Among his original contributions, Merleau-Ponty's (1945/1962) claim that embodiment and the preconscious (or unreflective) level of meaning giving in everyday life are intimately connected is especially noteworthy. In this regard, he wrote of the "body-subject," a notion that was intended to overcome the dualism inherent in the idea of a "mind/body" relationship. Furthermore, he conceived of the relationship between the "body-subject" and the world in terms of a dialogue that gives rise to perception. In his last work he deepened the notion of the relationship between the world and the body by speaking of it as an "intertwining," that is, an interpenetration (Merleau-Ponty, 1964/1968). Given these interests, it is not surprising that Merleau-Ponty's influence in psychology has been more in the area of theory and research than in psychotherapy. For example, the influence of Merleau-Ponty and of Husserl are evident in the work of Amedeo Giorgi (e.g., 1970), who has articulated a new foundation for psychology that he views as a "human" rather than a natural science.

A Dialogical Philosophy: Martin Buber

While Merleau-Ponty referred to dialogue, this notion is central to the work of Martin Buber, where it has a deeper meaning. Buber (1878–1965) is probably the best-known existentialist philosopher outside Europe. As one of his biographers has noted, "In the English-speaking world acceptance of some form of

Buber's ideas is almost axiomatic" (R. G. Smith, 1967, p. 38); he has certainly had a tremendous influence on theology, philosophy, and education as well as on psychiatry, particularly in North America. (See also chapter 6 for further discussion of Martin Buber.)

For Martin Buber (1923/1958), it is meaningless to speak of human reality except in terms of relations since "through the Thou a man becomes I" (p. 28). That is, in Buber's view, we become fully human insofar as we enter deeply into reciprocal relations with other human beings, regarded not as means to an end (I-it relationships), but as ends in themselves (I-Thou relationships) (see the discussion of Buber in chapter 6). Buber's remarkable analysis of the fundamental character of the human encounter—the interplay between distance and relationship (Buber, 1951/1965)—and his emphasis on the human encounter as the context for becoming and realizing oneself have influenced numerous psychotherapists, including Carl Rogers. In analyzing the notions of distance and relationship, Buber shows how the capacity of humans to stand apart from and to be at a distance from the world and others is also precisely what makes it possible for us to enter into relationship; these two terms presuppose each other.

When Buber came to the United States for the second time in 1957, he had a remarkable public discussion with Rogers about the nature of the therapeutic relationship that continues to be the subject of debate and analysis (Cissna & Anderson, 1994; Friedman, 1994). Although they disagreed about the extent to which there can be mutuality in the therapist-client relationship, they agreed about the importance of the quality of the relationship for therapeutic progress. This debate served to bring Buber's thought to the attention of many other American psychotherapists.

EXISTENTIAL-PHENOMENOLOGICAL PSYCHIATRY IN EUROPE

The Founders: Jaspers, Binswanger, Boss, Straus

Karl Jaspers (1883–1969), philosopher and psychiatrist, insisted on a passionately involved and concretely realized philosophizing. Jaspers authored *General Psychopathology* (1913/1963), which "stands out as one of the seminal works in the psychiatric literature" (Stierlin, 1974, p. 218), and without which "objective phenomenology could not have achieved the position in psychopathology which it now holds" (Spiegelberg, 1972, p. 173).

The engaging style of Jaspers's *Philosophy* (1932/1969–1971) exemplifies his insistence that "genuine philosophizing must well up from a man's individual existence and address itself to other individuals to help them to achieve true existence" (Kaufmann, 1975, p. 22). As an outspoken critic of the Nazis, Jaspers lost his professorship from 1937 until the close of the war.

Ludwig Binswanger (1881–1966) also made vital contributions to the E-P movement. Early in his career Binswanger concluded that Freud's approach, suggesting that all behavior is meaningful, had much to offer. Even after Binswanger grew more critical of psychoanalysis, he remained convinced that its therapeutic techniques were valuable in many cases. Nonetheless, he disagreed with Freud, who inferred that hidden processes have priority over observed phenomena, that instincts provide the primary motivation for human behavior, and that it is fruitful to conceptualize the person in terms of a "psychic apparatus" (Spiegelberg, 1972; Brice, 1978). Binswanger's main criticism of psychoanalysis is based on his concern that it views the patient in mechanistic and reductionistic terms.

In order to interpret Freud's theory and to bridge the gap between psychoanalysis and a biologically based psychiatry, Binswanger needed a theoretical foundation "to demonstrate that the symptoms of disease with which psychiatry deals refer to facts in the fellow-human area of sympathy and intercourse" (Binswanger, 1958b, p. 228). This statement, written in 1945, presupposed a number of principles Binswanger had drawn from philosophy in developing his phenomenological anthropology. He first turned to Husserl's notion of intentionality and unbiased description. Then, after 1927, Binswanger was strongly influenced by Heidegger, whose notion of "being-in-the-world" appeared to provide a more fundamental interpretation of human relatedness than Husserl's intentionality.

On this basis Binswanger provided a reinterpretation of Freud, an articulation of a phenomenological anthropology (*Daseinanalyse*) as a new foundation for psychiatry, and his penetrating analysis of various psychiatric cases. These efforts, including the case of Ellen West (Binswanger, 1958a), firmly established E-P within the social sciences. Binswanger also wrote a book describing his almost thirty-year friendship with Freud (Binswanger, 1956/1957), whom he greatly admired as a humanist while opposing him as a natural scientific thinker. Finally, Binswanger, influenced by Max Scheler and Buber's philosophy, sought to develop a more adequate conception of the interpersonal than was present in either Freud's or Heidegger's work. He centered his writing on "we-love," which he claimed is a fundamental human experience characterized by a sense of timelessness, at-homeness, and participation in a shared world of meaning (Binswanger, 1942).

Binswanger introduced the writing of Heidegger to Medard Boss (1903–1991), a fellow Swiss psychiatrist. The two later parted ways, and Boss became the "authorized" psychiatric interpreter of Heidegger's philosophy. After the war, Boss met Heidegger, and a close collaboration ensued (Moss, 1978).

Boss wrote that he "aspires to greater empiricism and 'objectivity' than that which the natural scientist can achieve"; this requires one to "adhere to the immediately given objects and phenomena of man's world, to remain with man's undistorted perceptions" (Boss, 1957/1963, p. 59). In his first text (1947/1949), a Heideggerian-based analysis of six cases of sexual deviance, he attacked Freud's libido theory while providing an existential alternative. He interpreted perverted modes of sexuality as desperately inadequate, yet nonetheless real, attempts to move from a confined existence to a freer and more genuine togetherness with other persons. After successfully lecturing in the United States, Boss revised a collection of German articles for the English text *Psychoanalysis and Daseinanalysis* (1957/1963). In *Existential Foundations of Medicine and Psychology* (1971/1979), Boss attempted to show the need for the physician or therapist to be aware of the overall existential situation of the patient.

Erwin Straus (1891–1975) also established himself as a major advocate of phenomenological psychiatry on both sides of the Atlantic. (See chapter 29 on Straus in part II of this volume). He made his impact through publishing numerous works, organizing the Lexington Conferences on Pure and Applied Phenomenology, deeply influencing many of the psychologists who studied with him (e.g., C. Fischer, W. Fischer, R. Griffith, and J. Lyons), and giving lectures at various universities. Straus (1969) was critical of Husserl's and Heidegger's neglect of the human body. He also opposed the reductionistic treatment of sensory experience by contemporary science and sought to demonstrate that sensory experience is a form of communication between person and world (Straus, 1935/1963). Moreover, there is a unity of sensing and movement; we are in the world and we take a stand over and against it. In addition, there is a perceptual-knowing relationship in which we are grounded in objects and sensory experience at the same time that we transcend them.

The Next Generation: van den Berg, Frankl, and Laing

J. H. van den Berg (b. 1914) is another phenomenologist who has received recognition around the world. In his book *A Different Existence* he speaks of having "an unshakable faith in the everyday observation of objects, of the body, of the people around him and of time" (van den Berg, 1972, p. 77). In this classic work van den Berg examines a patient's experience through the fourfold aspects of existence (body, others, time, and world), critiquing the interpretations of neurosis that rely on Freudian defense mechanisms. He affirms intentionality and the possibility of developing a genuine understanding of psychopathology.

Perhaps his most original idea is that of "metabletics," in his own words, historical psychology. He asserts that human "nature" is not fixed but alters as the human condition changes. For example, van den Berg examines psychiatric phenomena such as neurosis and the unconscious within a historical context. He concludes that these phenomena are of recent historical origin. Furthermore, they are symptomatic of contemporary social shifts that lead to chaos. "If the groups of society are in disorder, then the result to the individual is . . . unconsciousness" (1963/1974, p. xi).

Viktor E. Frankl (1905–1997) is another well-known existential psychiatrist. His understanding of life was profoundly affected by his internment in a German concentration camp in World War II, where he came to see the sustaining power of life purpose (Frankl, 1963). Frankl rejected the psychodynamic reductionism of both Freud and Adler, claiming that "our most powerful longing is not the longing for pleasure . . . or for power. . . . instead, it is the longing for meaning" (Weisskopf-Joelson, 1978, p. 277). He created Logotherapy, or healing through meaning. Frankl (1948/1965) claimed that neurotic and even psychotic symptoms arise when people experience their lives as meaningless. Healing constitutes realized meaning in the creative, experiential, and attitudinal realms.

R. D. Laing (1927–1989), Britain's most celebrated existential psychiatrist, is often associated with Sartre and wrote an endorsed overview of Sartre's philosophy from 1950 to 1960 (Laing & Cooper, 1964). (See chapter 22 on Laing in part II of this volume.) Yet it would be a mistake to regard Laing primarily as a follower of Sartre. In *The Divided Self* (1960) Laing drew freely from virtually every E-P philosopher and European psychiatrist mentioned in this chapter.

Laing's primary agenda in *The Divided Self* (1960), *Sanity, Madness, and the Family* (with Esterson, 1964), *Self and Others* (1961), and *The Politics of the Family* (1971) was to make intelligible disturbed behavior in terms of the patient's relationships with others. In *The Divided Self* (1960) Laing introduced the concept of "ontological insecurity," the schizophrenic patient's deep sense that his or her very existence is threatened. Many of the "symptoms" of schizophrenia are seen as ways through which the ontologically insecure person protects himself or herself from being misunderstood or attacked by others.

Frankl, Laing, Straus, and van den Berg have had as much influence in North America as in Europe. Since the end of World War II the United States and Canada have become more receptive to E-P thought. In addition, numerous North American thinkers have made original contributions to this movement, as we will show.

EXISTENTIAL-PHENOMENOLOGICAL PSYCHOLOGY IN AMERICA

Philosophical and Psychological Beginnings

While existential phenomenology is a distinctly European movement born out of a particular period of political turbulence and cultural upheaval, America has also generated its seminal existentialists and phenomenologists, who laid the groundwork for the import of the E-P movement in the wake of World War II. For example, one of America's foremost philosophers, William James (1842–1910), was exploring E-P alternatives to the scientific method as Husserl groped toward his phenomenology. Gordon Allport claims that had James's ideology been integrated into the mainstream, "it might have served as the foundation for an American school of phenomenology" (Linschoten, 1968, p. 31). James was atypical of his time. Plagued by recurrent illness and severe depression, he traveled throughout Europe in search of bodily cures and "an intellectually honest way to affirm freedom" (Brennan, 1968, p. 45) and alleviate mental suffering. He "dragged himself out of depression by deciding that his first act of will would be to believe in the freedom of the will" (Grattan, 1962, p. 152).

James, who asserted that reality is that which is directly experienceable, was known as a radical empiricist. Other phenomenological motifs, including a primitive notion of intentionality and a respect for description as a scientific procedure, exist as well. However, during James's lifetime the intellectual community in America remained unsympathetic to these themes and assimilated only his more overtly scientific works; indeed, he was adopted by the early behaviorists as a precursor (Bjork, 1983).

Although the philosopher John Dewey (1859–1952) was not a phenomenologist, there are obvious phenomenological motifs in his thinking as well. In his writings on education (e.g., Dewey, 1938), he insisted that educational reform must be based on a careful consideration of the actual experiences of children. Kestenbaum (1977) argues that there are important similarities between Merleau-Ponty and Dewey: they agreed on the "primacy of experience" and "were united in their opposition to (1) dualism of any kind, (2) that sort of intellectualism which would reduce all experience of knowing, and (3) scientism" (p. 7).

Only through the Great Depression, the threat of territorial invasion in World War II, and the advent of the nuclear age did American citizens' experiences of the alienation, disintegration of traditional values, and attendant anxiety begin to mirror what Europeans had earlier known. European-trained philosophers such as Marvin Farber and psychologists such as Gordon Allport and Robert MacLeod began encouraging colleagues to explore the E-P movement (May, 1969a). In addition, some European immigrants fleeing Fascist oppression had been trained in Gestalt psychology using the phenomenological method (e.g., Kurt Koffka, Wolfgang Köhler) or were within the E-P movement (e.g., Paul Tillich, Erwin Straus). Still others already working in the United States and expressing an affinity with E-P's concerns were European born and trained, among them Andras Angyal, Helm Stierlin, Adrian van Kaam, Henri F. Ellenberger, and Rudolf Allers. In the 1940s a contingent of grass-roots phenomenologists and existentialists were also calling for a more experiential approach to psychology and psychotherapy. Among these were Donald Snygg, his colleague Arthur W. Combs, and Carl Rogers.

Psychologist Ulrich Sonnemann (1954) wrote, "Existentialism steers towards a rediscovery of spontaneous man [sic] in his world" (p. 372). Such exploration and rediscovery were characteristic of the American E-P movement as a whole from 1949 to 1958. While European E-P scholars of this time were actively building upon earlier foundations, their American counterparts were in many ways still in the process of establishing the basic groundwork. Consequently, many scholars turned to Europe for direction. This resulted in multiple critiques and examinations of noteworthy pioneers such as Sartre, Binswanger, and Jaspers (e.g., Alfred Stern, *Sartre: His Philosophy and Psychoanalysis*, 1953; the translation of Karl Jaspers, *Reason and Existenz*, by William Earle, 1955; and Jacob Blauner, "Existential Analysis: Ludwig Binswanger's Daseinanalyse," 1957).

Throughout the 1940s American phenomenologists Donald Snygg (1904–1967) and Arthur Combs (b. 1912) made significant contributions to the growth of psychology. In multiple cowritten works they argued for the development of a phenomenological system of psychology that was true to subjective experience. In

their efforts toward this goal, Snygg and Combs sought to identify basic human
needs and clarify the relationship between these subjectively experienced needs
and human actions. These authors contended that the most basic human need
was for the preservation and enhancement of the phenomenal, that is, the experienced, self. Furthermore, they proposed, "All behavior is determined by the
phenomenological field at the moment of action" (Snygg & Combs, 1949, p.
45), suggesting that present perceptions rather than "objective" events govern
behavior. The phenomenological field, which is the situation as experienced by
the person, is always in flux, and the person is constantly seeking adjustment.
Accordingly, Snygg and Combs (1950) called into question the concept of coping
mechanisms such as regression, as well as the acceptance of other mechanistic
and explanatory constructs, which they viewed as an "attempt to explain mystery
with greater mystery" (p. 526).

Efforts were also made to further clarify the relationship between existentialism
and psychotherapy. Among the significant contributors were Edith Weigert's
article, "Existentialism and Its Relations to Psychotherapy" (1949), Ulrich Sonnemann's book *Existence and Therapy* (1954), and Rolf Muus's article "Existentialism and Psychology" (1956). In her article Weigert presented an overview of
the early E-P movement and indicated applications to psychology by contrasting
Heidegger's notion of care with Binswanger's idea of love. Sonnemann and Muus
both provided introductions to psychology and existential analysis, with the latter
examining the strong emphasis on personal experience in the writings of Kierkegaard, Jaspers, and Sartre.

The Emergence of E-P Psychology as a Major Force

While essential groundwork was being laid through the further elucidation of
philosophical understandings, the American E-P movement did not expand significantly from the late 1940s to the early 1950s. However, in the late 1950s two
events markedly spurred the growth of American E-P psychiatry and psychotherapy. The first was Martin Buber's 1957 participation in the William Alanson
White Memorial Lectures and his famous discussion with Carl Rogers. As has
already been suggested, Buber has had a considerable impact on American psychiatrists, including authors Leslie H. Farber (1912–1981), Ivan Boszormenyi-
Nagy, and Lyman Wynne at the National Institute of Mental Health (Friedman,
1984).

The second pivotal event was the 1958 publication of *Existence*, a collection of
previously untranslated papers by European E-P psychiatrists with introductory
essays by May and Ellenberger (May, Angel, & Ellenberger, 1958). William
Barrett's *Irrational Man* (1958), an introduction to existentialism, also came out
that year. The unexpected popularity of these books led to further E-P translations, a surge of psychotherapist interest in the movement, and more original E-P
writing by American authors. In the next few years a spate of associations spon-
soring journals and periodicals sprang up, and in 1962 a doctoral program in E-P
psychology was established at Duquesne University in Pittsburgh.

Along with *Existence*, a ground-breaking psychological work was published by the sociologist Helen Lynd (1894–1965). In *On Shame and the Search for Identity* (1961) she forcefully argued that psychoanalytic and behavioral theories and methods are inadequate to the study of a phenomenon as pervasive and subtle as shame. Anticipating some of the critiques soon to be made by phenomenological psychologists, Lynd decried the dogmatic reliance on preconceived methods of inquiry (especially experimentation and "objective" observation) as well as the hegemony of abstract and often categorical concepts, typically based on positivistic philosophy. In her own sensitive and incisive analysis, Lynd skillfully drew upon literary and biographical representations of experiences of shame.

The works of Andras Angyal, viewed by Maslow (1965) as "consistent with the existential-phenomenological approach" (p. vi), were also beneficial in revealing "the simpler structures beneath the surface" (p. v) of human experience. Andras Angyal, a Hungarian-born psychologist and psychiatrist, is, in the words of Neil Friedman (1982), "a neglected genius." After immigrating to the United States, Angyal spent many years as the research director at Worcester State Hospital, during which time he explored schizophrenic hallucinations in relation to hypnotic states and kinesthesis (a person's experience of bodily movement). At a later date Angyal went into private practice.

Angyal also developed a holistic personality theory that was founded upon a very careful and empathic reading of the way the client experiences existence at a very fundamental level. Angyal's findings are presented in *Foundations for a Science of Personality* (1941) and further clarified in *Neurosis and Treatment: A Holistic Theory* (1965). Angyal contended that each human being is motivated by the principles of mastery (autonomy) and homony (love). These motivations govern the personality. Furthermore, the personality as a whole is dominated by a healthy or a neurotic pattern. Therefore, the individual may attempt to obtain mastery and homony through either system, depending on which pattern is dominant.

Angyalian therapy then begins as a "demolition of the neurosis" and a "reconstruction of the (dormant) system of health" through holistic insight, which the therapist helps to facilitate. The next stage becomes a "struggle for decision," in which the movement of health must become strong enough to defeat the neurotic paradigm. The last stage of therapy involves two components: "getting well" and "staying well" (N. Friedman, 1982, p. 86).

Charlotte Bühler (1893–1974), an eminent German-born scholar and psychologist, also had a deep-seated interest and resolute desire to explore human experience. These interests led her to become an international leader and spokesperson for the humanistic movement. She also made momentous contributions through research, teaching, and publications pertaining to child psychology, clinical psychology, psychotherapy, psychological testing, life-cycle studies, and values and life goals (Bugental, 1975/1976).

Prior to immigrating to the United States to avoid Nazi persecution, Bühler participated in the Munich Phenomenological Circle to discuss Husserl's phenomenology (Misiak & Sexton, 1973). Throughout her writings an underlying connection to E-P psychology is revealed, with a clear emphasis placed on intentionality as developed by Brentano, Husserl, and May, and a concern for studying human life in a way that does justice to its experiential, creative, and adaptive aspects (C. Bühler, 1969, 1971).

Charlotte Bühler's famous husband, psychologist, psychiatrist, and scholar Karl Bühler (1879–1963), also made noteworthy contributions to psychology (for an overview, see Bugental, 1966). Among these multiple contributions, he is acknowledged for challenging behaviorism's dismissal of inner experience as well as the failure of psychoanalysis to do justice to human creativity (Wegrocki, 1966). His own work was highly integrative; he was open to a variety of theoretical perspectives and valued diverse psychological methods (K. Bühler, 1930; Murphy, 1966).

Bühler's desire to explore research through introspective methods may be linked to his earlier immersion in Husserl's phenomenology through participation in the Munich Phenomenological Circle, as well as his studies with Carl Stumpf and Oswald Külpe. But this influence was not just one way. Husserl wrote to Karl Bühler in 1927, indicating that he had read his work with the greatest interest (Spiegelberg, 1982).

The Development of an E-P Clinical Tradition

Undoubtedly the "most influential native American spokesman for an existential phenomenology" (Spiegelberg, 1972, p. 158) has been psychotherapist Rollo May (1909–1994), first editor of *Existence* (1958) and a prolific author. While enrolled at Union Theological Seminary, he met Paul Tillich (1886–1965), a recent immigrant and later his primary mentor. Tillich's work, while not strictly existential, as he stressed the need for understanding human beings in terms of their nature (essence) as well as their freedom (existence), reflects the thought of Kierkegaard, Nietzsche, and Heidegger.

After enrolling at Columbia University to study clinical psychology, May developed tuberculosis. His growing sense of "personal responsibility for the fact that it was I who had the tuberculosis" (May, 1972, p. 14) served as the impetus for his doctoral dissertation, published as *The Meaning of Anxiety* (1950). *Man's Search for Himself* (1953) shows May's continued concern with existential issues and thinkers. By the time *Existence* (May, Angel, & Ellenberger, 1958) appeared, May had identified himself with the E-P movement (Spiegelberg, 1972). He continued to expand and clarify his views through writing, often through the exploration of polarities (*Love and Will*, 1969b; *Power and Innocence*, 1972; *Freedom and Destiny*, 1981). In one of his most recent books, May (1991) returned to one of his ongoing interests, the importance of myth. He developed the thesis "that contemporary therapy is almost entirely concerned, when all is surveyed, with the problems of the individual's search for myths" (p. 9).

May focused upon the fundamental relations between selfhood and anxiety and selfhood and guilt. He viewed the self as an experiencing center of being that,

when threatened with nonbeing, attempts to preserve centeredness by retrenchment, a kind of contraction away from the world and its challenges. Therapy,
then, involves an expansion of awareness and self and a courageous release of
potential in the context of genuine client-therapist encounter (Bilmes, 1978; May
1958a). In a book completed just before his death, Rollo May and coauthor Kirk
Schneider gave a detailed articulation of the relevance of existential psychology
for a wide variety of clinical situations and issues, including the treatment of
trauma and cross-cultural psychology (Schneider & May, 1995).

Another American therapist profoundly affected by the E-P movement is
James F. T. Bugental (b. 1915; see chapter 16 on Bugental in part II of this
volume). A former associate clinical professor of psychiatry at Stanford University
and past president of various psychological associations, Bugental defines his therapeutic orientation as existential-humanistic. He chooses an existential framework
for humanism on the basis of its experiential validity, ability to illuminate the
human condition, flexibility, and nonreductionist emphasis. In *The Search for Authenticity* (1965), *The Search for Existential Identity* (1976), and *The Art of the
Psychotherapist* (1987), E-P concerns such as authenticity, choice, tragedy, and
transcendence are aired.

Eugene T. Gendlin (b. 1926), former student of and collaborator with Carl
Rogers, is associate professor of psychology at the University of Chicago, founding
editor of the journal *Psychotherapy: Theory, Research, and Practice*, and author of
several books and articles on experiential psychotherapy. Gendlin investigates the
effectiveness of therapy through an understanding rooted in existential works.
This foundation helped him to sharpen Rogers's concept of the self as a process
of experiencing. Gendlin is able to explicate his experiential approach in a philosophically foundational manner (*Experiencing and the Creation of Meaning*,
1962), as well as in a more concrete way (*Focusing*, 1981; *Let Your Body Interpret
Your Dreams*, 1986).

One of the most recent and influential contributors to American E-P psychotherapy is Irvin D. Yalom (b. 1931), author of *Existential Psychotherapy* (1980)
and *The Theory and Practice of Group Psychotherapy* (1985) and coauthor of *Every
Day Gets a Little Closer* (1974). Yalom received his M.D. from Boston University
and is currently professor of psychiatry at Stanford. Yalom views existential psychotherapy as a dynamic psychotherapy. He emphasizes "conflict that flows from
the individual's confrontation with the givens of existence" (Yalom, 1980, p. 8)
(death, freedom, isolation, meaninglessness). Psychopathology is the result of
"anxiety and its maladaptive consequences [in response] to these four ultimate
concerns" (Yalom, 1980, p. 485).

Numerous other contributions have been made to psychotherapy within the
E-P tradition. Notable among them are Barton's (1974) comparative analysis of
Freud, Jung, and Rogers, Hycner's (1991) presentation of psychotherapy within
a dialogical perspective, van Deurzen-Smith's (1988) text on the practice of existential counseling, and Moustakas's (1988) discussion of the relationship between philosophical phenomenology and psychotherapy. In addition, a number

of authors have written about "experiential psychotherapy." Although this term has been used, with multiple meanings, by various authors, it is evident that their work is closely related to the E-P tradition. Mahrer (e.g., 1983) has written extensively about experiential psychotherapy, and Felder and Weiss (1991) have published an overview of the experiential tradition developed in Atlanta under the leadership of Carl Whitaker, John Warkentin, and others. (For an overview of experiential and phenomenological psychotherapy, see Moss, 1989b.)

In addition, several psychologists have attempted to spell out the implications of E-P psychology for clinical practice. Keen (1970) argues for the relevance of existential psychology for psychopathology, in part by providing an existential reinterpretation of Freud. Another psychologist, Joseph Lyons (1963, 1973), has both critiqued the natural scientific conception of the human and articulated an experience-based perspective for understanding abnormal and normal human behavior. In the area of psychological assessment, little has been done by phenomenologists, with the almost singular exception of Constance Fischer (1985). She has developed "the individualized approach," which is remarkable in its humanistic ethos, theoretical coherence, and clinical value. Central to this approach is the recognition that "the client's experience of his or her situation must be taken into account. The assessor's own experience also is inevitably involved—a historical/cultural context, professional training, personal background and so on" (C. T. Fischer, 1989, p. 165).

Theory and Research Developments in E-P Psychology

So far, the reader may have the impression that E-P psychology is primarily relevant to clinical psychology, an impression that a review of a classic text like *Existence* (May, Angel, & Ellenberger, 1958) would only confirm. However, this is far from the truth. In fact, the contributions of E-P psychology to theoretical and research psychology are so extensive (although less widely known) that we can only discuss them in a summary fashion.

Adrian van Kaam's (1966) book *Existential Foundations of Psychology* provides a well-articulated vision of a theoretical and empirical psychology based on the concepts of E-P philosophers such as Martin Heidegger. He argues that specific psychological theories (in his terms, "differential psychologies"), such as psychoanalysis and behaviorism, are simultaneously powerful and reductionistic. Biologically oriented psychology, for example, frequently conceives of the person merely as an organism. In van Kaam's view only existential psychology is sufficiently comprehensive and faithful to the reality of human existence to provide a context within which the findings of all the differential psychologies can be brought together in a meaningful way.

Van Kaam (1959) also provided an early example of a phenomenologically based research dissertation, "the experience of feeling understood," that was accepted by a traditional psychology department. In 1962 he founded the doctoral program at Duquesne University, which soon became known as the primary center for phenomenological psychology in North America (D. Smith, 1983).

Amedeo Giorgi, van Kaam's successor as chair of the Duquesne Psychology Department and currently at the Saybrook Graduate School and Research Institute in San Francisco, wrote what was to become a highly influential foundational text of psychology, one that is cited in virtually every phenomenological psychological dissertation in North America. Many qualitative researchers throughout the Western world frequently draw from his instrumental expertise as well.

Giorgi received his training in experimental psychology but turned to phenomenological philosophers, especially Husserl and Merleau-Ponty, when his experience in an applied setting convinced him that a psychology based in natural science was not responsive to the realities of everyday life. In his *Psychology as a Human Science*, Giorgi (1970) critiques mainstream psychology for not doing justice to complex human phenomena, its lack of holistic methods, and its uncritical adoption of the *approach* (i.e., the implicit philosophy) underlying the natural sciences. Psychology conceived as a human science, in contrast, would be based on three suppositions: fidelity to the phenomenon of humans as persons, special concern for uniquely human phenomena, and recognition of the primacy of human life as relational.

In subsequent work, Giorgi has carried out phenomenological research on phenomena such as learning and memory (e.g., 1975a; 1989), based on a systematically conceived model of data analysis (1975b; 1985). An overview of Giorgi's method of data analysis is provided by Polkinghorne (1989, pp. 53–55). Basically, Giorgi's aim is to provide procedures that guide researchers to look carefully and systematically at the descriptions collected, express their implicit psychological meaning, and articulate the structure of each description (a portrait of the essential constituents of each account and their interrelationship) as well as the general structure of the phenomenon as revealed by all the descriptions collected. In other words, the general structure articulates what these descriptions most basically have in common. Giorgi is consistent in emphasizing that this process of analysis requires imagination and discernment; it cannot be done mechanically.

By describing concretely how phenomenological research can actually be done, Giorgi has helped numerous researchers and doctoral students to make the practice of phenomenological psychology a reality rather than just a hope. He has also demonstrated to the larger (and typically skeptical) psychological community that human science psychology can be as rigorous and as intersubjectively valid as psychology based on natural science principles.

In addition to Constance Fischer and Anthony Barton, previously mentioned, a number of faculty members at Duquesne have made significant scholarly contributions. Richard Knowles has provided an existential reading of Erik Erikson's developmental theories in his *Human Development and Human Possibility* (1986). William Fischer (e.g., 1974, 1988, 1991) has written extensively about the experience of anxiety, analyzing firsthand accounts in order to arrive at a structural interpretation of this central human experience. In the area of social psychology, Rolf von Eckartsberg (1932–1993) has developed an ecological and existential approach that is mindful of how all human action is situated within a cultural, historical, and spiritual context (e.g., 1981, 1993). He has also been a pioneer in utilizing a dialogical approach to research, one that explicitly acknowledges an intersubjective and linguistic basis for scientific understanding (von Eckartsberg, 1986, 1989). Edward Murray (1986, 1987) has argued strongly for the centrality of imaginative thinking in human existence and has elaborated on its importance for psychotherapy, personality integration, and religion.

There are numerous scholars who have been influenced by the Duquesne tradition. For example, Wertz (1982, 1987) has published a number of studies and theoretical discussions on perception understood from an E-P perspective. He has also made significant contributions to the issue of methodology in the human sciences, most notably with his frequently cited article on reliability in psychological research (Wertz, 1986). At the State University of West Georgia, another center for E-P and humanistic psychology, Aanstoos has focused his scholarship on thinking. On the basis of an empirical study of chess players and philosophical considerations, Aanstoos (1983, 1987) has demonstrated that a computational model of thinking is unable to account for everyday problem solving.

In terms of a broad, scholarly examination of nonpositivistic alternatives for psychology and other social sciences, Donald Polkinghorne's *Methodology for the Human Sciences* (1983) has been quite influential. Polkinghorne, who was originally associated with the Saybrook Institute, a center for humanistic research and education in psychology, looks at the philosophical roots of the human science tradition (e.g., Wilhelm Dilthey) and provides an overview of current trends and methods in qualitative research. In a subsequent book Polkinghorne (1988) notes, as have many others in psychology, "I have not found the findings of academic research of much help in my work as a clinician" (p. ix), and suggests that understanding human life in terms of narrative structure, story, and meaning giving might be a remedy for this discrepancy between research and practice. In a similar vein, Howard (1991) advocates that psychology recognize the centrality of the notion of storytelling and suggests that we understand "psychopathology as instances of lifestories gone awry; and psychotherapy as exercises in story repair" (p. 187).

One of the best-known practitioners of the narrative approach to research is the Harvard-based psychiatrist Robert Coles. An eloquent and prolific writer who has published close to forty books, Coles (e.g., 1964, 1967a, 1967b, 1977, 1978, 1990) has done much to tell the stories of the lives of children in America. Although he is clearly cognizant of the E-P tradition, as is shown by his occasional references to Heidegger, Kierkegaard, and phenomenology, he is not formally associated with this tradition. Nonetheless, anyone who looks closely at his work and his thoughtful discussions of issues of method will note that he is deeply immersed in the lives of the people he tries to understand, alert to the subtle ways in which the observer's preconceptions get in the way of attending to lived experience, continually engaged in adjusting his method to fit his subject matter, and adept in revealing the structure of various experiences through the use of contrasting descriptions. For example, in writing about children of migrant workers, Coles (1967a) helps us to understand the nature of the world in which they live by showing how different it is from middle-class children who have a bed and a room of their own.

Clark Moustakas (1990), well known for his contributions to humanistic psychology, has developed what he calls a "heuristic" approach to research that is rooted in phenomenology, but also emphasizes the importance of "a direct, personal encounter with the phenomenon being investigated" (p. 7). He has also published a very useful text on phenomenological research methods (Moustakas, 1994).

Faculty involved in the graduate program in E-P therapeutic psychology at Seattle University have developed an innovative dialogical phenomenological method in the process of studying phenomena such as forgiveness, humility, and social activism. The essence of the dialogical method is that researchers work collaboratively in small groups, fostering faithfulness to the phenomenon through open dialogue among the researchers in relationship to the data, rather than adhering to a set of explicitly spelled-out procedures (for an overview, see Halling, Kunz, & Rowe, 1994).

In the last decade there has also been a developing hermeneutical tradition in psychology. Hermeneutics originally concerned itself with the question of how one can adequately interpret written texts, but has more recently taken on the general question of the nature of interpretation, whether within the humanities or the social sciences. Obviously, interpretation is key in psychotherapy, assessment, and research. This tradition is closely aligned with phenomenology; psychologists interested in hermeneutics typically draw on Heidegger (1927/1962) and Gadamer (1960/1989), who was a student of Heidegger. Packer and Addison's (1989) text provides a good introduction to hermeneutics and includes examples of its application to research.

E-P Psychology in Canada

Over the last two decades there has also been a great deal of activity in E-P psychology in Canada. Again, we can give only a brief overview of selected material. One of Canada's pioneers of phenomenological and hermeneutical psychology, Lewis Brandt, is intimately familiar with European psychological developments, especially in Germany. In his 1982 book *Psychologists Caught* Brandt looks at various approaches to psychology and questions whether any of them can account for the activity that they themselves carry out, that is, theorizing and attempting to explain human behavior. He concludes that most psychologies fail this test and challenges the conventional wisdom that cognitive behaviorism is a significant departure from traditional behaviorism.

York University in Toronto has become something of a center for human science psychology, even though the adherents of this orientation, among its faculty as well as students, remain a minority. At York, Malcolm Westcott (1988) has studied the experience of human freedom (and of restriction), drawing upon philosophical sources and providing a synthesis of empirical and phenomenological research. His book includes a balanced critique of positivistic psychology. David Rennie (Rennie, 1992; Rennie & Toukmanian, 1992) has shown that qualitative research based on the grounded-theory perspective has much to contribute to the study of the psychotherapy process.

There are several faculty members at the University of Alberta at Edmonton who are working within a phenomenological tradition and are encouraging doctoral students to follow in their footsteps. John Osborne (1987, 1990) has written both about the nature of learning and E-P methodology. Max van Manen (1990) has written a guide to human science research for education and the social sciences, with an emphasis on social application.

EXISTENTIAL PHENOMENOLOGY AND HUMANISTIC PSYCHOLOGY

Though we have sought to demonstrate throughout this chapter that existential-phenomenological psychology is a distinctive approach for addressing the human condition, we also believe that there are large areas of philosophical and clinical agreement between existential-phenomenological psychology and humanistic psychology. These two traditions are both part of what is often referred to as "the Third Force" in psychology. Wandersman, Popen, and Ricks (1975) suggest that they share a commitment to "human psychology which is distinct from models accounting for animal or mechanical behavior" (quoted in DeCarvalho & Krippner, 1993, p. 64).

In joint efforts to establish a human psychology that moves beyond biological reductionism and depersonalization, the Third Force has endeavored to develop a new paradigm that is able to encounter human beings in all their complexity and uniqueness while simultaneously facilitating genuine understanding. The humanistic works of Allport, Maslow, and Rogers are representative of efforts to overcome the positivistic aspects of the natural science movement. Like Giorgi and May, proponents of the E-P movement, Allport, Maslow, and Rogers acknowledge the weaknesses inherent in imitating the natural scientific approach. Allport (1968) warns, "Physicalistic and deterministic theories tend so to restrict our science as to render it incapable of having fruitful bearing upon practical life" (p. 19).

Similarities between the humanists and E-P psychologists can be confirmed in several other areas as well, as has been shown by DeCarvalho and Krippner (1993). For example, Allport advanced the idea of "systematic eclecticism," which, like existentialism, seeks to address the total human experience, as evidenced by one's relation to one's self, others, and the world in which one lives. A strong correlation can also be drawn between Maslow's (e.g., 1969, chap. 10) concept of "Taoist objectivity," which "stresses careful observation of a noninterfering sort" (p. 96) in regard to experience, and Husserl's phenomenological method, which aims to "get back to the things themselves."

In addition, E-P tenets can be seen in the intersubjective approach proposed by Rogers. By emphasizing the importance of the subjective experience of the client and prioritizing the relationship between the clinician and the client, Rogers (e.g., 1973) firmly aligns himself with the intersubjective approach integral to E-P psychology and the transcendent possibilities suggested in Buber's "I-thou" (1923/1958) dynamics.

As a whole movement, humanism has been most successful in calling into question the dominant paradigms underlying the medical and behavioral models of psychology. These movements—characterized by reductionism, mechanization, dehumanization, and the artificial splitting of subjective and objective realities—have been shown to be incomplete and nonreflective of the human condition. However, the gains in awareness and practice that have been catalyzed by humanistic psychology, especially in the arena of clinical psychology (Giorgi, 1992), are once more being challenged through the introduction, across the United States, of bureaucratically based, short-term/managed care with an emphasis on preconceived behavioral objectives, the reemphasis on the medical model, the hegemony of the American Psychiatric Association's (1994) diagnostic manual, and the American Psychological Association's controlling influence in such areas as accreditation of doctoral programs in clinical psychology. As a result, one may wonder how influential humanistic and E-P psychology will be in the future.

At the same time, it is evident that Third Force psychologists are responding to these trends within psychology. For example, humanistically and E-P–oriented graduate psychology programs have come together to form the Consortium for Diversified Psychology Programs. Under the leadership of Clark Moustakas, this group works to promote and protect academic freedom and diversity in graduate clinical education and training (Simpkinson, 1990).

Nonetheless, in order to go beyond being merely a protest movement, humanistic psychology will need to squarely confront the twofold challenge that presently demands its attention. At one level, this challenge exists internally and is evidenced by the absence of an explicit theoretical foundation that is distinctly humanistic. In addition, there are marked inconsistencies that exist in the methodology proposed to study and genuinely understand human experience. Although humanistic psychologists want to study the whole person, typically they have used traditional research methods to do so. At an external level, humanistic psychology must address the trends toward mandated short-term/managed care and positivistic assumptions still evident in much of contemporary psychology and in the medical model.

Although the multiple perspectives within the Third Force are unified in their desire to remain true to lived human experience, the means to this end are much less clear. This lack of direction and the tendency to be overly eclectic consequently weaken the movement. Moustakas (1985) highlights this dilemma, claiming, " 'Humanistic' does not have any more exact meaning in 1985 than it did in 1959, but rather, continues to unfold in meaning according to one's conception and values regarding freedom, science, faith, human nature, human experience, humanness, and human being" (p. 6). This absence of theoretical agreement has impeded the movement's ability to develop dynamic systematic methodologies that are recognized by more traditional psychologies. Giorgi (1992) convincingly argues that the lack of a positive method or an adequate conception of the person is the primary reason that humanistic psychology has not yet made strong inroads into the academic world. Rogers (1985) seconds "the need for new models of science more appropriate to human beings" (p. 9). Yet while Rogers gives undivided support for the growth in experientially based methodologies, he fails to fully grasp the possibility and necessity of developing critical noneclectic methods that are qualitative and reflective of human experience, but nonetheless rigorous and systematically consistent.

To surmount these obstacles, proponents of humanistic tenets could benefit by developing and embracing foundations that are uniquely expressive of the full spectrum of human experience and fully cognizant of the intersubjective realm that transcends the positivistic limitations of subject-object duality. Giorgi (1992) aptly claims that "humanistic psychology has not let that articulated sense of being human inform its scientific practice in a theoretically radical way" (p. 428). Clearly, the inadequacies and inconsistencies at the theoretical and methodological level directly impact the humanistic movement's ability to thoroughly address the challenges that we have mentioned.

One helpful example of how a phenomenologically based approach can be used to foster humanistic goals of understanding of the person and growth-oriented, respectful intervention, as well as to counter some of the limitations of the medical model, has been provided by Peters (1995). He argues that the biological perspective on physical problems proceeds as if the disease were unrelated to the individual. This view, then, cannot account for differences in disability among people with equivalent physical pathologies, nor does it provide insight into issues around "treatment compliance." In contrast, Peters documents how phenomenological methods bring to light how a particular problem (e.g., rheumatoid arthritis) disrupts a person's sense of self and world and show how the consequent level of disability is a function of patients' social context and manner of interpreting and coping with their illness.

Phenomenological thinkers can also be useful to the humanistic movement insofar as they address basic issues, such as the relationship between mind and body. As we have shown, Merleau-Ponty (1942/1963, 1945/1962) has addressed this issue in a thoughtful and highly sophisticated manner, drawing extensively on clinical literature.

We started this chapter with a quote from the preface to Merleau-Ponty's (1945/1962) classic work *Phenomenology of Perception*. It seems especially fitting to return to this preface as we conclude this chapter since much of Merleau-Ponty's work was animated by the same spirit that is alive in contemporary humanistic and E-P psychology. In attempting to identify what is distinctly human, Merleau-Ponty (1945/1962) wrote:

I am the absolute source, my existence does not stem from my antecedents, from my physical and social environment; instead it moves out towards them and sustains them. . . . Scientific points of view, according to which my existence is a moment of the world's, are always both naive and at the same time dishonest, because they take for granted, without explicitly mentioning it, the other point of view, namely that of consciousness, through which from the outset a world forms itself round me and begins to exist for me. (p. ix)

REFERENCES

Aanstoos, C. (1983). A phenomenological study of thinking. In A. Giorgi, A. Barton, & C. Maes (Eds.), *Duquesne studies in phenomenological psychology* (Vol. 4, pp. 244–256). Pittsburgh, PA: Duquesne University Press.

Aanstoos, C. (1987). A critique of the computational model of thought: The contribution of Merleau-Ponty. *Journal of Phenomenological Psychology, 18*(2), 187–200.

Allport, G. (1968). *The person in psychology: Selected essays*. Boston: Beacon Press.

American Psychiatric Association. (1994). *Diagnostic and statistical manual of mental disorders* (4th ed.). Washington, DC: Author.

Angyal, A. (1941). *Foundations for a science of personality*. New York: Commonwealth Fund.

Angyal, A. (1965). *Neurosis and treatment: A holistic theory*. New York: J. Wiley.

Barnes, H. E. (1953). Introduction. In J. P. Sartre, *Existential psychoanalysis* (H. E. Barnes, Trans.) (pp. 1–40). New York: Philosophical Library.

Barrett, W. (1958). *Irrational man: A study in existential philosophy*. Garden City, NY: Doubleday & Company.

Barton, A. (1974). *Three worlds of therapy*. Palo Alto, CA: National Press Books.

Bilmes, M. (1978). Rollo May. In R. S. Valle & M. King (Eds.), *Existential-phenomenological alternatives for psychology* (pp. 290–294). New York: Oxford University Press.

Binswanger, L. (1942). *Grundformen und erkenntnis menschlichen daseins* [Basic forms and knowledge of human existence]. Zurich: Niehans.

Binswanger, L. (1957). *Sigmund Freud: Reminiscences of a friendship* (N. Guterman, Trans.). New York: Grune & Stratton. (Original work published 1956)

Binswanger, L. (1958a). The case of Ellen West. In R. May, E. Angel, & H. F. Ellenberger (Eds.), *Existence: A new dimension in psychiatry and psychology* (pp. 237–364). New York: Basic Books.

Binswanger, L. (1958b). Insanity as life-historical phenomenon and as mental disease: The case of Ilse. In R. May, E. Angel, & H. F. Ellenberger (Eds.), *Existence: A new dimension in psychiatry and psychology* (pp. 214–236). New York: Basic Books.

Bjork, D. W. (1983). *The compromised scientist: William James in the development of American psychology*. New York: Columbia University Press.

Blauner, J. (1957). Existential analysis: Ludwig Binswanger's Daseinsanalyse. *Psychoanalytic Review, 44*, 51–64.

Boss, M. (1949). *Meaning and content of sexual perversions* (L. L. Abell, Trans.). New York: Grune & Stratton. (Original work published 1947)

Boss, M. (1963). *Psychoanalysis and daseinsanalysis* (L. B. Lefebre, Trans.). New York: Basic Books. (Original work published 1957)

Boss, M. (1979). *Existential foundations of medicine and psychology* (S. Conway & A. Cleaves, Trans.). New York: Aronson. (Original work published 1971)

Brandt, L. W. (1982). *Psychologists caught: A psycho-logic of psychology.* Toronto: University of Toronto Press.

Brennan, B. P. (1968). *William James.* New York: Twayne Publishers.

Brentano, F. (1874). *Psychologie vom empirischen standpunkt* [Psychology from an empirical perspective]. Leipzig: Dunker & Humblot.

Brice, C. W. (1978). Ludwig Binswanger. In R. S. Valle & M. King (Eds.), *Existential-phenomenological alternatives for psychology* (pp. 300–307). New York: Oxford University Press.

Buber, M. (1958). *I and thou* (2nd ed.) (R. G. Smith, Trans.). New York: Scribner. (Original work published 1923)

Buber, M. (1965). Distance and relation. In M. Friedman (Ed.), *Martin Buber: The knowledge of man* (pp. 59–71). New York: Harper Torchbooks. (Original work published 1951)

Bugental, J.F.T. (1965). *The search for authenticity: An existential-analytic approach* to psychotherapy. New York: Holt, Rinehart & Winston.

Bugental, J.F.T. (Ed.). (1966). Symposium on Karl Bühler's contributions to psychology. *Journal of General Psychology, 75,* 181–219.

Bugental, J.F.T. (1975/1976). Toward a subjective psychology: Tribute to Charlotte Bühler. *Interpersonal Development, 6,* 48–61.

Bugental, J.F.T. (1976). *The search for existential identity.* San Francisco: Jossey-Bass.

Bugental, J.F.T. (1987). *The art of the psychotherapist.* New York: Norton.

Bühler, C. (1969). Humanistic psychology as an educational program. *American Psychologist, 24*(8), 736–742.

Bühler, C. (1971). Basic theoretical concepts of humanistic psychology. *American Psychologist, 26*(4), 378–386.

Bühler, K. (1930). *The mental development of the child.* London: Routledge & Kegan Paul.

Cissna, K. N., & Anderson, R. (1994). The 1957 Martin Buber–Carl Rogers dialogue, as dialogue. *Journal of Humanistic Psychology, 34*(1), 11–45.

Coles, R. (1967). *Children of crisis: Vol. 1. A study of courage and fear.* Boston: Little, Brown.

Coles, R. (1971a). *Children of crisis: Vol. 2. Migrants, sharecroppers, mountaineers.* Boston: Little, Brown.

Coles, R. (1971b). *Children of crisis: Vol. 3. The south goes north.* Boston: Little, Brown.

Coles, R. (1977a). *Children of crisis: Vol. 4. Eskimos, Chicanos, Indians.* Boston: Little, Brown.

Coles, R. (1977b). *Children of crisis: Vol. 5. Privileged ones.* Boston: Little, Brown.

Coles, R. (1990). *The spiritual life of children.* Boston: Houghton Mifflin.

DeCarvalho, R., & Krippner, S. (1993). The problem of method in humanistic psychology. *Methods,* pp. 51–68.

Dewey, J. (1938). *Experience and education.* New York: MacMillan.

Felder, R. E., & Weiss, A. G. (1991). *Experiential psychotherapy.* Lanham, MD: University Press of America.

Fischer, C. T. (1985). *Individualizing psychological assessment.* Monterey, CA: Brooks/Cole.

Fischer, C. T. (1989). Personality assessment. In R. S. Valle & S. Halling (Eds.), *Existential-phenomenological perspectives in psychology* (pp. 157–178). New York: Plenum.

Fischer, W. F. (1974). On the phenomenological mode of researching being-anxious. *Journal of Phenomenological Psychology, 4,* 405–423.

Fischer, W. F. (1988). *Theories of anxiety* (2nd ed.). Washington, DC: University Press of America.

Fischer, W. F. (1991). The psychology of anxiety: A phenomenological description. *The Humanistic Psychologist, 19*(3), 289–300.

Frankl, V. E. (1963). *Man's search for meaning.* Boston: Beacon Press.

Frankl, V. E. (1965). *The doctor and the soul* (2nd ed.) (R. Winston & C. Winston, Trans.). New York: Vintage. (Original work published 1948)

Friedman, M. (1984). *Contemporary psychology: Revealing and obscuring the human.* Pittsburgh, PA: Duquesne University Press.

Friedman, M. (1994). Reflections on the Buber-Rogers dialogue. *Journal of Humanistic Psychology, 34*(1), 46–65.

Friedman, V. N. (1982). Holistic insight and focusing: Angyal and Gendlin. *Journal of Humanistic Psychology, 22*(3), 83–91.

Gadamer, H. G. (1989). *Truth and method* (2nd rev. ed.) Trans. revised by J. Weinsheimer & D. G. Marshall). New York: Crossroad. (Original work published 1960)

Gendlin, E. T. (1962). *Experiencing and the creation of meaning.* New York: Free Press.

Gendlin, E. T. (1981). *Focusing.* New York: Bantam.

Gendlin, E. T. (1986). *Let your body interpret your dreams.* Chicago: Chiron.

Giorgi. A. (1970). *Psychology as a human science.* New York: Harper & Row.

Giorgi, A. (1975a). An application of phenomenological method in psychology. In A. Giorgi, C. Fischer, & E. Murray (Eds.), *Duquesne studies in phenomenological psychology* (Vol. 2, pp. 82–103). Pittsburgh, PA: Duquesne University Press.

Giorgi, A. (1975b). Convergence and divergence of qualitative and quantitative methods in psychology. In A. Giorgi, C. Fischer, & E. Murray (Eds.), *Duquesne studies in phenomenological psychology* (Vol. 2, pp. 72–81). Pittsburgh, PA: Duquesne University Press.

Giorgi, A. (1985). Sketch of a psychological phenomenological method. In A. Giorgi (Ed.), *Phenomenology and psychological research* (pp. 8–22). Pittsburgh, PA: Duquesne University Press.

Giorgi, A. (1989). Learning and memory from the perspective of phenomenological psychology. In R. S. Valle & S. Halling (Eds.), *Existential-phenomenological perspectives in psychology* (pp. 99–112). New York: Plenum.

Giorgi, A. (1992). Whither humanistic psychology? In F. J. Wertz (Ed.), *The humanistic movement in psychology: History, celebration, and prospectus* [Special issue]. *Humanistic Psychologist, 20*(2–3), 422–438.

Grattan, C. H. (1962). *The three Jameses: A family of minds.* New York: New York University Press.

Halling, S., Kunz, G., & Rowe, J. O. (1994). The contributions of dialogical psychology to phenomenological research. *Journal of Humanistic Psychology, 34*(1), 109–131.

Heidegger, M. (1962). *Being and time* (J. Macquarrie & E. Robinson, Trans.). New York: Harper & Row. (Original work published 1927)

Howard, G. S. (1991). Culture tales: A narrative approach to thinking, cross-cultural psychology, and psychotherapy. *American Psychologist, 46*(3), 187–197.

Hubben, W. (1962). *Dostoevsky, Kierkegaard, Nietzsche, and Kafka*, New York: Collier.

Husserl, E. (1970a). *The crisis of European sciences and transcendental phenomenology* (D. Carr, Trans.). Evanston, IL: Northwestern University Press. (From original work published 1936)

Husserl, E. (1970b). *The logical investigations* (J. N. Findlay, Trans.). New York: Humanities Press. (Original work published 1900)

Hycner, R. (1991). *Between person and person: Towards a dialogical psychotherapy.* Highlands, NY: Gestalt Journal.

Jaspers, K. (1955). *Reason and existenz* (William Earle, Trans.). New York: Noonday Press. (Original work published 1953)

Jaspers, K. (1963). *General psychopathology* (J. Hoening & M. W. Hamilton, Trans.). Chicago: University of Chicago Press. (Original work published 1913)

Jaspers, K. (1969–1971). *Philosophy* (Vols. 1–3). (E. B. Ashton, Trans.). Chicago: University of Chicago Press. (Original work published 1932)

Jones, E. (1953–1957). *The life and work of Sigmund Freud 3 vols.* New York: Basic Books.

Kaufmann, W. (1967). Friederich Nietzsche. In P. Edwards (Ed.), *The encyclopedia of philosophy* (Vols. 5 & 6) (pp. 504–514). New York: Macmillan.

Kaufmann, W. (1975). Introduction. In W. Kaufmann (Ed.), *Existentialism from Dostoevsky to Sartre* (rev. ed.) (pp. 11–51). New York: New American Library.

Keen, E. (1970). *Three faces of being: Toward an existential clinical psychology.* New York: Appleton-Century-Crofts.

Kestenbaum, V. (1977). *The phenomenological sense of John Dewey: Habit and meaning.* Atlantic Highlands, NJ: Humanities Press.

Kierkegaard, S. (1941). *Sickness unto death* (W. Lowrie, Trans.). Princeton: Princeton University Press. (Original work published 1849)

Kiesel, T. (1979). A prefatory guide to readers of *Being and time.* In F. Elliston (Ed.), *Heidegger's existential analytic* (pp. 13–20). The Hague: Mouton.

Knowles, R. T. (1986). *Human development and human possibility: Erikson in the light of Heidegger.* Lanham, MD: University Press of America.

Laing, R. D. (1960). *The divided self.* London: Tavistock.

Laing, R. D. (1961). *Self and others.* London: Tavistock.

Laing, R. D. (1971). *The politics of the family and other essays.* New York: Pantheon.

Laing, R. D., & Cooper, D. (1964). *Reason and violence: A decade of Sartre's philosophy* (1950–1960). London: Tavistock.

Laing, R. D., & Esterson, A. (1964). *Sanity, madness, and the family.* London: Tavistock.

Linschoten, H. (1968). *On the way toward a phenomenological psychology* (A. Giorgi, Ed.). Pittsburgh, PA: Duquesne University Press.

Lowrie, W. (1970). *A short life of Kierkegaard.* Princeton: Princeton University Press.

Lynd, H. (1961). *On shame and the search for identity.* New York: Wiley.

Lyons, J. (1963). *Psychology and the measure of man.* New York: Free Press.

Lyons, J. (1973). *Experience: An introduction to a personal psychology.* New York: Harper & Row.

Mahrer, A. (1983). *Experiential psychotherapy.* New York: Brunner Mazel.

Malantschuk, G. (1971). *Kierkegaard's thought.* Princeton: Princeton University Press.

Maslow, A. H. (1965). Foreword to A. Angyal, *Neurosis and treatment: A holistic theory* (pp. v–vii). New York: Viking Press.

Maslow, A. H. (1969). *The psychology of science: A reconnaissance.* Chicago: Henry Regnery Co.

May, R. (1950). *The meaning of anxiety*. New York: Ronald Press.

May, R. (1953). *Man's search for himself*. New York: W. W. Norton.

May, R. (1958a). Contributions of existential psychotherapy. In R. May, E. Angel, & H. F. Ellenberger (Eds.), *Existence* (pp. 37–91). New York: Basic Books.

May, R. (1958b). The origins and significance of the existential movement in psychology. In R. May, E. Angel, & H. F. Ellenberger (Eds.), *Existence* (pp. 3–36). New York: Basic Books.

May, R. (1969a). *Existential psychology* (2nd ed.). New York: Random House.

May, R. (1969b). *Love and will*. New York: W. W. Norton.

May, R. (1972). *Power and innocence*. New York: Delta.

May, R. (1981). *Freedom and destiny*. New York: Delta.

May, R. (1991). *The cry for myth*. New York: W. W. Norton.

May, R., Angel, E., & Ellenberger, H. F. (Eds.). (1958). *Existence: A new dimension in psychiatry and psychology*. New York: Basic Books.

Merleau-Ponty, M. (1962). *Phenomenology of perception* (C. Smith, Trans.). New York: Humanities Press. (Original work published 1945)

Merleau-Ponty, M. (1963). *The structure of behavior* (A. L. Fisher, Trans.). Boston: Beacon Press. (Original work published 1942)

Merleau-Ponty, M. (1968). *The visible and the invisible* (A. Lingis, Trans.). Evanston, IL: Northwestern University Press. (Original work published 1964)

Misiak, H., & Sexton, V. S. (1966). *History of psychology: An overview*. New York: Grune & Stratton.

Misiak, H., & Sexton, V. S. (1973). *Phenomenological, existential, and humanistic psychologies: A historical survey*. New York: Grune & Stratton.

Moss, D. (1978). Medard Boss. In R. S. Valle & M. King (Eds.), *Existential-phenomenological alternatives for psychology* (pp. 308–323). New York: Oxford University Press.

Moss, D. (1981). Phenomenology and neuropsychology: Two approaches to consciousness. In R. Valle & R. von Eckartsberg (Eds.), *The metaphors of consciousness* (pp. 153–166). New York: Plenum.

Moss, D. (1982). Distortions in human embodiment: A study of surgically treated obesity. In R. Bruzina & B. Wilshire (Eds.), *Phenomenology: Dialogues and bridges: Selected studies in phenomenology and existential philosophy, Vol. 8* (pp. 253–267). Albany: State University of New York Press.

Moss, D. (1989a). Brain, body, and world: Body image and the psychology of the body. In R. S. Valle & S. Halling (Eds.), *Existential-phenomenological perspectives in psychology* (pp. 63–82). New York: Plenum.

Moss, D. (1989b). Psychotherapy and human experience. In R. S. Valle & S. Halling (Eds.), *Existential-phenomenological perspectives in psychology* (pp. 193–213). New York: Plenum.

Moustakas, C. (1985). Humanistic or humanism? *Journal of Humanistic Psychology, 25*(3), 5–12.

Moustakas, C. (1988). *Phenomenology, science, and psychotherapy*. Cape Breton, Canada: Family Life Institute.

Moustakas, C. (1990). *Heuristic research: Design, methodology, and applications*. Newbury Park, CA: Sage.

Moustakas, C. (1994). *Phenomenological research methods*. Thousand Oaks, CA; Sage.

Murphy, G. (1966). Karl Bühler and the psychology of thought. In J.F.T. Bugental (Ed.), Symposium on Karl Bühler's contributions to psychology. *Journal of General Psychology, 75,* 188–195.

Murray, E. (1986). *Imaginative thinking and human existence.* Pittsburgh, PA: Duquesne University Press.

Murray, E. (Ed.). (1987). *Imagination and phenomenological psychology.* Pittsburgh, PA: Duquesne University Press.

Muus, R. (1956). Existentialism and psychology. *Educational Theory, 6,* 135–153.

Nordentoft, K. (1978). *Kierkegaard's psychology* (B. Kirmmse, Trans.). Pittsburgh, PA: Duquesne University Press. (Original work published 1972)

Osborne, J. W. (1987). A human science study of learning about learning. *Journal of Humanistic Psychology, 27,* 485–500.

Osborne, J. W. (1990). Some basic existential-phenomenological research methodology for counsellors. *Canadian Journal of Counselling, 24*(2), 79–91.

Ott, H. (1993). *Martin Heidegger* (A. Blunden, Trans). New York: Basic Books. (Original work published 1988)

Packer, M. J., & Addison, R. B. (Eds.). (1989). *Entering the circle: Hermeneutic investigation in psychology.* Albany: State University of New York Press.

Paskow, A. (1991). Heidegger and Nazism. *Philosophy East and West, 41*(4), 522–528.

Peters, D. J. (1995). Human experience in disablement: The imperative of the ICIDH. *Disability and Rehabilitation, 17*(3/4), 135–144.

Polkinghorne, D. (1983). *Methodology for the human sciences.* Albany: State University of New York Press.

Polkinghorne, D. (1988). *Narrative knowing and the human sciences.* Albany: State University of New York Press.

Polkinghorne, D. (1989). Phenomenological research methods. In R. S. Valle & S. Halling (Eds.), *Existential-phenomenological perspectives in psychology* (pp. 41–60). New York: Plenum.

Rennie, D. L. (1992). Qualitative analysis of client's experience of psychotherapy: The unfolding of reflexity. In S. G. Toukmanian & D. L. Rennie (Eds.), *Psychotherapy process research: Paradigmatic and narrative approaches* (pp. 211–233). Newbury Park, CA: Sage Publications.

Rennie, D. L., & Toukmanian, S. G. (1992). Explanation in psychotherapy process research. In S. G. Toukmanian & D. L. Rennie (Eds.), *Psychotherapy process research: Paradigmatic and narrative approaches* (pp. 234–251). Newbury Park, CA: Sage Publications.

Rockmore, T. (1992). *On Heidegger's Nazism and philosophy.* Berkeley: University of California Press.

Rogers, C. R. (1973). My philosophy of interpersonal relationships and how it grew. *Journal of Humanistic Psychology, 13*(2), 3–15.

Rogers, C. R. (1985). Toward a more human science of the person. *Journal of Humanistic Psychology, 25*(4), 7–24.

Sadler, W. A. (1969). *Existence and love.* New York: Scribner.

Sartre, J.-P. (1948a). *The emotions: Outline of a theory* (B. Frechtman, Trans.). New York: Philosophical Library. (Original work published 1939)

Sartre, J.-P. (1948b). *The psychology of imagination.* New York: Philosophical Library. (Original work published 1940)

Sartre, J.-P. (1953). *Existential psychoanalysis* (H. E. Barnes, Trans.). New York: Philosophical Library. (Original work published 1940)

Sartre, J.-P. (1965). *Being and nothingness* (H. E. Barnes, Trans.). New York: Citadel Press. (Original work published 1943)

Schneider, K. J., & May, R. (1995). *The psychology of existence: An integrative, clinical perspective.* New York: McGraw-Hill.

Sheehan, T. (1988, June 16). Heidegger and the Nazis. *New York Review of Books*, pp. 38–47.

Sheehan, T. (1993, January 14). A normal Nazi. *New York Review of Books*, pp. 30–35.

Simpkinson, C. H. (1990, March/April). Alternative psychology programs: Fight for licensing. *Common Boundary*, pp. 22–25.

Smith, D. (1983). History of the graduate program via existential-phenomenology at Duquesne University. In A. Giorgi, A. Barton, & C. Maes (Eds.), *Duquesne studies in phenomenological psychology* (Vol. 4, pp. 259–315). Pittsburgh, PA: Duquesne University Press.

Smith, R. G. (1967). *Martin Buber.* Richmond, VA: John Knox Press.

Snygg, D., & Combs, A. (1949). *Individual behavior.* New York: Harper.

Snygg, D., & Combs, A. (1950). The phenomenological approach and the problem of "unconscious" behavior: A reply to Dr. Smith. *Journal of Abnormal and Social Psychology, 45*(3), 523–528.

Sonnemann, U. (1954). *Existence and therapy: An introduction to phenomenological psychology and existential analysis.* New York: Grune & Stratton.

Spiegelberg, H. (1972). *Phenomenology in psychology and psychiatry.* Evanston, IL: Northwestern University Press.

Spiegelberg, H. (1982). *The phenomenological movement* (3rd ed.). The Hague: Martinus Nijhoff.

Stern, A. (1953). *Sartre: His philosophy and psychoanalysis.* New York: Liberal Arts Press.

Stierlin, H. (1974). Karl Jaspers' psychiatry in the light of his basic philosophic position. *Journal of the History of the Behavioral Sciences, 10*(2), 213–226.

Straus, E. W. (1963). *The primary world of senses* (J. Needleman, Trans.). Glencoe, IL: Free Press. (Original work published 1935)

Straus, E. W. (1969). Psychiatry and philosophy. In M. Natanson (Ed.), *Psychiatry and philosophy* (pp. 1–83). New York: Springer-Verlag.

van den Berg, J. H. (1972). *A different existence.* Pittsburgh, PA: Duquesne University Press.

van den Berg, J. H. (1974). *Divided existence and complex society.* Pittsburgh, PA: Duquesne University Press. (Original work published 1963)

van Deurzen-Smith, E. (1988). *Existential counselling in practice.* Newbury Park, CA: Sage Publications.

van Kaam, A. (1959). Phenomenal analysis: Exemplified by the study of the experience of "really feeling understood." *Journal of Individual Psychology, 15*, 66–72.

van Kaam, A. (1966). *Existential foundations of psychology.* Pittsburgh, PA: Duquesne University Press.

van Manen, M. (1990). *Researching lived experience: Human science for an action sensitive pedagogy.* Albany: State University of New York Press.

von Eckartsberg, R. (1981). Maps of the mind: The cartography of consciousness. In R. S. Valle & R. von Eckartsberg (Eds.), *The metaphors of consciousness* (pp. 21–93). New York: Plenum.

von Eckartsberg, R. (1986). *Life-world experience: Existential-phenomenological research approaches in psychology.* Lanham, MD: University Press of America.

von Eckartsberg, R. (1989). The social psychology of person perception and the experience of valued relationships. In R. S. Valle & S. Halling (Eds.), *Existential-phenomenological perspectives in psychology* (pp. 137–154). New York: Plenum.

von Eckartsberg, R. (1993). The person's psychocosm and the stream of consciousness. *Methods,* pp. 5–30.

Wegrocki, H. J. (1966). Introduction. In J.F.T. Bugental (Ed.), Symposium on Karl Bühler's contributions to psychology. *Journal of General Psychology, 75,* 181–188.

Weigert, E. (1949). Existentialism and its relations to psychotherapy. *Psychiatry, 12*(4), 399–412.

Weisskopf-Joelson, E. (1978). Viktor E. Frankl. In R. S. Valle & M. King (Eds.), *Existential-phenomenological alternatives for psychology* (pp. 274–284). New York: Oxford University Press.

Wertz, F. (1982). Findings and value of a descriptive approach to everyday perceptual process. *Journal of Phenomenological Psychology, 13*(2), 169–195.

Wertz, F. (1986). The question of the reliability of psychological research. *Journal of Phenomenological Psychology, 17*(2), 181–205.

Wertz, F. (1987). Cognitive psychology and the understanding of perception. *Journal of Phenomenological Psychology, 18*(2), 103–142.

Westcott, M. (1988). *The psychology of human freedom.* New York: Springer-Verlag.

Wolin, R. (1991). *The Heidegger controversy: A critical reader.* New York: Columbia University Press.

Wundt, W. (1902). *Outline of psychology* (C. H. Judd, Trans.). New York: Gustav E. Steckert.

Yalom, I. (1980). *Existential psychotherapy.* New York: Basic Books.

Yalom, I. (1985). *The theory and practice of group psychotherapy* (3rd ed.). New York: Basic Books.

Yalom, I., & Elkin, G. (1974). *Every day gets a little closer.* New York: Basic Books.

9

Feminist Psychology and Humanistic Psychology

HENDRIKA VANDE KEMP AND
TAMARA L. ANDERSON

HUMANISM AND FEMINISM

Humanism and feminism share an emphasis on "the expansive growth of the individual toward wholeness, . . . toward encompassing the whole spectrum of human potentialities" that requires us to "reach out to other individuals in love and compassion" (Nevill, 1977/1978, pp. 81, 82). The social psychologist B. Lott (1991) notes that "a feminist perspective is not only compatible with the history, objectives, and emphases of social psychology, but necessary for its continued vitality. In view of social psychology's humanist roots and its 'nurturist' and 'social optimist' tenets, it is not surprising that feminist scholarship has flourished within it" (p. 505). Both feminists and humanists are interested in the social forces that limit human potential and compassion, and both groups address significant social issues. Humanistic psychology and feminist psychology are also indebted to related movements such as feminist theology, family psychology, and Marxist philosophy, whose influence will be implicit and explicit in the exploration that follows.[1]

FEMINIST MOVEMENTS IN AMERICAN CULTURE

One of the great weaknesses of feminist psychologists is their isolation from feminist theologians. Despite the fact that these groups have little interaction, there is great convergence in their work, and we adopt here the categories Van Leeuwen (1988) used to characterize feminist theologians.[2] These categories order the historical data and help to link feminists from various disciplines. Although the present review incorporates only occasional contributions of feminist theologians, it reflects the immersion of its authors in the literature of both theological and psychological feminism.

Liberal Feminism

Liberal feminism is rooted in "the Enlightenment commitment to individual autonomy and faith in human reason" (Van Leeuwen, 1988, p. 171), and follows Mill (1869/1970), who argued that "access to middle-class British economic, educational, and political institutions should be on the basis of individual human merit, and not gender" (Van Leeuwen, 1988, p. 171). This group, focused on "status politics" (Rossi, 1973, p. 473), includes both Enlightenment feminists such as Mill and Harriet Martineau and "moral crusader feminists" (p. 247) such as Lucretia Mott, Elizabeth Cady Stanton, Susan B. Anthony, and Lucy Stone, with the latter group most directly responsible for political and social reform. In the nineteenth century there was "overlap and continuity" between the evangelical religious revivals and "moral reform, abolition, temperance, and woman's rights" (p. 273), all movements with a distinct humanistic flavor. Stanton, who was personally involved in these overlapping movements, launched feminist theology when she published the two-part *The Woman's Bible* in 1895 and 1898.

Marxist Feminism

Marxist feminism is "at heart a *conflict* theory of society" that explicates women's oppression "in class terms," reducing it primarily to economic oppression (Van Leeuwen, 1988, p. 173). Marxist feminists focus on what Christians regard as "the fallenness of social institutions" and consider "the cause of this corruption to be the domination of capitalist economic structures" (p. 174). Historically this group also had two branches: the "radical" group, which included Friedrich Engels and Emma Goldman, provided theoretical underpinnings; the "reform" group, which included Jane Addams, Margaret Sanger, and Charlotte Gilman, pursued amelioration through legislative and civic reforms. Marxist feminists deplore the individualism and narcissism connected with American capitalism and focus especially on class-related issues that apply particularly to women. Their arguments are central to discussions of gender issues in family therapy, as individual welfare and responsibility come into conflict with family welfare (Doherty & Boss, 1991). This approach to feminism easily exposes major inconsistencies in feminist philosophy. Christians pinpoint the individualism and narcissism inherent in the prochoice movement. Baumrind (1975) challenges the proabortion feminists, whose argument is a special case of "ethical universalism, which permits, in certain contexts, acts that are normally regarded as morally reprehensible" (p. 43), on the basis of the Marxist principle that "ideals of right and justice are justified by how far they serve the common good and advance progress in society" (Baumrind, 1978a, p. 68). Baumrind supports legalized abortion, but recognizes it as an exception to the general rule of murder, as a form of justifiable homicide. Baumrind (1978b) also comments on the "child liberation" movement, observing that "the only right entirely consistent with their position which these child liberators never demand for children is what anti-abortionists call the right-to-life" (p. 181). Many feminist psychologists find such arguments objectionable, but these issues demonstrate that feminism on its own can appear to be remarkably unhumanistic, as it permits powerful adults (both male and female) to make life-and-death choices of personal convenience.

Contributions of Liberal and Marxist Feminists

Katz (1991) highlights contributions of psychologists to feminist reforms during various time periods relative to the founding of the Society for the Psychological Study of Social Issues (SPSSI) in 1937. Early liberal feminism resulted in the rights of women to vote (1919/1920), to own property, and to receive custody of children in cases of divorce. In religious circles it led to the ordination of women as deaconesses, elders, and clergy (Angel, 1991). Prior to 1930 women were a strong force in "the mental hygiene, mental testing, progressive education, and child welfare movements" (Katz, 1991, p. 667), and they contributed to the development of settlement houses and the education and employment of girls. Through the efforts of Emma Goldman and Margaret Sanger, women acquired ready access to contraception, a gain with its own costs. "The invention of the Pill made millions for the drug companies, made guinea pigs of all [women], and made [women] all the more 'available' as sexual objects" (Morgan, 1970, p. xxxi).

SPSSI, which was founded by men, soon attracted social-activist psychologists who "helped legitimize the use of research for the solution of social problems" (Katz, 1991, p. 669); by the late 1930s women comprised about one-third of SPSSI's members, although women "social activists were more visible outside SPSSI" (p. 669). After the founding of the National Council of Women Psychologists (NCWP) in 1941 (Carrington, 1951), it was the major venue for feminist psychology: NCWP worked with the American Psychological Association (APA) and American Association for the Advancement of Psychology (AAAP) on "War Services to Children, . . . peace-planning committees, and a variety of research on women's issues including postwar gender roles, the political role of women in helping to pass the proposed amendment of women's rights, the selection of women workers in war industries, and the problems of black women in Harlem" (Katz, 1991, p. 670).

Later, feminism brought about political reforms also sought by the civil rights movement (Freeman, 1975), and both were reinforced by humanism, with its ability to see each "person" as unique and valuable and its concerns about the lack of adequate civil rights. A thread of purposefulness provided a connection between the formalization of the humanistic psychology movement, the civil rights activities of the 1960s, and the women's movement; these movements cooperated to "promote social activism toward the goal of societal change" (Worell & Etaugh,

1994, p. 448). Foci of concern in the 1960s and 1970s included cross-cultural psychology and ethnic issues, globalization, gay and lesbian rights, antiwar protests (which fed directly into the men's movement), and an interest in posttraumatic stress and the special toll that war exacts on men. The role that women psychologists played in these movements is explored by Rossi (1973), O'Connell and Russo (1980), Stevens and Gardner (1982), Katz (1991), and Bohan (1992).

Radical Feminism

Radical feminists emphasize economic differences between men and women as *sexual* classes (Van Leeuwen, 1988, p. 175), placing patriarchy rather than capitalism at the root of oppression. Much of feminist literature is devoted to a discussion of the role of patriarchy in the suppression of women's rights, focusing on such issues as the power differential between men and women and its effect on socialization, the dynamics of privation and privilege, women's health, interpersonal relationships within hierarchical power structures, strategies for women's empowerment, and "shifting attributions of responsibility and blame from victim to perpetrator" (Worell & Etaugh, 1994, p. 447). Whether it is true that the establishment of patriarchy is subsequent to an original matriarchal or partnership/egalitarian model, as some feminist scholars argue (Capra, 1982; Edwards & Kluck, 1980; Eisler, 1987; Milbrath, 1988), many cultures did develop enduring patriarchal structures.

Lerner (1986) suggests that men's control of women's sexuality and procreativity was an important step toward the formation of private property and class society: the appropriation of female capabilities provided men with a status-enhancing commodity. Women attained their first gender-defined role when they were exchanged, as their fathers' property, in marriage transactions. Such "subordination of women by men provided the conceptual model for the creation of slavery" (p. 89). Once one group is regarded as inferior, other groups can be similarly stigmatized and enslaved. Inequality has predictable consequences: "Once a group is defined as inferior, the superiors tend to label it as defective or substandard in various ways. These labels accrete rapidly" (J. B. Miller, 1986, p. 6). The dominant group assigns to subordinates jobs that it does not want to perform, simultaneously suggesting that the subordinates are incapable of performing the duties of the dominant group.

When such tactics are unchallenged, the system maintains homeostasis, but a significant disruption can result in the type of destabilization brought on in women's roles by World War II. While the men were at war from 1941 to 1945, women in the United States replaced men in the factories so successfully that after the war role distinctions and expectations would never be the same: Women were fiercely reluctant to give up their newly acquired skills and freedom. Later, oral contraceptives allowed women the opportunity and decision-making power of whether to have children, pursue a career, or both, and created the new role of the corporate woman.

Patriarchal systems clearly contain the blueprint for women's subordination, though many feminists regard the patriarchal analysis as inadequate. Thus Coward (1983) argues that reliance on the patriarchy concept to explain sex differences offers a polarization that impedes the actual understanding of family, sexual relations, and sexual characteristics. Van Leeuwen (1988) also rejects the view of the "radical feminists who so strongly located the roots of patriarchy in female biology and socialization as to insist that only when both are virtually eliminated will there be gender justice. This is a more extreme expression of the liberal feminists [sic] emphasis on androgyny—so extreme as to want to 'debiologize' even childbearing" (p. 176).

Postradical or Differentiating Feminism

Differentiating feminists "plead for a more nuanced understanding of both maturity and immaturity which takes the differential life experiences of men and women seriously without ranking them in terms of moral superiority" (Van Leeuwen, 1988, p. 177). This group argues that the very real differences between women and men may "result from a complex blend of nature, nurture, and free choice. But whatever their origin, they are important in their own right, and must be restudied and reinterpreted by women working on their own theoretical terms" (p. 177). This group includes such well-known developmental theorists as Gilligan (1982) and Chodorow (1978). Differentiating feminism has been criticized by those who demonstrate that autonomy and interpersonal connectedness are not antithetical (Berlin & Johnson, 1989) and by those who fear that it risks substituting gynocentrism for androcentrism (Unger, 1988).

HUMANISTIC CONTRIBUTIONS OF FEMINIST PSYCHOLOGY

Psychological Theory and Women

By the 1970s the psychology of women had passed through four historical stages (Alpert, 1978). Through the 1960s it focused on the psychology of sex differences, with specific concerns about sexual development and incidental concerns about sex differences. In the late 1960s the focus shifted to the psychology of women, with an interest in understanding why women were understood as "inferior" and how this related to women's subordinate social status. Especially critical were the findings on the relationship between sex roles and mental illness (Hafner, 1986) and the "striking relationship between marital status and mental illness . . . accounted for by the higher rates of illness for married women" (Carmen, Russo, & Miller, 1981). In the 1970s the focus shifted to the sex roles and behavior of both men and women, leading eventually to the psychology of gender and the psychology of men (Levant & Pollack, 1995; L. Silverstein & Phares, 1996). This contributed to the literature such concepts as sex-role conflict and sex-role strain (Hafner, 1986) and gender failure (Sheinberg & Penn, 1991). Psychologists explored the biological, sexual, social, and cultural components of sex roles and their socialization; examined specific sex-role issues such as maternal employment and dual-career families; and critically examined methodology in the field. By the late 1970s the focus shifted to "the psychology of the sexual self-fulfilling prophecy" (Alpert, 1978, p. 967), and research focused on the "illusion of sex differences" (p. 967), stereotypes, Pygmalion effects, and gender-identity formation. The later stages of this history involve taking seriously both the psychology of women and "all the human experience" (Torrey, 1987, p. 159), thus defining feminism as humanism. Humanistic psychology contributed by positively valuing traditionally feminine qualities such as caring, genuineness, and empathy, offering an alternative to the misogynistic historical tradition that regarded women as histrionic and essentially evil and often labeled them as witches (Levack, 1992). Bernstein and Russo (1974) suggested that a new phase of the movement should be focused on the women of psychology, and feminist historians have begun to document the work of women psychologists (Bohan, 1992; Corey-Seibold, 1982; O'Connell & Russo, 1980; Stevens & Gardner, 1982). Most recently, feminists have begun to explore "questions of metatheory, epistemology, and method in feminist psychology" (Marecek, 1989, p. 368).

Women's Lives and Experience

A major contribution of feminist psychology is its spotlight on women as distinct from men (Worell & Etaugh, 1994): It regards women as legitimate targets for research; studies women without applying male norms; explores the various ways in which women themselves represent a variety of unique groups; encourages questions and methods "that are grounded in personal experiences of women researchers" (p. 446) and explores issues that are "relevant to women's lives, such as rape, incest, sexual harassment, reproductive processes, sexual decision-making, employment segregation, discrimination" (p. 446); emphasizes within-sex variations as more significant than between-sex differences; studies women in their natural context to avoid "context-stripping" (p. 447); attends "to women's strengths and capabilities as well as their problems" by studying resilience and competence (p. 447); and interprets "observed gender differences in the context of power dynamics and women's expected socialized role behaviors rather than as differences embedded in biology" (p. 447). The interest in women's lives and experiences has included questions about the ways that ethnicity interacts with gender (Comas-Díaz, 1991). Despite these efforts, "the fundamental belief in the normalcy of men, and the corresponding abnormality of women, has remained virtually untouched" (Tavris, 1992, p. 17; Caplan & Caplan, 1993), despite the fact that very few significant sex differences exist: "The failure to take into account situational context, social role, and historical circumstances has led even feminist psychologists to overestimate the importance of personality as an explanation of behavior" (Unger, 1988, p. 127). Also relevant to women's experience is the fact that their contributions have been "distorted or omitted through the use of terminology presumed to be generic" (C. Miller & Swift, 1976, p. 36). The APA addressed this first by adopting "guidelines for nonsexist language" in 1977 (APA, 1983, p. 43); an official policy on nonsexist language was adopted by the APA Publications and Communications Board in 1982 and incorporated into the 1983 *Publication Manual.*

Women in Therapy

Clinical psychology, like academic and research psychology, has marginalized women. The APA's Task Force on Sex Bias and Sex Role Stereotyping in Psychotherapeutic Practice (1978) identified four categories of problematic therapist behavior: "(1) fostering traditional sex roles, (2) bias in expectations and devaluation of women, (3) sexist use of psychoanalytic concepts, and (4) responding to women as sex objects, including seduction of female clients" (p. 1122). The task force recommended "13 general guidelines for ethical and effective psychotherapy with women" (p. 1122) that reflect multiple humanistic assumptions. Feminist psychologists challenged diagnostic labels such as "paraphilic rapism, self-defeating personality disorder, and late luteal phase disorder" (Marecek & Hare-Mustin, 1991, p. 525), opposed the inclusion of homosexuality in the DSM-III, and "noted that definitions of normal sexual functioning are based on an implicit model of male sexual gratification" (p. 525); they helped introduce into the *Ethical Standards of Psychologists* (APA, 1977, 1981, 1992) prohibitions "against sexual contact between therapist and client" and "against sexual harassment of students and employees" (p. 525). "Feminists have also voiced strong concerns about possible misprescribing and overprescribing of psychoactive drugs for women" (Marecek & Hare-Mustin, 1991, p. 526). They have contributed a variety of feminist therapies, ranging from the consciousness raising of the 1960s to sex-role resocialization, feminist psychoanalysis, feminist family therapy (Luepnitz, 1988), and "ethical principles for gender-fair family therapy" (Nutt, 1991). Noting the isomorphism between supervision and psychotherapy, Kaiser (1992) applied to supervision the humanist/feminist principles of accountability, personal awareness, trust, and an understanding of power and authority and how these are affected by gender. Kaiser's understanding of ethical relationships blends the contextual therapy model of Boszormenyi-Nagy (1987) with Noddings's (1984) theory of ethical caring.

Women's Health

Feminist psychologists have been concerned about multiple aspects of women's physical and psychological health. Travis, Gressley, and Crumpler (1991) review this literature, highlighting the role of religious leaders Ellen White, Mary Baker Eddy, and Aimee Semple McPherson in transforming the medical model. Special feminist concerns itemized by these reviewers include reproductive choice, AIDS, and health policy and planning. Feminist psychology has contributed to health psychology an interest in prevention, locus of control and compliance, social support, and coping. Feminists and humanists alike challenge the victim blaming and self-blaming that is implicit in much of the recent psychoneuroimmunology movement and the illusion that there are no forces greater than the human will (Vande Kemp, 1990).

Violence against Women and Children

Violence against women and children has been a special concern of feminists, who are interested in understanding the societal, cultural, and political structures that undergird physical, emotional, and sexual abuse (Horton & Williamson, 1988; Scully, 1990; Trible, 1984). Rape—by strangers, acquaintances, dates, and husbands—has been one specific concern. The first marital-rape law was enacted in 1979, but the notion that rape by a spouse constitutes a mere "domestic dispute" or "incident" lingers (Glasman & Neale, 1994). Despite these significant legal changes, feminist scholars (Fuller, 1995) are concerned about the decriminalization of rape by psychologists who regard rape as a form of individual psychopathology rather than a symptom of societal dysfunction. Courts still routinely blame rape victims rather than rapists (Tavris, 1992), basing their decisions on outmoded psychoanalytic models of gender and sexuality (Edwards, 1981; Temkin, 1987). Rape victims are revictimized when their attractiveness, style of dress, sexual history, and marital status are considered relevant information during a trial (Amir, 1971; Pollard, 1992). Battered women are victimized when the legal system searches for extenuating circumstances leading up to a beating (Edwards, 1981; Tavris, 1992): feminists have responded to this by articulating the battered-wife and battered-child syndromes as forms of diminished responsibility in cases of domestic violence that lead to homicide. In addition, feminist efforts have led to the passage of sexual-predator laws and more nuanced definitions of dual-role relationships (APA, 1992). However, power dynamics continue to manifest themselves in various forms of sexual exploitation of which women are the primary victims (Gabbard, 1989).

Feminist psychologists have been especially concerned about child sexual abuse (for extensive bibliographic material, see de Mause, 1991). This phenomenon has exposed great deficiencies in psychoanalytic theory and the ways in which patriarchal power structures have rendered women and girls invisible and voiceless (Eurich-Rascoe & Vande Kemp, 1997). Freud redefined the actual accounts of abuse as illusions created by the "power of internal fantasy and of spontaneous childhood sexuality" (Masson, 1984, p. xxii). The nearly universal acceptance of this Freudian theory led to the mistaken notion that children's sexuality mirrors adult sexuality, and the concomitant failure to develop a realistic theory of childhood sexual development to facilitate research on the long-term effects of childhood sexual abuse (Davis-Stephenson, 1990). When children are regarded as seductive, psychologists are likely to overlook the social forces that lead to child abuse just as they overlook the social forces supporting rape. Baumrind (1994) argues that "escalating child maltreatment in the United States is symptomatic of society's 'forgotten half' of our citizens, with the primary causes and cures of child maltreatment attributable primarily to social-structural rather than to psychological factors" (p. 360). Her humanism is evident in her conclusion that "battering, sexual abuse, and psychological mistreatment, serious as they are, are not as worthy of public outrage as the social policies in the United States that contribute to the neglect of the welfare of children and their mothers, especially in inner-city, ethnic communities where homelessness, grinding poverty, racism, poor health care, untreated substance abuse in women of child-bearing age, adolescent prostitution, and children having children all persist" (p. 366).

Child sexual abuse is clearly connected with the development of dissociative identity and borderline personality disorders, with reduced marriage rates, and with a variety of posttraumatic syndromes. Many psychologists still blame mothers (or victims) for the sexual abuse perpetrated by fathers. This diffusion of perpetrator responsibility is viewed as a consequence of women's status as "other" in society and men's need to construct a reality that aligns with their view of sexual violence (Tavris, 1992). Unger (1988) has noted that "if there is disagreement about the construction of a particular reality, the males in the situation are likely to have the power to define that reality" (p. 134), and women often "have little opportunity to validate alternative versions of reality" (p. 134). Thus women are not only victimized, but also subtly mystified, so that they question their own reality testing.

The Troubled Embodiment of Women

In our society, women often experience guilt about embodiment itself that is revealed in a wide variety of symptoms and attitudes (Fine-Thomas, 1995). Embodiment disorders often surface as eating disorders, and 90% of eating disorders appear in women and girls who live primarily in industrialized societies where thinness is associated with success (APA, 1994; Chernin, 1985). Body-image distortions and eating disorders are created by media influences (B. Silverstein, 1986), sex-role tensions, and certain enmeshed familial structures (Bruch, 1985; Garner & Garfinkel, 1980). The fashion and plastic-surgery industries reinforce these forces, so that multiple factors operate to create guilt and shame about embodiment (Fine-Thomas, 1995).

FEMINIST CONTRIBUTIONS TO RESEARCH METHODOLOGY AND ETHICS

Understanding of Research Participants

Humanistic and feminist psychologists deplore the subtle indignity inherent in understanding the human research participant as a " 'determined' being, subject to the controlling influences of assorted variables" (Jourard, 1967, p. 109). Jourard (1967) characterized the experimenter-subject relationship as an encounter that mystifies by withholding information, engaging in other forms of deception, and limiting the subject's vocabulary (i.e., depriving subjects of ordinary language). The research psychologist "tries to impersonate a machine by depersonalizing himself. He tries to be invisible or 'constant.' He seldom tries to find out from his subject just how that person experiences him, the researcher, either perceptually or in his fantasy" (p. 111). Jourard contrasts this with *dialogue*, the encounter that reveals. The process described by Jourard is a "movement away from reflexivity, from a time when author, experimenter, and subject could be the same person" (Budge & Katz, 1995, p. 219). Feminist psychologists prefer communal methods that rely on "the cooperation of the researcher and subjects, [and] the personal participation of the researcher" (Peplau & Conrad, 1989, p. 393). The report of the Division 35 Task Force on Guidelines for Nonsexist Research in Psychology (McHugh, Koeske, & Frieze, 1986) pointed out the "dangers in excluding respondents from participation in making decisions about research applications that affect them, in failing to inform or support respondents seeking advice, and in failing to explicate assumptions and misgivings about the research for professional audiences for fear of appearing 'subjective' " (p. 880). This problem was resolved by adopting the principle that feminist psychologists do not turn subjects into "objects to be manipulated by the researcher" (Worell & Etaugh, 1994, p. 446) but engage in "collaborative efforts with research participants" (Worell, 1990, p. 4). The new editorial policy of *Psychology of Women Quarterly* (*PWQ*) replaces "the term 'subjects' with alternatives such as participants, respondents, women, men, individuals" (p. 4), a policy reflected in the 1994 APA *Publication Manual* and illustrated in the work of Baumrind (1971), who believed that the quality of her research benefited because most of her subjects "viewed themselves as collaborators rather than objects and, therefore, took care to behave thoughtfully and with integrity" (p. 896). Related to the personal qualities of participants is a concern about how to designate and assess the impact of the various members of the research team (Lott, 1991). McHugh et al. (1986) note that the roles of "experimenter, confederate, and target" all affect the "response, performance, and behavior of the participants," and "multiple experimenters (confederates and targets)" must be incorporated "to vary the sex composition of the group" in order to analyze and counterbalance effects (p. 889). Denmark, Russo, Frieze, and Sechzer (1988) are concerned about unexplained variance that may result from "potential interactions of sex and race or other variables" (p. 583). Researchers tend to employ "participants as data sources only" and seldom "report consent, debriefing or feedback; authors generally described participants but not data collectors and setting, . . . and seldom acknowledged participants" (Walsh-Bowers, 1995). Even in *PWQ* (Walsh, 1989) fewer than half of authors used "human-centered titles" (p. 439). This problem has not yet been addressed in formal journal policies, nor has the fact that "the standard citation style [initials only] may function to perpetuate myths about women's lack of participation in the production of knowledge" (Crawford & Marecek, 1989, pp. 481–482).

Research Ethics and a Critique of Deception

Diana Baumrind pioneered the critique of research ethics, taking a stance closely related to radical feminism and joining those who challenge "the tenets of traditional scientific inquiry" (Worell & Etaugh, 1994, p. 446). Baumrind's (1964) reaction to Milgram (1963) mirrors the feminist critique of traditional research and lays the groundwork for her systematic metaethics, her study of moral development, and a larger literature on the ethics of deception (Adair, Dushenko, & Lindsay, 1985). Baumrind argues that Milgram's research is characterized by the very dehumanizing processes it was designed to investigate, and she uses Milgram's work as a paradigm case for the problem of deception in social science research. Her analysis unfolds a rich range of concerns central to feminist psychology.

Baumrind's Critiques of Milgram

Baumrind (1964) specifically denounces Milgram for violating the human dignity and rights of his subjects by not protecting their security and self-esteem, thereby contributing to their insecurity, alienation, and hostility. She condemns the detached impersonality in Milgram's reports of his subjects' emotional distress and his facile assurance that "these tensions were dissipated before the subject left the laboratory" (p. 422). She herself "would expect a naive, sensitive subject to remain deeply hurt and anxious for some time, and a sophisticated, cynical subject to become even more alienated and distrustful" (p. 423), and believes that the subjects' distress was "at what the experimenter was doing to them as well as from what they were doing to their victims" (p. 423).

Methodological problems that reduced the impact of Milgram's research included his use of a nonrepresentative sample and his ignoring the "special quality of trust and obedience" (Baumrind, 1964, p. 421) and the "set" subjects bring to the experimental setting (p. 423). Milgram's research design lacked ecological validity because it had no convincing parallel with the "subordinate-authority relationship demonstrated in Hitler Germany" (p. 423). The research setting exerted "dissonant demands," creating ambiguity and an unnatural "sense of unreality and absurdity" (Baumrind, 1966, p. 11). Baumrind notes, along the line of the social constructionist feminists (Crawford & Marecek, 1989), Milgram's failure to understand that the "meaning persons give a situation is contextual and purposive and dependent upon factors that the experimenter may not even be aware of, such as the strangeness of the situation from the perspective of the subject" (Baumrind, 1985, p. 170). Milgram had no warrant for labeling the behavior of his paid volunteer subjects as "shockingly immoral" or applying to them the term "destructive obedience" (Baumrind, 1966, p. 3): their behavior might as easily be explained by value hierarchies in which cooperation, loyalty, and knowledge took precedence over charity and compassion. It would be more accurate to apply the term "destructive obedience" to the experimenter's confederates. These concerns are further elaborated in Baumrind's metaethics.

Baumrind's Metaethics and Systematic Critique of APA's Code of Ethics

Baumrind served as a resource person to APA's ad hoc Committee on Ethical Standards in Psychological Research and published three explicit commentaries on APA's (1973) *Ethical Principles in the Conduct of Research with Human Participants*. She was deeply concerned about intentional deception, "the withholding of information in order to obtain participants, concealment in natural settings, manipulation in field experimentation, and deceptive instructions and manipulations in laboratory research" (Baumrind, 1979, p. 1). Most researchers use a cost-benefit analysis that legitimizes the suspension of the right to informed consent, to open and honest dealings, to protection from physical and mental distress and loss of self-esteem, and to clear and fair contractual agreement. "By codifying the bases upon which the recognized rights of subjects can be suspended, [the code] serves as a declaration of the rights of the experimenter as much as a statement of the obligations of the experimenter to the subject" (Baumrind, 1972, p. 1083).

Four Theories of Justification

Baumrind employs four classic theories of ethical justification to untangle the web of experimental deception. *Obedience* theories, which appeal to dogma and subordinate human autonomy to the Creator of Truth (Baumrind, 1975), are acceptable only if they can be stated as the natural theological (and humanistic) principle "that man's highest spiritual aspirations must accord with his highest potential and be in harmony with the laws of his own nature and the external world" (p. 41). Baumrind (1985) rejects as dogmatic and inhumane *deontological* theories (both Kantian and Aristotelian) that ground choice in intuitively given obligations, "without regard to any balance of good over evil for self, society, or the universe" (p. 167). She is most disturbed by *act-utilitarianism*, in which ethical choices emerge from a cost-benefit analysis applied to a specific experimental design, because such an analysis is relativistic, subjective, nongeneralizable, unaware of fundamental minority rights, and ignorant of long-range costs. Baumrind favors *rule-utilitarianism*, "the view that an act is right if, and only if, it would be as beneficial to the common good in a particular social context to have a moral code permitting that act as to operate under a rule that would prohibit that act" (p. 167).

Baumrind (1971) insists that even noble scientific ends do not "justify the use of means that in ordinary transactions would be regarded as reprehensible" (p. 890). The APA code takes for granted certain moral dilemmas created when the researcher weighs the potential benefit to science or humankind against the subject's right not to be "deceived, manipulated, and demeaned" (p. 890). Ordinary risk/benefit analyses weigh the benefit *to the subject* against the cost *to the subject*, whereas the ethics code weighs the benefits *to humankind* against the cost *to the subject*, erroneously assuming that a researcher "is *equally* culpable if when faced with but the two alternatives, he chooses to violate the basic human rights of subjects in preference to using a less rigorous experimental method" (p. 891). Baumrind argues that investigators should never "engage in research that permits only two possible alternatives: *deceptive debriefing* . . . or *inflicted insight*" (p. 892). It is, in fact, a moral "duty insofar as possible to avoid provoking situations which create conflicts of obligation" (Baumrind, 1975, p. 51).

Costs of Deception

Harm Done to the Subject

In self-report studies on social-psychological experiments, 20% of subjects report harm, and "the proportion is highest for deception research" (Baumrind, 1985, p. 169). Baumrind (1966) considers it critical that the researcher not be allowed to abdicate responsibility for negative effects simply by "pointing to the responsibility of the subject for his own actions" (p. 8). Milgram robbed his subjects of agency, or internal locus of control, by deceiving them about their options. Autonomous subjects might "freely agree to incur risk, inconvenience, or pain, but a subject whose consent has been obtained by deceitful and fraudulent means has become an object for the investigator to manipulate" (Baumrind, 1985, p. 169). Feminists might add that meaningful consent can never be given in situations characterized by unequal power (Gabbard, 1989). Milgram behaved irresponsibly in not anticipating consequences that included "formation of neurotic defensive maneuvers, symptom formation, and alteration of character" (Baumrind, 1966, pp. 6–7). Physical stress and pain (the usual concerns of ethics committees) are ultimately less harmful than "cynicism, anomie, and hopelessness" (Baumrind, 1975, p. 56) in subjects, who thereby lose "trust in themselves and the investigator and, by extension, in the meaningfulness of life itself" (Baumrind, 1971, p. 888). College students are especially vulnerable to such effects, as their developmental task is exactly that of "setting one's own standards, of formulating guides to living" (Paula Lozar, quoted in Baumrind, 1975, p. 59). Researchers are morally obligated to use "the tools and standards of the profession . . . to test hypotheses concerning subjects' welfare" (Baumrind, 1971, p. 895) before an experiment is done, "since *evidence* of aftereffects can by definition be obtained only *after* the subject has already been harmed" (Baumrind, 1966, p. 6).

Baumrind also specifically addresses Milgram's efforts (1977, pp. 92–149) to prove that his subjects were not harmed by evidence from a simple questionnaire

item to which 80% of his subjects responded that "they were glad to have participated in the experiment" (Baumrind, 1985, p. 168). This "fact" is not logically
equivalent to having sustained no harm, nor can the 80% nullify "the harm the
minority of subjects report they have suffered" (p. 169). It is illogical for Milgram
to accept at face value the judgments of persons he himself described as "destruc-
tively obedient." Denial of harm may involve complex mechanisms: "reduction of
cognitive dissonance, identification with the aggressor, and masochistic obedience" (p. 168). It is no surprise that deceived subjects "tend to affirm their agency
by denying that they have allowed themselves to be treated as objects" (p. 169).
Nor is harm to subjects mitigated by debriefing, which does not "nullify the wrong
done participants by deceiving them and may not even repair their damaged self-
image or ability to trust adult authorities" (p. 172). We can make the public less
vulnerable if we publish our principles in public sources and provide copies to "all
prospective research subjects prior to obtaining their consent" (Baumrind, 1971,
p. 894). Researchers should routinely invite subjects to evaluate their work, so
that proposed violations of the ethical code are approved by both professional
peers and the peers of prospective subjects (Baumrind, 1975); such evaluations
always "include persons with a wide range of explicit values among those who
design and evaluate the results of experiments dealing with controversial subjects"
(Baumrind, 1990, p. 25).

Milgram's empirical effort to establish that his subjects were not harmed illustrates a problem inherent in the APA ethics code, which "appeals to conventional
rather than post-conventional standards" (Baumrind, 1975, p. 48). The APA
committee aimed "to determine, crystallize, and make explicit" the "prevailing
viewpoint among American psychologists regarding ethical standards for research" (Cook et al., 1972, p. i). Baumrind appeals to centuries of moral philosophy to argue that moral principles cannot be determined by consensus: In
attempting to honor the "values and interests of all factions," the APA code in
fact violates "certain fundamental tenets of each" (Baumrind, 1966, p. 15). What
can be tested empirically are the premises on which a researcher's value judgments
are based: Baumrind's (1990) own "personal values concerning adolescent sexuality" (p. 25) challenge national policy on grounds that can be stated in terms of
testable hypotheses. Thus empirical science can contribute to the identification
of harmful practices and the development of ethical codes, but this is done by
testing hypotheses rather than by sampling opinions.

Harm Done to the Profession

Intentional deception in research compromises the integrity of the profession
and exhausts the pool of naïve subjects, increasing the probability that subjects
will guess at the experiment's true purpose and "assign idiosyncratic meaning"
rather than "buy the experimenter's cover story," thus making it unlikely that the
instructions create a "uniform psychological reality" (Baumrind, 1985, p. 170).
Deception jeopardizes community support for research as suspicious subjects suspect psychologists "of being tricksters" and respond by playing the role they think

is expected. Investigators who use deception undermine their "commitment to truth" and trade short-term gains "for the cumulative costs of long-term deterioration" in their "ethical sensibilities and integrity" and damaging their credibility (p. 169).

Harm Done to Society

Intentional deception in the laboratory undermines trust in authority and respect for experts. There is no ethical system "which condones deceit, lie telling, and the breaking of contracts" (Baumrind, 1975, p. 15), because "belief in the coherence of the universe cannot be maintained without contract" (p. 16), and civilization is eroded when powerful role models, with legitimate authority, are permitted to break implicit or explicit contracts. Baumrind (1979) rightly notes that "most of us in our everyday relationships do not deliberately mislead others about what we intend to do, make promises we intend to break, or in other ways violate the respect to which all fellow humans are entitled" (p. 2); we have no justification for suspending these rules in our research procedures. Similar arguments apply to the use of deception in family therapy, especially to the use of paradoxical intention and its variations (Doherty & Boss, 1991).

In this chapter we have surveyed the contributions of liberal feminism, Marxist feminism, radical feminism, and postradical or differentiating feminism. We have summarized the humanistic contributions of feminist psychology in the domains of psychological theory and women, women's lives and experience, women in therapy, women's health, violence against women and children, and the troubled embodiment of women. Feminist contributions to research methodology and ethics were examined in detail, with a focus on the work of Diana Baumrind, the psychologist chosen for the accompanying case study. Feminists and humanists have added a new perspective to the understanding of research participants and of research ethics. Baumrind's critique of Milgram stands as a case study in humanist psychology by one of psychology's prominent women. From a dialectic materialist perspective, Baumrind provides a metaethics, a theory of ethical justification, and a critique of APA's ethics code that complement the humanist and feminist positions. A summary of the costs of deception—to subjects, the profession, and society—provides a transition to the case study that follows.

NOTES

1. The authors wish to thank Catherine Smith and Michele Winterstein, who helped plan various portions of this chapter; Dan Palomino, who assisted in tracking down bibliographic material; and Quinn Fox, for his excellent summary of the language problem.

2. Due to the severe length restrictions on this chapter, we will reference recent reviews of relevant literature rather than cite all specific historical references. The reader will find extensive bibliographic material in these reviews. We also focus only on developments in the United States.

REFERENCES

Adair, D. G., Dushenko, T. W., & Lindsay, R. C. (1985). Ethical regulations and their impact on research practice. *American Psychologist, 40*(1), 59–72.

Alpert, J. (1978). The psychology of women: What should the field be called? *American Psychologist, 33*, 965–969.

American Psychiatric Association. (1994). *Diagnostic and statistical manual of mental disorders* (4th ed.). Washington, DC: Author.

American Psychological Association. (1973). *Ethical principles in the conduct of research with human participants.* Washington, DC: Author.

American Psychological Association. (1977). *Ethical standards of psychologists* (revised). Washington, DC: Author.

American Psychological Association. (1981). *Ethical standards of psychologists* (revised). Washington, DC: Author.

American Psychological Association. (1983). *Publication manual of the American Psychological Association* (3rd ed.). Washington, DC: Author.

American Psychological Association. (1992). Ethical principles of psychologists and code of conduct. *American Psychologist, 47*, 1597–1611.

American Psychological Association. (1994). *Publication manual of the American Psychological Association* (4th ed.). Washington, DC: Author.

Amir, M. (1971). *Patterns in forcible rape.* Chicago: University of Chicago Press.

Angel, A. (1991). Ordination of women. In J. D. Douglas (Ed.), *New 20th-century encyclopedia of religious knowledge* (2nd ed.) (pp. 875–876). Grand Rapids, MI: Baker Book House.

Baumrind, D. (1964). Some thoughts on ethics of research: After reading Milgram's "Behavioral study of obedience." *American Psychologist, 19*, 421–423.

Baumrind, D. (1966). *Further thoughts on ethics after reading, Milgram's "A reply to Baumrind."* Unpublished manuscript, Institute of Human Development, Berkeley, CA.

Baumrind, D. (1971). Principles of ethical conduct in the treatment of subjects: Reactions to the draft report of the Committee on Ethical Standards in Psychological Research. *American Psychologist, 26*, 887–896.

Baumrind, D. (1972). Reactions to the May 1972 draft report of the Ad Hoc Committee on Ethical Standards in Psychological Research. *American Psychologist, 27*, 1083–1086.

Baumrind, D. (1975). Metaethical and normative considerations governing the treatment of human subjects in the behavioral sciences. In E. C. Kennedy (Ed.), *Human rights and psychological research: A debate on psychology and ethics* (pp. 37–68). New York: Thomas Y. Crowell.

Baumrind, D. (1978a). A dialectical materialist's perspective on knowing social reality. In W. Damon (Ed.), *Moral development. New directions for child development; vol. 2.* (pp. 61–82). San Francisco: Jossey-Bass.

Baumrind, D. (1978b). Reciprocal rights and responsibilities in parent-child relations. *Journal of Social Issues, 34*, 179–196.

Baumrind, D. (1979). IRBs and social science research: The costs of deception. *IRB: A Review of Human Subjects Research, 1*(6), 1–4.

Baumrind, D. (1985). Research using intentional deception: Ethical issues revisited. *American Psychologist, 40*, 164–174.

Baumrind, D. (1990). Doing good well. In C. B. Fisher & W. W. Tryon (Eds.), *Ethics in applied developmental psychology* (pp. 17–28). Norwood, NJ: Ablex.

Baumrind, D. (1994). The social context of child maltreatment. *Family Relations, 43*, 360–368.

Berlin, S., & Johnson, C. (1989). Women and autonomy: Using structural analysis of social behavior to find autonomy within connections. *Psychiatry, 52*, 79–95.

Bernstein, M., & Russo, N. F. (1974). The history of psychology revisited; Or, up with our foremothers. *American Psychologist, 29*, 130–134.

Bohan, J. S. (1992). *Re-placing women in psychology: Readings toward a more inclusive history.* Dubuque, IA: Kendall/Hunt.

Boszormenyi-Nagy, I. (1987). *Foundations of contextual therapy: Collected papers of Ivan Boszormenyi-Nagy.* New York: Brunner/Mazel.

Bruch, H. (1985). Four decades of eating disorders. In D. M. Garner & P. E. Garfinkel (Eds.), *Handbook of psychotherapy for anorexia nervosa and bulimia* (pp. 7–18). New York: Guilford Press.

Budge, G. S., & Katz, B. (1995). Constructing psychological knowledge: Reflections on science, scientists, and epistemology in the APA *Publication Manual. Theory and Psychology, 5*, 217–231.

Caplan, P. J., & Caplan, J. B. (1993). *Thinking critically about research on sex and gender.* New York: HarperCollins.

Capra, F. (1982). *The turning point: Science, society, and the rising culture.* New York: Bantam Books.

Carmen, E. H., Russo, N. F., & Miller, J. B. (1981). Inequality and women's mental health: An overview. *American Journal of Psychiatry, 138*, 1319–1330.

Carrington, E. M. (1951). History and purpose of the International Council of Women Psychologists. *American Psychologist, 7*, 100–101.

Chernin, K. (1985). *The hungry self: Women, eating, and identity.* New York: Perennial Library.

Chodorow, N. (1978). *The reproduction of mothering: Psychoanalysis and the sociology of gender.* Berkeley: University of California Press.

Comas-Díaz, L. (1991). Feminism and diversity in psychology: The case of women of color. *Psychology of Women Quarterly, 15*, 597–610.

Cook, S. W., Hicks, L. H., Kimble, G. A., McGuire, W. J., Schoggen, P. H. & Smith, M. B. (1972, May). Ethical standards for research with human subjects: Published for review and discussion. *APA Monitor, 3*(5), i–xix.

Corey-Seibold, M. (1982). Psychology's foremothers: Case studies of six women who shaped the development of American psychology. *Dissertation Abstracts International, 43*-03B, 850. (University Microfilms No. AAC #8217690).

Coward, R. (1983). *Patriarchal precedents: Sexuality and social relations.* Boston: Routledge & Kegan Paul.

Crawford, M., & Marecek, J. (1989). Feminist theory, feminist psychology: A bibliography of epistemology, critical analysis, and applications. *Psychology of Women Quarterly, 13*, 477–491.

Davis-Stephenson, C. (1990). The construction of childhood sexuality: A symbolic interactionist perspective. *Dissertation Abstracts International, 51*-04B, 2057. (University Microfilms No. DEX-90–08–536).

Denmark, F., Russo, N. F., Frieze, I., & Sechzer, J. A. (1988). Guidelines for avoiding sexism in psychological research: A report of the Ad Hoc Committee on Nonsexist Research. *American Psychologist, 43*, 582–585.

Doherty, W. J., & Boss, P. G. (1991). Values and ethics in family therapy. In A. S. Gurman & D. P. Kniskern (Eds.), *Handbook of family therapy* (Vol. 2, pp. 606–637). New York: Brunner/Mazel.

Edwards, J. N., & Kluck, P. (1980). Patriarchy: The last universal. *Journal of Family Issues, 1*, 317–337.

Edwards, S. M. (1981). *Female sexuality and the law.* Oxford, UK: Robertson.

Eisler, R. (1987). *The chalice and the blade: Our history, our future.* San Francisco: Harper & Row.

Eurich-Rascoe, B. L., & Vande Kemp, H. (1997). *Femininity and shame: Women, men, and giving voice to the feminine.* Lanham, MD: University Press of America.

Fine-Thomas, W. R. (1995). Ontic gender guilt and sexual identity in women. *Dissertation Abstracts International, 56*, B1697. (University Microfilms No. AAC 9523648).

Freeman, J. (1975). *The politics of women's liberation: A case study of an emerging social movement and its relation to the policy process.* New York: David McKay.

Fuller, P. (1995). The social construction of rape in appeal court cases. *Feminism and Psychology, 5*, 154–161.

Gabbard, G. O. (Ed.). (1989). *Sexual exploitation in professional relationships.* Washington, DC: American Psychiatric Press.

Garner, D. M., & Garfinkel, P. E. (1980). Socio-cultural factors in the development of anorexia nervosa. *Psychological Medicine, 10*, 647–656.

Gilligan, C. (1982). *In a different voice: Psychological theory and women's development.* Cambridge, MA: Harvard University Press.

Glasman, C., & Neale, A. (1994). Rape: A changing climate. *Women: A Cultural Review, 5*, 290–294.

Hafner, R. J. (1986). *Marriage and mental illness: A sex-roles perspective.* New York: Guilford Press.

Horton, A. L., & Williamson, J. A. (Eds). (1988). *Abuse and religion: When praying isn't enough.* Lexington, MA: Lexington Books.

Jourard, S. (1967). Experimenter-subject dialogue: A paradigm for a humanistic science of psychology. In J. F. Bugental (Ed.), *Challenges of humanistic psychology* (pp. 109–116). New York: McGraw-Hill.

Kaiser, T. L. (1992). The supervisory relationship: An identification of the primary elements in the relationship and an application of two theories of ethical relationships. *Journal of Marital and Family Therapy, 18*, 283–296.

Katz, P. (1991). Women, psychology, and social issues research. *Psychology of Women Quarterly, 15*, 665–676.

Lerner, G. (1986). *The creation of patriarchy.* New York: Oxford University Press.

Levack, B. P. (Ed.). (1992). *Articles on witchcraft, magic, & demonology: Vol. 10. Witchcraft, women, and society.* Hamden, CT: Garland.

Levant, R., & Pollack, W. S. (Eds.). (1995). *A new psychology of men.* New York: Basic Books.

Lott, B. (1991). Social psychology: Humanist roots and feminist future. *Psychology of Women Quarterly, 15*, 505–519.

Luepnitz, D. A. (1988). *The family interpreted: Feminist theory in clinical practice.* New York: Basic Books.

Marecek, J. (Ed.). (1989). Theory and method in feminist psychology. *Special Issue: Psychology of Women Quarterly, 13*, 367–491.

Marecek, J., & Hare-Mustin, R. T. (1991). A short history of the future: Feminism and clinical psychology. *Psychology of Women Quarterly, 15*, 521–536.

Masson, J. M. (1984). *The assault on truth: Freud's suppression of the seduction theory.* New York: Farrar, Straus & Giroux.

de Mause, L. (Ed.). (1991). The sexual abuse of children [Special issue]. *Journal of Psychohistory, 19*, 123–243.

McHugh, M. C., Koeske, R. D., & Frieze, I. H. (1986). Issues to consider in conducting nonsexist psychological research: A guide for researchers. *American Psychologist, 41*, 879–890.

Milbrath, L. W. (1988, July). *Making connections: The common roots giving rise to the environmental, feminist, and peace movements.* Paper presented at the meeting of the International Society for Political Psychology, Tel Aviv, Israel.

Milgram, S. (1963). Behavioral study of obedience. *Journal of Abnormal and Social Psychology, 67*, 371–378.

Milgram, S. (1977). *The individual in a social world: Essays and experiments.* Reading, MA: Addison-Wesley.

Mill, J. S. (1970). The subjection of women. In A. S. Rossi. (Ed.), *Essays on sex equality: John Stuart Mill and Harriett Taylor Mill* (pp. 123–242). Chicago: University of Chicago Press. (Original work published 1869)

Miller, C., & Swift, K. (1976). *Words and women: New languages in new times.* Garden City, NY: Doubleday.

Miller, J. B. (1986). *Toward a new psychology of women* (2nd ed.). Boston: Beacon Press.

Morgan, R. (Ed.). (1970). *Sisterhood is powerful: An anthology of writings from the women's liberation movement.* New York: Random House.

Nevill, D. D. (1978). Feminism and humanism. In I. D. Welch, G. A. Tate, & F. Richards (Eds.), *Humanistic psychology: A source book* (pp. 81–82). Buffalo, NY: Prometheus. (Original work published 1977)

Noddings, N. (1984). *Caring: A feminine approach to ethics and moral education.* Berkeley: University of California Press.

Nutt, R. L. (1991, Summer). Ethical principles in gender-fair family therapy. *Family Psychologist, 7*(3), 32–33.

O'Connell, A. N., & Russo, N. F. (Eds.). (1980). Eminent women in psychology: Models of achievement. *Special Issue: Psychology of Women Quarterly, 5*, 5–144.

Peplau, L. A., & Conrad, E. (1989). Beyond nonsexist research: The perils of feminist methods in psychology. *Psychology of Women Quarterly, 13*, 379–400.

Pollard, P. (1992). Judgements about victims and attackers in depicted rapes: A review. *British Journal of Social Psychology, 31*, 307–326.

Rossi, A. (Ed.). (1973). *The feminist papers: From Adams to de Beauvoir.* New York: Oxford University Press.

Russo, N. F., & O'Connell, A. N. (1980). Models from our past: Psychology's foremothers. *Psychology of Women Quarterly, 5*, 11–54.

Scully, D. (1990). *Understanding sexual violence: A study of convicted rapists.* London: HarperCollins.

Sheinberg, M., & Penn, P. (1991). Gender dilemmas, gender questions, and the gender mantra. *Journal of Marital and Family Therapy, 17*, 33–44.

Silverstein, B. (1986). The role of the mass media in promoting a thin standard of bodily attractiveness for women. *Sex Roles, 14*, 519–532.

Silverstein, L., & Phares, V. (Eds.). (1996). Fathering and feminism. *Psychology of Women Quarterly, 20*, 1–77.

Stevens, G., & Gardner, S. (1982). *The women of psychology* (2 vols.). Cambridge, MA: Schenkman.

Task Force on Sex Bias and Sex Role Stereotyping in Psychotherapeutic Practice. (1978). Guidelines for therapy with women. *American Psychologist, 33*, 1122–1123.

Tavris, C. (1992). *The mismeasure of woman: Why women are not the better sex, the inferior sex, or the opposite sex.* New York: Simon & Schuster.

Temkin, J. (1987). *Rape and the legal process.* London: Sweet & Maxwell.

Torrey, J. (1987). Phases of feminist re-vision in the psychology of personality. *Teaching of Psychology, 14*, 155–160.

Travis, C. B., Gressley, D. L., & Crumpler, C. A. (1991). Feminist contributions to health psychology. *Psychology of Women Quarterly, 15*, 557–566.

Trible, P. (1984). *Texts of terror: Literary-feminist readings of biblical narratives.* Philadelphia: Fortress Press.

Unger, R. K. (1988). Psychological, feminist, and personal epistemology: Transcending contradiction. In M. M. Gergen (Ed.), *Feminist thought and the structure of knowledge* (pp. 124–141). New York: New York University Press.

Vande Kemp, H. (1990). Character armor or the armor of faith? Reflections on psychologies of suffering. *Journal of Psychology and Christianity, 9*, 5–17.

Van Leeuwen, M. S. (1988). Christian maturity in light of feminist theory. *Journal of Psychology and Theology, 16*, 168–182.

Walsh, R. T. (1989). Do research reports in mainstream feminist psychology journals reflect feminist values? *Psychology of Women Quarterly, 13*, 433–444.

Walsh-Bowers, R. (1995). The reporting and ethics of the research relationship in areas of interpersonal psychology, 1939–1989. *Theory and Psychology, 5*, 233–250.

Worell, J. (1990). Feminist frameworks: Progress and prospects. *Psychology of Women Quarterly, 14*, 1–6.

Worell, J., & Etaugh, C. (Eds.). (1994). Transformations: Reconceptualizing theory and research with women. *Special Issue: Psychology of Women Quarterly, 18*, 443–651.

10

Biofeedback, Mind-Body Medicine, and the Higher Limits of Human Nature

DONALD MOSS

THE BIRTH OF BIOFEEDBACK, 1969

A new interdisciplinary paradigm emerged throughout the late 1960s, unifying developments from the diverse fields of psychology, neurophysiology, cybernetics, and medicine, culminating in a number of key publications in the final year of the decade. In 1969 Neal Miller published an article in *Science* on "Learning of Visceral and Glandular Responses." Elmer Green was senior author for two classic articles in the same year, "Self-Regulation of Internal States" (in *Progress of Cybernetics: Proceedings of the First International Congress of Cybernetics*) and "Feedback Technique for Deep Relaxation." Charles Tart also published his edited compendium *Altered States of Consciousness* (Tart, 1969), including several articles on feedback techniques or operant conditioning modifying neurophysiological processes.

In the same year key publications in systems theory and cybernetics gave wider dissemination to new concepts of feedback within systems, which were to be critical in understanding self-regulatory phenomena. Ludwig Van Bertalanffy contributed a chapter to *General Systems Theory and Psychiatry* (Gray, Duhl, & Rizzo, 1969); and Herbert Simon published *The Sciences of the Artificial* (1969).

Biofeedback as a model and technique was ready to be born: A scientist applies sensitive electronic instruments to provide meaningful information about physiologic processes to an animal or human subject. In turn, the subject gains greater awareness and control over the physiology and self-regulates more effectively. Biofeedback, the providing of information back to a subject about life processes, contributes a powerful new tool for self-mastery, research, and clinical intervention.

In October 1969 the Biofeedback Research Society was formed and held its first meeting in Santa Monica, California, at the Surfrider Inn, and the phenomenon of biofeedback officially received its name. We will return to this institutional history of biofeedback as a profession after reviewing several of the research and clinical foundations of biofeedback.[1]

THE ORIGINS OF BIOFEEDBACK

The contributions of many earlier researchers and practitioners can be cited as forerunners of biofeedback. Edmund Jacobson commenced research at Harvard in 1908 and throughout the 1920s and 1930s worked to develop progressive muscle relaxation as an effective behavioral technique for the alleviation of neurotic tensions and many functional medical disorders (Jacobson, 1938). He used crude electromyographic equipment to monitor the levels of muscle tension in his patients during the course of treatment. The German Johann Schultz contributed autogenic training in the 1930s, a discipline for creating a deep low-arousal condition with a pervasive quieting effect on the autonomic nervous system (Schultz & Luthe, 1959). B. F. Skinner, Albert Bandura, Joseph Wolpe, and others extended the operant training principles of the animal laboratory into a refined science of behavior therapy and behavior modification through instrumental learning (Skinner, 1969; Bandura, 1969; Wolpe & Lazarus, 1966). The building blocks were in place for a science of self-regulation by the 1960s.

The scientific emergence of biofeedback is a good example of synchronicity. A number of independent areas of scientific work converged and overlapped until a community of researchers recognized their common ground. Kenneth Gaarder points out that biofeedback was not so much a discovery as it was "an awareness which emerged from the Zeitgeist" (Gaarder, 1979). Many researchers of the 1950s and 1960s can be cited as independent founders of biofeedback. I will highlight here the early work on electroencephalograph (EEG), visceral learning, electromyography, and incontinence.

Operant Control of EEG and the Pursuit of Alpha States

In the late 1950s Joe Kamiya studied the phenomenon of internal perception or the awareness of private internal experiencing. Serendipitously, he discovered that a subject could learn through feedback to reliably discriminate between alpha- and beta-dominant cortical states, and then further demonstrated that a subject could learn to produce such alpha or beta brain states on demand (Kamiya, 1969, 1994; Gaarder & Montgomery, 1977, p. 4). Kamiya's continuing work on voluntary production of alpha states coincided with the dawning countercultural interest in altered states of consciousness and the emergence of a new interest in

Eastern religions, the psychology of consciousness, and transpersonal psychology (Moss & Keen, 1981; de Silva, 1981).

This was the era in which Timothy Leary was attracting media attention by encouraging youth to use LSD to discover new levels of human consciousness. In August 1969 the renowned social psychologist Richard Alpert, renamed Ram Dass, gave a presentation to the annual meeting of the Association for Humanistic Psychology on "The Transformation of a Man from Scientist to Mystic."

Alpha brain states are most closely associated with a creative, open awareness or with a receptive, meditative state. Kamiya's research gave birth to a new humanistic dream of human beings learning to cultivate a spiritually awakened state within a relatively short time frame and through the guidance of electronic monitoring. Now human beings could explore higher states of consciousness without psychedelic drugs.

A host of EEG studies and optimistic clinical reports followed. In 1967 Les Fehmi undertook a series of experiments on producing brain synchrony in humans in hopes of enhancing the clarity and scope of information processing. In another example of serendipity, Fehmi discovered that he dramatically increased his own alpha production after he "gave up on the task" out of frustration at being unable to increase alpha. Further study of voluntary enhancement of alpha brain states, including studies of relaxation and imagery, led Fehmi to highlight a broadened, diffuse state of awareness. Fehmi contends that this nonfocused, non-goal-oriented attentional state serves to release physiological tensions, soften interpersonal relating, and optimize physiological functioning and health. Out of this program of research Fehmi developed his Open Focus model for training individuals in a learned, meditative attentional style (Fehmi & Fritz, 1980; Fehmi & Selzer, 1980; Fehmi, in press). On a more philosophical level, Fehmi characterizes the human being as *Homo qui attendit quomodo attendit*, or the species that can attend to and choose its own style of attention (in press).

The research on alpha brain-wave production and meditative spiritual awareness found a ready audience in the popular press. A new industry emerged, offering "alpha training units," primitive biofeedback instruments, to assist the meditatively oriented individual in enhancing alpha states.

The scientifically minded community became increasingly skeptical. Ancoli and Kamiya (1978) critiqued the methodological weaknesses and inconsistencies of many of the early studies on alpha feedback training. They found the quality and length of training inadequate in many studies and criticized researchers for neglecting to monitor such critical variables as the social interactions between experimenter and subject, and instructional set (1978, pp. 179–180). In 1979 Basmajian declared that "alpha feedback is still a mystery but it is not an acceptable treatment method" (1979, p. 1).

The basic principle that brain processes can be brought under voluntary control remains exciting, and the scientific evidence for this principle continues to mount four decades later. Further, the interest never entirely faded in pursuing meditative, alpha-dominant states of mind conducive to some kind of spiritual integration. Today's EEG feedback or neurofeedback movement, however, has also been encouraged by additional pragmatic applications of brain-wave control.

Eugene Peniston's impressive 1989 report on successful outcomes in treating alcoholics with a program based on enhancing alpha/theta-range cortical activity sparked a flood of interest that altered states of consciousness could, after all, have benefit for personal growth and recovery (Peniston & Kukolski, 1989). Similarly, a series of methodologically cautious reports by Joel Lubar suggested that schoolchildren diagnosed with atttention deficit and hyperactivity disorder could enhance their attentional capacities through selective EEG training in theta suppression and enhancement of beta-range cortical activity (Lubar, 1989, 1991; Lubar & Shouse, 1977).

The neurofeedback movement of the late 1980s and 1990s continues some of the evangelistic fervor and methodological carelessness of the 1960s alpha movement. The advances in instrumentation and computer signal processing in three decades, however, make possible an impressive degree of precision in electroencephalographic measurement and real-time feedback.

Visceral Learning and the Dream of Controlling One's Own Health

Neal Miller, Leo DiCara, and their colleagues carried out a series of dramatic animal experiments in the 1960s demonstrating the operant conditioning of a variety of internal autonomically regulated physiologic processes, including blood pressure, cardiac function, and intestinal activity (Miller & DiCara, 1967; Miller, 1969, 1978). Prior to their research physiologists generally assumed that organisms have control over bodily functions governed by the central nervous system (or "voluntary nervous system"). The internal physiological processes controlled by the autonomic (or "involuntary") nervous system were regarded as operating beyond conscious awareness or control.

Miller and DiCara used animals paralyzed by curare so that the animals could not produce the desired visceral changes through voluntary activity mediated by the central nervous system. In this paralyzed state their animal subjects were still able to change their visceral functions. A group of thirsty dogs were trained to salivate more (or to salivate less) to obtain water. Curarized rats were even able to change their EEG.

Many of Neal Miller's experiments on curarized animals have not been successfully replicated, but his animal studies spurred further investigations extending the same operant model of visceral learning to human subjects (Miller & Dworkin, 1974). More importantly, Miller's research inspired the hope that biofeedback can enable a human being to take a more active role in recovering and maintaining health. Further, it encouraged the dream that human beings can aspire to previously unimagined levels of personal control over bodily states, reaching unprecedented states of wellness and self-control.

John Basmajian and the Control of a Single Motor Unit

The skeletal muscles have long been known to be under the human being's conscious control through the central nervous system. Human locomotion is based on this conscious control. The individual carelessly pictures the destination and begins to move. In that same moment his or her central nervous system fluidly organizes multiple components of muscular activity into a "kinetic melody" that effectively carries the individual to the goal. Hundreds and even thousands of "motor units" (each motor unit comprised of many muscle fibers) are recruited into one such activity or movement.

A variety of diseases, injuries, and pathological conditions undermine this muscular integration, and rehabilitation of muscle pain and functional motor deficits is challenging at best. In many cases injury destroys the sensorimotor pathway linking brain and muscle, while the muscle fibers themselves remain structurally intact, but without coordination. Even the healthy individual shows little precise awareness of, or control over, individual motor units in the muscles. There is no proprioceptive sensation to guide the acquisition of control of such microscopic areas of muscle function.

John V. Basmajian began a program of research in the 1950s to test the outer limits of voluntary control over the skeletal muscles. Basmajian utilized surface electrodes over the muscle and visual (oscilloscope) and auditory feedback to the subject (Basmajian, 1967). Ultimately he demonstrated that almost any subject could establish conscious control and training of a single motor unit within a muscle within a brief time. On one occasion he monitored the muscle functions of a television interviewer. This interviewer insisted that he would learn the motor control while simultaneously conducting the interview for television cameras. Basmajian discouraged this bravado, yet the interviewer persisted and mastered the motor control with feedback while carrying out the half-hour interview (Brown, 1980).

Basmajian's research and the thousands of investigations that have followed have established the powerful role that surface electromyography can play in physical therapy, neuromuscular reeducation, and pain treatment (Moss, Kasman, & Fogel, 1996). The applications range from relieving a tension headache to rehabilitating foot drop after a stroke. Further, Basmajian's work provides convincing support for the basic biofeedback model. If an external device is able to provide the human subject with precise information about physiological processes, then the individual's control over these bodily processes can be increased. Even those muscles (or other organ functions) that have been damaged by injury or disease process may be brought under some form of compensatory control once electronic feedback is provided to the individual. The biofeedback instrument creates a functional substitute (an external feedback loop), replacing the body's original internal feedback and self-regulatory process.

Arnold Kegel, O. H. Mowrer, and Incontinence

One less glamorous area of clinical biofeedback practice antedates the rest of the biofeedback movement by at least two decades. In 1947 California gynecologist Arnold Kegel invented the perineometer to assist his gynecological patients in controlling urinary leakage. John Perry and Leslie Talcott (1988, 1989) point out that the perineometer meets all of the definitions of a biofeedback device, including the ten-point definition of biofeedback proposed by Mark Schwartz (Schwartz & associates, 1987). The perineometer is an instrument inserted into the vagina that measures muscle contraction and provides the patient with immediate feedback to guide her enhanced control of urine. The use of this device enhances self-regulation and avoids personal embarrassment, social stigma, and costly and often ineffective surgical procedures. Kegel also introduced the now widely used Kegel exercises, but it is noteworthy that the Kegel exercises are more effective when their use is accompanied by perineometric feedback. John Perry points out that the only book on biofeedback ever to reach the *New York Times* Bestseller List was *The G Spot and Other Recent Discoveries about Human Sexuality* (Ladas, Whipple, & Perry, 1982), which includes discussion of the Kegel exercises and the perineometer.

The field of incontinence treatment also produced another contender for the earliest biofeedback device. O. Hobart Mowrer, a respected psychological researcher, described the use of a bedwetting alarm in a 1938 article. The simple device detected wetting, sounded an alarm, and awakened the child and parents (Mowrer & Mowrer, 1938). This immediate feedback triggered awakening, reflex sphincter contraction, and detrusor muscle relaxation. Through a process of classical conditioning, the internal cues presented by the filling bladder take over to stimulate the same response sequence (Collins, 1973). Many children rapidly learn to self-monitor and self-regulate. The process becomes automatic for most children, to the extent that they sleep through the night without incident.

These early innovations in daytime and nighttime incontinence treatment have borne fruit with dramatic personal consequences for many individuals. The U.S. Agency for Health Care Policy and Research published practice guidelines for adult urinary incontinence in 1992, recommending biofeedback as the first choice of treatment (Whitehead, 1995). Research reports show a similar efficacy for biofeedback with fecal incontinence (Whitehead & Drossman, 1996). These procedures produce a tremendous boon in personal esteem because the individual can once again lead an active life without shame or fear. Further, incontinence is one of the most frequent reasons many older adults are placed prematurely in nursing-home care, and effective treatment preserves the personal dignity of independent living.

The Rapid Application of Biofeedback Techniques

The work of the previously mentioned pioneers in biofeedback was not the only research being done. Reports of biofeedback applications to a variety of medical and emotional disorders proliferated rapidly in the 1960s and 1970s. I will cite just a few of these investigations. Barry Sterman (1986) demonstrated that EEG-guided training of a specific sensorimotor rhythm over the sensorimotor cortex could suppress some epileptic seizures. Bernard Engel (1973) reported operant control of cardiac arrhythmias. Chandra Patel (1975) reported on the use of both yoga and biofeedback in hypertension. Elmer Green, Dale Walters, and Joseph Sargent reported on the use of self-regulation training for migraine headache (Sargent, Walters, & Green, 1973). Thomas Budzynski, Johann Stoyva, and Charles Adler (1970) reported on the effects of feedback-induced muscle relaxation on tension headaches.

A SCIENCE OF SELF-REGULATION

By 1975 the field of biofeedback had established a number of effective treatment protocols for tension headache, migraine, lower-back pain, temporomandibular disorders, hypertension, Raynaud's disease, incontinence, and a number of other functional disorders. The basic instrumentation triad of the electromyograph (EMG), thermal feedback, and the galvanic skin response (GSR) meter had emerged as the "workhorses" of the biofeedback clinic. The EMG measures the electrical potential of muscle fibers and proved to be useful for general relaxation training, the treatment of headaches and muscular pain, and neuromuscular education. Thermal feedback measures skin temperature, especially finger temperature, and proved useful as an indirect measure of vasoconstriction or vasodilation and blood flow. Thermal feedback proved useful for migraine headache, Raynaud's disease, hypertension, and general autonomic relaxation. The galvanic skin response meter (GSR, also referred to as a skin conductance or electrodermal activity meter) measures electrical changes in the skin associated with sympathetic nervous arousal. The GSR proved useful as an adjunct to psychotherapy and behavior therapy, measuring anxiety and cognitive/emotional threat reactions (Fuller, 1977). A variety of additional feedback modalities proved useful for special applications: the feedback EEG (electroencephalograph), measuring electrical activity on the cortex of the brain; the pneumograph, measuring respiration rate and pattern; the photoplethysmograph, measuring heart rate and blood pulse volume; the perineometer, discussed earlier; and a variety of other devices (Schwartz & associates, 1995). This same time period of the 1960s and 1970s also saw the articulation of a number of concepts framing a new approach to health, wellness, and the actualization of higher human potential.

Mind-Body Medicine

Humanistic psychology dramatically emphasized the unity of body and mind. Fritz Perls introduced a number of body-awareness exercises into Gestalt therapy, as did the Reichian and other body-therapy schools. Biofeedback took this emphasis on a mind-body unity to a new level and created a mind-body medicine. The "psychophysiological principle" was formulated in a variety of ways. Elmer Green and his associates expressed it as follows: "Every change in the physiological state is accompanied by an appropriate change in the mental-emotional state, conscious or unconscious, and conversely, every change in the mental-emotional state, conscious or unconscious, is accompanied by an appropriate change in the physiological state" (Green, Green, & Walters, 1970b, p. 3). Body and mind are one, and the pursuit of health requires a holistic, biopsychosocial approach (Green & Shellenberger, 1991).

Ian Wickramasekera and colleagues have proposed that current applied psychophysiological methods can serve as a bridge between the traditional biomedical model and the biopsychosocial model in family medicine and primary care (Wickramasekera, Davies, & Davies, 1996). Over 75% of patients visiting a primary-care physician present with physical symptoms related to psychosocial and behavioral factors. George Engel (1977) called for a biopsychosocial model for medicine two decades ago, but this challenge remains unfulfilled. Wickramasekera cites a variety of interrelated mind-body techniques—biofeedback, hypnosis, and cognitive behavior therapy—as effective tools for addressing a variety of stress-related disorders and somatization disorders. Psychophysiological assessment and psychophysiological monitoring using sophisticated electronic biofeedback instruments can play a critical role in effective interventions with medical patients (Wickramasekera, Davies, & Davies, 1996, pp. 223–229).

Dysponesis

George Whatmore and Daniel R. Kohli (1974) used EMG feedback to teach patients to relax muscle groups and developed the concept of dysponesis, misplaced effort, as a common neurophysiological factor in many functional disorders. Many individuals facing stressful situations respond by dramatically increasing efforts in the same old directions and drawing on the same old strategies and habits. The result is a misplaced waste of effort and energy. The concept of dysponesis takes this problem of "doing more of the same" to a neurophysiological level. In the face of stress the individual engages in maladaptive muscular efforts, breathing patterns, and autonomic arousal, producing only illness and fatigue. The promise of biofeedback is to increase awareness of such dysponetic habits and to provide an avenue to new, more healthful behavioral and physiological habits.

The Stress Response and the Relaxation Response

Hans Selye's (1956) ground-breaking research on stress demonstrated that the human response to stress is an adaptive biological response with impact on the entire organismic system. Cognitive attention to an approaching threat triggers an alarm and mobilization response preparing the body for emergency action. The stress response activates the limbic or emotional brain and the hypothalamus, which then stimulate large portions of the sympathetic nervous system and the endocrine system. The result is a flood of stress hormones (including ACTH), elevated blood sugar, and hyperarousal of many internal organs and functions. The individual will notice elevated heart rate, tense musculature, rapid respiration, and a variety of intense emotional states. This adaptive response prepares the individual to flee or fight the threat. In ideal circumstances the threat passes and the individual can return to a more relaxed psychophysiological state.

In modern human society, however, the individual is exposed to chronically stressful work and family environments, the individual perseverates in thinking about the problems, and neither mind nor body return to the original resting state. This is the basis for many functional medical and psychiatric disorders. The body and mind enter a state of fatigue, exhaustion, and loss of adaptability. Many specific components in the stress response have a temporary adaptive effect, but a debilitating effect over time. Under stress, for example, the pituitary gland releases vasopressin, which contracts the walls of the arteries, raising blood pressure. Over time this vasoconstriction contributes to chronic and life-threatening hypertension. The immune system also can become depleted and unable to protect one from disease.

More recent research has shown that the so-called stress response is really more complex than first recognized. The autonomic nervous system does not respond as one single unit; rather, a variety of divergent patterns occur in different individuals, some, for example, affecting the cardiovascular system in various ways, others affecting the upper or lower gastrointestinal tract, and others the musculoskeletal system. Both sympathetic and parasympathetic nervous system activation patterns play a role in the multiple forms of the human stress response (Gevirtz, 1996).

Herbert Benson (1975) established that just as there is a human stress response with negative effects on the body, there is also a relaxation response with a healing or restorative impact on the human physiology and mind. Benson began by investigating transcendental meditation and its effects on physiology. The effects were the exact opposite of the stress response: a decrease in sympathetic activation, a reduction in stress-hormone levels, lowered heart rate and blood pressure, relaxed musculature, and emotional calm. Benson reviewed the literature on Eastern meditation, Christian mysticism, and relaxation practices and found that most approaches shared a common formula with three elements: a quiet environment, cultivation of a passive mental attitude ("letting go"), and the use of a mental device to focus attention. Benson then developed a nonreligious form of meditation based on these three elements and discovered similar effects on quieting physiological arousal. Benson hypothesized that this "relaxation response" (as he called the psychophysiological state) appears to underlie the beneficial effects of many schools of Eastern and Western meditation, yoga, and relaxation-skills training.

Benson's research showed the clinical benefits of cultivating the relaxation response in lowered blood pressure, reduced anxiety, smoking cessation, and reduced drug and alcohol dependence. The relaxation response provides a conceptual framework for one of the major contributions of biofeedback. Providing immediate physiological feedback enhances the acquisition of a relaxation response, with immediate benefits for a number of functional medical disorders.

THE INSTITUTIONAL HISTORY OF BIOFEEDBACK

Academic departments of neurophysiology, physiological psychology, and sleep research and a few medical institutions such as the Veterans' Administration and the Menninger Foundation supported much of the new research on feedback mechanisms controlling physiological processes. Kenneth Gaarder identifies two critical meetings that preceded the Santa Monica conference and supported the networking that culminated in the Biofeedback Research Society. First, an annual Veterans Administration research meeting took place in Denver in 1968, and several feedback researchers were in attendance: Thomas Budzynski, Kenneth Gaarder, Thomas Mulholland, Barry Sterman, and Johann Stoyva. In April 1969 the American Association for Humanistic Psychology and the Menninger Foundation cosponsored a Conference on Altered States of Consciousness in Council Grove, Kansas, bringing together researchers working on many aspects of consciousness in relation to health. The work reported at Council Grove reflected the mood of the 1960s, including research on meditation, psychedelic drugs, mysticism, and extrasensory perception. Elmer Green was one of the prime movers for the conference, and Barbara Brown, Kenneth Gaarder, Joe Kamiya, Gardner Murphy, and Johann Stoyva were in attendance.

The Santa Monica Conference and the Biofeedback Research Society

In 1969 a triad of Kenneth Gaarder, Gardner Murphy, and Barbara Brown formed a core committee to organize a single unifying conference to focus the growing interest in the concept of feedback. Several colleagues encouraged and supported the concept of a larger conference and the establishment of a new scientific society. Barbara Brown did most of the logistical work for the conference, set up the scientific program, and later was elected as the first president. The conference was held on October 20–22, 1969, at the Surfrider Inn in Santa Monica, California.

The conference program was organized into a series of research reports and panels on the following issues: conditioning and the control of autonomic functions, muscle feedback, EEG feedback, feedback and states of consciousness, methodologies of feedback, feedback—theory and the future, feedback techniques in experimental animals, and clinical applications of feedback concepts. The word *biofeedback* was not listed anywhere in the program, and one of the controversial issues of the program was the debate over what to call this new research and treatment technique as well as what to call the organization. The terms *self-regulation, auto-regulation*, and *feedback* were all proposed. Finally, the technique of "biofeedback" was named and the Biofeedback Research Society was formed.

The presenters listed in the program included John Basmajian, Barbara Brown, Thomas Budzynski, Leo DiCara, Les Fehmi, Elmer Green, Joe Kamiya, Thomas Mulholland, Gardner Murphy, Barry Sterman, Johann Stoyva, Charles Tart, and George Whatmore, among others. Joe Kamiya observes that the group that gathered in Santa Monica was fascinating in its diversity, ranging from "the hardest nosed operant conditioners to those in white robes" (Kamiya, 1994). The Eastern spiritual influences were strong, as was the humanistic emphasis on the unfolding of new levels of human potential. The pursuit of alpha cortical states as a pathway to spiritual awareness especially drew the interests of transpersonal psychologists and meditators. Yet methodology and rigorous psychophysiological research received equal emphasis. Biofeedback seemed to be a meeting point where high technology and the higher levels of consciousness could meet.

After the conference at Santa Monica the broadly focused new Biofeedback Research Society continued to evolve, becoming the Biofeedback Society of America in 1976 and the Association for Applied Psychophysiology and Biofeedback (AAPB) in 1988. The development of a panoply of clinical techniques for a variety of health problems increased the clinical emphasis of the society. A greater emphasis developed on research documenting clinical efficacy of biofeedback techniques with a variety of clinical problems.

Biofeedback and Applied Psychophysiology Today

Today the Association for Applied Psychophysiology and Biofeedback, headquartered in Wheat Ridge, Colorado, supports a peer-reviewed journal publishing scientific articles and a news magazine and fosters basic scientific work by recognizing outstanding research papers at the annual conference. A variety of sections and interest groups have developed within the association for individuals pursuing special interests in EEG feedback ("neurofeedback"), surface EMG applications, technology, education, nursing, pediatric applications, respiratory physiology, and applied psychophysiology in family medicine.

Diversity continues to characterize the organization, which remains multidisciplinary and continues to combine the poetic and the empirical in its annual programs. The 1996 annual meeting in Albuquerque, New Mexico, featured keynote speakers on (1) the frontiers of brain-imaging technology, (2) transpersonal medicine, (3) the psychophysiology and behavioral treatment of hypertension, (4) the development and control of childhood asthma, (5) recent advances in spinal-cord rehabilitation, and (6) "Why do African Americans suffer illness and die at a higher rate than other Americans?"

As this list of topics illustrates, both the scientific foundations and the clinical breadth of the biofeedback movement have grown steadily since 1969. The term *biofeedback* is frequently criticized as too narrow, since biofeedback practitioners also engage in a variety of other treatment interventions drawing on psychophysiological principles, but without specific use of a biofeedback instrument. The concepts of applied psychophysiology, clinical psychophysiology, and behavioral health may more broadly capture the spirit of the field today.

The majority of biofeedback practitioners today are health care providers involved in a daily clinical practice; this includes physicians, psychologists, nurses, social workers, physical and occupational therapists, and several other disciplines. Clinical biofeedback today offers a diversity of clinical procedures and protocols with applications to a wide range of disorders.

Today's vigorous EEG biofeedback movement, or neurotherapy movement, provides examples of the diversity of today's clinical biofeedback. Many substance-abuse therapists apply Eugene Peniston's treatment protocol for training recovering alcoholics to produce higher magnitudes of alpha and theta brain activity while utilizing imagery techniques for self-transformation and rehabilitation (Peniston & Kukolski, 1989). Other neurotherapists follow Joel Lubar's or Michael Tansey's protocols for training children with attention deficits to alter dominant brain rhythms and enhance academic attention (Lubar, 1991). Others apply Barry Sterman's (1986) EEG protocols to suppress convulsive neural activity and control epilepsy. Additional EEG applications and treatment protocols emerge regularly for disorders ranging from multiple personality to closed head injury. According to an AAPB publication (Shellenberger, Amar, Schneider, & Turner, 1994, pp. 2–3), the clinical efficacy of biofeedback has been demonstrated for the following disorders: anxiety disorders, attention deficit and hyperactivity, cerebral palsy, chronic pain, enuresis, epilepsy, essential hypertension, headache (migraine, mixed, and tension types), incontinence (fecal and urinary), insomnia, irritable bowel syndrome, motion sickness, myofascial pain syndrome, neuromuscular disorders, rectal pain and rectal ulcer, Raynaud's disease, rheumatoid arthritis pain, stroke, and temporomandibular joint (TMJ) disorders.

In a recent publication Schwartz and associates categorized biofeedback applications according to the quality of outcome research supporting each application. Schwartz and associates (1995, pp. 108–109) report that abundant empirical research has demonstrated biofeedback's efficacy for the following disorders: tension-type headache, migraine headache, Raynaud's disease, urinary and fecal incontinence, essential hypertension, nocturnal enuresis, and dyschezia. At least some research supports good outcomes with insomnia, anxiety disorders, chronic pain, ADD and ADHD, functional nausea and vomiting, irritable bowel syndrome, motion sickness, asthma, bruxism and temporomandibular disorder (TMD), tinnitus, phantom limb pain, and secondary Raynaud's symptoms. Additionally, there are case reports of positive outcomes for biofeedback with writer's cramp, esophageal spasm, occupational cramps, blepharospasm, dysmenorrhea, visual disorders, some dermatologic disorders, diabetes mellitus, fibromyalgia, and menopausal hot flashes.

Professional Standards

Today AAPB has a sister organization, the Biofeedback Certification Institute of America (BCIA), also headquartered in Wheat Ridge, Colorado, which serves to assure the standards of care in the clinical practice of biofeedback. BCIA has established a basic blueprint of knowledge and skills regarded as essential to the practice of clinical biofeedback. BCIA now grants certification in three areas—biofeedback, stress management, and EEG biofeedback—based on didactic educational prerequisites, supervised personal training, supervised clinical practice, and a comprehensive examination.

BIOFEEDBACK TODAY AND THE SEARCH FOR HUMAN POTENTIAL

Several figures in the field have expressed a concern that biofeedback's transformation into a health profession treating sick individuals has led the field astray from the original dream of a human being guided by technology into a higher realization of human potential (Kamiya, 1994; Kall, 1994; Peper, 1994). According to Rob Kall, the vision of biofeedback involves re-creating wholeness, balance, and health, rather than merely eliminating symptoms. At its best, biofeedback "opens people's vision, dissolves inner barriers, illuminates paths to greater potential, opportunity, capacity for happiness, and ability to share with and contribute to others" (1994, p. 30).

The excitement of enhancing personal control and self-direction is never entirely lost even in the most mundane clinical procedures. Clinicians frequently report that patients utilizing biofeedback instruments have reported "eureka" experiences: "You mean that when I change my thoughts, my heart slows down and my heart rate and breathing come into balance?" or "I can do it! I can warm my own hands with my own mind. And I don't ever have to have headaches again."

Nevertheless, the critics remain justified in their concerns. The original visionaries never intended biofeedback to be an entirely practical affair. Barbara Brown, a founder and first president of the Biofeedback Research Society, proclaimed that biofeedback could give to the human being a *new mind* and a *new body* (1974). Later she imaged this new mind as a *supermind* with expanded consciousness and unlimited potential (Brown, 1980). Kenneth Pelletier showed that the mind can slay human health, but with the guidance of biofeedback, autogenic training, and meditative practices this same human mind can become the basis for a new holistic and creative adaptation for the healthy individual (1977).

If we are to be faithful to this original vision of Barbara Brown, Kenneth Pelletier, Elmer Green, and many others, it is essential that the approach, concepts, and techniques of biofeedback remain available for education, spiritual discovery, self-awareness, and personal growth and never become entirely medical. The biofeedback research tradition remains a part of the humanistic quest for human freedom, self-regulation, and personal and spiritual renewal.

NOTE

1. The author is grateful to Joe Kamiya, Kenneth Gaarder, and Francine Butler for assistance in drafting the historical overview.

REFERENCES

Ancoli, S., & Kamiya, J. (1978). Methodological issues in alpha biofeedback training. *Biofeedback and Self-Regulation, 3*(2), 159–183.

Bandura, A. (1969). *Principles of behavior modification.* New York: Holt, Rinehart & Winston.

Basmajian, J. V. (1967). *Muscles alive: Their functions revealed by electromyography.* 2nd ed. Baltimore: Williams & Wilkins.

Basmajian, J. V. (1979). *Biofeedback: Principles and practice for clinicians.* Baltimore: Williams & Wilkins.

Benson, H. (1975). *The relaxation response.* New York: William Morrow.

Brown, B. (1974). *New mind, new body.* New York: Harper & Row.

Brown, B. (1977). *Stress and the art of biofeedback.* New York: Harper & Row.

Brown, B. (1980). *Supermind: The ultimate energy.* New York: Harper & Row.

Budzynski, T. H., Stoyva, J. M., & Adler, C. (1970). Feedback-induced muscle relaxation: Application to tension headache. *Journal of Behavior Therapy and Experimental Psychiatry, 1*, 1–14.

Butler, F. (1993, June). Personal correspondence.

Collins, R. W. (1973). Importance of the bladder-cue buzzer contingency in the conditioning treatment for enuresis. *Journal of Abnormal Psychology, 82*(2), 299–308.

de Silva, P. (1981). Two paradigmatic strands in the Buddhist theory of consciousness. In R. S. Valle & R. von Eckartsberg (Eds.), *The metaphors of consciousness* (pp. 275–285). New York: Plenum.

Engel, B. T. (1973). Clinical applications of operant conditioning techniques in the control of cardiac arrhythmias. *Seminars in Psychiatry, 5*(4), 433–438.

Engel, G. L. (1977). The need for a new medical model: A challenge for biomedicine. *Science, 196*, 129–136.

Fehmi, L. G. (in press). Attention to attention. In R. Kall (Ed.), *Applied neurophysiology and brain biofeedback.* Trevose, PA: FUTUREHEALTH.

Fehmi, L. G., & Fritz, G. (1980, Spring). Open focus: The attentional foundation of health and well being. *Somatics*, pp. 24–30.

Fehmi, L., & Selzer, F. (1980). Biofeedback and attention training. In S. Boorstein (Ed.), *Transpersonal psychotherapy* (pp. 314–337). Palo Alto, CA: Science and Behavior Books.

Gray, W., Duhl, F. J., & Rizzo, N. D. (Eds.). (1969). *General systems theory and psychiatry*. Boston: Little, Brown.

Fuller, G. D. (1977). *Biofeedback: Methods and procedures in clinical practice*. San Francisco: Biofeedback Press.

Gaarder, K. (1979). Unpublished manuscript on the founding of the Biofeedback Society of America.

Gaarder, K. R., & Montgomery, P. S. (1977). *Clinical biofeedback: A procedural manual*. Baltimore: Williams & Wilkins.

Gevirtz, R. (Chair). (1996, March). *The stress response is not unidimensional.* Symposium at the Annual Meeting of the Association for Applied Psychophysiology and Biofeedback, Albuquerque, New Mexico.

Green, E., & Green, A. (1977). *Beyond biofeedback*. New York: Delacorte Press.

Green, E., Green, A. M., & Walters, E. D. (1970a). Self-regulation of internal states. In J. Rose (Ed.), *Progress of cybernetics: Proceedings of the First International Congress of Cybernetics, London, 1969* (pp. 1299–1318). London: Gordon & Breach Science Publishers.

Green, E., Green, A. M., & Walters, E. D. (1970b). Voluntary control of internal states: Psychological and physiological. *Journal of Transpersonal Psychology, 2*, 1–26.

Green, E., Walters, E. D., Green, A., & Murphy, G. (1969). Feedback technique for deep relaxation. *Psychophysiology, 6*(3), 371–377.

Green, J., & Shellenberger, R. (1991). *The dynamics of health and wellness: A biopsychosocial approach*. Fort Worth: Holt, Rinehart, & Winston.

Jacobson, E. (1938). *Progressive relaxation*. Chicago: University of Chicago Press.

Kall, R. (1994, Summer). Heart, spirit, and human potential section proposed for AAPB. *Biofeedback Newsmagazine, 22*(2), 30.

Kamiya, J. (1969). Operant control of the EEG alpha rhythm. In C. Tart (Ed.), *Altered states of consciousness* (pp. 507–515). New York: Wiley.

Kamiya, J. (1994, February). Personal correspondence.

Ladas, A., Whipple, B., & Perry, J. D. (1982). *The G spot and other recent discoveries about human sexuality*. New York: Holt, Rinehart & Winston.

Lazarus, R. S. (1990). Stress, coping, and illness. In H. S. Friedman (Ed.), *Personality and disease* (pp. 97–120). New York: Wiley.

Lazarus, R. S. (1991). *Emotion and adaptation*. New York: Oxford University Press.

Lubar, J. F. (1989). Electroencephalographic biofeedback and neurological applications. In J. V. Basmajian (Ed.), *Biofeedback: Principles and practice for clinicians* (3rd ed.) (pp. 67–90). Baltimore: Williams & Wilkins.

Lubar, J. F. (1991). Discourse on the development of EEG diagnostics and biofeedback treatment for attention-deficit/hyperactivity disorders. *Biofeedback and Self-Regulation, 16*, 201–225.

Lubar, J. F., & Shouse, M. N. (1977). Use of biofeedback in the treatment of seizure disorders and hyperactivity. In B. B. Lahey & A. E. Kazdin (Eds.), *Advances in clinical child psychology* (pp. 203–265). New York: Plenum Press.

Miller, N. E. (1969). Learning of visceral and glandular responses. *Science, 163*, 434–445.

Miller, N. E. (1978). Biofeedback and visceral learning. *Annual review of psychology, 29*, 373–404.

Miller, N. E., & DiCara, L. (1967). Instrumental learning of heart rate changes in curarized rats: Shaping and specificity to discriminative stimulus. *Journal of Comparative
and Physiological Psychology, 63*, 12–19.

Miller, N. E., & Dworkin, B. (1974). Visceral learning: Recent difficulties with curarized
rats and significant problems for human research. In P. A. Obrist, A. H. Black, J.
Brener, & L. V. DiCara (Eds.), *Cardiovascular psychophysiology* (pp. 312–331). New
York: Aldine.

Moss, D. (1994, March). Twenty-five years of biofeedback and applied psychophysiology.
In D. Moss (Ed.), *Twenty-fifth anniversary yearbook* (pp. 3–6). Wheat Ridge, CO:
Association for Applied Psychophysiology and Biofeedback.

Moss, D., Kasman, G., & Fogel, E. (Eds.). (1996). Physical medicine and rehabilitation
[Special Issue]. *Biofeedback Newsmagazine, 24*(3).

Moss, D., & Keen, E. (1981). The nature of consciousness. In R. S. Valle & R. von
Eckartsberg (Eds.), *The metaphors of consciousness* (pp. 107–120). New York:
Plenum.

Mowrer, O. H., & Mowrer, W. M. (1938). Enuresis: A method for its study and treatment. *American Journal of Orthopsychiatry, 8*, 436–459.

Patel, C. (1975). 12-month follow-up of yoga and bio-feedback in the management of
hypertension. *Lancet, 1*, 62–65.

Pelletier, K. R. (1977). *Mind as healer, mind as slayer.* New York: Delta.

Peniston, E. G., & Kukolski, P. J. (1989). Alpha-theta brainwave training and beta-
endorphin levels in alcoholics. *Alcoholism: Clinical and Experimental Research, 13*,
271–279.

Peper, E. (1994, November). *The future of applied psychophysiology.* Panel discussion at the
Midwestern Regional Conference on Behavioral Medicine and Biofeedback, Grand
Rapids, MI.

Perry, J. D., & Talcott, L. B. (1988, May). *The bastardization of Dr. Kegel's exercises.* Presentation to the Northeast Gerontological Society, New Brunswick, NJ.

Perry, J. D., & Talcott, L. B. (1989, March). *The Kegel perineometer: Biofeedback twenty
years before its time.* Presentation to the Annual Meeting of the Association for
Applied Psychophysiology and Biofeedback, San Diego, CA.

Sargent, J. D., Walters, E. D., & Green, E. E. (1973). Psychosomatic self-regulation of
migraine headaches. *Seminars in Psychiatry, 5*(4), 415–428.

Schultz, J., & Luthe, W. (1959). *Autogenic therapy.* New York: Grune & Stratton.

Schwartz, M., & associates. (1987). *Biofeedback: A practitioner's guide.* New York: Guilford.

Schwartz, M., & associates. (1995). *Biofeedback: A practitioner's guide* (2nd ed.). New York:
Guilford.

Selye, H. (1956). *The stress of life.* New York: McGraw-Hill.

Shellenberger, R., Amar, P., Schneider, P., & Turner, J. (1994). *Clinical efficacy and cost
effectiveness of biofeedback therapy: Guidelines for third party reimbursement.* Wheat
Ridge, CO: AAPB.

Simon, H. (1969). *The sciences of the artificial.* Cambridge, MA: MIT Press.

Skinner, B. F. (1969). *Contingencies of reinforcement: A theoretical analysis.* New York:
Appleton-Century-Crofts.

Sterman, M. B. (1986). Epilepsy and its treatment with EEG feedback therapy. *Annals of
Behavioral Medicine, 8*, 21–25.

Tart, C. (Ed.). (1969). *Altered states of consciousness.* New York: Wiley.

Whatmore, G. B., & Kohli, D. R. (1968). Dysponesis: A neurophysiologic factor in functional disorders. *Behavioral Science, 13*(1), 102–124.

Whatmore, G. B., & Kohli, D. R. (1974). *The physiopathology and treatment of functional disorders.* New York: Grune & Stratton.

Whitehead, W. E. (1995, March/April). Biofeedback benefits patients with stress and urge incontinence. *National Psychologist, 8B,* 11.

Whitehead, W. E., & Drossman, D. A. (1996). Biofeedback for disorders of elimination: Fecal incontinence and pelvic floor dyssynergia. *Professional Psychology: Research and Practice, 27*(3), 234–240.

Wickramasekera, I., Davies, T. E., & Davies, S. M. (1996). Applied psychophysiology: A bridge between the biomedical model and the biopsychosocial model in family medicine. *Professional Psychology: Research and Practice, 27*(3), 221–233.

Wolpe, J., & Lazarus, A. A. (1966). *Behavior therapy techniques.* New York: Pergamon Press.

Beyond the Person: Spiritual and Transpersonal Psychologies

Chapters 11 and 12 move beyond the original territory of humanistic psychology to explore spiritual dimensions of human being. Spiritual and transpersonal viewpoints emphasize that we cannot understand the individual human person without understanding that human person's relationship and need for connection with God or a spiritual realm.

From the beginning humanistic psychology was critical of the failure of psychoanalytic and behavioral psychology to affirm art, culture, religion, and the higher aspirations of human life (see chapter 2 on psychoanalytic reductionism and behavioristic determinism). Existential psychology and humanistic psychology were welcomed and nurtured in several religiously oriented universities, including Duquesne University in Pittsburgh, the University of Seattle in Washington, and Louvain University in Belgium. Many spiritually oriented authors recognized that this new humanistic picture of the human being converged with or paralleled spiritual perspectives more closely than did Freudian or behavioristic psychologies (Powell, 1969; Carter & Narramore, 1979). Many spiritual authors also referred to Carl Jung's work, especially his *Modern Man in Search of a Soul* (1933), as providing a psychological viewpoint sympathetic to both humanistic values and religious experience.

Nevertheless, a number of humanistic psychologists and several authors within religious circles were dissatisfied with the approach of humanistic psychology to the spirit. Morton Kelsey (1986), writing from a Christian perspective, credited humanistic psychologists, especially Carl Rogers, with putting Jesus' message into effect: "Jesus' radical idea of the value of every human being and the importance of unconditional love as the most important transforming power in the world" (Kelsey, 1986, p. 31). Yet Kelsey also believed that this humanistic view was incomplete because the much-valued love was viewed as something located entirely within the person and radiating from one person to the other (Kelsey, 1986, p. 30). In the Christian religious worldview, in contrast, the person who loves also abides within a divine love that is as real as the physical world (1 John 4:16). In each traditional religious worldview—Christian, Jewish, Islamic, Hindu, and Buddhist—there is recognition of a spiritual reality that transcends the individual person and can have a powerful impact on the growth and healing of an individual, once the person commits to open himself or herself to the spiritual world. There is also within religious worldviews an emphasis that the human being has a spiritual nature and spontaneously yearns for transcendence or spiritual fulfillment. St. Augustine, in the late fourth century, wrote in his *Confessions*, "Thou hast formed us for Thyself, and our hearts are restless till they find rest in Thee" (Augustine, 1980, book 1, p. 3).

Of course, not all humanistic psychologists have chosen to follow Maslow into a transpersonal orientation. Albert Ellis criticizes the "evils of transpersonal and mystical humanism" and labels them as dogmatic, absolutist, and antihumanistic (Ellis, 1992, p. 350). Ellis prefers the orientation of secular humanism, which recognizes that human life is full of ambiguities, indeterminacies, and tensions, and places the responsibility for each individual's existence on that person's shoulders. Rollo May challenged many of the excesses in transpersonal psychology, especially the apparent offer of easy or guaranteed solutions to age-old human dilemmas (May, Krippner, & Doyle, 1992). James Bugental calls himself a "dedicated agnostic," yet acknowledges an openness to the spiritual dimensions of human existence. (See chapter 24 on Rollo May and chapter 16 on James Bugental in part II of this volume.) Nevertheless, transpersonal psychology for many remains a natural and necessary development from humanistic psychology's openness to the fullness of human experience.

Chapter 11 introduces Christian humanistic psychology. The authors begin by highlighting humanistic perspectives visible within Christian spiritual traditions since the early centuries of the Christian era. They clarify the relationship between revealed religious truths and empirical scientific knowledge. The authors also overview current efforts by Christian psychologists to bridge theological and psychological viewpoints and to introduce a life-affirming, Christ-centered perspective on personal growth and healing.

Chapter 12 introduces the Fourth Force school of transpersonal psychology. Abraham Maslow was the founder of humanistic psychology; his self-actualization model served as the core theory of the Third Force. Maslow was also the pioneer who moved humanistic psychology into spiritual territory, founding the Fourth Force or "transpersonal psychology." In the course of his research on self-actualizing persons, Maslow encountered repeated references to transcendent experiences. He came to regard his original humanistic approach as inadequate to address the spiritual experiences of these individuals and called for a new psychology "centered in the cosmos rather than in human needs and interest" (1968, p. iv). Maslow expressed this shift to a transpersonal perspective by adding a new higher level to his famous hierarchy of basic human needs, showing that the human being evolves beyond self-actualization and personal growth toward self-transcendence.

Transpersonal psychology transcends any single religious viewpoint and is deliberately both scientific (empirical) and spiritual in orientation. Transpersonal psychologists have entered into a dialogue with a variety of world religions, seeking to discover within each implicit psychological principles and models for spiritual growth. Carl Jung paved the way for this dialogue decades earlier, commenting in a 1942 address on the central role of myths, religious symbols, and religious archetypes in understanding human experience and healing human pain. He remarked that we are "forced to go back to pre-Christian and non-Christian conceptions, and to conclude that Western man does not possess the monopoly of human wisdom and that the white race is not a species of *Homo sapiens* specially favored by God. Moreover we cannot do justice to certain collective contemporary phenomena unless we revert to the pre-Christian parallels" (1942/1966, p. 82). Transpersonal psychologists have also undertaken a number of empirical investigations of spiritual and paranormal experiences.

REFERENCES

Augustine. (1980). The confessions of St. Augustine (J. G. Pilkington, Trans.). In W. J. Oates (Ed.), *Basic writings of Saint Augustine* (Vol. 1) (reprint ed.). Grand Rapids, MI: Baker Book House.

Carter, J. D., & Narramore, B. (1979). *The integration of psychology and theology: An introduction.* Grand Rapids, MI: Zondervan.

Ellis, A. (1992). Secular humanism and rational-emotive therapy. *Humanistic Psychologist, 20,* 349–358.

Jung, C. G. (1933). *Modern man in search of a soul.* New York: Harcourt, Brace.

Jung, C. G. (1966). General problems of psychotherapy. VI. Psychotherapy and a philosophy of life. In *Collected works of C. G. Jung* (Vol.16). (pp. 76–84). Princeton: Princeton University Press. (Original work published 1942)

Kelsey, M. (1986). *Christianity as psychology: The healing power of the Christian message.* Minneapolis: Augsburg Publishing House.

Maslow, A. (1968). *Toward a psychology of being* (2nd ed.). New York: Van Nostrand Reinhold.

May, R., Krippner, S., & Doyle, J. (1992). The role of transpersonal psychology in psychology as a whole: A discussion. *Humanistic Psychologist, 20,* 307–317.

Powell, J. (1969). *Why am I afraid to tell you who I am?* Niles, IL: Argus.

11

Christian Humanistic Psychology

J. HAROLD ELLENS AND DONALD E. SLOAT

THE HISTORICAL ORIGINS OF A CHRISTIAN HUMANISTIC PSYCHOLOGY

The foundations of a Christian humanistic psychology were firmly laid by the Greek and Latin church fathers in the first five centuries of the common era (Hornblower & Spawforth, 1996; Roberts & Donaldson, 1965–1968; Schaff, 1956–1964). Irenaeus (130–202 C.E.), bishop of Lyon, developed the first thoroughgoing Christian theological anthropology[1] and promulgated a soundly psychological view of humankind, influenced by Platonic transcendentalism and Aristotelian empiricism. He conceptualized the whole of the created world and its history as a process of redemptive divine self-manifestation and considered human persons and personalities as the epitome of that divine economy. History was a psychotheological enterprise in Irenaeus's view, in that it was the unfolding self-actualization of the entire cosmos, with full-orbed (fully developed and perfected) humans appearing as the crowning outcome of the entire divine economy. For Irenaeus, Jesus of Nazareth came to be called the Christ of God because in him was realized the highest potential of human nature and thus of all creation. Jesus Christ is the paradigmatic redemptive divine achievement, for in him humanity came and comes to its full potential in God's design. In this perspective Irenaeus set the course for early Christian psychological and theological thought along a trajectory that was deepened and expanded by Tertullian (160–240 C.E.), Athanasius (293–373 C.E.), and Augustine (354–430 C.E.) (Augustine, 1956). Behind both Irenaeus's psychology and theology lay the conviction that God's glorious concept for human destiny is a fully alive human being. Clearly he meant to set before us the notion that the essence of being human is the potential and destiny to actualize the full-orbed self in its material and spiritual, mundane and transcendent dimensions. Thus he laid the foundation stone for what has come to be known as humanistic psychology.

Thomas Oden has disclosed the contribution of these early Christian thinkers to the development of theological and psychological anthropology[2] and thus to the art and science of psychology in his book on classical pastoral psychology (Oden, 1984). The scientific worldview of the modern era, with its empirical perspective and positivist philosophy, made an enormously valuable contribution to our understanding of the created world and our ability to meet its challenges for the good of humankind. However, that kind of positivistic science has been progressively called into question over the last quarter-century as being deficient in providing a wholistic understanding of human nature in particular and of the transcendent dimensions of the universe in general.

As humanistic psychology is a concerted effort to solve the problem that psychology tends to reduce humans to mere material organisms, so Christian theology and psychology have attempted to take adequate account of the entire world of the human psyche and spirit, including the capacity for transcendental ideation and experience. Humanistic psychology is bent upon taking seriously the comprehensive sphere of human experience in thinking, feeling, willing, imagining, relating, perceiving, and ordering meaning. This is a project for understanding persons in body, mind, psyche, and spirit so as to give full credence to all functions of the material and spiritual quest of humans for growth, meaning, and actualization. Christian psychology, which is crucially shaped and illumined by that anthropology derived from biblical theology, is one form of humanistic psychology in the sense that it is one of the many sources from which humanistic psychology can draw insight regarding the full-orbed function of the immanent and transcendent quest and expression of the human nature and spirit.

The tradition of Christian psychological insight and perspective is an unbroken line from the Patristics to the present moment. That tradition is expressed in one degree or another in the provisions of the medieval theology for the confessional and its absolution ceremony, the work of Friedrich Schleiermacher, the transcendentalism of William James, the theological interpretation of psychoanalytic psychodynamics by Anton Boisen, and the psychodynamic psychotheologies of Seward Hiltner, Wayne Oates, John Patton, Charles Gerkin, Don Browning, Peter Homans, Donald Capps, John Powell, Howard Clinebell, J. Harold Ellens, and Donald Sloat. This chapter presents some of the significant factors in the development of Christian perspectives on psychology in recent decades and demonstrates the way in which they reflect the theologies and anthropologies that stand behind them.

PSYCHOLOGY AND THEOLOGY, PSYCHE AND SOUL

The Historical Relationship of Psychology and Christian Theology

Psychology in the Western world has devolved into a largely secular enterprise despite the fact that it arose from religious notions of human personality and from theological roots. The idea of a Christian psychology is nonetheless problematic for most people who are serious about both Christian religion and psychological science, since the term implies that Christian ways of looking at the human psyche produce a different science than that of secular psychology. This seems, on the face of it, to be an absurd and unacceptable notion. However, the distinctive qualities of a set of Christian perspectives on the data and science of psychology have added a great deal that is valuable to a comprehensive psychological understanding of human persons as spiritual, as well as cognitive and affective, beings, as capable of reaching for, and indeed reaching, transcendent connections and meaning, as well as adapting to the mundane internal and external environments with which humans function on this planet. Moreover, the research of Christians who work in the field of psychology and have attempted to explore the ways in which Christian theological and anthropological perspectives legitimately illumine the field has made significant contributions to the science of psychology and the art of psychotherapy (Myers, 1980; Malony, Papen-Daniels, & Clinebell, 1988). Some have even been willing to use the term *Christian psychology* for what they have done (McDonagh, 1982; Myers, 1978).

The Foundations of a Christian Humanistic Psychology in Early Christian Thought

It is clear that like Irenaeus, the later church fathers developed their Christian perspectives on human nature in terms of the theological, philosophical, and psychological constructs of the Greco-Roman world. That was their world, and they were not embarrassed by it; indeed, they celebrated its superb achievements in all of these fields. Hellenistic culture carried with it into the Christian era all the benefits of the scientific and humanistic achievements of the ancient world. With Justin Martyr (100–165 C.E.), the church fathers discerned that all truth was God's truth, no matter who found it, how, or where (Roberts & Donaldson, 1962–1968, vol. 1, pp. 159–303). Thus they built their Christian worldviews in terms of the constructs available to them. Two constructs that were crucial to their theological and psychological anthropologies were the Greco-Roman and, consequently, New Testament concepts of psyche and pneuma. The former referred primarily to what we today call the psychological dimension of a human being, and the latter referred essentially to what we would call the spiritual or transcendental dimension. In biblical and Hellenistic thought these two were not in apposition or opposition to each other. Particularly in the Hellenistic ideas in the New Testament, for example, in the Christology of the Gospel of John and in Pauline anthropology, as well as in Neoplatonism, the two terms were at least somewhat overlapping and at most of a unitary and corollary nature and function.

The Secularization of the Psyche in the Modern Era

The secularization of the psyche is a uniquely modern and Western scientific phenomenon and has led to the creation of psychology as a discipline distinct from theology and philosophy. The language of the discipline has been desacralized, as it were. In the Old Testament, the Hebrew community used the term *nephesh* to describe the whole human person with inner and outer, psychospiritual and material characteristics. This concept of the self was approximately comparable to the combination of psyche and pneuma in the New Testament. *Nephesh* is often translated as "soul," meaning the whole person, "a living soul," as in "the entire ship's crew of sixteen souls was lost in the storm."

Nephesh and soul have come to have almost exclusively transcendent connotations, so secularizing psychological perspectives have shifted to the term *self.* This contemporary emphasis upon the self and the development of self psychology as a subdiscipline involved an attempt to recover the original wholism of psychology's roots while avoiding the supposedly questionable scientific nature of things transcendent and spiritual.[3] Thus developed the trajectory to humanistic psychology.

The Institutional Development of a Professional Community Dedicated to Christian Perspectives on Psychology

This trajectory led to a secularized wholism that left unsatisfied a large community of psychologists whose life's meaning intricately and intimately involved legitimate personal experience of spirituality and transcendent connection. They perceived that the secular wholism was a fine achievement, but that it was incomplete. It failed to take into consideration a large world of phenomenological data about the spiritual and transcendent human functions that was obviously integral to an honest and thoroughgoing anthropological and, hence, psychological wholism. They felt that theology as a science and an art needed the illumination of psychology in order to be sound and complete, and psychology as a science and an art needed the comparable and corollary illumination of theology to achieve that same integrity. Thus the interface of psychology and theology was deemed essential to the comprehensiveness and the unity of truth in a sound discipline of psychology.

In 1954 a group of Christian professionals trained and practicing in the fields of psychology and psychiatry met at Calvin College in Michigan to establish what is known today as the Christian Association for Psychological Studies (CAPS). It was the founders' intent that the Christian community should explore in a systematic way the manner in which our actual ontological relationship with God, as well as our psychological perception, experience, or projection of that relationship, interfaces with our state of health. The founders shared a conviction that the human being's relationship with God is definitive for his or her psychological and spiritual well-being, as well as a suspicion that this relationship might also impact heavily on one's physical well-being. Moreover, it became clear from the kinds of papers read at convocations of CAPS during its early decades that members of CAPS also shared an understanding that sometimes the nature of our personal religion or spirituality, our posture before the face of God, can create or expand pathology, while sometimes our real or perceived relationship with God, the Bible, our faith tradition, and our theology enhances health in body, mind, and spirit.

It was not the concern of the founders to drag the psychologically aware community, or indeed any part of the communities of faith and science, into the questionable processes of mysticism, subjective pietism, parapsychology, spiritism, or the occult. The founders intended, rather, to explore why it seemed to be at least heuristically and perhaps even empirically evident that wholistic health involves the self-actualization of the full range of grand potentials for growth with which God has invested humans by creating us, through our evolutionary development, in God's unique design, with body, mind, psyche, and spirit.

During the last four decades such other associations as the Christian Scientific Affiliation, the American Association of Christian Therapists, the Society of Pastoral Theology, the American Association of Pastoral Counselors, the Association for Practical Theology, and the Association for Clinical Pastoral Education have pursued endeavors similar to those of CAPS. These enterprises in the investigation of the interface of psychology and theology have been served effectively by such professional journals as the *Bulletin of CAPS*, the *Journal of Psychology and Christianity*, the *Journal of Psychology and Theology*, *Pastoral Psychology*, *Christian Scholar's Review*, and the like. Their cause was championed further by such major graduate institutions as the Fuller Graduate School of Psychology in Pasadena and the Rosemead Graduate School of Psychology in La Mirada, California, as well as by the psychology departments at many Christian colleges. In these institutions significant basic research was carried out on the scientific discovery, definition, and quantification of the psychodynamics of spirituality and religious behavior as well as on the spiritual and theological implications of scientific psychological data.

DIVISIONS AND CONTROVERSIES WITHIN THE CHRISTIAN PSYCHOLOGICAL COMMUNITY

By 1974, when CAPS moved to the national scene and undertook plans for publication of a professional journal and scientific monographs, it had become clear that there were at least two communities in this quest for Christian perspectives on psychology and spirituality.[4] On the one hand, there flourished the more conservative evangelical community with such noted scholars as John D. Carter (Carter & Narramore, 1979), Bruce Narramore, H. Newton Malony (Malony, 1977), David G. Benner (Benner, 1985, 1987, 1988), David G. Myers (1978, 1980), and many others. On the other hand, the more progressive mainline Protestant community has been represented over the years by such scholars as Seward Hiltner, Don S. Browning (Browning, 1987; Browning, Jobe, & Evison, 1990), LeRoy Aden (Aden, Benner, & Ellens, 1992; Aden & Homans, 1968), Colin Brown, Wayne Oates, Liston Mills, John Patton, Brian Childs, J. Harold Ellens (Ellens, 1982), Rodney Hunter (Hunter, 1990), Ralph Underwood, James Lapsley, Donald E. Sloat (Sloat, 1986), and many others.

The Influence of Anton Boisen

Hiltner, Browning, Aden, Oates, Brown, Mills, and others had been influenced significantly by their experience with the person and work of Anton Boisen (1876–1965) (Aden & Ellens, 1990). Boisen knew psychology from the inside out. He was a trained theologian who had

five psychotic episodes in his life, three of them severe enough to require hospitalization. The first disturbance was the most intense, and it started Boisen on a journey—we might even say an obsession—that lasted the rest of his life. It began unpretentiously. Boisen, then forty-four, was unemployed, and because he had time on his hands he decided to rework his personal statement of belief which had been required by the Presbyterian church. This process of religious reflection triggered a flood of ideas, ideas of grandeur and world destruction, of life and love sacrificed for the strong.

Three weeks after hospitalization, Boisen emerged from the acute phase of the psychosis as quickly as he had sunk into it. The agenda for his life was set—to study acute mental disturbances of the functional type in order to increase both our understanding of them and our ability to minister to those experiencing them.

Gradually, Boisen developed a core of ideas that became the hallmark of his work. He believed that certain forms of mental illness, especially those marked by anxiety, were not bad in themselves but instead were problem-solving attempts to unify the personality around more enduring values. He found that disturbances are usually precipitated by immediate situations, but under the surface lingers a deeper, more important problem, specifically a sense of failure for not living up to introjected standards and, therefore, a sense of isolation from "the fellowship of the best."

Raised to its highest level, the fellowship of the best is represented in the idea of God. Thus some forms of mental illness can be a profound and productive experience, equivalent in some respects to a religious experience, an experience of radical upheaval and spiritual healing. What is interesting is that unlike Sigmund Freud and others, Boisen did not focus on psychotherapy but on mental illness itself as a means of healing.[5] (Aden & Ellens, 1990, pp. 11–12)

Boisen's influence has persisted in the progressive mainline Christian scholars until now, compelling them to work out their psychotheological models in the context of scientific *theological* concepts. The evangelical community, however ironically, was more directly dependent upon the world of secular psychology for its orientation and tended to work out its psychotheological models in the context of those scientific *psychological* claims.

Progressive and Evangelical Voices within Contemporary Christian Psychology

Two interesting issues arose out of the different but corollary tracks pursued by these two Christian communities in the quest for a Christian wholistic psychology. The first was that the evangelical community did not speak to or read the works of the progressive community. Neither did the mainline scholars read the evangelicals or dialogue significantly with them. Moreover, the evangelicals generally came to this quest for what they called the integration of psychology and theology from the side of scientific psychology, having been trained primarily as professional psychologists, mostly at the doctoral level. On the other hand, the progressives came to the inquiry from the side of scientific theology, having been trained primarily as professional theologians teaching in pastoral psychology departments of graduate theological faculties. Therefore, the evangelicals did not trust the progressives because they thought that they did not know scientific psychology and were working mainly with an intuitive popularization of the field. The progressives did not trust the evangelicals because they thought that they did not know scientific theology and were working mainly with an intuitive and primitive Sunday school religion or the dogmatic categories and language of fundamentalism.

The Emergence of Dialogue

Both sides were in error, of course. Actually, such scholars as Hiltner, Browning, Homans, and the like were heavily trained in psychoanalytic and psychodynamic psychology. Moreover, increasingly from 1980 forward the evangelicals had command of contemporary theological perspectives and constructs and had been moderately informed of current developments in biblical studies. Generally speaking, they were also honest with the data. Moreover, it must be said that the evangelicals began to read the positions of and take seriously the dialogue with the progressives before the latter began to take them seriously. Don Browning was one of the first progressives who by 1985 recognized that his colleagues needed to be reading the evangelical publications as thoroughly as the evangelicals had begun to read theirs. Today the dialogue between the two communities flows freely, so that the names *evangelical* and *progressive* that once distinguished them are becoming less and less useful at the levels of academic, clinical, and research operations.

The Integration of Psychology and Theology: Problems with the Integration Paradigm

There has been a central problem, however, in the framework within which the evangelical community has tended to conceptualize the relationship between psychology and theology because of its use of the term *integration* to describe the desired interface. To think of the matter as integration suggests a certain inherent disparity between psychology and theology that must be overcome by force-fitting them together somehow. That begs the question. Since both, done properly, are legitimate sciences with the same required rigor, the same human subject, and therefore similar or overlapping databases, even though psychology and theology operate within different universes of discourse, there can be no inherent disparity. Both intend to move along a course of scientific integrity to the end product of disclosing truth about human nature and function. Both depend upon empirical and heuristic data and methods. Each has its own forming and informing history and its own paradigms; each depends upon theory formation that must respond with integrity to the scientific constraints upon theory development and testing; and each must respond with integrity to its respective database.

It is quite clear that what we in the Christian community have been seeking for the last half-century or more regarding this matter is a model that helps us understand authentically the relationship between the scientific disciplines of psychology and theology, together with the relationship of their applied arts and the worldviews they afford us. We have been seeking a model that affords us an interface of mutual illumination between these disciplines, both of which have as their primary investigative arena and subject what Gerkin calls, quite helpfully and imaginatively, the living human document (Gerkin, 1984).

A theological and philosophical problem lay just beneath the surface of the integration paradigm. This problem is readily apparent when the integration model is compared with the paradigm of a mutually illumining interface between psychology and theology. In the integration model there is always the danger that the equivalence of truth disclosed by both disciplines is not adequately insisted upon or is only tacitly acknowledged. The evangelical community frequently has seen the interface as one in which psychology must be drawn under the authority of theology, implying that the truth value of the data produced by psychology has a lesser valence or less immediate relevance and less ultimacy than the truth value of the insights of theology. To put this simply, the evangelical community has been plagued with the assumption or claim that the truth of the Bible is more truthful than the truth of psychology and is more important as a self-manifestation of the nature and behavior of God and, therefore, of humans.

The scholars of the progressive community of Christians have contested this way of thinking vigorously and consistently. They have done so on the theological grounds that God reveals proximate and ultimate truth in both nature and in grace, in creation and in Scripture, in our world of work experience and in our world of faith experience, and God does not speak with a forked tongue. God's two books, the evidence of the material world and the evidence of the spiritual testimony of the historic believing community in history, namely, the Bible and the theological tradition of the Church, are inherently in agreement insofar as they are truthful. The progressive community of scholars also contested the evangelical integration paradigm and its risk of an impaired notion of truth on the philosophical grounds that all truth as truth has equal valence, though it may have varied priority of application, depending upon the situation. If one is bleeding from the jugular, the truth about blood pressure may be the most important truth relevant to that situation. If one is lost in the grief and confusion of a life that seems meaningless and hopeless, the biblical truth about God's unconditional grace, a truth that can be empirically demonstrated to have radically changed people's lives in that situation, is obviously the most important truth relevant to that situation. But both truths have equal valence as truth. Both are God's truth in the ultimate sense of the word. Under the rubrics of the progressive community's spiritually and scientifically rich philosophical tradition, scientific inquiry into theology and spirituality stands on equal footing with scientific inquiry into the natural and social sciences, and vice versa.

There is a second theological problem implied in the integration model, and it is related to the one just discussed. It is the notion that the revelation of truth in the material world is not merely different in value or valence from that of Scripture but that what we see through the text of the Bible and what we see through the science of psychology represent two radically different realms of ontological reality, the world of the natural and of the supernatural. These terms have become largely nonfunctional in the thought world of the progressive community, though there has been an increased use of such terminology as "material and transcendent worlds" as the positivism of the Enlightenment thinking has come under fire in recent decades. Such terminology is meant to address the wholistic concerns of humanistic psychology with adequate and honest recognition of the psychosomatic and psychospiritual phenomena in human experience without reductionist resort to models that imply that the world of the former is inherently discontinuous with the world of the latter and vice versa.

Postmodern Perspectives: The Impossibility of a Value-free Scientific Objectivity

The insights of the postmodern era regarding the impossibility of achieving a valueless scientific objectivity are crucial here, namely, the realization that all scientific theory development is born, in the first place, out of assumptions that are to some degree driven or shaped by one's religious, theological, or value-laden predisposition. All the data one acquires, therefore, is not, strictly speaking, empirical data or objective rationality but rather the formulations of reason within the bounds of religion (Wolterstorff, 1976). This is true, for example, whether we examine the empirical research of behaviorist psychology or the heuristic research of theological analysis and reflection.

In his article entitled "Integration of Psychology and Theology," Carter, a professional psychologist from the evangelical community, addressed this issue as follows:

In an historical sense, the integration of current thought forms with Christianity has been the intellectual task of the Christian theologian and pastor beginning with the apologists in the second century, continuing with Augustine's *City of God*, Thomas Aquinas' *Summa*

Theologica, and Calvin's *Institutes*. In the post-Reformation period the task of integration became one of relating the emerging sciences with a Christian theological worldview. The task was continued by Kepler, Newton, and many others with the rapid developments in science. The stress on integrating science and Christianity was particularly strong in such nineteenth century American theologians as McCosh, Porter, and Upham. With the emergence of psychology as a separate discipline at the end of the nineteenth century some integration was incorporated into the early psychology of religion texts of James and Starbuck, although a shift of focus from integration to psychology of religion can be clearly seen. However, the antireligious bias of the early developers of psychology such as Freud and Watson coupled with the strong materialistic and physicalistic emphases of twentieth-century philosophy of science led to an eclipse of the experience-oriented areas of study such as the psychology of religion. (Carter, 1990, pp. 584–585)

Carter acknowledged that the quest for a sound understanding of the interface of psychology and theology gained its greatest momentum from the progressive community and from such enterprises in that arena as the pastoral care movement from Boisen onward and the development of scholarly interest in the psychology of religion from William James forward. In *The Integration of Psychology and Theology*, a 1979 monograph he coauthored with Bruce Narramore, Carter addressed such undesirable constructs as an integration in which theology absorbs psychology or in which psychology absorbs theology, so to speak. He emphasized the importance of taking both seriously as independent disciplines; however, on the issue of the valence of truth from various sources, he continued the evangelical claim that ultimately the word of the Bible takes precedence over all other forms or sources of truth. This misguided notion fails to acknowledge that if there seems to be a tension or conflict between the truth received from the Bible, theology, or our spiritual experience, on the one hand, and the truth received from empirical or heuristic psychological research or from any of the natural or social sciences, on the other, the dissonance must arise from our having read the Bible or the other scientific data incompletely or incorrectly. In such a case, the remaining task is to do better scientific work in theology and biblical studies or better scientific work in the natural and social sciences, or both.

In his 1990 dictionary article on the integration of psychology and theology mentioned earlier, Carter's position is discernibly matured. There he declares:

Integration does not imply that psychology and theology are creating a new discipline out of the other two. Rather, it assumes that the phenomena of psychology and theology are not in conflict because they are integral with the unity of truth. This unity is of necessity to [*sic*] God's truth since God is the author of all.

Integration can be conceptualized in terms of the figure of a diamond with three levels. The first level is abstract and conceptual and examines the metaphysical assumptions behind various psychological concepts and theories for this unity with theology. Since truth is one, there is ultimately only one set of explanatory principles, that is, the world and humankind, which science and psychology study, are in harmony with theology. In theological terms general and special revelation are in agreement because God is the author of both. Integration seeks to discover that harmony. At the second level there is an equal emphasis on both psychology and theology, while their distinctive methods are recognized. Psychology tends to be empirical and theology rational in their research. The difference in their content is not fused, nor is one reduced to the other forming a psychologized theology or a theologized psychology. Both are affirmed, including their difference, but the dynamic equivalence of their respective concepts is recognized where it exists. The third level of integration is experience and behavior. Psychology and theology converge at the points of experience because every person thinks, wills, feels, and behaves. The concepts used to explain this process—thought, choice, anxiety, guilt, values, and action—are simultaneously part of psychology and Christian theology, especially pastoral theology, because persons are fundamentally a part of both. Thus the unity or integration appears again as in the first level, but at the third level it is in experience. Finally, the three levels of integration are not separate but form a dynamic whole or Gestalt which involves the principles behind both disciplines, study of both disciplines, and awareness of one's experience in psychology as well as one's spiritual context. (Carter, 1990, p. 585)

One can say, then, that secular biophysically oriented psychology has attempted to account for human function and experience on a material plane. Humanistic psychology wishes to take account additionally of the volitional and transpersonal nature of human function and experience. Christian psychology or, more properly, psychology viewed from a Christian perspective is profoundly concerned to understand and describe the function and experience of the human organism and person in terms of a Christian worldview. This means understanding human beings in a way that takes seriously into account the human quest and achievement of transcendent experience and connection. Any explanation of the nature, function, and meaning of humanness is incomplete unless it acknowledges the reality of the human longing for God, the actual experience of God's presence in our lives, and our experiential connection with God. Psychology in Christian perspective is an endeavor to develop a psychological and theological anthropology that can account for these phenomenological givens, and that can account as well for the full range of other relevant information inherent to the discipline of psychology.

Whether one approaches the study and understanding of the living human document through the perspective of secular and materialist psychology, humanistic psychology, or psychology in a Christian perspective, the enterprise always begins from a faith perspective. Regardless of the worldview within which one conducts science, the process of the scientific investigation begins with a set of assumptions, a belief system. Valueless science is impossible. This is not a disadvantage so long as one's assumptions and value system are announced up front. Once this honest acknowledgment takes place, it is possible for such different, though not inherently antipathetic, perspectives as secular, humanistic, or Christian psychological worldviews and such different, though not inherently disparate, disciplines as psychology and theology to mutually illumine each other with their differing worldviews and value systems and with their differing, though often overlapping, databases.

A MODEL OF MUTUAL SCIENTIFIC ILLUMINATION

The Relationship between Christian Theology and Secular Psychology

A mutually illumining interface between scientific disciplines suggests what Ellens calls a perspectival model of their relationship (see a similar discussion of this in Ellens, 1982, 1997a, and 1997b). Seward Hiltner and his colleagues would have approved that terminology. This model implies three principles necessary to scientific and psychospiritual integrity. First, it must be acknowledged that both theology and psychology are sciences in their own right, stand legitimately on their own foundations, and, read carefully, are two equivalent sources of illumining truth. Speaking theologically or religiously, we would say that they are two equivalent sources of God's self-revelation, in creation and Scripture. Conversely, speaking psychologically, we would say that they are two equivalent subjects of scientific study, assessment, and description. They are not inherently alien. When they seem at odds, paradoxical, or disparate in some way, the basis must lie in one of four kinds of dysfunction. Either we have failed, first, to read the Bible or do theology well enough, or we have failed to investigate the science of psychology thoroughly enough. Or, second, we have distorted the science of the theological or natural world by arbitrary dogmatism, not properly constrained by sound investigation of God's word as discovered in the scientific truth that is evident in creation or in the Bible. Or, third, we have drawn erroneous conclusions in either of these investigations and have not allowed each of the scientific disciplines to illumine the other adequately, honestly, or thoroughly. Or, fourth, we have started in either or both disciplines with faith assumptions, value judgments, or belief systems that are erroneous and hence unwarranted and dysfunctional in pursuit of truth.

Schuurman (1977, 1980) and Jaki (1978, 1980) have independently developed the claim that, given the nature of the human mind and personality, it is imperative to recognize that the mutual illumination of all scientific disciplines is essential to a full-orbed and honest achievement in any one of them. Schuurman was a professor of philosophy at Eindhoven Institute of Technology and a lecturer at the Free University of Amsterdam, while Jaki was a Benedictine priest and professor at Seton Hall. Their significant contributions participated in or stimulated a rich spate of interdisciplinary studies over the last two decades, and the flow seems not to be abating, holding great promise for the new millennium.

In his recent article in *Christian Scholar's Review*, Padgett (1996) puts it similarly. Though his model of the mutual illumination of distinct sciences fails to clarify with adequate crispness the scientific nature of theology, his observations are worth noting. He declares:

In order to develop this "mutuality model" of the relationship between science and theology [*sic*],[6] we must look more closely at the nature of explanation. Explanation is an important, even central, idea in the quest for knowledge and understanding. This in turn raises the question of the nature of explanation in science and theology. Such an approach to the theology-science dialogue will afford us the opportunity to explore theological explanation in contrast to other kinds. In this way we can develop a model of mutual learning and edification between theology and science in the development of a coherent worldview. The process of this intellectual exploration will lead us to three conclusions: (1) theological explanation is similar to explanation in the natural and social sciences, in that it develops models for a causal explanation, positing certain entities, with certain natures, powers, and relationships. (2) Theology assumes the findings of other disciplines in its explanatory scheme, and as such the natural and social sciences influence theology. In the same way the findings of theology may send us back to the other disciplines to rethink the basis of our scientific conclusions, and change our mind. (3) A consideration of the nature of levels of explanations, or explanatory schemes (also called "paradigms"), leaves an open place for a two-way dialogue that can and should take place between theology and the other disciplines. . . . Our model, then, is of theology and the sciences having a mutual dialogue, each discipline learning from the other, as we seek a fully adequate philosophy of life that is both true and satisfies our ethical/existential needs. (Padgett, 1996, pp. 15–16, 25)

The second principle necessary to a thoroughgoing scientific and psychospiritual integrity is this. The criterion of soundness in theory formation or practical application of the illumination the sciences of psychology and theology bring to each other is not the effectiveness with which our psychological insights fit in with our theological worldview or our theological insights fit in with our psychological worldview, but rather whether they make discernible claims upon each other in a way that either requires modification of the other or makes the thoroughgoing understanding of the other plainer, more evident, more complete, or more coherent with the data. Perhaps this has to do with the manner in which one discipline exacerbates or resolves problems in the internal coherence of the other. Psychological data, insights, paradigms, or worldviews may be helpful, for example, in illumining a theological or anthropological construct by enlarging the perception of the internal coherence of that construct or of the biblical text or human characteristic from which it arises; or psychology may resolve problems in the internal coherence of that construct; or it may disturb the supposed coherence of the construct or its purported relation to its database. This may enlarge the understanding of what the coherent message of the theological construct is or ought to be. Conversely, theological data, insights, paradigms, or worldviews may do a similar thing to psychological anthropology and understanding of the living human document in its functions, possibilities, and needs. Theology may helpfully illumine the internal coherence or lack thereof in a person or in the psychological construct with which the scientist approaches or understands the person. This may discernibly enhance the healing progress of a living human document, that is, the patient in the clinical process. Or theological illumination may resolve problems or impasses in the process of the therapy, or may disturb the presumed progress only to lay bare deeper needs, coherences, or incoherences. Similar contributions can be made by theology shedding its light on the theoretical processes of psychological research, enhancing the understanding of humans about which both sciences are concerned to take accurate account.

The third principle at stake here is the imperative that responsible function in the perspectival model, providing mutual illumination between psychological and theological sciences, requires a posture on the part of the scientist and practitioner that holds as true the notion that each respective science has legitimate light to bear on the other and that that light is the light of truth, insofar as we can apprehend it, expressed in the perceptions and understanding possessed by the scholar. This means that the scholar perceives herself or himself as a midwife of the truth, not merely a manipulator of data.

An illustration of the way in which psychological insight can illumine a theological perception may be seen in a recent *New York Times Magazine* article by Jack Miles (1995b). In that article about the story of Jesus' birth in Matthew 1–2 and Luke 1–2, Miles points out that the enduring attractiveness, spiritual gratification, and meaning-inducing truth of that story resides less in its theological sublimity and narrative elegance and more profoundly in its ability to connect with and vitalize archetypal percepts rooted deeply in the human psyche.

Wayne Rollins observes that "the particular truth that Miles finds subliminally activated in the crowds who find themselves drawn back to church at Christmas time is 'first and last the story of an infant to whom mysterious greatness is promised but who is found fleeing death from virtually the first moment of His life' . . . so that 'the story of the slaughter of the innocents and the infant Messiah's flight by night is far closer to the emotional center of the Christmas story than the manger' " because it is far closer to our deepest perceptions of the most fundamental fact of our selfhood and our existence (Rollins, 1997, p. 163). Carl Jung observed in this regard that when we speak in primordial images, we connect with the center of the psyche of humankind; we lift the idea we are sharing out of the occasional and transitory into the realm of transcendent and eternal meaning, transmuting personal destiny into universal destiny. We evoke those forces of hope and certainty that "have enabled humanity to find a refuge from every peril and to outlive the longest night" (Jung, 1922/1966, p. 82).

The biblical story is a paradigm of the human psychological odyssey. As such, it asserts an inherent union of experience in our history and God's, at least metaphorically. Jack Miles (1995a) articulately suggests this, as well, in his Pulitzer Prize–winning *God, a Biography*. The import of this has been worked out rather well by John Cobb and the process theologians (Cobb, 1969, 1982; Cobb & Gamwell, 1984; & Cobb & Griffin, 1976). Or, as Ellens has expressed this elsewhere,

The import of this centers in the realization that life for God, as Spirit, however mythically or ontologically we conceive of it, and the life of the human psyche cut across each other at such substantive levels as to affect the description and definition of both. Presumably the only thing we can know about God or the meaning and content of our God-talk is what we can understand through the perceptions and projections of the human person. So any theology about God, us, and the world is heavily dependent upon the cognitive and affective apperceptive processes of human beings. Thus to employ theology for insights regarding any reality requires the employment of a useful and warrantable anthropology and, therefore, a sound psychology. Conversely, to employ a proper psychology in the pursuit of truth also requires a useful and warrantable anthropology and, therefore, I claim, a sound theology.

Psychology and theology are, thus, inevitably interlinked regardless of what the immediate focus or concern of either is. Hence, whether we are exploring the biblical text or the living human document, the mutual illumination of psychology and theology is imperative because a properly enlightened anthropology is required for both. Moreover, the mutual illumination undoubtedly takes place precisely in the anthropology which is formed or forming in, which functions in, and which informs each discipline. Since both disciplines deal with the psycho-spiritual domains, either of these which ignores the other is not adequately serious about itself. (Ellens, 1997a, pp. 201–202)

Psychological Illumination of Theological Research

Rollins (1997) presents a helpful paradigm highlighting ten key ways in which psychology illumines theology and biblical studies. First, psychology aids our understanding of the biblical text and biblical interpretation as part of a psychic process in which both conscious and unconscious factors are at work in fashioning meaning. Viewed in their aspects as human works, religion and religious texts reflect the psychological structure of human personality. Second, psychology urges upon us the awareness that our understanding of the Bible and theology engages our conative, moral, intuitive, spiritual, sensual, and affective functions, as well as our intellectual functions. Third, psychology impresses us with the polyvalence of biblical and theological or religious symbology. Fourth, Jungian psychology particularly demonstrates the archetypal depth of biblical or religious images and stories. Fifth, psychology teaches us to recognize the many levels of meaning a text can evoke in readers and the different modes of actualizing a text one may encounter. Sixth, psychology illumines and clarifies the psychodynamic factors at work in a text. "A psychological-critical approach can assist the biblical scholar in identifying psychological dynamics at work in the context, structure, textual placement, and communal history of the text, whether myth or legend, court history or gospel story, psalm or wisdom saying, apocalyptic vision or epistle" (Rollins, 1997, p. 163). The nature of the author, the implied or intended audience, the intended suasion, and the redactionary layers of the text are also aspects of the text's very nature and message that are fraught with psychodynamic factors crucial to the understanding of the text and its theological or religious meaning and function. Seventh, psychological insight into biblical personality characterizations and types is essential to any responsible biblical hermeneutic. Eighth, psychological description and analysis of biblical religious phenomena are valuable in understanding them and their import for today. For example, psychology deepens our understanding of such constructs as sin, guilt, forgiveness, grace, salvation, redemption, rebirth, conversion, inspiration, glossolalia, visions, demon possession, and ritual practices. Ninth, a proper understanding of the biblical or theological phenomena requires a psychocritical analysis of biblical effects on individuals, communities, and cultures in the past and present. Tenth, the effort to reclaim biblical psychology as a rubric in biblical scholarship is aided by dialogue with current models of the self from the psychological disciplines. Such dialogue is inherent to honest work in theology and biblical studies. These ten factors assume that the models psychology has developed for understanding the living human document are applicable cross-culturally and thus also cross-generationally and over the millennia. Thus today's models can be used to illumine a text that was written two or three millennia ago.

The Biblical Illumination of Psychological Practice

Such notions about how psychology illumines theology are most useful, and the list could and should be extended significantly. Comparably, one could and should construct a similar paradigm describing the multiple ways in which theology and biblical studies can illumine psychology and bring essential understanding to psychology's approach to the "living human document." Elsewhere Ellens has identified eight biblical concepts and twelve practical applications demonstrating this crucial illumination without which psychology cannot be thoroughly accountable in its approach, understanding, and treatment of human life and behavior. These concepts and applications are explored in his recent article in *Pastoral Psychology* (Ellens, 1997a) and his book *God's Grace and Human Health* (Ellens, 1982).

The biblical concepts include the biblical theology of human personhood and the notions of alienation, sin or sickness, discipline, grace, wounded healers, mortality, and celebration. The practical application of these concepts in psychological research or clinical practice might look something like this: First, theology and biblical studies illumine the identity of the patient as a person before the face of God. Second, they affirm the patient's destiny as a self-actualization of the *imago Dei*, the image of God. Third, they assure the patient that he or she is ultimately secure before the face of God because of the radical nature of unconditional grace, and that he or she may also realize an immediate, practical security before God. These three applications imply a fourth, that the patient has inherent dignity as a creature of God despite his or her illness. Fifth, theology and biblical studies assure the therapist that he or she need not take ultimate responsibility for the patient, but must merely incite a finite growth process. Sixth, they emphasize that the patient, as a person before the face of God, will find his or her self-esteem affirmed in the therapeutic process. Seventh, biblical perspectives give the patient permission to give up situation-inappropriate or neurotic anxiety. Eighth, biblical constructs of personhood, grace, and the inherent relationality of healthy humans affirm that the dynamics of transference and countertransference produce energy useful for healing; one need neither repress nor run in fear from these dynamics.

Ninth, the Christian therapist embodies, expresses, and perhaps even announces God's inviolable grace, indicating the transcendental reality that life may be pursued in a context of cherishing goodwill. Whether in health or illness, one need not focus one's life on defeating threat. Tenth, biblical perspectives affirm that growth is the objective and purpose of existence. Eleventh, in theological perspective, both the therapist and the patient are in the process of illness and growth, and neither needs to play God in therapy or in life. Twelfth, mortality is acceptable since the biblical worldview offers the opportunity for relief from the terminal panic and the existential threat of ultimate meaninglessness that stand as a specter behind all pathology. Undoubtedly this taxonomy can be extended greatly and perhaps refined usefully. Increasingly, understanding the enterprise of doing psychology from a Christian perspective, or of doing Christian psychology, means for the Christian community in general that we take seriously these two paradigms for the mutual illumination that theological and psychological science can bring to one another.

A Formal Model for the Scientific Interface of Psychology and Theology

As we draw together the strands woven rather intricately in the development of this chapter, it seems clear that the interface between psychology and theology can be located, as implied earlier, in a specific function of the scientific enterprise, namely, in the theological anthropology and psychological anthropology at play in these sciences. An anthropological concept of the nature of humanness is the common database of psychological and theological science. Moreover, it seems clear that the most crucial factor in each anthropology is the personality theory with which one is working (Maddi, 1996). Moreover, such an anthropology and personality theory will be at play in each of the sciences and their associated arts, at each level of the interface, namely, at the data-collection level, the theory-development level, the research-methodology level, and the operationally applied level. One might speculate, as well, about the way in which this interface is also a significant function intrapersonally for the scientist in each science, and about the significance of that intrapersonal interface for the scientist's work.

CONCLUSION

Christian psychology or, more properly, psychology in a Christian perspective is a construct that holds out a potentially generative challenge for the scholarly world of the twenty-first century, indeed for the millennium that is taking shape ahead of us. This challenge will need to be taken up by concerned and thoughtful theoreticians in the academic and research arenas as well as by insightful and able professionals in the pastoral and clinical communities. The method, shape, and trajectory for such development are now relatively clear and can be illustrated readily at all levels of the work. It is urgent that we elaborate models and enlist them for more effective outcomes in the formation of worldviews and operational practice that more productively form and inform our society and cultures.

The modes and methods for mutual scientific illumination in the interface between psychology and theology are an example of the broader requirement for such mutual illumination among all the sciences in the formation of an honest and wholistic worldview. Anything less than this kind of bifocal and multidimensional vision of a quest for truth is irresponsible and can only lead to our unfortunate and unnecessary loss.

APPLYING THIS CHAPTER TO EVERYDAY LIFE: TWO CURRENTS IN THE STREAM

Although the average Christian in the pew is not intensely aware of the progressive and conservative scholars' debates, his or her life is nevertheless touched by the practical effects that reach congregations through pastor, church, and mass media. As one might expect, there are two popular streams of thought that correspond to the two major scholarly divisions in this dialogue.

There are many conservative evangelical Christians who distrust psychology and believe that Scripture has all the answers to questions of psychospiritual meaning or psychological and spiritual distress. They see psychology and especially the notion of *humanistic psychology* as a sacrilegious venturing of secular forces into transcendental spiritual territory. They become suspicious of any serious inquiry into the psychological side of the living document. When they consider psychological treatment, one of their primary concerns is how to pursue emotional wholeness without losing their faith or alienating God in the healing process.

One distressed fundamentalist Christian woman summed up this dilemma very accurately as she observed her situation as a patient in a psychiatric hospital. "If I do everything they are telling me to do to get better, I will have to turn my back on God!" She obviously did not believe that "all truth is God's truth." She viewed psychological truth as antithetical to biblical truth, and her healing was blocked in a very serious manner. She might even find some Christian therapists who would agree with her and encourage her to avoid psychotherapy in favor of meeting all her needs through the biblical revelation centered in Jesus Christ.

More likely, however, she would find trained Christian therapists with a progressive viewpoint who are convinced that biblical truth and psychology illumine each other in the crucial ways indicated earlier. Such therapists would claim that humans are designed as relational beings, and that one's psychological and spiritual functions must be engaged in a grace-based relationship with another person's psychospiritual character for healing to occur. This human, healing relationship creates a space for God's work toward redeeming and developing the fully orbed human beings that God intended and designed.

She may have trouble trusting this approach, however, because she has been taught to distrust truth that does not come from the Bible. She experiences the tension between the progressive and the conservative perspectives, but she may not be able to articulate the dilemma. Suppose she is suffering from codependence, exhaustively giving of self in order to receive validation and love. When she reads a "secular" book on codependence and it makes sense, she thinks, "That sounds like me!" Experientially, she resonates with the truth of psychology. Then she is reminded of biblical injunctions to "turn the other cheek," "go the extra mile," and "share Christ's suffering" and becomes both confused and frightened. She is straddling the gap between the conservative and progressive perspective. From her vantage point, she sees no possible resolution. Unfortunately, her dilemma is made worse by the pseudoscience of such Christians in the psychological and theological professions as J. H. Boyd,[7] Jay Adams, and John McArthur who, with little theological understanding, employ their professional stature to play loosely with psychological and theological/spiritual terms, concepts, and research methods to promote their own erroneous views about the Bible and salvation.[8]

The secularization of the pneuma into the self in our society has prompted some evangelical Christians operationally to turn against their needy selves and their own humanity in the name of being spiritual. Society's secularization of "humanism" has intensified this split and the subsequent dilemma. Consequently, the sincere Christian who wants to find serious psychological help within the Christian community may find contradictory and confusing ideas about what "Christian counseling" or therapy really is. This state of affairs is an unacceptable irresponsibility on the part of so-called Christian counselors who devalue psychology because of an erroneous nomistic and literalist view of Scripture.

Changes within the Church

The progressive Christian and mainline Christian denominations began moving away from this dilemma in the 1920s. Even the evangelical Christian community's acceptance of the recovery movement in the late 1980s signaled a change in many conservative churches. The true nature of the human condition was more openly addressed than ever before. In sharp contrast to the 1950s and 1960s when many evangelical Christians were wondering if serious Christians could have emotional problems, the Christian recovery movement openly acknowledged the presence of human psychospiritual sickness, dysfunction, and failure, requiring healing and redemption. In addition, the concept of spiritual abuse was openly discussed as the pain and damage wreaked by legalism, rigid literalist views of Scripture, and magical notions of God and Christian doctrine were openly identified and addressed. Many churches began offering support groups for alcoholics, drug addicts, and persons suffering from codependence, sex addictions, spiritual abuse, and the like. The major publishing houses began printing many practical resources that presented an interface and synthesis between the biblical truth and psychology. In the last two decades there has been a growing acceptance that psychology has a legitimate place in the evangelical Christian's life. Moreover, in the secular field the spiritual or transcendental dimension of human experience is beginning to receive more attention.

Practical Issues for Healing

Ultimately, each person is responsible for his or her own healing and must choose the direction for this healing. How does one go about accomplishing this, making sense of all the theological and psychological talk? What about the Christians who learned while growing up that they had better watch how they act or think lest they bring down God's wrath upon themselves and their families? How can Christians clean up their lives without fearing God's watchful eye? How can individuals face their true humanity without feeling rejected by God in the process? In our quest to be like Christ, can we develop our true humanness without fearing divine judgment?

The answer to each of these dilemmas lies in developing trust and celebrating our authentic humanness as the ultimate expression of God's work in the universe. In pursuing such a personal transformation, two wide-ranging principles can provide guidance.

Rewriting One's Personal Theology

Many conservative, hurting Christians, such as the psychiatric patient mentioned earlier, have misinformation or skewed perceptions on both the theological and psychological issues. Therefore, in the course of personal healing, the damaged Christian must work on two levels: the psychological and spiritual. Because incorrect spiritual beliefs can interfere with emotional healing, the first principle is rewriting one's personal theology. This takes time and must be done with a knowledgeable therapist or pastoral counselor. Although there is insufficient space to describe the process thoroughly here, the following common example may be useful.

Suppose a person from a dysfunctional family presents himself or herself for therapy. Part of the healing involves identifying and resolving the pain the parents caused. The evangelical Christian may protest, "I cannot express anger toward my parents! It is a sin against the commandment that requires that I honor them!" In this case, before emotional healing can occur by means of the truth of psychology, the individual's personal theology must be rewritten to allow the legitimate expression of pain about the parents, in keeping, by the way, with the strong biblical injunction about truthfulness. The patient needs to become able to discover that this kind of honesty about the truth of the parents, together with the ultimate achievement of the capacity to forgive them, is the real "honoring of parents" of which the Bible speaks. Denial of their true human realities is not an honoring of them. As stated earlier, when there seems to be a discrepancy between the biblical revelation and psychological truth, we may suspect misinterpretation on one side or the other, and corrections must be made. Rewriting one's theology involves correcting the spiritual beliefs that interfere with healing and replacing them with more accurate, health-oriented, theological insights and biblical truth.[9]

Grace: The Radical Option

A thorough biblical perception of grace needs to be firmly in place as the foundation for personal psychospiritual growth and wholeness. This principle is radical because it is not characteristic of the human mind to conceive of grace as a viable, realistic option (Ellens, 1989, p. 4). In fact, of all the religions in the history of humankind only Judaism (along with Christianity by inheritance) has developed this perception of God and spirituality epitomized in the biblical message regarding the healing power of grace.

Grace is the overall theme of Scripture and has its ultimate expression in the person and life of Jesus Christ. Understanding and applying this radical concept is the foundation for understanding all of what God intends to accomplish in the living human document. The biblical notion of grace is the linchpin holding in union the truth of psychology with the truth of Scripture. By understanding and living in grace, one can benefit from all of God's truth without fearing one's humanness (Sloat, 1990). Allison summarizes the essence of grace this way:

Whatever responsibility we face, whatever there is within us that is tragically not what it should be, whatever evil we think of ourselves, our mutual hope, our common faith and our Christian commitment is that there is no rejection. Rebuke, repentance, responsibility, and restitution, yes; but rejection, no! No matter how evil we may feel that we are, God reckons us good in Jesus Christ. This is what is good about the Good News. (Allison, 1972, p. 50)

As the truth of this Good News begins to soak in, we are able to see the freedom grace brings Christians. Being reckoned as good, Christians do not have to stifle their humanity—their thinking, willing, feeling, and doing—in order to please God or earn his approval. There is no longer any "master list" of sins, no inventory of all the do's and don'ts of any particular Christian group. We need not live in fearful avoidance of such a master list in order to prove that we are fine and deserving Christians (Sloat, 1986, pp. 104–110). Since God already knows us to be human and dysfunctional, God is not surprised or unsettled by our sin, sickness, or dysfunction. Through Christ, God has counted us good and whole.[10]

As Allison aptly points out, Christians continue to be accountable for their actions (1972, pp. 34–51). Living under grace does not absolve them of all responsibility, but God certifies through Christ that they will not be rejected as they work out the damaged, darker sides of their lives. "Rebuke, repentance, responsibility, and restitution, yes; but rejection, no!" (Allison, 1972, p. 50).

The good news is that grace provides the security affording a safe matrix for our lives as we move toward maturity, making our mistakes and committing our sins as we go. The good news is that we are free to let ourselves experience all of ourselves as we live. Healthy Christian motivation derives from the open-ended freedom to grow in grace and not from the fear of the threat requiring us to "measure up." The more we are motivated by fear, the sicker we get. The more we are motivated by freedom to grow, the healthier we get. Christianity is not a law to be labored under, nor a responsibility to be reckoned up. It is an invitation to love and be loved, an invitation to be seized, and an opportunity to be celebrated.

God has counted us as acceptable, as we are, in spite of ourselves, so we do not have to split the "bad" parts of ourselves away in an erroneous attempt to live before the face of God looking clean and scrubbed up. We can apprehend God and count upon God to apprehend and accept us just as we are because the message of grace declares that we are reckoned as perfect (Micah 7:18–20). "God's Grace: The Radical Option" succinctly summarizes God's radical grace in the following passage: "God can't remember that you're a sinner. God honestly thinks that you are a saint, so you are free for self-actualization, free for growth, free to be and to become with alacrity and with abandon" (Ellens, 1989, p. 7).

NOTES

1. [Editor's note]. A theological anthropology is a theory of human nature within a larger philosophy of God, man, and world.

2. [Editor's note]. A psychological anthropology is a philosophy and understanding of human nature within the context of a specific theory of psychology.

3. Many Christian scholars prefer to use the spellings "wholism" and "wholistic" rather than wholism and wholistic, in order to indicate that their sense of the "whole" is broader, including spiritual dimensions and theological perspectives, as well as the solely psychological perspectives of previous "wholistic" theories. See Westberg (1979) for a clarification of this usage.

4. [Editor's note]. There were at least three such scientific communities, if one also considers the community of Catholic psychologists, theologians, and philosophers, similarly but separately pursuing the study of the linkages between psychology, spiritual growth, and the humanistic traditions within Christianity. One center for such research, at Duquesne University, was initially called the Institute of Man and later renamed the Center for the Study of Formative Spirituality. Its journal featured especially such works of Adrian van Kaam as his five-volume series *Formative Spirituality* entitled, respectively, *Fundamental Formation* (1983), *Human Formation* (1985), *Formation of the Human Heart* (1986), *Scientific Formation* (1987), and *Traditional Formation* (1992). The journal, published in New York by Crossroads, was known originally as *Humanitas* and is now known as *Studies in Formative Spirituality*. It has published a rich variety of existential and humanistic investigations of spiritual life and growth.

5. [Editor's note]. Boisen's ideas parallel those of R. D. Laing, the British phenomenological psychiatrist, who argued that madness is a kind of existential *metanoia* by means of which the individual sheds his or her earlier, more constricting modes of being and is

reborn to a more open and authentic way of life. See the discussion of Laing's existential psychoanalysis in chapter 22 in part II of this book.

6. The present authors challenge the dichotomy which Padgett implies between science and theology, because they propose that theology can be conducted in a methodologically sophisticated scientific manner. Ellens and Sloat propose that the primary tension or dichotomy is between a science of psychology and a science of theology.

7. J. H. Boyd, for example, is chairman of psychiatry and chairman of ethics at Waterbury Hospital, a teaching hospital affiliated with Yale Medical School, and was formerly an ordained Anglican clergyman. Among his publications on these matters are *Affirming the Soul: Remarkable Conversations between Mental Health Professionals and an Ordained Minister* (1994a), *Soul Psychology: How to Understand Your Soul in Light of the Mental Health Movement* (1994b), *Reclaiming the Soul: The Search for Meaning in a Self-centered Culture* (1995a), "The Soul as Seen through Evangelical Eyes, Part I. Mental Health Professionals and the Soul" (1995b), and "Part II. On the Use of the Term Soul" (1995c), and "An Insider's Effort to Blow Up Psychiatry" (1996).

8. Similarly destructive impact upon evangelical Christians comes from such iconoclastic sources as W. K. Kilpatrick, an academic educational psychologist from Boston College, who has written such books as *Psychological Seduction: The Failure of Modern Psychology* (1983), and Professor Paul Vitz, who wrote *Psychology as Religion: The Cult of Self Worship* (1977).

9. Paul Tournier's 1968 book *A Place for You* provides a helpful guide for resolving the tensions between psychology and Scripture in one's own life.

10. This stands in radical contrast to the unchristian and unbiblical theology of J. H. Boyd, who erroneously claims: "Most important . . . we will face a Judge. My experience is that when lay people hear about the soul, their first thought is . . . that they will face a Judge. . . . This is the cornerstone, or capstone upon which . . . an evangelical self-concept is built. It is a time-honored wisdom in the evangelical world that emphasis upon our judgment by Christ, with an implied risk of hell, is central to keeping us aware that we are accountable" (1996, p. 230).

REFERENCES

Aden, L., et al. (1968). *The dialogue between theology and psychology* (P. Homans, ed.). Chicago: University of Chicago Press.

Aden, L., Benner, D. G., & Ellens, J. H. (Eds). (1992). *Christian perspectives on human development*. Grand Rapids, MI: Baker.

Aden, L., & Ellens, J. H. (Eds). (1990). *Turning points in pastoral care: The legacy of Anton Boisen and Seward Hiltner*. Grand Rapids, MI: Baker.

Allison, C. F. (1972). *Guilt, anger, and God: The patterns of our discontents*. New York: Seabury Press.

Augustine. (1956). Confessions. In P. Schaff (Ed.), *Nicene and post-nicene fathers* (Series 1, Vol. 1, pp. 45–175). Grand Rapids, MI: Eerdmans.

Benner, D. G. (Ed.). (1985). *Baker encyclopedia of psychology*. Grand Rapids, MI: Baker.

Benner, D. G. (Ed.). (1987). *Psychotherapy in Christian perspective*. Grand Rapids, MI: Baker.

Benner, D. G. (Ed.). (1988). *Psychology and religion*. Grand Rapids, MI: Baker.

Boyd, J. H. (1994a). *Affirming the soul: Remarkable conversations between mental health professionals and an ordained minister*. Cheshire, CT: Soul Research Institute.

Boyd, J. H. (1994b). *Soul psychology: How to understand your soul in light of the mental health movement*. Cheshire, CT: Soul Research Institute.

Boyd, J. H. (1995a). *Reclaiming the soul: The search for meaning in a self-centered culture*. Cleveland: Pilgrim Press.

Boyd, J. H. (1995b). The soul as seen through evangelical eyes. Part I. Mental health professionals and the soul. *Journal of Psychology and Theology, 23*(3), 151–160.

Boyd, J. H. (1995c). The soul as seen through evangelical eyes. Part II. On the use of the term soul. *Journal of Psychology and Theology, 23*(3), 161–170.

Boyd, J. H. (1996, Fall). An insider's effort to blow up psychiatry. *Trinity Journal, 17*, 223–239.

Browning, D. S. (1987). *Religious thought and the modern psychologies: A critical conversation in the theology of culture*. Philadelphia: Fortress.

Browning, D. S., Jobe, T., & Evison, I. A. (Eds). (1990). *Religious and ethical factors in psychiatric practice*. Chicago: Nelson-Hall.

Carter, J. D. (1990). Integration of psychology and theology. In R. J. Hunter (Ed.), *Dictionary of pastoral care and counseling* (pp. 584–585). Nashville: Abingdon.

Carter, J. D., & Narramore, B. (1979). *The integration of psychology and theology*. Grand Rapids, MI: Zondervan.

Cobb, J. B., Jr. (1969). *God and the world*. Philadelphia: Westminster.

Cobb, J. B., Jr. (1982). *Process theology as political theology*. Philadelphia: Westminster.

Cobb, J. B., Jr., & Gamwell, F. I. (Eds). (1984). *Existence and actuality: Conversations with Charles Hartshorne*. Chicago: University of Chicago Press.

Cobb, J. B., Jr., & Griffin, D. R. (1976). *Process theology: An introductory exposition*. Philadelphia: Westminster.

Ellens, J. H. (1982). *God's grace and human health*. Nashville: Abingdon.

Ellens, J. H. (1989). God's grace: The radical option. *Perspectives, 4*(9), 4–8.

Ellens, J. H. (1997a). The Bible and psychology: An interdisciplinary pilgrimage. *Pastoral Psychology, 45*(3), 159–162.

Ellens, J. H. (1997b). The interface of psychology and theology. *Journal of Psychology and Christianity, 16*(1), 5–17.

Gerkin, C. V. (1984). *The living human document*. Nashville: Abingdon.

Griffin, D. R., & Altizer, T.J.J. (Eds.). (1977). *John Cobb's theology in process*. Philadelphia: Westminster.

Hornblower, S., & Spawforth, A. (Eds.). (1996). *The Oxford classical dictionary*, 3rd ed. New York: Oxford University Press.

Hunter, R. J. (Ed.). (1990). *Dictionary of pastoral care and counseling*. Nashville: Abingdon.

Jaki, S. L. (1978). *The road of science and the ways to God*. Chicago: University of Chicago Press.

Jaki, S. L. (1980). (1984). *Cosmos and creator*. Chicago: Regnery gateway.

Jung, C. G. (1953–1978). *The collected works of C. G. Jung*. New York: Pantheon Books; Princeton: Princeton University Press.

Jung, C. G. (1966). On the relation of analytical psychology to poetry. *Collected works of C. G. Jung* (Vol. 15, pp. 65–83). New York: Pantheon Books. (Original work published 1922)

Kilpatrick, W. K. (1983). *Psychological seduction*: New York: T. Nelson Publishers.

Maddi, S. R. (1996). *Personality theories, a comparative analysis* (6th ed.). Pacific Grove, CA: Brooks/Cole.

Malony, H. N. (Ed.). (1977). *Current perspectives in the psychology of religion*. Grand Rapids, MI: Eerdmans.

Malony, H. N., Papen-Daniels, M., & Clinebell, H. (Eds.). (1988). *Spirit-centered wholeness: Beyond the psychology of self*. Lewiston, NY: Mellen.

McDonagh, J. M. (1982). *Christian psychology: Toward a new synthesis*. New York: Crossroad.

Miles, J. (1995a). *God, a biography*. New York: Knopf.

Miles, J. (1995b, December 24). Jesus before he could talk. *New York Times Magazine*, pp. 28–33.

Myers, D. G. (1978). *The human puzzle*. San Francisco: Harper & Row.

Myers, D. G. (1980). *The inflated self*. New York: Seabury Press.

Oden, T. C. (1984). *Care of souls in the classic tradition*. Theology and Pastoral Care Series (Vol. 4) (D. S. Browning, Series Editor). Philadelphia: Fortress.

Padgett, A. G. (1996, Fall). The mutuality of theology and science: An example from time and thermodynamics. *Christian Scholar's Review, 26*(1), 12–35.

Roback, A. A. (1961). *History of psychology and psychiatry*. New York: Philosophical Library.

Roberts, A., & Donaldson, J. (Eds.). (1965–1968). *The ante-Nicene fathers* (Vols. 1–10). Grand Rapids, MI: Eerdmans.

Rollins, W. G. (1997). The Bible and psychology: New directions in biblical scholarship. *Pastoral Psychology, 45*(3), 163–179.

Schaff, P. (Ed.). (1956–1964). *Nicene and post-Nicene fathers* (Series 1, Vols. 1–14; Series 2, Vols. 1–14). Grand Rapids, MI: Eerdmans.

Schuurman, E. (1977). *Reflections on the technological society*. Toronto: Wedge Publishing Foundation.

Schuurman, E. (1980). *Technology and the future: A philosophical challenge*. Toronto: Wedge Publishing Foundation.

Sloat, D. E. (1986). *The dangers of growing up in a Christian home*. Nashville: Thomas Nelson.

Sloat, D. E. (1990). *Growing up holy and wholly: Understanding and hope for adult children of evangelicals*. Brentwood, TN: Wolgemuth & Hyatt.

Tournier, P. (1968). *A place for you*. New York: Harper & Row.

Tracy, D., & Cobb, J. B., Jr. (1983). *Talking about God: Doing theology in the context of modern pluralism*. New York: Seabury.

Vitz, P. (1977). *Psychology as religion: The cult of self-worship*. Grand Rapids, MI: Eerdmans.

Westberg, G. E. (1979). *Theological roots of wholistic health care*. Hinsdale, IL: Wholistic Health Centers, Inc.

Wolterstorff, N. (1976). *Reason within the bounds of religion*. Grand Rapids, MI: Eerdmans.

Transpersonal Psychology: The Fourth Force

ARTHUR HASTINGS

THE DEVELOPMENT OF TRANSPERSONAL PSYCHOLOGY

Abraham Maslow and the Fourth Force

Just as Abraham Maslow was a key figure in the establishment of humanistic psychology, he played a central role in the emergence of what he called the Fourth Force, transpersonal psychology. As Maslow continued his research on self-actualizing persons, it led him to reports of transcendent experiences and transcendent values that did not easily fit into either the humanistic or the mainstream psychology paradigms. His initial assumption, probably based on his training in classical psychology, was that peak experiences and metavalues were a part of the biologically based personality. But Maslow recognized that in peak experiences the universe was perceived in a manner reaching beyond biological needs, and individuals went beyond their personal interests to be altruistic, to engage in service to others, and to transcend the individual personality. The self was not the ultimate touchstone.

In his 1968 book *Toward a Psychology of Being* Maslow wrote of a "Fourth Psychology, transpersonal, transhuman, centered in the cosmos rather than in human needs and interest, going beyond humanness, identity, self-actualization, and the like" (p. iv). Maslow viewed this new psychology as a naturalistic, empirical one, but nevertheless believed that it could provide a life philosophy and value system bigger than ourselves to which people could commit themselves. In particular, his studies of peak experiences and metavalues implied a transpersonal level of being. In peak experiences there is a direct experience of the Being nature of the universe. The universe may be seen as a whole, capturing the individual's entire attention, independent of practical functions or needs. There may be a sense of oneness, of beauty and goodness per se (Maslow, 1968). Maslow noted that these seem to be factual qualities of the universe, characteristics that were previously hidden or overlooked. Maslow recognized the difficulty of validating these qualities as facts. Subjective certainty is not enough, he noted. There must be some pragmatic test of the truth of the claims. Nevertheless, he accepted the reality of the peak experience and the reality of the changes that peak experiences produce in those involved.

These experiences, he postulated, are the basis of religions and values. The person who experiences a peak state communicates it to others, often as a vision of a finer and higher reality. Others take the vision as a revelation and organize it into a religion. Maslow spelled out this scenario in his 1964 book *Religions, Values, and Peak-Experiences*.

Another consequence of Maslow's studies of self-actualizers was his postulation of metavalues, or Being values. These are deep values held by self-actualizers and are perceived as intrinsically real. In his interviews of self-actualizing persons, Maslow (1968, 1971) identified fourteen metavalues: wholeness, perfection, completion, justice, aliveness, richness, simplicity, beauty, goodness, uniqueness, effortlessness, playfulness, truth, and self-sufficiency. The similarity of these to Platonic forms is evident; in fact, Maslow wrote to a friend that he lived in the world of Platonic essences (1968, p. xxi). The metavalues are highly abstract, but can function as motivations. They are values that go beyond the ego, and Maslow made a case that they are as necessary to mental health as vitamins are to physical health.

Maslow's investigations led him to areas of perception and experience not included in the usual conceptions of the personality in psychology. In humanistic psychology the self was viewed as holistic, with an emphasis on emotional wholeness, creativity, interpersonal expression, and richness of growth and potential. In mainstream psychology the focus was on personality traits and dynamics. Maslow, however, speculated about a transpersonal level of the universe larger than personal identity, yet providing meaning and significance to the individual and contributing to optimal health and well-being. He avoided attributing religious meanings to this level of experience, yet recognized that it involves a transcendence from a doing level of self to the level of being.

Sutich and the Palo Alto Group

Maslow was in correspondence with Tony Sutich, editor of the *Journal of Humanistic Psychology*. Sutich and a small group had been meeting in the Palo Alto, California, area to discuss developing themes in humanistic psychology. Members of this group began to recognize areas of experience that seemed to go beyond the interests of humanistic psychology, perhaps forming a next stage. These areas were articulated as ultimate values, altered states of consciousness, and experiences that somehow transcend the ego and everyday personality.

In discussions with Maslow it became evident that these common interests could be formulated as a new psychology. A conversation between Maslow and Stanislav Grof suggested the word *transpersonal*, which seemed the right term to use, meaning that which is beyond or transcends the personality. The word *transpersonal* had been used before. C. G. Jung referred to *Überpersonlicht* (beyond or higher than the personal) in 1929, and the philosopher, artist, and astrologer Dane Rudhyar used the word *transpersonal* the same year. The psychologist Ira Progoff began using the word about 1964. However, there was as yet no systematic concept of psychology built around these uses of the label. The new founding group adopted transpersonal as a conceptual umbrella for their new field of interest.

At first they simply referred to the transpersonal orientation, and everyone in the group was expected to have personal interest in transpersonal or spiritual exploration. Then the term *psychology* was added to identify the area as a field. The Tibetan lama Chogyam Trungpa visited Sutich and commented that these levels of the mind were studied in Tibetan Buddhism, and the field of psychology was the one that had the best Western language for them.

Growth of the Field

The *Journal of Transpersonal Psychology* was established in 1969, with Sutich as editor. Other staff members were Michael Murphy, James Fadiman, Harriet Francisco, Miles Vich, and Sonja Margulies. In 1975 Miles Vich became editor and has continued to the present. In 1972 the growing group established the American Association for Transpersonal Psychology, which soon became simply the Association for Transpersonal Psychology. The journal and the association, with its annual conferences held on the West Coast, have been the core institutions for the transpersonal field.

In 1979 the International Transpersonal Association (ITA) was established by Stanislav Grof and other professionals to further the growing international interest. The ITA sponsors transpersonal conferences around the world, usually biennially.

While there are many specifically transpersonal groups, there is still a lively interest in transpersonal matters among humanistic psychologists. Many of them believe that the transpersonal is a part of humanistic experience, rather than a separate domain. The *Journal of Humanistic Psychology* frequently publishes articles on transpersonal topics, and the humanistic division of the American Psychological Association includes a transpersonal interest group.

In 1976 the journal *ReVision* was founded, edited initially by Ken Wilber. This publication has a stronger emphasis on philosophical and theoretical writing, while the humanistic and transpersonal journals tend to cover research, experiential reports, and clinical and other applications of the field.

ORIGINS OF TRANSPERSONAL IDEAS

The transpersonal orientation came from many streams of thought and experience—philosophy, religion, and psychology—that provided conscious and unconscious roots for the flowering of the movement in the second half of the twentieth century.

Transcendentalism

The American transcendental movement began in the 1830s in New England. Its most prominent figures were Ralph Waldo Emerson, Henry David Thoreau, and Walt Whitman. Emerson lectured and wrote on the tenets of the movement: the underlying transcendent oneness of all, the Oversoul, which was within every individual; the importance of self-reliance rather than following tradition or outside authority; a reverence for nature; and the value of intuition over empiricism. Emerson rejected orthodox religion and urged ministers to acquaint people firsthand with the Divine. He spoke of transcendent forms such as Justice, Beauty, Love, Goodness, and Power. He believed these to be in the depths of spiritual nature, just as Maslow found similar Being values in the motives of the self-actualized. Emerson was interested in Oriental religion and wrote on Buddhism. Themes that later appeared in transpersonal psychology can be found in Emerson's *Nature, The Oversoul, Self Reliance*, and other essays.

Thoreau, attempting to live the transcendentalist beliefs practically, immersed himself in nature and in being self-reliant. Thoreau's valuing of Nature as a reflection of the Divine presages the contemporary concern with deep ecology. Thoreau's book *Walden* has been a major influence in American thought, and the empirical, behavioral psychologist B. F. Skinner ironically gave his fictional utopian community the name Walden Two.

The poet Walt Whitman provided a third facet of the new thought of the transcendental movement, an acceptance of the body. In *Leaves of Grass*, he wrote:

> I am the poet of the Body;
> I am the poet of the Soul.

Body and spirit were to be experienced with equal delight. Sexual energy—the body electric—was relished and reverenced as joyful.

I do not know the extent of interest in the transcendental movement among the founders of transpersonal psychology. Maslow studied Emerson as a historical self-actualizing person, so he was clearly familiar with Emerson's life and thought. Thoreau's transpersonal qualities have been discussed in the transpersonal literature. The transcendentalists traced their worldview to the European idealist school of philosophy, holding that ideas and intuitions have reality of their own and are not just derivative from empiricism; the same point of view can be found in transpersonal psychology. In any case, the transcendental movement contributed its intellectual beliefs and their practical expressions to American—and Western—culture, and transpersonal psychology presents for our time many of the same perspectives. William James's conception of the unconscious included many of the qualities of transcendental intuition. In the 1960s and 1970s many American youth reflected in their lives the ideas of the transcendentalists, who more than one hundred years earlier rejected civil authority, lived in communes, founded their own schools, urged a life of simplicity, cultivated intuition, pursued spiritual understanding, and celebrated their bodies.

William James

While William James was not a direct founder of transpersonal psychology, his psychological and philosophical ideas are predecessors of transpersonal theory. His *Varieties of Religious Experience* (James, 1902/1936) was essentially the first study of religious experience as a psychological process, not as a theological one. He did not explain away religion as pathology, but as a contact with a transmarginal region of experience. The term *transmarginal* comes from F. W. H. Myers and means the dimension of the self beyond the conscious ego and through which the spiritual manifests itself. James concluded that our consciousness is a small and limited part of a wider consciousness, and that around our conventional awareness, separated by a thin boundary, lie other types of consciousness giving access to further realities and knowledge. This was not simply an abstract conclusion; he based it on his investigations of religious experience, his personal experience with the psychedelic gas nitrous oxide, and his research on psychical phenomena. A pragmatist, James insisted that findings be based on evidence, and that what is directly experienced should not be rejected or ignored, even if it does not fit the prevailing fashion of scientific theory. Many of James's interests resurface as themes in transpersonal psychology: peak and spiritual experiences, the effects of psychedelic substances on consciousness, and the processes of psychic communication and subtle energies.

For James, consciousness was the most important element of psychology. "My experience is what I agree to attend to," he wrote, in a phrase reminiscent of Patanjali's yoga sutras, in which attention leads to absorption in the object of meditation, be it a deity or the bliss of oneness. James's analysis of the "stream of consciousness" will be recognized by those who observe their inner experience, and his suggestions of how it can be directed by attention and will are still valuable tools of personal growth.

However, James did not believe that consciousness was a substance or a thing, in contrast to some current transpersonalists and yogic philosophy. He said that it was a quality of experience. Nor did he firmly support the validity of psychic phenomena; he remained somewhat favorable, but undecided. Nevertheless, he was critical of so-called scientists who maintained their views rigidly and rejected any experience or evidence that pointed to other possibilities. Today there are still skeptics and true unbelievers who consider transpersonal ideas to be superstition, emotional fanaticism, and unscientific. Some of the critiques are constructive, while others embody the same blindness that James criticized.

Besides *The Varieties of Religious Experience* James wrote a still-impressive two-volume *Principles of Psychology* and professional papers on many related topics, including parapsychology and philosophy. After his death his approach to psychology declined in influence as behaviorism emerged. When the transpersonal movement developed, it renewed interest in the spirit of William James. A 1990 "Principles of Psychology Congress" in Amsterdam celebrated the hundredth anniversary of the publication of James's best-known work and included many presentations on topics in transpersonal psychology and the psychology of consciousness. Fadiman and Frager (1994) credit him as the founding figure in the psychology of consciousness.

Humanistic Psychology

The transpersonal movement built on the foundations of humanistic psychology in several ways. Transpersonal psychology is also a psychology with a vector, with an emphasis on mental health and optimal well-being. The human being is assumed to be basically good and oriented toward growth, including not just the self, but also the transcendent levels beyond the personal state. In asserting that there are peak and transcendent experiences, there is also the implicit position that these are worth seeking, just as humanistic psychology holds that human potential is worth exploring and achieving.

Like humanistic psychology, the transpersonal approach includes the grounding of ideas in experience. Personal integration of the material through experiential work is essential. As in humanistic psychology, there are seminars, training programs, groups, workshops, and other activities for personal learning, experience, and practice of transpersonal orientations. Those interested in transpersonal psychology often have personal interests in spiritual traditions and religious practices. Robert Frager has delineated how transpersonal psychology draws from and integrates these domains of experiential humanistic psychology, the psychology of consciousness, and the study of spiritual traditions and practices (Frager, 1989). His article is also an excellent introduction to the field. A fine introductory collection of transpersonal articles and essays is found in *Paths beyond Ego* by Roger Walsh and Frances Vaughan (1993a), which builds on their earlier (and also worthwhile) compilation *Beyond Ego* (Walsh & Vaughan, 1980). The most comprehensive and many-faceted reference is *Textbook of Transpersonal Psychiatry and Psychology*, edited by Scotton, Chinen, and Battista (1996).

DEFINITIONS OF TRANSPERSONAL PSYCHOLOGY

The most permissive definition of the field is given by Roger Walsh and Frances Vaughan: transpersonal psychology is the study of transpersonal experiences and phenomena—their nature and implications (Walsh & Vaughan, 1993a,

1993b). This leaves only the task of defining transpersonal experiences. These experiences are usually defined as going beyond the ordinary sense of identity or personality to encompass wider dimensions of the psyche and the cosmos. This can include experiences of intense love, enhanced perception, a sense of merging into a more comprehensive identity, spiritual and religious experiences, psychic awareness, and the wide range of events that Maslow categorized as peak experiences (Vich, 1992).

Other definitions suggest that transpersonal means optimal health and well-being, holistic development of the self, and the psychology of transformation. In a survey of forty definitions of transpersonal, Lajoie and Shapiro (1992) synthesized this definition: Transpersonal psychology is concerned with the study of humanity's highest potential and with the recognition, understanding, and realization of unitive, spiritual, and transcendent experiences.

TRANSPERSONAL EXPERIENCES

Beginning with Maslow, transpersonal psychologists have recognized that certain experiences of mystics, meditators, and religious devotees have transpersonal qualities—that is, they bring the self into a state that transcends individual ego boundaries. William James had observed that this was true of religious conversion, that it brought (at least in some cases) the person into contact with a greater reality, one that was inspiring and that made his or her existence more meaningful.

In the past, such experiences were generally the province of religions. In psychology these phenomena were treated as exaggerated developments of normal processes, such as fantasy, or as by-products of pathological processes, such as migraine phenomena, organic brain disorders, or psychosis. Maslow regarded transpersonal experiences as natural and healthy, rather than pathological. James had said the same of conversion and mystical experiences, that they were not pathological per se, though an individual could have mental disturbances with or without a religious experience.

Peak experiences (also called transpersonal, mystical, or spiritual) cover a broad range of phenomena, from simple feelings of peace and absorption in nature to inner states that transcend time, space, identity, and physical reality. There is no one typical experience, and there may be images, ESP, voices, forms, nonforms, visions, and physical effects as part of the encounter. These are reported by many people, not just mystics or contemplatives, self-actualizers, or even humanists and transpersonal psychologists. They appear to be natural parts of human experience. There are no solid data on their frequency and distribution, but their phenomenology and effects in spiritual traditions and the general public have been discussed, studied, and, to some extent, empirically researched.

There are several suggested models to encompass these experiences. Maslow initially felt that they were instinctual, built into the biological system in some way. This viewpoint has found little acceptance in the transpersonal field, though in a negative sense reductionist critics of mystical states have claimed that transpersonal experiences are simply neuropathology (Group for the Advancement of Psychiatry, 1976). This reductionist viewpoint was answered by Deikman (1977), who states that this viewpoint does not address the levels of transcendent and intuitive experience, which are quite different from pathological sensory modalities. Ken Wilber has offered a developmental model in which transpersonal experiences emerge from levels of inner developmental structure ranging from a pantheistic identification with nature, based on telepathic or psychic awareness, to absolute unity at the developmental level of identification with an absolute oneness underlying all reality (Wilber, 1980; Wilber, Engler, & Brown, 1986). As discrete states of consciousness, peak experiences can be described as varying along dimensions of time, identity, perception, and other systems of the self (Tart, 1975a). Most religions provide models that are consistent with their particular belief system, usually of a divine or spiritual reality, a deity, or of a metaphysical system, mingled with cultural and social attitudes of the time. However, each religious tradition appears to have an implicit psychology of these transpersonal states and experiences. For example, St. Teresa described her inner experiences in the Christian tradition in great detail, with several elements that will be familiar to transpersonal psychologists. Charles Tart has edited a volume of essays on the implicit psychology in various spiritual teachings (Tart, 1975b).

The assumption in transpersonal psychology is that these experiences are not just normal, but also desirable. Their worth may be expressed as a part of the holistic growth of the individual, as a developmental level beyond the personal, or as an inspiring contact with a higher reality that transcends the personality and the ego identity, which then guides the self. Psychiatrist Stanislav Grof reports that psychotherapy using the psychoactive substance LSD progresses toward an increasing experience of these transpersonal states by the client, and such experiences become more frequent as personal psychodynamic issues and traumatic events are resolved. This is also true for intensive nonpsychedelic therapy (Grof, 1980) and potentially for any therapeutic work that moves through the levels of the self.

However, transcendent experiences may precipitate a crisis for unprepared individuals, resulting in a spiritual emergency, perhaps requiring therapeutic assistance (Grof & Grof, 1989). In contrast to some religions in which immersion in profound, ecstatic experiences is the goal, many transpersonal psychology professionals hold that the qualities of the experiences should be brought into everyday life, transforming the self in the world. This parallels the Zen Buddhism principle that there are two paths to enlightenment, one involving intense spiritual experiences and the other a gradual growth of spiritual qualities.

The metaphysics of these experiences has not yet been dogmatized in transpersonal psychology. There is a general tolerance of multiple metaphysical facets that may conflict when they are taken out of context. For example, Buddhist psychology holds that there is no self, whereas the Christian psychology holds the opposite. Yoga generally emphasizes a concentrative meditation, while Zen advocates an openness practice. Transpersonal psychologists may draw from any of these systems without discounting the others. There is a sense that different individuals require different paths to transpersonal growth, and that no one system will suit all persons.

MEDITATION PRACTICES

Transpersonal psychology is not limited to theory and research, but is a practice discipline. Transpersonal psychologists are expected to be interested and motivated in personal work with transpersonal experiences, values, and actions. This does not mean that one has to be saintly; I do not notice saintliness in my colleagues or myself. But sincerity is expected.

Transpersonal psychology is not value free, as behaviorism claims to be. Like depth psychology and humanistic psychology, transpersonal psychology holds that some values and traits are positive and healthy and should be sought by individuals and society. The developmental levels postulated by transpersonal psychology can and should be facilitated, though not forced.

For this reason, there has been considerable exploration of practices that lead in transpersonal directions. The most prevalent practice is that of meditation, which has received considerable attention and research in transpersonal and mainstream psychology (Shapiro & Walsh, 1984). At a simple personality level, there is ample evidence that it relaxes, reduces stress, facilitates creative processes, and often improves personal and work relationships. However, most studies have been conducted on short-term meditation practice and rarely touch on the possible transpersonal effects of the practice, which may develop with extended practice or retreats ranging from three weeks to three years.

There are a few studies of deeper meditation practice. Early EEG studies of experienced yogi practitioners and Zen monks showed that meditation shifted brain waves to alpha levels (Anand, Chhina, & Singh, 1961; Kasamatsu & Harai, 1966). Dan Brown and Jack Engler (Brown & Engler, 1986) gave Rorschach inkblot tests to beginning, intermediate, advanced, and enlightened master meditators in South Asia. They found striking changes in the responses at different experience levels, suggesting that meditation practice changes the perceptions and associations of the meditators as they progress. For example, longer-term meditators tend to see the inkblots as energy patterns rather than representational figures. In terms of emotional impulses, long-term meditators still retain such elements as sexual and aggressive feelings, but do not attribute much significance to them. In a study of Western meditators, Jack Kornfield (1979) found that initial practitioners reported surges of emotions, physical sensations, disruptive mental states, and other reactions as they began to meditate. As practice continued (in a three-month retreat, for example), these preliminary experiences decreased and periods of calmness began to prevail.

There are many forms of meditation besides the basic sitting practice. Christian prayer, Sufi dancing, walking meditation, chanting, Jewish davening, and tantric energy practices are all methods that may open the self to transpersonal contact.

OTHER TRANSPERSONAL PRACTICES

Dreams

Working with dreams or within dreams holds potential for transpersonal development. Dream analysis is an accepted therapeutic modality in most psychotherapy schools, including Freudian, Jungian, and Gestalt. Exploring the meanings of dreams—representational and symbolic—gives information about emotions, relationships, memories, and the concerns of living. Dreams also offer artistic creative expression, problem solving, technical innovations, and novel concepts. Beyond this, dreams also give access to transpersonal experiences: peak experiences, near-death experiences, ESP, inner guides, intuitive insights, and inspirations have been experienced in dreams. Thus it seems that dreamwork can be used for many levels of growth, from dealing with emotional and personality issues to higher levels of functioning and to transpersonal growth and related issues (Faraday, 1974; Jung, 1961; Taylor, 1983, 1992).

Two recent developments in dream theory and practice are of interest to transpersonal psychologists. The first is dream incubation, a practice that goes back to ancient times. In dream incubation the dreamer requests a dream on a topic, question, or theme. This may be done through a ritual, a verbal phrase or other focused intention, or a verbalized formulation (Delaney, 1988; Garfield, 1974; Reed, 1976). Dreamers report that dreams respond with scenarios, symbols, and themes relevant to the request. Incubated dreams can be directed toward personality issues or extended to transpersonal requests.

The second dream "rediscovery" is of lucid dreaming, that is, the experience of being consciously awake in a dream, indeed, usually more vividly and lucidly than usual. This is found in yogic and Buddhist traditions and in anecdotal dream reports, but had not been given credence by skeptical conventional dream researchers. In the 1970s the reality of waking ego consciousness within dreaming was demonstrated by Stephen LaBerge (1985). Lucid dreams give the opportunity to work within the symbolism of dreams, for example, by confronting a threatening figure or by intentionally opening to transpersonal experiences within the dream (LaBerge & Rheingold, 1990; Tart, 1989).

Journaling

Another practice with transpersonal potentials is journaling and writing. In the forms of diaries, autobiographies, letters, poetics, and self-analysis, written self-reflections have been a common part of inner work leading to transpersonal growth. In the spiritual traditions the writings of St. Teresa of Avila and St. John of the Cross in Christianity, poetry of Kabir and Rumi in Islam, and the songs of Milerepa in Buddhism are well known. There are many first-person accounts of spiritual practice, altered states, and transformative experiences. These self-reflections and reports have value in themselves for integrating and deepening the experiences. Psychologist Ira Progoff (1975) developed a powerful method of journaling that he named the Intensive Journal, but journaling does not necessarily need instructions; people write about their lives for themselves and others in many ways.

Drugs

Psychoactive substances, usually from plants, have been used in many religious ceremonies and practices to produce an altered state of consciousness that gives access to transpersonal experience. Wine in Greek religion, soma (perhaps a mushroom derivative) in early Hindu tradition, ayahuasca in South American shamanism, and peyote in Native American ceremonies have all been used within cultural contexts and rituals that direct the experience. In contemporary times there are no mainstream religious organizations that use such substances to produce religious states of consciousness (the Native American church is legally allowed to use peyote cactus in ceremonies).

Perhaps the best-known study of the religious effects of a psychedelic drug is by Pahnke (1963; Pahnke & Richards, 1969), who found that individuals who had taken LSD in a religious setting reported effects that met the criteria of mystical experiences (contrasted with a control group). A follow-up study of the participants twenty-five years later indicated that the experiences had important, positive effects on the lives of those who had taken the drug (Doblin, 1991). When William James tried nitrous oxide (laughing gas) at the turn of the twentieth century, his experiences led him to observe that there are many potential forms of consciousness beyond our normal waking consciousness (in Walsh & Vaughan, 1993a). As a transpersonal practice, such drugs are not advisable because of their illegal status and the lack of a supportive system in therapy or spiritual direction for the experiences.

Near-Death Experiences

Over the centuries people have given accounts of physically "dying," continuing to have consciousness, traveling to a nonearthly place (e.g., a place of light, a beautiful landscape, a temple), having experiences there, and then returning to their body to continue their life. In current language this is called a near-death experience (NDE), and there is a growing body of writing and research on these experiences, which are reported by adults and children and by religious and non-religious individuals. While the data cannot directly prove or disprove the reality of the nonphysical realm reported by the individuals, there is strong evidence that the person was conscious and in an out-of-the-body state during the clinical death (Sabom, 1982). Regarding the effects of the experience, Kenneth Ring (1980) studied individuals who had NDEs and found that their attitudes, beliefs, and behaviors were significantly changed by the impact of the experience, equivalent to the effects of mystical and peak experiences. The changes included increased appreciation for nature and ordinary life; more compassion, tolerance, and patience for others and interest in helping them; less interest in material things and material success; much more interest in purpose and meaning in life; higher consciousness and self-understanding; increased belief in a life after death; and increased spiritual interests, more of a universal nature rather than denominational.

The most obvious explanation of an NDE is that what the person reports is really a contact with a nonphysical realm, interpreted or modified by the cultural and personal belief systems to some extent. No doubt most people who have had an NDE hold this belief, as do many researchers. This conclusion is controversial, and other explanations given for the experience hold that it is a fantasy created to ease death, a hallucination caused by drugs or lack of oxygen, or some brain program triggered by crisis or fear (some "NDEs" have occurred in the absence of near death). None of these have been very satisfactory counterexplanations, and all have little evidence or theory to support them. In my opinion, the most adequate explanation is still the obvious one, which requires some stretching or replacement of the conventional paradigm.

This chapter mentions only a few practices and phenomena that are relevant to transpersonal psychology. Others include physical disciplines with transpersonal dimensions, such as aikido and tai chi (Frager, 1989), artistic expression, past life memories (Woolger, 1987), ceremonial and ritual experiences, psychic functioning, and a variety of altered states of consciousness.

TRANSPERSONAL THERAPY

Several assumptions are common to all transpersonal therapies. One basic belief is in the experiential reality of the transcendent levels of experience and the value of them for human development. Michael Washburn (1988) describes this transpersonal level of growth as reconnecting with the dynamic ground of the self. Ken Wilber (1980) describes it as turning inward to identify with subtle causal and ultimate realms of reality. Whatever the framework, transpersonal therapists assume that one goal of therapy is to facilitate growth of the self toward these higher levels of experience. In other words, the purpose of therapy is to increase conscious awareness and move toward enlightenment.

A further assumption is that there is a natural, spontaneous movement toward wholeness. The psyche moves toward a larger sense of self. There is an intrinsic tendency for the person to want to be healthy, to learn, and to bring all parts of the self together. The therapist's work is to help remove obstacles and fixations so the individual can move toward greater awareness and freedom. Bryan Wittine (1989) has articulated these and other transpersonal assumptions in therapy.

In transpersonal therapy all levels of the spectrum are addressed, the egoic, the existential, and the transpersonal. The ego level of the personality is that of work, relationships, everyday living, hopes, fears, and self-identity. The existential level brings forward the values of the choices that we make and our relation to others and to the great issues of meaning, purpose, and authenticity. Transpersonal levels bring the client to identification with the One Self, to service for others in loving ways, to experiencing interpersonal connections at deeper levels, and to expanded awareness and intuition.

An important assumption is that people have purposes and values (Maslow's being values) in their lives that go deeper than everyday activities. Frances Vaughan (1979; also in Walsh & Vaughan, 1980) writes that there are three dimensions to transpersonal therapy: context, content, and process. The context is the attitude of the therapist—the assumptions that have just been described. Even when there is no mention of the transpersonal, the therapist can be transpersonal in her or his assumptions, and this establishes a transpersonal context for therapeutic work.

In terms of content, transpersonal experiences can be the subject of therapy. The therapist provides support and guidance in these growth processes. Transpersonal issues such as dilemmas of compassion, truth, loss of limiting ego identity, and fears of the transcendent may emerge in therapy. As the person moves outside of any limiting paradigms, there may be experiences of extrasensory perception, visions, channeling, past life memories, perceptual changes, subtle body energies, out-of-the-body experiences, synchronicities, and mythological projections. The transpersonal therapist will consider these experiences as potential contributors to the growth of the individual, neither rejecting them as fantasy or pathology nor treating them as signs of enlightenment.

A transpersonal therapist can draw on many therapeutic processes that come from transpersonal practices. Perhaps the best known are imagery and visualization. Therapists may also work with dreams or journaling or suggest meditation. Asking clients to draw or sculpt a feeling or an experience of the self allows powerful expressions through nonverbal modes that bypass the ego and the limitations of language. Working as a therapist with these levels of growth is best done if the therapist has personally explored the transpersonal realm.

TRANSPERSONAL THEORY

The most influential theorist in transpersonal psychology is Ken Wilber (see chapter 30 on Ken Wilber in part II of this volume). Wilber's developmental model in *The Atman Project* (Wilber, 1980; Wilber, Engler, & Brown, 1986) has the advantage of meshing with developmental psychology and extending it to transpersonal growth. Wilber says that people move through three life stages: prepersonal, personal, and transpersonal growth. The prepersonal stage begins at birth, before a personality is developed. From birth to adolescence the task is to build a personality. In the personal stage the individual's task is to use the personality in work, relationships, and mature life in the world. In the transpersonal stage, usually beginning in adult life, the person begins to move beyond the external world and explore the inner reaches of the self and spiritual realities. The ultimate purpose is to attain the state of oneness or unity with the consciousness of the universe. Wilber contends that the growth toward these levels of being is a natural movement of the self, an inward arc in contrast to the outward arc that relates to the external world.

Wilber presents a second model of transpersonal experience in *The Spectrum of Consciousness* (1977) and *No Boundary* (1981). Here Wilber presumes the identity of the self with absolute oneness as the natural state of consciousness. But the self is kept from this Oneness by boundaries that split it into limited bands, like colors of a spectrum. As we experience self, there is a boundary that creates a Persona and a Shadow (using Jungian terms). When these two bands are reunited to become the whole Ego, there is a further barrier between the Ego and the Body. This boundary drops to create the integrated Body-Mind. The person then integrates the Biosocial band (relation to others), the Existential (meaningful connection with the universe), and the Transpersonal.

Wilber's powerful insight here is that schools of psychotherapy speak to healing these splits, but usually are limited to one band, depending on the interests of the founder. Psychoanalysis, for example, addresses the split between the persona and the unconscious, while Reichian body therapy attempts to integrate the body with the ego. The schools are useful in what they address, but of little use to the splits they ignore. Wilber considers the spiritual traditions to be the ones dealing with the split between the self and the ultimate reality.

Obviously Wilber is devoted to categories and hierarchies and theorizes from a mental plane, but there is no denying the brilliance and influence of his conceptual models. The Atman model bridges transpersonal with mainstream psychology in ways that can be applied and tested (though little research has been conducted along these lines). The Atman model can be compared with the models of Loevinger, Piaget, and other developmental psychologists and calls attention to valid areas of human growth. Wilber's limitations are those of any hierarchical theory: the world is more complex than the theory, and exceptions are the rule (Rothberg, 1986). We may also note that transpersonal experiences occur to children during the prepersonal stage as well as in the third stage of the model. Also, the transpersonal sometimes manifests like an intrusion from another realm into human experience, rather than as a process of growth. Washburn and Wilber have debated these issues (Washburn, 1990; Wilber, 1990). Wilber's most recent developmental formulation presents an evolutionary model of individual and social systems, each with an inner and outer dimension (Wilber, 1995).

Another transpersonal model comes from the therapy system of psychosynthesis, developed by psychiatrist Roberto Assagioli (1965). In his model a higher self is a mediator between the personality and the divine. There is first an integration (synthesis) of the parts of the personality, and then a synthesis with the higher self. While Assagioli personified the higher self as somewhat separate from the personality, contemporary practitioners tend to consider the higher self to be an intrinsic part or quality permeating the self.

Michael Washburn suggests a different transpersonal model in *The Ego and the Dynamic Ground* (1988). Washburn conceives the self to have an intrinsic creative energy, a natural reservoir of dynamic potential that includes transpersonal qualities. As the Ego develops, this dynamic ground is repressed in the service of structure, form, linear process, and cultural-consensus reality. However, when the Ego matures and becomes less defended (or when crisis cracks the shell), the Ground begins to emerge again in the person's life, and the task becomes one of coming into a relationship with this dynamic level of energy and creativeness. Washburn calls his theory a spiral model, in contrast to the ladder model of Wilber. Washburn's conceptualization tends to be more congruent with Western spiritual traditions, for example, Christianity, while Wilber's model draws more from the psychology of Eastern traditions.

The transpersonal movement in psychology has parallels in other academic and scientific fields, including anthropology, philosophy, parapsychology, and physics. It offers an expanded or alternate paradigm for the understanding of the person and of our relationships with each other and the universe. The transpersonal paradigm holds that we are not separate from one another nor from sources of higher love, insight, and being. The transpersonal paradigm challenges us to study and explore the transpersonal and spiritual dimensions of the person and to find ways to cultivate these levels of being.

REFERENCES

Anand, B. K., Chhina, G. S., & Singh, B. (1961). Some aspects of electroencephalographic studies in yogis. *Electroencephalography and Clinical Neurophysiology, 13*, 452–456.

Assagioli, R. (1965). *Psychosynthesis.* New York: Hobbs, Dorman.

Brown, D., & Engler, J. (1986). The stages of mindfulness meditation: A validation study. Part I. Study and results. The stages of mindfulness meditation. Part II. Discussion. In K. Wilber, J. Engler, & D. Brown (Eds.), *Transformations of consciousness* (pp. 161–217). Boston: New Science Library/Shambhala.

Deikman, A. (1977). Comments on the GAP report. *Journal of Nervous and Mental Disease, 165*, 213–217.

Delaney, G. (1988). *Living your dreams.* San Francisco: Harper & Row.

Doblin, R. (1991). Pahnke's "Good Friday Experiment": A long-term follow-up and methodological critique. *Journal of Transpersonal Psychology, 23*(1), 1–28.

Fadiman, J., & Frager, R. (1994). *Personality and personal growth* (3rd ed.). New York: HarperCollins.

Faraday, A. (1974). *The dream game.* New York: Harper & Row.

Frager, R. (1989). Transpersonal psychology: Promise and Prospects. In R. S. Valle & S. Halling (Eds.), *Existential-phenomenological perspectives in psychology* (pp. 289–309). New York: Plenum.

Garfield, P. (1974). *Creative dreaming.* New York: Ballantine.

Grof, S. (1980). *LSD psychotherapy.* Pomona, CA: Hunter House.

Grof, S., & Grof, C. (Eds.). (1989). *Spiritual emergency.* Los Angeles: J. P. Tarcher.

Group for the Advancement of Psychiatry. (1976). *Mysticism: Spiritual quest or psychic disorder?* Publication 9(97). New York: Author.

James, W. (1936). *The varieties of religious experience.* New York: Random House Modern Library. (Original work published 1902)

Jung, C. G. (1961). *Memories, dreams, reflections.* New York: Random House.

Kasamatsu, A., & Harai, T. (1966). An electroencephalographic study on the Zen meditation (Zazen). *Folia Psychiatrica et Neurologica Japonica, 20,* 315–336.

Kornfield, J. (1979). Intensive insight meditation: A phenomenological study. *Journal of Transpersonal Psychology, 11*(1), 41–58.

LaBerge, S. (1985). *Lucid dreaming.* Los Angeles: J. P. Tarcher.

LaBerge, S., & Rheingold, H. (1990). *Exploring the world of lucid dreaming.* New York: Ballantine.

Lajoie, D. H., & Shapiro, S. I. (1992). Definitions of transpersonal psychology: The first twenty-three years. *Journal of Transpersonal Psychology, 24*(1), 79–98.

Maslow, A. (1964). *Religions, values, and peak-experiences.* Columbus: Ohio State University Press.

Maslow, A. (1968). *Toward a psychology of being* (2nd ed.). New York: Van Nostrand Reinhold.

Maslow, A. (1971). *The farther reaches of human nature.* New York: Viking.

Pahnke, W. (1963). *Drugs and mysticism: An analysis of the relationship between psychedelic drugs and the mystical consciousness.* Unpublished doctoral dissertation, Harvard University, Cambridge, MA.

Pahnke, W., & Richards, W. (1969). Implications of LSD and experimental mysticism. *Journal of Transpersonal Psychology, 1*(2), 69–102.

Progoff, I. (1975). *At a journal workshop.* New York: Dialogue House Library.

Reed, H. (1976). Dream incubation: A reconstruction of a ritual in contemporary form. *Journal of Humanistic Psychology, 4,* 52–70.

Ring, K. (1980). *Life at death.* New York: Coward, McCann, & Geoghegan.

Rothberg, D. (1986). Philosophical foundations of transpersonal psychology: An introduction to some basic issues. *Journal of Transpersonal Psychology, 18*(1), 1–34.

Sabom, M. (1982). *Recollections of death: A medical investigation.* New York: Harper & Row.

Scotton, B., Chinen, A., & Battista, J. (Eds.). (1996). *Textbook of transpersonal psychiatry and psychology.* New York: Basic Books/HarperCollins.

Shapiro, D., Jr., & Walsh, R. (Eds.) (1984). *Meditation: Classic and contemporary perspectives.* New York: Aldine.

Tart, C. T. (1975a). *States of consciousness.* New York: E. P. Dutton.

Tart, C. T. (1975b). *Transpersonal psychologies.* New York: Harper & Row.

Tart, C. T. (1989). *Open mind, discriminating mind.* San Francisco: Harper & Row.

Taylor, J. (1983). *Dream work.* New York: Paulist Press.

Taylor, J. (1992). *Where people fly and water runs uphill.* New York: Warner.

Valle, R. S., & Halling, S. (Eds.). (1989). *Existential-phenomenological perspectives in psychology.* New York: Plenum.

Vaughan, F. (1979). Transpersonal psychotherapy: Context, content, and process. *Journal of Transpersonal Psychology, 11*(2), 101–110.

Vich, M. A. (1992). Changing definitions of transpersonal psychology. *Journal of Transpersonal Psychology, 24*(1), 99–100.

Walsh, R., & Vaughan, F. (Eds.). (1980). *Beyond ego.* Los Angeles: J. P. Tarcher.

Walsh, R., & Vaughan, F. (Eds.). (1993a). *Paths beyond ego.* Los Angeles: J. P. Tarcher.

Walsh, R., & Vaughan, F. (1993b). On transpersonal definitions. *Journal of Transpersonal Psychology, 25*(2), 199–207.

Washburn, M. (1988). *The ego and the dynamic ground.* Albany: State University of New York Press.

Washburn, M. (1990). Two patterns of transcendence. *Journal of Humanistic Psychology*, *30*(3), 84–112.

Wilber, K. (1977). *The spectrum of consciousness*. Wheaton, IL: Quest Books.

Wilber, K. (1980). *The Atman project*. Wheaton, IL: Quest Books.

Wilber, K. (1981). *No boundary*. Boston: Shambhala.

Wilber, K. (1990). Two patterns of transcendence: A reply to Washburn. *Journal of Humanistic Psychology*, *30*(3), 113–136.

Wilber, K. (1995). *Sex, ecology, spirituality: The spirit of evolution*. Boston: Shambhala.

Wilber, K., Engler, J., & Brown, D. (Eds.). (1986). *Transformations of consciousness*. Boston: Shambhala.

Wittine, B. (1989). Basic postulates for a transpersonal psychotherapy. In R. Valle & S. Halling (Eds.), *Existential-phenomenological perspectives in psychology* (pp. 269–287). New York: Plenum.

Woolger, R. (1987). *Other lives, other selves*. New York: Dolphin Doubleday.

The Heritage and the Promise of Humanistic and Transpersonal Psychology

Humanistic psychology is now four decades old and stands on the threshold of a new developmental challenge: to accomplish a deep-reaching renewal or face irrelevance. Humanistic psychology was born in a confrontation with the scientific deficiencies of 1950s-era psychology and with the cultural and spiritual deficiencies of American society of that time. Today there are once again far-reaching deficiencies both in psychology and in American and world culture. The challenge of humanistic psychology today is twofold: (1) to address the lingering irrelevance of much psychological theory and research to pressing human problems and (2) to attempt to ameliorate the anguish of existence in a global village, where individuals around the world, linked by instantaneous electronic communication, watch war and ethnic cleansing unfold on the evening television news.

Chapter 13 presents an argument for the continued need for a humanistic and transpersonal psychology. The idealistic world-changing ambitions of humanistic psychology remain merely a hope, and the world is as much in need of humanization as it was in Maslow's day.

Chapter 14 describes the vitality discernible in humanistic psychology, but also the challenges it must face, including the task of overcoming the legitimate accusations of its critics. This chapter also addresses the renewed mission and direction of the humanistic psychology of the twenty-first century.

13

The Continuing Need for a Humanistic and Transpersonal Psychology

DONALD MOSS

Why now? Why in the year 1998 do we undertake a comprehensive new volume on humanistic and transpersonal psychology? Aren't humanistic and transpersonal psychologies intellectual children of the late 1950s and the 1960s? Aren't they also in a certain sense mere cultural by-products of the social ferment of the 1960s? The hippies and gurus of the 1960s, the social and sexual experimentation, and the pursuit of altered states of consciousness through drugs and meditation—haven't these phenomena had their time in American life and been rejected as too destructive? Haven't the politics of 1960s radicalism become a dirty word in American political dialogue? If the 1950s were banner years for existential and humanistic psychology, as our chapter on existential-phenomenological psychology maintains, then why are we still in 1998 presenting a new book to sum up this movement? We will address these questions by reviewing the progress in psychology and the parallel progress in American/Western culture, and the gaps that still remain.

THE IMPACT OF THE HUMANISTIC CRITIQUE ON PSYCHOLOGY

All of the objections just spelled out are in one sense correct, yet they also miss the point. The shortcomings within the American psychology of the 1950s that gave birth to humanistic psychology have in many respects been addressed and resolved. The primary critique of humanistic psychology in the 1950s and 1960s was that American scientific psychology lacked the measure of the fully alive human being. The concepts and images of human behavior latent in psychological theories, laboratory research, and textbooks failed to give recognition to the higher potentials of the human being, the individual's consciousness of the world, his or her vision of the future, and free choices to create his or her own future.

The concepts of psychology in 1958 seemed to be derived from, and seemed more suitable to, a rat in a Skinner box, a mental patient with his or her delusions, or a developmentally disabled person with behavior problems. Within each school of psychology, both theory and research seemed to reduce the full breadth of human experience to one simplistic dimension of behavior, instinct, or, in general, causality. Psychology no longer seemed suited to approach the creative human being as the source of art, science, and democracy. When B. F. Skinner, the foremost behaviorist of the era, conceived of a utopian society, he proposed to do so in terms that left freedom and dignity out of the picture and focused on the behavioral and social engineering that might manipulate individuals into a healthier society (Skinner, 1948, 1953, 1971).

However, the winds of change swept through the science of psychology. The refusal of radical behaviorism to give place in its theory and research to thinking, emotion, and perception has been addressed. Cognitive-behavioral approaches have supplemented behaviorism, both in textbooks and in the clinic (Meichenbaum, 1977; Turk, Meichenbaum, & Genest, 1983; Lazarus, 1991). Further, phenomenological (Moss, 1989, 1992), constructivist (Gergen, 1985, 1991; Rychlak, 1993), and religious (Jones, 1994) perspectives are given credence regularly by mainstream articles and authors, and experiential therapy has become an empirical approach with its own outcome studies (Gendlin, 1981; Mahrer, 1983). Roger Sperry (1993, p. 878) asserts that the "cognitive, mentalist, or consciousness revolution" has been the most radical turnaround in the history of psychology. One-dimensional theories, which explain all phenomena by the same cause, no longer have much credibility within psychology. Psychology has been forced to recognize that the neglected dimensions of human experience return to haunt one. William James's early recognition of a "pluralistic universe," in which all dimensions interact but no single dimension explains or contains all the others, seems to have won out (James, 1909, 1912; Robinson, 1993). Conceptual discussion in psychology now abounds with hybrid terms, reflecting an attempt at systematic thinking, inclusiveness, and comprehensiveness. For example, Richard Lazarus (1991, p. vii) speaks of a "cognitive-motivational-relational" theory; G. L. Engel (1977) speaks of a "bio-psycho-social model"; and Vittorio Guidano (1987, 1991) speaks of a "unitary, developmental, process-oriented model."

In psychoanalysis the conceptual explanation of all behavior by reference to unconscious drives and to the psychosexual complexes of the first three years and the attempt to reduce the work of the creative artist to its instinctual basis (for example, Freud's study of Leonardo) have given way to a new psychoanalysis based in a deeper awareness of culture, society, language, "object relationships," and the self (Lacan, 1968; Kernberg, 1975; Kohut, 1977, 1984; St. Clair, 1986). The humanistic, existential, and sociological critiques of Freud found their mark, and today's analysts are as likely to read James Masterson, Margaret Mahler, or Heinz Kohut as Freud.

Similarly, Maslow's critique that psychology must not base its understanding of normal and gifted persons on the case studies of abnormal and mentally ill behavior has been accepted. There is an entire body of research now on creativity and the lives of the gifted or highly functioning person (Torrance, 1969; Horowitz & O'Brien, 1985; Wallace, 1985; Feldman, 1982; Clark, 1988; Csikszentmihalyi, 1990). Even the study of abnormal states and conditions has benefited from closer investigation of those individuals who show the resilience to "overcome a cruel past" (Higgins, 1994).

In summary, the psychology of the 1990s is a much more comprehensive and inclusive science than was the psychology of 1950. The problem of fragmentation remains, with many subdomains within psychology failing to take into account the rethinking and conceptual breakthroughs of other areas. Nevertheless, the field of psychology as a whole, as represented by the American Psychological Association in its polyglot multiplicity and diversity, is a much richer house with windows and doors flung wide open. It would appear that so many schools of psychological theory and research have accepted elements of the humanistic critique that there is hardly any longer a need for a separate humanistic psychology.

This all seems true, and yet there remains a problem. Although psychology has addressed many of the conceptual deficits identified in the original humanistic psychology movement and has wrestled with many of the personal issues raised in the heyday of existential psychology, the existential and cultural problems raised so long ago appear only to have deepened and taken on a more ugly turn. I will highlight several examples in turn in order to accent the continued need for the same kind of humanistic and existential searching begun four decades ago.

THE CRISIS IN VALUES IN WESTERN SOCIETY

The crisis in values addressed by humanistic psychology has only deepened today and become more graphic in everyday life. In the 1960s and 1970s Erich Fromm and Carl Rogers highlighted the breakdown of external religious belief and cultural values and offered us instead the quiet, inner voice of the humanistic conscience (Fromm, 1964, 1973; Rogers, 1977). However, that still inner voice remains unheard, and we now face a crisis of human beings without any form of conscience whatsoever.

Most days the newspaper provides horrifying examples of American children whose actions show no apparent regard for the value of a human life. On October 13, 1994, two gang members in Chicago, ages ten and eleven, dropped Eric Morse, a five-year-old acquaintance, from a fourteenth-floor window because he refused to steal candy as he had been ordered to do. Both boys already had criminal records, and both reported that their fathers were in prison. Eric's eight-year-old brother looked on horrified and struggled with the gang members, but his efforts could not save his brother. One month earlier, on September 1, eleven-year-old Robert "Yummy" Sandifer, also of Chicago, was shot by two fellow gang members because he had shot and killed a fourteen-year-old girl and drawn too much police attention to their gang. Problems with violent youth are not specific to Chicago nor even to the United States. According to one recent estimate, children bring about 270,000 guns to school each day in America (Sautter, 1996, p. 55). In 1991, about 430,000 violent crimes occurred in and around American schools (Sautter, 1995, p. 54). The English and Swedish peoples have been equally shocked in recent years by the brutally violent and senseless crimes committed by their children, and in Bosnia, Afghanistan, Rwanda, and all too many other hot spots, children carry weapons on behalf of ethnic hatreds, nationalistic passions, and age-old religious intolerance.

Human life seemed to lose value in the 1950s, and well-mannered middle-class individuals described their existential malaise and ennui to psychotherapists and discovered new perspectives for meaning in life in the existential literature of Camus and Sartre. Today the loss of meaning is more nuclear and devastating and shows up in an utter degradation of existence for large groups of persons. Individuals on television talk shows discuss their sexual relationships with parents, children, animals, and multiple partners. The rate of birth outside of marriage in the entire population skyrocketed to about 27% in 1990, and the breakdown of marriages has reached 50% (Wilson, 1994). In 1990, 57% of black babies were born to nonmarried mothers. Approximately 50% of American children now reside in "nontraditional families," including single-parent homes, stepfamilies, living-together arrangements with one or both natural parents, or separation from both parents. Some 27% of high-school students think about suicide in the course of one calendar year. Marriage, the family, privacy, personal dignity, and respect for human life all show a pervasive breakdown.

One can protest that neither psychology nor any other professional discipline can single-handedly reverse such serious cultural and social problems. However, many humanistic psychologists did in fact raise just such messianic hopes that a new understanding of the human being would enable psychologists to remake modern human life. Abraham Maslow, Carl Rogers, William Schutz, and Sidney Jourard all at various times and with varying perspectives announced hopes for a new social order. Jourard, for example, emphasized the value of a pluralistic society at the close of the preface to the second edition of his classic, *The Transparent Self*:

If America and, indeed, the Western world, become "pluralistic" societies, then they will indeed be places suitable for "transparent selves." I dedicate this new edition of *The Transparent Self* to the passionate, and I hope, unbloody quest for social structures in which all who are of goodwill can live in harmony and mutual confirmation. (Jourard, 1971, p. vi)

Similarly, Leo Buscaglia, in his 1978 volume *Personhood*, proclaimed his personal belief in the social transformations possible when one individual pursues self-actualization:

Each of us still has within us that which is necessary to remake the world. The principle motivational force necessary to accomplish this requires only our personal commitment to dedicate ourselves to the process of living our lives fully, not only to exist in life, but to experience it totally. (Buscaglia, 1978, p. 135)

If we take such idealistic goals seriously, then we must conclude that the task of remaking society remains incomplete, and that the original optimism of the humanistic psychologists was naïve and simplistic. Individual transformation is of infinite value, but social transformation and values change remain difficult. The challenge remains unmet, and if humanistic psychology is to contribute further to improving the Western way of life, it must discover a more realistic and seasoned approach, informed by past failures.

In the last three decades psychology has succeeded richly in conceptual and research breakthroughs, but has failed to make an adequate difference at the everyday level of human beings and their daily existence. Psychology has been a success in the laboratory and the classroom, but a failure in life.

Psychology has successfully investigated the process by which human beings attribute linguistic labels and cognitive meaning to events. Psychology has not succeeded in showing teen single mothers how to convey either meaning or wisdom to young boys and girls growing up in a violent society. Psychology has successfully studied the impact of violent television programming on subsequent behavior. Psychology has not succeeded in reducing the sensationalistic violence of television and other mass media. Psychology has successfully identified factors enhancing emotional bonding between parent and child in the first hours of life. Psychology has not succeeded in eliminating brutal child and spousal abuse, murder of children by parents, and murder of parents by children. Psychology has successfully documented the artificiality of mind-body dichotomies and has rejected the false compartmentalization of medical problems into physical or mental. Psychology has not succeeded in integrating its own services with those of medicine, nor has it reduced the needless expense and suffering of patients who shuttle back and forth helplessly between specialists in medicine and psychology.

THE CONTINUING SEARCH FOR MEANING

Evangelical Christianity is on the rise today, gathering increasing numbers of adherents and promulgating the belief that Jesus Christ has and is the answer, the one way, the one truth, and the one life. The churches growing most rapidly are those that emphasize a direct personal relationship with Christ, an immediate and radical challenge to one's personal way of life, and a direct experiential encounter with the present reality of the gospel. Spiritualistic schools from East and West and "new-age" philosophies continue to emerge and draw adherents, offering an experience of the spirit and not just an abstract sermon or catechism.

Nevertheless, the evidence is glaring that many Americans and Western Europeans still lack direction and live lives of quiet desperation. Many youths escalate their anger and violence, lashing out at an adult world in which they feel no part. Many blacks and Hispanics continue to lash out at a white world that offers them no place. Seeking meaning and affiliation, teens of all colors and ethnic origins join gangs, identify themselves with their colors, and pride themselves on violence without hesitation. Ruthless, destructive, and self-destructive actions serve as a cheap substitute for a sense of real personal or spiritual direction.

Large numbers of individuals in Western societies turn to cults in a quest for meaning and life direction. For some, this is a developmental stage, a temporary search for absolutes on the way to the ambiguities of adult life. For others, it is a lifelong journey for a spiritual way of life amid the materialism of the prosperous West. Traditional monasteries and new cult communities continue to attract individuals to live apart, in the age-old image of retreating into the deserts and lonely places at the edges of civilization. The "desert fathers" began this journey and began the Western movement of monasticism—living apart—when they began to move into the deserts of Egypt and Asia Minor in the fourth century (Merton, 1960).

Occasionally, however, we see bloody results of bad choices—misguided dedication to false prophets. In November 1978, 912 followers of Jim Jones committed suicide together in Jonestown, Guyana. In May 1985, 11 members of the MOVE organization died during a police bombing and assault on their armed stronghold. In April 1993, America watched on television as David Koresh and 86 followers died a fiery death during a federal assault on the Branch Davidian compound. In October 1994, 53 followers of Luc Jouret and his Order of the Solar Temple died in Quebec Province and Switzerland in an apparent combination suicide/murder.

THE ANTAGONISM BETWEEN RELIGION AND PSYCHOLOGY

In the years since humanistic psychology raised its critique, mainstream psychology has opened its doors once again to spirituality and religious perspectives (Jones, 1994). Yet there are also growing forces within American religion that newly reject psychology as godless, secularistic, and humanistic.

On the one hand, many pastors turn for their inspiration in sermon writing to the psychological self-help literature. The ideas of Alcoholics Anonymous, including the concept of a twelve-step recovery process, the surrender to a higher power, and the need to make a fearless moral inventory of one's errors, lend themselves easily to religious application. Similarly, the psychological concepts of self-esteem, self-disclosure, and positive mental attitude have wide currency in sermons and in the religiously oriented self-help book market (Powell, 1969, 1978; Schuller, 1969, 1977). At present one of the most energetic movements of renewal within evangelical Christian circles is called Promise Keepers, a movement bringing large gatherings of men—60,000 men gathering together in football stadiums and other familiar sites—to discover an experiential peak experience of enthusiasm and moral rebirth, rediscovering maleness, one's role as father, and commitment.

On the other hand, conservative religious figures, both preachers and authors, have declared the labels "secular humanism" and "new age" synonymous with godless, pagan, and anti-Christian. It is not unusual in more conservative communities for a patient to drop out of psychotherapy suddenly, even though the patient was progressing rapidly, because the therapist has recommended a relaxation skill, a meditation tape, or a relevant book that the patient's pastor then condemns as godless or new age. The reason for the cessation of therapy becomes clear when the patient approaches his or her physician or managed-care gate-keeper and requests a "real Christian therapist."

The antagonism of conservative religious groups against humanistic psychology takes many forms. Many figures within humanistic and transpersonal psychology have studied Eastern and other world religions extensively to discover the unrecognized kinship among the spiritual traditions of mankind, to disclose those substantial contributions that other spiritual traditions might have to make to Western religions, and to identify the psychological insights and understanding implicit in such religious systems (de Silva, 1979; Watts, 1961; Tart, 1975). The dialogue with the East—with Buddhist and Hindu approaches—follows the pathway opened originally by such deeply religious Christian figures as Thomas Merton, who died while visiting a Buddhist monastery.

Instead of joining in this interested dialogue with other religions, however, many conservative Christian forces have chosen to condemn all such dialogue once again as "new age," "humanistic," and "godless." Their response has been the age-old conservatism of rejecting the unfamiliar as dangerous; the Inquisition is born again at the revival tent.

Many conservative Christians lack historical perspective and do not realize that the "new humanism" of Erasmus of Rotterdam, Thomas More of England, and their colleagues in the sixteenth century was the original movement making biblical texts accessible in the language of the common man. Modern humanism began as an effort to achieve a fuller appreciation of human nature in the light of both biblical texts and classical Greek philosophy. Erasmus desired to combine what he called "good letters," the study of classical Greek philosophy, with what he called "sacred letters," or biblical scholarship. His preface to his new edition of the New Testament in 1516 expressed the wish that "every woman might read the Gospel and the Epistles of St. Paul . . . [and] . . . that these were translated into each and every language." The pursuit of humanism historically has not been antagonistic to either religion or spirituality.

Both psychology and humanistic psychology are frequently blamed for the social excesses of the past three decades. Humanistic psychology, with its emphasis on self-actualization, is portrayed as advocating a selfish life for the "me generation." There were self-oriented excesses in the humanistic movement, and at times there was a failure to attend to the more traditional values of relationship and community. Christopher Lasch, in *The Culture of Narcissism* (1979), criticized the "awareness movement" for contributing to the individual's self-oriented isolation:

Even when therapists speak of the need for "meaning" or "love," they define love and meaning simply as the fulfillment of the patient's emotional requirements. It hardly occurs to them—nor is there any reason why it should, given the nature of the therapeutic enterprise—to encourage the subject to subordinate his needs and interests to those of others, of someone or some cause or tradition outside himself. (Lasch, 1979, pp. 42–43)

At the extreme the result was narcissistic self-preoccupation at the expense of other persons (Solomon, 1989). The Gestalt therapist Fritz Perls's famous verse about relationships is frequently cited as an example of giving the momentary encounter a higher priority than commitment, integrity, or responsibility:

> I do my thing, and you do your thing.
> I am not in this world to live up to your expectations
> And you are not in this world to live up to mine.
> You are you and I am I,
> And if by chance we find each other, it's beautiful.
> If not, it can't be helped. (Perls, 1973, p. 4)

Self-actualization was not originally intended to mean only narcissistic self-gratification. The highly self-actualized individuals studied by Abraham Maslow included such individuals as Eleanor Roosevelt, who was best known for her selfless dedication to the needs of others. Later Maslow also focused on individuals who not only served others altruistically, but also reported an explicit sense of self-transcendence, including such persons as Martin Buber, Albert Schweitzer, and Albert Einstein (1971, p. 270). The "farther reaches of human nature," as Maslow titled one of his books, include the surpassing and transcending of self in the narrow sense. Maslow defined self-actualization as "experiencing fully, vividly, selflessly, with full concentration and absorption . . . the person is wholly and fully human" (1971, p. 44). Maslow moved in the course of his own life's work beyond the viewpoint of humanistic psychology, which he himself had created, to espouse a transpersonal psychology with a conscious dedication to the cultivation of spirituality: "I consider Humanistic, Third Force Psychology to be transitional, a preparation for a still "higher" Fourth Psychology, transpersonal, transhuman, centered in the cosmos rather than in human needs and interest, going beyond humanness, identity, self-actualization and the like" (Maslow, 1968, p. iii). It is time for humanistic psychology and its close cousin transpersonal psychology to again find their voice, to defend themselves against misinformed condemnations, and to enter into a dialogue with genuine religious forces.

THE SPLIT BETWEEN SCIENCE AND THE ARTS

There is a recurrent tension in our culture between science and the arts and the sets of values associated with each. Writing at the time of humanistic psychology's birth, Sir Charles P. Snow deplored the chasm developing between two great traditions that together had contributed to the best achievements in Western humanity. In his influential 1959 work *The Two Cultures and the Scientific Revolution*, he described the first tradition of the arts and humanities as more and more separated from the second tradition of the sciences and engineering, to such an extent that each tradition had become a separate culture with its own distinct modes of understanding and communication. Each culture was isolated within its own paradigms of thought, preferences of tools, and familiar vocabulary and literature, thus forming barriers to those wishing to communicate across the differences. Few individuals would remain citizens of both cultures and freely move back and forth. This situation, according to Snow, was deplorable and denied each tradition access to the best fruits of the other.

We may utilize Snow's two-culture model as an image to illuminate a parallel situation within psychology. Scientific psychologists have long prided themselves on their break with philosophy and theology, citing the superstitions, unexamined assumptions, and irrational submission to authority of many traditional philosophical and religious schools. Similarly, scientific psychologists have viewed themselves as part of the rigorous laboratory tradition of the empirical natural sciences and have rejected as unscientific the often intuitively based insights of poetry, art, and literature. Even many branches of psychology have been rejected as inadequately scientific because their cognitive subject matter was not amenable to empirical observation or measurement, or because their methods, such as introspection or dialogue, were not those of the physical sciences.

The origins of humanistic psychology in European existentialism involved extensive literary and philosophical foundations. The father of modern European existentialism, the Danish theologian Søren Kierkegaard, believed that literature and philosophy provide many keys to understanding human existence; he also believed that many literary forms offer better means of expressing such understanding than do objective essays. Kierkegaard and later the French philosopher Jean-Paul Sartre experimented with a variety of literary genres—dialogues, stories, novels, and drama—as forms of "indirect communication" about human experience.

The European existential psychiatrists turned as extensively to philosophy and literature as they did to more traditional sources of clinical psychiatric knowledge. Ludwig Binswanger was a close friend and disciple of Freud, but found a deeper kinship with the German phenomenological philosophers Edmund Husserl and Martin Heidegger. Medard Boss involved Heidegger in an ongoing seminar with psychiatrists and other physicians. Eugene Minkowski found much of the basis for his understanding of "lived time," time as humanly experienced, in the French philosopher Henri Bergson. Erwin Straus found perhaps his greatest guide in plumbing the depths of human experience to be the great German man of letters, Goethe; Straus turned as well to Shakespeare and the classical Greek philosophers.

Humanistic psychology, as it emerged in the 1950s, involved a renewed attention to the humanistic traditions of the arts and humanities as alternative modes of understanding human experience. For example, after graduating from Oberlin College, Rollo May traveled to Greece and studied painting. Thereafter he entered Union Theological Seminary and studied with the existential theologian Paul Tillich. Throughout his career May drew on the richness of literature, theology, philosophy, and the arts to reach a deeper understanding of the human being. James Bugental, another early leader in the "Third Force" and the first president of the Association for Humanistic Psychology, formulated the fundamental principles of a humanistic psychology in a 1963 article and placed emphasis on a convergence of science and the humanities (Bugental, 1963).

The growth of humanistic psychology in the United States was also associated with a rising interest in the European existential novels and plays. Jean-Paul Sartre and Albert Camus are the names most closely linked with existentialism, but a careful search found existential themes throughout literature. A 1963 publication, *The Existential Imagination*, sought to portray the essence of existentialism through excerpts from literary classics (Karl & Hamalian, 1963). The selections began with Shakespeare's *King Lear*, moved through Dostoevski's *Brothers Karamazov* (especially highlighting the moving scene with the Grand Inquisitor) and Tolstoy's *Memoirs of a Lunatic*, and eventually included passages from Sartre, Samuel Beckett, Albert Moravia, and Ilse Aichinger.

Since the 1950s psychology has given attention to the split between science and the arts, and many articles and conference presentations have emphasized that the arts and literature represent legitimate means of understanding human existence. The movement of archetypal psychology has also gathered momentum in the United States, taking its inspiration from Carl Jung (1961) and James Hillman (1977, 1979), but drawing extensively on mythology, art, and literature for its central images. Nevertheless, the rift remains, and literature and the arts continue to need the advocacy that humanistic psychology has provided.

THE TRIVIALIZATION OF EXISTENTIAL PERSPECTIVES IN LIFE AND PSYCHOLOGY

One could convincingly argue that humanistic psychology has been co-opted and bought out by the McDonalds and Burger King equivalents within the psychological enterprise. Humanistic psychologists are one more set of names on the multiple-choice quizzes of general psychology. Humanistic psychology receives its chapter in the personality theory textbooks and its lecture in the history and systems courses. Humanistic and existential psychotherapy are two more modalities to be checked off on the insurance-company credentialing forms. All of this represents progress, but with a possible cost. Humanistic psychology originally sought authenticity in each moment, but has been trivialized. If the salt should lose its savor, how then will life be seasoned?

Further, the sociological and careerist forces shaping vocational behavior in our society tend to place an emphasis on achievement, productivity, and a product or outcome, and these influences operate as effectively on psychologists as on other occupational groupings. The psychologist with "existential leanings" too easily becomes preoccupied with writing publishable articles for peer-reviewed journals on existential themes and with placing these articles in the best existential journals. The pursuit of writing, talking, and theorizing about existence can become a substitute for truly grappling with the anguish and horror of human existence in their darkest forms.

In another sphere, social and economic forces have produced a trivialization of the impact of psychotherapy. The cost of health care has escalated unconscionably, and there is a fairly widespread perception of the medical community as a collection of greedy, profit-oriented individuals, little interested in the patient's personal well-being and preoccupied with extravagant lifestyles. In actuality, medical salaries have escalated relative to those of other occupational groups. Physicians and other health care providers, including psychologists, have for several decades enjoyed a relative affluence and a social status not shared by their professional peers in many other countries. The result has been efforts in both the private sector and the legislatures to contain medical costs and to remove barriers to competition. One of the most radical changes produced by this movement has been the emphasis on "managed care." Patients can no longer simply make their own decisions as to which health care provider to use or which procedure to undergo. Preauthorizations, "gate keeping" of services, and a specific limitation on how much treatment each individual can receive are now common practice.

Managed care is now extending its influence over mental health services at an accelerating rate. This movement compels psychotherapists toward a utilitarian focus on problems and solutions and toward "brief therapy" and "solution-oriented therapy." On the one hand, this effort frequently suits the patient's preferences quite well, since many patients accept "mental" help reluctantly and are eager to return to self-sufficiency and self-direction. Brief-therapy research has produced many strategies that focus the therapist's and patient's energies more effectively toward bringing about those changes the patient most desires. On the negative side, however, psychotherapy, which was once a reflective retreat from the pressures of work and life, is now one more arena in which both doctor and patient are supposed to concentrate on a goal-oriented and efficient use of time with a measurable outcome.

PSYCHOLOGY STILL FAILS TO ADDRESS THE ANGUISH OF EXISTENCE

Psychology has seemed to address Maslow's insistence that a psychology based only on the study of mentally ill persons and rats could not take the full measure of a human being's dignity. Yet the research and practice of psychology still seem to bog down in a focus on trivial and tangential phenomena.

In 1994 Frank Farley, in his presidential address to the American Psychological Association, echoed concerns similar to Maslow's and warned of the danger they present for psychology's future and the future of mankind:

We stand very close to being a discipline concerned with relatively superficial problems: the anxieties and fears of otherwise healthy people; how's my self-esteem today; the science of memory for simple material; and so on. These are important things to do but I sense the world doesn't have the time. . . . There are bigger problems. . . . How can one person deliberately inflict heinous physical pain and death upon another in torture, often for strictly ideological purposes? (Farley, 1996, p. 775)

If psychology cannot help understand and reduce human horror, we will have failed our original promise. (Farley, 1996, p. 775)

Further, Farley insisted that psychology is increasingly in need of spirituality— "deep feelings about soul and eternity." He voiced his plea to psychology finally as follows:

My dream is of a psychology of meaning in the broadest sense, uplifting, ennobling, placing the mystery of life in a context, and most importantly, showing the road to generosity and love. We should accept no less. (Farley, 1996, p. 776; Martin, 1994, p. 12).

Thomas Moore struck a similar chord in 1992 when he announced that the great malady of the twentieth century is "loss of soul." He turned to medieval and Renaissance studies and the archetypal psychology of Carl Jung and James Hillman to uncover a new art that he calls "care of the soul," emphasizing practical ways to foster soulfulness in everyday life. He especially called for an end to the dangerous split between psychology and spirituality (Moore, 1992, pp. xi–xx).

Along with Farley's appeal for a psychology of meaning and Moore's call for a reunification of spiritual practice and psychotherapy, we might also appeal for a return to a fuller appreciation of tragedy and the tragic. Many of the most brilliant contributors to existential and humanistic psychology, such as Søren Kierkegaard, William James, and Rollo May, have been melancholic individuals, struggling to find a reason for their own life to continue and well attuned to the tragic side of human life. William James, writing over ninety years ago, called such individuals the "serious minded" or "morbid minded" souls (James, 1902/1961). They are troubled by the dark, irrational, and unseen side of the world and acutely aware of their own deficiencies and limitations. Conscious of the often tragic consequences of well-intended actions, the morbid-minded individual doubts the ultimate attainability of human yearnings. Such persons arrive at an ultimate faith in the value of this life only by means of a struggle with doubt and sin. Life is ultimately embraced and affirmed, but with a full recognition of its warts and creases.

KIERKEGAARD'S PROPHETIC VOICE

As has so often been true in humanistic psychology, we may benefit here from returning to the melancholic Dane. Søren Kierkegaard was a man of letters, social critic, and theologian in nineteenth-century Copenhagen. He spent his life passionately combatting what he called "the system," which included (1) the German Hegelian dialectical philosophy, which claimed too neatly to include all of life, (2) the established church, which seemed to reassure too many Christians into a comfortable and complacent assurance that their eternal salvation was already taken care of by previous generations and a matter of little concern, and (3) the comfort and complacency of bourgeois, middle-class life, which seemed too laden with routine and comforts and too devoid of challenge to remain vital. He described the average bourgeois individual as like the peasant who falls asleep in his wagon and is carried along mindlessly by the horse who follows his own habits and direction.

Kierkegaard saw his role as that of waking up sleeping and complacent individuals and of challenging them to face existence in its immediate reality, unsheltered by predigested philosophy, religion, or socialization. Kierkegaard conceptualized this challenge to each individual in Christian, theological terms. There is no "disciple at second hand," he wrote. The challenge to the would-be Christian in 1846 was no different than the original task for the individual meeting Jesus Christ in the first century. Each must come to terms himself or herself with the immediate challenge to his own personal existence. God has made "his covenant with men equally difficult for every human being in every time and place; equally difficult, since no man is able to give himself the condition, nor yet is to receive it from another" (Kierkegaard, 1844/1962, p. 134; Kierkegaard, 1846/ 1941).

Leaving aside the theological/Christian context, one finds a parallel with the present-day situation of psychology, almost forty years after the humanistic movement first burst forth within psychology. There is no "psychologist at second hand." The task of humanizing both psychology and society and of opposing the dehumanizing influences within both science and our culture confronts the psychologist today just as it did forty years ago. All of those deep existential and personal challenges facing the generation of the 1950s, in the era of Elvis Presley and Ozzie and Harriet, are returning to haunt us in a magnified form. We cannot rest on the breakthroughs and achievements of the past four decades of psychologists. Rather, we must face the eternal dilemmas of personal existence—human suffering, good and evil, beauty and degradation, and man's (and woman's) inhumanity to man—all over again and work out solutions for our times.

Kierkegaard elaborated his approach in a book about his authorship: "In all eternity it is impossible for me to compel a person to accept an opinion, a conviction, a belief. But one thing I can do: I can compel him to take notice. . . . By obliging a man to take notice I achieve the aim of obliging him to judge" (Kierkegaard, 1859/1962, p. 35). Throughout his work Kierkegaard confronted a myriad of self-soothing defenses by which individuals preserve their sleepy complacency: "Was this your consolation that you said: One does what one can? Was this not precisely the reason for your disquietude, that you did not know within yourself how much it is a man can do? . . . no earnest doubt, no really deep concern, is put to rest by the saying that one does what one can" (Kierkegaard, 1843/1959, pp. 347–348). If Kierkegaard were to address the annual conference of the American Psychological Association, his message might be expressed as follows: "Awaken, and look around you. The job is never done and it is ours. Look directly into the anguish and pain and joy of existence, and address it now. That is the task of a humanistic psychology."

REFERENCES

Brown, R. (Ed.). (1994). *Children in crisis. The Research Shelf, 66*(1). New York: H. W. Wilson Company.

Bugental, J.F.T. (1963). Humanistic psychology: A new breakthrough. *American Psychologist, 18*, 563–567.

Buscaglia, L. F. (1978). *Personhood: The art of being fully human.* Thorofare, NJ: Charles B. Slack.

Clark, B. (1988). *Growing up gifted.* Columbus, OH: Charles E. Merrill.

Csikszentmihalyi, M. (1990). *Flow: The psychology of optimal experience.* New York: Harper & Row.

de Silva, P. (1979). *An introduction to Buddhist psychology.* London: Macmillan.

Engel, G. L. (1977). The need for a new medical model: A challenge for biomedicine. *Science, 196*, 129–136.

Farley, F. (1996). From the heart: APA presidential address. *American Psychologist, 51*(8), 772–776.

Feldman, D. H. (Ed.). (1982). *Developmental approaches to giftedness and creativity.* San Francisco: Jossey-Bass.

Fromm, E. (1964). *The heart of man: Its genius for good and evil.* New York: Harper & Row.

Fromm, E. (1973). *The anatomy of human destructiveness.* Greenwich, CT: Fawcett Premier Books.

Gendlin, E. T. (1981). *Focusing.* New York: Bantam.

Gergen, K. (1985). The social constructionist movement in modern psychology. *American Psychologist, 40*, 266–275.

Gergen, K. (1991). *The saturated self: Dilemmas of identity in contemporary life.* New York: Basic Books.

Guidano, V. (1987). *Complexity of the self: A developmental approach to psychopathology and therapy.* New York: Guilford.

Guidano, V. (1991). *The self in process.* New York: Guilford.

Higgins, G. O. (1994). *Resilient adults: Overcoming a cruel past.* San Francisco: Jossey-Bass.

Hillman, J. (1977). *Re-visioning psychology.* New York: Harper Colophon.

Hillman, J. (1979). *The dream and the underworld.* New York: Harper Colophon.

Horowitz, F. D., & O'Brien, M. (Eds.). (1985). *The gifted and talented: Developmental perspectives.* Washington, DC: American Psychological Association.

James, W. (1902/1961). *The varieties of religious experience.* London: Collier Macmillan.

James, W. (1909). *A pluralistic universe: Hibbert lectures at Manchester College on the present situation in philosophy.* New York: Longmans, Green.

James, W. (1912). *Essays in radical empiricism.* New York: Longmans, Green.

Jones, S. L. (1994). A constructive relationship for religion with the science and profession of psychology. *American Psychologist, 49*(3), 184–199.

Jourard, S. (1971). *The transparent self.* (2nd ed.). New York: Van Nostrand Reinhold.

Jung, C. G. (1961). *Memories, dreams, reflections* (R. Winston & C. Winston, Trans.). New York: Random House.

Karl, F. R., & Hamalian, L. (1963). *The existential imagination.* New York: Fawcett.

Kernberg, O. (1975). *Borderline conditions and pathological narcissism.* New York: Jason Aronson.

Kierkegaard, S. (1843/1959). *Either/Or, vol. 2* (W. Lowrie, Trans.). Princeton: Princeton University Press.

Kierkegaard, S. (1844/1962). *Philosophical fragments, or a fragment of philosophy* (D. F. Swenson, Trans.). Princeton: Princeton University Press.

Kierkegaard, S. (1846/1941). *Concluding unscientific postscript* (D. F. Swenson & W. Lowrie, Trans.). Princeton: Princeton University Press.

Kierkegaard, S. (1859/1962). *The point of view for my work as an author* (W. Lowrie, Trans.). New York: Harper & Row.

Kohut, H. (1977). *Restoration of the self.* New York: International Universities Press.

Kohut, H. (1984). *How does analysis cure?* (A. Goldberg with P. E. Stepansky, Eds.). Chicago: University of Chicago Press.

Lacan, J. (1968). *The language of the self.* Baltimore: Johns Hopkins University Press.

Lasch, C. (1979). *The culture of narcissism.* New York: W. W. Norton.

Lazarus, R. S. (1991). *Emotion and adaptation.* New York: Oxford University Press.

Mahrer, A. (1983). *Experiential psychotherapy: Basic practices.* New York: Brunner/Mazel.

Martin, S. (1994). Farley sums up his '93–'94 presidential year. *APA Monitor, 27*(10), 12.

Maslow, A. H. (1968). *Toward a psychology of being* (2nd ed.). New York: Van Nostrand Reinhold. (1st ed. 1962).

Maslow, A. H. (1971). *Farther reaches of human nature.* New York: Viking.

Masterson, J. F. (1981). *The narcissistic and borderline disorders: An integrated developmental approach.* New York: Brunner/Mazel.

Meichenbaum, D. B. (1977). *Cognitive-behavior modification: An integrative approach.* New York: Plenum.

Merton, T. (Trans.) (1960). *The wisdom of the desert: Sayings from the desert fathers of the fourth century.* New York: New Directions.

Moore, T. (1992). *Care of the soul: A guide for cultivating depth and sacredness in everyday life.* New York: HarperCollins.

Moss, D. (1981). Phenomenology and neuropsychology: Two approaches to consciousness. In R. S. Valle & R. von Eckartsberg (Eds.), *The metaphors of consciousness* (pp. 153–166). New York: Plenum.

Moss, D. (1989). Psychotherapy and human experience. In R. Valle & S. Halling (Eds.), *Existential-phenomenological perspectives in psychology* (pp. 193–213). New York: Plenum.

Moss, D. (1992). Cognitive therapy, phenomenology, and the struggle for meaning. *Journal of Phenomenological Psychology, 23*(1), 87–102.

Moss, D. (in press). The patient's experience: A phenomenological, structural understanding of posttraumatic stress disorder. In D. Miller (Ed.), *Handbook of posttraumatic stress disorder*. New York: Plenum.

Perls, F. (1973). *Gestalt therapy verbatim*. Moab, UT: Real People Press.

Powell, J. (1969). *Why am I afraid to tell you who I am?* Niles, IL: Argus Communications.

Powell, J. (1978). *Unconditional love*. Niles, IL: Argus Communications.

Pribram, K. H. (1981). Behaviorism, phenomenology, and holism in psychology: A scientific analysis. In R. S. Valle & R. von Eckartsberg (Eds.), *The metaphors of consciousness* (pp. 141–151). New York: Plenum.

Robinson, D. N. (1993). Is there a Jamesian tradition in psychology? *American Psychologist, 48*(6), 638–643.

Rogers, C. (1977). *Carl Rogers on personal power: Inner strength and its revolutionary impact*. New York: Delacorte.

Rychlak, J. F. (1993). A suggested principle of complementarity for psychology: In theory, not method. *American Psychologist, 48*(9), 933–942.

St. Clair, M. (1986). *Object relations and self psychology: An introduction*. Monterey, CA: Brooks/Cole.

Sautter, R. C. (1996). Standing up to violence. In S. E. Kender (Ed.), *Crime in America* (pp. 45–67). New York: H. H. Wilson.

Schuller, R. (1969). *Self-love: The dynamic force of success*. Old Tappan, NJ: Spire Books.

Schuller, R. (1977). *Peace of mind through possibility thinking*. Garden City, NY: Doubleday.

Skinner, B. F. (1948). *Walden Two*. New York: Macmillan.

Skinner, B. F. (1953). *Science and human behavior*. New York: Macmillan.

Skinner, B. F. (1971). *Beyond freedom and dignity*. New York: Knopf.

Snow, C. (1959). *The two cultures and the scientific revolution*. New York: Cambridge University Press.

Solomon, M. F. (1989). *Narcissism and intimacy: Love and marriage in an age of confusion*. New York: W. W. Norton.

Sperry, R. W. (1993). The impact and promise of the cognitive revolution. *American Psychologist, 48*(8), 878–885.

Staats, A. W. (1991). Unified positivism and unification psychology: Fad or new field? *American Psychologist, 46*(9), 899–912.

Tart, C. T. (Ed.). (1975). *Transpersonal psychologies*. New York: Harper & Row.

Torrance, E. P. (1969). *Creativity*. San Rafael, CA: Dimensions.

Turk, D. C., Meichenbaum, D. B. & Genest, M. (1983). *Pain and behavioral medicine: A cognitive-behavioral perspective*. New York: Guilford.

Vandenberg, B. (1991). Is epistemology enough? An existential consideration of development. *American Psychologist, 46*(12), 1278–1286.

Wallace, D. B. (1985). Giftedness and the construction of a creative life. In F. D. Horowitz & M. O'Brien (Eds.), *The gifted and talented: A developmental perspective* (pp. 361–385). Washington, DC: American Psychological Association.

Watts, A. (1961). *Psychotherapy east and west*. New York: Pantheon.

The Promise and Hope of Humanistic Psychology

DONALD MOSS

What is the present condition and what is the future of humanistic psychology? What is the significance of humanistic psychology (and transpersonal psychology) for psychology as a whole and for the well-being of humankind? Has humanistic psychology already contributed the best that it has to contribute? Or can it hope to provide new energies and ideas for scientific psychology and for humankind in the new millennium? This chapter will first address concerns about the survival of humanistic psychology and then identify the promise of humanistic psychology for the future.

THE CRISIS OF HUMANISTIC PSYCHOLOGY

The opening chapters of the present book emphasize that humanistic psychology began as a protest in a double sense, first, against the affluent and economically expansive, but bland culture of 1950s-era America, and second, against the failure of behavioral and Freudian psychologies to address the essence of humanness. Amedeo Giorgi, a pioneer in humanistic and especially phenomenological psychology in the United States, addressed the "crisis of humanistic psychology" in articles in 1987 and again in 1992. Giorgi insists that humanistic psychology must now come through with positive contributions or become no more than a footnote to the history of science. Others before have voiced this concern: "Rogers . . . warned us early on that if humanistic psychology turned out to be only a protest movement, its effects would be only temporary" (Giorgi, 1992b, p. 423). According to Giorgi, humanistic psychology originally offered three promises to the community of psychologists: "the human potential promise,

the promise of a better image of the human person, and the promise of better
and more relevant research" (1992b, p. 423). Failing to fully live up to these
promises, humanistic psychology now faces a crisis.

Giorgi sees humanistic psychology as having best fulfilled the promise of discovering higher human potential, but with a greater impact on the culture at large
than on the community of psychology. He also credits humanistic psychology
with putting pressure on psychologists to clarify their implicit models and assumptions about human nature, so that today psychologists are more cautious
about extrapolating from rats to humans. However, Giorgi critiques the failure
of humanistic psychologists to link their new concepts of "human" with the strong
humanistic traditions of antiquity and the Renaissance. Finally, Giorgi sees the
deepest failures of humanistic psychology in its inability to establish and promote
a new humanistic research paradigm, especially because much of the research
effort of humanistic psychologists has been frittered away in studies using methodologies based on the natural sciences that are not congruent with the topics
they are investigating (Giorgi, 1992b, 1987). We will return later in this chapter
to Giorgi's concern with the weaknesses of the research tradition in humanistic
psychology. (See also chapter 19 on Giorgi in part II of this book.)

Other humanistic psychologists may place the emphasis differently than Giorgi,
but they seem to agree that we face a crisis in contemporary humanistic psychology, if not in contemporary humanness. Arons (1992) points out that many
of the original idealistic aspirations of humanistic psychology have gone astray or
disclosed a dark side: "The popularized inner search crested in the late 1970's,
effectively terminating at Jonestown and its narcissism, almost immediately and
symmetrically replaced by Heritage U.S.A. and greed" (Arons, 1992, p. 172).
Further, the creativity that was set loose like a wildfire in the 1960s seems to have
since been tamed by computer-science models and co-opted by business-oriented
entrepreneurship models (Arons, 1992, p. 172). Arons sees an insidious trend in
which the meaninglessness of the 1950s was succeeded by the "back and forth
meanings" of the 1960s through the 1980s and now is culminating in a new
"meanness" in the 1990s.

Ultimately, humanistic psychology's original social and cultural critique carries
a message that has outlived the 1950s and 1960s. Man's inhumanity to man has
not vanished, only deepened, in the 1990s. The world, including the average
American community, is not a better place to raise a child than it was before
humanistic psychology began its world-changing efforts. Humanistic psychology
reechoes the older spiritual message that one does not live by bread alone. However, humanistic psychology's original answers to the crises in postmodern life
now seem either naïve or insufficient. The twin humanistic challenges of remaking
psychology and remaking our humanness remain.

REMAKING THE PROFESSION

Humanistic and transpersonal psychologies are not museum pieces. Humanistic and transpersonal psychologies have transformed psychology as a whole,

gaining credibility for the study of consciousness, emotional life, human self-determination, and spiritual experience. Cognitive and experiential psychology, phenomenological perspectives, and self psychology are all established elements within the discipline of psychology. Both in its research focus and in its methodologies, the mainstream of psychology is now a broader river, thanks to the hard work of humanistic psychologists.

Beyond this success in changing the rest of psychology, humanistic psychology and transpersonal psychology themselves continue to thrive. They are active, vibrant streams within that large river of psychology. Graduate students on many campuses across North America and abroad continue to undertake innovative dissertation projects investigating a bewildering variety of topics derived from the theories and methods of humanistic psychology. A recent visit with students from the Saybrook Institute, for example, found one graduate student eagerly discussing his research on the neuroimmune-system effects of Eastern meditative breathing practices and a would-be doctoral candidate brainstorming about how she might study the psychophysiological accompaniments of personal transformation aided by a visualization process (Moss, 1996).

Further, in nearly five decades the movement of humanistic psychology has developed a healthy array of diverse independent academic and institutional supports to sustain its momentum (DeCarvalho, 1992). Psychology departments with programs or concentrations in humanistic psychology include Sonoma State College in California, the State University of West Georgia, Saybrook Institute, Duquesne University, the University of Seattle, the University of Quebec at Montreal, Union Graduate School, the Fielding Institute, the Center for Humanistic Studies, and many other programs listed in the *Directory of Humanistic-Transpersonal Graduate Programs in North America*, an official publication of Division 32 of the American Psychological Association (APA) (Arons, 1996; see also deCarvalho, 1992, pp. 129–130).

A variety of professional associations also support the work of humanistic psychology. The Association for Humanistic Psychology (AHP), originally the American Association for Humanistic Psychology, was founded in 1962 and today has chapters in several European countries, Israel, India, Iceland, and Central and South America. AHP sponsors an annual national conference, international conferences, and the *Journal of Humanistic Psychology*. Division 32, the Humanistic Psychology Division within the APA, was formed after some controversy in 1971 and actively sponsors many educational activities and a divisional journal, the *Humanistic Psychologist*.

Both AHP and Division 32 of APA provide an organizational home for many psychologists with a transpersonal orientation. Both the *Journal for Humanistic Psychology* and the *Humanistic Psychologist* publish articles on transpersonal topics. There has been a Transpersonal Psychology Interest Group in APA since 1975, but to date efforts to establish a Division of Transpersonal Psychology have failed. Articles on transpersonal topics are also published in two transpersonally oriented journals, *ReVision*, founded in 1976, and *Transpersonal Review*, founded in 1995. The interested reader may also wish to consult the many information-packed articles in the special 1992 double issue of *The Humanistic Psychologist* titled "The Humanistic Movement in Psychology: History, Celebration, and Prospectus" (Wertz, 1992). The guest editor, Frederick J. Wertz, filled this special issue with a wealth of information on institutions, journals, and organizations supporting humanistic psychology.

In 1964 many of the founders of humanistic psychology—Gordon Allport, James Bugental, Abraham Maslow, Carl Rogers, Rollo May, and others—gathered at Old Saybrook, Connecticut, for a conference on the theoretical foundations of the new Third Force psychology (DeCarvalho, 1992, p. 127). This event is regarded by many as the real moment of birth for humanistic psychology. Plans are currently under way for a "New Saybrook Conference" to take place in 1998, probably at the State University of West Georgia, to rededicate and redirect the movement of humanistic psychology.

REMAKING THE HUMAN PERSON

Technologies for Personal Change

The four decades of humanistic psychology have produced an impressive technology for personal change. The many personal and body-awareness exercises of Gestalt therapy, the sensitivity-training practices of the T-group movement, the self-disclosure principles of Sidney Jourard, and the accumulated practices of the Rolfing and other body-therapy movements are just a few of the powerful strategies designed to enable human beings to accomplish dramatic increases in personal awareness and equally dramatic changes in emotional and behavioral habits. The American landscape has been transformed as these personal-change technologies have spread through our culture. From the 1960s, when middle-class housewives gathered in each other's homes for "consciousness raising," through the present, when classes on meditation, assertion, and self-esteem are available in most local churches and YMCAs, American culture has become richer by the addition of these basic life-enhancing skills.

Business environments have also benefited from an increased emphasis on optimal interpersonal environments, employees' self-esteem, and the cultivation of human potential in the workplace. It remains true today that the average employee responds better to an invitation and opportunity to actualize his or her productive potential within the company's pursuits of growth and profits than to purely externalized financial-incentive systems. Humanistic messages of encouragement and affirmation lie at the heart of effective motivational campaigns for individual employees and business teams.

Many of the popular motivational systems of the past two decades have relied on at least some aspects of humanistic psychology's Maslowian-Rogerian core principles (Covey, 1989; Peters & Waterman, 1982; Peters & Austin, 1985). Stephen Covey, in his most widely read work, cites Erich Fromm and challenges individuals to give up the illusory pathway of quick fixes and to undertake the difficult but rewarding process of true personal growth and change (Covey, 1989, pp. 35–40). Tom Peters tells us that true leadership consists in creative, symbolic (and we might say humanistic) uses of attention; the effective leader is a "cheerleader, enthusiast, nurturer of champions, hero finder, wanderer, dramatist, coach, facilitator, and builder" (Peters & Austin, 1985, p. 311). Even efforts to "reengineer the corporation," which sound strictly functional and antihumanistic, succeed in part because they bring the decision-making functions closer to the employees and work teams that carry out the basic work of the company (Hammer & Champy, 1993). As William Byham emphasizes in his popular book *Zapp: The Lightning of Empowerment* (1988), reengineering also reenergizes the human potential of employees who suddenly find that their business organization empowers their new initiatives and creativity instead of frustrating and blocking them. Jan Carlzon (1987) applied these reengineering principles to Scandinavian Airlines, redefining middle managers as facilitators to assist front-line personnel in doing their jobs. The energy this process unleashed turned the financially ailing airline around. One of Carlzon's principles is cited at the opening of the book: "Giving someone the freedom to take responsibility releases resources that would otherwise remain concealed" (1987, p. xv).

The educational profession has also drawn extensively on humanistic psychology and its concepts in seeking to optimize the classroom environment and to cultivate the individual student's spontaneous desire to learn (Rogers, 1969, 1983). Whoever has seen the spontaneous curiosity and delight of the four-year-old child piecing together the words on a picture book must be deeply troubled by the alienation and apathy of too many of today's middle-school students. What part does our educational approach play in this deadening of once-lively human interest?

Rogers's concepts of unconditional positive regard, congruence, and empathy continue to bear fruit in the classroom. When each individual student feels accepted, "prized," and valued by the teacher, and when each student perceives the teacher as genuine, interested, and understanding the child's perspective, the conditions for both learning and personal growth are optimal. Even in today's "outcomes"-oriented classroom, these basic humanistic principles provide the interpersonal foundation for a positive classroom environment.

Tom Peters, whose *In Search of Excellence* and *A Passion for Excellence* have deeply influenced both educators and corporate leaders, conveys a deeply humanistic vision of the educational process and the leadership process. In a powerful chapter on "Excellence in School Leadership," Peters and his coauthor Nancy Austin quote a number of educators from successful American secondary schools and elaborate a number of critical principles of humanistic school leadership (Peters & Austin, 1985, pp. 465–489). According to Peters and Austin, we must provide an educational climate of caring, seek strategies to turn every child into a winner, treat children as adults, with dignity and respect, and find ways to help each child experience himself or herself as part of the school community or, better yet, of the school family.

A Humanistic Ethos and Value System

Humanistic psychology continues to convey a vision of personal growth and personal integrity that captures the imagination of individuals in the most diverse sectors of contemporary life, from graduate students of management and industrial engineering to idealistic high-school psychology students. The vision of humanistic psychology conveys an implicit and explicit ethical framework of increasing importance in a society where many individuals have lost their rootedness in religious traditions. Whether an individual chooses to remain rooted in traditional religion, borrows from the world religions in a daily cultivation of meditative practices, or embraces the skepticism and agnosticism of "secular humanism," the ethical contributions of humanistic psychologists remain of lasting significance.

Abraham Maslow, Carl Rogers, Erich Fromm, and Rollo May, among others, have criticized the value-free outlook of much of modern science and have called on psychologists to clarify the ethical dilemmas facing each human being. Individuals need to discover a new "high ground" on which to stand, and these humanistic authors have each sought a basis in humanistic studies to clarify what that high ground is and where it can be found.

Maslow and Rogers each described ethical aspirations in the human being as flowing spontaneously from the process of self-actualization and growth, as something innate to human nature (DeCarvalho, 1991). Maslow discovered a fairly consistent set of core values among those persons he identified as higher-functioning or more self-actualized, regardless of social class, education, or creed, including such virtues as autonomy, self-acceptance, spontaneity, and the capacity to love deeply. His sample included such persons as Albert Schweitzer, Jane Addams, and Eleanor Roosevelt. Maslow, therefore, regarded these values as inherent humanistic virtues, derivative of the person's growth toward self-actualization.

Carl Rogers also emphasized an innate spontaneous aspiration toward higher values, evident as soon as we are able to create the "necessary and sufficient conditions" for spontaneous inwardly directed growth. Rogers optimistically assumed that once we assist the individual to overcome inward and outward obstacles to freedom, he or she will spontaneously move to become what he or she truly is, that is, to actualize his or her innate identity. Rogers, like Fromm and Maslow, believed that we can trust such positive self-actualization to lead to positive moral behavior.

Like Maslow and Rogers, Erich Fromm described the humanistic conscience as an inward and spontaneous urging toward positive actions that develops in the course of productive living. Fromm, however, emphasized that this humanistic conscience is especially based on the experience of social solidarity with other human beings. Fromm's socialist views and his immediate personal experiences with Nazism and fascism in Europe prevented any naïveté about automatic goodness in human beings. Fromm was one of the first to describe the human retreat from freedom, in which individuals abdicate any responsibility for the mass evil in which they participate (1941). Fromm also continued his entire life to search for a deeper understanding of the roots of human destructiveness through extensive research on individual personality, sociological forces, genetics, and animal behavior (1973). (See chapter 18 on Fromm in part II of this book.)

Diana Baumrind also developed a radically social perspective on humanistic ethics, influenced by the Catholic Worker movement and the philosophy of personalism. Baumrind emphasized an ethics based on "reasonable relatedness," right conduct in relation to others, and a reconciling of divergent social interests (Baumrind, 1992). The reader is referred to chapter 15 on Baumrind in part II of this book for a more complete elaboration of Baumrind's ethical theory.

Otto F. Bollnow was a German educator and philosopher close to the existential, phenomenological, and humanistic traditions that so strongly influenced humanistic psychology. In an essay on educating the human character toward peace, Bollnow made comments relevant to this debate on humanistic ethics (1966/1987). He observed that it is not enough to develop concepts or theories of peace, which may have little lingering impact on character. For Bollnow, the roots of true ethical progress lie in reshaping the foundations of character.[1] According to Bollnow, we must seek a way to provide individuals, especially in their formative years, with opportunities that "awaken an insight, or call forth an experience" (1966/1987, p. 87). Just as the person who has once vividly perceived the mathematical relationship that 2 times 2 equals 4 will never be able to perceive otherwise, Bollnow believed that there are moral experiences that transform the person in an irrevocable manner. He mentioned a number of experimental approaches in Germany toward creating such moral experiences, including cooperative voluntary service projects similar to the American Vista Volunteers or Peace Corps programs, which provide young people with a sense of solidarity beyond parochial boundaries. Bollnow, like Maslow and Rogers, believed that such experiences can only awaken what has already been laid out in human nature, yet he believed that within that broad compass of what is humanly possible, ethical education can prevail: "Whoever has once experienced the deep satisfaction involved in a self-surrendering activity, is thereby irrevocably transported beyond the conditions of a purely passive and hedonistic life" (1966/1987, p. 87).

Rollo May spent much of his career highlighting a variety of human ethical challenges. His choice was never to simplify or to offer facile reassurance. Life, in May's view, is difficult and complex, and the wonders of modern psychology cannot make it less so. May doubted that human beings always or automatically "grow" toward higher decisions. May meditated at length on the human capacity for good and evil and believed that each person must come to terms with the "daimonic" in his or her own personality or risk acting out this evil mindlessly (May, 1969). May studied the human valuing process phenomenologically and emphasized the never-ending work of becoming an aware, responsible, and moral adult. He felt that the true ethical task of humanistic psychology was not to provide reassuring or soothing guidelines for human action, which might lull the individual to an ethical sleep, but rather to prick the conscience and awaken the sleeping soul (DeCarvalho, 1991).

REMAKING THE SOCIAL WORLD: FACING THE CRITICS OF HUMANISTIC PSYCHOLOGY

Humanistic psychology has from the beginning inspired social activism. Howard (1992) has identified social activism and the pursuit of human self-determination as two of the pillars of humanistic psychology. Yet, as chapter 13 has reminded us, the world is not necessarily a more humane place after four decades of humanistic social activism. The critiques by Lasch (1979) and Solomon (1989) of the humanistically oriented movement for personal and political liberation were cited in chapter 6. To recap briefly, Lasch asserts that the drive for greater sexual freedoms, undertaken for the humanization of individuals, has had a dramatic backlash effect, depersonalizing sex and disconnecting physical release from deeper intimacy. Similarly, Solomon observes that self-assertion, while intended to enhance personal development, can deteriorate into a primitive form of narcissism and entitlement. Lasch (1979) interpreted many of the ideas of humanistic psychology as an extension of nineteenth-century individualism, culminating in an isolation of the self, self-absorption, and self-indulgence.

Conservative commentators have continued to critique the excesses of social liberalism, including many concepts and attitudes central to the humanistic movement. Bork (1996) expressed a conservative critique of the liberal political heritage and highlighted its dangers for American culture. He traced the rise of liberalism in European history and identified its central trends as a movement away from social restraint and toward a growing emphasis on individuality. Bork asserted that the liberating force of liberalism had historically been held within broad limits by religion, traditional morality, and the law until the 1960s, when these bulwarks against excess dissolved and the full force of individual liberation produced cultural chaos. Among the destructive anticultural trends Bork identified are a coarsening of popular entertainment, the celebration of sex and violence, and a rejection of all normative standards.

We could elaborate on the many similar criticisms of the political and social principles associated with humanistic psychology. However, the consistency of such critiques and the acknowledged failure of many social experiments and many governmental programs seemingly based on humanistic principles challenge us to a reassessment of both the values and the assumptions of humanistic theories. Positive, well-intentioned goals pursued by misguided means can still cause intense, widespread human suffering. To have one's heart in the right place is no excuse for failing to recognize that many long-favored solutions have failed. In summary, one of the challenges for a revitalized humanistic psychology is to recognize which of its own core political beliefs reflect personal prejudice based on the sociological accidents of humanistic psychology's birth in the turbulent 1960s, and which principles have stood the test of time and closer scrutiny.

It would be presumptuous in this context to provide "the answers" to this need for a revitalization of humanistic psychology. Rather, this author believes that we may benefit from performing a "phenomenological reduction" on our assumptions about humanistic social change, loosening our attachment to specific beliefs and favored solutions, and opening ourselves both to new visions and to critical and objective means of reviewing the real impact of future social experiments. Humanistic psychology remains tied to the tradition of scientific psychology and would do well to continually assess and measure the impact of our social activism and community interventions.

We can also recognize now that the vision of remaking the world in a perfectly humane mold was naïve. Rollo May cited Carl Jung's observation that "the serious problems of human life are never solved, and if it seems that they have been solved, something important has been lost" (May, 1969, p. 308). The challenge for humanistic psychology in the future will be to recognize the eternal problems and address them anew, with new strategies, in the new century. The poor may always be with us, and the hungry may always hunger, but we need not walk complacently away from our fellow humans.

Further, the humanistic challenge of remaking the world must in the future be revisioned in global terms. Making a more comfortable and self-actualizing life for middle-class suburban Americans while the inner cities of America or the ethnic enclaves of Bosnia or Rwanda are engulfed in violence and brutality is not only self-centered but short sighted. We must take seriously the words of the poet John Donne that "no man is an island" and "no man stands alone." A humanistically oriented civilization, a civilization that cares about and nurtures the humanity of its citizens, will endure only as long as it actively addresses the problems and suffering of its least citizen and its farthest neighbor. This can no longer mean paternalism, an external imposition of a perceived "superior" group's solutions onto a perceived "inferior" group, but it must mean conceiving community in the broadest and most global terms.

REMAKING PSYCHOLOGY: SUSTAINING A VITAL RESEARCH TRADITION

Abraham Maslow was trained at Cornell University and the University of Wisconsin at Madison in the strongest traditions of experimental psychology and behaviorism. Shortly after earning his Ph.D. he became dissatisfied with the predominant reliance on laboratory and animal studies in American psychology (DeCarvalho, 1992, pp. 112–114). Later he became critical of the reliance on abnormal and psychologically disturbed individuals for much of the research and theory on human behavior (Maslow, 1962, 1969). Maslow became convinced that a central mission of humanistic psychology must be to revolutionize research because the behavioristic and experimental model of psychological research explicitly shut out too much of the personhood of the highly functioning human beings he wished to understand. Maslow criticized the tendency of natural scientific research to impose its categories, preconceptions, and measurements prior to any real understanding of a phenomenon. Instead, he endorsed a more phenomenological approach with a greater receptiveness to experiencing phenomena as they present themselves (Maslow, 1969).

This chapter began with a reference to Amedeo Giorgi, a pioneer in the development of a research approach and method based on a humanistic recognition of the uniqueness of the human species and of each human being. Giorgi believes that the greatest and potentially fatal failure of humanistic psychology is its inability to discover and rally around a research methodology that is appropriate and adequate to investigate human beings in their full existential breadth. Too much psychological research has involved the investigation of trivial phenomena that are easier to adapt to laboratory experiments and/or to statistical research design.

Giorgi has criticized humanistic psychologists for paying lip service to the need for a new humanistic approach to research and then falling into the rut of using the same quantitative and experimental research methods based on the natural sciences. Giorgi believes that many well-intentioned humanistic researchers fall prey to the seductive arguments of "philosophical naturalism," which holds that human beings, as biological organisms with evolutionary, emergent properties such as consciousness and will, can still be studied by the same natural scientific methods as animals. (The reader may also return to chapter 8 in the present volume for Halling and Carroll's discussion of the problem of research method in humanistic psychology.)

Even the revered founders of humanistic psychology are vulnerable to methodological criticism. Sidney Jourard, for example, conducted research on self-disclosure that inspired hundreds of later studies. Yet review of Jourard's works shows that he spent more time surveying and measuring the impact of self-disclosure than he did on reaching a phenomenological understanding of what self-disclosure actually involves. The danger here, like that with intelligence and IQ tests, is that psychologists too quickly settle for tacit, never-articulated operational definitions, such as "Self-disclosure is what Jourard's Self-Disclosure Questionnaire measures." Then the rush for results leads to a multiplicity of studies based on the same quantitative measures and unexamined operational definitions. Yet as chapter 6 showed, at least two studies have suggested that inconsistencies in the literature on the impact of self-disclosure may be due to internal inconstencies within the questionnaire (Raphael & Dohrenwend, 1987) or to failure of the scale to measure the kind of self-disclosure to which Jourard's theory referred (Bayne, 1977).

Giorgi has spent much of his career developing and refining a "human science approach" that uses qualitative research methods, derived originally from phenomenological psychology, that are useful for the investigation of a variety of human experiences and situations. The emphasis of this human science approach is to reach an understanding of human action and experience, not an explanation. Giorgi's concern is with a contextual illumination of a human situation, not a causal reference to mechanisms (Giorgi, 1970, 1990, 1992a). (See chapter 19 on Giorgi in part II of this volume for a more detailed exposition of Giorgi's approach to research.)

Davidson (1992) and Polkinghorne (1992) have echoed Giorgi's insistence that humanistic psychology must seek renewal through greater focus on research methods congruent with the humanity of the research subject. Davidson concluded that "while humanistic psychology has been strong on imagination, it can only benefit from a sustained and serious consideration of method. . . . Science may liberate as much as constrict" (1992, pp. 152–153). Similarly, Polkinghorne criticized the failure of humanistic psychology to have sufficient impact on American academic psychology and asserted that "the particular task of humanistic psychology, because it is part of the organization of American psychologists, is to bring methodological changes within the discipline" (1992, p. 236; 1983).

There is also an international association dedicated to the development and propagation of qualitative methodologies, International Human Science Research (IHSR). IHSR, coordinated by the Department of Psychology at Seattle University, publishes a newsletter and sponsors annual conferences. The 16th annual conference in 1997 was held in Trondheim, Norway, and the 17th in 1998 in Sitka, Alaska. IHSR has supported a fruitful networking of humanistically oriented researchers in Europe, the Americas, and now worldwide.

At this time there remain a number of research traditions within humanistic psychology with obvious convergencies and divergencies. A look at the research culture at the leading graduate programs in humanistic psychology shows this diversity and encourages hope in the vitality of both humanistic psychology and transpersonal psychology.

Duquesne University's Department of Psychology has supported an aggressive research program since 1964, utilizing a variety of empirical phenomenological methodologies advanced by Adrian van Kaam, Amedeo Giorgi, William Fischer, Constance T. Fischer, and Rolf von Eckartsberg (see Giorgi, Fischer, & von Eckartsberg, 1971; Giorgi, Fischer, & Murray, 1975). A 1990 department publication lists over one hundred pages of books, articles, chapters, and dissertations by Duquesne psychology students and faculty, most of them phenomenological investigations (Knowles, Lydon, & Peiritsch, 1990). A supplement produced in 1996 lists thirty-two years of phenomenologically oriented doctoral dissertations (Duquesne University, 1996). A sampling of titles, along with author and year, provides some impression of the breadth of the doctoral research (dissertations, theses, and articles in this section will be cited only by title, author and year, based on the sources cited): "Being Disappointed: A Phenomenological Psychological Analysis," Michael P. Daehn, 1988; "The Use of Diazepam in an Effort to Transform Being Anxious," Patricia E. Deegan, 1983; "The Lived Experience of Returning to Heroin Use after a Period of Abstinence," Priscilla Friday, 1992; "Experiencing the Sacred in Everyday Life: An Empirical Phenomenological

Study," Will Adams, 1993; "The Movement from Unsuccessful to Successful Smoking Cessation: An Empirical Phenomenological Study of Self-initiated Change," Josef F. Tybl, 1993; "Allergic Reaction: A Phenomenological Study of Persons' Participation in Disease," Peggy Moody, 1992; and "Psychospiritual Developmental Paths for Women Who Have Difficulty Praying to Masculine Images of the Divine: A Phenomenological-Dialogal Study," Kathleen Mulrenin, 1995.

West Georgia College (now the State University of West Georgia) began a master's program in humanistic psychology in the late 1960s under the guidance of Mike Arons and the strong influence of Maslow's orientation. A list compiled by Christopher Aanstoos (1996) shows master's theses on humanistic topics from 1968 through 1991, and a supplementary list (Rice, 1996) shows master's theses through the time of compilation. Topics are diverse from the beginning, reflecting the full range of interests within humanistic psychology, from hypnotic susceptibility and religious experience to "myths of the Aquarian age." Methodologies sound predominantly quantitative at first, including such titles as "Determination of Factorial Composition of a Purported Measure of Self-Concept to Determine Feasibility of Further Development and Validation as a Self-Concept Measure," Charles E. Kennedy, 1970, and "Blink Rate of Cerebral Palsied, TMR, EMR, and Normal Children as Related to Intelligence Test Scores," Mary Ann Watson, 1972. Over the decades more specifically qualitative and phenomenological methodologies are evident, although empirical studies on the outcome of various clinical, psychophysiological, and experiential interventions also appear. A sampling of recent theses includes "Using Electromyographic Biofeedback in the Battle against Alcoholism," Victor R. Gonzales, 1988; "The Therapeutic Wilderness Experience," John Stephen Cockerman, 1989; "Rape from the Rapist Point of View," Jeffery T. Coalson, 1992; and "Alternative Healing and Cancer Patients: A Literary Review," Jennifer D. Reese, 1995.

Seattle University has a master's program in existential-phenomenological therapeutic psychology. The master's program does not include a thesis, but the faculty is active in research and has developed a dialogical phenomenological method that can be applied to topics ranging from forgiveness to social activism. Recent faculty publications (Halling, 1996) include "The Theory and Practice of Dialogal Research," Steen Halling, 1991; "When the Other Falls from Grace: A Phenomenological Analysis of Interpersonal Disillusionment," Steen Halling, 1996; "Integrating Political Societal Concerns in Psychotherapy," Lane Gerber, 1990; and "The Recovery of Will in Persons with AIDS," Kevin Krycka, 1997.

The faculty at the Saybrook Institute has supported an eclectic approach to research, exposing students to a wide range of both quantitative and qualitative research methods and encouraging dissertation research drawing on any methodology that can be shown to be congruent with its topic. A sampling of recent Saybrook dissertations and master's theses shows this broad eclecticism in topic and method (Saybrook Institute, 1996): "A Psychosocial and Psychoneuroimmunological Study of Patients with Rheumatoid Arthritis," Roberta Provenzano, 1994; "The Phenomenology of the Experience of Critical Thinking," Lyn Freeman, 1994; "Perspectives of a Public Sector Strike: An Ethnographic Field Study," Robert Hammer, 1995; "The Effects of a Specialized Three-Part Breathing Technique on Human Health: A Psychophysiological-bioenergetic Perspective," Ranjie Singh, 1995; and "Contemporary Spiritual Dream Reports: Their Content and Significance," Kira Lynn Casto, 1996.

Methodology: Uniformity or Diversity

Giorgi advocates a unification of humanistic psychology around a qualitative approach to research. He has cited many practical examples showing how human phenomena are grossly distorted by natural scientific investigative procedures (1970, 1987). From the beginning, however, humanistic psychology has been characterized by its open-mindedness and eclecticism. The strength of humanistic psychology has been diversity, and never uniformity. The reigning principle in human scientific discussion of research, following Maslow, Rogers, and Giorgi, remains that the research method must be congruent with the phenomena under investigation. Humanistic psychologists pursue a diverse and expansive range of human phenomena, ranging from obvious experiential topics such as the structure of emotional experiencing through the complex psychophysiological investigations of the neuroimmune effects of specific cognitive-behavioral practices to the clinical effectiveness of various therapeutic interventions.

Paul Ricoeur, the French scholar of phenomenology and hermeneutics, has commented that many of the phenomena of human behavior call for a *mixed discourse*; that is, we find ourselves at the interface between objective biological processes and lived, experiential processes (Ricoeur, 1970, 1974). At such moments we stand at the crossing point between divergent systems of interpretation and explanation (Ricoeur, 1970). Maurice Merleau-Ponty also situated behavior at the middle point between objective processes and subjective phenomena (Merleau-Ponty, 1942/1963).

An entire investigation may lie at an interface point, calling for a mixture of methodologies. We may consider, for example, an investigation of the changing field of consciousness when a subject is guided by electronically mediated neurofeedback to cultivate an altered, alpha-theta–dominant brain state (Peniston & Kukolski, 1989; Moss, in press). In such an investigation the researcher utilizes a computer to perform an immediate real-time quantitative algorithm, often a fast-Fourier transform, to monitor and visually display the cortical activity to the subject. Then the subject's own descriptions of his or her altered mode of experiencing can be subjected to a careful, qualitative, phenomenological analysis. Finally, the impact of this neurofeedback training over time on several subjects' successful abstinence from alcohol and drug use must be tracked and measured quantitatively to demonstrate clinical effectiveness and cost-effectiveness for our evidence-oriented and economically minded health care managers.

A review of the dissertation and thesis titles cited earlier demonstrates that this example of an investigation calling for a mixed methodological discourse is quite common. The mission of today's humanistic psychology appears to demand a continued reliance on an eclectic combination of innovative qualitative descriptive methods, objective psychophysiological methods, and rigorous quantitative methods that measure the objective impact of a variety of humanistic and transpersonal interventions.

Chapter 6 of this volume discussed the research of James Pennebaker and his colleagues, who began with the familiar humanistic concept that self-disclosure is beneficial for personal well-being and utilized a creative and methodologically precise series of investigations to illuminate the true complexity of self-disclosure. Pennebaker's 1995 anthology *Emotion, Disclosure, and Health* is a beautiful example of a multidisciplinary and multimethodological approach to illuminating a single phenomenon. The volume combines physiological investigations of the impact of self-disclosure on the body with hermeneutic discussions of the varying cultural meanings of self-disclosure.

Remaking Scientific Method and Remaking the Social World: Knowledge and Social Interest

Positivistic sciences, including those psychologies that emphasize empirical investigation designed along the lines of the natural sciences, typically conceptualize science in isolation as the simple pursuit of a truth that is understood as an objective, neutral fact. In contrast, the European school of critical theory, steeped in the historical and political insights of Hegel, Marx, and their twentieth-century heirs, emphasizes the linkages among methodology, knowledge, theory, and social action. Jürgen Habermas (1968/1971) asserts that a theory of knowledge is already a social theory and highlights the emancipatory consequences of scientific knowledge. Habermas maintains that the positivistic idea of a pure methodological objectivity is based on a historical forgetfulness of the intertwining of scientific methodology with the "objective self-formative process of the human species" (Habermas, 1968/1971, p. 5). In other words, human beings create their sciences in the image of that human society that they are in the process of constructing. Knowledge and social interest are originally one. Research is in part a handservant to social action. Research in this sense falls squarely at the center of humanistic psychology, with its original emphasis on social action and human liberation (Howard, 1992).

The German philosopher Hegel, in his "dialectic of the beautiful soul" in his *Phenomenology of Mind* (1807/1967, pp. 644–679), illustrated the dangers of choosing purity over active involvement. An individual may preserve himself or herself from personal evil by withdrawing and maintaining a pervasive detachment from the hustle and bustle of life.[2] In detachment, the moral conscience becomes self-satisfied and complacent, turns in upon itself, and lives in fear of "sullying the magnificence of its interior by action" (Hegel, 1807/1967, p. 666; Lauer, 1993, p. 253). However, the individual who defines his or her purity by such detachment becomes a tacit accomplice in the greater evils of the world, failing to face the challenges and missions of his or her larger situation. In Hegel's ethical philosophy, knowledge and the duty for action are paired. The beautiful soul will not risk action, but prefers to talk and adopt beautiful attitudes: "instead of acting it proves its righteousness by the expression of excellent attitudes" (Hegel, 1807/ 1967, p. 671; Lauer, 1993, p. 254). Similarly, humanistic psychology sacrifices too much when it refuses all quantitative methodologies because this step isolates humanistic psychology from many of the pressing questions of modern life, including such questions as the neurobiological roots of violence, the relative efficacy of clinical techniques, and the real outcomes of interventions for social change.

It is not only the subject matter of an investigation that should decree the methodology, but also the questions posed in the investigation and the potential action that the research empowers. This discussion does not imply that all research should be subordinated to immediate practical objectives. The decades of Nazi and Soviet misuse and perversion of the sciences show the dangers of subordinating science too closely to political or social objectives. Habermas has acknowledged the value of the myth of methodological purity in sustaining the autonomy of the sciences: The myth has minimized the political exploitation or external direction of the sciences (Habermas, 1968/1971, p. 315). Nevertheless, when an entire program of research draws in upon itself, into a methodological elegance without consequence, alarm bells should sound. Psychology in our century has too often pursued methodological sophistication at the risk of existential irrelevance; humanistic psychology must be careful to avoid the same temptation.

The larger action context of research also has immediate methodological consequences. For example, a researcher seeking to understand the meaning of an eating disorder for an individual would do well to apply phenomenological methods and to interrogate the experience of such an individual. However, a researcher seeking to prove to the federal Food and Drug Administration that a specific medication reduces binging in a clinically efficacious and cost-effective way will do well to rely on double-blind controlled studies with a quantitative data analysis. Phenomenological methods neither aim at nor produce evidence of causal linkages (Hollon, 1996, p. 1026). The individual's account of his or her experience with a medication, for example, is subject to the same kind of misattributions that mark verbal report and personal inference in general. Unfortunately, the average person has no accurate knowledge of what most contributed to his or her improvement (Nisbett & Ross, 1980; Nisbett & Wilson, 1977; Hollon, 1996).[3]

Both qualitative and quantitative research can serve social action. Wertz (1985), for example, utilized a phenomenological descriptive method to illuminate the experiences of individuals who had been criminally victimized. Such a phenomenological study sparks action because it successfully draws attention to individuals who suffer the unintended consequences of social policy. Similarly, a number of phenomenological investigations of clinical and social phenomena—retirement, the death of a child, obesity, and AIDS—have increased the understanding for the experiences and needs of the individuals involved, with potential consequences for clinical intervention and social action (Brice, 1991; Hornstein & Wapner, 1984; Moss, 1992; Murphy, 1992). The diversity of issues facing humanistic psychology in today's troubled world dictates the need for a variety of methodologies, both qualitative and quantitative. Humanistic psychology dare not risk irrelevancy. I believe that we must risk impurity in methodology in order to have a broader impact on the social and cultural evils of our time.

THE EMERGING SHAPE OF HUMANISTIC PSYCHOLOGY

A final question facing humanistic psychology is whether to remain a separate room within the house of psychology or to seek greater impact on the entirety of psychology and life. The history of humanistic psychology to date shows evidence of both processes: Humanistic psychology has contributed basic concepts and perspectives to the rest of psychology, with its greatest impact on clinical/therapeutic psychology and personality theory. At the same time, humanistic psychology has tended to become one more closed room in psychology, with separate division, meetings, journals, and adherents. This latter process of compartmentalization creates the danger of lessening humanistic psychology's impact on the profession as a whole, rendering it marginal or irrelevant. The great founders of humanistic psychology addressed their most moving books not only to the entire field of psychology, but also to the educated layperson.

Following the same Hegelian principles cited earlier, this author sees comfort but also danger in any compartmentalization of humanistic psychology. It is too comfortable to talk only to sympathetic audiences, to publish one's research only in sympathetic journals, and to apply oneself only to those topics and applications familiar already within humanistic circles. We must do more than cultivate our own "beautiful souls" (Hegel, 1807/1967); both our profession and our world are in continuous need of transformation.

All of the institutional supports delineated in this chapter—the journals, schools, and associations—are necessary and helpful to the survival and prosperity of humanistic psychology. However, we dare not contain the fire and vigor of humanistic theory and action in such small rooms or narrow channels. The mandate of humanistic psychology must remain one of enunciating its humanizing message over and over again in new contexts within psychology and the surrounding world. Humanistic psychology will be most meaningful if it sparks the conscience and awareness of industrial psychologists, psychophysiologists, social psychologists, neuroscientists, and others throughout psychology, and if it inspires change as well in other specialties throughout education, the health professions, and the larger world of educated persons. It is my hope that this book will aid in that never-ending mission.

NOTES

1. The origin of the English word *ethics* lies in the Greek root *ethos*, referring to human character (Lauer, 1993, p. 17n).

2. Hegel's historical reference for the "beautiful soul" was the movement of German romanticism, especially figures such as Novalis. Humanistic psychology has frequently been compared to the romantic movement, both for its idealistic aspirations and its occasional naïveté.

3. Elsewhere Giorgi (1986, 1989) demonstrates conceptually and empirically the positive significance of verbal reports for research.

REFERENCES

Aanstoos, C. M. (1996). *M. A. theses completed at West Georgia College.* Personal communication.

Arons, M. (1992). Creativity, humanistic psychology, and the American zeitgeist. *Humanistic Psychologist, 20*(2–3), 158–174.

Arons, M. (Ed.). (1996). *Directory of humanistic-transpersonal graduate programs in North America* (5th ed.). Carrollton, GA: Psychology Department, State University of West Georgia.

Baumrind, D. (1992). Leading an examined life: The moral dimension of daily conduct. In W. M. Kurtines, M. Axmitia, & J. L. Gewirtz (Eds.), *The role of values in psychology and human development* (pp. 256–280). New York: John Wiley.

Bayne, R. (1977). The meaning and measurement of self-disclosure. *British Journal of Guidance and Counseling, 5*(2), 159–166.

Bollnow, O. F. (1966/1987). *Crisis and new beginning (Krise und neuer Anfang).* (D. Moss, Trans.). Pittsburgh, PA: Duquesne University Press.

Bork, R. H. (1996). *Slouching towards Gomorrah: Modern liberalism and American decline.* New York: Regan Books.

Brice, C. W. (1991). What forever means: An empirical existential-phenomenological investigation of maternal mourning. *Journal of Phenomenological Psychology, 22*(1), 16–38.

Byham, W. C. (with Cox, J.) (1988). *Zapp: The lightning of empowerment.* New York: Harmony Books.

Carlzon, J. (1987). *Moments of truth.* New York: Harper & Row.

Covey, S. (1989). *The seven habits of highly effective people.* New York: Simon & Schuster.

Davidson, L. (1992). Philosophical foundations of humanistic psychology. *Humanistic Psychologist, 20*(2–3), 136–157.

DeCarvalho, R. J. (1991). *The founders of humanistic psychology.* New York: Praeger Publishers.

DeCarvalho, R. J. (1992). The institutionalization of humanistic psychology. *Humanistic Psychology 20*(2–3).

Duquesne University. (1996, May). *Dissertation titles.* Duquesne University, Department of Psychology, Pittsburgh, PA.

Fromm, E. (1941). *Escape from freedom.* New York: Farrar & Rinehart.

Fromm, E. (1973). *The anatomy of human destructiveness.* Greenwich, CT: Fawcett Premier Books.

Giorgi, A. (1970). *Psychology as a human science.* New York: Harper & Row.

Giorgi, A. (1986). Theoretical justification for the use of descriptions in psychological research. In P. Ashworth, A. Giorgi, & A. deKoning, *Qualitative research in psychology* (pp. 3–22). Pittsburgh, PA: Duquesne University Press.

Giorgi, A. (1987). The crisis of humanistic psychology. *Humanistic Psychologist, 15*, 5–20.

Giorgi, A. (1989). An example of harmony between descriptive reports and behavior. *Journal of Phenomenological Psychology, 20*(1), 60–88.

Giorgi, A. (1990). A phenomenological vision for psychology. In W. J. Baker, M. E. Hyland, R. van Hezewizk, & S. Terwee (Eds.), *Recent travels in theoretical psychology, vol. 2* (pp. 27–36). New York: Springer Verlag.

Giorgi, A. (1992a). The idea of human science. *Humanistic Psychologist, 20* (2–3), 202–217.

Giorgi, A. (1992b). Whither humanistic psychology? *Humanistic Psychologist, 20*(2–3), 422–438.

Giorgi, A., Fischer, W. F., & von Eckartsberg (Eds.). (1971). *Duquesne studies in phenomenological psychology,* vol. 1. Pittsburgh, PA: Duquesne University Press.

Giorgi, A., Fischer, W. F., & Murry, E. (Eds.). (1975). *Duquesne studies in phenomenological psychology,* vol. 2. Pittsburgh, PA: Duquesne University Press.

Giorgi, A., Knowles, R., & Smith, D. L. (Eds.). *Duquesne studies in phenomenological psychology,* vol. 3. Pittsburgh, PA: Duquesne University Press.

Habermas, J. (1968/1971). *Knowledge and human interests* (J. J. Shapiro, Trans.). Boston: Beacon Press.

Halling, S. (1996). Personal communication.

Hammer, M., & Champy, J. (1993). *Reengineering the corporation: A manifesto for business revolution.* New York: HarperCollins.

Hegel, G.W.F. (1807/1967). *The phenomenology of mind* (J. B. Baillie, Trans.). New York: Harper Torchbook.

Hollon, S. D. (1996). The efficacy and effectiveness of psychotherapy relative to medications. *American Psychologist, 51*(10), 1025–1030.

Hornstein, G. A., & Wapner, S. (1984). The experience of the retiree's social network during the transition to retirement. In C. Aanstoos (Ed.), *Exploring the lived world: Readings in phenomenological psychology. West Georgia College Studies in the Social Sciences, 23*, 119–136.

Howard, G. (1992). Projecting humanistic values into the future: Freedom and social activism. *Humanistic Psychologist, 20*(2–3), 260–272.

Knowles, R. T., Lydon, J. A., & Peiritsch, J. D. (1990). *List of publications of the Department of Psychology.* Duquesne University, Pittsburgh, PA.

Lasch, C. (1979). *The culture of narcissism: American life in an age of diminishing expectations.* New York: W. W. Norton & Co.

Lauer, Q. (1993). *A reading of Hegel's "Phenomenology of spirit"* (2nd ed.). New York: Fordham University Press.

Maslow, A. H. (1962). *Toward a psychology of being.* New York: Van Nostrand.

Maslow, A. H. (1969). *The psychology of science: A reconnaissance.* Chicago: Henry Regnery Co.

May, R. (1969). *Love and will.* New York: W. W. Norton & Co.

Merleau-Ponty, M. (1963). *The structure of behavior* (A. L. Fisher, Trans.). Boston: Beacon Press. (Original work published 1942)

Moss, D. (1992). Obesity, objectification, and identity: The encounter with the body as an object in obesity. In D. Leder (Ed.), *The body in medical thought and practice* (pp. 179–196). Dordrecht, The Netherlands: Kluwer Academic Publishers.

Moss, D. (1996 August). Personal communication with Saybrook students.

Moss, D. (in press). Phenomenology, applied psychophysiology, and behavioral medicine. In R. Kall (Ed.), *Applied neurophysiology and brain biofeedback*. Trevose, PA: FUTUREHEALTH.

Murphy, J. (1992) The body with AIDS: A post-structuralist approach. In D. Leder (Ed.), *The body in medical thought and practice* (pp. 155–176). Dordrecht, The Netherlands: Kluwer Academic Publishers.

Nisbett, R. E., & Ross, L. (1980). *Human inference: Strategies and shortcomings of social judgment*. Englewood Cliffs, NJ: Prentice-Hall.

Nisbett, R. E., & Wilson, T. D. (1977). Telling more than we can know: Verbal reports on mental processes. *Psychological Review, 84*, 231–259.

Peniston, E. G., & Kukolski, P. J. (1989). Alpha-theta brainwave training and beta-endorphin levels in alcoholics. *Alcoholism: Clinical and Experimental Research, 13*, 271–279.

Pennebaker, J. W. (Ed.). (1995). *Emotion, disclosure, and health*. Washington, DC: American Psychological Association.

Peters, T., & Austin, N. (1985). *A passion for excellence: The leadership difference*. New York: Warner.

Peters, T., & Waterman, R. H. (1982). *In search of excellence*. New York: Warner.

Polkinghorne, D. E. (1983). *Methodology for the human sciences*. Albany: State University of New York Press.

Polkinghorne, D. E. (1992). Research methodology in humanistic psychology. *Humanistic Psychologist, 20*(2–3), 218–242.

Raphael, K. G., & Dohrenwend, B. P. (1987). Self-disclosure and mental health: A problem of confounded measurement. *Journal of Abnormal Psychology, 96*(3), 214–217.

Ricoeur, P. (1970). *Freud and philosophy: An essay on interpretation*. New Haven: Yale University Press.

Ricoeur, P. (1974). *The conflict of interpretations: Essays in hermeneutics*. Evanston, IL: Northwestern University Press.

Rice, D. (1996). *Theses, 1991–present*. Department of Psychology, University of West Georgia, Carrollton, GA.

Rogers, C. R. (1969). *Freedom to learn*. Columbus, OH: Charles E. Merrill.

Rogers, C. R. (1983). *Freedom to learn for the 80's*. Columbus, OH: Charles E. Merrill.

Saybrook Institute. (1996). *A complete list of dissertations produced from 1974 to the present, including author, degree granted, chair of committee, date of graduation, and title*. Saybrook Institute, San Francisco, CA.

Solomon, M. F. (1989). *Narcissism and intimacy: Love and marriage in an age of confusion*. New York: W. W. Norton.

Wertz, F. (1985). Method and findings in a phenomenological psychological study of a complex life-event: Being criminally victimized. In A. Giorgi (Ed.), *Phenomenology and psychological research* (pp. 155–216). Pittsburgh, PA: Duquesne University Press.

Wertz, F. (1992). The humanistic movement in psychology: History, celebration, and prospectus. *Special Issue: The Humanistic Psychologist, 20*(2–3).

Part II

Biographical and Critical Essays on Central Figures in Humanistic Psychology and Transpersonal Psychology

15

Diana Baumrind: Researcher and Critical Humanist

HENDRIKA VANDE KEMP

Diana Baumrind (b. August 23, 1927) is explicitly neither humanist nor feminist, but her writings suggest ways in which both humanistic and feminist psychology lack essential aspects of humanism.[1] She is a vocal critic of professional research ethics and moral development theory, identifying dehumanizing elements in the American Psychological Association's (APA) code of ethics, deploring the use of deception in social psychological research, and discerning vital deficiencies in Lawrence Kohlberg's model (Kohlberg, 1973). She is also an articulate critic of research methodology and misapplied statistical techniques.

BRIEF SYNOPSIS OF CAREER

Diana Blumberg was the first of two daughters born to Hyman and Mollie Blumberg, a lower-middle-class couple residing in one of New York's Jewish enclaves.[2] In childhood Diana had a strong intellectual friendship with her father, an atheist who retained a strong sense of Jewish cultural tradition. Diana deeply admired the political activism of her uncle, Isadore Blumberg, and his wife, Hannah (Levine). Hyman and Isadore, sons of Eastern European immigrants, were educated at City College and developed anti-Zionist and pro-Soviet philosophies. Diana affirmed their aspirations, captured in the Soviet anthem "The Internationale" and the Soviet slogan of justice, "From each according to his ability and to each according to his need." The young Hyman was a poet and journalist who joined his peers in a left-wing political activism that struggled for the recognition of unions and equal rights for minorities. Isadore was an organizer for the Transport Workers' Union and later for the Teachers' Union. After the McCarthy

Diana Baumrind (Photo courtesy of Diana Baumrind).

inquisition expelled him from the unions, he became a widely recognized advocate for the mentally ill. Blumberg schooled his niece in the principles of dialectical materialism and imprinted her with his concern "to empower the disenfranchised and underrepresented." He "stood up to the early witchhunters of the '30s" and supported his nephew by marriage, David Lubell (husband of Diana's sister Doris), in his resistance to the Senate Subcommittee on Internal Security in 1953. He was, however, not an anarchist, believing that "socialism without democracy was unthinkable."

Diana, the eldest in an extended family of female cousins, inherited the role of eldest son, which allowed her to participate in serious conversations about philosophy, ethics, literature, and politics. Diana resisted all attempts to limit her personal rights on the basis of her being a child or a woman. Her childhood self was "not very educable" because she was unwilling to accommodate to all the required social conventions and much preferred classes that allowed her to express her own point of view. In her teens Diana supplemented her personal education in Marxist philosophy and economics by attending night classes at the Worker's School, a series of speakers and roundtable discussions that took place after 1933 at the *Catholic Worker* newspaper office and House of Hospitality in the slums of

New York (Miller, 1982). Here Diana met two celebrity Communists whose left-wing activism strongly reflected the values of the Blumberg brothers (Belfrage, 1973; Navasky, 1980). One was Pete Seeger, prolabor and anti-Fascist songwriter and founder (in 1945) of the People's Songs trade union who was indicted for contempt when he remained silent before the House Committee on Unamerican Activities in 1961. The other was the African-American bass-baritone, actor, and labor and civil rights activist Paul Robeson, whose Soviet sympathies cost him his passport, and thereby his living, from 1950 to 1958. During these years, with the Holocaust spreading a dark cloud over American Jews, Diana heard numerous challenges to racism and working-class oppression. Always rebellious, she joined the Communist party and was an active and open member for fifteen years.

Diana was led to the all-women Hunter College of the City of New York by a variety of circumstances that included family finances, a strong belief in public education, and, because of her "intentional nonconformity" during her earlier school years, grades too low to be competitive for the few slots available to Jews and women at most private colleges. She completed her A.B. in philosophy and psychology in 1948. Diana's teachers—many of them closet Marxists—reinforced her social consciousness and strengthened her philosophical grounding in dialectical materialism. One Hunter teacher was the philosopher John Somerville, who later edited *Soviet Studies in Philosophy*, served as president of the Society for the Philosophical Study of Dialectical Materialism, lectured in Soviet-bloc countries, and labored with UNESCO for human rights. Another radical and influential Hunter instructor was the experimental social psychologist Bernard Frank Riess, who had studied the "effect of economic security, class-membership, and affiliation with workers on attitude towards the rôle of the intellectual in social change" (Riess, 1940, p. 461).

During these years Diana was also influenced by Otto Klineberg, a humanist par excellence whose graduate study in anthropology led him to ask how psychologists could "speak of *human* attributes and *human* behavior when they knew only one kind of human being" (Klineberg, 1974, p. 166). Klineberg's careful research on selective migration and racial stereotypes challenged American racism and eugenics programs, and such cross-cultural sensitivity inspired Baumrind's criticism of professional ethics as she presented a variety of contemporary systems of moral judgment—each equally valid, each based on different value hierarchies—that might guide the psychologist (Baumrind, 1985). Such sensitivity also runs through her critique of Kohlberg's moral judgment theory as she points out the consequences of the deontologists' "intolerant and parochial denigration of so-called lower level thinking" (Baumrind, 1975, p. 91).

Newly married, Baumrind left New York in 1948 for graduate school at the University of California's Berkeley campus, where she studied developmental, clinical, and social psychology and earned the M.A. (1951) and Ph.D. (1955). She arrived in time to witness the events of 1949–1950, the year when the university regents required faculty to sign a loyalty oath. E. C. Tolman chaired the nonsigners' Group for Academic Freedom, took the case to the American Association of University Professors in 1950, and led the legal battle of the nonsigners in *Tolman v. Underhill* (Gardner, 1967). Many Berkeley professors modeled personal convictions and professional interests that strengthened Baumrind's Marxist and humanitarian convictions. Among them was the group that conducted the classic Berkeley research project on anti-Semitism and the authoritarian personality (Adorno, Frenkel-Brunswik, Levinson, & Sanford, 1950). Baumrind's other teachers included Egon Brunswik (who impressed upon her the importance of idiographic research), Leo Postman, and conformity researchers David Krech and Richard S. Crutchfield. Krech no doubt had a special influence. The Jewish, Soviet-born Isadore Krechevsky anglicized his name (to David Krech) in order to escape the pervasive effects of anti-Semitism (Krech, 1974). He was a member of, and temporary newsletter editor for, New America, a "Marxist revolutionary organization" (p. 235), and his signed protest after witnessing the 1937 Memorial Day Massacre on a picket line at the Republic Steel Corporation plant cost him posts at the Universities of Chicago and Colorado. He reluctantly signed the loyalty oath.

Baumrind completed her thesis (1955) on structured and unstructured discussion groups under Hubert Coffey, a student of Kurt Lewin and a nonsigner of the loyalty oath. Coffey was not only an influential teacher, but also a close personal friend who served as Baumrind's mentor, protector, and role model of humanity. Coffey was the original codirector, with Saxton Pope, of the Group Therapy Research Project, funded by the National Institute of Mental Health (NIMH), that culminated in the publication of Timothy Leary's (1957) interpersonal classic. From 1955 to 1958 Baumrind completed a clinical residency at the Cowell Hospital/Kaiser Permanente and was a fellow under the NIMH grant investigating therapeutic change, extending her leadership research to therapy groups (Baumrind, 1959) and families. In her family-socialization research, she focuses on a structured (authoritative) parental leadership style that couples directive elements of the authoritarian style with responsive elements of the democratic style. Baumrind regarded Leary as a superb clinician, and her philosophy of a social self, though grounded in dialectical materialism, also contains elements of interpersonal psychology, social psychology, and the philosophy of personalism, which in personality theory refers specifically to the theory of Stern (1935/1938), but denotes any theory asserting "that the individual person as a patterned entity must serve as the center of gravity for psychology" (Allport, 1961, p. 553). This differs from the vernacular psychological definition Baumrind (1978a) linked with Buddhism and Christianity: "the idea that the life and integrity of the person remain of greater value than any object or function which the person may be called upon to serve" and that "persons are of unconditional value" (p. 11). Baumrind is deeply indebted to the literature of Christian mysticism (Underhill, 1911/1961) and Christian romantic love (e.g., Lewis, 1936, 1942; Williams, 1943). Baumrind's atheism is inconsistent with the theism in mainline personalism, although she is indebted to MacMurray's (1961) classic in the Christian personalist tradition (Baumrind, 1992, p. 272).

Elements of Baumrind's formal education meshed with the philosophical core of the Catholic Worker movement, whose cofounders (Peter Maurin and Dorothy Day) followed the radical personalism of Emmanuel Mounier, founder in 1932 of *L'Esprit*, "a group of French intellectuals who tried to engage religion with the great social and moral issues of the day" (Piehl, 1982, p. 69) and offered an alternative to existentialism and Marxism. The Catholic Workers were committed to "satisfying and socially useful labor, a rejection of all forms of violence and coercion, and a personal detachment from material goods" (p. 97). Baumrind (1990) denounced both market materialism (a focus on achievement and the attainment of goods) and mechanistic materialism (i.e., reductionism), linking these to sacrifices of scientific integrity as researchers "subordinate [the] quest for knowledge to [the] quest for funds or social approval" (p. 22). The Catholic Workers also deplored the bureaucratic or impersonal treatment of others, a concern evident in Baumrind's (1964) critique of Milgram (see chapter 9 in this volume). Just as Dorothy Day believed that love should lead to personal responsibility, service to one's neighbors, and the transformation of society, Baumrind (1992) argues that "justice and compassion [are] implicit in true self-interest" (p. 268). She continues to read the *Catholic Worker* and believes that "given the proper material conditions all human beings could embody their projected image of the divine."

By 1960 Baumrind affiliated with the Institute of Human Development, where she still directs the Family Socialization and Developmental Competence Project. Baumrind chose the research focus, with its often demoralizing time and energy-consuming fund-raising stressors, because it provided the flexible hours required for the mothering of her three daughters. Baumrind (1980) regards mothering as a "primary commitment [that] cannot be shared, "although the care itself can and should be. Someone must, when no one else will, provide the attention, stimulation, and continuous personal relationship without which a child is consigned to psychosis, psychopathy, or marasmus. . . . If society grants a woman the power of life and death over the fetus, it thereby binds her morally to the life she gives birth to" (p. 645).

Baumrind's work from 1960 to 1966 was funded by an NIMH grant. Further grants of nearly $3.5 million funded Baumrind's studies on family socialization, developmental competence, and adolescent risk taking and resulted in approximately three dozen publications. Baumrind is a recipient of the G. Stanley Hall Award from APA's Division 7 (1988) and the Research Scientist Award from NIMH (1984–1988).

THE CENTRALITY OF RESPONSIBILITY

A central humanistic affirmation that unifies Baumrind's work on research design, socialization, moral development, and professional ethics is the assertion of responsible relatedness, an attitude that regards individual rights and respon-

sibilities as inextricable, and moral actions as determined "volitionally and consciously" (Baumrind, 1992, p. 256). This assertion flows out of Baumrind's
Marxist belief "in the possibility of creating a moral world." Her sense of responsibility in turn flows out of her atheism:

> Because God does not exist it is the responsibility of human beings to perform all the acts
> of creation, compassion, and justice assigned by theists to God. A heavy responsibility
> indeed! If human beings are masters of our own destiny, then our responsibility (to our
> species, all sentient beings, and our shared environment) cannot be evaded. (Baumrind,
> personal communication, January 24, 1995)

For Baumrind, self-actualization depends on "right conduct in relations with
others" (1992, p. 258); altruistic actions "*reconcile* the interests of self and other"
(p. 266). Baumrind asserts that "prudential, partisan considerations are a necessary
ingredient of moral judgments and moral conduct" because they are most likely
to "motivate congruent conduct" (p. 265). In opposition to the moral universalists,
she asserts that "impartiality is not superior morally to *enlightened partiality*. Partiality allows conflicts of interest to be identified, debated, and negotiated by
individuals, or by the elected representatives of communities, with divergent interests" (p. 266). This enlightened partiality is much like the multidirected partiality of the contextual therapist, the therapist's "ability to maintain [a] genuine
interest in eliciting the mutually exclusive and incompatible interests and aspirations of each and every family member" (Boszormenyi-Nagy & Krasner, 1986,
p. 52). Baumrind applied these principles, worked out in the context of moral
judgment theory, in her specific critique of Milgram (see chapter 9 in this volume)
and of APA's research ethics.

Responsibilities of the General Researcher

Early in her career, Baumrind (1959) challenged therapists to analyze their
cases systematically and invite "verification from professional colleagues" (p. 341).
Clinical researchers must make any "private definition of adjustment" explicit and
connect this to theoretical constructs that are operationally defined and "measure
improvement" rather than mere change (p. 342), are in actuality stable and unidimensional (as assumed by our statistical techniques), have "important adaptive
consequences," and "offer clarification and unity to diverse behavioral measurements" (p. 343). Baumrind's incisive reasoning is already apparent as she targets
the unjustified leap clinicians often make "from test scores" to "traits, to constructs" (p. 343) and pleads for better construct and content validation and the
production of a "nomological network, . . . an interlocking set of propositions relating to an aspect of mental activity" (p. 346). She also identifies the problems
inherent in evaluating *change* scores in tests designed specifically to measure *stable*
traits. Baumrind (1960) employed these principles in a critique of the Group
Therapy Research Project, concluding that the interpersonal system suffered from

"logical and methodological inconsistencies" (p. 396) compounded by imperfect reliability, sampling errors, and the inappropriate application of inferential statistics, leading to misleading statements "for which there is only trivial evidence" (p. 401).

These methodological criticisms reveal a deep concern for intellectual honesty that surfaces in Baumrind's methodological critique of Milgram and her discussion of "specious causal attributions" (1983). Providing a penetrating analysis of correlation and causation, Baumrind argues that some sociologists employ a definition of causality that is neither "logically sound" nor suited to "the solution of key social problems" (p. 1291) because it diverges markedly from the position of the public and social policy planners, who understand causality as "a *necessary* connection or intrinsic bond embedded in the very nature of things" (Baumrind, 1990, p. 24). No matter how humanistic their motives, psychologists lose their credibility, and thereby their humanism, when they "endorse by [their] complicity unrealistic expectations by policy makers of what [their] efforts can produce" (p. 23). They also reduce the dignity of individuals when their research designs assume that persons are "interchangeable" or "identical with themselves over time" (Baumrind, 1985, p. 172). These methodological critiques are grounded in Baumrind's philosophical materialism, the notion that "every idea must be tested by comparison with objective reality" (Baumrind, personal communication, January 24, 1995).

Responsibilities of the Moral Judgment Theorist

Baumrind (1992) also critiques moral judgment theories and the many "sources of discrepancy between moral judgments and the moral actions they claim to govern" (p. 260). She challenges moral theorists such as Kohlberg (1973), who accord a more privileged status to "abstract moral principles" than to "social rules and conventions" (p. 260), and she insists that "so-called lower level conventional reasoning, because it is situated in time and space, has clearer implications . . . than post-conventional reasoning, which is directed to a hypothetical prototypic other" (p. 260). What matters far more than cognitive ability is the affective and conative involvement of individuals, who must "implicate themselves" in their judgments and be prepared to act on their ethical values (p. 264). Here Baumrind echoes Gilligan's (1982) observation that "hypothetical dilemmas . . . divest moral actors from the history and psychology of their individual lives" (p. 100). Baumrind similarly rejects the notion that "the moral dimension of social cognition or conduct should exclude the practical consequences for self" because this requires "of human beings when they behave morally that they become alienated from their own subjective natures," an assertion that is "inhumane and unrealizable" (p. 265). In a compassionate statement that epitomizes Baumrind's humanism, she states:

The exclamation "I am only human" should provide the reason to coordinate one's conduct with one's values and not the excuse for failing to do so. Human insufficiencies will assure that our reach exceeds our grasp without reaching for ideals that are intrinsically unrealizable. One may not leap from "is" to "ought." But one can argue that what cannot be, in the sense of being contrary to human nature . . . ought not to be espoused. (p. 266)

Responsibilities of the Socialization Researcher

Baumrind (1991) is also deeply concerned about developmental behavior genetics and its emphasis on nature over nurture. She questions the logic of the typical research design and the validity of environmental measures and feels that "cultural and genetic determinism both undermine the attribution of personal responsibility to the individual as a moral agent" (p. 387). Genetic attributions for child behavior "undermine parents' belief in their own effectiveness, whereas parents' attribution of responsibility for their children's outcomes to parents' own actions is associated with more effective caregiving, which in turn is associated with more positive child outcomes" (Baumrind, 1993, p. 1300). If we believe that environment influences behavior, "we have an obligation to determine what kind of environment is truly human" (Baumrind, 1990, pp. 26–27), even if doing so costs us social disapproval.

One example is Baumrind's concern about adolescent sexuality and her judgment that the National Research Council's (1987) report failed to create a more humane environment because it focused on pregnancy prevention and ignored the devastating consequences of venereal diseases and the documented health risks of birth-control pills. Baumrind (1982) notes that promiscuous recreational sex is a moral problem because of the "possible trivializing and desacralizing of human love and human life" (p. 1402), a statement that evokes both spirituality and humanism, despite Baumrind's avowed atheism. Bringing additional developmental research to bear on ethical issues, Baumrind (1978b) challenges the child-liberation movement and its focus on equality in parent-child relations, asserting that "parents have a social and moral duty to commit themselves to the welfare of the child, while the child has a duty to conform to parental standards" (p. 193). Here she aligns herself with a number of other psychologists who reject the view, often espoused by humanists, "of society as necessarily oppressive and inhibiting of human individuality, creativity, and self-determination, and who regard conformity vs. individuality as a necessary and desirable social dialectic" (p. 185). In an eloquent discourse on adolescent alienation, Baumrind (1987) again reveals both spiritual and humanistic concerns as she pleads for parents to take responsibility for teaching to their adolescent offspring those "values about which there is social consensus" (p. 118). Alienation can be prevented only by teaching that emphasizes our natural embeddedness in the social environment and the construction of "self in interaction with nonself" (p. 108). These statements on responsibility are foundational to Baumrind's metaethical theory and her ethical critiques.

A second example is Baumrind's (1995) examination of the nature-nurture interface and its social policy implications in relation to homosexuality:

For the individual, the attribution of no choice puts pressure on the convert to homosexuality to remain within the fold, and on the heterosexual to not explore same-gender sex. Politically, the attribution of no choice proscribes legal or moral censure, because persons cannot be held responsible for behaviors they cannot control. If being gay or lesbian is genetic, it ceases to be a sin. If sexual orientation, like race and gender, is immutable, then courts are obliged to protect nonheterosexuals from discrimination.(p. 135)

Baumrind "emphasizes choice rather than genetic or environmental determinism in developing a nonheterosexual or heterosexual identity," and she prefers "the term *sexual preference* to *sexual orientation*" (p. 135). She believes that choice involves not only sexual attraction, but also "attitudes toward convention, an affinity for enacting or rejecting gender role demands and expectations, and for socializing primarily with those who share one's affinity" (p. 135). Arguments for acceptance should be based not on "the basis of renunciation of choice, but rather on the basis of respect for people's right to behave as they choose in their private lives, for the social contributions nonheterosexual people have made, and on appreciation of diversity in culture and lifestyle" (p. 135).

It is clear from Baumrind's writing that responsible relatedness undergirds all her more specific principles. In her moral development theory and metaethics, she rejects approaches that value rationalization over personal involvement and those that favor individual human existence over the communal good. In her family-socialization and adolescent risk-taking research, she rejects the stance of humanists who see socialization as detrimental to self-actualization; affirms a balance between the feminist values of nurturance, intimacy, and interconnectedness and the masculine values of agency and self-assertion; and refuses the child-liberation movement by challenging parents to take an authoritative nurturing stance that includes the inculcation of societal values. In her critique of research ethics (see chapter 9 in this volume) she summons social psychologists to an ethical posture that recognizes the dignity and intentionality of persons and takes responsibility for any violation of what we affirm as inalienable human rights. In her criticism of research design and statistical procedures, she abhors self-deception in researchers who pretend to unwarranted certainty and deceive the public and their colleagues with misleading statements. Throughout, she is unwavering in her commitment to what she understands as humanism and courageous in her challenge to insincere orthodoxies, whether these be embodied in "McCarthy red-baiting," "gender feminism," or "rationalizations for mistreating participants to promote sanctity of scientific method" (Baumrind, personal communication, January 24, 1995).

NOTES

1. I am grateful to the many persons who assisted in the preparation of this chapter: Dan Palomino, my administrative assistant, attended to the tedious details of bibliographic accuracy; a transcribed interview with Vivian Makosky provided many biographical details;

and Diana Baumrind's patient encouragement provided the motivation to continue. I am also indebted to Howard Gadlin, my dissertation chair at the University of Massachusetts/ Amherst, for first acquainting me with the virtues of Marxism.

2. For factual details I rely on Diana Baumrind's *Vita*, published biographical entries, and the transcript of Makosky's 1984 interview for a yet-to-be-published book on *Prominent Women in Psychology*. Quotations not otherwise cited come from Makosky's interview, a personal letter from Diana Baumrind (January 24, 1995), from the comments made by Diana Baumrind and her brother-in-law, David Lubell, at the memorial service for Isadore Blumberg on December 5, 1993, and from Blumberg's obituary published in the *New York Times* on October 5, 1993.

REFERENCES

Adorno, T. W., Frenkel-Brunswik, E., Levinson, D. J., & Sanford, R. N. (1950). *The authoritarian personality*. New York: Harper.

Allport, G. W. (1961). *Pattern and growth in personality*. New York: Holt, Rinehart & Winston.

Baumrind, D. (1955). *Some personality and situational determinants of behavior in a discussion group*. Unpublished doctoral dissertation, University of California, Berkeley.

Baumrind, D. (1959). Conceptual issues involved in evaluating improvement due to psychotherapy. *Psychiatry, 22*, 341–348.

Baumrind, D. (1960). An analysis of some aspects of the "interpersonal system." *Psychiatry, 23*, 395–402.

Baumrind, D. (1964). Some thoughts on ethics of research: After reading Milgram's "Behavioral study of obedience." *American Psychologist, 19*, 421–423.

Baumrind, D. (1975). It neither is nor ought to be: A reply to Wallwork. In E. C. Kennedy (Ed.), *Human rights and psychological research: A debate on psychology and ethics* (pp. 83–102). New York: Thomas Crowell.

Baumrind, D. (1978a). Nature and definition of informed consent in research involving deception. *The Belmont Report: Ethical principles and guidelines for the protection of human subjects of research* (and *Appendix*, Vol. 2, pp. 1–71). DHEW Publication No. [OS] 78–0014. Washington, DC: National Commission for the Protection of Human Subjects of Biomedical and Behavioral Research.

Baumrind, D. (1978b). Reciprocal rights and responsibilities in parent-child relations. *Journal of Social Issues, 34*, 179–196.

Baumrind, D. (1980). New directions in socialization research. *American Psychologist, 35* 639–652.

Baumrind, D. (1982). Adolescent sexuality: Comment on Williams' and Silka's comments on Baumrind. *American Psychologist, 37*, 1402–1403.

Baumrind, D. (1983). Specious causal attributions in the social sciences: The reformulated stepping-stone theory of heroin use as exemplar. *Journal of Personality and Social Psychology, 45*, 1289–1298.

Baumrind, D. (1985). Research using intentional deception: Ethical issues revisited. *American Psychologist, 40*, 164–174.

Baumrind, D. (1987). A developmental perspective on adolescent risk-taking in contemporary America. In W. Damon (Ed.), *New directions for child development: Adolescent health and social behavior, 37* (pp. 93–126). San Francisco: Jossey-Bass.

Baumrind, D. (1990). Doing good well. In C. B. Fisher & W. W. Tryon (Eds.), *Ethics in applied developmental psychology* (pp. 17–28). Norwood, NJ: Ablex.

Baumrind, D. (1991). To nurture nature. *Behavioral and Brain Sciences, 14*, 386–387.

Baumrind, D. (1992). Leading an examined life: The moral dimension of daily conduct. In W. M. Kurtines, M. Azmitia, & J. L. Gewirtz (Eds.), *The role of values in psychology and human development* (pp. 256–280). New York: John Wiley.

Baumrind, D. (1993). The average expectable environment is not good enough: A response to Scarr. *Child Development, 64*, 1299–1317.

Baumrind, D. (1995). Commentary on sexual orientation: Research and social policy implications. *Developmental Psychology, 31*, 130–136.

Belfrage, C. (1973). *The American inquisition, 1945–1960.* Indianapolis: Bobbs-Merrill.

Boszormenyi-Nagy, I., & Krasner, B. (1986). *Between give and take: A clinical guide to contextual therapy.* New York: Brunner/Mazel.

Gardner, D. P. (1967). *The California oath controversy,* Berkeley: University of California Press.

Gilligan, C. (1982). *In a different voice: Psychological theory and women's development.* Cambridge, MA: Harvard University Press.

Klineberg, O. (1974). Otto Klineberg. In G. Lindzey (Ed.), *A history of psychology in autobiography* (Vol. 6, pp. 161–182). Englewood Cliffs, NJ: Prentice-Hall.

Kohlberg, L. (1973). *Collected papers on moral development and moral education.* Cambridge, MA: Harvard University Press.

Krech, D. (1974). David Krech. In G. Lindzey (Ed.), *A history of psychology in autobiography* (Vol. 6, pp. 219–250). Englewood Cliffs, NJ: Prentice-Hall.

Leary, T. (1957). *Interpersonal diagnosis of personality: A functional theory and methodology for personality evaluation.* New York: Wiley.

Lewis, C. S. (1936). *The allegory of love: A study in medieval tradition.* Oxford: Clarendon Press.

Lewis, C. S. (1942). *A preface to "Paradise Lost."* Oxford: Oxford University Press.

MacMurray, J. (1961). *The form of the personal: Vol. 2. Persons in relation.* London: Faber & Faber.

Miller, W. D. (1982). *Dorothy Day: A biography.* San Francisco: Harper.

National Research Council. (1987). *Risking the future: Adolescent sexuality, pregnancy, and childbearing.* 2 vols. Washington, DC: National Academy Press.

Navasky, V. S., (1980). *Naming names.* New York: Viking.

Piehl, M. (1982). *Breaking bread: The "Catholic Worker" and the origin of Catholic radicalism in America.* Philadelphia: Temple University Press.

Riess, B. F. (1940). The role of the intellectual in social change. *Psychological Bulletin, 37*, 461.

Stern, W. (1938). *General psychology from the personalistic standpoint* (H. D. Spoerl, Trans.). New York: Macmillan. (Original German edition 1935)

Underhill, E. (1961). *Mysticism: A study in the nature and development of man's spiritual consciousness.* New York: Dutton. (Original work published 1911)

Williams, C. (1943). *The figure of Beatrice: A study in Dante.* London: Faber & Faber.

16

James F. T. Bugental: Continuity and Change

STEEN HALLING

> The rock bottom concern of each human being is the simple but profound
> fact of being alive. Life is the question we all face; living is the answer each
> one of us gives.
>
> —Bugental, 1990, p. xi

It is impossible to begin to do justice to a productive person's accomplishments
in a lengthy biography, let alone in a few pages. James Bugental has made an
enduring contribution as therapist, thinker, and professional to the world of humanistic and existential psychology. Since he continues to write, teach, and conduct workshops, this contribution is still evolving. As the subtitle of this chapter,
"Continuity and Change," suggests, I will focus my discussion around a theme
that is central in most of James Bugental's work. As Bugental mentions in his
latest book, *Intimate Journeys* (1990), this theme is also evident in his life. Commenting on the differences between the Jim Bugental of the mid-1960s and of
the late 1980s, he himself notes, "but in the course of preparing this book I have
come to realize how much continuity, even sameness, exists" (p. xiv).

BRIEF BIOGRAPHY

James Bugental was born in Fort Wayne, Indiana, on Christmas Day, 1915.
He describes his parents as resilient people who "bounced back with new optimism" (Stearn, 1991, p. 182) after numerous disappointments and setbacks, many
of them associated with the hardship of the Great Depression. His father, Richard

James F. T. Bugental (Photo courtesy of James F.
T. Bugental).

Francis Bugental, was a contractor; his mother, Hazel Jeanette (née Veness), had wanted to become a concert pianist but ended up working as a music teacher. Their relationship was a difficult and stormy one given their differences in class background as well as temperament, leaving the young Bugental with much apprehension about conflict and anger (Bugental & Russell, 1990).

Bugental received his associates degree from Glendale Junior College in California and his B.A. from Texas West State College; he earned his M.A. in sociology at George Peabody College in 1941. He worked in public personnel administration for the U.S. Civil Service Commission and the Tennessee Department of Personnel from 1941 to 1944 and was at the Lawson Army General Hospital in Atlanta as a psychologist and noncommissioned officer from 1945 to 1946. By the time he entered the doctoral program in clinical psychology at Ohio State University, he had considerable clinical and teaching experience.

After his graduation in 1948, Bugental moved to Los Angeles, where he taught as an assistant professor at the University of California at Los Angeles. He also conducted psychotherapy as a partner in Psychological Services Associates, which he founded with his close friend Alvin Lasko in 1953. By 1955 he had left his faculty position because of the constant infighting and the resistance to humanistic psychology at UCLA and was in full-time private practice (Bugental & Russell, 1990). The late 1960s were a period of difficult and painful transition for Bugental and for his family. He was divorced in 1967 and remarried in 1968, the same year he moved to northern California to become a consultant at the Educational Policy Research Center at the Stanford Research Institute, a position he held for three years. In two of his books Bugental (1976, 1990) vividly describes how difficult this period of change and termination was for him and for some of his patients. After the move to northern California, he continued to do long-term, intensive psychotherapy until 1987.

Throughout his professional life Bugental has given numerous workshops and invited presentations throughout North America, as well as overseas, and continues to be involved in the education of psychologists as an adjunct faculty member at institutions such as the Saybrook Institute and the California School of Professional Psychology. He has published over a hundred articles and book chapters, as well as ten books, including *The Search for Authenticity* (1965b) and *The Art of the Psychotherapist* (1987).

In addition to his therapeutic and academic work, James Bugental has been highly influential as a leader in his profession and the humanistic movement within psychology. While at UCLA he acted as legislative lobbyist for the State Psychological Association (Bugental & Russell, 1990). Subsequently, he was the first president of the Association for Humanistic Psychology (1962–1963), as well as president of the California State Psychological Association (1960–1961) and the Southern California Psychological Association (1955–1956). As an editor, he brought together the contributions of major humanistic thinkers in *Challenges of Humanistic Psychology*, published in 1967.

CONTRIBUTIONS TO HUMANISTIC PSYCHOLOGY AND PSYCHOTHERAPY

Orientation to Psychology

While he was a graduate student, James Bugental was initiated into psychology as an objective science, which was "fascinating, gave me a sense of new power, taught me much *about* people, but never really brought me to know others—or myself" (1987, p. 17; emphasis in original). His graduate teachers were caring and humane, yet he found that most of them regarded psychology as a discipline that, in imitation of the physical sciences, necessitated the objectification of its subject matter.

Bugental's interest in the subjective was evident in his dissertation (1948), where he examined psychotherapy protocols to determine patients' attitudes toward self and not-self and the relationship between the two. Later he was to regard his early attempts to arrive at inner experience through objective analysis as naïve (Bugental, 1987). Nonetheless, he did have the advantage of doing his work at Ohio State University, where, given the influence of George Kelly's construct psychology and Victor Raimy's interest in the "self" (both were on his dissertation committee), there was at least some possibility of exploring human experience.

In those early years he aligned himself with the self-concept theory of personality, which "holds that the behavior of the individual is primarily determined by and pertinent to his phenomenal field and, in particular, that aspect of the field which is the individual's concept of himself" (Bugental, 1950, p. 483). He advocated the use of what he termed the W-A-Y (who are you) technique as a method for helping counselors and other professionals to assess a person's self-concept. In several publications (e.g., Bugental, 1950, 1952) based on his dissertation, he presented an "objective" methodology for analyzing client statements. Yet as early as 1955 Bugental (1962) approvingly quoted Snygg and Combs's call for a phenomenological (or experiential) perspective in psychotherapy.

By the early 1960s Bugental was an established figure within humanistic psychology. Not only was he the first president of the Association of Humanistic Psychology (AHP), but his article "Humanistic Psychology: A New Breakthrough" (Bugental, 1963) became one of the sources for AHP's first policy statements (deCarvalho, 1992). Bugental (1963) believed that humankind was on the verge of a new era because of the emergence of a new paradigm, championed by humanistic psychology, that would foster a new evolution in human consciousness. This paradigm viewed the person holistically, rejected the medical model as a guiding principle for psychotherapy, valued integration of perspectives rather than specialization, and saw practitioners rather than researchers as pioneers in advancing psychological understanding. Bugental (1963) optimistically anticipated a convergence of science and the humanities resulting in "a tremendous outpouring of new awareness about ourselves in the world" (p. 567).

For Bugental (1964b), humanistic psychology provides "a broader conception of human experience" (p. 25) within which the contributions of other views within psychology can find a place. Thus throughout his writings on psychotherapy, Bugental (e.g., 1965b, 1987) acknowledges the value of his own psychoanalytic therapy and training and the critical importance of concepts such as transference, countertransference, and resistance. In fact, Bugental credits his own psychoanalysis with helping him to write in a more personal style (Bugental & Russell, 1990). However, he eschews Freudian metapsychology, instead placing these concepts within an existential perspective, where the person is understood in terms of intentionality rather than causality and subjectivity rather than drive theory (Bugental, 1987).

Bugental consistently identifies his orientation as existential-humanistic rather than just humanistic. In an article coauthored with his wife, Elizabeth Bugental, they explain how the existential and humanistic traditions converge in their work:

We approach clients with the implicit (and often explicit) question, "What are you making of the fact of your being alive?" We are not assumptionless—to our minds a self-deception and an impossibility—but we endeavor to remain close to our clients' lived lives. As humanistically oriented psychotherapists, we value the realization of each person's potential, and we insist upon the ultimate capacity of individuals to cope with their own concerns. (Bugental & Bugental, 1984a, p. 51)

Although his exposure to existential thought has been primarily through secondary sources, especially the writings of Rollo May, there is no doubt that his views are in many respects those of an existentialist. The existential influence is particularly evident in those areas where he disagrees with his fellow humanists Carl Rogers and Abraham Maslow, who, along with May and George Kelly, are the thinkers who have influenced him the most. First, he strongly emphasizes the presence of tragedy in human life (e.g., Bugental, 1965b, 1989). Second, he disputes the assumption of many humanistic psychologists that humans are innately good: "Man [*sic*] is. Not man is good or man is bad" (Bugental 1965b, p. 143). Finally, he resists the genetic and environmental determinism implicit in some of Maslow's and Rogers's writings. Human choice, he believes, is a key element both in the creation of "human nature" and in the movement toward health or neurosis (e.g., Bugental, 1965a, 1978, 1987, 1990).

His relationship to transpersonal psychology is ambiguous. Bugental (1987, p. 197) questions whether the term "transpersonal" makes sense (how can one study what is beyond the personal?). Yet he clearly recognizes the spiritual dimension of human existence. As a doctoral student he attended the Episcopal church for a time during a period of personal turmoil and anxiety (Bugental & Russell, 1990; Stearn, 1991). A number of years later, although he was no longer affiliated with any church, he nonetheless used religious terms to describe aspects of the psychotherapy process, referring to clients' "search for the God hidden within them." Of those who are able to plumb the depth of their own being, he writes, "They return with the sense of having touched God" (1971, pp. 33, 36). Bugental has summed up the change in his own view in this area: "Subtly my clients are converting me from a dedicated agnostic into a kind of believer who does not know what it is he believes but daily becomes more convinced that there is something more in which we do well to believe and on which we do well to rest our efforts" (1987, p. 198).

Key Issues

Bugental's theory and practice have for the most part centered on life-changing psychotherapy with reasonably functional and committed clients. Typically he has worked intensively with them for two to four years with meetings at least twice weekly. Along with others within the existential tradition (e.g., Yalom, 1980), he regards neurosis as a flight from the basic givens of life and the anxieties they entail (for example, we are finite, separate yet related, and forced to make choices with limited information) into inauthenticity or unawareness. The ultimate "threat we try to conceal from ourselves is non-being" (Bugental, 1964a, p. 201), but in so doing we lose the vitality of the very life that we are trying to preserve. As we become alienated from ourselves and our basic feelings, we may end up speculating about the underlying motives of our behavior, essentially treating ourselves as if we were intriguing objects rather than having direct knowledge of our wants, desires, and fears (Bugental, 1965b). As Bugental (1990) laments, in resonance with the suffering of one of his patients, "I don't want to have wasted so many years in hiding my own self" (p. 239).

The path back to authenticity, that is, living with some measure of awareness and acceptance of one's subjectivity, the contingencies of life, and one's own decisions, is, of course, far from easy. Hence therapists meet resistance from their patients. Bugental fruitfully broadens the concept of resistance. He asserts that resistance is just one particular manifestation of the way in which the patient defends himself or herself against the threats that life brings (e.g., analyzing problems rather than confronting them). Further, "Resistance is also that which makes possible the ways in which the patient does have life" (Bugental & Bugental, 1984b, p. 543). Unless the therapist's interventions take into account the client's attachment to the security provided by a familiar concept of self and the world and recognize how therapy threatens such a concept, therapy is likely to fail (Bugental, 1987).

Although Bugental is attentive to the therapeutic relationship and acknowledges that the personality of the therapist is crucial, he does not view the relationship as the agent of change as much as the medium in which therapeutic change occurs. Instead, he asserts that therapy "is a philosophic venture. It is not the treatment of an illness. It is daring to confront self and world" (1965b, p. 42). Change requires the increased mobilization of the committed patient, and therefore interventions of the therapist have the goal of "heightening the patient's feeling of being the author from which his behavior flows" (1965b, p. 119). Consistent with his philosophical rejection of determinism, Bugental (1990) reminds us that therapy is a struggle the success of which ultimately depends on the client's willingness to risk reconnecting with his or her "inner sensing."

APPRAISAL

It is obvious that James Bugental has made substantial contributions to existential and humanistic psychology. Perhaps one of his most distinctive contributions has been to provide us with vivid descriptions of the process of intensive psychotherapy. As Attneave (1977) has pointed out, we rarely get case reports that tell us what the therapist is thinking and feeling, and even more rarely do we get reports that are as candid as those that James Bugental has written. Here is a committed and skilled therapist who also makes mistakes, gets carried away by his own convictions, struggles with countertransference reactions, and acknowledges that the problems bewildering his patients are not theirs alone.

In an age where preoccupation with the procedural and the bureaucratic has led many psychologists to highlight the technical side of psychotherapy, Bugental the humanist reminds us that it is as much art and journey as it is science. He also affirms that it is possible for people to change at a deep level, not just to adapt or modify their behavior or their cognitions. Because of his eagerness to write in a way that "challenges the boundaries between textbooks and popular literature, between factual reporting and using fiction to portray deeper truths" (Bugental, 1988, p. 63), his stories and vision have reached a wide audience.

In articulating his theoretical position, Bugental has drawn on the existential (and phenomenological) tradition, giving him a broader range than many of his colleagues within humanistic psychology. Nonetheless, his theoretical presentations might be more cogent and faithful to experience had he drawn more deeply upon this tradition. For example, when Bugental (1987) characterizes subjectivity as an "inner, separate and private realm" (p. 7), he falls back into the very subject-object dualism that he attempts to overcome. Ironically, it is also a dichotomy about which he himself raises questions in one of his notes (Bugental, 1987, p. 305, chap. 9, note 1). The existential-phenomenological philosopher Martin Heidegger's (1927/1962) interpretation of existence as being-in-the-world emphasizes that authenticity as an appropriation of our personhood or "subjectivity" is not a matter of what we find within ourselves but of our basic stance toward others and the world. While Bugental's writings are replete with discussions of notions such as the "thrown" nature of the human condition, authenticity, and finitude, originally discussed by Heidegger, there are no references to Heidegger's work or the works of other European existential philosophers, with the exception of Martin Buber.

Notwithstanding such occasional theoretical lapses, Bugental provides his readers with rich insights into the human condition and clinical practice. In *The Art of the Psychotherapist* (1987), a book written primarily for clinicians, he presents a sophisticated integrative conceptual system for interpreting therapist-patient interactions and promoting deeper therapeutic exploration. Consistent with his emphasis on the personal, he warns his readers not to let his schema get in the way of their personal presence to patients. In most of his writings, it seems to me that Bugental succeeds in convincingly portraying psychology and psychotherapy as the study of personal change. One gets a sense of Bugental as someone who is genuine and serious about his work, but who does not take himself too seriously, who takes risks but who also is mindful of his responsibility to his patients and to himself. One can enjoy and learn from such a writer, with his wealth of experience as a psychotherapist, whether or not one agrees with him.

REFERENCES

Attneave, C. L. (1977). A credible journey. *Contemporary Psychology, 22*(1), 42–44.

Bugental, J.F.T. (1948). *An investigation of the relationship of the conceptual matrix to the self-concept.* Unpublished doctoral dissertation, Ohio State University.

Bugental, J.F.T. (1950). Investigations into the "self-concept": The W-A-Y technique. *Journal of Personality, 18*, 483–498.

Bugental, J.F.T. (1952). A method for assessing self and not-self attitudes during the therapeutic series. *Journal of Consulting Psychology, 16*, 435–439.

Bugental, J.F.T. (1962). A phenomenological hypothesis of neurotic determinants and their therapy. *Psychological Reports, 10,* 527–530.

Bugental, J.F.T. (1963). Humanistic psychology: A new breakthrough. *American Psychologist, 18,* 563–567.

Bugental, J.F.T. (1964a). The nature of the therapeutic task in intensive psychotherapy. *Journal of Existentialism, 5*(18), 199–204.

Bugental, J.F.T. (1964b). The third force in psychology: Basic postulates and orientation of humanistic psychology. *Journal of Humanistic Psychology, 4,* 19–26.

Bugental, J.F.T. (1965a). The existential crisis in intensive psychotherapy. *Psychotherapy: Theory, Research, and Practice, 2,* 16–20.

Bugental, J.F.T. (1965b). *The search for authenticity: An existential-analytic approach to psychotherapy.* New York: Holt, Rinehart & Winston.

Bugental, J.F.T. (Ed.). (1967). *Challenges of humanistic psychology.* New York: McGraw-Hill.

Bugental, J.F.T. (1971). The search for the hidden God. *Voices: The Art and Science of Psychotherapy, 7,* 33–37.

Bugental, J.F.T. (1976). *The search for existential identity.* San Francisco: Jossey-Bass.

Bugental, J.F.T. (1978). *Psychotherapy and process: The fundamentals of an existential-humanistic approach.* Reading, MA: Addison-Wesley.

Bugental, J.F.T. (1987). *The art of the psychotherapist.* New York: W. W. Norton.

Bugental, J.F.T. (1988). My writing "credo." *Journal of Humanistic Psychology, 28*(4), 63.

Bugental, J.F.T. (1989). Foreword. In R. S. Valle & S. Halling (Eds.), *Existential-phenomenological perspectives in psychology* (pp. ix–xi). New York: Plenum.

Bugental, J.F.T. (1990). *Intimate journeys: Stories from life-changing therapy.* San Francisco: Jossey-Bass/Macmillan.

Bugental, J.F.T., & Bugental, E. K. (1984a). Dispiritedness: A new perspective on a familiar state. *Journal of Humanistic Psychology, 24,* 49–67.

Bugental, J.F.T., & Bugental, E. K. (1984b). A fate worse than death: The fear of changing. *Psychotherapy, 21*(4), 543–549.

Bugental, J.F.T., & Russell, D. E. (1990). *A twentieth century life.* Unpublished manuscript. Santa Barbara: University of California Oral History Program.

DeCarvalho, R. J. (1992). The institutionalization of humanistic psychology. *Humanistic Psychologist, 20*(2–3), 124–135.

Heidegger, M. (1962). *Being and time.* New York: Harper & Row. (Original work published 1927)

Stearn, M. B. (1991). James F. T. Bugental. In *Portraits of passion: Aging: Defying the myth* (pp. 181–184). Sausalito, CA: Park West Publishing.

Yalom, I. D. (1980). *Existential psychotherapy.* New York: Basic Books.

17

Moshe Feldenkrais and Functional Integration

PAUL SHANE

LIFE

Functional integration, as an approach to the improvement of human somatic and psychological functioning, was developed by Moshe Feldenkrais (1904–1984), a Russian-born physicist, judo master, mechanical engineer, and educator. He reportedly left home at the age of thirteen and traveled to Palestine, where he worked as a laborer, cartographer, and mathematics tutor. While living in Palestine, he became interested in gymnastics, soccer, and jiujitsu. Later, Feldenkrais moved to France to study at the Ecole des Travaux Publiques de Paris, from which he graduated with a degree in mechanical and electrical engineering. He earned his doctorate in physics from the Sorbonne, where he assisted Frédéric Joliot-Curie, a Nobel Prize winner, for his research into nuclear energy. While in Paris, Feldenkrais studied judo under Jigaro Kano, the creator of that martial arts form, and received his black belt in 1936. During World War II he worked in antisubmarine warfare for the British Admiralty and patented a number of components related to sonar detection.

Feldenkrais suffered a crippling injury to both knees while playing soccer during his Palestine years. Unfortunately, his sea duty during World War II aggravated the condition of the knees. The surgeons he consulted advised him that he should have had an operation years earlier and that he would probably need a cane or crutch after surgery (Shafarman, 1998). Feldenkrais's scientific mind refused to accept such a grim and perfunctory prognosis. Through a combination of positive attitude, curiosity, persistence and effort, he experimented with his own body and learned to walk again. It was out of this experience, as well as from his study of judo and mechanics, that he developed the seminal principles for neuromuscular rehabilitation which were to become known as the Feldenkrais Method.

Feldenkrais's wife was a pediatrician, and observations of her patients also contributed to his conceptual framework. He observed babies in her office and noticed that toddlers (like Judo masters) walked with a low center of gravity, maintained relatively low and uniform muscle tension, and distributed their weight throughout the skeleton (Shafarman, 1998). He concluded first that movement, as a learned behavior, is organized through the nervous system, and second, that theoretically one could learn to move more comfortably at any age. Stimulated by his own rehabilitation and intrigued by his observations of children, Feldenkrais studied neurophysiology, psychology, and other health-related fields. Upon his return to Israel in 1949, he continued to develop his ideas and refine his techniques into a coherent system.

THEORY, PRACTICE, AND RESEARCH

Feldenkrais (1949) denied the primacy of instinct over human psychological functioning and argued instead for the importance of learning, imagination, muscular patterning through neurological functioning, and attitude development. His two fundamental premises are the following:

First, that maturity means that the individual has learned to bring to bear upon the present circumstance only those parts of the previous experience that he consciously deems necessary. The immature person cannot stop himself from restoring the whole situation where only an element of it is associated with the present. Second, that to reeducate, perfectly and successfully, a person such as the one described, by psychiatric methods alone, is a forlorn hope. Such treatment cannot have any lasting effect. The psychiatrist will treat emotional instability, will make him relive the old trauma of childhood, and will obtain an apparent improvement, restoring possibly failing potency, etc., but so long as no radical change of the nervous and body patterns has been wrought, any sharp change of environment, any new shock, or simply time will, by dint of the unchanged muscular and attitudinal patterns, reinstate the whole situation, and bring back the old manner of doing with only minor differences in detail, every time treatment is given up. (Feldenkrais, 1949, p. 154)

Feldenkrais based his approach upon the idea that human development, on a physical and psychological level—what he called the level of "maturity," a state of mental and emotional health marked by a stable, integrated personality—cannot be achieved by psychological intervention alone but needs to be augmented by concomitant changes in the neuromuscular system. Feldenkrais's method is based on reeducating muscular movement and enhancing kinesthetic awareness. Both are achieved by dividing physical movements into increasingly smaller increments. Feldenkrais hypothesized that patterning and repetition of these incremental movements would create new neural connections between the motor cortex and the muscular system.

Feldenkrais held a monist view of the human body with a holistic perspective on human movement. One of the most remarkable aspects of the Feldenkrais approach is its perception of the interrelationships among moving, sensing, feeling, and thinking. These interrelationships are difficult to communicate given the restrictions of everyday language. Feldenkrais was extremely sensitive to language and, as his students attest, always chose his words carefully when teaching and working with clients (Shafarman, 1998). Problems such as pain are almost always, from the perspective of functional integration, based on doing—that is, concrete action—rather than on vague states of being or having, which the unquestioned use of everyday language unconsciously reinforces (Shafarman, 1998). Feldenkrais was suspicious of medical diagnoses because diagnoses are often comprised of vague or ambiguous terms compounded by the unexamined use of language on the part of patients. These careless linguistic habits reinforce the patients' habitual ways of experiencing their bodies.

The problem of pain illustrates both Feldenkrais's holistic view of the body and his emphasis on the role of the client's language. Typically, patients will comment that "I have back pain," which suggests that pain is a kind of foreign object that is possessed by the person or that possesses the person. Pain, however, is an experience and not an object. By the same token, many people tend to identify with their diagnoses such as "I am paranoid," when in reality they refer to a reoccurring pattern of experiencing their self in relation to the world. "Stress" and anxiety also can illustrate how Feldenkrais's monistic thinking transcends dualism. Human beings tend to experience what is labeled as "anxiety" when breathing shallowly and rapidly, and when tightening muscles in the neck and upper chest. Learning to move more skillfully enables a "stressed out" person to function in a more relaxed and comfortable way (Shafarman, 1998).

Theory

Goldfarb (1990) provides a systemic approach to examining the theoretical and practical aspects of the Feldenkrais method. Goldfarb proposes that cybernetic theory may provide the basis for understanding the functioning of the sensorimotor loop and the role of perceptual learning in rehabilitation, including the relationship of perception, action, and intention. Goldfarb's cybernetic model provides a tentative, although promising, map showing how movement limitations, physical disabilities, and chronic pain can be successfully addressed by an educational approach. His study includes case histories that illuminate the theoretical issues.

Description of the Procedure

Functional integration is applied in two formats. The first is in private sessions in which a movement teacher works with the client by giving movement cues in the form of very gentle touch or by verbal directions. The second form is "awareness through movement" (ATM) and is taught in a group setting. In this context the student practitioners initiate their body movements solely by verbal instructions from the group leader. An ATM session usually lasts from thirty to sixty minutes and tends to consist of gradual, easy movements that slowly increase in range and complexity. Although Feldenkrais himself described twelve fundamental exercises in his most famous book, *Awareness through Movement* (Feldenkrais, 1977), ATM lessons now literally number in the thousands and range from minute movements of the hands, eyes, or even just the lips to others that are larger and more "dancelike" involving lying on the floor, sitting, standing, or moving about the room. Both formats are based on Feldenkrais's theory that movement, especially movement initiated and explored with conscious awareness, generates new information in the form of sensation and perception that the nervous system may use to slowly reorganize itself. The guiding rationale is that precisely executed movements are awareness explorations that engage the student with the cognitive, sensory, motoric, and imaginative aspects that are all involved in using one's body. The emphasis throughout both formats is to assist the student to discover which movements are more easily performed and to accept the resulting qualitative shifts in experience. In this way students learn through increased awareness to abandon formerly habitual ways of moving—ways that often create undue stress and strain—and to use new patterns that result in enhanced flexibility and coordination.

Research

Feldenkrais practitioners maintain that anyone, regardless of age, may benefit from their method. Loosely speaking, it would appear that they are correct, but five distinct groups appear to find the most benefit and practical application: the elderly, actors and musicians, those with chronic pain problems, the severely disabled, and sports enthusiasts.

The Elderly

Wildman (1995), in an informal report, observed significant changes when he applied ATM lessons to a group of elderly students. He noted that this group held common attitudes that neither their physical pains could be alleviated nor their physical mobility could be enhanced. In the first session, most participants had to be helped to take a position on the floor, but by the tenth no assistance was necessary. Other changes he observed were that individual awareness of one's body increased and that the students were able to perform former motions (e.g., sitting down onto a chair) much more easily, gracefully, and without the assistance of others.

Performing Artists

In working with performing artists such as dancers, actors, and musicians, Feldenkrais practitioners essentially teach that the body itself is an instrument that supports the performance of art, and so how one uses one's body affects the quality of one's performance. The idea is that the way one "organizes" one's physical self while sitting, standing, or breathing influences the activity one wishes to engage in. For example, in the case of a stringed-instrument player, the operations of one's back, belly, chest, and shoulders all influence how the instrument is played. In the course of their careers string players commonly experience carpal tunnel syndrome, thoracic outlet syndrome, shoulder bursitis, elbow tendonitis, stiff neck, low-back pain, and other physical complaints. These are often accepted as inevitable "occupational injuries" without any recognition that such conditions stem from *how* the player uses his or her body. Since the movement patterns can be improved, these conditions can be prevented or, once they occur, alleviated.

The essential idea that Feldenkrais teachers try to impart to their artist-clients is that all motion, no matter how small, in some way affects the whole body. Continuing the example of the stringed-instrument player, consider the violinist. To play the violin requires hand-finger precision, speed, force, and pressure control. But one cannot concentrate solely on the fingers of the hand since the fingers are connected with the hand, wrist, forearm, elbow, shoulder and chest, and even, functionally speaking, with the supporting structures of the pelvis, legs, and feet.

Sullivan (1987) observes that the training of the actor's body to improve theatrical performance has always been a topic of debate in the history of theater, but it was not until the eighteenth century that interest began to shift from vocal training to a program that included movement training and movement skills. A study of the current theater reveals changing attitudes with respect to the use of movement both in training and performance. In addition to the contributions of Konstantin Stanislavski, Vsevolod Meyerhold, and Jerzy Grotowski, three non-theater practitioners have had a strong influence on the attitudes of movement training for the modern actor: Rudolf Laban and his Effort/Shape theory of modern dance and his system of movement choreography, F. M. Alexander's method of postural and movement improvement, and Moshe Feldenkrais and functional integration.

Chabora (1994) studied the developments in the field of neuropsychology since 1966 that have influenced training available for actors. She found that the advances in hemispheric lateralization and specialization research begun by Roger Sperry in 1966 as well as the application of this neuropsychological research to "self-use systems" that have been incorporated into actor-training curriculums over the past several decades are highly significant as modern trends. The main self-use systems she found are the Alexander technique, Sweigard's ideokinesis, and functional integration. Chabora's descriptive study also identified a cyclical pattern of how neuropsychological research has been and can be applied to self-use training for actors.

According to Tabish (1995), current brain research provides empirical evidence that suggests the validity of the premises underlying brain-hemisphere theories of learning. The actor's mind and body are in fact a mind-body unity that is readily accessible and responsive to external and internal physical manipulation. While kinesthetic engagement is only one technique for the actor, knowing what it is, why it enhances ease and expressiveness of performance, and how it can be consciously controlled and applied serve the pedagogy behind actor training.

Stress Reduction

Because functional integration teaches ease of movement and the reduction of effort through conscious awareness, it seeks to change unconscious, habitual movement patterns that create physical stress. In this regard, it may have great potential application in the work force where people have confined their movements to a small repertoire of repetitive behaviors—working on an assembly line, sitting at a desk, or using a computer and a telephone. With this idea in mind, Casola (1990) designed a specialized stress-reduction program incorporating Feldenkrais and yoga movements as well as other mind-body practices that can be performed while sitting at one's desk.

The Chronically Disabled

Ofir (1993) found that functional integration had positive results when applied to two subjects with traumatic brain injury and may have great potential value in physical rehabilitation. Ofir reports that the physical recovery of the first subject was remarkable in that she regained some 85% of her functional physical activities and continued to improve to such an extent that her formal physical rehabilitation program has been discontinued and her cognitive remediation program maintained. The second subject responded positively to the treatment program and was improving in accordance with expectations until a serious medical complication of unknown etiology caused a partial regression that, at the time of his report, was not fully overcome. Ofir's data support the application of functional integration as a valuable physical rehabilitation method for the remediation of physical disability sustained as a result of brain injury.

Sports Enthusiasts

Functional integration can potentially be of value anywhere, at any time, and in any way a person uses her or his body. Such potential applicability for functional integration, as in other forms of somatic education and therapy, is of great note in the area of athletic performance. Functional integration appears to be making some inroads in this area, as two recent articles in the popular health press may indicate. Pear (1993) reported the idea that an athlete who moves incorrectly hampers his or her ability to perform and is potentially at greater risk of sustaining injury. Her article includes descriptions of three methods in body movement reeducation, the Rolfing, Feldenkrais, and Alexander techniques, that a professional or amateur athlete may use to improve movement efficiency. Rhodes (1995), in another article in the popular press, reports on five "mind-body" workouts that may be natural matches with five different sports: yoga for runners, the Alexander technique for swimmers, Pilates exercises for skiers, tai chi for hikers, and functional integration for cyclists. While this is an admittedly narrow application of the Feldenkrais Method, it highlights the positive application of neuromuscular repatterning in sports and the growing awareness of such ideas in the mind of the general public.

Training of Feldenkrais Instructors

The training of Feldenkrais instructors is guided by the Feldenkrais Guild, an international organization whose training programs are supervised by the Guild Training Board. The guild has regional centers in many countries, including the United States, Austria, Belgium, Canada, France, Germany, Israel, Italy, the Netherlands, Norway, Sweden, Switzerland, and the United Kingdom. To become a Feldenkrais teacher, one must complete between 800 and 1,000 hours of training over a three-to four-year period. A directory of approved practitioners in the United States and informational materials are available from the Feldenkrais Guild of North America, 524 Ellsworth St. SW, P.O. Box 489, Albany, Oregon 97321. (Phone 800–775–2118)

NOTE

The author is indebted to contributions made by Steve Shafarman during the development of this article. Shafarman, a Feldenkrais practitioner and graduate student at Fielding Institute, began studies with Moshe Feldenkrais in 1976 and was his assistant and appointment secretary during Feldenkrais's last trip to the United States in 1981. Shafarman is the author of *Awareness Heals: The Feldenkrais Method for Dynamic Health* (Reading, MA: Addison-Wesley, 1997).

REFERENCES

Casola, A. (1990). *Less stress through awareness.* Unpublished doctoral dissertation, Union Institute, Cincinnati, OH.

Chabora, P. D. (1994). *A descriptive study of the application of research in neuropsychology to self-use training for actors.* Unpublished doctoral dissertation, Michigan State University, East Lansing.

Feldenkrais, M. (1949). *Body and mature behaviour: A study of anxiety, sex, gravitation, and learning.* New York: International Universities Press.

Feldenkrais, M. (1977). *Awareness through movement: Health exercises for personal growth.* New York: Harper & Row.

Goldfarb, L. W. (1990). *Articulating changes.* Unpublished master's thesis, San Jose State University, San Jose, CA.

Goldfarb, L. W. (1995). *Understanding standing*. Unpublished doctoral dissertation, University of Illinois, Urbana-Champaign.

Ofir, R. D. (1993). *A heuristic investigation of the process of motor learning using the Feldenkrais (RTM) method in physical rehabilitation of two young women with traumatic brain injury*. Unpublished doctoral dissertation, Union Institute, Cincinnati, OH.

Pear, M. J. (1993, March). All the right moves. *Women's Sports and Fitness, 15*(2), 28–30.

Rhodes, M. (1995, February). Complementary exercise. *Women's Sports and Fitness, 17*(1), 45–50.

Shafarman, S. (1997). *Awareness heals: The Feldenkrais method for dynamic health*. Reading, MA: Addison-Wesley.

Shafarman, S. (1998, March 27). Personal communication.

Sullivan, C. N. (1987). *Movement training for the actor: A twentieth-century comparison and analysis*. Unpublished doctoral dissertation, University of Colorado, Boulder.

Tabish, D. R. (1995). *Kinesthetic engagement technique: Theories and practices for training the actor*. Unpublished doctoral dissertation, University of Pittsburgh, Pittsburgh, PA.

Wildman, F. (1995, March). Anti exercise for the older and wise. *Advance for Physical Therapists, 6*(9), 7–21.

18

Erich Fromm: Humanistic Psychoanalysis

DANIEL BURSTON

THE MAN AND HIS LIFE

Born on March 23, 1900, in Frankfurt, Germany, Erich Pinchas Fromm (1900–1980) became the most widely read psychoanalyst of his day, authoring such best-sellers as *Escape from Freedom* (1941), *Man for Himself* (1947), *Psychoanalysis and Religion* (1950), *The Forgotten Language* (1951), *The Sane Society* (1955), *The Art of Loving* (1956), *Sigmund Freud's Mission* (1959), *Zen Buddhism and Psycho-analysis* (with Suzuki and de Martino, 1960), *The Heart of Man* (1964), and many others.

Childhood Roots in Judaism

Though Fromm is widely admired for his lively and accessible writing style, which is readily intelligible to people from all backgrounds and walks of life, it is impossible to understand Fromm personally without appreciating his Jewish roots and his lifelong preoccupations with the work of Karl Marx and Sigmund Freud. Erich's mother, Rosa, and his father, Naphtali, were both descended from a long line of rabbis, and in keeping with his family name—Fromm means "pious" in German—he studied with some of the leading religious scholars of his day, including Rabbi Nehemia Nobel and Rabbi Zalman Baruch Rabinkow. As a result, by his late teens, Fromm had the opportunity to converse with such luminaries as Franz Rosenzweig, Martin Buber, Gershom Scholem, Ernst Simon, and S. I. Agnon.

Moreover, and more importantly, Rabbi Nobel and Rabbi Rabinkow left a deep

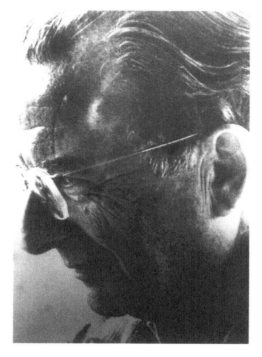

Erich Fromm (Photo courtesy of Daniel Burston).

impression on Fromm. In their different ways, they combined a traditionalist approach to religious observance with a great personal and intellectual openness to others' traditions and ideas—Nobel being steeped in Goethe, the German Enlightenment, and the great neo-Kantian Hermann Cohen, and Rabinkow being steeped in socialism, Hasidism, and Kaballah. These two traits that his teachers shared, namely, deep rootedness in tradition combined with great openness, originality, and syncretism, shaped Fromm's attitudes toward socialism and psychoanalysis in later life. To the end of his days, Fromm meditated on Scripture, and in moments of great exaltation or sorrow he would spontaneously break into a Hasidic song or dance, often to the merriment or embarrassment of friends and passersby (Funk, 1983).

Humanistic Studies

While Fromm was immersed in religious studies during his teenage years, he also studied history, philosophy, and literature. Moreover, as he recalled, his interest in social psychology was kindled by the events surrounding World War I. As Germany prepared for war, Fromm noted with dismay that many of his friends and teachers were swept up in the prevailing war hysteria. As the war wore on, he felt a deepening sense of doubt and betrayal at the official lies and propaganda churned out by the German newspapers. When the war ended, Germany was in ruins, and Fromm, now eighteen, was desperate to understand more about the roots of human destructiveness, a preoccupation that would stay with him for the remainder of his life (Fromm, 1962). As a result, during the 1960s and 1970s Fromm would write extensively on human destructiveness, challenging the rival orthodoxies of Freud and B. F. Skinner in provocative and illuminating ways.

Training in Psychoanalysis

Four years later, at the age of twenty-two, Fromm received his doctorate in sociology under Alfred Weber's supervision at Heidelberg. The subject of his dissertation was the function of talmudic law in three Jewish communities: the Orthodox, Reform Jewry, and the Karaites. Fromm was toying with the idea of becoming a rabbi, but at twenty-four he met his first analyst and later his first wife, Frieda Reichmann, a progressive Jewish psychiatrist trained by Kurt Goldstein and Hanns Sachs. A formidable person in her own right, Fromm's first wife would go on to achieve considerable recognition in the United States under her married name of Frieda Fromm-Reichmann. With her assistance, Fromm's training analysis with Wilhelm Wittenberg commenced at age twenty-five in Munich and was followed by a year under Karl Landauer back in Frankfurt, after which point he finally relinquished his Orthodox Jewish observances. He finished his training with two more years under Hanns Sachs and Theodor Reik in Berlin, returning to Frankfurt shortly thereafter (Funk, 1983).

PSYCHOANALYSIS AND POLITICS

Marxist and Socialist Viewpoints in the Psychoanalytic Movement

Although Fromm trained with the steadfast Freudian loyalists, his real sympathies lay with Freud's loyal opposition, or those independent-minded analysts who tried to reconcile their fidelity to Freud with other influences and ideas, but who attempted to remain within the analytic mainstream (Burston, 1991, chap. 1). When Fromm began writing in the late 1920s, Freud's loyal opposition could be divided into two camps, the Marxists and the non-Marxists. The non-Marxists were somewhat dispersed geographically and were so strikingly individual in many ways that one hesitates to call them a "group." But their number included analysts like Sandor Ferenczi, Georg Groddeck, Karen Horney, Ludwig Binswanger, and Paul Schilder, among others. (Groddeck and Horney, in particular, were close personal friends of Erich and Frieda.)

By contrast, the left-leaning analysts included Wilhelm Reich and his followers, other participants in Otto Fenichel's *Kinderseminar*, and a sprinkling of Viennese and Hungarian analysts like Bruno Bettelheim and Paul Gero, who were periph-eral players in Fenichel's circle (Jacoby, 1983). During the late 1920s and early 1930s the intellectual center of gravity for this group was Berlin. Here again, however, characterizing Freud's left-wing loyal opposition as a "group" is prob-lematic because despite various collaborative efforts, they fought bitterly and ex-pressed their differences with a cold and furious pedantry rooted as much in left-wing sectarianism as in the jealous, fratricidal atmosphere Freud cultivated among his less independent followers (Burston, 1991).

In retrospect, it is interesting to note that Fromm was the only one among them with an academic, rather than a medical, background. In 1927, at the in-vitation of Max Horkheimer, he became the director of social psychology at the Frankfurt Institute for Social Research, a left-leaning scholarly enclave that would eventually have a massive impact on postwar intellectual life in the United States and Europe. Fromm was the only psychoanalyst at the institute and, in the course of his duties there, conducted a posthumously published empirical study of pro-fascist tendencies of German workers (Fromm, 1984)—the forerunner, in fact, for *The Authoritarian Personality* by Theodor Adorno and his collaborators (Bur-ston, 1991).

Although Fromm was a follower of Reich's for about a year, Reich and he quarrelled prior to Fromm's appointment to the Frankfurt Institute (Burston, 1991; Eros, 1992), and Fromm had no respect for Fenichel whatsoever. One of the differences between Reich and Fromm was Reich's involvement with the Communist party, which Fromm and his associates, notably Max Horkheimer and Herbert Marcuse, viewed with deep suspicion (Jay, 1973; Eros, 1992). An-other divisive issue was Freud's libido theory, which Reich retained (in modified form), but which Fromm soon abandoned.

In any case, Freud's left-wing opposition, such as it was, was fragmented and dispersed by the events preceding World War II and the flight of European émi-grés to America. The events and processes that caused their fragmentation are too complicated to relate in detail here. Suffice it to say that though he avoided the sterile controversies between Reich and Fenichel, in 1938 Fromm left the Frank-furt Institute for Social Research (now operating in exile at Columbia University). His departure was triggered by, among other things, disagreements about the issue of fidelity to Freud. As Fromm later recalled, Horkheimer, who had supported him initially, was now deeply displeased with his criticisms of Freud. Immediately after Fromm's departure, Theodor Adorno joined the institute (Jay, 1973).

Meanwhile, having moved to America in 1933, Fromm set up practice in New York, where he became a regular member of Harry Stack Sullivan's Zodiac Club, socializing with Sullivan, Karen Horney, Clara Thompson, Ruth Benedict, Ralph Linton, Margaret Mead, and Abram Kardiner, among others. Fromm divorced Fromm-Reichmann, now an associate of Sullivan's, in 1940 and after an an-guished and abortive romance with Karen Horney married his second wife, Henny Gurland, in 1944 (Funk, 1983).

Postwar Orthodoxy: Fromm Increasingly Isolated

In the war's immediate aftermath, as the Cold War took hold, innovative and independent-minded analysts were increasingly enveloped by (and answerable to) a resurgent orthodoxy that swept psychoanalysis in the United States during the late 1940s, 1950s, and early 1960s, when McCarthyism ran rampant, and pressures for mindless conformity in America were prevalent and intense. In this climate of opinion, Reich became a staunch anti-Communist and a great admirer of Dwight D. Eisenhower, while Otto Fenichel managed to conceal his Marxist past (Jacoby, 1983) and aligned himself with the orthodox analytic establishment. Fromm, undeterred, made no secret of his socialism, but was angrily attacked by Fenichel for his "revisionist" views on psychoanalytic theory.

Other attacks from the left came from Theodor Adorno, who was about to embark on *The Authoritarian Personality* (Jay, 1973, chap. 3), and from another Frankfurt Institute alumnus, Herbert Marcuse. Marcuse had come to Freud somewhat after World War II and had evidently hoped to find in Freud a "revolutionary" philosopher who would revive his flagging faith in the possibilities of radical social transformation (Jay, 1973). As far as I know, Fromm never bothered to respond to Fenichel or Adorno publicly, but the debate between Fromm and Marcuse, which began in 1955, was a long and bitter one, indicating that Fromm attributed much more importance to Marcuse's attack than the ones that preceded it (Burston, 1991). Indeed, in retrospect, it was more important, as most of the New Left intelligentsia sided with Marcuse after 1968, dismissing Fromm as an idle conformist, an assessment that has contributed to the comparative neglect of Fromm ever since.

FROMM'S MOVE TO MEXICO

After his ejection from the International Psychoanalytic Association, Fromm was made clinical director of the William Alanson White Institute in New York City. He held this position from 1946 to 1950, though in the fall of 1949 Fromm and Gurland moved to Mexico in the hopes of arresting or reversing Gurland's rheumatoid arthritis. As it turned out, however, they were not successful, and she died early in 1952. Fromm was devastated, but at the invitation of the government, he decided to stay on in Mexico and to found the Mexican Institute of Psychoanalysis, which he directed until 1967, when a heart attack prompted a retreat to Locarno, Switzerland, to recuperate for several months (Burston, 1991).

In the intervening decade and a half, from 1952 to 1967, Fromm led a varied and active life. In December 1953 Fromm married his third wife, Anis Freeman, an American woman, who was his constant companion and helped design their magnificent home in Cuernavaca. Erich and Anis solicited help in planting and landscaping their garden from the noted Zen scholar D. T. Suzuki. Suzuki lived in a small hut on their property throughout much of 1959 and taught Fromm about Buddhism and meditation.

While deepening his familiarity with Asian art and ideas, Fromm was also immersing himself in the culture of his newly adopted home. In 1955 and 1956 Fromm, who had taught anthropology with Ralph Linton in 1947, joined Lorette Cenourne for an intensive postgraduate seminar on the religion, economics, and history of pre-Columbian cultures in Central America. With this new knowledge now firmly in his grasp, from 1957 to 1963 Fromm and his associates conducted a massive study of a Mayan peasant village, Chiconcuac, in which he gathered all available historical and anthropological data on the 162 households and conducted detailed psychological testing, face-to-face interviews, and naturalistic observation on a day-to-day basis. The findings, published as *Social Character in a Mexican Village* (Fromm & Maccoby, 1970/1996), is a much-neglected classic in the history of social psychology.

FAME, SOCIAL ACTIVISM, AND THE THIRD FORCE

During his immersion in Mexican culture Fromm continued to live and teach for three months a year in the United States. For most of this time he stayed in New York, but he also spoke and taught for brief periods all around the country. This was the time of Fromm's greatest fame and popularity, and he used his reputation to further the causes of nuclear disarmament, civil rights, and, in due course, the anti–Vietnam War movement. Through his books, pamphlets, and public lectures, Fromm acquired a vast and varied readership and came to the attention of psychologists around the world. In 1963, during an inaugural address for the new building for the Mexican Institute of Psychoanalysis, Fromm spoke of the rise of a Third Force in psychology, psychiatry, and psychoanalysis (Fromm, 1963/1975), though strangely enough he did not engage in dialogue with Abraham Maslow, Carl Rogers, or Rollo May, who, incidentally, was an analysand of his. Despite his rejection of (and by) orthodox psychoanalysis, Fromm maintained that most humanistic and existential psychologists failed to grasp the vital core of Freud's work or were simply too harsh or dismissive toward him. Finally, as I noted in *The Legacy of Erich Fromm* (1991), the words "humanism" and "humanistic" have somewhat different connotations for Europeans and Americans, and Fromm remained decidedly European in outlook throughout his entire life.

In 1967, after a hectic odyssey of public speaking engagements in the United States, Fromm suffered a heart attack and in the course of his recovery in Locarno began to withdraw from public life. In 1968 his popularity slowly began to wane as the rise of the counterculture and the New Left brought many new ideologues into the limelight, among whom were his old adversary Marcuse and the existential psychoanalyst R. D. Laing. Nevertheless, in 1969 Fromm began work on his last big best-seller, *The Anatomy of Human Destructiveness* (1973), a massive and engrossing study that wove his clinical, sociological, and philosophical erudition together with recent findings in genetics, ethology, and neurophysiology. It was an impressive effort. Around this time Fromm began to take a deep interest in Theravada Buddhism and to cultivate a warm and extensive correspondence with one of its greatest living exponents, Nyanaponika Mahathera.

FROMM'S HUMANISTIC VISION OF PSYCHOANALYSIS

To Have or To Be?, published in 1976, was Fromm's last effort to synthesize the psychoanalytic and spiritual traditions that had informed his life and work with the kind of humanistic social criticism that had first brought him into the public eye in *The Sane Society* (1955). *Greatness and Limitations of Freud's Thought*, published in 1980, is a testament to Fromm's creative ambivalence toward Freud. On the one hand, Fromm is unsparing in his criticism of Freud's mechanistic materialism, his muddled metapsychology and theory of the instincts, his incorrigible sexism, and his authoritarian tendency to turn psychoanalysis into a set of dogmatic precepts rather than an open and evolving field of inquiry. On the other hand, his veneration for Freud is also plain throughout and is evidenced, among other things, in his lifelong project of distilling and expanding the essential core of Freud's thought, which he regarded as humanistic, while discarding those elements that are reductionistic, parochial, or outdated. This attitude of Fromm's, which I term "Freud piety," not only estranged him from many humanistic and existential-phenomenological theorists and practitioners, it also created friction in his relations with Harry Stack Sullivan and Karen Horney. As a result, to the end of his life, Fromm was deeply displeased with the "neo-Freudian" or "cultural school" labels that were used to group him and his former associates together, and he took every opportunity of reminding readers that he felt much closer to Freud than they.

FROMM'S ATTITUDE TOWARD MARX: SOCIALIST HUMANISM

By contrast with his relationship to Freud, Fromm's attitude toward Karl Marx was more forgiving and, as a result, less realistic. Indeed, one could say that while his basic attitude toward Freud never wavered, despite shifts in emphasis over the years, his attitude toward Marx became decidedly less critical with the passage of time. In *The Sane Society* (1955), for example, where Fromm introduced the concept of alienation as a major social problem in the industrialized world, he drew up an illuminating catalog of Marx's errors and oversights and called attention to authoritarian features of Marx's personality and leadership style that fostered the emergence of Leninism and Stalinism later on. His assessment here was quite sound. However, in *Marx's Concept of Man* (1961), Fromm shifted the blame for subsequent developments entirely from Marx's shoulders and, like Trotsky, faulted others for the alleged distortions and deviations from Marx's original message.

Still, *Marx's Concept of Man* was a timely and important book that fostered a revival of socialist humanism in North America and around the world. It contributed enormously to the burgeoning literature on alienation, an idea first thematized in Hegel's *Phenomenology of Spirit* and developed systematically in Marx's *Economic and Philosophic Manuscripts* of 1844. Borrowing from the early, humanistic Marx, Fromm noted that the way in which we are constrained to fulfill our material needs and aspirations in a competitive, materialistic, and technologically dominated society is often profoundly at odds with our existential needs for self-actualization and solidarity with other human beings. This socially patterned discrepancy, which is seldom fully conscious, gives rise to the frequent violation and eventual constriction of our "humanistic conscience," resulting in many varieties of anguish and self-estrangement.

FROMM'S THEORY OF HUMANISTIC CONSCIENCE

Fromm's theory of humanistic conscience is obviously at variance with Freudian theory. In classical Freudianism the part of the personality that corresponds with conscience is supposedly the superego. The superego allegedly consists of unconscious representations of our parents, whose ethical ideas and prohibitions are internalized in childhood. According to Freud, when we act in conformity with these internalized prohibitions and standards of conduct, we feel good about ourselves. When we transgress or violate these ideal standards, even in fantasy, our self-esteem suffers.

However, in many instances, Freud noted, we violate our internalized ethical norms not in fact, but in fantasy, and in many instances, as a result of repression, we are not even aware of our fantasies, being estranged from the real nature of our desire and guilt laden for no apparent reason. Alternatively, the guilt feeling itself is also repressed and masked with self-punishing behavior. This is neurotic guilt. Ideally, however, the superego is a vital part of our psychological organization. Without it, presumably, we would engage in all kinds of antisocial behavior because we lack sufficient "social feelings" (Adler, Reich) to govern our conduct spontaneously. In other words, conscience, while necessary to our social existence, is not a primary part of our instinctual equipment, but a product of socialization that helps curb our antisocial proclivities.

According to Fromm, however, Freud misunderstood conscience. In Fromm's estimation, there are actually two kinds of conscience. The authoritarian conscience, as Fromm called it, corresponds with the Freudian superego. It represents the sum of internalized prohibitions that the individual acquires in the process of socialization, and runs on the principle of obedience. It makes the individual feel guilty for violating standards that are imposed externally, from without, so to speak, and rewards the individual for conforming to social roles and expectations (Fromm, 1947).

By contrast, Fromm believed, the humanistic conscience develops spontaneously in the process of productive living (Fromm, 1947) and is based on the principle of solidarity (Fromm, 1951). It represents the response of the whole person to people and situations based on reverence for life. Subjectively, the humanistic conscience is experienced as a kind of call to act in accordance with the interests of humanity and decency—an ethical imperative that may flatly contradict or override conventional beliefs and prejudices, promoting disobedience or nonconformity, even if the penalties are high.

When a person fails to act in accordance with his or her humanistic conscience, according to Fromm, he or she is troubled by existential guilt, not neurotic guilt, and the only way to resolve that person's problem, finally, is to bring the underlying ethical conflict into consciousness and to act in accordance with the promptings of his or her "better selves." If the person lacks the ability or the courage to do so, he or she will become neurotically impaired.

For example, take an armed guard in a Nazi concentration camp who develops an ulcer or some mysterious gastrointestinal disorder that requires immediate rest and reassignment elsewhere. He is diagnosed correctly by an army psychiatrist as suffering from a psychosomatic complaint, but because of his circumstances, he dares not admit to his employers or coworkers—or, indeed, to himself—that his work sickens him, that the guilt he feels or, more accurately, represses is "eating him up inside." His neurotic disability is a "compromise formation." It falls well short of open disobedience, but absolves him of further responsibility in the death and degradation of countless innocents. The question now is: Is this man, who is poorly adapted to his surroundings, sicker or healthier than his nonneurotic coworkers? Can neurosis be a symptom of "health," so to speak (Burston & Olfman, 1996)?

This last example is admittedly quite extreme and is intended to put the pertinent issues in bold relief. For something a little closer to home, take a gifted writer who cannot earn much in his artistic calling and so goes to work for a newspaper or publisher that publishes mediocre material or has a political agenda that he secretly deplores. He is quite successful initially, but after several months he gets insomnia and starts to drink excessively, so that his job peformance is suddenly impaired, and he is sacked. Alternatively, consider a young woman who falls deeply in love with a man from a different racial, ethnic, or class background, but eventually succumbs to parental pressure to drop the engagement because he does not live up to their expectations. She gives in to their wishes, but becomes grief stricken, hysterical, and anorexic afterwards, ruining her chances of finding another mate. In either of these instances, a Freudian might diagnose unresolved Oedipal issues, latent masochism, the death instinct, and so on. But according to Fromm, these are the stigmata of self-betrayal. In addition to criticizing Freud's theory of conscience, Fromm took issue with several elements of the Freudian outlook, which are summarized briefly here.

Motivation

In addition to their instinctual drives, human beings are motivated primarily by two existential strivings: (1) the need to belong or affiliate oneself, to be related to others at any cost, and (2) the need to individuate, or to actualize one's full emotional and intellectual potential. These needs are often profoundly at variance, and society often strengthens the former at the expense of the latter (Fromm, 1941).

Socialization

Like Reich, Fromm believed that human beings are not naturally as egocentric or antisocial as Freud imagined, and that many of the personality traits that Freud thought natural or instinctive are actually the products of faulty or excessive socialization—that socialization is the cause, and not the cure, for many undesirable character traits (Fromm, 1955).

Character

Fromm believed that character structure is a crystallized pattern of dynamic adaptations to one's cultural and social surroundings that acts as a substitute for animal instincts. However, it does not follow any preordained psychosexual progression, as Freud imagined. Fromm felt that character structure is formed and modified, not just in childhood, but throughout the human life span (Fromm, 1947).

Unconscious

Fromm allowed that the unconscious mind contains the infantile, aggressive, and sexual components that Freud said are excluded from consciousness. But Fromm, like Carl Jung or, indeed, Carl Rogers, thought that the unconscious mind is capable of insights into reality that are quicker, deeper, and more certain than our conscious judgment, and that it may contain hidden resources of strength, as well as strivings toward maturity, integration, and love (Fromm, 1962, 1963/1975).

Love and Hate

According to the logic of Freud's libido theory, love of self (narcissism) and love of others (object love) are mutually exclusive. Similarly, he argued that the death instinct can cathect the self in masochism or be directed outwards at others in sadism. While recognizing the depth and danger of narcissism (Fromm, 1964), Fromm argued that genuine self-love and love of others are conjunctive, as are self-hatred and hatred of others (Fromm, 1947; Fromm, 1956).

Having said that, however, it is important to remember that Fromm was not a benign optimist or a Pollyanna, as many critics allege. On the contrary, he was always alert to the tragic dimension of human life—to the inevitability of death and the fact that no one, however fortunate or favored, ever realizes his or her full human potential. Toward the end of his life, he became increasingly pessimistic about our prospects for sane living, or indeed, for mere survival in the twenty-first century. Nevertheless, despite his diminished energy and hopefulness, as the end drew near, he always lived and worked in the name of life and would wish to be remembered that way.

REFERENCES

Burston, D. (1991). *The legacy of Erich Fromm*. Cambridge, MA: Harvard University Press.
Burston, D., & Olfman, S. (1996). Freud, Fromm, and the pathology of normalcy. In M. Cortina & M. Maccoby (Eds.), *A prophetic analyst: Erich Fromm's contribution to psychoanalysis* (pp. 301–323). New York: Jason Aronson.
Eros, F. (1992). Wilhelm Reich, Erich Fromm, and the analytical psychology of the Frankfurt school. In M. Kessler & R. Funk (Eds.), *Erich Fromm und die Frankfurter Schule* (pp. 69–73). Tübingen: Francke Verlag.
Fromm, E. (1941). *Escape from freedom*. New York: Holt, Rinehart & Winston.
Fromm, E. (1947). *Man for himself*. New York: Holt, Rinehart, & Winston.
Fromm, E. (1950). *Psychoanalysis and religion*. New Haven: Yale University Press.
Fromm, E. (1951). *The forgotten language*. New York: Rinehart.
Fromm, E. (1955). *The sane society*. Greenwich, CT: Fawcett Premier Books.
Fromm, E. (1956). *The art of loving*. New York: Bantam Books.
Fromm, E. (1961). *Marx's concept of man*. New York: Frederick Ungar.
Fromm, E. (1962). *Beyond the chains of illusion*. New York: Simon & Schuster.
Fromm, E. (1964). *The heart of man: Its genius for good and evil*. New York: Harper & Row.
Fromm, E. (1973). *The anatomy of human destructiveness*. Greenwich, CT: Fawcett Premier Books.
Fromm, E. (1975). Humanism and psychoanalysis. *Contemporary Psychoanalysis, 11*(4), 396–406. (Original publication 1963)
Fromm, E. (1976). *To have or to be?* Greenwich, CT: Fawcett Premier Books.
Fromm, E. (1980). *Greatness and limitations of Freud's thought*. New York: Harper & Row.
Fromm, E. (1984). *The working class in Weimar Germany*. Cambridge, MA: Harvard University Press.
Fromm, E., & Maccoby, M. (1970/1996). *Social character in a Mexican Village*. Reprint edition. New Brunswick, NJ: Transaction Publications.
Funk, R. (1983). *Erich Fromm*. Hamburg: Rowohlt Taschenbuch Verlag.
Jacoby, R. (1983). *The repression of psychoanalysis.*: Otto Fenichel and the political Freudians. New York: Basic Books.
Jay, M. (1973). *The dialectical imagination*. Boston: Little, Brown.
Suzuki, D. T., Fromm, E., & de Martino, M. F. (1960). *Zen Buddhism and psychoanalysis*. New York: Harper & Row.

19

Amedeo Giorgi and the Project of a Human Science

FREDERICK J. WERTZ AND
CHRISTOPHER AANSTOOS

BIOGRAPHICAL BACKGROUND

A Discrepancy between Expectations and the Field of Psychology

Having begun college as an English major, Amedeo Giorgi (b. 1931) decided to make psychology his field after having read William James's (1950/1890) *Principles of Psychology* (Giorgi, 1984). In such undergraduate courses as physiological psychology, statistics, and tests and measurements, the field clashed with the expectations that Giorgi had derived from James. In his graduate study of psychophysics, perception, sensation, statistics, and physiology, Giorgi continually felt that the essence of psychological problems was left untouched. Knowledge of physics, physiology, probability theory, and so on seemed superior to the psychological knowledge achieved. He had a vague sense that psychology was leaning too heavily on the achievements of the natural sciences and that psychological problems were not being directly attacked.

After defending his dissertation at Fordham University in May 1957, Giorgi continued to experience discrepancies between academic psychology and its true calling. In his work as a research psychologist at Dunlap and Associates on military and industrial problems, the gap between academic psychology and the demands of the real world came to the fore. Giorgi found that success required general, intelligent problem solving rather than control and manipulation in laboratory experimentation. Giorgi also felt uncomfortable with the inability of psychology to deal squarely with human beings; the primary concern in

Amedeo Giorgi (Photo courtesy of Amedeo Giorgi).

"human-machine" relationships was to fit the human to the machine. Human experience was either not considered at all or was minimized as much as possible.

Returning to academia to teach at Manhattan College, Giorgi found himself presenting the material critically and being unable to believe that the limits of knowledge were due to psychology's youth as a science. His inescapable conclusion was that something was fundamentally wrong with psychology: The access to the psychological was blocked, and the approach to the subject matter was counterproductive.

The Discovery of an Alternative Orientation

At the suggestion of a former classmate, Giorgi met with Adrian van Kaam, who discussed the value of phenomenology and existentialism for psychology. Despite his initial skepticism, Giorgi intensely studied this tradition and was asked by van Kaam to join the Duquesne psychology faculty in the fall of 1962 in order to work out an integration of phenomenology and psychological research.

In an attempt to approach such fundamental phenomena as attention, perception, and learning in a way Giorgi called "systematic" rather than experimental, he began with a study of the history of psychology. Giorgi became aware of an "alternative" or "dissenting" tradition internationally protesting the status quo in virtually every period, including writers such as Franz Brentano, Wilhelm Dilthey, Edmund Husserl, James Ward, George Frederick Stout, F. C. Bartlett, Edgar Rubin, David Katz, Alfred Binet, Georges Politzer, William McDougall, and Gordon Allport. However, this "tradition of founders" had not achieved agreement among themselves and had not established a cohesive and unified worldwide institution. Hence there was no geographical or historical continuity of any alternative.

THE PROBLEMS OF PSYCHOLOGY AS A NATURAL SCIENCE: THE IMPORTANCE OF APPROACH

Giorgi was impressed by an article written by Bentley (1930), who called for psychology to shed its extrinsic influences and find its own true perspective in order to finally dispel the fragmentation and confusion in the field (Giorgi, 1984). In his first book, *Psychology as a Human Science* (1970), Giorgi focuses on the psychologists' conception of the nature of psychology and science in a historical way in order to move "Third Force" psychology from its focus on clinical and personality issues to more fundamental disciplinary concerns.

The Root of Psychology's Problems

Giorgi recounts the persistence of complaints about psychology's lack of unity, lack of consistent direction, failure to investigate meaningful phenomena, failure to do justice to the whole person, and irrelevance. All these problems, along with psychology's inability to resolve recurrent theoretical controversies, in Giorgi's view, stem from psychology's inappropriate attempt to be a natural science, which fails to provide psychology with a proper and central relationship to its subject matter that would provide unity, consistency, comprehensivity, and relevance. On the contrary, the natural science approach inevitably engenders fragmentation, exclusion of important phenomena, loss of a sense of the whole person, irrelevance, and remoteness from life. For instance, topics are limited to what is measurable; experimentation isolates variables from the whole; and hypothetical thought proliferates theoretical fragmentation. This orientation involves the unexamined and uncritical adoption of the presuppositions that psychology must be experimental, reductionistic, deterministic, positivistic, quantitative, genetic, predictive, and independently observing.

The Importance of Approach in Psychology

Giorgi's analysis leads him to delineate the essential role of approach, beyond method and subject matter, in the constitution of science. By "approach" Giorgi refers to what Thomas Kuhn called "paradigm" but adds more, including the entire taken-for-granted worldview of the scientist. Because the presuppositions that make up the natural science approach are philosophical, Giorgi challenges the idea that by adopting the methods of the natural sciences, psychology could be autonomous from philosophy. Psychology cannot solve its disciplinary problems by refining or even changing its methods as long as it is driven by a philosophy not suited to its subject matter. In phenomenological philosophy, Giorgi finds an orientation that does not seek homogeneity among the sciences and provides general directives for fresh, self-critical investigations into foundational concepts and appropriate methods for psychology.

A Fresh Start: Phenomenology and the Lifeworld

In Giorgi's view, sciences most fruitfully begin by first studying the subject matter and only subsequently asking the question of what it would mean to be scientific and what methods achieve the best knowledge. But where to begin? Giorgi went to what phenomenologists call "the lifeworld," the world of everyday life that precedes and is the implicit ground of all sciences. There psychology should be faithful to the human being as a person, show a special concern for uniquely human phenomena, accord a primacy to relationships over isolated elements, and involve an engaged attitude on the part of the investigator. Further, Giorgi asserted that the proper subject matter for psychological science is the "structures of intentionality" found in those person-work situational unities that give rise to meaning.

UNIQUE RESEARCH METHODS FOR HUMAN SCIENCE

Rather than taking any one method, or even a set of methods, for granted, Giorgi calls for the fresh and at times innovative development of and justification for methods in each unique research project. In order to highlight the reflectivity that should be a part of the researcher's activities, Giorgi prefers to speak of the praxis rather than mere "practice."

From the Laboratory to the Lifeworld

Giorgi's first research projects replicated other studies, for example, in learning and memory, utilizing classical experimental paradigms (e.g., Giorgi, 1967b, 1975; Colaizzi, 1971). But rather than limiting the data collection and analysis to measured performance, Giorgi analyzed descriptions of the experimental situation provided by the experimental subjects in order to gain further insight into the psychological processes involved. For instance, these studies supplemented the knowledge of nonsense-syllable learning by providing analyses of the qualitatively different learning strategies used and the various manners in which experience is organized in different phases of the learning process.

However, Giorgi was not satisfied with these studies inasmuch as laboratory tasks imposed by the experimenter provide no access to knowledge of the psychological processes involved in everyday life. In order to overcome this problem, Giorgi began to take phenomena of interest to experimental psychologists and to study a lifeworld situation in which they could be more faithfully known than the artificiality of the laboratory would allow. For instance, McConville (1974) took up the problem of the perceptual judgment of horizontal lines, but rather than using the rod-and-frame task, he collected descriptions from golf players and analyzed their experience of the slopes of golf courses during play.

Inasmuch as even these studies presuppose definitions of research problems from the standpoint of the psychologists, they too fall short of maximal fidelity to life as it is lived outside of the psychologist's agenda. Giorgi therefore invited research participants to describe their psychological life in a more open-ended way in order to allow the psychological researcher to define the phenomena, theoretical problems, and other issues with less prejudiced access to the actual lives of persons. For instance, in a study of anger, participants might be asked simply to describe situations in which they were angry, and the researcher's role would be to identify and elaborate the structure of anger as it presents itself in such descriptions of everyday life. Giorgi contends that the most important research problems and most suitable experimental situations should follow from direct contact with the lifeworld.

The Researcher's Choice Points and Options

Giorgi argues for a widening in the range of options that may be appropriate for a given research project. The essential choice points are the research problem or question, the research situation, the research participants, the data constitution, analytic procedures, and the expression of findings (Giorgi, 1983).

At each of these choice points, Giorgi advocates widening the alternatives for the psychological researcher so as to make greater fidelity to the researched phenomenon possible. For instance, in the area of data, Giorgi calls for concrete and ultimately verbal descriptions, utilizing ordinary language of everyday life. Participants offer descriptions either orally or in writing and either in an interview or in solitude. The task may be relatively open ended or very elaborate and specific. Description may be simultaneous or retrospective and may be constituted from the first-person perspective or from the viewpoint of an other.

The expression of findings may take many forms. It may aim at formulating knowledge of a single case, a typical psychological structure, or a general, even universal, structure. These findings are expressed in ordinary language. When psychological jargon is used, it is used descriptively, and the researcher is careful to clarify its concrete meaning in the research findings in contrast to theoretical implications a term might carry in other contexts. The report may be discursive, including narrative, or utilize tables and diagrams; it may be brief and telegraphic or elaborate. In any case, the inclusion of participants' voices and abundant use of their descriptions is essential to presentation for the purpose of informing readers of the nature of the procedures, giving them a better understanding of the context within which the findings emerged, and so that they may provide critical checks and balances.

Qualitative Analytic Procedures

Given his concern with systematic rigor and accountability in research, Giorgi was careful to identify the steps of his qualitative analytic procedures in his early research efforts (Giorgi, 1975). Although he was describing what he had done in a particular study of learning rather than prescribing general procedures, these same steps have been employed in other contexts by Giorgi himself (1985a, 1989b) and by a diverse array of other researchers. In our view, Giorgi has identified essential steps for qualitative data analysis: openly reading the description, demarcating changes in meaning (or "meaning units") as they appear to the researcher, reflecting on the psychological significance of each meaning unit, and summarizing the findings in an integrated, cohesive statement. He has articulated and ordered the operative intentionalities that constitute any qualitative psychological analysis. We have elaborated these procedures even further and demonstrated their unacknowledged but essential presence in diverse existential-phenomenological research (Wertz, 1983a, 1983b) as well as in the qualitative research of the psychoanalytic tradition (Wertz, 1987).

Justification of Methods: The Problems of Validity and Reliability

Giorgi accepts the burden of rigorous accountability, but he affirms Kuhn's emphasis on the difficulties of communication that arise between different scientific paradigms (Giorgi, 1988). In order to communicate, educate, and remain consistent with his own approach, Giorgi's strategy is to radically reflect on the essential scientific demands underlying traditional research principles and then to freshly rethink how a phenomenological perspective would address these. The typical result is that if one is able to successfully shift paradigms, it becomes clear that the phenomenological methods have problems and difficulties of their own, but that these difficulties can be addressed and resolved, just as is the case for experimental methods.

One must first understand basic paradigm differences in order to properly approach these issues. Giorgi (1966) cleared much of the basic ground in distinguishing experimentation from research, quantity from quality, measurement from grasping meaning, analysis from explication, determined reactions from intentional subjects, identical repetition from essential theme, and independent from participant observer. One must respect the aim and focus of research that aims at the qualitative structures of psychological life so as to explicate the meanings of intentional activities according to their essential themes from the standpoint of an engaged researcher.

Giorgi has been careful to address criticisms that other psychologists voice in opposition to phenomenological procedures. For instance, Giorgi (1986c) theoretically justifies the potential adequacy of verbal description. In a later article (Giorgi, 1989a), he confronts such critics of verbal data as Nisbett and Wilson (1977) and empirically demonstrates their value for phenomenological research. Giorgi has also written extensively on how traditional aspirations of the researcher such as "standardization," "manipulation," "observation," and "measurement" must not be considered essential for phenomenological psychology but imply scientific values that the phenomenologist fulfills in a way that is more appropriate for psychology (Giorgi, 1986b, 1994). In addressing concerns of reliability and validity, Giorgi (1988) formulates the principle of proper evidence for knowledge claims given the contingency and corrigibility of the empirical order. He shows how phenomenological procedures insure that knowledge claims are genuinely data based and remain within the limits of the data given. Phenomenological criteria are stricter than those of quantitative research in that all empirical data as well as all imaginable data must be consistent with knowledge statements, which must be substantiated not merely in a probability estimate concerning the aggregate but in each individual case.

EMPIRICAL AND THEORETICAL ADVANCES

Specific Psychological Subject Matter

In contrast with psychology's study of highly abstracted phenomena under laboratory conditions, Giorgi has investigated phenomena that are concretely lived in the world, from traffic flow to artistic creativity to moral sense. However, his major projects have attempted to challenge mainstream psychology by researching topics it takes to be foundational. Giorgi aims "to show that problems of sensation, perception, memory, etc. all could be radicalized by using the phenomenological approach if we had a genuinely appropriate method" (Giorgi, in Aanstoos, 1996, p. 16). The result is that even psychology's most mechanistically understood processes can reveal an irreducibly human depth. Because this research program was primarily conceived as a demonstration of the efficacy of phenomenological methodology, these investigations have not been carried through completely; there is "about five percent done and ninety-five percent to do" (Giorgi, in Aanstoos, 1996, p. 16). Nevertheless, Giorgi has made some important and original findings, especially in the areas of learning, memory, and imagination.

Giorgi has devoted his most intense attention to learning over more than two decades (Giorgi, 1967b, 1986a). In an early study of serial learning using lists of letters and words but with a phenomenological addition, the analysis of participants' experience, Giorgi found that while the aggregate behavioral data showed no statistically significant difference in difficulty between lists of meaningful words and nonsense syllables, not a single subject experienced them as equally difficult. Relative difficulty depended upon the strategy each subject adopted. This finding led Giorgi to affirm the importance of distinguishing the psychological reality from the physical stimulus and to demonstrate the priority of the former in psychological activities. Giorgi showed the key role of the subjects' experience in shaping performance, a role that is veiled when only the behavioral data are considered (Giorgi, 1967a, 1967b).

Giorgi next moved beyond the laboratory in order to study learning as it oc-curred naturally in everyday activities such as making yogurt and driving a car (1975, 1985a). In discerning the essential structures of learning, Giorgi discovered that learning is not merely the acquisition of knowledge, but also the application of this knowledge to attain a "new way of perceiving" (1975, p. 97) that emerged through subjects' discovery of a discrepancy between their previous assumptions and the emergent situation (1985a, p. 65). In other words, learning is essentially an experience of engagement with something "new" that reorganizes experience by breaking through the previous assumptive world and reverberates so that it can be built upon again. Giorgi thus related the subject's knowledge, behavioral ap-plication, and attitude, concluding that "learning is the relationship between each of these so-called contents and the experiential-behavioral history of the subject" (1975, pp. 97–98).

Another discovery that Giorgi has repeatedly emphasized about learning is its essential interpersonal context (1975, p. 98; 1985a, pp. 67–68). From the actual or virtual presence of a learned other to the social contexts in which the learning is confirmed in application, Giorgi has noted that it is a "radically inter-human phenomenon" (1975, p. 98). As he also notes, this important dimension has re-mained only implicit in many laboratory settings.

Giorgi's research on the imagination can be reviewed more briefly here, yet in this context he has also advanced an understanding that eluded mainstream ap-proaches. He conducted two phenomenological studies, utilizing descriptions gathered from other subjects (1987a) and from himself (1987b). Giorgi described imaginal experiencing as a constructive dialectic between an ideal and its empirical variations (Giorgi, in Aanstoos, 1996, pp. 22–23). This dialectic contrasts with cognitive psychology's usual conception of the imagination as the apprehension of a "thinglike" image. Cognitivism's preoccupation with "the image alone, with-out contextualization, is too narrow to capture the total imaginary experience. . . . to work on just a focus without context is ultimately to indulge in abstraction" (Giorgi, 1987a, p. 39). As Giorgi discovered instead, in a "meaningful relationship between present reality and the imagined events . . . [r]eality lacks are fulfilled by the irreal presences of the imagination, and these presences are psychologically meaningfully related to the gaps in reality" (Giorgi, 1987a, p. 41).

In summary, with respect to his research on key psychological processes, Giorgi is pushing beyond psychology's usual elementistic, mechanistic, and reductionistic conceptions. He does this by seeing within these very basic processes such essen-tial dialectical dimensions as context. In following these insights, Giorgi has elucidated four essential constituents of consciousness itself: sociality, historicity, meaning attribution, and expression (Giorgi, in Aanstoos, 1996). Giorgi's vision of the person-as-a-whole-in-context is his most important research-based insight and will undoubtedly be his most enduring legacy. Giorgi has also succeeded in establishing phenomenological psychology as an empirical research science that provides original psychological knowledge.

Implications for a Definition of Psychology

Giorgi believes that good research and knowledge come first and answers to fundamental disciplinary questions about subject matter and method in general follow. Premature attempts to define and set limits on psychology have led to poor knowledge and disciplinary confusion. After having engaged in his own psychological research, Giorgi has not hesitated to speak out on such perplexing disciplinary issues as the possibility of unity in psychology, the nature of psychological subject matter, and the essential ingredients of science.

The Problem of Unity in Psychology

Giorgi has taken strong positions in the debate about the unity of psychology. He acknowledges the pluralistic character of historical and contemporary psychology but argues that this pluralism arises from theoretical confusion and an inappropriate idea of science. If these were overcome, psychology could achieve unity. Giorgi (1985c, 1985d) clearly indicates that by unity he does not mean homogeneity or the absence of differences but rather "concinnity," which integrates diverse parts under a single idea. Giorgi believes that psychological work can be diverse and yet theoretically coherent, offering complementary knowledge of the various facets of the whole of psychological life. But this principle calls for clarity with respect to the meaning of psychology, a setting of limits on what constitutes psychological subject matter that renders the discipline distinctive, that is, one discipline different from and yet related to other sciences.

A Science of Paraobjective/Paralogical Meaning

Based on his psychological research, Giorgi (1982, 1985d, 1990, 1993) has attempted to formulate the essential character of the psychological. Giorgi (1982) concludes that the psychological lies between the physical and the rational and therefore cannot be conceptualized in physicalistic or rationalistic categories. He calls the psychological "paraobjective" and shows how it demands descriptions of its meaningful structures. Put otherwise, the psychological is "more than biological and less than logical" (Giorgi, 1985d; p. 55). The regularities of the psychological sphere, which Giorgi later calls "paralogical," cannot be deduced or induced but can be intuited and described, the most appropriate descriptor being its meaning (Giorgi, 1990). The most interesting and relevant psychological meanings are contextual and typical rather than universal.

A Broadened Definition of Science

Giorgi (1994) argues that the demands of psychological subject matter and the meaning of science could be resolved by conceiving of a meaning of science that would properly apply to and do justice to human existence. Science, for Giorgi, is methodical, systematic, general, and critical. To be methodical means to use procedures that are rigorously designed in relation to research problems and phenomena as well as being clearly spelled out for maximum accountability and intersubjectivity. Science is systematic in that the various constituents of the discipline's knowledge are conceptually interrelated in an intelligible order. As general, scientific knowledge goes beyond the situation in which it is achieved. Science is critical in that it attempts to address relevant challenges and to acknowledge its limits. Science is not defined in this context by a particular style of theorizing or by particular research methods. Liberating the meaning of science from its historically powerful natural science instantiation opens the possibility to develop an original and appropriate production of knowledge specially designed for human subject matter.

IMPACT ON THE FIELD

Giorgi has been an activist visionary, building, safeguarding, and nurturing a humanistic perspective within and beyond mainstream psychology. His tireless efforts as a teacher, editor, and organizer have been instrumental in securing the institutional forums for the continuing vitality of the humanistic movement.

His quarter-century tenure at Duquesne University was largely responsible for its becoming recognized as "the capital of phenomenological psychology in the New World" (Misiak & Sexton, 1973, p. 62). While there, he supervised many doctoral students who have since gone on to distinguished academic careers of their own. After Duquesne, Giorgi went to the Saybrook Institute in San Francisco, where he introduced descriptive phenomenological methods and again directed numerous dissertations. In his next post, at the University of Quebec at Montreal, Giorgi served as a key catalyst for the coalescence of a doctoral program in humanistic psychology. In his current position, as dean at Saybrook Institute, he remains pivotal in shaping a humanistic psychology doctoral program. Giorgi has left his mark on three of the most important centers for educating the next generation of the humanistic movement.

Giorgi has also contributed enormously to the field through his publishing efforts. In addition to his own prolific writing, Giorgi has devoted himself to disseminating others' work as an editor. He has edited or coedited seven books on phenomenological psychology and qualitative research (Ashworth, Giorgi, & deKoning, 1986; Giorgi, 1985b; Giorgi, Barton, & Maes, 1983; Giorgi, C. Fischer, & Murray, 1975; Giorgi, W. Fischer, & von Eckartsberg, 1971; Giorgi, Knowles, & Smith, 1979; Linschoten, 1968). He was also the founding editor of the *Journal of Phenomenological Psychology* and served in that capacity for twenty-five years. This publication remains the leading outlet for phenomenological psychology.

A third area of Giorgi's impact has been within scholarly societies. As a past president of two divisions of the American Psychological Association (Humanistic, and Theoretical and Philosophical), he has persistently advanced the continuing presence of a human science approach. His inspirational example has served to bring many of his former students to APA, where he has arranged many symposia and paper presentations. Several students have subsequently gone on to become division presidents, program chairs, and journal editors in their turn.

Giorgi has also been active with philosophical societies, such as the Merleau-Ponty Circle and the Society for Phenomenology and Existential Philosophy, sometimes as the only psychologist. In these, he and his students have consistently inculcated a cross-fertilizing dialogue between philosophy and psychology. For philosophers, Giorgi provides the concrete research contexts within which philosophical ideas that are otherwise sometimes too abstract can find their grounding. For psychologists, he nurtures a philosophical depth and sophistication too often lacking in the field.

In addition to his support of psychological and philosophical societies, Giorgi also saw the need for interdisciplinary forums for researchers using diverse qualitative approaches that often have more in common with colleagues in neighboring disciplines than with the mainstream of their own fields. Giorgi helped found the Human Science Research Association (HSRA) following a conference at the University of Michigan in 1982. This group has met annually since then, bringing together scholars primarily from psychology, pedagogy, philosophy, nursing, and sociology, but also including researchers from urban history, religious studies, political science, geography, and the arts (see Aanstoos & Arons, 1985). Giorgi also founded a smaller, European-based group, the International Association for Qualitative Research, in 1983. It met every two years through the 1980s for an in-depth examination of research methodologies and applications and resulted in two noteworthy books (Ashworth, Giorgi, & deKoning, 1986; van Zuuren, Wertz, & Mook, 1987). This smaller group merged with HSRA to create a new international organization, International Human Science Research (IHSR), whose recent meetings in Denmark, Canada, Sweden, Holland, South Africa, Norway (the 1997 IHRS meeting), and the United States, including Alaska (the 1998 meeting), reflect a growing community of human science researchers worldwide. Scholars from Asia, Eastern Europe, and South America are participating in increasing numbers.

Giorgi himself has long recognized the importance of both the interdisciplinary and the international outreaches. He has often served as a visiting professor to schools of nursing and education, in addition to psychology, in such places as Brazil, New Zealand, Sweden, and South Africa. One could fairly say that Giorgi is the movement's ambassador-at-large.

One must look beyond these sorts of immediate activities to Giorgi's most important impact: his vision of psychology as a human science. He has opened the field beyond its confinement in a narrow scientism to the fullness of the lifeworld (Giorgi, 1970). Only in time will the extent of this impact be manifest because, as Giorgi often reiterates, this work is far from complete. In recent years, Giorgi himself has become more pessimistic about the factual state of affairs in psychology. The cognitive revolution's atavistic retention of mechanistic presuppositions even as it overturned the old behaviorist hegemony has left many humanistic psychologists disillusioned with the prospect of more fundamental change. It would seem that the humanistic challenge to bring psychology back to experience, mounted with such intensity in the 1960s, has been co-opted by newer machine models of cognition in which consciousness is understood as information processing. In contrast to Giorgi's more radical paradigmatic change, this shift is only putting the old wine into new bottles.

But while Giorgi has become less hopeful of an imminent shift within psychology toward an authentically human science, he remains the optimist he has always been about psychology's ultimate possibilities. Most leading theoreticians have abandoned the hope for any comprehensive, unifying conceptual foundation for psychology. They pessimistically concede that it is an inherently fractured discipline (Royce, 1976, p. 2; Hilgard, 1987, pp. vii, viii, 803; Koch & Leary, 1985, p. 2; Koch, 1985, p. 29; Kendler, 1987, p. 457). Giorgi likewise notes this factual disunity: "It is clear to most astute observers of the field that psychology's . . . precise meaning and its place among the other sciences are still to be determined in a manner acceptable to the majority of psychologists" (Giorgi, 1985d, p. 46). Giorgi continues to insist that it is through the recovery of what is distinctive about humanity that psychology can attain its elusive vitality and unity. He remains unswervingly devoted to that goal.

REFERENCES

Aanstoos, C. M. (1996). Reflections and visions: An interview with Amedeo Giorgi. *Humanistic Psychologist, 24*, 3–27.

Aanstoos, C. M., & Arons, M. (1985). Report on the 1984 Human Science Research Conference. *Journal of Humanistic Psychology, 25*, 125–127.

Ashworth, P. D., Giorgi, A., & deKoning, A. J. (1986). *Qualitative research in psychology*. Pittsburgh, PA: Duquesne University Press.

Bentley, M. (1930). A psychology for psychologists. In C. Murchison (Ed.), *Psychologies of 1930* (pp. 95–114). Worcester, MA: Clark University Press.

Colaizzi, P. F. (1971). Analysis of the learner's perception of the learning material at various stages of the learning process. In A. Giorgi, W. Fischer, & R. von Eckartsberg (Eds.), *Duquesne studies in phenomenological psychology* (Vol. 1, pp. 101–110). Pittsburgh, PA: Duquesne University Press.

Giorgi, A. (1966). Phenomenology and experimental psychology: II. *Review of Existential Psychology and Psychiatry, 6*(1), 37–50.

Giorgi, A. (1967a). The experience of the subject as a source of data in a psychological experiment. *Review of Existential Psychology and Psychiatry, 7*, 169–176.

Giorgi, A. (1967b). A phenomenological approach to the problem of meaning and serial learning. *Review of Existential Psychology and Psychiatry, 7*, 106–118.

Giorgi, A. (1970). *Psychology as a human science: A phenomenologically based approach*. New York: Harper & Row.

Giorgi, A. (1971). A phenomenological approach to the problem of meaning and serial learning. In A. Giorgi, W. F. Fischer, & R. von Eckartsberg (Eds.), *Duquesne studies in phenomenological psychology* (vol. 1). Pittsburgh, PA: Duquesne University Press.

Giorgi, A. (1975). An application of phenomenological method in psychology. In A. Giorgi, C. Fischer, & E. Murray (Eds.), *Duquesne studies in phenomenological psychology* (Vol. 2, pp. 82–103). Pittsburgh, PA: Duquesne University Press.

Giorgi, A. (1982). Issues relating to the meaning of psychology as a science. In G. Floistad (Ed.), *Contemporary philosophy: A new survey* (Vol. 2, pp. 317–342). The Hague: Martinus Nijhoff.

Giorgi, A. (1983). Concerning the possibility of phenomenological psychological research. *Journal of Phenomenological Psychology, 14*, 129–169.

Giorgi, A. (1984). The "unfinished business" of psychology. In D. P. Rogers (Ed.), *Foundations of psychology: Some personal views* (pp. 18–34). New York: Praeger.

Giorgi, A. (1985a). The phenomenological psychology of learning and the verbal learning tradition. In A. Giorgi (Ed.), *Phenomenology and psychological research* (pp. 23–85). Pittsburgh, PA: Duquesne University Press.

Giorgi, A. (Ed.). (1985b). *Phenomenology and psychological research*. Pittsburgh, PA: Duquesne University Press.

Giorgi, A. (1985c). Theoretical plurality and unity in psychology. *Psychological Record, 35*, 177–181.

Giorgi, A. (1985d). Towards the articulation of psychology as a coherent discipline. In S. Koch & D. E. Leary (Eds.), *A century of psychology as science* (pp. 46–59). New York: McGraw-Hill.

Giorgi, A. P. (1986a). A phenomenological analysis of descriptions of concepts of learning obtained from a phenomenological perspective. *Publikationer fran institutionen for pedagogik*, Goteborgs Universitet, *Fenomenografiska Notiser, 4*, 18–77.

Giorgi, A. (1986b). The role of observation and control in laboratory and field research settings. *Phenomenology and Pedagogy, 4*(3), 22–28.

Giorgi, A. (1986c). Theoretical justification for the use of descriptions in psychological research. In P. Ashworth, A. Giorgi, & A. deKoning, *Qualitative research in psychology* (pp. 3–22). Pittsburgh, PA: Duquesne University Press.

Giorgi, A. (1987a). Phenomenology and the research tradition in the psychology of the imagination. In E. Murray (Ed.), *Imagination and phenomenological psychology* (pp. 1–47). Pittsburgh: Duquesne University Press.

Giorgi, A. (1987b). Problems in self-descriptive research as exemplified in a phenomenological analysis of imaginative experiences. In F. van Zuuren, F. Wertz, & B. Mook (Eds.), *Advances in qualitative psychology* (pp. 41–52). Berwyn, PA: Swets.

Giorgi, A. (1988). Validity and reliability from a phenomenological perspective. In W. J. Baker, L. P. Mos, H. V. Rappard, & H. J. Stam (Eds.), *Recent trends in theoretical psychology* (pp. 167–176). New York: Springer-Verlag.

Giorgi, A. (1989a). An example of harmony between descriptive reports and behavior. *Journal of Phenomenological Psychology, 20*(1), 60–88.

Giorgi, A. (1989b). One type of analysis of descriptive data: Procedures involved in following a scientific phenomenological method. *Methods*, pp. 39–61.

Giorgi, A. (1990). A phenomenological vision for psychology. In W. J. Baker, M. E. Hyland, R. van Hezewizk, & S. Terwee (Eds.), *Recent trends in theoretical psychology* (Vol. 2, pp. 27–36). New York: Springer-Verlag.

Giorgi, A. (1993). Psychology as the science of the paralogical. *Journal of Phenomenological Psychology, 24,* 63–77.

Giorgi, A. (1994). The idea of human science. In F. J. Wertz (Ed.), *The humanistic movement: Recovering the person in psychology* (pp. 89–104). New York: Gardner Press.

Giorgi, A., Barton, A., & Maes, C. (Eds.). (1983). *Duquesne studies in phenomenological psychology* (Vol. 4). Pittsburgh, PA: Duquesne University Press.

Giorgi, A., Fischer, C., & Murray, E. (Eds.). (1975). *Duquesne studies in phenomenological psychology* (Vol. 2). Pittsburgh, PA: Duquesne University Press.

Giorgi, A., Fischer, W., & von Eckartsberg, R. (Eds.). (1971). *Duquesne studies in phenomenological psychology* (Vol. 1). Pittsburgh, PA: Duquesne University Press.

Giorgi, A., Knowles, R., & Smith, D. (Eds.). (1979). *Duquesne studies in phenomenological psychology* (Vol. 3). Pittsburgh, PA: Duquesne University Press.

Hilgard, E. R. (1987). *Psychology in America.* New York: Harcourt Brace Jovanovich.

James, W. (1950). *The principles of psychology.* (Vols. 1–2). New York: Dover. (Original work published 1890)

Kendler, H. H. (1987). *Historical foundations of modern psychology.* Chicago: Dorsey Press.

Koch, S. (1985). Foreword. In S. Koch & D. E. Leary (Eds.), *A century of psychology as science* (pp. 7–35). New York: McGraw-Hill.

Koch, S., & Leary, D. E. (1985). Introduction. In S. Koch & D. E. Leary (Eds.), *A century of psychology as science* (pp. 1–6). New York: McGraw-Hill.

Linschoten, H. (1968). *On the way toward a phenomenological psychology: The psychology of William James,* (A. Giorgi, Ed.). Pittsburgh, PA: Duquesne University Press.

McConville, M. (1974). *Perception in the horizontal dimension of space: An empirical phenomenological study of the perceptual experience of spatial orientation in a life-world situation.* Unpublished doctoral dissertation, Duquesne University, Pittsburgh, PA.

Misiak, H., & Sexton, V. S. (1973). *Phenomenological, existential, and humanistic psychologies: A historical survey.* New York: Grune & Stratton.

Nisbett, R. E., & Wilson, T. (1977). Telling more than we can know: Verbal reports on mental processes. *Psychological Review, 84,* 231–259.

Royce, J. R. (1976). Psychology is multi-: methodological, variate, epistemic, world view, systemic, paradigmatic, theoretic, and disciplinary. In W. J. Arnold (Ed.), *1975 Nebraska Symposium on Motivation: Conceptual foundations of psychology* (pp. 1–64). Lincoln: University of Nebraska Press.

van Zuuren, F. J., Wertz, F. J., & Mook, B. (1987). *Advances in qualitative psychology: Themes and variations.* Berwyn, PA: Swets; Lisse, Netherlands: Swets & Zeitlinger.

Wertz, F. J. (1983a). From everyday to psychological description: Analyzing the moments of a qualitative data analysis. *Journal of Phenomenological Psychology, 14*(2), 197–241.

Wertz, F. J. (1983b). Some components of descriptive psychological reflection. *Human Studies, 6*(1), 35–51.

Wertz, F. J. (1987). Common methodological fundaments of the analytic procedures in phenomenological and psychoanalytic research. *Psychoanalysis and Contemporary Thought, 9*(4), 563–603.

20

On Psychology as a Person-Centered Science: William James and His Relation to the Humanistic Tradition

EUGENE IRVINE TAYLOR, JR.

Humanistic psychology has both a long and a short history, depending on whom you read.[1] Some writers trace its origins back to the Greeks, claiming Plato rather than Aristotle as their forebear; others are enamored with the humanist tradition of the European Renaissance.[2] Still others, although many fewer, restrict the term to mean that movement in American psychology that flourished as a viable form of academic discourse between 1941 and 1969.[3] Although these are, of course, somewhat arbitrary dates, 1941 was the year Carl Rogers first articulated the client-centered approach in psychotherapy, and 1969 was that fateful moment when humanistic psychology as an academic outgrowth of personality theory fractionated into several major streams. There were three major ones: the first was transpersonal interest in altered states of consciousness; the second was experiential body work; and the third was political psychology. The result was that humanistic psychology appeared to disappear as an academic endeavor and instead became absorbed into the American counterculture movement, where it still seems to flounder, only half-alive today.[4]

In the present writer's opinion, while wandering around in the humanist past of Western philosophy allows us to give wide scope to all the possible meanings of humanistic psychology, confining ourselves to the meaning of the term in the immediate past allows us to get a better perspective on the place of humanistic psychology and transpersonal psychology within the larger context of American academic psychology. When we do that, we discover some extraordinarily important but overlooked historical connections. The most obvious of these link the humanistic and transpersonal psychologists of the 1960s and 1970s to the personality-social psychologists of the 1930s and 1940s in a uniquely American

William James, 1899–1900. (By permission of the Houghton
Library, Harvard University).

tradition that actually encompasses most of psychology and that emanates originally from the work of the American philosopher and psychologist William James.

LIFE AND WORK

William James, is a figure not normally associated by mainstream psychologists
with the more recent movement called humanistic psychology, and he is known
to most younger humanistic psychologists, if he is known at all, only in a general
way. James was born in 1842 into a distinguished literary circle that included his
father, Henry James, Sr., an independently wealthy philosopher of religion and
noted Swedenborgian, and Ralph Waldo Emerson, William's godfather, close
family friend, spiritual mentor, and foremost voice of New England transcendentalism, the first uniquely American literary aesthetic to develop independent of
European roots.

Reared under unconventional circumstances and without much formal school-
ing, William and his younger brother Henry, who later became a famous novelist,
received their education from the great art museums and libraries of Europe, from
direct contact with leading literary, philosophic, and scientific minds of the mid-
nineteenth century who knew their father, and, above all, from lively and some-

times heated conversations at the James family dinner table.[5] Henry James, Sr., whose other vocation was raising his five children, required that every one of them know how to observe and draw their own conclusions. Indeed, far from simply knowing about just one or two subjects, the younger Jameses were expected to have an opinion about everything.

After trying his hand at painting under the Barbizon stylist William Morris Hunt in the late 1850s, when the family lived in Newport, Rhode Island, in 1861 William James suddenly entered the Lawrence Scientific School at Harvard to pursue a major in chemistry. He switched to medicine in 1864 and graduated with the M.D. from Harvard Medical School in 1869.[6] His chief scientific interest at this time was in the area of evolutionary psychology, namely, applying the doctrine of natural selection to understanding the role of personal consciousness in the biological evolution of the species.[7]

After recovery from a severe personal crisis in 1870 that involved the direction his life would subsequently take, James began teaching anatomy and physiology at Harvard in 1873. He taught the first course called physiological psychology, founded the first laboratory devoted to experimental psychology in an American university in 1875, and granted the first Ph.D. in the new scientific psychology to G. Stanley Hall in 1878.[8] Eventually, in 1888, he rose to the rank of full professor of philosophy. He became Harvard's first full professor of psychology in 1889, in anticipation of *The Principles of Psychology*, which appeared in 1890. *The Principles* is a definitive two-volume work that wrested the study of consciousness from the control of the abstract philosophers and helped launch psychology as a discipline in the domain of the natural sciences. The focus of this work was the study of psychology as a cognitive science of consciousness.

While James's reputation in the new science soon became international, during the period of the 1890s he developed a sophisticated metaphysics, later called radical empiricism, that grounded psychology in the phenomenology of immediate experience rather than the laboratory measurements and cognitive models of the scientific reductionists developing at the time. While he had interests in new areas of psychology for many years, the 1890s were also the period when James made his most visible contributions to the development of fields such as educational psychology, abnormal psychology, psychical research, and the psychology of religion. Indeed, scientific evidence collected from these fields fueled his metaphysics of radical empiricism, which he, in turn, developed into a trenchant critique of experimentalism in psychology and in science generally.[9]

In 1892 James published a shortened one-volume version of his *Principles* called *Psychology: Briefer Course*, which became a standard textbook in colleges and universities for the next two decades. In 1896 he delivered a series of Lowell Lectures on exceptional mental states, outlining a dynamic theory of the subconscious, which effectively launched what came to be known over the next twenty years as the Boston school of psychotherapy.[10] In 1897 he published his first major work in philosophy, *The Will to Believe*. He followed this in 1898 with a major statement launching the American philosophical movement of pragmatism, the idea that beliefs are always tested by their consequences. In 1899 he produced *Talks to Teachers on Psychology and to Students on Some of Life's Ideals*, a work that applied the new principles of psychology to the field of education. In 1902 he published *The Varieties of Religious Experience*, the Gifford Lectures on Natural Religion at Edinburgh, which helped launch the field of pastoral counseling and is still the most widely used text in psychology of religion courses in the United States.[11]

The years after 1902 have been labeled James's preeminent philosophical period. In 1907 he published *Pragmatism*, his 1906 Lowell Lectures, perhaps his most well-known work by the general reader; and in 1909 he produced *A Pluralistic Universe*, a vigorous defense of each individual's unique worldview. Other volumes also followed: *The Meaning of Truth* came out in 1909, followed by his *Problems in Philosophy* (1911), an attempt at a synthetic statement of his own system, and his *Essays in Radical Empiricism*, (1912) published posthumously, an incomplete effort to articulate the core of his philosophical metaphysics.

When James died in 1910, it was generally acknowledged that a major figure of international importance had passed from the scene. Nevertheless, his influence continued to radiate out in many directions. Subsequently, behaviorists, Gestalt psychologists, phenomenologists, and even cognitive scientists have all claimed him as their predecessor. Indeed, in 1990, on the centenary celebration of the publication of his *Principles of Psychology* (1890), numerous authors agreed that there is not much in academic psychology that has advanced beyond his original ideas. Meanwhile, the Jamesian influence in humanistic psychology has only recently become a focus of attention.[12]

JAMES AND HUMANISTIC PSYCHOLOGY

Humanistic psychology is inextricably linked to the Jamesian tradition in American psychology in three important ways: historically, intellectually, and spiritually.[13] Historically, the great personality-social psychologists of the 1930s and 1940s represented the Jamesian legacy during the era dominated by the experimental rat runners, while additional evidence shows that humanistic psychology grew directly out of this same personality and motivational psychology by the 1950s. Intellectually, during his own era James tried to broaden psychology to become a person-centered science by the variety of subjects he investigated and by his metaphysics of radical empiricism, which he developed as a critique of reductionistic laboratory science. Humanistic psychologists clearly carried on the same discussions beginning with Abraham Maslow in the 1950s and extending to Amedeo Giorgi by the early 1970s, during the era when humanistic psychology still remained a viable form of academic discourse. Spiritually, not only might James be considered the godfather of humanistic psychology, but his legacy also might still become a guiding light for the potential renaissance of a humanistic perspective in American psychology that is yet to come.

THE HISTORICAL LINEAGE

In both the general and the specific sense, both James and the humanistic psychologists who followed him half a century later were functionalists—the single most important idea, if there is one, that characterizes the history of American psychology. Functionalism refers in a Darwinian context to the inherent relationship between the organism and the environment, as in the perennial nature-nurture controversy that keeps surfacing or in such themes as culture and personality. It refers to the relationship between ideas and acts, as in the relation of cognitions to behavior or between dynamic forces of the unconscious that define what we observe in the field of consciousness. It also refers to the pragmatic value of beliefs and ideas—not only that ideas are tested by their consequences, but that mutually incompatible systems of thinking can still be of equal value if they lead to the same consensually validated social ends. Pragmatism, optimism, and eclecticism are the three primary characteristics of functionalism as a uniquely American movement.

Following the functionalist outlook, most American psychologists believe that it is possible to have a variety of different viewpoints all represented side by side. For William James, this meant that psychology studied the mystery of the person, while science was but a tool and not an end to that understanding. In fact, we would need all the different tools we could get to understand who we were. This view came to represent the Jamesian tradition in American psychology.

Historically, however, in order to get funds for research and to create new jobs, American students returning with their new Ph.D.'s fresh from the experimental laboratories in Germany between 1880 and 1910 had to make a case for how their brand of laboratory psychophysics was more scientific than the reigning Jamesian view. They did this by establishing laboratories in the newly built graduate schools in American universities on the premise that psychology was a reductionistic enterprise like the rest of the natural sciences because they could quantify the structure of consciousness.[14]

Following the German laboratory ideal, American experimentalists gained control of the epistemology that would govern psychological discourse. Here they established the experimental method as the standard by which to judge legitimate knowledge in psychology. According to this ideal, which we still hear touted today, experimental evidence collected in the laboratory to prove scientific theories could then be applied to real life so that science could be extended from theory and research into the domain of controlled social engineering. James, however, remained the champion of the "ever not quite," the great desideratum, the larger picture of things that the puny little experiments of science could never grasp. The mystery of the person always remained at the center of his psychology, so that functionalism for him always meant the relation of personal consciousness to the world around us. His view of functionalism was actually closer to what clinical rather than experimental psychologists do today, and is still closer to the humanistic and transpersonal emphasis on immediate experience.

After James's death in 1910, however, functionalism became just another school of thought next to structuralism, behaviorism, and mental testing. Meanwhile, the Gestalt tradition of German laboratory science, Freudian psychoanalysis from Vienna, and the French schools of psychopathology also flourished in an eclectic mix that still reflected the broad, uniquely American Jamesian outlook even if

James himself was not there to lead it.[15] A period of repression followed, however, in which experimentalism gradually gained the upper hand.

By the 1930s the academic laboratory science of psychology had become totally dominated by the theories of the behaviorists, who had fallen heir to the university laboratories of the earlier generation of psychophysicists.[16] Nevertheless, the Jamesian tradition soon reemerged in the form of the macropersonality theorists—psychologists interested, as James was, in the self, the will, personality, and consciousness, but who also followed in the new vein of their own times. Among them, there was Henry A. Murray, clinical psychologist at Harvard, Melvillian, friend of both Jung and Freud, and founder of the field of experimental personology, the multivariate assessment of the personal at many different levels of complexity. There was Gordon Allport, pioneer in personality-social psychology, psychologist of religion, and specialist on rumor and prejudice, whose focus was on the development of normal, healthy individuals. There were Gardner and Lois Murphy, personality psychologists and parapsychological investigators who opened the field of experimental social psychology, helped launch parapsychology as a university-based experimental enterprise, contributed to the psychoanalytic study of children, investigated non-Western psychologies, and were instrumental in developing the voluntary control of internal states program in biofeedback research at the Menninger Clinic.[17]

From the 1930s to the 1950s, these and other courageous psychologists carried on the larger Jamesian agenda of studying the whole person, going against the grain of a thirty-year era of scientific investigation in academic psychology that strongly resisted their work and instead focused exclusively on laboratory measurements of the white rat. In many different instances their careers suffered because they were judged by the more dominant experimental and reductionistic standards of their time as being "unscientific." Yet, significantly, the personality-social psychologists exerted an enormous influence for their small numbers. They helped disseminate psychoanalysis into the humanities and social sciences, fed major developments in the burgeoning field of clinical psychology, and always kept the person in focus as the proper object of scientific study in psychology.

Humanistic psychology as we know it today was a direct historical outgrowth of the Jamesian tradition represented by these macropersonality theorists. One of the key events suggesting this lineage was the Old Saybrook Conference, held in the fall of 1964 in Old Saybrook, Connecticut. At this conference Abraham Maslow, Carl Rogers, James Bugental, Clark Moustakas, Charlotte Buhler, and Rollo May, all recognized pioneers in humanistic psychology, met with Henry A. Murray, Gordon Allport, Gardner Murphy, George Kelly, and others, and the torch was passed from the older personality-social psychologists to the leaders of the new humanistic movement in American psychology.

However, while many continually refer to it, until recently no one has done the kind of thorough archival investigation required to reconstruct the events and personalities involved with the Old Saybrook Conference. Chief among recent discoveries has been not only a large cache of original documents on every aspect of the meetings, including the original grant proposals, letters of invitation, and even railroad schedules of arriving guests, but also the unpublished keynote address, delivered by Henry A. Murray.[18]

In his address Murray clearly associated more than a quarter of a century of his own work on personology with the new humanistic psychology. He cogently articulated where psychology had come from, and he defined the window of opportunity for the humanistic movement at that time. Failure of the "unity in science movement" among the academic learning theorists, the waning influence of both psychoanalysis and behaviorism, and the general deregulation of American psychology as a reductionistic academic discipline all contributed to the opening of a more expansive era than the one that had preceded. Murray proposed that humanistic psychologists should leap into this temporary breach, and he gave a bold twelve-point program to reorient psychology toward its original Jamesian trajectory as a person-centered science.

There are, of course, numerous other instances of the historical connections between William James and the personality psychologists of the 1930s and 1940s and between humanistic psychologists and the older tradition of personality-social psychology. The point is, however, that this history has yet to be fully reconstructed and therefore is little known and remains underrecognized, even by humanistic psychologists themselves.

THE INTELLECTUAL LINEAGE

As far as a lineage of ideas goes, in the late nineteenth century William James stood for a psychology of individual differences, the evolutionary function of consciousness, and an eclectic and open-minded approach to the study of the person, as many of the humanistic psychologists of the 1950s and 1960s did as well. Probably during no other time in the history of American psychology did the person occupy so central and open a place in the scientific development of the discipline as in these two periods.[19] While the humanistic view of psychology is closer to us in historical time and therefore more fresh in our minds, James's career and outlook, while it has been worked over endlessly, remains broken up and exists in pieces, carved out by the limits of the specialized disciplines that only look at part of his work each time that they approach him.

The center of James's intellectual vision for psychology, however, can only be understood, in my opinion, by considering as a whole his metaphysical position. In his philosophy of pragmatism James argued that beliefs are always tested by their consequences, and that radically different and apparently incompatible truth statements that lead to similar outcomes are for practical purposes of equal value. Pluralism, by which James meant noetic pluralism, argued for personality as an ultimate plurality of states of consciousness, the majority of which could be unified around the transcendent, mystical experience. Unity within the individual did not invalidate the small but very important differences between people, however, since each person's conception of ultimate reality could be different, but still lead to the same consensually validated way of behaving. Radical empiricism, actually the core of James's metaphysics, presumed that the basic subject matter of psychology was pure experience in the immediate moment, before the differentiation of subject and object. In this way, consciousness, for James, did not exist as an independent entity, but was always a function of someone's experience, which had to be specified.[20]

Clinical and personality-social psychologists who followed James have also not been well studied historically.[21] There is some general agreement, however, that they promoted the reality of unconscious processes, projective exploration of the unseen, the study of motives, values, myths, the reality of psychic events, identification of the basic traits of character, the deep connection between psychology and the humanities, the voluntary control of internal states, and an emphasis on normal, healthy personality development and the importance of an active spiritual life.[22]

Humanistic psychologists, building not entirely unwittingly on this Jamesian legacy, developed concepts of the self-actualizing personality, a client-centered approach to psychotherapy, and a growth-oriented theory of motivation; they also emphasized the existential nature of the psychotherapeutic hour.[23] In addition, they developed an important literature on the psychology of science and on the phenomenology of the science-making process.[24] Collectively, these remain some of the major themes of the Jamesian legacy in American psychology.

THE SPIRITUAL LINEAGE

The Jamesian legacy in American psychology shows every sign of not only having had an impact, but also being still quite alive and well. One need only look at the diversity of the annual program of the American Psychological Association, the large counterculture movement in psychotherapy that is driving the current spiritual revolution in popular thought, the current human science movement, or just what psychologists actually do as opposed to what the textbooks say they should be doing in both research and therapy. In all these endeavors we see that an eclectic, functional psychology in the way James envisioned it continues to flourish. There is also some evidence to suggest that James's ideas on radical empiricism are being resuscitated as a strategy to interpret the humanistic implications of the neuroscience revolution. At its base, neuroscience is a biological revolution about consciousness, but one that is generating important philosophical implications that are now being more widely discussed—the very subject on which James focused throughout his rich and varied career as a psychologist.[25]

Humanistic psychologists might well consider the recent call to reclaim their legitimate place in the history of American academic psychology and to inform themselves about the potential implications of radical empiricism as part of their own intellectual legacy if they wish to have something significant to say in reshaping present-day psychology.[26] At the very least, a more acute historical examination of their own past might position them to contribute to the biology of transcendence, to a more forward-looking neuroscientific understanding of consciousness, or to the outlines of a possible depth psychology to come.

Whether they do so or not, James still remains a spiritual godfather to the humanistic movement, the promulgator of a uniquely American native psychology, and a figure whose ideas represented one of the only two times in the history of American psychology when the discipline was truly a person-centered science. Contemporary developments seem to be telling the humanistic psychologists to take heed. That which once was may yet come again, but in a form more relevant to contemporary concerns. The question remains, as James might have put it, "In the present state in which humanistic psychologists find themselves, will they be prepared to lead such a psychology of the future?"

NOTES

1. At present, there is no definitive history of humanistic psychology. In the 1960s and 1970s attempts to define its shape appeared, such as Frank Goble's *The Third Force* (1970), but these were largely popular accounts by writers untrained in history. Specific articles in the *Humanistic Psychologist* and the *Journal of Humanistic Psychology*, either by protagonists of the movement or by graduate students, have appeared sporadically (Wertz, 1994; Taylor, 1992b). History of psychology texts will sometimes contain a section on humanistic psychology, but these remain largely incomplete. There are several biographies or individual studies, among them Hoffman's *The Right to Be Human: A Biography of Abraham Maslow* (1988), Kirschenbaum's *On Becoming Carl Rogers* (1979), Gaines's *Fritz Perls: Here and Now* (1979), Furlong's biography of Alan Watts, *Zen Effects* (1986), and Walter Truit Anderson's *Upstart Spring* (1983). The only published works to date by an academic press are Roy Jose DeCarvalho's *The Founders of Humanistic Psychology*, a text that is not really a continuous narrative, is not based on archival sources, and, as well, contains serious interpretive flaws because the author was not familiar with the larger history of American academic psychology; a more reliable but completely overlooked study is Misiak and Sexton (1973). Consequently, the historical picture that does exist is largely anecdotal and remains a recycling of the same stereotyped and uncorroborated information.

2. Compare Rychlak (1988) with Smith (1982).

3. See Taylor and Kelley (1994) and Taylor and Lowe (1995).

4. This is, of course, appearance only. Humanistic psychologists maintain an active division in the American Psychological Association, and the Consortium for Diversified Graduate Psychology Programs continues to function and is even presently lobbying for the right to credential alternative programs in psychology.

5. The definitive biography remains Ralph Barton Perry's two-volume Pulitzer Prize–winning *Thought and Character of William James* (1935). The only chronological work is still Gay Wilson Allen's *William James: A Biography* (1967). There have been a number of family portraits; the two most interesting are F. O. Matthiessen, *The James Family* (1947), and R.W.B. Lewis, *The Jameses: A Family Narrative* (1991). It should also be pointed out that not all the James children received the same educational opportunities. See Strouse (1980) and Maher (1986), for instance. Habegger (1994) provides a good biography of the father, Henry James, Sr.

6. The sudden shift in vocation and resulting suicidal crisis ten years later has been the subject of numerous investigations, among them J. W. Anderson (1982) and Feinstein (1984).

7. James and Darwin continue to be an active subject of interest for psychologists. See Taylor (1990) and Richards (1987).

8. There continues to be a dispute over the status of Hall's doctorate. Recently, scholars have maintained that the first Ph.D. in the new experimental science was awarded by Hall to Joseph Jastrow in 1886 at Johns Hopkins.

9. See Taylor (1996b).

10. See Taylor (1982, 1994a, 1994b).

11. See Taylor (1995b).

12. For an overview of psychologists' opinions of James, see the appendix in Taylor (1996b).

13. For a statement on James's connections to classical Eastern psychology, existentialism and phenomenology, personality-social psychology, and psychical research, see Taylor (1991, 1996a).

14. See Leary (1980).

15. See Angell (1988) and Owens and Wagner (1992).

16. Wozniak (1993).

17. I have documented James's influence on these psychologists in Taylor (1992b).

18. Taylor (1995a) presents a reconstruction of the previously lost and unpublished keynote address, recently discovered in Murray's papers and presented at the 27th annual meeting of the Cheiron Society (International Society for the History of the Behavioral and Social Sciences), Bowdoin College, Brunswick, Maine.

19. I would characterize this era of the personality-social psychologists as one of active and relentless repression by the experimentalists, who remained in control of the professional societies, journals, and departments of psychology throughout the United States.

20. See Taylor and Wozniak (1996) for a look at James's seminal articles on radical empiricism from 1904 and a collection of essays in the ten years following by psychologists and philosophers demonstrating that only a few really understood what he was saying.

21. The greater emphasis of historians in psychology as a whole is to focus on the nineteenth-century German experimental laboratory tradition, the history of Watsonian behaviorism, Galton, Cattell, and the history of IQ testing, the neobehavioral laboratory psychology of Hull, Tolman, Spence, and Skinner, and now, cognitive psychology (see Taylor, in press b).

22. See, for instance, Murray et al.'s *Explorations in Personality* (1938), Allport's *Personality* (1937), and Murphy's *Personality* (1947).

23. See Maslow's *Motivation and Personality* (1954), Rogers's *Client-centered Therapy* (1951), and May, Angel, and Ellenberger's *Existence* (1958), for instance.

24. Maslow (1966), Giorgi (1970), and Child (1973). A strong case can also be made for the Jamesian influence on European existentialism and phenomenology, an influence that reentered American psychology through the humanistic movement in the 1950s and 1960s and came to light in the form of existential-phenomenological psychotherapy. Current interest in deconstructionism and contextualism in human science has some roots in this Jamesian lineage. See the appendix of Taylor (1996b), Child (1973), Polkinghorne (1990), and Herzog (1995).

25. James has had a direct influence on such researchers as Sperry, Pribram, and Crick, for instance. See Taylor (1995a, 1995b), the appendix of Taylor (1996b), and Taylor (1997).

26. Wertz (1994) and Taylor (1997).

REFERENCES

Allen, G. W. (1967). *William James: A biography*. New York: Viking.
Allport, G. W. (1937). *Personality: A psychological interpretation*. New York: Holt.
Anderson, J. W. (1982). "The worst kind of melancholy": William James in 1869. *Harvard Library Bulletin, 30*(4), 369–386.
Anderson, W. T. (1983). *The upstart spring: Esalen and the American awakening*. Reading, MA: Addison-Wesley.
Angell, J. R. (1988). The province of functional psychology. In L. T. Benjamin, Jr. (Ed.), *A history of psychology: Original sources and contemporary research* (pp. 324–332). New York: McGraw-Hill.
Child, I. (1973). *Humanistic psychology and the research tradition: Their several virtues*. New York: John Wiley.
DeCarvalho, R. J. (1991). *The founders of humanistic psychology*. New York: Praeger.
Feinstein, H. (1984). *Becoming William James*. Ithaca, NY: Cornell University Press.
Furlong, M. (1986). *Zen effects: The life of Alan Watts*. Boston: Houghton Mifflin.
Gaines, J. (1979). *Fritz Perls: Here and now*. Millbrae, CA: Celestial Arts.
Giorgi, A. (1970). *Psychology as a human science*. New York: Harper & Row.
Goble, F. G. (1970). *The third force: The psychology of Abraham Maslow*. New York: Grossman.
Habegger, A. (1994). *The father: A life of Henry James, Sr*. New York: Farrar, Straus, & Giroux.
Herzog, M. (1995). William James and the development of phenomenological psychology in Europe. *History of the Human Sciences 8*(1), 29–46.
Hoffman, E. (Ed.). (1996). *Future visions: The unpublished papers of Abraham Maslow*. Thousand Oaks, CA: Sage Publications.
Hoffman, E. (1988). *The right to be human: A biography of Abraham Maslow*. Los Angeles: J. P. Tarcher.
James, W. (1890). *The principles of psychology* (2 vols.). New York: Henry Holt.
James, W. (1897). *The will to believe*. New York: Longmans, Green.
James, W. (1899). *Talks to teachers on psychology and to students on some of life's ideals*. Cambridge, MA: Henry Holt & Co.
James, W. (1902). *The varieties of religious experience*. New York: Longmans, Green.
James, W. (1907). *Pragmatism*. New York: Longmans, Green.
James, W. (1909). *A pluralistic universe*. New York: Longmans, Green.
James, W. (1909). *The meaning of truth, a sequel to Pragmatism*. New York: Longmans, Green.
James, W. (1911). *Some problems of philosophy, a beginning of an introduction to philosophy*. New York: Longmans, Green.
James, W. (1912). *Essays in radical empiricism*. New York, Longmans, Green.
Kirschenbaum, H. (1979). *On becoming Carl Rogers*. New York: Delacorte Press.

Leary, D. (1980, September). *William James, psychical research, and the origins of American psychology*. Paper presented at the 88th annual meeting of the American Psychological Association, Montreal, Canada.

Lewis, R.W.B. (1991). *The Jameses: A family narrative*. New York: Farrar, Straus, & Giroux.

Maher, J. (1986). *Biography of broken fortunes: Wilkie and Bob, brothers of William, Henry, and Alice James*. Hamden, CT: Archon Books.

Maslow, A. H. (1954). *Motivation and personality*. New York: Harper & Row.

Maslow, A. H. (1966). *The psychology of science: A reconnaissance*. New York: Harper & Row.

Matthiessen, F. O. (1947). *The James family: Including selections from the writings of Henry James, Senior, William, Henry, and Alice James*. New York: A. A. Knopf.

May, R., Angel, E., & Ellenberger, H. F. (Eds.). (1958). *Existence: A new dimension in psychiatry and psychology*. New York: Basic Books.

Misiak, H. K., & Sexton, V. S. (1973). *Phenomenological, existential, and humanistic psychologies: A historical survey*. New York: Grune & Stratton.

Murphy, G. (1947). *Personality: A biosocial approach to origins and structures*. New York: Harper.

Murray, H. A., Barret, W. G., Langer, W. C., Morgan, C. D., Homburger, E., & others. (1938). *Explorations in personality*. New York: Oxford University Press.

Owens, D. A., & Wagner, M. (Eds.). (1992). *Progress in modern psychology: The legacy of American functionalism*. Westport, CT: Praeger.

Perry, R. B. (1935). *The thought and character of William James* (2 vols.). Boston: Little, Brown.

Richards, R. J. (1987). *Darwin and the emergence of evolutionary theories of mind and behavior*. Chicago: University of Chicago Press.

Rogers, C. R., (1951). *Client-centered therapy: Its current practice, implications, and theory*. Boston: Houghton Mifflin.

Polkinghorne, D. E. (1990). Psychology after philosophy. In R. N. Williams & J. E. Faulconer (Eds.), *Reconsidering psychology: Perspectives from continental philosophy* (pp. 92–115). Pittsburgh, PA: Duquesne University Press.

Rychlak, J. F. (1988). *The psychology of rigorous humanism* (2nd ed.). New York: New York University Press.

Smith, M. B. (1982). Psychology and humanism. *Journal of Humanistic Psychology, 22*, 44–55.

Strouse, J. (1980). *Alice James, a biography*. Boston: Houghton Mifflin.

Taylor, E. I. (1983). *William James on exceptional mental states*. New York: Scribner's.

Taylor, E. I. (1990). William James on Darwin: An evolutionary theory of consciousness. *Annals of the New York Academy of Sciences, 602*, 7–33.

Taylor, E. I. (1991). William James and the humanistic tradition. *Journal of Humanistic Psychology, 31*(1), 56–74.

Taylor, E. I. (1992a). Biological consciousness and the experience of the transcendent: William James and American functional psychology. In R. Wozniak (Ed.), *Mind and Body: René Descartes to William James* (pp. 53–56). Bethesda, MD: National Library of Medicine and the American Psychological Association.

Taylor, E. I. (1992b). The case for a uniquely American Jamesian tradition in psychology. In M. Donnelly (Ed.), *Reinterpreting the legacy of William James: APA Centennial William James Lectures* (pp. 3–28). Washington, DC: American Psychological Association Press.

Taylor, E. I. (1992c). Transpersonal psychology: Its several virtues. In F. Wertz (Ed.), *The humanistic movement in psychology: History, celebration, and prospectus [Special issue].* *Humanistic Psychologist, 20* (2–3), 285–300.

Taylor, E. I. (1994a). A metaphysical critique of experimentalism in psychology: Or "Why G. Stanley Hall waited until William James was out of town to found the APA." In H. E. Adler & R. Rieber (Eds.), *Aspects of the history of psychology in America, 1892–1992* [Centenary volume honoring the 100th anniversary of the founding of the American Psychological Association, published by the American Psychological Association and the New York Academy of Sciences]. *Annals of the New York Academy of Sciences, 727,* 37–62.

Taylor, E. I. (1994b). Radical empiricism and the conduct of research. In W. Harman & J. Clark (Eds.), *New metaphysical foundations of modern science* (pp. 345–374). Sausalito, CA: Institute of Noetic Sciences.

Taylor, E. I. (1995a, February). Radical empiricism and the new science of consciousness. *History of the Human Sciences, 8*(1), 47–60.

Taylor, E. I. (1995b). The transcendent experience. *One Hundredth Anniversary Issue* [Special issue]. *Prabuddha Bharata, Journal of the Ramakrishna Vedanta Society, Calcutta,* 100(2), 14–22.

Taylor, E. I. (1996a). William James and transpersonal psychiatry. In B. Scotton, A. Chinin, & J. Battista (Eds.), *Textbook of transpersonal psychiatry and psychology* (pp. 21–28). New York: Basic Books.

Taylor, E. I. (1996b). *William James on consciousness beyond the margin.* Princeton: Princeton University Press.

Taylor, E. I. (1997). *"What is man, psychologist, that thou art so unmindful of him?" A note on the historical relation between classical personality theory and humanistic psychology.* Paper presented at the 28th annual meeting of Cheiron, the International Society for the History of the Behavioral and Social Sciences, Bowdoin College, Brunswick, Maine.

Taylor, E. I. (in press a). An intellectual renaissance of humanistic psychology? *Journal of Humanistic Psychology.*

Taylor, E. I. (in press b). William James on the demise of positivism in American psychology. In R. Rieber & K. Salzinger (Eds.), *Psychology: Theoretical-historical perspectives* (2nd ed.). Washington, DC: American Psychological Association.

Taylor, E. I., & Kelley, M. (1994). *Major events and personalities in the history of humanistic psychology: A conceptual outline.* The History of Humanistic and Transpersonal Psychology Project, Saybrook Institute, San Francisco.

Taylor, E. I., & Lowe, T. (1995). *An historical outline of transpersonal psychology, based on an analysis of primary texts, relevant secondary literature, and oral history interviews.* The History of Humanistic and Transpersonal Psychology Project, Saybrook Institute, San Francisco.

Taylor, E. I., & Wozniak, R. H. (Eds.). (1996). *Pure experience: The response to William James.* Bristol, England: Routledge/Thoemmes.

Wertz, F. (Ed.). (1994). *The humanistic movement: Recovering the person in psychology.* Lake Worth, FL: Gardner Press.

Wozniak, R. H. (1993). *Theoretical roots of early behaviourism: Functionalism, the critique of introspection, and the nature and evolution of consciousness.* London: Routledge/Thoemmes.

21

Sidney Jourard: Disclosing to Ourselves and Others

DON RICE

> Every maladjusted person is a person who has not made himself [herself]
> known to another human being and as a consequence does not know himself
> [herself] . . . provides for himself [herself] a cancerous kind of stress . . . pro-
> ducing the wide array of physical ills that have come to be recognized as the
> province of psychosomatic medicine.
>
> —Jourard, 1971, p. 32

In his book *The Transparent Self*, Sidney Jourard states, "We need to devote our best scientific talent to intensive investigation of the psychophysiological mechanisms which are brought into play when people have their faith and confidence inspired by supposed healing symbols and rituals" (p. 79). He goes on to suggest that a person's self-disclosures are the equivalent of the numbers on a thermometer. Therefore, a doctor or nurse presenting herself to a patient as warm, understanding, and willing to listen will actually hasten the healing process in the patient. While many patients will not feel significantly different after having their blood pressure read, they will report feeling better after disclosing to an interested health care professional (Jourard, 1971).

Jourard's assertion equates self-disclosure with physical and psychological health. For Jourard, the healthy personality is one that is capable of disclosing to itself and others (Jourard, 1968, 1971). Much of what is written today about the relationship between personality and health and mind-body interaction was anticipated by Jourard at least a quarter of a century ago. He proposed that a new field of science and medicine be developed that links mind and body in a way previously not understood (Rice, 1995).

While Jourard's writings covered a variety of topics, including counseling, psychotherapy, personality theory, and spirituality, the central issue of self-disclosure and its importance for psychological and physical well-being is a constant theme throughout his writings. Today, support for Jourard's contention that self-disclosure is equated with health and healing is found in popular writings of mind-body researchers such as Herbert Benson (1975), Larry Dossey (1982), Jeanne Achterberg and Frank Lawlis (1992), Dean Ornish (1990), and Joan Borysenko (1988). For example, Borysenko has suggested that to be healthy, we must have an interpersonal connectedness that allows us to be vulnerable and trusting of ourselves so that we can fully learn to trust others. Other researchers have found self-disclosure related to improved immune functioning (Pennebaker, Kiecolt-Glaser, & Glaser, 1988).

I allude to this research to illustrate the more visible impact of Jourard's works. However, besides exploring the meaning of self-disclosure for health and personal growth, Jourard was interested in broader questions of how psychology, and humanistic psychology in particular, can communicate its findings in a way that would promote personal growth (Jourard, 1968). Therefore, my aim in this chapter is to examine Jourard's pioneering studies in self-disclosure and to survey his views on humanistic psychology, psychotherapy, and what it means to be human.

BRIEF BIOGRAPHY

Childhood in Canada

Sidney M. Jourard was born on January 21, 1926, in Mount Dennis, a working-class suburb of Toronto where his father owned a small clothing business. In an article entitled "On Becoming a Psychotherapist," he describes himself as feeling like an outsider during his years of growing up because his family was the only Jewish family living in the area (Jourard, 1994). He further describes himself as possessing a tremendous amount of energy as a child, often running three to five miles simply to dissipate his excess energy. He portrays his years between twelve and sixteen as lonely, lacking any friends except one "chum" in whom he could confide. However, despite these feelings of loneliness, he was in many ways a typical Canadian kid active in a variety of sports, including hockey, skiing, football, soccer, and baseball, to name a few. This love for physical activity was equally balanced with a love for reading. In Jourard's words, "I read anything and everything in orgies" (1994, p. 184).

Education in Psychology

While working on a farm during the summers of 1942 and 1943, Jourard decided to go to college. Not knowing what he wanted to study, he selected "social and philosophical studies" as a beginning college program. However, by the end of his first year he had selected psychology as a major. Thinking that he had found a subject that would answer many personal questions he was struggling with at the time, he soon learned that much of what he was studying in psychology was irrelevant to his personal life. As he states: "I was not remotely interested in sensation and perception, and the intricacies of learning theory. I was looking for myself" (Jourard, 1994, p. 185).

Despite his disenchantment with undergraduate psychology at the University of Toronto, Jourard completed his degree and entered the master's program. Upon completing that program, Jourard went to the University of Buffalo to obtain his Ph.D. It was there that he felt a revival of his interest in psychology. He says: "I was involved in receiving counseling and psychotherapeutic help as part of my training and for personal reasons. I found psychology becoming more interesting but I still didn't quite fit" (Jourard, 1971, p. 9).

Feeling some trepidation over not having any interest in what his colleagues were investigating, Jourard began researching those things that interested him. Primarily he wanted to understand the problems he was experiencing in his own life. Having had some exposure to psychoanalytic thinking while at Buffalo, he decided to do his dissertation on ego strength. To avoid doing the typical experiments with rats so characteristic of most psychology departments, he was able to pursue research on people's attitudes toward their bodies, an interest he had held for quite some time (Jourard, 1971).

A Psychology of Self-Disclosure

After graduating with his Ph.D. in 1950, Jourard took a position with Emory University in Atlanta. He stayed there for five years before accepting a position at the University of Alabama at Birmingham. It was at Birmingham that he began his studies in self-disclosure. In 1958 Jourard joined the faculty of the University of Florida's Department of Psychology. While there, he continued his research in self-disclosure and other aspects of humanistic research. He remained at Florida until his death on December 2, 1974.

Jourard was a member of the American Psychological Association and the Association for Humanistic Psychology. Every year of his professional career, Jourard made presentations at the annual meetings of the American Psychological Association and the Association for Humanistic Psychology. He played a key role in helping to expand the Association for Humanistic Psychology as an international organization (Harari, 1975).

Beyond his many journal publications and chapters in edited works, books written by Jourard include *Personal Adjustment* (1958), *Healthy Personality* (1974), *The Transparent Self* (1964; second edition, 1971), and *Disclosing Man to Himself* (1968). His works have been translated into Dutch, Japanese, Spanish, and French. The Jourard Collection is stored in the library archives at the State University of West Georgia, Carrollton, Georgia.

JOURARD'S ORIENTATION TO PSYCHOLOGY

Jourard's orientation to psychology can be traced literally to his experiences growing up. He describes himself as having a fascination with human differences and a robust interest in himself. This fascination with his own experiences would later lead to his interests in such disciplines as existentialism, phenomenology, humanism, and personalism. He suggested that these disciplines allow psychologists to use "their experience of themselves as persons as a guide to exploring and understanding the experience of others" (Jourard, 1968, p. 3). Jourard was opposed to the mechanistic view that the psychology of the 1950s had of human beings. However, he was not opposed to "scientific psychology." What he saw emerging was a "scientifically informed psychology of human persons" (Jourard, 1968, p. 4). For Jourard, the psychology of the 1940s, 1950s, and early 1960s had reached its limits in understanding human nature. Therefore, he was attracted to the emerging movement in humanistic psychology, whose primary spokespersons were Abraham Maslow and Carl Rogers. However, I should note that Jourard began his research in self-disclosure before he became aware of the name "humanistic psychology" (Jourard, 1974). As he states:

In 1957 I began to study self-disclosure. This was before I ever heard of anything called humanistic psychology. I was trained in experimental as well as clinical psychology, and a program of research has always been part of my view of the practice of my profession. I chose self-disclosure as a subject for scientific study because I began to wonder what we knew about the conditions under which people would reveal personal information to others. . . . I soon discovered that one of the most powerful correlates, if not determiners, of one person's self-disclosure was self-disclosure from the other person in the dyad. (Jourard, 1974, p. 358)

To understand the person beyond the objectification of the experimentalists, Jourard (1968) proposed that humanistic psychology begin rigorously investigating such questions as the following:

What are the outer limits of human potential for transcending biological pressures, social pressures, and the impact on a person of his past conditioning? What developmental and interpersonal and situational conditions conduce to courage, creativity, transcendent behavior, love, laughter, commitment to truth, beauty, justice, and virtue? These questions themselves, and even my proposal that we address them, once struck me as less than manly, as tender-hearted and sentimental. I would never have dared pose them to most of my mentors during my undergraduate and graduate-student days. (Jourard, 1968, p. 7)

Jourard (1974, p. 359) also pointed out that humanistic psychology could be defined "as an effort to disclose man and his situation to himself," to discover the influences on his or her experiences and actions. He went on to say that a humanistic psychology should study how various social rules produce conformity in people so that a person could make an informed choice about whether or not he or she wants to conform (Jourard, 1971). In other words, Jourard suggested that humanistic psychology focus its research on issues that help people understand themselves, others, and their environments as opposed to the limiting stated goals of "scientific psychology" that seek to manipulate and control behavior.

KEY ISSUES

Self-Disclosure and Physical Health

Self-disclosure and the role it plays in human research and psychotherapy is the central theme throughout Jourard's writings and research. As I stated earlier, he equated one's ability to disclose with mental and physical health. "Being sick is a temporary respite from the dispiriting conditions of our existence up to the onset of the illness," states Jourard (1971, p. 77). Whether mental or physical, illness may be one of the many ways in which people express protest against a way of life that will not support wellness. Healthy people, on the other hand, when they find life to be dull, frustrating, or tedious, pay attention to their all-is-not-well signals and change what they are doing.

This perspective on health and illness by Jourard reflects the sentiments expressed by the philosopher and theologian Paul Tillich (1981) when he said that "health in the dimension of self-awareness (disclosing to himself) shows the dialectical structure of life processes most clearly. The processes of psychological growth demand self-alterations in every moment, in receiving reality, in mastering it, in being united with parts of it, and in changing it" (p. 56). Thus to understand health and illness, comprehending the essential and existential nature of the individual is necessary. To gain this level of understanding of the other person, the therapist (or researcher) must invite disclosure. As Jourard (1974, p. 358) has emphasized, the self-disclosure of one party is one of the most powerful forces for eliciting the openness of another party to the relationship.

The Dyadic Principle

In the research setting, Jourard (1969, 1971) found that when subjects are interviewed about aspects of their personal lives, they are more forthcoming with information when the interviewers first disclose something of themselves. Disclosure by the interviewers also eases the interview process because the subjects tend to feel comfortable early in the interview situation. Likewise, in psychotherapy the therapist's attempt to manipulate a client to cause change in his or her behavior only begets manipulation from the client. However, when the therapist appropriately discloses, the client discloses.

As Jourard (1971, pp. 141–142) states, "When a therapist is committed to the task of helping a patient grow, he functions as a whole person. . . . if he [the therapist] spontaneously and honestly conveys his thoughts and reactions, I believe he is not only communicating his concern, but he is also in effect both inviting and reinforcing kindred uncontrived behavior in his patient." Hence when we look at the relationship between self-disclosure and health, particularly a healthy personality, Jourard and Lasakow (1958) have found that self-disclosure is both a symptom of and a means to achieve a healthy mind and body.

Somatic disclosure, the term used by Jourard to describe the experience of becoming fully aware of one's body, can be an index of psychological and physical health (Jourard, 1994). Following the lead of body-oriented psychotherapists such as Wilhelm Reich and Alexander Lowen, Jourard asserts how social and cultural influences or what we might call the "normalization" process can affect one's body. Somatic perception, a person's awareness of how his or her body is responding to a situation, is an important part of one's consciousness (Jourard, 1994, p. 143). The healthy person, one who is capable of disclosing to herself or himself and others, is aware of the dispiriting influences that tend to drain the body of its vitality and can make adjustments.

"I will argue," says Jourard, "that the loss of the capacity for somatic perception . . . is a factor in the self-induction of physical and psychological breakdown. If a person cannot discern how his relationships with others, and his physical regimen are affecting him as an embodied being, then he will continue living lethal or pathological life-styles" (1994, p. 144). Given these sets of circumstances, Jourard (1971, p. 77) asks the question, "Why aren't we sick all of the time?" Or what is it that the person who seldom becomes ill does differently than the one who is often sick? The answer is found in the capacity of the former to find ways of life that permit him to be and to disclose himself to himself and to others.

APPRAISAL: THE ENDURING INFLUENCE OF SIDNEY JOURARD

A Medicine of Mind and Body

It is my opinion that the importance of Jourard's contributions is just being realized, particularly in the new "mind-body" approaches to health care. In 1971 Jourard wrote that "the failure of health scientists to study how healing is promoted by placebos, Christian Science, chiropractic, and the symbols of medical know-how is a fantastic oversight" (p. 79). He went on to suggest that since we know that healing is rooted in the biological structure of the organism and not in drugs or surgery, we need to identify what might loosely be called a "healing reflex."

Jourard's suggestion anticipated a new field of science and medicine that links mind and body in a way heretofore not understood. This bridge between what we might refer to as science and spirit is often described by such terminology as psychoneuroimmunology, holistic medicine, behavioral medicine, and psychosomatic medicine. Jourard's (1971) call for a program or field of study devoted to understanding such phenomena as faith healing, placebo effect, and spontaneous remission was realized when psychologist Robert Ader and immunologist Nicholas Cohen discovered that the immune system could be trained like a reflex (Ader & Cohen, 1975). Subsequently, many investigators have substantiated and expanded their work (e.g., Pert, 1986).

Jourard's understanding that healing is rooted in the biological structure of the organism is consistent with the view held by Patricia Norris (1988), director of the psychoneuroimmunology unit of the Menninger Clinic. She points out that we have a clearly established cybernetic feedback loop between the central nervous system and the immune and other systems of the body. As a result, not only do psychological/emotional/eidetic states affect the systems of the body in this loop, but the systems of the body in turn influence psychological states.

A Biopsychological Model of Health and Illness

Jourard addresses an issue, however, that includes and extends beyond the biopsychological model of health and illness. What Jourard proposes is an interpersonal understanding of health and illness, an existential understanding, and a transpersonal view. At the interpersonal level, disclosure by a patient to an attentive health care professional has been found to produce positive effects in the direction of healing. The patient's ability to disclose or, at least, the ability of the health care professional to elicit disclosure by appropriately disclosing something of herself or himself leads to growth and better self-awareness in the patient.

Therefore, once a person is open to disclosure, he or she becomes aware of the sociocultural influences that do not support physical and psychological wellness. Thus the existential dimension of finding life challenging and satisfying is addressed by Jourard. He asserts that "a more subtle factor in the production and maintenance of physical health is morale or spirit. . . . If a person finds life challenging . . . his body works better and he resists infectious illness better" (Jourard, 1974, p. 135).

This statement by Jourard forecast the research of Suzanne Kobasa (1982), a pioneer in attitudes and health. Her research shows that certain mind states contribute to health and hardiness. In Kobasa's subjects, the factors most predictive of healthy coping were what she refers to as the three Cs: challenge, the perception of a threat or change as a challenge; control, the ability to do something about a situation versus a feeling of victimization; and commitment, the sense of purpose in life that there is something important to accomplish. The three Cs that Kobasa deems the hardiness factor are the basis for resilience and resistance to disease and exposure to brutal circumstances.

In the transpersonal realm, Jourard speaks of "spirit and wellness." He states that

spirit has been a nagging and persistent problem to the scientific world. To the non-scientific world spirit is considered real and an essential part of being human. We speak of people as spirited—meaning that they are vital, enlivened or in short healthy. Healing involves not only the body, but also the mind, the emotions, and the spirit. (Jourard, 1971, p. 80)

Thus Jourard (1971) asks the question, what inspirits a person? His answer is that "psychotherapists, physicians, quacks, and witch-doctors all can attest that confidence of the patient in the powers of the healer must be inspired if the healing rituals are to work" (p. 85). Again we find contemporary researchers addressing these issues. Joan Borysenko (1990), a cell biologist, now focuses her research on the spiritual/mystical aspects of healing. Larry Dossey (1989), a respected physician, writes about transpersonal healing. Herbert Benson (1975), a Harvard cardiologist, has done extensive research on the positive effects of meditation, the structure of voodoo deaths, and the relaxation response.

While I am not suggesting that these researchers were directly or indirectly influenced by Jourard's work, I am suggesting that Jourard asked questions more than a quarter of a century ago that researchers are exploring now. More important, he added a research dimension to humanistic psychology that allowed us to understand ourselves and others without violating the integrity of the person. As Jourard (1971, p. 236) concluded, self-disclosure is a measurable facet of our being and our behavior, and understanding of its conditions and correlates will enrich our understanding of ourselves in wellness and in disease.

REFERENCES

Achterberg, J., & Lawlis, G. F. (1992). Human research and studying psychosocial interventions for cancer. *Advances, 8*(4), 2–4.

Ader, R., & Cohen, N. (1975). Behaviorally conditioned immunosuppression. *Psychosomatic medicine, 37*, 333–340.

Benson, H. (1975). *The relaxation response.* New York: Avon.

Borysenko, J. (1988). *Minding the body, mending the mind.* New York: Bantam.

Borysenko, J. (1990). *Guilt is the teacher, love is the lesson.* New York: Warner Books.

Dossey, L. (1982). *Space, time, and medicine.* Boston: New Science Library.

Dossey, L. (1989). *Recovering the soul.* New York: Bantam.

Harari, C. (1975). Sidney Marshall Jourard: A tribute. *Newsletter, Division of Humanistic Psychology.* Division 32, American Psychological Association, *2*(3), 1.

Jourard, S. M. (1958). *Personal adjustment: An approach through the study of healthy personality.* New York: Macmillan.

Jourard, S. M. (1968). *Disclosing man to himself.* Princeton: Van Nostrand.

Jourard, S. M. (1969). The effects of experimenters' self-disclosure on subjects' behavior. In C. Spielberger (Ed.), *Current topics in clinical and community psychology* (pp. 109–150). New York: Academic Press.

Jourard, S. M. (1971). *The transparent self* (2nd ed.). New York: Van Nostrand Reinhold.

Jourard, S. M. (1974). *Healthy personality.* New York: Macmillan.

Jourard, S. M. (1994). *Sidney M. Jourard: Selected writings* (M. Lowman, A. Jourard, & M. Jourard, Eds.). Marina del Rey, CA: Round Right Press.

Jourard, S. M., & Lasakow, P. (1958). Some factors in self-disclosure. *Journal of abnormal and social psychology, 56*, 91–98.

Kobasa, S. (1982). The hardy personality: Toward a social psychology of stress and health. In G. Sanders (Ed.), *Social psychology of health and illness* (pp. 147–163). Hillsdale NJ: Lawrence Erlbaum.

Norris, P. (1988). Clinical psychoneuroimmunology. In J. V. Basmajian (Ed.), *Biofeedback: Principles and practice for clinicians* (pp. 567–580). Baltimore: Williams & Wilkins.

Ornish, D. (1990). *Dr. Dean Ornish's program for reversing heart disease.* New York: Ballantine.

Pennebaker, J. W., Kiecolt-Glaser, J. K., & Glaser, R. (1988). Disclosure of traumas and immune function: Health implications for psychotherapy. *Journal of Consulting and Clinical Psychology, 56,* 239–245.

Pert, C. (1986). The wisdom of the receptors: Neuropeptides, the emotions, and body-mind. *Advances, 3*(3), 8–16.

Rice, D. L. (1995). The transparent self as a key to health? Jourard's contribution to today's understanding of mind-body relationships. *Somatics, 10*(2), 10–12.

Tillich, P. (1981). *The meaning of health.* Richmond, CA: North Atlantic Books.

22

Ronald Laing: Existentialism and Psychoanalysis

DANIEL BURSTON

Ronald David Laing was born on October 7, 1927, in Glasgow, Scotland. At age thirty-two Laing published *The Divided Self* (1960), a classic in existential psychiatry. In the following decade he published *Self and Others* (1961), *Sanity, Madness, and the Family* (Laing & Esterson, 1964), *The Politics of Experience* (1967b), and *Knots* (1970), which made him into one of the most popular and controversial intellectuals in the latter part of the twentieth century. Though he was trained as a psychoanalyst, Laing's primary commitment was to existential phenomenology. Over the years he delivered scathing attacks on psychiatry, behaviorism, and psychoanalysis, hinting that the practice of psychotherapy must be grounded in a deeper conception of human being than these various approaches make allowance for.

EARLY YEARS IN GLASGOW

Ronald David Laing was born at 21 Ardbeg Street in the Govanhill district of Glasgow. He was the only child of David Park McNair Laing and Amelia Elizabeth (née Kirkwood) Laing, a quiet Presbyterian couple of the lower middle class. Judging from his autobiography, Ronald Laing lacked for playmates, and as a result his early childhood was bereft of the kind of companionship most children crave and expect (Laing, 1985). Moreover, there were deep family tensions. David's relatives heartily disapproved of Amelia, and both David and Amelia openly detested their own fathers. In fact, David often fought fiercely with his father, John, in young Ronald's presence, sometimes inflicting serious injuries (Laing, 1976, pp. 4–5).

Ronald D. Laing in the last decade of his life
(Photo courtesy of Kirk J. Schneider).

Another noteworthy feature of Laing's childhood was the strange relationship between Ronald and his mother. For reasons no one can fathom, Amelia managed to conceal her pregnancy from her entire family until the very day of delivery, suggesting that whatever maternal pride she felt was overshadowed by prudery and shame and/or a perverse need to keep others in the dark. After his birth, Laing reports, Amelia went into a precipitous "decline." Judging from Laing's recollections and the testimony of his late aunt Ethel, David's sister, Amelia was a devious person, strongly inclined to pathological jealousy and character assassination. Other features of her behavior were even more alarming. For example, when Amelia traveled downtown, she took lengthy and elaborate detours around certain districts to avoid the malign influence of persons supposedly hostile to herself who lived in the neighborhoods concerned. Years later, when Laing had achieved worldwide recognition, Amelia adopted the habit of sticking pins into an effigy of her son, which she called a "Ronnie doll."[1] Whether this profoundly hostile gesture was intended as an act of magical retribution, like voodoo, or just as a joke—which seems doubtful—the malevolent feelings and intentions expressed in her bizarre behavior are too palpable to be ignored.

Reading Laing's memoirs and pondering the impressions of others, one gets the distinct impression that Ronald was not a wanted child. Nevertheless, it seems likely that Amelia felt constrained to conduct herself in ways that conformed to prevailing cultural expectations of what a mother should feel toward her offspring. As a result, while sending Ronald clear messages that she did not want him or respect his needs and feelings, she also had to disavow the real content of these communications, disguising them as love. Moreover, to live up to her (culturally reinforced) image of what a mother should be, she not only had to deceive herself about her real feelings and intentions, but had to make her son, her spouse, and all concerned experience the ostensible meaning or motives behind her actions as the real ones—what Laing later termed an *interpersonal defense* (Laing, 1971).

Arguably, the resulting confusion could have driven a weaker boy to madness or into severe developmental arrest. In order not to be engulfed by a sense of unreality and despair, young Ronald Laing had to acquire a strong oppositional identity grounded in attitudes of distrust and defiance, which were seldom expressed openly until adolescence. He never really "got over" his youthful oppositionalism. Nor could he, perhaps. Instead, in later life he tried to cultivate it productively by championing the cause of the mad. In any case, it is no accident that Laing's first book, *The Divided Self*, thematized the problems of ontological insecurity experienced by people whose needs, feelings, and experiences are consistently nullified in early childhood (Laing, 1960). Nor is it a coincidence that in *The Facts of Life*, some sixteen years later, Laing speculated that the majority of people are actually unwanted at the moment of their birth, if not, indeed, at the moment of conception (Laing, 1976).

Laing's relationship to his father was more positive, on balance, than his relationship to his mother. David Laing was an engineer in the Royal Tank Corps and Royal Air Corps. His career as a military and weapons man—which he evidently came to loathe—preceded his employment with the Corporation of Glasgow, which he took up shortly after Ronald's birth, and where he remained for the rest of his working life. In addition to his professional career, which was a source of great pride, David Laing was the principal baritone for the Glasgow University Chapel choir. Besides the usual church choir repertoire, he had a penchant for Italian opera and Victorian ballads. Eyewitnesses report that during Ronald's teens and early twenties, David Laing welcomed Ronald's friends into their home with great warmth and generosity and engaged them in musical pastimes and singalongs, with Ronald at the piano. (Amelia made herself scarce or was openly unfriendly to Ronald's friends.) Like his father, Ronald Laing achieved a professional level of competence in music without pursuing it as a career. (He received his licentiate in piano from the Royal Academy of Music at age fourteen.)

PHILOSOPHY, MEDICINE, AND PSYCHIATRY

Education

At school Laing was a gifted pupil who excelled in classics. However, school did not satisfy his intellectual hunger, and at the age of fourteen he resolved that he would read everything in the local library from A to Z and so encountered

Kierkegaard, Marx, Nietzsche, and Freud for the first time. At seventeen Laing enrolled in Glasgow University. While he read as widely as ever, he went on to specialize in medicine. One thing that emerges vividly from his recollections of that time is his urgent need to embrace, explore, and ultimately reject the dogmatic certainties of his elders—religious, political, and scientific. By the age of twenty-two he was deeply immersed in Continental philosophy, having worked his way systematically through Nietzsche, Husserl, Heidegger, Sartre, Merleau-Ponty, Jaspers, Wittgenstein, and Camus (Laing, 1985).

Training in Psychiatry

After a brief apprenticeship in neurosurgery at the Glasgow and Western Scotland Neurosurgical Unit at Killearn in 1950, Laing decided to specialize in psychiatry. In fact, he hoped to work with Jaspers in Basel, but the army and the Korean War soon scuttled his plans. Laing spent 1951–1953 as an army psychiatrist whose chief task was to differentiate those soldiers who were truly disturbed from malingerers. Despite rigid prohibitions on communicating with patients unless absolutely necessary, Laing found ways of developing a rapport with some of the inmates by sitting quietly with them in their padded cells, a move construed by his superiors as a dedicated research effort. In a sense, of course, it was. Laing was anxious to discover how these miserable, frightened, and deeply confused people experienced the world, and how they would respond given the chance to communicate freely. One of the hallmarks of Laing's approach was that he did not demand anything from the patients, whether silence or speech, and that he did not interrogate them as a conventional psychiatrist would have. On the contrary, he maintained a relaxed and nonthreatening posture in their presence and allowed them to open up or unravel their thoughts, feelings, and fantasies at their own pace.

Laing left the army in 1953 and went to work at the Royal Gartnavel Hospital and Southern General Hospital, where he worked under Angus McNiven, a humane psychiatrist, and Ferguson Rodger, who was keen to try innovative approaches. With Rodger's support and encouragement Laing spent several months living with his patients on the wards and conversing with them at every opportunity. Moreover, he continued to experiment with unconventional treatments and to get surprisingly good results.

PSYCHOANALYSIS AND EXISTENTIAL-PHENOMENOLOGY

In 1954 Rodger brought Laing to the attention of an Edinburgh colleague, J. D. Sutherland, then director of the Tavistock Clinic in London. With the help of Sutherland, his successor John Bowlby, and Charles Rycroft, Laing came to London in 1956 to train as a psychoanalyst. During his analysis with Rycroft he worked as the registrar of the Adult Services Section at the Tavistock Clinic and completed his first book, *The Divided Self* (Rycroft, 1990; Sutherland, 1990).

During Laing's last year of training at the London Psychoanalytic Institute, his imminent graduation was obstructed by the Training Committee, which demanded that he repeat his last year of classes and supervision. However, Rycroft, along with Marion Milner and D. W. Winnicott, Laing's clinical supervisors, leapt to Laing's defense, and he graduated on time in 1960. It seems likely that Laing's characteristic ambivalence toward psychoanalysis was already in evidence and played an appreciable role in exacerbating this ordeal. Though Rycroft, Milner, and Winnicott were clearly pleased with Laing's lack of dogmatism and his intellectual independence, Laing's leanings toward existential phenomenology were not to everyone's taste (see, e.g., Brierley, 1961; Freeman, 1961). Indeed, throughout the 1960s Laing denounced the reification inherent in the natural science approach to psychology and reproached Freud for aligning his discipline with this orientation to insure a measure of respectability for his new "science" (Laing, 1961, 1967b). In its place he proposed the adoption of a rigorous "science of persons" (Laing, 1960) or, alternatively, an "interpersonal phenomenology" (Laing, 1967b) that, while perhaps allowing for the existence of "the unconscious," owed at least as much to Hegel, Kierkegaard, Dilthey, Husserl, Heidegger, Buber, and, above all, Sartre as it did to Freud and his followers (Burston, 1994, 1996).

A NEW PSYCHIATRY OF PERSONS AND ANTIPSYCHIATRY

In 1958 John Bowlby introduced Laing to Gregory Bateson's double-bind theory of schizophrenia, which Laing incorporated into his second book, *Self and Others* (Laing, 1961, chap. 7). Thoroughly intrigued with Bateson's approach, Laing engaged another Glasgow native, Aaron Esterson, in an intensive phenomenological study of more than one hundred families of diagnosed schizophrenics in the London area. In 1962, while this work was in progress, Laing traveled to meet Bateson and his coworkers in Palo Alto (and elsewhere across the United States) with a grant from the Tavistock Clinic. In 1964 Laing and Esterson published the results of their study in a brilliant and deeply disturbing book, *Sanity, Madness, and the Family* (Laing & Esterson, 1964). That same year Laing published another book, *Reason and Violence: A Decade of Sartre's Philosophy, 1950–1960*, with South African psychiatrist David Cooper, who later coined the term "anti-psychiatry" (Cooper, 1967, Introduction). Laing always rejected the "anti-psychiatry" label, but regrettably it stuck, and in the ensuing years friends and detractors alike would think of him as an anti-psychiatrist.

THE PHILADELPHIA ASSOCIATION

In 1965 Laing, Esterson, Cooper, and a small group of friends and supporters founded the Philadelphia Association, a charitable foundation devoted to the creation of therapeutic communities for people suffering from mental and emotional crises. The founders of the Philadelphia Association were committed to the idea that a psychotic breakdown is not a symptom of genetic abnormality or neurological disorder per se, but is an existential crisis and therefore potentially an attempt to reconstitute the self in a more authentic and integrated way. Furthermore, they argued, professional and patient roles, as implemented and understood in mainstream psychiatry, were not conducive to the process of cure. In fact, the roles and procedures commonly used preclude a genuine understanding of the psychotic as a person and tend to confirm the mad in their sense of powerlessness and isolation.

To remedy this situation, Laing and his associates set up therapeutic households that provided those suffering acute distress and disorientation asylum from the world outside, free from the stigma of diagnosis and the traumas of involuntary treatment. The most famous (and controversial) of these households was Kingsley Hall in London's East End, which ran from 1965 to 1970. As his first marriage to Anne Hearne disintegrated, Laing himself moved in there, only to leave in December 1966 to launch other projects. Meanwhile, Kingsley Hall acquired a life of its own and became an integral part of the whole London scene until it finally closed in 1970.

RONALD LAING AND ERICH FROMM

In February 1967 Laing published *The Politics of Experience*. Though not his best book, perhaps, it was certainly the most popular, selling millions of copies in campuses and bookstores all across North America and Europe. Thanks to this book, Laing's reputation eclipsed that of Erich Fromm, and in the decade that followed he became the most widely read psychoanalyst in the world. Like Fromm, Laing reached people in all walks of life and achieved far more recognition outside his own profession than he did inside it. That being so, it is interesting to note that there are profound parallels in their critique of the concept of adaptation and the psychology of normality, as Fromm later acknowledged (Fromm, 1970, 1992).

Long before Laing, Erich Fromm had expressed grave skepticism about the use of adaptation to society as a criterion of mental health (Fromm, 1955, 1956). Indeed, Fromm wrote extensively about the widespread atrophy of the ability to think critically and to feel deeply and authentically in the face of pervasive "social filters" acquired in the process of socialization (Suzuki, Fromm & deMartino, 1960). Unlike the Freudian censorship, which alienates people from the experience of their own desires, but was construed as a purely intrapsychic "agency" or process, Fromm's social filters were conceived of as logical and linguistic categories that are embedded in and diffusely distributed through the culture as a whole and that shape and constrain our experience of ourselves, others, and the world, filtering out raw, primitive elements and experiences of transcendent oneness and harmony with humanity and the cosmos (Suzuki, Fromm, & deMartino, 1960).

At the risk of oversimplifying somewhat, it can be said that Laing argued that mad people have lost their conventional social filters and regressed to a level of experience that precedes the acquisition of rudimentary distinctions between inner and outer, real and imaginary, good and bad, and so on, but that their anguish and confusion may herald an inner voyage, termed *metanoia*, that under optimal circumstances can result in the emergence of a more authentic and integrated way of being-in-the-world. Meanwhile, their alienation from the world around them stands in stark contrast to the statistically normal forms of self-alienation that are usually deemed sane. Unfortunately, Laing maintained, what are usually described as normal experiences or ways of being are really so many forms of pseudosanity, a product of radical estrangement from the "inner" world and mysterious ground of Being.

A DISENCHANTMENT WITH POLITICS

In July 1967 Laing participated in the "Dialectics of Liberation Conference" at the Roadhouse in Chalk Farm, London. The event lasted for two weeks and included most of the leading left-wing and counterculture thinkers and activists of the day among its list of speakers (Cooper, 1967). Though Laing had identified himself as a left-leaning intellectual until that point, he was extremely disenchanted by this experience and in 1968 began to distance himself from political events, issues, and alliances. This distancing process registers indirectly in his next best-seller, *Knots* (Laing, 1970), which, unlike *The Politics of Experience*, steered clear of social criticism altogether. Indeed, Laing's thought was now taking on a decidedly mystical and otherworldly character. Throughout 1968, 1969, and 1970 Laing studied Hindu and Buddhist authors and the work of Mircea Eliade and Robert Graves; he became obsessed with the Gnostic notions of "Pleroma" and "Creatura"—a concurrent preoccupation of Bateson's (Bateson, 1972), and before him, of course, of C. G. Jung's (Jung, 1963).

Toward the end of 1970 Laing was a bit burnt out and weary of being in the public eye. Accordingly, in 1971 he took himself, his companion, Jutta Werner, and their two children to Ceylon (now Sri Lanka) and India for a year, during which time he studied Buddhist meditation at the Kanduboda Meditation Center, near Delgoda. For almost eight weeks he meditated for seventeen hours a day under the guidance of an elderly Sinhalese monk, the Venerable Sumatipalo Thera. Toward the end of September Laing and his family left Sri Lanka for Madras and thence for New Delhi, where he stationed his family while he visited the Buddhist monastery at Bodgaya. From there, in November, they journeyed to Almora in Uttar Pradesh, where they stayed for six or seven months while Laing spent many hours in the company of a largely silent, near-naked swami— Gangotri Baba—in a wooded crevice one mile from nearby Nani-Tal.

In late March or early April 1972 Laing took his leave of Gangotri Baba and journeyed to Banaras and thence to London. After his return Laing planned a whirlwind speaking tour of the United States, which lasted from November 5 to December 8 and was chronicled in part by Peter Mezan (in Evans, 1976). After his American tour he started developing a new angle on the theory and practice of psychotherapy. Laing's new angle, however, was not new at all. As Laing himself confessed, he derived his inspiration for this phase of his work from a variety of sources, including Otto Rank, Francis Mott, E. G. Howe, and Arthur Janov. Last but not least, he borrowed from American midwife Elizabeth Fehr, who introduced him to the practice of rebirthing. Rather than blazing a path into unknown territory, as he had done previously, Laing was now following in their footsteps. Perhaps Laing hoped that by putting an original spin on their work, he could capitalize on the emerging craze for birth-oriented therapies that followed Arthur Janov's best-seller *The Primal Scream* (Janov, 1970). Perhaps he hoped that he could use this new approach on himself to gain some leverage against his own inner demons and perplexities. Evidence for this idea comes from the late William Swartley, who toured Europe in the fall of 1975 and, in a newsletter to his colleagues and patients, informed them that while in London,

I spent an afternoon with Ronnie Laing. . . . Ronnie showed me the galley proof of his next book [*The Facts of Life*], which will assure him a role in the history of psychotherapy as the discoverer of the "implantation primal" (my term, not his), similar to the status of Otto Rank with the birth trauma. Reviewers opinions will vary from concluding that he has finally gone completely mad to speculating that the whole book is some type of mystic message. In any case, Ronnie had a lot of trouble attaching himself to the wall of his mother's uterus eight days after his conception. . . . All that was clear is that Ronnie had such a will to be born . . . that he overcame her strong reluctance to the idea. (Swartley, 1975, p. 1)

Judging from Swartley's testimony, *The Facts of Life* (Laing, 1976) was an attempt to provide a theoretical rationale for Laing's conjectures about his own prehistory.[2] In view of Laing's early development, this fantasy, qua fantasy, makes a certain amount of sense. Much of Amelia's behavior after he was born was thoroughly invalidating and might have been annihilating had it not been for young Ronald's determination to survive. Nevertheless, how he (or anyone else) could ever know what transpired in Amelia's uterus eight days after conception is obviously open to question.

What is most troubling about this personal theory is its apparent literalism. During the 1960s Laing laid considerable emphasis on the hidden truth of fantasy. Understood in context, neurotic fantasies or psychotic delusions can become intelligible as symbolic representations of actual states of affairs in the person's social surroundings, past and present, that have been rendered opaque or invisible to others through mystification. In the present instance, however, Laing was not treating his fantasy as a meaningful codification of an as-yet-undisclosed familial or existential dilemma, but as a historical event or process that he "remembered." He attributed a measure of sentience to "himself" as a zygote. This approach runs counter to his own early position circa 1960. In *The Divided Self*, for example, Laing wrote:

Under usual circumstances, the physical birth of a new living organism . . . inaugurates rapidly ongoing processes whereby within an amazingly short time the infant feels real and alive and has a sense of being an entity, with continuity in time and a location in space. In short, physical birth and biological aliveness are followed by the baby becoming existentially born as real and alive. (Laing, 1960, p. 41 of 1965 edition)

In Laing's initial estimation, then, existential birth, or the emergence of the self, is something that follows the process of birth, not something that precedes it. But the later Laing went on to endow zygotes with memory and, by implication, a certain psychological subjectivity. Instead of being a definitive act that precedes the emergence of the interpersonal field, birth was now construed as "implantation in reverse" (Laing, 1976). If Laing hoped that his new departure would buttress his waning popularity or sagging financial fortunes, he was sadly mistaken. *The Facts of Life* (Laing, 1976) did poorly, as did *The Voice of Experience* (Laing, 1982), which is much more balanced and circumspect with regard to the epistemic status of intrauterine "memories" than its predecessor.

THE FINAL YEARS

In the meantime Laing's relationship with some of his colleagues in the Philadelphia Association grew strained. Many of them regarded his rebirthing phase as an unwelcome departure from his earlier work, or as a cynical attempt to win converts or to make an easy buck from people who wanted a quick fix, rather than a therapeutic approach that takes discipline and reflection from therapist and patient alike. As tensions in the Philadelphia Association mounted, Laing and Jutta Werner, who had lived together since 1965 and had married in 1974, experienced an acute marital crisis in 1981. The following year the Philadelphia Association refused to endorse Laing as its chairman any longer. After a year of fruitless efforts to have himself reinstated, Laing finally left the Philadelphia Association in 1983 as he began composing his *Wisdom, Madness, and Folly: The Making of a Psychiatrist* (Laing, 1985), an autobiographical sketch that covers the first twenty-seven years of his life. In view of all the pain and disappointment that hounded him that year, it is a remarkably lucid and moving statement, despite some notable oversights, omissions, and factual errors here and there.

In 1985 Laing joined up with his former secretary, Margarite Romayn-Kendon, who was his companion for the remainder of his life. They moved to Going, Austria, in the summer of 1987. In 1988 Laing met American psychologist Robert Firestone, who invited Laing and Margarite to join Firestone and his wife on their yacht in the Mediterranean. In the midst of a heat wave, on August 23, 1989, Laing, always a fierce competitor, succumbed to a massive heart attack in the middle of a tennis match. Rumor has it that he was winning.

A summary this brief could never do justice to the depth or diversity of Laing's thought. Accordingly, in fairness to Laing, I should add that in his own mind, at any rate, he always remained an existentialist and always believed that a person-centered psychology can be methodologically rigorous without aping the non-human sciences. At his worst Laing was weird, bombastic, and self-indulgent. At his best, however, he was an extremely lucid and compassionate theorist of interpersonal experience, a genius of our time.

NOTES

1. I suppose there is a danger that some readers might mistakenly infer that because she believed in magic, or appeared to, Amelia Laing was an ignorant, uneducated, or primitive sort of person. This is far from true, which makes this anecdote all the more illuminating and disturbing.

2. William Swartley's collective papers are available care of the Scott Library at York University in North York, Ontario.

REFERENCES

Bateson, G. (1972). *Steps to an ecology of mind*. New York: Ballantine Books.

Bowlby, J. (1990). Interview with the author.

Brierley, M. (1961). [Review of *The divided self*]. *International Journal of Psychoanalysis, 42*, 288–291.

Burston, D. (1991). *The legacy of Erich Fromm*. Cambridge, MA: Harvard University Press.

Burston, D. (1994, March). *Laing's existentialism*. Address to the 12th Annual Simon Silverman Conference, Duquesne University, Pittsburgh, PA.

Burston, D. (1996). *The Wing of madness: The life and work of R. D. Laing*. Cambridge, MA: Harvard University Press.

Cooper, D. (Ed.). (1967). *The dialectics of liberation*. Harmondsworth, England: Penguin.

Evans, R. (1976). *R. D. Laing: The man and his ideas*. New York: E. P. Dutton.

Freeman, T. (1961). [Review of *The divided self*]. *British Journal of Medical Psychology, 34*, 79–80.

Fromm, E. (1955). *The sane society*. Greenwich, CT: Fawcett Premier Books.

Fromm, E. (1956). *The art of loving*. New York: Bantam Books.

Fromm, E. (1970). *The crisis of psychoanalysis*. New York: Holt, Rinehart & Winston.

Fromm, E. (1992). *The revision of psychoanalysis*. Boulder, CO: Westview Press.

Janov, A. (1970). *The primal scream*. New York: Delta Books.

Jung, C. G. (1963). *Memories, dreams, reflections*. New York: Vintage Books.

Laing, R. D. (1960). *The divided self*. London: Tavistock, Penguin Books edition, 1965.

Laing, R. D. (1961). *Self and others*. London: Tavistock, Penguin Books edition, 1971.

Laing, R. D. (1967a). Family and individual structure. In P. Lomas (Ed.), *The predicament of the family: A psycho-analytical symposium* (pp. 107–125). London: Hogarth Press.

Laing, R. D. (1967b). *The politics of experience*. New York: Pantheon.

Laing, R. D. (1971). *The politics of the family and other essays*. New York: Pantheon.

Laing, R. D. (1970). *Knots*. Harmondsworth, England: Penguin Books.

Laing, R. D. (1976). *The facts of life*. New York: Pantheon Books.

Laing, R. D. (1982). *The voice of experience*. New York: Pantheon Books.

Laing, R. D. (1985). *Wisdom, madness, and folly: The making of a psychiatrist*. New York: McGraw-Hill.

Laing, R. D., & Cooper, D. (1964). *Reason and violence: A decade of Sartre's philosophy, 1950–1960*. New York: Humanities Press.

Laing, R. D., & Esterson, A. (1964). *Sanity, madness, and the family.* Harmondsworth, England: Penguin Books edition, 1970.

Rycroft, C. (1990). Interview with the author.

Sutherland, J. (1990). Interview with the author.

Suzuki, D. T., Fromm, E., & deMartino, M. F. (1960). *Zen Buddhism and psychoanalysis.* New York: Harper & Row.

Swartley, W. (1975). Newsletter. Unpublished manuscript. Scott Library, York University, North York, Ontario.

23

Abraham Maslow: Yesterday, Tomorrow, and Yesteryear

MIKE ARONS

HISTORICAL MASLOW

No individual is more fully identified with humanistic psychology than Abraham H. Maslow. He was the great synthesizer who gave "visionary body"—an inspirational coherence—to this orientation. That coherence centers around the question "What does it mean to be fully human?" or, put in the idiom of his field, "What is psychological health?" He treated this question primarily in motivational and personality terms. Given the radical nature of Maslow's question in a discipline and social climate estranged from such questions, and given his inspirational model of a self-actualizing human being, Maslow's historical place would seem assured. But Western progressivistic history devours its parents in feeding from them. How does Maslow stand currently? What will his place be in the future?

MAN, CONTEXT, AND PROJECT

Abraham Harold Maslow (1908–1970) was the son of Russian Jewish immigrants. Raised in Brooklyn, New York, he was steeped in a model of the American dream, its hope, and its opportunity for happiness. His father was a barrel maker. He became a world-renowned psychologist. His mother was highly superstitious, a disposition that, as he recalled, only challenged him to daily test her ritualistic taboos. This was the child scientist. But his childhood was also culturally grounded in the Jewish ethical tradition and its sense of *Menschlichkeit*, a quality of self-sufficiency and responsibility. Maslow would come to give a special combined sense to happiness, "mensch-hood," and ethics, while expanding psychology's model of science (Maslow, 1972).

Abraham Maslow (upper right), with faculty and students from the Brandeis University Humanistic Psychology program, early 1950s. Top row, left to right: James Klee, Kurt Goldstein, Richard Held, Ricardo Morant, and Abraham Maslow. (Photo courtesy of Mike Arons and the Department of Psychology, University of West Georgia).

As a youth he was very shy and quite neurotic, yet so bright that in college he "knocked the top off" his Professor Thorndike's intelligence test. He was also a student of wide-ranging interests. When his father asked what he intended to study in college, he replied, "Everything" (Fadiman & Frager, 1984, p. 374). Later almost everything showed up compatibly integrated in his works. The most influential of these was *Toward a Psychology of Being* (Maslow, 1962/1968). Drawing foundational insights across fields, times, and cultures and reconfiguring them in psychological terms, Maslow sketched the heuristic rudiments for a vision of what the human being could be at his or her best. Although he was often criticized as an "American optimistic existentialist," he died in 1970 while developing a psychology of evil as part of his project exploring *The Farther Reaches of Human Nature* (Maslow, 1971).

SELF-ACTUALIZING PSYCHOLOGY

Filling a "Huge Gaping Hole": Dialogue and Research

Maslow denied that he was an optimist and fully acknowledged the validity of those psychologies dominating his day that stressed the darker and diminished sides of the human. He, in turn, addressed what was being left out of psychology.

To sense what is left out, one must bring psychology into the greater debate about humanness. This was a holistic perspective that psychology had rejected in the process of distancing itself from philosophy and the humanities, that is, the "pre-sciences," in the interest of identifying with the "hard sciences."

Maslow, the man who was interested in everything, had since his youth been in dialogue with Jefferson, Aristotle, Spinoza, Bergson, and other thinkers of the Western past who had reflected on the question of what makes a human complete. Maslow's creative mind joined to these eternal flames sparkling neo-Freudian insights of Rank, Jung, Horney, and Adler, along with those of Gestaltists and ego psychologists such as Wertheimer and Allport, all in the creation of a new psychology of "self-actualization." This evolving psychology was given body in the organismic physiology of Kurt Goldstein; cultural reach in social anthropology such as that of Ruth Benedict; a meaningful languaging in the semiotic theories of S. I. Hayakawa; value support in the axiology of R. S. Hartman; and a practical grounding in the human condition by the philosophy of existentialism (Maslow, 1959; Hartman, 1967). All this intellectual timber, lit by Maslow, was empirically oxygenated by the newly opening research into creativity. The transcendent spiritual dimension emerged as Maslow's insights began to overlap those of Lao-Tzu, Buddha, and others of the Eastern tradition. All of this was in a remarkable quest to fill what Maslow called a "huge gaping hole in the field of psychology" (Maslow, 1968, 1970).

What was missing in the reductionistic, "mechano-morphic," value-free psychology of his day was the human subject, taken on its own terms, in all its complexity and wholeness. Psychology of Maslow's day was harnessed to physics-emulating scientific methods, and its practice areas were locked into the medical model. This psychology had typically inquired into the human psyche via laboratory animals or via the psychologically distressed humans who came for therapy or, given the convenience, through introductory psychology students. Maslow, by contrast, chose to study humans at their recognized best. His subjects were culturally respected individuals, such as Albert Schweitzer, who stood out for their creativity, insight, and moral and spiritual leadership and wisdom. He called these select subject models "self-actualizers."

Mending the Cartesian Split

By the mid-twentieth century, in industrialized America, the shortcomings of the Cartesian mind-body split—an infrastructural fixture of modern rationalism—were being symptomatically experienced in the society as segmentalization, identity crisis, and conformity (Fromm, 1947). In a constitutional (church-state) version of that Cartesian split, spiritual matters had been implicitly consigned to religion. The main schools of psychology of the day, behaviorism and psychoanalysis, were reductionistically materialistic. The science of psychology was value free.

Psychology's understanding of psychological health in this period was gauged in terms of a lack of debilitating symptoms, or "good social adjustment." The theoretical grounding for these normative presuppositions was a "homeostasic" or "tension (anxiety) reduction" model. These deficiency-oriented views accounted only poorly, if at all, for the uniqueness of individuals, human dignity, nobility, or spirituality. They failed to speak of love or even of the creative spirit that generates science. Maslow's psychology was to become an account of human potential that neither reduced the spiritual (although he rarely used that term) to the biological or social, nor the biosocial to the spiritual. Ultimately Maslow's approach, in expanding consciousness, allowed the biosocial and the spiritual each to illuminate one other.

D and B Needs, Values, and Motivational States

Maslow spoke of a needs hierarchy because in hierarchical fashion, beginning with the basic biological needs, some needs are prepotent to others. Unless they are satisfied, they preclude the others' emergence. These needs distinctions, representing base and summit of his hierarchy, he nicknamed D or Deficiency needs, for basic biological needs, and B or Being needs, for self-actualizing needs. Intermediary, crossing the D and B at the center of the hierarchy, were ego and social needs. Each of these need levels roughly corresponds to value distinctions, expressed motivationally. One would do anything—extrinsically, instrumentally— in order to breathe, or would use any instrumental means necessary and available in order to secure safety or even social recognition. The Being level, however, is increasingly characterized by intrinsic motivation. Thus one exercises a talent or skill simply because one is endowed with it, for its own sake. It cries out to be exercised and actualized. Once that talent is actualized, a sense of inner security (satisfaction), social recognition, and self-esteem may follow. Likewise, in B cognition one seeks knowledge and understanding for their own sake, including artistic or scientific knowledge and self-knowledge, because, as the Hellenistics emphasized, our full humanness calls for this (Maslow, 1968).

While the lower or basic needs are more familiarly recognizable as instinctual (in the animal biological sense), Maslow regarded the entire path of opening toward the being needs, the pull toward human wholeness and fulfillment, as "instinctoid." This is an instinctlike quality in the sense that one is drawn to follow one's specieswide and individual nature. Unlike instinct, however, the instinctoid can be more easily overwhelmed or inhibited, for example, by social forces or failure to get beyond D-level needs.

D-level needs, often experienced at the lower stages of development as impossibly oppositional, contradictory, and conflictual, may be recognized by an individual functioning at the B level, to use Bergson's musical metaphor, as point and counterpoint, or consonant and dissonant variations on one's whole life's theme. Even one's conflicts and the symptoms of pathology can be viewed at the B level in similar growth-oriented terms and, so recognized, can serve as indices and insightful grounds for more healthy development. Reciprocally, this unifying consciousness achieved by self-actualizers (even when it is unified by paradox) allows for a greater, more natural, more ironic, and more playfully deployable range of creative variations in daily life (Maslow, 1968).

CREATIVE, SPIRITUAL, AND ETHICAL

Creative Grumbles

Maslow's self-actualizers were creative not only (or even necessarily) in the talent and external-product sense. They and their lifestyles were themselves ongoing creative productions. Maslow's own attempt at reconciliation of the mind-body problem was an example of the creative consciousness and lifestyle characteristic of his self-actualizers. These self-actualizers welcomed diversity, ambiguity, contradiction, and even chaos as heuristic precursors to new, original, and more clarifying ways of gleaning reality. These S-A subjects were not without complaints or symptoms, but their grumbles were B grumbles, their tensions part of the adventure, like those of an artist struggling to get her painting just right, not D grumbles of the person struggling simply to survive, reduce impinging discomforts, or adapt to a given way of construing social reality.

Peak and Transcendent Experiences

The self-actualizing process, with its creative transformations, not uncommonly leads to a moment of peak experiencing, experiencing that in a powerful, time-free moment reveals life's unitary substrata, the ocean of the individual waves, or, in Eastern terms, the "ta ta ta" of Being. Although these moments and their unitary glimpses into reality's deeper relationships are typically furtive, they are reported more frequently by self-actualizers and leave on their lives a powerful impact, characteristically resulting in more enduring states of broadly raised consciousness and ethical comportment that Maslow called "plateau experiences" (Maslow, 1968, 1971).

Ethical Transformation

These transformative experiences transpose one's ethical consciousness accordingly. Maslow's self-actualizing subjects were ethical models, persons compassionately concerned with humanity and life as a whole. Yet they had a strong sense of themselves, their autonomy, and their special need for privacy. The contradiction here is only apparent. "The achievement of self-actualization (in the sense of autonomy) paradoxically makes more possible the transcendence of self, and of self-consciousness and of selfishness. It makes it *easier* for the person to be homonous, i.e., to merge himself as part of the larger whole than himself"

(Maslow, 1968, p. 212). Maslow attempted to formulate these B-level insights of his self-actualizers into the power of synergy in society, or in "eupsychian" terms, that is, the "good society" making and made by "good individuals" (Maslow, 1965).

ZEITGEIST

Maslow came to write as an insider-outsider of psychology and addressed his message to an era that was about to burst into a cultural revolution or, more accurately, a countercultural revolution. His psychology gave considerable intellectual and spiritual support to that revolution. It credentialed and, in today's terms, empowered it, much as Enlightenment and romantic philosophy served to empower the French Revolution. His writings offered a biopsychologically based foundation for the presupposition of human dignity, rationally implied in Enlightenment philosophy, while they simultaneously helped empower a post-rational zeitgeist. Seen in today's terms, Maslow was both modernist and postmodernist.

His thinking in several ways joined and served to inspire a historical wave. First, it gave a central coherence to a number of emerging strands of thought, past and present, Western and Eastern, modern and postmodern, both inside and outside of psychology. Maslow brought these strands together under the name of, first, "Third Force psychology," then "humanistic psychology," and still later "humanistic-transpersonal psychology."

Maslow's psychology had substantial impact on personality, motivation, and developmental theories. Beyond these fields, Maslow's paradigm—proposing a motivational ground beyond deficiency and a new understanding of psychological health—served to spark the development of clinical, counseling, and organizational-development psychologies and to give a new value centering to educational psychology. Maslow's work relegitimized such terms as "consciousness," which for years under behaviorism had been ruled out of order. Reborn, the concept of consciousness offered conceptual support for the emergence of many forms of cognitive psychology. Maslow's contribution also served psychology by fostering diversity within a field previously concentrated on doctrinaire, reductionistic schools and has helped to reopen the field methodologically from its narrowest, most positivistic self-definition of science.

Second, Maslow's thinking directly supported extradisciplinary dialogue and activities in a wide range of areas through organizations and journals that he personally helped establish, or that were established in support of the humanistic paradigm. Among the former are the (American) Association for Humanistic Psychology and the Association for Transpersonal Psychology, along with their journals and newsletters. Among the latter are Division 32—the Humanistic Psychology Division of the American Psychological Association, the Consortium for Diversified Programs in Psychology (CDPP), and the Human Science Research Association (HSRA). HSRA merged with the International Association for Qualitative Research to form International Human Science Research (IHSR). IHSR stresses the kinds of qualitative research that, in Maslow's eyes, were necessary to render the science of psychology adequate to its human subject matter. CDPP represents the many schools and psychology programs that developed around the humanistic and transpersonal psychology orientation (Arons, 1996). Missing from this list of schools and programs, which counts nearly forty institutions, is the Department of Psychology at Brandeis University, the first humanistic psychology program, which was established and chaired by Maslow himself in the 1950s. Its ultimate fall back into conventionality was one of his greatest disappointments (Maslow, 1979, vols. 1 and 2, pp. 255, 258, 873, 964–965).

Third, Maslow's thinking was one, but a significant, expression of a greater wave or zeitgeist that at its peak in the 1960s and 1970s was being described by various, sometimes overlapping names such as "the human-potential movement," "the new consciousness," and the "counterculture revolution." This zeitgeist served as historical midwife to a variety of significant social (consciousness) movements. It supported the development of growth centers and a wide range of new psychological approaches and experiential techniques intended to foster authentic relationships and expanding consciousness.

This social zeitgeist went well beyond Maslow and psychology, and he certainly neither identified with nor accepted it in its entirety. Maslow recognized some of his own concepts being misinterpreted, reified, and misused. He leveled criticisms at his students about the directions some of this revolution was taking, including expressions of narcissism, anti-intellectualism, and antiscience. For Maslow (1968), scientific psychology ("only science can progress") was not an enemy. Rather, it needed to be vastly expanded to adequately support study of the human subject on its own terms. Development of human science research since Maslow's day would have pleased him. However Maslow felt about it, virtually all dimensions of this 1960s social zeitgeist embraced and drew intellectual and spiritual power from his psychology. Concerning this wide-ranging influence, George Leonard (1983, p. 326) wrote:

Abraham Maslow has done more to change our view of human nature and human possibilities than has any other American psychologist of the past fifty years. His influence, both direct and indirect, continues to grow, especially in the fields of health, education and management theory, and in the personal and social lives of millions of Americans.

CHANGING CRISES: MASLOW AND HIS ZEITGEIST AT THE GATES OF THE THIRD MILLENNIUM

Values-Ethics Crisis

What is Maslow's future role and relevance? Although times have changed since his era, Maslow's place in future dialogue seems assured. In the judgment of this writer, this assurance is based not only on his past but on the potential contribution of his model. This is true despite the criticism currently aimed at his views from a variety of contemporary sources. Maslow's future contribution centers around values and ethics. Maslow had much explicitly to say about values, and this value orientation implies much about ethics. A central problem of our times is a crisis in values and ethics (Marx, 1992), which many see as related to a chaotic historical stage of passage from a modern to a postmodern epoch. If chaos is pregnant with order, as much of the creativity literature leads us to believe, there will likely be much of Maslow in whatever new ethical order emerges.

Maslow proposed a fulfillment philosophy—from a contemporary psychological frame of reference—that joins a pantheon of fulfillment philosophies across times and cultures, including modern and ancient rationalisms, Western religions, and Eastern spiritual systems. All are called forth into dialogue to address today's values-ethics crisis. Maslow's theory, like other fulfillment philosophies, including ancient eudaimonic,[1] Christian, Western Enlightenment rationalist, and Eastern enlightenment traditions, implies both values and ethics.

In Maslow's viewpoint "good" implies "whole"; this equation is shared in common with many fulfillment philosophies. That is, wholeness and fulfillment are in themselves a good. Yet Maslow's approach also differs from many modern rationalistic and Christian traditions in that the very process of becoming whole (the self-actualizing process) implies an evolving ethical consciousness. One acts ethically because within the very process of fulfillment, one comes to see (recognize) the intrinsic linkage of one's own and others' interests. In contrast, one can remain quite unfulfilled and unenlightened in many Christian and modern rationalistic traditions and yet be expected to follow the ethical rules that are derived from higher metaphysical or divine principles.

In this intrinsic linkage between the "telos" of fulfillment and the evolution of ethics, Maslow shares much with the Hellenistic ancients. Most important, Maslow's and the Western ancients' eudaimonic models of fulfillment are grounded in personal experience and are not derived from abstract principle. For instance, in reflecting on experience, the Hellenistic ancients discovered that happiness is a special valued end rather than a means. The triad of intuition, reason, and experience—the basis for ancient self-inquiry—reveals that we seek health, wealth, power, and longevity for the happiness they promise. We do not seek happiness in order to attain the others. Happiness is the valued end. All of the others may be means toward that end.

Maslow and the Western Ancients

Beyond this establishment of special ends (happiness, self-actualization, and so on), which we have called fulfillment, the path of fulfillment is itself existential. That is, one's self, one's understandings, and one's sense of ethics are all transformed in this process. Note the essential eudaimonic structure of the Hellenistic ancients, which we can find in many viewpoints from the third century B.C. to third century A.D.:

1. One finds oneself in a state of dissatisfaction.
2. Dissatisfaction prods one to open the "first virtue" of self-questioning.
3. This inquiry joins in its interest a tandem of intuition and reason.
4. The first matter to undergo scrutiny is one's own inculcations (conditioning and unexamined assumptions).
5. This scrutiny is undertaken in a search to discern and fulfill one's own unique nature (each individual has his or her own path to take).
6. The search, to use contemporary terms, deconstructs or relativizes the previously accepted truths, opening up states of confusion, contradiction, paradox, and even chaos.
7. The path of inquiry that had begun as a search in self-interest arrives in process at a recognition that one's own interest is not alien to that of the species. One's own interests are also those of others, of the "polis" (or community), and of humanity at large.
8. From this path of insight develops an intrinsic ethic.
9. The process terminates in the sense of a completion, self-sufficiency, fulfillment, and wisdom. The result is the good or virtuous soul (Annas, 1993).

Points of Commonality and Dimensions Introduced by Maslow

Maslow's own fulfillment (self-actualizing) model shares much with the ancient Western eudaimonic one, notably the following:

1. The path is experiential.
2. The path is unique to the person's nature, yet this path also opens onto a specieswide (natural) pathway.
3. One's own interests come to be seen as joining those of others. That is, there is a joint path of good (full) humanness, good (ethical) humanness, and good person/good society.
4. There is an experienced sense of fulfillment (e.g., "my cup runneth over").

What Maslow's model adds to this ancient structural skeleton is both a psychological and a spiritual dimension. In the sphere of the psychological, Maslow brings into the fulfillment debate virtually all contemporary psychology insights (Freudian, post-Freudian, creativity, developmental, physiological, and so on). As to the spiritual, during the Hellenistic period other "esoteric" traditions took up the issues we now consider spiritual and even mystical. Indeed, Christianity emerged in the heart of that period. Maslow's contemporary opening to the spiritual, which he sees as inherent to the fulfillment process, is at the gateway to Eastern and transpersonal psychologies.

Maslow, the Transpersonal, and the Postmodern

As regards the values-ethics crisis and the unique contribution Maslow could make, on the one hand, Eastern and transpersonal psychologies go considerably farther than the ancients, or even Maslow, in linking fulfillment to ethics. An individual following an Eastern spiritual path comes to recognize more than one's own interest in others' interests, indeed comes to actually see one as other. This is part of a consciousness process in which one goes beyond what comes to be recognized as the illusion of separate selfhood.

Given this advance of Eastern and transpersonal psychologies over Maslow and the ancients in the ethical sphere, should we not consider Maslow and the ancients as rendered obsolescent? Do not the Eastern philosophies then have a better ethical answer? The problem here is that as one moves more into the spiritual one enters into a sphere of esoteric ethics, an ethics for the illuminated, which is often understood as an immunity to normal ethical requirements. This sort of ethical elitism, justified or not on its own terms, does not fully respond to the range of ethical concerns for a population as a whole. Thus, for instance, Taoist and Buddhist spiritual paths in China were complemented in the everyday ethical sphere by Confucianism.

Maslow's model, on the other hand, speaks to the whole range of human need and value states and does so from vantage points that include the biophysiological, sociological, anthropological, and, of course, psychological as well as spiritual. The very criticisms raised by some transpersonal psychologists—and raised for other reasons by the postmodern deconstructionists—that Maslow is too concerned with ego states ("core self") imply Maslow's potential centrality in a values-ethics debate that in our day has at core Rodney King's question: How can we best live with one another, in timely context, and with our environment?

Criticisms of Maslow from postmodern (deconstruction) sources, like those of transpersonalists, ironically bolster Maslow's stock in the future values-ethics dialogue. Not only does the postmodern critique deconstruct core self (here as a remnant of romanticism), but also hierarchy, progress, teleology, and meta-narratives, all identifiable modernisms to be found in Maslow (Delueuze, 1996). The problem with this postmodern critique of Maslow as far as values-ethics issues are concerned is that postmodern deconstruction is itself most vulnerable in the sphere of values and ethics. Its deconstructive processes are regressive and nihilistic. Moreover, having deconstructed most modern institutional supports, including the very rationalistic moorings underpinning modern ethics, deconstructionists have left a void that seems best potentially filled by a philosophy like Maslow's that is ironically both and neither modern and postmodern. For example, Maslow's self is not something fixed, but is in transformation, and its self-image passes through all the ambiguity, diversity, and irony that have come to characterize postmodern thought itself. Likewise, the understanding of telos, hierarchy, progress, and the story, like that of the self, is altered in meaning in the self-actualizing process. All these concepts deconstruct in the self-actualizing process.

On the other hand, Maslow's fulfillment model cannot be seen as merely deconstruction. Deconstruction is part of a process of self-reflection: the process of honestly looking within. Deconstruction in Maslow's self-actualizing process is also a form of reconstruction. Put differently, this looking-within process is itself transformative. Implicit to this transformation, existential meaning is given to what previously were seen merely as abstractions. For instance, our American Constitution, inspired by the rational Enlightenment, merely (and that is all it can do) guarantees the "right to . . . pursuit of happiness." Maslow provides (1) a realization process for this abstract right to the pursuit of happiness and (2) a vision of what happiness means, all this intrinsically implicating ethics and spirituality. Expressed differently, by putting existential meat on the dry bones of modern rationalism, Maslow stands between the modern and postmodern precisely by being identified with both and therefore being a values-ethics arbitrator for both. If Maslow's promise to the present and future dialogue lies largely in the sphere of contributions to values and ethics, that dialogue itself should have a major impact both on Maslow's field of psychology and on a world in rapid transformation.

MASLOW'S IMPACT ON PSYCHOLOGY

Academic and Theoretical

With much indebtedness to Maslow, the academic field of psychology has moved from the dominance of a few reductionistic schools to an eclectic diversity. While this status ends the school wars of the past, at least these schools had each claimed some unitary, albeit reductionistic, model of the human being. The current status of eclecticism only highlights the fact that psychology now lacks a nonreductionistic working model of full humanness. In order to accommodate full humanness, such a model must be value laden and must account for the spiritual. It is hard to imagine any attempt to construct such a working model that could circumvent Maslow.

Clinical and Practice

Maslow's thinking has also significantly supported the burgeoning of clinical psychology. However, as recognized in the very term *clinical*, this sphere of psychological practice has been aligned with a medical or deficiency-oriented practice model. There have always been questions of the appropriateness of the medical model for humanistic-transpersonal practice. For instance, in the ethics sphere, there are different ethical considerations in the doctor-patient relationship than in the person-to-person relationship, and still additional differences between those who come for symptom relief and those, on the other hand, in search of self-actualizing or spiritual services.

Moreover, other issues are currently coming to the fore, such as issues implied in outcome studies, licensure and credentialing issues, and health care politics and economics. These issues raise a major question: Is there not in the wings awaiting center stage a new vocation, a soul-doctor vocation centered, as it were, on the eudaimonic institutes of the ancients, on the full development of being human? In fact, such a vocation is already emerging around the edges of conventional practice under such rubrics as alternative, holistic, mind-body, spiritual, or transpersonal psychologies. In Europe we encounter philosophical or humanistic counseling. Dialogue relevant to such a new vocation can hardly avoid the issues raised by Maslow and his particular contributions.

THE CHANGING WORLD

Postindustrial society both joins and separates people in ways never before experienced. Even communications technology—cyberspace—connects and separates in a way that the family or downtown cafe table does not. Ten million Americans already work from their homes. The global economy internationalizes in some ways that Maslow had wished for, yet it is often ruthlessly driven by bottom-line profit values. The postmodern educational institution distances instructor from student and student from student even as it joins them. All productions—communication, commercial, technological, and educational— while affording greater liberty of action, do not necessarily guarantee greater freedom. We speak of freedom here as understood by Herbert Read as the opening of internal insight, or by Maslow as the engendering of the best conditions for self-society actualization. The issues of authenticity, alienation, and identity, which were originally raised in another time and context by existentialists, along with issues of values, ethics, and spirituality, now reemerge to relevance as reality becomes increasingly an imitation simulacrum of itself.

Our culture and times, for all their wonders, have yet to assure the distinction that Alan Watts made between money and wealth (1960, 1970). While at once exciting and frightening in prospect, the ethos and ambience of this emerging zeitgeist can hardly be characterized as "eupsychian." It appears that there is still a huge gaping hole to be filled. Is Maslow's instructional job complete? Or is there another earth-moving debate in prospect that extends even beyond the reaches of cyberspace, one between Abraham Maslow and those who have now taken up the spade?

NOTE

1. [Editor's note]. Eudaimonics (or eudemonics) is the theory and art of pursuing happiness.

REFERENCES

Annas, J. (1993). *The morality of happiness.* New York: Oxford University Press.

Arons, M. (Ed.). (1996). *Directory of humanistic-transpersonal graduate programs in North America* (5th ed.). Carrollton: Psychology Department, State University of West Georgia.

Arons, M. (1997). *Deconstruction and fulfillment: Two pulls on the human sciences.* Manuscript submitted for publication.

Arons, M., & Harari, C. (1993–1994). *An oral history of humanistic psychology, video interviews with longtimers.* Archives, Division 32, American Psychological Association, Washington, DC.

Delueuze, G. (1996, May). La conditions de la question qu'est ce que la philosophie? Philosophie et Postmodernite. Special Issue, *Pretetaine* (Journal of the "Institut de Recherches Sociologiques et Anthropologiques (IRSA), Université Paul Valery, Monpellier, France), *5*, 19–25.

Fadiman, J., & Frager, R. (1984). Abraham Maslow and self-actualization psychology. In R. Frager & J. Fadiman (Eds.), *Personality and personal growth* (2nd ed.) (pp. 370–400). New York: Harper & Row.

Fromm, E. (1947). *Man for himself.* Greenwich, CT: Fawcett Premier Books.

Hartman, R. S. (1967). *The structure of value: Foundations of scientific axiology.* Carbondale: Southern Illinois University Press. (Original work published in Spanish, *La estructura del valor*, 1959).

Kramer, J., & Alstad, D. (1993). *The guru papers: Masks of authoritarian power.* Berkeley, CA: North Atlantic Books.

Laski, M. (1961). *Ecstasy: A study of some secular and religious experiences.* London: Cresset Press.

Leonard, G. (1983, December). Abraham Maslow and the new self. *Esquire,* pp. 326–336.

Marx, W. (1992). *Towards a phenomenological ethics: Ethos and the life-world.* Albany: State University of New York Press.

Maslow, A. H. (Ed.). (1959). *New knowledge in human values.* New York: Harper & Row.

Maslow, A. H. (1964). *Religions, values, and peak-experiences.* Columbus: Ohio State University Press.

Maslow, A. H. (1965). *Eupsychian management: A journal.* Homewood, IL: Irwin.

Maslow, A. H. (1966). *The psychology of science: A reconnaissance.* New York: Van Nostrand.

Maslow, A. H. (1968). *Toward a psychology of being* (2nd ed.). New York: Harper & Row. (Original work published 1962).

Maslow, A. H. (1970). *Motivation and personality* (rev. ed.). New York: Harper & Row.

Maslow, A. H. (1971). *The farther reaches of human nature.* New York: Viking.

Maslow, A. H. (1972). *Being Abraham Maslow, a 16mm film.* Richfield, NJ: Filmmakers Library, Sterling Films.

Maslow, A. H. (1979). *The journals of A. H. Maslow.* (Vols. 1–2.) (R. J. Lowry, Ed.). Monterey, CA: Brooks/Cole.

Maslow, A. H. (1965). *Eupsychian management: A journal.* Homewood, IL: Irwin.

Watts, A. (1960). *The spirit of Zen.* New York: Grove.

Watts, A. (1970). *Does it matter?* New York: Pantheon.

24

Rollo May: Liberator and Realist

KIRK J. SCHNEIDER

In 1994, Rollo May (1909–1994) and I shared the excitement of completing our text, *The Psychology of Existence: An Integrative Clinical Perspective* (1995). We shared our delight over the book, our attraction to its overall design, and our hopes for its timeliness. Two days later, Rollo died. To the best of my ability, I will now convey what I view as the heart of Rollo's teachings. These observations will not be formal or exhaustive, but they will deeply reflect my experience of Rollo as person and thinker.[1]

Rollo Reese May was interested in the big questions about life, the basic issues. This is what existentialism is all about. Drawing from the intimate observations of phenomenology, existential psychology addresses that which is central and vital to human experience: who are we, what are we, why are we? May's response to these queries was that our condition is complex in many ways and paradoxical. We are not this or that but this *and* that, and our basic paradox is that we are free yet limited or destined. Freedom is the capacity to choose (attitudes or actions), while destiny is the limitation or structure placed on those choices by culture, genes, and cosmic fate (May, 1981).

The paradox between freedom and limitation runs through every one of May's major ideas and is central to his approach to therapy. Whenever there was one-sidedness, wherever there was complacency, May was there to upend them. Whenever complexity and ambiguity emerged, on the other hand, May was there to affirm them.

There was a line that May attributed to his great friend and teacher Paul Tillich that just as well could have applied to May himself: He brought "doubt to the faithful and faith to the doubters" (May, 1987, p. 114). This is a tremendously

Rollo May (Photo courtesy of Kirk J. Schneider).

significant phrase—really a credo—that guided May's outlook on life. Those who were smug or overly certain about a position, May used to say, could use doubt. In fact, they needed it to give their positions credibility. Those who were cynical, on the other hand, or who had lost hope needed faith—the answer yes to the absurd, or abandon before the improbable. May was that rarest of thinkers, one who could genuinely hold the contradictoriness of our nature despite temptations to defuse it. We are doomed and yet live on in some sense, May would assert. Life may ultimately be absurd, and yet it may also be ultimately meaningful, he would elaborate. The challenge to us is to take both of these notions in, to affirm them as required, and to fashion something of value from them, something enduring.

BACKGROUND

Childhood and Schooling

In his own life, Rollo May was familiar with both that yawning chasm of despair and the response necessary to bridge it, to carry on in spite of it. A brief glance at his background will serve to illustrate. May was born in 1909 in the tiny

Rollo May with Kirk Schneider (Photo courtesy of Kirk J. Schneider).

midwestern town of Ada, Ohio. Soon after he was born, the family moved to another remote locale called Marine City, Michigan. May was the second of six children of Victorian and traditionally religious parents. To illustrate the isolation that May felt during this period, he once recalled his and his siblings' reaction while traveling to a neighboring town: "The children literally ran and hid behind their mother, so fearful and unused to strangers were they" (Bilmes, 1978, p. 55).

Yet May did not become entrenched in this timorous mentality. In fact, in a pattern that he was to effectively maintain throughout his life, he dramatically transformed himself. By the time he enrolled in college, for example, he became editor of his school newspaper. Soon afterward, he wrote an article that was so controversial that he was expelled from the school. He then moved on to complete his B.A. in English at one of the most liberal institutions in the country, Oberlin College, in Ohio. For May, the world began opening up, and he was eager to meet it.

Personal Searching

May traveled to Greece and taught at the American College in Salonika. He spent three years there and carefully studied the culture's history, literature, and myths. He also spent time traveling, painting, and attending seminars by the renowned psychoanalyst Alfred Adler. Yet as he eloquently describes in his book *My Quest for Beauty* (1985), he also became "exhausted" during this period of his life. He became obsessed with his book and intellectual duties, and neglectful, increasingly, of social and spiritual involvements, of opportunities to be whole: "I had what is called, euphemistically, a nervous breakdown," he observed. "I had to find some new goals and purposes to relinquish my moralistic, somewhat rigid way of existence" (p. 8).

Again, May's "dark night" gave way to a fruitful reassessment, a summoning of courage, and a "bright dawn." With renewed vigor, he realized how precious life was, how significant ordinary events could be, and how essential it was to be open in one's life, to develop choice.

Yet another challenge to May's way of being came some ten years later when he contracted tuberculosis. Hovering near death, May was able, arduously and over an eighteen-month trial, to claim life. It was "not until I developed some 'fight,'" he said, "some sense of personal responsibility for the fact that it was I who had the tuberculosis, an assertion of my own will to live, . . . [that I made] . . . lasting progress" (quoted in Bilmes, 1978, p. 55).

In future years, May continued to demonstrate this resilient pattern. It happened in the early 1950s when, as president of the New York State Psychological Association, he fought the medical establishment for psychology licensure laws. It happened when he co-edited the controversial book *Existence* (May, Angel & Ellenberger, 1958) and firmly allied himself with existentialism. It occurred yet again when he criticized members of his own organization (the Association for Humanistic Psychology) for excesses in the human-potential movement, and still again when he wrote his controversial best-seller *Love and Will* (1969), which challenged the mentality of sexual caprice in our own culture. Most recently, it occurred when May challenged what he viewed as extremes in the transpersonal psychology movement and felt unduly counterattacked by some in that movement (May, 1986, 1989; May, Krippner, & Doyle, 1992). Finally, it occurred before my own eyes during May's latest, and ultimately fatal, struggle. In total defiance of conventional expectations during this period, May would repeatedly surprise me (and others) with his infectious humor, elaborate recollections, and profound reveries.

THERAPEUTIC APPROACH

Freedom and Wholeness

With regard to therapy, Rollo May's aim was to set clients free, to help them become whole (May, 1981). By freedom (and wholeness) May did not at all mean doing or being anything one wanted to do or be; he meant engaging in paradox and finding the most meaningful directions, values, and choices within the most suitable limits (or design) of one's being. Holism, for May, meant optimizing our contradictoriness, our limitations as well as our freedom.

Problems occur, in May's view, whenever we cut off our freedom or destiny. He called such one-sidedness "neurotic" (May, 1981). For example, guilt or anxiety or depression become neurotic if they neglect hope, creativity, and possibility (freedom); likewise, zest, boldness, or power become neurotic if they neglect (social or moral) consequences, natural (or existential) anxieties of living, and limits.

As I indicated, May's approach to therapy was integrative, always tailored to the whole human being as I have earlier defined wholeness. First, he would use presence to understand a given person—presence being defined as careful, bodily attunement to who this person is before me right now, what his region of freedom and choice is (including the freedom to limit himself), and what his region of compulsion and capitulation is.

May used a variety of techniques to help a person find wholeness, but techniques that fit the person and not the other way around. For example, he might use a cognitive or analytic interpretation with the person, but only because that interpretation made sense at the moment. For example, he might say, "You see me like your father right now." But he would not equate that interpretation with the whole person or his total experience. The whole person was likely to see May as much more than his father and see his problem as much more than being oppressed by his father, as being oppressed in the world in some way, which included the way he felt with his father, with May, with the culture, with his boss, with his creativity, with his sense of being, and so on.

Therefore, May saw repression and resistance much more broadly than did the psychoanalysts. He saw them as involving much more than conflicts with past social prohibitions, sexual instincts, or past attachments versus separations, and rather as the more general and profound conflict between present limitations versus freedoms to be in all our various capacities (May, 1958, 1981, 1983).

This essential difference explains why the thrust of May's therapy was experiential, beyond words or discussion. He invited (and challenged) clients to see the contexts for their isolated fears or behaviors, which are before life and which are immediate, direct, or bodily. For example, beyond observing that the client saw May as his father, he might ask what else the client saw in his relationship with May, or what else the client was feeling currently; or he might observe how the client's body looked, or encourage the client to embody (or act out within the container) his present feelings—all in the service of opening the client to the fullness of his experience before life and the cosmos, not merely before past or isolated contents (Schneider & May, 1995). Out of this experiential contact with his denied side—in this case the client's ability to defy and transcend the smallness of his world—came a more substantive meaning, purpose, and commitment in the client's life. I want to be clear that the denied side could also be the client's destined aspects and his inability to integrate limits. In this case, May might not only talk about what limits had meant to the client as a child, but also would explore with him how he experienced limits in the here and now, and through their relationship.

Case Illustration

The classic "Case of Mercedes: Black and Impotent," from *Power and Innocence* (1972), is a palpable demonstration of Rollo May's approach. In this case, a repressed and lethargic young African-American woman (who denied the "free-dom" side of her existence more than the destined) harbored great resentment toward her mother for allowing her stepfather to force her into a life of debauchery and prostitution. Mercedes could not acknowledge this resentment (because she was terrified of it), and as a result she lived a shrunken life in terms of her ambitions, her relationship with her husband, and her pregnancies, which would repeatedly miscarry. The reason for these miscarriages, according to May, was her fear of her mother and stepfather killing her baby to preserve her income from prostitution.

May worked with Mercedes for months to contact and experience her fuller self, in this case her rage. He did this partially through helping her to stay present to her aggressive dream imagery, but the biggest breakthrough occurred when May himself spontaneously acted out her rage before her. He called her mother a so and so, and he acted out her fury toward her stepfather. This, in turn, helped Mercedes to experience her rage and to stay present to the implications of that rage. These implications eventually led to a rejuvenated marriage, a renewed ca-reer, and a baby.

The Nucleus of May's Approach

In summary, Rollo May's approach to therapy can be characterized by five points: (1) a focus on freeing the client within the natural and self-imposed limits of living; (2) an emphasis on freedom and limitation before life versus isolated behavioral or childhood conflicts as the fundamental context to be addressed; (3) a stress on techniques that fit the person rather than merely the practitioner, or, correlatively, avoidance of equating the technique with the whole person; (4) a stress on experiential contact (including that facilitated by the therapeutic rela-tionship) to promote optimal healing; and (5) a stress on experiential awareness (or one's whole bodily understanding) prior to insight, decision, and commitment.

IMPLICATIONS OF ROLLO MAY'S WORK FOR THE FUTURE

The embracing of life's paradoxes and the maximizing of freedom are Rollo May's prime psychological legacies. Currently, there are three major threats to these legacies: scientistic reductionism; psychospiritual absolutism; and postmod-ern relativism (Schneider & May, 1995). Before addressing these threats, an im-portant caveat is in order. May concurred with many aspects of the latter positions, but what he could not countenance was their extremity (as he viewed it) and their neglect, thereby, of life's complexity.

The first threat, scientistic reductionism, is strikingly evident today. Managed care, the standardizing and manualizing of psychotherapy, and the quantitative-experimental tradition in psychology have become formidable mainstream allies. As a result, there is less and less room for May's existential-humanistic perspective, and fewer scholars capable of promoting it (Norcross, Alford, & DeMichele, 1992).

While transpersonal and postmodernist psychologies ostensibly oppose reductionistic trends, ironically, they have spawned new reductions. For example, some in the transpersonal movement embrace psychospiritual absolutism (or the equation of human with deific consciousness). Within this frame, moreover, life's ambiguities are resolvable, and limits dispensable (see Schneider, 1987, 1989, and 1993, for an elaboration).

Certain segments of postmodernism, on the other hand, tout the baselessness of such universalist claims and solely uphold relativist positions (Sampson, 1993). No point of view is inherently privileged over any other view, according to postmodernists, and there are no sacred positions.

For Rollo May, however, there is a stance between relativist and universalist polarities. Our great task, he implied, is the existential task: to acknowledge both relative and universalist positions, carefully craft responses to them, and test them in the marketplace of experience.

These criteria, formulated eloquently by a favorite of May's, William James (1842–1910), are challenging indeed. While many scholars may sympathize with them, few, it seems, will stake reputations on them. However, among those who uphold them today are the handful of organizations and scholars who identify themselves as either existential-humanistic or phenomenological. Saybrook Institute (where I teach a course on May, and where May was a founding member), the State University of West Georgia, Duquesne University, Union Institute, and Seattle University are among the most prominent institutional representatives of these perspectives, and James Bugental, Irvin Yalom, Maurice Friedman, Amedeo Giorgi, and Tom Greening are among their most visible spokespersons. There are also professional organizations, such as the Association for Humanistic Psychology (which May helped to found) and Division 32 of the American Psychological Association, that affirm May's philosophy.

Will the handful of groups and individuals carrying Rollo May's legacy forward survive? Will mainstream psychology pay him more than token attention? These are trying questions. But the larger question, in my view, is just beginning to be posed by May's successors: will society change? Will culture and the vast socioeconomic machine that fuels it open themselves to Rollo's insights? For those of us who remain, this is the next frontier.

NOTE

1. This chapter is partially drawn from my article, "The Heart of Rollo May," *Review of Existential Psychology and Psychiatry* (in press).

REFERENCES

Bilmes, M. (1978). Rollo May. In R. Valle & M. King (Eds.), *Existential-phenomenological alternatives for psychology* (pp. 54–60). Oxford: Oxford University Press.

James, W. (1967). *Pragmatism and other essays.* New York: Washington Square Press. (Original work published 1907)

May, R. (1958). Contributions to psychotherapy. In R. May, E. Angel, & H. Ellenberger (Eds.), *Existence: A new dimension in psychiatry and psychology.* New York: Basic Books.

May, R. (1969). *Love and will.* New York: W. W. Norton.

May, R. (1972). *Power and innocence.* New York: W. W. Norton.

May, R. (1981). *Freedom and destiny.* New York: W. W. Norton.

May, R. (1983). *The discovery of being.* New York: W. W. Norton.

May, R. (1985). *My quest for beauty.* New York: W. W. Norton.

May, R. (1986). Transpersonal or transcendental? *The Humanistic Psychologist, 14*(2), 87–90.

May, R. (1987). *Paulus.* Dallas, TX: Saybrook Press.

May, R. (1989). Answers to Ken Wilber and John Rowan. *Journal of Humanistic Psychology, 29*(2), 244–248.

May, R., Angel, E., & Ellenberger, H. (1958). *Existence: A new dimension in psychiatry and psychology.* New York: Basic Books.

May, R., Krippner, S., & Doyle, J. (1992). The role of transpersonal psychology in psychology as a whole: A discussion. *The Humanistic Psychologist, 20*(1), 307–317.

Norcross, J., Alford, B., & DeMichele, J. (1992). The future of psychotherapy: Delphi data and concluding observations. *Psychotherapy, 29*(1), 150–158.

Sampson, E. (1993). Identity politics: Challenges to psychology's understanding. *American Psychologist, 48*(12), 1219–1230.

Schneider, K. (1987). The deified self: A "centaur" response to Wilber and the transpersonal movement. *Journal of Humanistic Psychology, 27*(2), 196–216.

Schneider, K. (1989). Infallibility is so damn appealing: A reply to Ken Wilber. *Journal of Humanistic Psychology, 29*(4), 470–481.

Schneider, K. (1993). *Horror and the holy: Wisdom-teachings of the monster tale.* Chicago: Open Court.

Schneider, K. J., & May, R. (1995). *The psychology of existence: An integrative, clinical perspective.* New York: McGraw-Hill.

25

Fritz Perls and Paul Goodman: When Ahasuerus Met Erasmus

PAUL SHANE

This chapter contains two short biographical sketches of Fritz Perls and Paul Goodman, two of the three cofounders of Gestalt therapy. Certainly, both Perls and Goodman would each warrant his own chapter, but their profiles are combined here to emphasize the importance of their meeting. This is done for two reasons. The first is that their collaboration was a highly unlikely union of two very gifted individuals of divergent backgrounds and personalities. This collaboration not only gave form and substance to the theory of Gestalt therapy, but also resulted in several polarized tensions inherent within its theory and practice. These tensions reflected their differing viewpoints and have remained paradoxically both problematic and fruitful in the development of Gestalt therapy to this day. The second reason to view these individuals together is that their meeting and collaboration in the late 1940s on *Gestalt Therapy* (Perls, Hefferline, & Goodman, 1951) marked a watershed in their respective personal lives and careers.

FREDERICK FRITZ PERLS (1893–1970)

Childhood in Berlin

Frederick Perls was born on July 8, 1893, in a Jewish ghetto outside of Berlin. His father was a wine salesman for the Rothschild Company. Growing up, Fritz was a youngster who liked to roughhouse and was ill disciplined and rebelliously unruly. His parents, as the marriage progressed, were mainly alienated from one another. Perls's father, Nathan, was an inveterate womanizer, stingy with money, and abusive toward young Fritz. When Nathan was home, which apparently was

Frederick "Fritz" Perls (Photo courtesy of the
Gestalt Journal Press).

not very often, he was either unavailable, tending to seclude himself in his study,
or, when he came out, would frequently berate his son. A favorite term used when
referring to Fritz was *Stück Scheisse* (a piece of shit) (Shepard, 1975).

Fritz was expelled from grade school for his poor grades and unruly behavior,
but later entered another school where he fortunately became interested in theater.
This experience was valuable for Perls's development because it brought him the
opportunity of studying under the legendary director Max Reinhardt. Following
this positive experience, he raised his grades to such a high level that he eventually
entered the University of Berlin to study medicine.

World War I: Experiences at the Front

Perls's studies were interrupted by the outbreak of World War I. Even though
he suffered from a bad stoop and an elongated heart, Perls volunteered with the
Red Cross and, as the war progressed and conscription standards fell, was eventually taken into the army and assigned as a medic to a poison-gas attack battalion.
Being subjected to anti-Semitism by both the officers and the enlisted men, he
was constantly given hazardous assignments while in the trenches. He was

wounded on several occasions and came near to death many times (Shepard, 1975). To try to recapture the utter horror of gas warfare in the trenches, Perls once shared a small anecdote describing a gas attack.

Hour after hour passes. Last night the attack was called off. What about tonight? Hour after hour passes. I am not very tense, sitting in my dug-out and reading some high brow stuff. Finally the wind conditions seem to be right. Open the valves! The yellow cloud creeps toward the trenches. Then a sudden swirl. The wind changed direction. The trenches are in zig-zag lines. We might get the gas into our trenches? And we did and the masks fail with many. And many, many, get slight to severe poison and I am the only medic and I have only four small oxygen flasks and everyone is desperate for some oxygen and clinging and I have to tear the flask away to give some comfort to another soldier.

More than once I was tempted to tear my mask off my sweating face. (Perls, 1969/1992, unpaginated)

Having seen death and destruction on an unimaginably barbaric scale, Perls became desensitized—numb, detached, and depersonalized from the war. Then it was called "shell shock"; now it would be classified as "posttraumatic stress syndrome." Yet at the same time, the horrors of combat Perls experienced, along with the sadistic authoritarianism and racial prejudice he was subjected to, fostered in him, as Shepard (1975) observed, a "tremendous humanitarianism coupled with a deep cynicism about human nature" (p. 27). This psychological polarity or existential theme would be seen throughout his life and career (Shepard, 1975).

Medicine and Bohemian Life

After the war an emotionally deadened Perls returned to Berlin to complete his studies and to attempt survival in the harsh economic times of postwar Germany. He associated himself with the bohemian class of writers and intellectuals—the counterculture and underclass of his day—and, completing his M.D. in 1921, began practicing neurology (Gaines, 1979). At this time, while involved with the Bauhaus intellectuals and artists, Perls encountered Salomo Friedlaender, the philosopher of the expressionist art movement, essayist, critic, and Nietzsche scholar (Shepard, 1975; Wheeler, 1991). Friedlaender's primary teaching, inspired by Nietzsche, was that of "creative indifference," more closely translated as "creative predifference." This the idea that all opposites define one another and that there is a neutral resting point—a "zero point"—from which differentiation occurs (Taylor, 1990). As Perls stated:

Friedlander brings forward the theory that every event is related to a zero-point from which a differentiation into opposites takes place. These *opposites* show *in their specific context* a great affinity to each other. By remaining alert in the centre, we can acquire the creative ability of seeing both sides of an occurrence and completing an incomplete half. By avoiding a one-sided outlook we gain a much deeper insight into the structure and function of the organism. (Perls, 1947/1969a, p. 15; emphases in the original)

Now a medical man and bohemian artist-intellectual, Perls entered psychoanalysis in 1926 with Karen Horney and later with Clara Happel in Frankfurt. He obtained an assistantship at the Institute for Brain-damaged Veterans headed by Kurt Goldstein and, at a seminar conducted by Goldstein and Adhemar Gelb, met his wife-to-be, Lore Posner. Lore, twelve years his junior, was a graduate student in Gestalt psychology, studying the visual perception of color contrasts under Adhemar Gelb. Perls continued his psychoanalytic supervision under Helene Deutsch and Edward Hitschmann in Vienna and then returned to Berlin to establish a private psychoanalytic practice. Perls and Lore married in 1930 (Gaines, 1979). Feeling that his own analysis was far from complete, he turned to Wilhelm Reich upon the advice of Karen Horney in 1930. Along with Reinhardt, Friedlaender, and Freud, Reich was a decisive influence upon Perls. At the time Reich, through his theoretical and technical innovations, as well as his political radicalism, was shifting psychoanalysis away from interpretation of past memories and toward direct confrontation with the patient's resistances, especially as they manifested in habitual muscular and vocal patterns. Reich was also at this time a member of the Communist party and advocated mass sexual education and freedom. Perls liked and respected Reich because, of all the analysts he had worked with, Reich seemed the most alive, the most outspoken, direct, and radically innovative (Shepard, 1975).

Such radical ideas and practices were soon to get Reich kicked out of both the psychoanalytic society and the Communist party, but they led to the development of his "character-analysis" approach, which earned him lasting fame (Sharaf, 1983). Reich's views of sexual freedom and body-oriented psychotherapy were also to influence Paul Goodman and thus created some common ground upon which Goodman and Perls could meet one another, although they approached Reich from very different directions (Stoehr, 1994; Wheeler, 1991; Widmer, 1980).

Emigration to South Africa and the Incubation of a New Therapy

By the mid-1930s Perls, his wife, Lore, and their infant daughter, Renate, were forced to flee Germany in the wake of Hitler's rise to power. Both Perls and Lore were members of the antifascist movement, leftists, and politically astute and foresaw the approaching danger. Perls left first to prepare the way for his wife and child, crossing the German border with only the equivalent of $25 hidden in his lighter. After a short, poverty-stricken stay in Holland, they relocated, thanks to Ernest Jones, Freud's biographer, to Johannesburg, South Africa, to establish a psychoanalytic institute. They remained there for more than a decade, waiting out the war and prospering as psychoanalysts.

Perls's South Africa period was immensely important in his professional development because it gave him a chance to practice, reflect on, and experiment with psychoanalysis. A singular influence on Perls's thinking was observing the breast-feeding and weaning of his infant daughter. In conversations with Lore about this phenomenon, Perls began drifting away from standard Freudian dogma that the resistances were invariably anal in nature and toward the notion that there was a distinct place for orality or the "oral instincts," as he called them (Wysong & Rosenfeld, 1982). The idea of orality—of aggressively biting into something, chewing it into solution, swallowing it into the belly, assimilating its nutrients, and expelling the unwanted—became a powerful metaphor for Perls for the psychological experience of encounter, experience, and learning. These ideas were first presented by him in 1936 at a psychoanalytic convention in Czechoslovakia and were met with rejection from the Freudian establishment. He returned to South Africa dejected but not defeated and gave the ideas fuller exposition in his first book, *Ego, Hunger, and Aggression* (1947/1969a). Just prior to the meeting, Perls visited Freud in hopes of gaining the master's blessing for a psychoanalytic institute in South Africa and of gaining Freud's acknowledgement of Perls's new contribution to psychoanalytic theory. But Freud, already old and very ill at this time, gave Perls a brief four minutes of his time. This apparent rejection by the great man was a wound that Perls would carry for the rest of his life. Freud's rejection of Perls may have caused Perls to reject Freud and to strike out on his own.

This striking out—probably more to the point, a striking back—came with the publication of *Ego, Hunger, and Aggression* (1947/1969a). In this early work, while still practicing from a psychoanalytic perspective, Perls adopted a biological, holistic, and existential approach. For indicative clues, the interested reader should pay particular attention to such chapter headings as "The Organism and Its Balance," "Past and Future," "Past and Present," "Hunger Instinct," "Mental Food," "The Split of the Personality," "Concentrating on Eating," "Sense of Actuality," and "Body Concentration." The third part of the book is entitled "Concentration Therapy," a term Perls borrowed from Reich. Another new influence on Perls, and one reflected in the pages of *Ego, Hunger, and Aggression* was the work of Jan Christiaan Smuts, author of *Holism and Evolution* (1926), a former field marshal, and then the prime minister of South Africa. Even though *Ego, Hunger, and Aggression* laid out an ambitious program—to revise Freudian "association psychology" in light of holism and Gestalt psychology—Perls's effort failed to achieve any theoretical consistency (Wheeler, 1991). Nevertheless, the kernels of his later ideas were present in the form of themes and principles that would preoccupy Perls for the remainder of his life.

Emigration to the United States: The Collaboration with Paul Goodman

With the war over and Smuts now out of office, Perls and Lore decided to emigrate once more, fearing a fascist backlash in South Africa with its spreading racist policies. Sponsored by Lore's brother and Karen Horney, Perls came to New York City in 1946. Perls quickly established a practice with the help of Erich

Fromm and was later joined by his wife, daughter, and new son, Steven (Gaines, 1979; Shepard, 1975; Wysong & Rosenfeld, 1982).

Upon arriving in New York City, Perls soon looked up Paul Goodman after meeting in a New York cafeteria with several anarchists who knew Goodman (Stoehr, 1994). The reason Goodman was on Perls's list of possible contacts was Goodman's positive essay about Reich that appeared in *Politics* magazine in July 1945. The meeting between Perls and Goodman was more portentous than either could have known at the time; Perls and Goodman needed one another. Perls had a working manuscript extending his oral concepts and Reichian-inspired "concentration" exercises and needed an editor, someone far more facile in English than himself, to rework and make the manuscript publishable. Goodman needed a practical framework within which to ground his anarchistic and Reichian-inspired organismic ideas and their libertarian social and political implications. The result of this star-crossed meeting was *Gestalt Therapy* (Perls, Hefferline, & Goodman, 1951).[1] The name "Gestalt therapy" was chosen after much debate. "Concentration therapy" was considered and then rejected; "existential therapy" was considered and then rejected because Jean-Paul Sartre's "nihilistic philosophy" was so much in vogue at the time. Over the misgivings of Lore Perls, Goodman and Perls elected to call it "Gestalt therapy" (Wysong & Rosenfeld, 1982). This is interesting in light of the fact that neither Perls nor Goodman were formally trained in Gestalt psychology, as was Lore Perls; their choice of "Gestalt" would eventually lead to a minor academic debate on the historical and intellectual lineage of Gestalt therapy extending through the present (see Henle, 1978; Litt, 1978; Sherrill, 1986).

The New York Institute and the Evolution of Gestalt Therapy

The book itself fared poorly in initial sales but served as a clarion call to a small and scattered group of disaffected intellectuals to begin rallying around a new psychotherapeutic philosophy. This group became the core of the New York Institute for Gestalt Therapy. Professional interest in Perls's ideas and work developed slowly. The first clinicians outside of New York came from Cleveland, and soon Perls was traveling there to teach and lead training groups. He was followed by Lore (now Americanized to "Laura"), Goodman, Isadore From, and Paul Weisz. As the 1950s progressed, Perls also made regular trips to Detroit, Toronto, and Miami.

Fritz Perls's ideas created a momentum, but as was typical for him, he left the actual organization and execution to others. In the case of the new institute, the responsibility fell by default to Laura. She continued to oversee the New York Gestalt Institute for the remainder of her life. But the institute itself caused problems for Perls. Surrounded by intellectually astute professionals and students, with Goodman at the forefront, Perls could not stand the competition and criticism. He thus fell from the limelight of center stage, something he found unbearable. Perls, now suffering from anginal pain, pulled up stakes to seek new ground elsewhere.

Wanderings, Esalen, and "Discovery"

Fritz Perls, feeling his age, experiencing heart problems, bitter about being unappreciated in New York as the great clinical innovator, and greatly disappointed that Gestalt therapy was not achieving the success he had hoped for, moved to Miami, Florida, ostensibly to bide his time waiting for death. For two years he lived alone in a small apartment, seeing a small group of patients and occasionally traveling to other cities to teach Gestalt therapy. In 1957 he fell in love again, which helped renew his vitality and sense of purpose (Shepard, 1975). But, still troubled by ghosts from the past, Perls began privately experimenting with psychedelic drugs. Marty Fromm, a former patient now turned girlfriend, witnessed his drug usage. According to her:

He [Perls] saw acid as a tool to get into his psychosis. He loved to use it, loved to become raving mad and get into his animal qualities. He loved to rant and rave and play act. He always had very violent tragedy-Queen experiences with huge sobbings and great traumas and memories and feelings—much of it about his father. But instead of being a tool to work through his psychosis, acid exacerbated his paranoia. (Shepard, 1975, pp. 89–90)

Perls's use of psychedelics must be kept in a historical perspective because, at this time, both the government and other clinicians were testing psychedelic drugs for applications in espionage and psychotherapy (see Lee & Shlain, 1985). If anything, the drug use attests both to Perls's personal courage and his underlying desperation. While the Florida sojourn was depressing and occasionally stormy, Perls slowly recovered both his physical and mental health. He moved again in 1959 to California at the invitation of Wilson Van Dusen to become a guest trainer at the Mendocino State Hospital. Later he practiced and taught for a short time in Los Angeles with James Simkin and, from there, traveled around the world to briefly study Zen in Japan and painting in Israel.

He returned to the United States in 1962 and landed at what was to become known as Esalen Institute, the first human-potential growth center. Clearly this turned out to be a classic case of "being in the right place at the right time" for Perls. When Esalen was "discovered" by the national media several years later, Perls and his seemingly miraculous method were catapulted to the front of the burgeoning human-potential movement. Besides Perls's technical brilliance, his radical ethics of here-and-now awareness and self-responsibility, as well as his cantankerous and lecherous reputation, drew the spotlight and quickly eclipsed his former colleagues in New York.

Perls, forever fond of theater and drama, was a natural showman and designed his teaching and practice around a kind of therapist-director, client-actor, and group-audience structure. Perls taught in the "workshop" format that consisted of a group of participants (the larger the better) of which each member would take turns working with him. The format led to the popularization of "the hot seat" and the "empty-chair" technique that became indelibly identified as Gestalt therapy and not just Fritz's preferred technique. Also, during this Esalen period, Perls began audiotaping and filming his workshops and making these tapes available for distribution and transcription into several books. These merely added to his already-dizzying fame. As Perls noted in his autobiography: "I am becoming a public figure. From an obscure lower middle class Jewish boy to a mediocre psychoanalyst to the possible creator of a "new" method of treatment and the exponent of a viable philosophy which could do something for mankind" (Perls, 1969/1992, unpaginated). As he can be heard to comment wryly on one of the audiotapes made during this time, "I have developed such a reputation that not even I can possibly live up to it." Perls had finally made it. Fritz Perls and Gestalt therapy had arrived. He was seventy-five years old.

Even though he began to mellow with success, old conflicts still troubled him. As had happened in New York, Perls found himself in competition (or, more accurately, put himself in competition) with other teachers at Esalen. After his experiences in Germany and South Africa, he feared a fascistic conservatism in the United States with the election of Richard M. Nixon. Perls purchased an aging motel on Lake Cowichan in British Columbia and established his own "Gestalt kibbutz" in 1969. It was to be his last home because a year later, while on a workshop tour and experiencing extreme flulike symptoms, he was hospitalized in Chicago. As he already knew, and as an autopsy later confirmed, Perls was suffering from advanced pancreatic cancer. He died of heart failure a few days later on March 14, 1970 (Gaines, 1979; Shepard, 1975).

Ahasuerus: The Wandering Jew

From Germany to Holland to South Africa to New York City to Florida to Japan to California to Canada and, finally, to his death in Chicago, it is with good reason that I liken Fritz Perls to Ahasuerus, the fabled Wandering Jew of medieval legend. This is hardly an original image and is possibly too sentimental, but there remains something fitting about it. Perls was a brilliant and courageous man, troubled, complex, and, in many ways, most unlovable. The image of him as the eternal wanderer is one that speaks of suffering, unceasing effort, an endless searching for home, and the eternal hope of finding it, but most of all, the promise of spiritual atonement and renewal.

PAUL GOODMAN (1911–1972)

Childhood in New York

Paul Goodman was born in New York City, the youngest of four children. His father was a fairly successful antique dealer who abandoned his family and left

Paul Goodman (Photo courtesy of Taylor Stoehr).

for Brazil with his mistress shortly before Goodman was born. Like Perls, Goodman grew up fatherless in a household of women, raised mainly by his sister and
three aunts. He was a bright and precocious child who discovered early on his
own proficiency with language and quickly became interested in art, especially
poetry. Stoehr (1994) comments:

To have been "born fatherless" was for Goodman the great shaping circumstance of his
life. Because he was a poet and a psychologist, he probably made more of this bad luck
than it deserved, but on the whole he did not pity himself. . . . It is tempting to believe
that Goodman's peculiar mix of respect for tradition and passion for the here and now
grew out of this fatherless childhood, always looking for a patrimony he could claim yet
unwilling to waive a particle of his autonomy. It made him especially sensitive to the crisis
our society would face at midcentury. (1994, p. 22)

Goodman was not just precocious with words but with intellectual ideas as well.
He discovered Freud while still in high school and studied the other psychoanalytical writers such as Otto Rank, George Groddeck, Karl Abraham, and Harry
Stack Sullivan (Goodman, 1977/1991). He was also precocious sexually and by
early adolescence identified himself as bisexual. As we will see again later, the

Paul Goodman, about 1955, in a group therapy session (Photo courtesy of Taylor Stoehr, with acknowledgment to Sam Holmes).

theme of erotic energy or "Eros," as he called it, runs through Goodman's writings and personal life in a constant rhythm.

Adult Years: Poetry, Philosophy, and Letters

Goodman majored in philosophy in college and was voted by his class as "best poet." Upon graduation, he began publishing essays in small literary and political magazines and, thanks to the help of his sister, with whom he still lived, began submitting brief synopses of French novels to the story department of Metro-Goldwyn-Mayer. Through a college friend doing graduate work at Columbia University, Goodman discovered the eminent philosophy professor Richard McKeon and began auditing his classes during the depression (Stoehr, 1994). Often he traveled to Cambridge to audit classes for free as well (Kaufman, 1972). It was through McKeon, a noted Aristotelian scholar (e.g., McKeon, 1941), that Goodman became interested in Aristotle. Certain ideas from Aristotle's natural philosophy recur perpetually throughout Goodman's writings. It was also during this time that Goodman became acquainted with Kant, John Dewey, and the anarchistic thinkers Kropotkin and Bakunin, as well as the great Taoist sages Lao-tzu and Chuang-tzu.

In the mid-1930s Goodman and his brother Percival, an architect, secured editorial positions on *Trend* magazine as cinema and architectural editors, respectively. Goodman also got a summer job as a dramatics counselor at a Zionist boys camp in Vermont, which would lead later to a fictionalized account, *The Break-up of Our Camp* (Goodman, 1949). Goodman was invited by McKeon in 1936 to teach in the "Great Books" program at the University of Chicago and prepare for his doctorate.

Marriages and Meanderings

Goodman moved to Chicago in 1936 and within a year met and fell in love with his first wife, a woman of rather bohemian tastes. Within three years of their common-law marriage, they had an infant daughter.

These new and deep attachments did not put an end to his promiscuous homosexual life. He settled once again into the pattern that went back to his childhood: a domestic hearth that was female dominated, stable, and monogamous, balanced against boyish exploits and homosexual adventuring away from home, sometimes comradely but more often casual and anonymous. (Stoehr, 1994, p. 28)

Goodman's homosexuality was not the problem; his lack of restraint and his refusal to keep his sexual pursuits off campus were his repeated downfall in academia and the literary world. He was fired from the University of Chicago for this reason, as he would be from a succession of other teaching positions in the future. Goodman refused to restrain himself with his students with highly rationalized arguments: He refused to give up his "right to fall in love" with his students; being an educator was inextricably grounded in Eros; and so on (Stoehr, 1994). Apart from his sexual escapades, Goodman's interest in youth and in the problems of adolescence continued for the remainder of his life.

Goodman returned to New York with a failed marriage but to several promising literary opportunities. His poetry and prose soon began appearing in small but prestigious journals such as *Partisan Review*. He completed his doctorate in 1940. His dissertation was published in 1954, thanks to help from friends, including McKeon, as *The Structure of Literature* (Goodman, 1954). By 1942 he had completed the first volume of his major comic *Bildungsroman The Empire City* (1959) and a book of Japanese Noh plays. However, the outbreak of World War II dashed his literary hopes. His Japanese book was untouchable, and he was blacklisted by *Partisan Review* because his essays were unpatriotically pacifist and critical of the capitalist system. During this period he remarried, again a common-law arrangement, only this time to a more stable but equally broad-minded woman with whom he fathered a second child, Mathew Ready. As the war progressed, the draft began including fathers, and Goodman was called up, only to experience rejection once again, but fortuitously so: "In 1945, even the Army rejected me as "Not Military Material" (they had such a stamp) not because I was queer but because I made a nuisance of myself with pacifist action at the examination and also had bad eyes and piles" (Goodman, 1977/1991, p. 218). His "pacifist action" during the induction examination consisted of smoking his pipe in a nonsmoking area, bothering the doctors and psychiatrists with his pacifist arguments, talking when he should have been silent, and, in general, just being a real "stinker case" (Stoehr, 1994). It was fortunate for Goodman that he was 4-F although his pacifist protest, however personally symbolic it might have been, did not have much political impact because the war was nearly over.

Wilhelm Reich, Sexual Politics, and Psychoanalysis

Goodman discovered Wilhelm Reich in 1945, wrote a favorable review of Reich's works, and linked Reich's work on sexual freedom with anarchistic thought. By this time Reich had emigrated to America after being forced out of Norway. Reich called Goodman in 1945 to come meet with him at his laboratory-home in Forest Hills, New York. As Goodman tells the story:

In 1945 Reich phoned and asked me to call on him. I was pleased and puzzled, and fondly hoped that this remarkable man would put me to some activity. (My need for such direction and permission is my problem.) But what he wanted was for me to "stop linking his name with anarchists or libertarians"—he had perhaps read a laudatory notice I had written of him in *Politics*, July 1945. I was astonished at his request; after all, I said, his main points were anarchist points and we needed him, and he never said anything we strongly disagreed with, though he made careless formulations. He denied my statements—it became clear that he had never read Kropotkin; charmingly his face fell in childlike surprise when I mentioned some pedagogic commonplace from *Fields, Factories, and Workshops*—I was immensely impressed by his openness to a simple feeling of surprise. "Really, Dr. Reich," I said finally, "what is it to you if we younger folk call you an anarchist or not?" He explained, this time to my dismay, that Neill in England would find it doubly hard to keep his upperclass kids in Summerhill, the progressive school, if the movement was tagged as anarchist *too*. My guess was that the doctor was suffering from the understandable paranoia of the refugee from Hitler. (Goodman, 1977/1991, p. 85)

Regarding Goodman's anarchism, it must be noted that he lived a very bohemian lifestyle, but "as an anarchist, he was more suggestively earnest than deeply serious" (Widmer, 1980, p. 144). That is, Goodman used the anarchistic-communitarian-libertarian position as a tool to analyze current social and political events and to espouse his own views on personal and civil freedoms. As Goodman described himself: "I am an anarchist not because I am 'individualist' or have an abiding faith in 'spontaneity,' but because I am communitarian and hope for the Commonwealth, whereas coercion and top-down direction make people fearful and stupid" (1966, p. 246).

In spite of Reich's admonishing Goodman, Goodman was determined to explore Reichian therapy farther, and he began to do so in 1946 with one of Reich's early students, Alexander Lowen. Goodman undertook therapy, however, in a typically contradictory way. He refused to enter into a formal relationship with Lowen as a "patient" and preferred instead to approach the Reichian method as a kind of "calisthenics" for releasing muscular "armoring" on a selectively applied basis (Stoehr, 1994). Goodman combined the Reichian "yoga," as he called it, with his own self-analysis through journal writings. His work with Lowen lasted about eighteen months, and thereafter he continued on his own, adding free association and dream analysis. Some of his writings from this period formed part of his novel *Parents Day* (1951), about his being fired for having sexual liaisons with his students. This work could only be printed in a limited run by a small printer because of its homosexual content, but became a kind of underground classic for the gay community (Stoehr, 1994).

After the war Goodman found work teaching night classes on the literary works of Franz Kafka to returning veterans. By synthesizing his interests in Kafka, Taoism, Freud, Reich, and Kierkegaardian existential theology, Goodman wrote a psychoanalytic analysis of Kafka, *Kafka's Prayer* (1947/1976). This particular book is of great interest because it contains seminal themes that Goodman would later elaborate in the second half of *Gestalt Therapy* (Perls, Hefferline, & Goodman, 1951).

Goodman's Encounter with Fritz and Laura Perls

It was at this time that Perls sought out Goodman for editorial assistance for his new book idea, and Goodman was drawn to both Perls and his wife, Laura. From Perls he gained views of Reich and Freud that were filtered through a handful of key concepts drawn from Gestalt psychology. The oral-aggression ideas struck Goodman instantly, and he immediately gave them social and political interpretations. From Laura, he gained a therapist and, later and perhaps more importantly, a close personal friend. Earlier Goodman had refused to accept the patient role with Alexander Lowen and like Freud had then undertaken a "self-analysis." This time, however, Goodman went to Laura Perls as a serious patient; his condition was desperate, as he was plagued by physical problems and suffered a deep and abiding despair over his failure as an artist. But instead of concentrating solely on the body or ruminating obsessively over past conflicts, Laura and Goodman focused on awareness in the present moment and on ways of supporting a livelier relationship to the world (Stoehr, 1994). Goodman's inner plight at this time is witnessed in his "Essay for My Fortieth Birthday," written in 1951 (Goodman, 1977/1991):

I always wrote with the hope of making money, at the same time as I jealously reserved the right to write "as I pleased," and I have hundreds of times had the sinking feeling of seeing a work become non-saleable under my pen. I have made almost no money by writing—I have been driven to, and learned, other expedients to achieve decent poverty— and now I have learned not to count on anything. . . . My works have no social audience. This is inevitably so because social groups are interested in the works that enhance their identity or solve their problems; but I am niggardly of enhancing the others or paying attention to their wants, just as I am niggardly with my own wants. (pp. 210–211)

Ironically, at about the time Goodman was writing these words, *Gestalt Therapy* (1951) was coming off the press. Even though that piece was also a commercial flop, it benefited Goodman financially. Perls had hired Goodman for editorial assistance for $500, a seemingly modest amount that nevertheless covered Goodman's rent in New York City for two years. The book also launched Goodman into a new, if sporadic, career as a psychotherapist (Stoehr, 1994).

Goodman's style of psychotherapy involved a combination of his playing the literary man, becoming the "differential friend," and enacting his own pursuit of authenticity in the present situation. No serious psychiatrically ill cases were ever referred to Goodman; he confined himself to working with those suffering from artistic blocks, career decisions, and garden-variety "neuroses." Clearly he had poor boundaries with his patients. Former lovers became clients, clients became lovers, and he even attempted therapy with his own brother. This nevertheless made Goodman more engaging and alive as a real person. Fritz Perls's boundaries were clearly too thick; for example, Perls once told a workshop group: "So if you want to go crazy, commit suicide, improve, get "turned on," or get an experience that will change your life, that's up to you. I do my thing and you do your thing" (Perls, 1969b, p. 75). Inversely, Goodman's boundaries were completely fluid. If a client in one of his groups was down on the floor weeping, Goodman would get down there and weep alongside of him. Goodman's style was that of a street philosopher or Taoist poet; he was, as Erving Polster described him, "a combination of the beatific and the outrageous" (Wysong & Rosenfeld, 1982, p. 54). Goodman valued bringing one's authenticity and humanness to the therapist's role; indeed, he viewed it as an obligation for the therapist to be a person and not just a persona.

A Modern Erasmus

Meanwhile, on the literary front, Goodman's great novel, *The Empire City* (1959), was finally published through a bit of luck and much help from his friends. It looked as if his ship had finally come in. He published some essays during this period and wrote a group of plays, but the latter productions were critically panned. Now Goodman was contracted to write a study on juvenile delinquency, *Growing Up Absurd* (1960). This was the piece that was to bring him fame and create a demand for his presence as a lecturer and speechmaker at antiwar, civil rights, and university-reform events. Even here, on the turbulent social scene of the 1960s, Goodman was uneasy. As a kind of "reluctant sage" to radical students and war protestors, Goodman would often berate his young and eager listeners, most of whom viewed him as the prototypical antiestablishment hero and pacifist-anarchist critic, that they lacked an appreciation of the cultural heritage of Western civilization. It must have been an amusing and uncomfortable meeting between those dedicated to the destruction of Western society, such as the SDS Weathermen, and Goodman, who conducted himself not as a radical but as a traditional "man of letters." It was during this late period that Goodman began to think of himself as a modern Erasmus—a humanist thinker and Renaissance man—working in a time of social and political upheaval.

Unfortunately, this last decade was marked by tragedy, despite a modicum of fame and, for once, a decent income brought by the lecture circuit. Goodman's son, Mathew Ready, was killed in 1967 during a mountaineering accident, dragging Goodman into deep mourning for several years. Goodman wrote in one of his "little prayers" (Goodman, 1972, p. 132) that his son had been "playing too happily" on a mountainside and "fell down and died." He acknowledged teaching his son to talk honestly, but failing to teach him the "cowardice and hesitation necessary to live a longer life unhappily." The end of Goodman's own suffering was nearing. Troubled for several years by an on-going heart condition, Goodman died of a heart attack at his little farm in North Stratford, New Hampshire on August 2, 1972.

THE ENCOUNTER OF FRITZ PERLS AND PAUL GOODMAN

The meeting between Fritz Perls and Paul Goodman was one between two men who shared common theoretical interests as well as glaring differences in their respective outlooks and personalities. Theirs was an uneasy alliance and, in some ways, more of a marriage of convenience. Perls was the idea man with the core practical concepts; Goodman was the writer who fleshed out the theoretical base and added a social perspective (Stoehr, 1994). Surprisingly, Perls gave Goodman almost free rein over the manuscript, even allowing him to pen the important theoretical exposition in the second half.

Perls was an innovative therapist who, dissatisfied with Freudianism, was deeply influenced by Reinhardt's dramatic techniques and the body-oriented approach of Wilhelm Reich, as well as by the practical implications of concepts gleaned from Friedlaender's creative indifference, biological holism, Zen Buddhism, and existential philosophy. He also borrowed a couple of key principles from Gestalt psychology. Perls developed from this grab bag of philosophies and clinical insights a special emphasis on awareness in the "here and now" of experience, a sensitivity to polarized conflicts within the personality, the urgency of incomplete gestalts of experience, and an almost fanatical devotion to independence and self-responsibility.

Goodman, on the other hand, was a classical scholar who was deeply influenced by Freud, Rank, and Reich—especially the political implications of their works—as well as by Aristotle, Kant, James, Dewey, Buber, and Taoism. Both figures were politically left of center, especially Goodman with his pacifism and anarchist communitarianism. Perhaps it is in the context of political and social thought that the meeting between Perls and Goodman can be most succinctly summarized. At the simplest level, Perls and Goodman can both be thought of as philosophers of freedom. For Perls, freedom meant an integrated personality—being fully present and spontaneously authentic in each moment—leading to a hyperindividualism and absolute personal independence. Truth, spontaneity, authenticity, self-responsibility, and independence were Perls's values and his ideals for "growth." These values are readily apparent in his private life and his style of psychotherapy. But when taken to an extreme, as Perls undoubtedly took them, they lead to a crass selfishness, callousness to others, and an almost schizoid stance in the world. Perls's "Gestalt prayer," while it may foster personal autonomy, also tends to negate intimate relationships. Goodman would have been (and probably was) aghast at Perls's pithy perversions of Gestalt therapy.

In this regard, Goodman stands in opposition to Perls. Goodman's problem, one he wrestled with throughout his life and writings, was how to exist as a healthy and authentic human "animal" spontaneously expressing one's impulses and needs in a society that by its hierarchical organization inhibits personal expression and freedom. Goodman identified the three Dilemmas:

The Dilemma of Political Action: We know that the behavior of our society is leading us to disaster, but the only way that we know how to behave, and that is available to us is the disastrous behavior of our society. The Dilemma of the Community: We who are alienated from the community cannot find the binding necessity to form a community of our own, yet we cannot live without some community or other. The Dilemma of our Society: If we conformed to the mad society, we became mad, but if we did not conform to the only society there is, we became mad. (Goodman, 1959, p. 407)

In his collaboration with Perls, Goodman was able to formulate his answer as to how to grow up as a healthy human in a culture that inhibits human nature. He dubbed this "the autonomous criterion of value." For Goodman the autonomous criterion of value involved a spontaneous engagement with the most urgent need or impulse that emerges naturally from one's own organismic functioning. The individual must engage this need-impulse in consciousness and express it through behavior following the organizational principle borrowed from Gestalt psychology of figure formation against an unstructured ground. Goodman hoped that by honoring the autonomous criterion of value, the human animal could recover the natural, the spontaneous, the playful, the passionate, the erotic, and the aggressive dimensions in human experiencing. These were Goodman's values, his ideals for health and growth. As can be seen, it was Goodman's interpretation of Perls's insights from Goodman's political standpoint of conservative anarchism that made the fundamental difference in their collaboration.

As Wheeler (1991) observes, the union of Perls and Goodman in *Gestalt Therapy* (1951) resulted in a positive and radical reevaluation of desire, although each of the two collaborators aimed at differing and often opposed ends. The fundamental difference between Perls and Goodman lies in their respective interpretations of "contact" at what they called the "organism-environment boundary" (Perls, Hefferline, & Goodman, 1951). Perls emphasized contact with what is in immediate awareness; this usually revolved around the organism-as-body and sought completion of "incomplete" gestalts of experience. Goodman, on the other hand, was more concerned with how the human organized his or her self around the need-impulse in relation to the immediate environment.

In Perls we see the personal and private; in Goodman, the social and public. In a sense, Perls used Freud and the Gestalt perceptual model to justify his notion of "oral aggression" as an individually oriented metaphor for human psychology and relationships. Goodman, following Aristotle, Buber, and the Tao, viewed human health and growth as occurring in the context of social relations.

Until now, Perls's popularization of Gestalt therapy through his own idiosyncratic practice and teaching has contributed to a historically lopsided application and understanding of the theory and potential of Gestalt therapy. Inversely, if we concentrate more on Goodman's theoretical articulation—a derivation more in line with Kurt Goldstein and Kurt Lewin—we discover that Gestalt therapy dovetails neatly with field theory and is a natural bridge to contemporary constructivist thought. But this line of thought would lead us too far afield from our present focus.

The meeting of Perls and Goodman in the pages of *Gestalt Therapy* produced a remarkable and revolutionary new formulation of psychotherapy. The book gave Perls the opportunity to turn his innovative ideas and techniques into a unified, formal approach to therapy and personal growth. Thus the book lent legitimacy to Perls's vision of psychotherapy and provided the impetus for him to establish his own school of thought. Goodman received the opportunity of framing his social and political views in a psychotherapeutic context. It gave both men the opportunity to formulate a radical critique of Freud and to articulate a viable alternative to psychoanalysis and behaviorism. Goodman was not fated to pursue a career as a psychotherapist. However, he carried the threads of the concerns he outlined in *Gestalt Therapy* throughout his later works, which, in turn, led to his popularity as a social activist. Both men later came to abhor one another personally. There is no doubt, however, that their meeting was a turning point in both of their lives and one of the single most important events in the creation of Gestalt therapy.

NOTE

1. [Editor's note] Ralph Franklin Hefferline was a psychologist engaged in experimental research at Columbia University when he collaborated with Perls and Goodman. Hefferline published a 1950 monograph on the experimental study of avoidance behavior and continued to publish a series of articles using an operant conditioning model to understand avoidance behavior, escape-avoidance conflicts, and the conditioning of a subject without his/her knowledge. The introduction to *Gestalt Therapy* (Perls, Hefferline, & Goodman, 1951, p. vii) first credits Hefferline with establishing the practical applications of the Gestalt model and then recognizes him as a full and equal collaborator. Hefferline published later on communication theory (1955a, 1955b) and continued work in experimental psychology, including collaborative work on the surface electromyogram waveform (1970). Even this later work on biofeedback echoed Gestalt themes. Hefferline conceptualized

biofeedback as a powerful tool, perhaps more powerful than Gestalt awareness exercises, to expand body awareness and self-awareness (Knapp, 1986).

REFERENCES

Bruno, L. J., Davidowitz, J., & Hefferline, R. F. (1970). EMG waveform duration: A validation method for the surface electromyogram. *Behavior Research Methods, Instruments & Computers, 2*(5), 211–219.

Gaines, J. (1979). *Fritz Perls: Here and now.* Millbrae, CA: Celestial Arts.

Goodman, P. (1949). *The break-up of our camp and other stories.* New York: New Directions.

Goodman, P. (1951). *Parents day.* Saugatuck, CT: 5 × 8 Press.

Goodman, P. (1954). *The structure of literature.* Chicago: University of Chicago Press.

Goodman, P. (1959). *The empire city.* Indianapolis: Bobbs-Merrill.

Goodman, P. (1960). *Growing up absurd: Problems of youth in the organized system.* New York: Random House.

Goodman, P. (1966). *Five years: Thoughts during a useless time.* New York: Brussel & Brussel.

Goodman, P. (1972). *Collected poems.* New York: Random House.

Goodman, P. (1991). *Nature heals: The psychological essays of Paul Goodman* (T. Stoehr, Ed.). Highland, NY: Center for Gestalt Advancement. (Original work published 1977)

Hefferline, R. F. (1950). An experimental study of avoidance. *Genetic Psychology Monographs, 42,* 231–234.

Hefferline, R. F. (1955a). Communication theory: I. Integration of arts and science. *Quarterly Journal of Speech, 41,* 223–233.

Hefferline, R. F. (1955b). Communication theory: II. Extension to intra-personal behavior. *Quarterly Journal of Speech, 41,* 363–376.

Henle, M. (1978). Gestalt psychology and Gestalt therapy. *Journal of the History of the Behavioral Sciences, 14*(1), 23–32.

Kaufman, M. T. (1972, August 4). A universal humanist. *New York Times,* p. 34.

Knapp, T. J. (1986). Ralph Franklin Hefferline: The Gestalt therapist among the Skinnerians, or the Skinnerian among the Gestalt therapists. *Journal of the History of the Behavioral Sciences, 22,* 49–60.

Lee, M. A., & Shlain, B. (1985). *Acid dreams: The CIA, LSD, and the sixties rebellion.* New York: Grove Press.

Litt, S. (1978). Fritz Perls and Gestalt therapy. *American Psychologist, 33*(10), 958–959.

McKeon, R. (Ed.). (1941). *The basic works of Aristotle.* New York: Random House.

Perls, F. S. (1969a). *Ego, hunger and aggression.* New York: Vintage. (Original work published 1947)

Perls, F. S. (1969b). *Gestalt therapy verbatim* (J. O. Stevens, Ed.). Moab, Utah: Real People Press.

Perls, F. S. (1992). *In and out the garbage pail.* Highland, NY: Center for Gestalt Advancement. (Original work published 1969)

Perls, F. S., Hefferline, R. F., & Goodman, P. (1951). *Gestalt therapy: Excitement and growth in the human personality.* New York: Julian Press.

Sharaf, M. (1983). *Fury on earth: A biography of Wilhelm Reich.* New York: St. Martin's Press.

Shepard, M. (1975). *Fritz*. New York: E. P. Dutton.

Sherrill, R. E. (1986). Gestalt therapy and Gestalt psychology. *Gestalt Journal*, *9*(2), 53–66.

Smuts, J. C. (1926). *Holism and evolution*. New York: Macmillan.

Stoehr, T. (1994). *Here, now, next: Paul Goodman and the origins of Gestalt therapy*. San Francisco: Jossey-Bass.

Taylor, S. (1990). *Left-wing Nietzscheans: The politics of German expressionism, 1910–1920*. Berlin: Walter de Gruyter.

Wheeler, G. (1991). *Gestalt reconsidered*. New York: Gardner Press.

Widmer, K. (1980). *Paul Goodman*. Boston: Twayne Publishers.

Wysong, J., & Rosenfeld, E. (1982). *An oral history of Gestalt therapy: Interviews with Laura Perls, Isadore From, Erving Polster, Miriam Polster*. Highland, NY: Center for Gestalt Advancement.

26

Laura Perls and Gestalt Therapy: Her Life and Values

ILENE AVA SERLIN AND PAUL SHANE

LAURA PERLS, A NEGLECTED FACTOR IN GESTALT THERAPY

The development of Gestalt therapy has been associated in the popular mind and in cultural myth with the aggressive, dramatic, and unusual personality of the late Frederick "Fritz" Perls. But now that enough time has passed, it is slowly coming to general consciousness within the field of psychotherapy that much of what was considered Gestalt therapy—that is, the "Fritz" style of working with the "empty chair" and the like—is but one particular form and that the other two codevelopers of Gestalt therapy, Laura Perls and Paul Goodman, made equally substantial although far-different contributions to its formulation, application, and dissemination.

The problem, at its simplest, is that Fritz Perls was Gestalt therapy's most successful promoter and proselytizer. In other words, he became more famous than either his wife or Goodman and so made a far larger impact, at least initially. This was primarily because of his wide traveling and public demonstrations—his weekend "circuses," as he called them—as well as through his published works, the audiovisual documentation of his workshops, and the prominent place he held at Esalen Institute during the glory days of the fledgling human-potential movement in the 1960s. In all fairness, Fritz was a brilliant, creative, and intuitive therapist as well as possessing a charismatic, courageous, and powerful personality. Esalen, for a time, became his own "bully pulpit" from which he preached the gospel of Gestalt therapy according to his own particular viewpoint. All of these things naturally made Gestalt therapy and Fritz Perls's way of practicing it syn-

Laura Perls (Photo courtesy of the Gestalt Journal Press).

onymous, but although he often liked to take credit for it, and perhaps this too is understandable because most certainly he was its primary inspiration and source of technical innovation, he did not work alone; there were also Laura Perls and Goodman.

In one respect, Fritz Perls's success in spreading his particular style of Gestalt therapy was based on being at the right place at the right time. The 1960s counter-culture emphasized freedom, liberation, and rebellion—"I do my thing and you do yours"—which dovetailed almost seamlessly with Fritz Perls's "Nietzschean" ideals of radical autonomy and individual growth. Laura Perls and Goodman, on the other hand, were personally and professionally more devoted to connection and community involvement; the ideals of Martin Buber and Lao-tzu, among others, were their respective touchstones.

Goodman, an author of fiction and political criticism in the anarchistic-communitarian vein, had studied Freud and was a devotee of Reichian therapy at the time he met Fritz and Laura Perls in 1949. Fritz Perls solicited Goodman to edit a manuscript for a new book on what he was calling at the time "concentration therapy," and Goodman later went into therapy with Laura Perls. Goodman, as opposed to Perls, is considered the chief theoretician of Gestalt therapy because he penned the second half of its 1951 manifesto, *Gestalt Therapy: Excitement and Growth in the Human Personality.* Goodman later attained fame equal to that of Fritz Perls through his social and political criticisms and became for a short time a spiritual leader for the antiwar, civil rights, and university-reform movements.

It is thus perhaps understandable that more is known about the flamboyant and charismatic Fritz Perls and Goodman, the Aristotelian social critic and Dutch uncle to the student protest movement, than about Laura Perls and her quiet and distinctly feminine contribution to the development of Gestalt therapy as well as her place in the history of humanistic psychology. Even though Laura Perls lived a full life and outlived both her husband and her dear friend, Goodman, by about twenty years, little has been written either by her or about her. Such lack of documentation, research interest, and public acknowledgment is not unusual from a historical point of view, as has been cogently observed by feminist literary critics. This is very sad, considering that Laura Perls's contribution to the development of Gestalt therapy as well as her influence as a teacher and trainer of psycho-therapists for almost forty years ranks her among the vanguard of pioneering female psychologists of the twentieth century along with such lights as Anna Freud, Lou Andreas-Salomé, Karen Horney, Aniela Jaffé, Marie-Louise von Franz, Frieda Fromm-Reichmann, Helene Deutsch, Virginia Satir, and others.

LIFE

In order to make a small effort toward remedying this situation, we devote the rest of our attention to examining the life and contributions of Laura Perls to Gestalt therapy. Given the limitations of available space, we will confine ourselves to focusing on the primary values she espoused as a teacher and a therapist.

Early Years

Lore (later Laura) Posner Perls was born in Pforzheim, Germany, a small town near Frankfurt and the Black Forest, on August 15, 1905. Her family was cultured, upper middle class, and Jewish, although largely assimilated. Her father, Rudolf Posner, earned his living as a jeweler, and Pforzheim was known for its jewelry trade. Hers was a warm, loving, and supportive family; her parents showed a keen interest in their daughter and encouraged her artistic development starting from the age of five, when she was first taught piano by her mother. She studied modern dance from the age of eight on and later eurhythmics and another school of modern dance related to the Eastern-influenced philosophy of Rudolf Steiner (Kudirka, 1992). This later dance experience and training, which included eu-rhythmics as well as the expressionistic dance theories of Rudolf von Laban and Mary Wigman, would play a significant role in her development as a therapist and in the formulation of Gestalt therapy in regards to movement and support functions of the human body (Serlin, 1992a, 1992b).

Laura Perls attended a classical gymnasium, which, at the time, was a very unusual choice for a girl, and she was the only female enrolled in the school. While there, she studied languages and became fluent in Greek, Latin, and French. She was particularly drawn to literature—she studied classical and mod-ern literature as well as German literature from the Middle Ages to the twentieth century—and began writing poetry and fiction, a practice she continued throughout her life. Upon graduation, she pressed on to the University of Frankfurt, which was, as she described it, one of the most avant-garde universities in Germany at the time and possibly in all of Europe (Kudirka, 1992). It was her intention to study law, and even though there were few women in the legal profession at that time, she felt drawn to it out of a growing social and political consciousness; she envisioned herself working with juveniles in the German court system (Humphrey, 1986).

But this was not to be, for, as she told the story, she was drawn into psychological studies after attending classes taught by Adhemar Gelb and being impressed by his literate and engaging style of lecturing. She was later to be even further influenced by Kurt Goldstein and Max Wertheimer (L. Perls, 1992). It was during a seminar conducted by Goldstein and Gelb in 1926 that she met Fritz Perls, a young medical student and World War I veteran who was deeply interested in theater and psychoanalysis (Gaines, 1979). Fritz Perls, who was older than she and a free, bohemian spirit, claimed that it was Laura who pursued him into marriage (F. Perls, 1992). But regardless of who pursued whom, Lore Posner married Fritz Perls in 1930 and several years later had their first child, Renate.

Even though at the time of their meeting Fritz Perls was for a brief time an assistant at Kurt Goldstein's neurological clinic for brain-damaged veterans, it was Laura Perls who several historians maintain was more deeply versed in Gestalt psychology. Besides being a student of Gelb, Goldstein, and Wertheimer, she explored the visual perception of color contrasts in her dissertation (Posner, 1932). While there has been much argument among historians of psychology about whether or not there is a valid connection between Gestalt psychology and Gestalt therapy, there can be no doubt that Laura was the living bridge between the two. Before formally studying psychoanalysis, Laura Perls already had firsthand experience as an analysand with an Adlerian psychoanalyst when she was sixteen (Humphrey, 1986). As she noted, she was a Gestalt psychologist first and came later to Freudian psychoanalysis, as opposed to Fritz Perls, who was trained in psychoanalysis first and only had a superficial brush with Gestalt theory (Wysong & Rosenfeld, 1982). While at the university, she studied psychoanalysis under Clara Happel, Otto Fenichel, and Karl Landauer. (Landauer was associated with Sandor Ferenczi and George Groddek and was later killed in a Nazi concentration camp.)

Intellectual Influences

Besides receiving a classical education as well as graduate study in clinical and Gestalt psychology, Laura Perls was deeply influenced by the existential and phenomenological philosophers. Much of Gestalt therapy as well as her own personal approach to psychotherapy reflects these intellectual sources. She reported that while in graduate school, she studied the works of Søren Kierkegaard, Edmund Husserl, Martin Heidegger, and Max Scheler and was a student of both Martin

Buber and Paul Tillich for a two-year period. While space does not permit a more detailed review of which ideas of these philosophers helped form the intellectual ground of Gestalt therapy, we do draw attention to the fact that Laura Perls attributed the formation of her style of psychotherapy to the personal and intellectual influences of Buber and Tillich (Kudirka, 1992). The importance of these two particular influences cannot be overstated, as she noted that

> Tillich and Buber were much more than what one usually thinks of as theologians. They were really psychologists. . . . They were interested in people, they were not talking about subjects. Listening to Buber and Tillich, you felt they were talking directly to you and not just about some *thing*. The kind of contact they made was essential in their theories. (L. Perls, 1992, pp. 21–22; emphasis in original)

Buber is noted for his idea of the transformative dialogue between the "I and thou"; Tillich, an existential Protestant theologian, later emigrated to the United States and inspired the existential approach of Rollo May (May, 1983). There is some question as to the depth of the relationship between Laura and Tillich, as Tillich is alleged to have told one interviewer that he did not formally meet Laura until sometime in the early 1960s at a cocktail party hosted by Paul Goodman (Wysong, 1996). But regardless, it will be seen later that the concept and value of human contact was central to Laura Perls's approach to Gestalt therapy.

Middle Years

As pointed out by Humphrey (1986), by the time she met Fritz Perls and began practicing psychoanalysis, Laura Perls had already been trained as a concert pianist, had a gymnasium education in languages and literature equivalent to that of an American undergraduate degree with dual majors, and had attended law school; she completed her training analysis and received her doctorate in 1932. It was during this year that she and Fritz Perls emigrated from Germany to Holland; being politically sensitive and somewhat active in leftist politics, they shrewdly assessed that the German political situation, although not desperate at that moment, was becoming increasingly worse. While living in abject poverty as refugees in Holland, they were approached by Ernest Jones, an American psychoanalyst and Freud's biographer, to establish a psychoanalytic institute in South Africa. They accepted and for the next fourteen years lived in relatively idyllic security and comfort in that country. They had a second child, Steven, and it was during this South African period that they both began slowly drifting away from orthodox Freudianism (L. Perls, 1992; Wysong & Rosenfeld, 1982).

That drift began with Laura Perls's experience and observations of nursing and weaning her children. She set these observations down into a series of informal notes and, naturally, discussed her experiences with her husband; they both began to become increasingly interested in the oral stage of development and the oral "instinct," as they termed it. These notes were later reworked by Fritz Perls into a lecture, "The Oral Resistances," that he gave at the 1936 International Psychoanalytic Conference at Marienbad. The presentation was a failure because it was too radical a departure from the Freudian dogma that all resistances are anal in origin (F. Perls, 1992). Disappointed and resentful but not discouraged, Fritz Perls returned to South Africa and began expanding the lecture into what would become the chapter on "Mental Metabolism" in his book *Ego, Hunger, and Aggression* (1969). Although she never received credit for it, Laura Perls claimed that she was instrumental in the development of this first book because she ghost-wrote two of its chapters, "The Dummy Complex" and "The Meaning of Insomnia" (L. Perls, 1992). The book itself, overall, was stylistically disjointed and theoretically weak, although it was filled with many keen therapeutic insights and observations (Wheeler, 1991). Twenty years later Perls would downplay its value by saying that the only reason he wrote it was to teach himself how to type (F. Perls, 1992).

Having spent fourteen years in South Africa, Laura Perls and her family were forced once again to emigrate for political reasons; the South African government was becoming more conservative, and apartheid, which was already in the culture, was becoming more rigidly legalized. This caused profound fears on their part of a swing toward fascism, and so they moved, thanks to sponsorship from Laura's brother and Karen Horney, to New York City in 1946–1947 (Wysong & Rosenfeld, 1982). It took less than six months for both Fritz and Laura Perls to establish full-time practices. As Fritz had been working on a manuscript for a new book and needed an editor to help carry it to completion, he sought out Paul Goodman because of his political writings about Wilhelm Reich (Stoehr, 1994). Within a year Goodman left Reichian analysis and became a trainee under Laura Perls.

From Lore Perls he had other kinds of things to learn, more in the realm of give-and-take. For the most part it was not ideas or intellectual gossip that passed between them, however much Lore knew about Gestalt psychology or Frankfurt existentialism or the first generation of Freudians. Rather Goodman came as a patient, ready to confide in her, and hoping for some relief from his sense of failure as a man and an artist. (Stoehr, 1994, p. 53)

With the publication of the 1951 treatise, *Gestalt Therapy*, Fritz and Laura Perls established a training institute in New York City, although he was soon to abandon it as well as his family for his life of wanderlust, as he could not abide the competition or criticism he experienced in both institutions (Gaines, 1979; F. Perls, 1992; Stoehr, 1994; Wysong & Rosenfeld, 1982). It remained up to Laura Perls and a core group of peers and students to support and maintain the New York institute, a task to which she devoted herself for the next forty years.

Professional Values

As space does not permit a full exposition of Laura Perls's influence on the development of Gestalt therapy, we will confine ourselves to discussing the key values underlying her work: contact and boundary, support, and style.

Value: Contact and boundary.

Following Latner (1992), contact can be defined as the awareness of difference organized in a figure-to-ground relationship at the boundary between the person and his or her environment. In the first formulation of Gestalt therapy, this contact boundary was envisioned as being almost like a physical organ in a metaphorical and functional sense representing conscious awareness (Perls, Hefferline, & Goodman, 1951). To Laura Perls's mind, contact and the boundary where it occurs were more a psychological and existential phenomenon than its original formulation as a biological metaphor:

Contact is made in any actual present situation, the only moment in which experience and change are possible. . . . It is the acknowledgment of, and the coping with, the *other*. The boundary where I and the other meet is the locus of the ego functions of identification and alienation, the sphere of excitation, interest and curiosity, or fear and hostility. (L. Perls, 1992, p. 131; emphasis in original)

Contact is the touchstone for therapeutic approach and strategy in Gestalt therapy its phenomenological form and experiential quality. As opposed to Fritz Perls, who concentrated mainly on the awareness of a person's contact with the primary object of experience—the primary Gestalt—Laura Perls also emphasized the quality of the client's contact with herself in the therapy situation. Laura Perls was much more apt to engage in looking at the relationship she and her client shared in the moment and used this as an important focus for interpersonal growth. Fritz Perls was more inclined to meet resistance with aggression or rejection (Gaines, 1979), whereas Laura Perls was more concerned with what she called the "psychology of give and take" (L. Perls, 1992); the difference in their personal styles doubtless reflects the respective influences of Nietzsche and Buber, but this is more speculation than verifiable assertion.

Value: Support.

Contact, as she so often pointed out in her teaching and therapy work, was made possible only through adequate *support*. That is, contact is a function of the amount of necessary and sufficient resources, internal and external, that can be mustered to enable the person to undertake the activity.

Support is everything that facilitates the ongoing assimilation and integration of experience for a person, a relationship or a society; primary physiology, upright posture and coordination, sensitivity and mobility, language, habits and customs, social manners and relationships, everything else that we have acquired and learned during our lifetime; in short, everything that we usually take for granted and rely on, even and particularly our hangups and resistances—the fixed ideas, ideals and behavior patterns which have become our second nature precisely because they were supportive at the time of their formation. (L. Perls, 1992, pp. 132–133; emphasis in original)

Support enables the person to contact what is and to realize the personal meaning and significance of the experience, the "aha!" of personal insight.

Contact is possible only to the extent that *support for* it is available. Support is the total background against which the present experience stands out (exists) and forms a meaningful Gestalt. For this is what meaning is: the relation of a figure to its ground. (L. Perls, 1992, p. 132; emphases in original)

Value: Style.

The ideas of contacting what is in immediate awareness supported by one's own resources or those of the environment, encountering the *other* and forming a relationship, and deriving personal meaning and insights from the experience of that relationship are, in their final analysis, derived from existential philosophy and aesthetic thinking. Laura Perls herself pointed out that "the basic concepts of Gestalt therapy are philosophical and aesthetic rather than technical" (L. Perls, 1992, p. 149). Her view derived not only from her own artistic background and philosophical study, but from her collaboration with Fritz Perls and Paul Goodman, both philosophically oriented artists.

People who got interested in psychology at one time were all, in a way, artists. There were not such great differences. They were artists. . . . At that time, psychology, and particularly psychotherapy, became an art and not really a science in spite of all the attempts to make it a science. The people who did it well, they were really artists. (Kudirka, 1992, p. 88)

From this view, we can see more clearly the background from which she often asserted that the practice of psychotherapy possesses an artistic component and can be considered an aesthetic, interpersonal event (Kudirka, 1992; Zinker, 1978, 1994). To Laura Perls, the difference between a good psychotherapist and a great one was not in technical skill, but in artistic sensitivity, in what Zinker (1994) calls the "good form" of the therapist-client encounter. Consequently, Laura Perls often talked more about "style" rather than "technique."

I think that's a great mistake [therapy as a technical skill]. In Gestalt Therapy, I think any technique is applicable that is existential and experiential. We are not involved in just one technique. I would rather talk about style than techniques. Every therapist develops his own style, as an integrated way of expressing and communicating. You use technically what you have available in yourself, through your own experience. (Kudirka, 1992, p. 89)

Final Years

Laura Perls had been in residence at the same address in New York City and teaching at the New York City Gestalt Institute since 1957. By 1981, with the onset of age and increasingly poor health, her daughter, Renate, became her primary caretaker. In May 1990, with her physical health steadily deteriorating, she undertook one final trip to her birthplace in the village of Pforzheim in Germany. Even though she had been forced to flee her homeland nearly sixty years before, Pforzheim always held a special place in her heart, and she often returned there throughout her life to visit childhood friends. It was in Pforzheim that Laura Perls died in July 1990. She went to her death as she had lived her life, honestly, unsentimentally, existentially. Her body lies buried along with those of her family in a little cemetery in Pforzheim, a particularly peaceful spot that she had loved since her childhood. It was there that she wanted to be placed between the grave of her father, Rudolf Posner, and that of Fritz Perls, reunited and resting at last with the two most important men of her life.

LAURA PERLS AND GESTALT THERAPY IN CONTEMPORARY PERSPECTIVE

Laura Perls lived a full life yet wrote very little, and so little has been written about her. Feminist critics have noted that there has long been a dearth of biographical material about women figures in history, and these same critics pose the question as to why women writers write less than men or, more pointedly, do not think that their own lives are apparently considered valuable enough in comparison to document. Female authors, for the most part, with the notable exception of Simone de Beauvoir, have tended to write novels rather than biography or autobiography. Heilbrun (1988) notes that women's lives were rarely considered interesting enough to deserve biographical analysis. The appearance of *Zelda* (Milford, 1970) marked a turning point in the rise of the female perspective, although Zelda Fitzgerald's voice was ultimately destroyed by her husband, F. Scott Fitzgerald, as "he had usurped her narrative" (Heilbrun, 1988, p. 12). In a similar vein, Spacks (1976) notes that feminine autobiography is typically marked by "woman's attitudes" as confessions of inadequacy. Spacks (1980, pp. 113–114) expands on this and other observations by analyzing the biographies of Dorothy Day, Eleanor Roosevelt, and Golda Meir and discovers a "rhetoric of *uncertainty*" as well as the tendency to attribute the woman's success to sources other than her own personal will, ambition, or talents; a calling, a higher power, or a significant male are named as typical explanations (Serlin, 1992b).

We see this apparently unconscious prejudice against women in the history of Gestalt therapy, as the latter has been inordinately skewed to the life and work of Fritz Perls. The past historical renderings of Gestalt therapy are, in our opinions, a bit imbalanced because they have not done justice to the influences of Laura Perls and Paul Goodman. Nor, in equal importance, do they do justice to the richness and complexity of what Gestalt therapy can and should be as practiced from a sense of appreciation for its aesthetic and philosophical subtleties, subtleties that come almost solely from the mind and heart of Laura Perls. We have sought to highlight the importance of her development, thought, style, and values; her intellect, teaching, and commitment are fundamental to the theory and practice of Gestalt therapy.

Contemporary feminist theory has sought to deconstruct the male discourse that tends to disempower women and their narratives. This means confronting one's anxiety in living without models or known narratives; it means standing alone and inventing oneself; it means having the courage to speak openly about anger and power. Finally, it means not only reading stories about women, but also writing about female impulses to knowledge and power, writing the narratives that women actually live (Serlin, 1992b). One of the authors (Serlin) began studying with Laura Perls in 1973 and has long been struck by the radical difference between her style of Gestalt therapy and that of Fritz Perls. Laura Perls was a dancer, a concert pianist, and a student of both Buber and Tillich; although she was a remarkable therapist and teacher, she was exceptionally modest about her talents and accomplishments and consequently wrote very little.

The present chapter can be seen as a small contribution toward correcting this historical and intellectual neglect of Laura Perls's role in the history of Gestalt therapy and in contemporary psychotherapy. Contact, support, stability, commitment, and rootedness were key words in the vocabulary of Laura Perls, and these principles are evident throughout her life, work, and death. Throughout her life she always valued friendship, established networks, and engaged in community involvement. While her husband, Fritz, traveled the world to popularize Gestalt therapy, Laura tended to focus on connection, cooperation, caring, and relationship. She gave Gestalt therapy a distinct and much-needed feminine voice, a contrapuntal voice to that of Fritz Perls, who spoke more of the joy of aggression and confrontation. Given his courageous personality, no-nonsense attitude toward life and growth, and tragic personal history, this is all quite understandable. In contrast, Laura practiced a slow, patient, and subtle way of following a client's intrapsychic and interpersonal process. Her work resulted in her giving spiritual birth to many generations of Gestalt therapists. Her creative involvement with her clients and students spanned continents and oceans. All of these activities form the essence of her feminine influence on Gestalt therapy. Laura Perls was not one who ever advised "letting go" of memories but strived to support their integration into the present, and so, for us and many others in the humanistic tradition, she will, despite death, "always be there," present, encouraging, and available in our hearts as the archetypal Old Wise Woman that she was in life.

REFERENCES

Gaines, J. (1979). *Fritz Perls: Here and now*. Millbrae, CA: Celestial Arts.

Heilbrun, C. (1988). *Writing a woman's life*. New York: Ballantine.

Humphrey, K. (1986). Laura Perls: A biographical sketch. *Gestalt Journal, 9*(1), 5–11.

Kudirka, N. (1992). A talk with Laura Perls about the therapist and the artist. In E.W.L. Smith (Ed.), *Gestalt voices* (pp. 85–92). Norwood, NJ: Ablex.

Latner, J. (1992). The theory of Gestalt therapy. In E. C. Nevis (Ed.), *Gestalt therapy: Perspectives and applications* (pp. 13–56). New York: Gardner Press.

May, R. (1983). *The discovery of being: Writings in existential psychology*. New York: W. W. Norton.

Milford, N. (1970). *Zelda*. New York: Harper & Row.

Perls, F. (1969). *Ego, hunger, and aggression: The beginning of Gestalt therapy*. New York: Vintage Books. (Original work published 1947)

Perls, F. (1992). *In and out the garbage pail*. Highland, NY: Center for Gestalt Advancement. (Original work published 1969)

Perls, F., Hefferline, R., & Goodman, P. (1951). *Gestalt therapy: Excitement and growth in the human personality*. New York: Julian Press.

Perls, L. (1992). *Living at the boundary* (J. Wysong, Ed.). Highland, NY: Center for Gestalt Advancement.

Posner, L. (1932). *Die Erscheinungen des simultanen Kontrastes und der Eindruck der Feld-beleuchtung*. Unpublished doctoral dissertation, University of Frankfurt am Main.

Serlin, I. (1977). Portrait of Karen: A Gestalt-phenomenological approach to movement therapy. *Journal of Contemporary Psychotherapy, 8*(2), 145–153.

Serlin, I. (1992a). In memoriam of Laura Perls. *Humanistic Psychologist, 19*(1), 105–113.

Serlin, I. (1992b). Tribute to Laura Perls. *Journal of Humanistic Psychology, 32*(3), 57–66.

Spacks, P. (1976). *Imagining a self*. Cambridge, MA: Harvard University Press.

Spacks, P. (1980). Selves in hiding. In E. C. Jelinek (Ed.), *Women's autobiography* (pp. 112–132). Bloomington,: Indiana University Press.

Stern, E. M. (1992). A trialogue between Laura Perls, Richard Kitzler, and E. Mark Stern. In E.W.L. Smith (Ed.), *Gestalt voices* (pp. 18–32). Norwood, NJ: Ablex.

Stoehr, T. (1994). *Here, now, next: Paul Goodman and the origins of Gestalt therapy*. San Francisco: Jossey-Bass.

Wheeler, G. (1991). *Gestalt reconsidered: A new approach to contact and resistance*. New York: Gardner Press.

Wysong, J. C. (1996, October 5). Personal communication to Paul Shane.

Wysong, J., & Rosenfeld, E. (1982). *An oral history of Gestalt therapy: Interviews with Laura Perls, Isadore From, Erving Polster, Miriam Polster*. Highland, NY: Center for Gestalt Advancement.

Zinker, J. C. (1978). *Creative process in Gestalt therapy*. New York: Random House.

Zinker, J. C. (1994). *In search of good form: Gestalt therapy with couples and families*. San Francisco: Jossey-Bass.

27

Carl Rogers: Client, Heal Thyself

DON RICE

> The best vantage point for understanding behavior is from the internal frame
> of reference of the individual himself.
>
> —Rogers, 1951, p. 483

Carl Rogers's client-centered approach probably has had more extensive impact
on the practice of counseling and psychotherapy than any other therapeutic approach. Moreover, this approach has influenced such diverse fields as education,
business, social work, and pastoral counseling (Rogers, 1970). One only has to
examine professional counseling/psychotherapy journals and textbooks to fully
appreciate the breadth of Rogers's influence. Many therapists and counselors of
various persuasions have either adopted the client-centered approach or modified
their methods to incorporate features of it that appeal to them. One reason for
the attraction to client-centered therapy among psychotherapists is its historical
ties to psychology rather than to medicine. While I cannot cover the magnitude
of Rogers's contributions in this brief chapter, I do wish to focus on a theme
present throughout his writings: the ability of the client to heal himself or herself.
For Rogers, a central hypothesis is that people have within themselves enormous
resources for constructive change when encouraged by a nonjudgmental, empathic
therapist (Rogers, 1951).

Carl Rogers (Photo courtesy of Barbara Temaner
Brodley with acknowledgment to Natalie Rogers).

BRIEF BIOGRAPHY

Early Years

Carl Rogers was born on January 8, 1902, in Oak Park, Illinois. He was the
fourth of six children reared in a close-knit family with strict and uncompromising
religious views. When Rogers was twelve, his father, a successful businessman,
moved the family to a farm he had purchased. It was this experience of growing
up on the farm that kindled within Rogers an interest in the biological and physical sciences. Rogers's interest in science was sustained through his graduation
from the University of Wisconsin in 1924, whereupon he entered Union Theological Seminary in New York to prepare for religious work. In one of his major
publications, *On Becoming a Person* (1961), Rogers discussed how his professional
thinking and personal philosophy were influenced by the liberal, philosophical
views offered at Union Theological Seminary. Later, he transferred to Teachers
College of Columbia University, where he took courses in the philosophy of

education under William Kilpatrick and was introduced to clinical psychology by Leta Hollingworth.

Studies in Psychology

Rogers earned his master's degree in 1928 and his doctorate in 1931 from Columbia. He served his internship at the Institute for Child Guidance, where he was exposed to the prevailing Freudian views. It was during this period that he became aware of the incompatibility between the scientific, statistical approaches to clinical psychology emphasized at Columbia and the speculative psychoanalytic approach practiced at the Institute for Child Guidance. After completing his internship, Rogers found employment as a psychologist at the Rochester Guidance Center, which was a division of the Society for the Prevention of Cruelty to Children in Rochester, New York.

Client-Centered Therapy: Rogers's Unique Approach

Rogers stayed in Rochester until 1940, when he accepted a full professorship in clinical psychology at Ohio State University. Disillusioned with the authoritarian nature of clinical work and with himself, he found renewed interest through his exposure to intellectually challenging graduate students. Rogers realized at this point that he had developed a distinctive position on counseling and psychotherapy, and he was compelled to make his views explicit in a book entitled *Counseling and Psychotherapy* (1942). After five years at Ohio State, Rogers moved to the University of Chicago as professor of psychology and executive secretary of the Counseling Center. He spent twelve productive years there further developing his client-centered method, cultivating a theory of personality, and conducting research in counseling and psychotherapy. Incidentally, Rogers felt that the distinction between counseling and psychotherapy was artificial (Rogers, 1961).

In 1957 Rogers accepted an appointment at the University of Wisconsin as professor of psychology and psychiatry. While there, he was involved in research on psychotherapy with schizophrenics. After five years at Wisconsin, he became a fellow at the Center for Advanced Study in the Behavioral Sciences at Stanford between 1962 and 1963. In 1964 he joined the staff of the Western Behavioral Sciences Institute as a resident fellow at La Jolla, California. In 1968 Rogers and a group of researchers working with him on a project for self-directed change in educational systems formed the Center for Studies of the Person in La Jolla (Rogers, 1969). Here Rogers and his associates held intensive group workshops for professional workers, business executives, educators, and persons who simply wanted to enhance their personal growth (Rogers, 1983). Rogers remained a resident fellow at the Center for Studies of the Person until his death in 1987.

Contributions to the Profession

Rogers was the president of the American Psychological Association (1946–1947) and a diplomate in clinical psychology of the American Board of Examiners in Professional Psychology. He authored more than one hundred journal articles and book chapters. Four of his books, *Counseling and Psychotherapy, Client-centered Therapy, Psychotherapy and Personality Change*, and *On Becoming a Person*, are significant in that they capture the essence of Rogers's attitude and approach to understanding the person as well as his suggestions for change.

ORIENTATION TO PSYCHOLOGY

Influences on Rogers's Approach

We can trace Rogers's initial orientation to psychology to his experiences at Teachers College, Columbia University, where he was influenced by the philosophy of John Dewey through the work of William H. Kilpatrick (Rogers, 1961). Dewey's influence on Rogers's thinking is clearly evident in his publication *Freedom to Learn* (Rogers, 1969). His earlier clinical training at Teachers College emphasized a rigorous scientific method with its requisite statistical proofs, underscored by the views of Edward Thorndike, which were prevalent at the time at Teachers College (Rogers, 1959). During this same period Rogers was exposed to Freudian psychoanalysis while doing an internship at the Institute for Child Guidance. Hence the basis for Rogers's orientation to psychology includes a mixture of Freudian psychoanalysis, scientific methodology, progressive educational thinking, and test and measurement approaches to clinical psychology.

Probably one of the most significant influences on Rogers's thinking was the work of Otto Rank. Although originally a disciple of Freud, Rank deviated from the orthodoxy of psychoanalysis, which he perceived as imposing its theoretical constructs on the client. Instead, he asserted that therapy is for the client, not the theory (Rank, 1936). Rank's position, which stresses the importance of clients expressing their personal will and taking charge of their lives, made an indelible impression on Rogers that provided the foundation for his client-centered therapy. According to Rogers (1959), Rank's thinking helped him formulate some of the therapeutic methods he was groping toward.

The fact that Rogers was influenced by widely differing views is vital to understanding the development of the client-centered approach to therapy. For instance, while at the University of Chicago, he was introduced to the philosophy of existentialism through his contacts with theological students. He found the writings of Martin Buber and Søren Kierkegaard to be particularly compatible with his client-centered perspective (Rogers, 1961). Elements of phenomenological thinking and Gestalt psychology as expressed by Kurt Lewin are evident in Rogers's approach. In his later years Rogers reported how he found certain Asian philosophies such as Zen and Taoism to be pertinent to the development of client-centered therapy (Rogers, 1980, 1983).

Thus Rogers's orientation to psychology does not follow any particular philosophy or previously held theory. As shown earlier, he did not have just one mentor. Instead, Rogers's thinking developed out of a continuing examination and re-examination of changing and broadening experiences with his clients. A meaningful experience for Rogers was "learning to live in an increasingly deep therapeutic relationship with an ever widening range of clients" (Rogers, 1961, p. 14). It was the client in process who constituted the basic data of learning for the development of client-centered thought.

Rogers's Personality Theory

From these experiences with his clients, Rogers developed a theory of personality (Rogers, 1951, 1959, 1961). Drawing from such personality theorists as Snygg and Combs (1949), Angyal (1948), Sullivan (1953), Maslow (1954), Standal (1954), and Gendlin (1962), Rogers suggested that what are fundamental to understanding both client-centered therapy and the personality are the concept of self and the concept of becoming or self-actualizing growth (Rogers, 1961). As Rogers (1961, p. 532) stated, his theory of self "is basically phenomenological in character and relies heavily upon the concept of self as an explanatory concept."

Fadiman and Frager (1976) point out that while a number of textbooks generally consider Rogers to be a "self" theorist, it is only that the self is crucial to Rogers's thinking. In other words, for Rogers, the self is the "I" or "me" that stands for awareness of one's being or functioning. It is a learned attribute constituting the individual's picture of herself or himself. In this perspective, the self is seen by Rogers as flexible and capable of growth and change. By viewing the self as having the capacity for growth and change, Rogers provides a symbiotic relationship between his theory of personality and the practice of client-centered therapy.

Rogers (1959, p. 194) has defined self-actualization as the "inherent tendency of the organism to develop all its capacities in ways which serve to maintain or enhance the organism." Like Maslow (1954), Rogers saw psychological growth of the person as essential to psychological health. Rogers (1962) characterized the self-actualizing person in the following manner:

I find such a person to be a human being in flow, in process, rather than having achieved some state. Fluid change is central in the picture. I find such a person to be open to all of his experience, sensitive to what is going on in his environment, sensitive perhaps most of all to the feelings, reactions, and emergent meanings which he discovers in himself. The fear of some aspects of his own experience continues to diminish, so that more and more of his life is available to him. . . . This process of healthy living is not, I am convinced, a life for the fainthearted. It involves the stretching and growing of becoming more and more of one's potentialities. . . . Yet the deeply exciting thing about human beings is that when the individual is inwardly free, he chooses this process of becoming. (pp. 31–32)

Thus, like his concept of the self, his emphasis on the tendency of the person to move toward self-actualization is congruent with the practice of client-centered therapy, which serves to facilitate the growth process.

Carl Rogers and Humanistic Psychology

Rogers's interest in the psychological growth of the individual identifies him with what has come to be known as humanistic or "Third Force" psychology (Severin, 1965). The other two major theoretical positions are psychoanalysis and behaviorism. However, unlike the latter two, humanistic psychology offers an optimistic view of the person. As Harper (1959) suggests, Rogers's perspective appropriated the American democratic tradition of equality between client and therapist. Its optimistic philosophy, which places emphasis on change and growth, is consistent with the tendency toward optimism in American culture.

KEY ISSUES

To reiterate a point made earlier, client-centered therapy places the responsibility of change not on the therapist, but on the client. However, the therapist must hold certain attitudes that facilitate change. According to Rogers (1951, p. 19), the effective counselor is one "who holds a coherent and developing set of attitudes deeply embedded in his personal organization, a system of attitudes which is implemented by techniques and methods consistent with it." Rogers found that the three attitudes or conditions that seem to be the most appropriate for successful therapy are the therapist's genuineness or congruence, the therapist's complete acceptance or unconditional positive regard for the client, and the therapist's accurate empathic understanding of the client's feelings and personal meanings (Rogers, 1951).

It is worth noting here that Rogers placed significance on attitudes and not techniques. In other words, it is the presence of these attitudes in the therapist more than the skill or technique that serves as the catalyst for change in the client. Taking these attitudes separately, genuineness or congruence refers to the attitude of openness on the part of the therapist. The therapist in the therapeutic relationship is transparent to the client. Hence the client is exposed to the "real" feelings of the therapist. Sometimes this can mean that the therapist may have to express negative feelings toward the client. For example, if the therapist is bored, she or he might voice this feeling to the client. However, the therapist conveys the message that this is not a judgment about the client but rather an honest statement about what the therapist is feeling at the time.

Unconditional positive regard is the ability of the therapist to communicate to her or his clients a sense of deep and genuine caring for them as persons (Rogers,

1959). It implies that the therapist will scrupulously avoid any behavior that is judgmental. When a therapist presents himself or herself as one who is uncontaminated with judgments or evaluations of thoughts, feelings, or behavior, it communicates to the client a feeling of empowerment for change and self-growth. The client is able to allow certain forbidden or unrecognized feelings to come into awareness because she knows that she is accepted for who she is. Moreover, the therapist grows in the process because he or she is able to see and accept his or her limitations as a consequence of the therapeutic interaction.

The quotation at the beginning of this chapter probably epitomizes the meaning of empathy. The ability of the therapist to accurately and sensitively understand the experience of the client from the point of view of the client might be the most demanding part of therapy (Rogers, 1959). To accomplish this kind of understanding of the client's experience, it is important for the therapist to go beyond the mere listening to the client's words and immerse herself or himself in the client's world. By keeping alert to nuances of feeling and making sure that she or he understands what the client is saying and feeling, even by interrupting if necessary, the therapist becomes an active participant in the therapeutic process. Likewise, the client experiences a profound sense of being understood that facilitates change and growth.

APPRAISAL

The contributions of Rogers are immense, to say the least. He once commented that he did not have a prominent place in psychology itself and could not care less. "But in education, and industry, and group dynamics and social work and the philosophy of science and pastoral psychology and theology and other fields my ideas have penetrated and influenced in ways I never would have dreamt" (Rogers, 1970, p. 507).

Indeed, Rogers was coy in his evaluation of his status within psychology. He is clearly recognized as one of the major founders of humanistic or Third Force psychology (Severin, 1965; Sutich & Vich, 1969).

Probably one of the more salient features of Rogers's work was his consideration for the importance of research. Unlike therapists before him, Rogers brought therapy out of the sanctity of the therapist's office and subjected it to the scrutiny of everyday experience. He and his colleagues were the first to record and transcribe client interviews in order to evaluate the outcomes of therapy. The most adequate studies have involved measuring the therapeutic relationships and its correlates, creating and using measures of the therapeutic process, measuring a variety of outcomes in clients as compared with matched control groups, and the investigation of personality predictions based on client-centered therapy (Rogers, Gendlin, Kiesler, & Truax, 1967).

A major criticism of client-centered therapy is that it places too much emphasis on the affective, emotional, feeling determinants of behavior while ignoring cognitive and rational factors. The subjective reports given by clients of their internal experiences may contain distortions and incomplete information. Another criticism addresses the issue of what is expected of the client. The client is expected to know what is best for himself or herself and to experience change within the "self," often described in loosely defined terms such as "actualizing," "becoming," "congruency," and "being."

While there is evidence indicating that client-centered therapy is effective with a wide range of individuals and problems (e.g., Rogers, Gendlin, Kiesler, & Truax, 1967), the evidence is not complete enough, particularly with respect to clients who assume little or no responsibility for their behavior. Finally, because client-centered therapy originated on college campuses, a disproportionately large number of clients were students. One could raise the question whether this group is representative of the general population. Since college students are typically bright and articulate and experience fewer severe emotional upsets, these factors could make them more amenable to the client-centered approach.

Despite these criticisms, Rogers's client-centered therapy continues to be a major force in the field of psychotherapy. It has given us a wealth of research findings that have enhanced our understanding of the person and the therapeutic process. As Rogers (1974, p. 116) stated:

It was the gradually formed and tested hypothesis that the individual has within himself vast resources for self-understanding, for altering his self-concept, his attitudes, and his self-directed behavior, and that these resources can be tapped if only a definable climate of facilitative psychological attitudes can be provided.

REFERENCES

Angyal, A. (1948). The holistic approach in psychiatry. *American Journal of Psychiatry, 105*, 178–182.

Fadiman, J., & Frager, R. (1976). *Personality and personal growth*. New York: Harper & Row.

Gendlin, E. T. (1962). *Experiencing and the creation of meaning*. New York: Free Press of Glencoe.

Harper, R. (1959). *Psychoanalysis and psychotherapy*. Englewood Cliffs, NJ: Prentice-Hall.

Maslow, A. (1954). *Motivation and personality*. New York: Harper.

Rank, O. (1936). *Will therapy*. New York: Alfred A. Knopf.

Rogers, C. R. (1942). *Counseling and psychotherapy: Newer concepts in practice*. Boston: Houghton Mifflin.

Rogers, C. R. (1951). *Client-centered therapy: Its current practice, implications, and theory*. Boston: Houghton Mifflin.

Rogers, C. R. (1959). A theory of therapy, personality, and interpersonal relationships, as developed in the client-centered framework. In S. Koch (Ed.), *Psychology: A study of a science*, vol. 3 (pp. 184–256). New York: McGraw-Hill.

Rogers, C. R. (1961). *On becoming a person*. Boston: Houghton Mifflin.

Rogers, C. R. (1962). Toward becoming a fully-functioning person. In J. Couch (Ed.), *Readings in human adjustment* (pp. 1–13). New York: Selective Academic Readings Press.

Rogers, C. R. (1969). *Freedom to learn.* Columbus, Ohio: C. E. Merrill Pub. Co.

Rogers, C. R. (1970). *Carl Rogers on encounter groups.* New York: Harper & Row.

Rogers, C. R. (1974). In retrospect: Forty-six years. *American Psychologist, 29,* 115–123.

Rogers, C. R. (1980). *A way of being.* Boston: Houghton Mifflin.

Rogers, C. R. (1983). *Freedom to learn for the 80's.* Columbus, OH: Charles E. Merrill.

Rogers, C. R., & Dymond, R. F. (Eds.). (1954). *Psychotherapy and personality change: Coordinated research studies in the client-centered approach.* Chicago: University of Chicago Press.

Rogers, C. R., Gendlin, E. T., Kiesler, D. J., & Truax, C. B. (1967). *The therapeutic relationship and its impact.* Madison: University of Wisconsin Press.

Severin, F. T. (1965). *Humanistic viewpoints in psychology.* New York: McGraw-Hill.

Snygg, D., & Combs, A. W. (1949). *Individual behavior: A new frame of reference for psychology.* New York: Harper.

Standal, S. (1954). *The need for positive regard: A contribution to client-centered therapy.* Unpublished doctoral dissertation, University of Chicago.

Sullivan, H. S. (1953). *The interpersonal theory of psychiatry.* New York: W. W. Norton.

Sutich, A., & Vich, M. (1969). *Readings in humanistic psychology.* New York: Free Press.

28

Ida P. Rolf and Structural Integration (Rolfing)

PAUL SHANE

LIFE AND THE DEVELOPMENT OF STRUCTURAL INTEGRATION

Ida Rolf (1896–1979) was born in 1896 in the Bronx Borough of New York City, New York. Her father was an electrical engineer, and while little is publicly known about her early years, it is known that she was educated at Barnard College and graduated in 1916. After receiving her Ph.D. in biochemistry from the College of Physicians and Surgeons of Columbia University, she found employment as a research associate at the Rockefeller Institute (now Rockefeller University) and began working in its chemotherapy and organic chemistry department (Feitas, 1978). While at the Rockefeller Institute, she was assigned to work on testing the effects on human connective tissue (fascia) of various antibiotic drugs that were created during World War I. By the early 1920s she took a sabbatical to study physics in Zurich, Switzerland, and, while there, began to study homeo-pathy as well.

Homeopathy is defined as a system based on the principle that a medicinal substance that closely re-creates the symptoms the patient is experiencing will help to relieve the conditions. This principle is a particularly ancient notion, having been described by both Hippocrates in ancient Greece and by the Ayur-vedic physicians in ancient India. Homeopathy was popularized in the West by Samuel Hahnemann (1755–1843) and was first introduced in America in 1825 (Chernin & Manteuffel, 1984).

Upon her return to the United States, Rolf began a long study of yoga under the noted American specialist in Tantric yoga, Pierre Bernard, in Nyack, New

York. Besides the natural sciences and these "alternative" therapies, Rolf was also interested in osteopathy. In her early adulthood, a horse's kick dislocated one of her ribs, and she was subsequently treated and cured through the ministrations of a blind osteopath, Thomas Morrison. Later, she and Morrison became friends, and she began to study the theory and practice of osteopathy.

To recapitulate her education and areas of study, Rolf began as a biochemist concentrating on the chemical structure of human connective tissue; her interest in yoga introduced her to the experiential study of human movement and joint mechanics; in homeopathy and osteopathy she became acquainted with physical problems, joint manipulation, and two alternative approaches to physical health.

What she lacked was the opportunity to practice the integration of these various areas of study, but this soon appeared in the form of everyday health problems in her family and friends. While at the Rockefeller Institute, by chance, she entered into a barter arrangement with a woman, a friend of a friend, who had fallen and subsequently lost partial use of her arms. This woman was a music teacher whom Rolf wanted to teach her children. The barter was that if Rolf could rehabilitate the music teacher to a point where she could teach again, then she would, in turn, train Rolf's children. Rolf began by applying basic yoga exercises, and soon the woman recovered; word-of-mouth referrals began appearing on Rolf's doorstep shortly thereafter (Feitas, 1978). One of these was a woman named Grace, and according to Rolf, it was through her work with Grace that structural integration was conceived:

Grace was a completely crippled woman. When she came to me, she was about forty-five. As a child of eight or so, she had been a great tomboy. She and a boy were diving off a roof of a pavilion . . . she went off the roof, not having told the boy she was going. He got mad and went after her. He went faster than she and, half-way down, he knocked her against the wall of the pool. She came out of it completely crippled with her back just bent over. . . . The day I started working with Grace was the day I really got Rolfing going. I would look at her and say, "This is in the wrong place," and I'd say, "Now, Grace, does this feel better this way, or does it feel better in the other direction?" And, she'd say, "That way," so we'd organize that corner. This went on for a couple of years, and in the end Grace picked her self up and went to California all by herself. That was when the first principle of Rolfing was really born—moving the soft tissue toward the place where it really belongs. (Feitas, 1978, pp. 9–10)

Entering into the 1940s, Rolf continued to practice and study. Two new areas she explored were the Alexander technique and the general semantics of Alfred Korzybski. By the 1950s she had increasing opportunities for teaching her methods to various osteopaths and chiropractors, but these early attempts proved unsatisfactory. These practitioners, trained in a different viewpoint, tended to see her work as a technique and not as a systematic approach (Feitas, 1978, p. 13). The turning point for her and her work came in the mid-1960s when she met Fritz Perls through one of her students and accepted an invitation to come to Esalen Institute in Big Sur, California, to give him treatments. Perls's rigorous schedule was taking its toll on his physical health; he was in his seventies at this time and for a number of years had been suffering from a heart problem. On her first visit, Rolf worked with Perls daily for about a week:

On that following Friday I gave him the seventh hour. And in the middle of the hour Fritz goes stark unconscious. I had a very bad two minutes, and I said to myself, "You bloody fool, taking a man who is dying of a heart failure, putting him through Rolfing, you deserved what you've got. See, the man's dead." And then I looked at him and I said, "Confound it, he's not dead. This is the picture of a man under anesthetic, not dying of heart failure." And so I said, "Well, I'll just wait and see what happens next, and pray to God he doesn't know where he's been."

But God was out to lunch. When Fritz came around, the first thing he said was something that indicated he knew perfectly well that he'd been unconscious. He said that he had once been injured by an anesthetist in surgery. When he had got out of the anesthetic he had accused the anesthetist of having injured him; the anesthetist said it was impossible. So you see, when I got into his neck, I began to raise that whole trip. After that he had some minor things which disappeared after a couple of months but he never had another bad heart attack. So, I came home, and I went back to Big Sur Christmas of that year to work with him again, and by this time his heart man was saying, "There's nothing wrong with your heart, I can't find anything wrong." He never was accused again after that of being a heart victim. (Feitas, 1978, pp. 16–17)

The original purpose of Esalen was to become a center for the study and application of Eastern philosophies, but it quickly became a melting pot, laboratory, and showcase for the new psychological growth techniques. Unexpectedly, through her success with Perls, Rolf found herself in the spotlight as well and in the midst of a new breed of student: hippies and hedonists, spiritual seekers, artists, and disaffected intellectuals. "At first, it was called Structural Integration. Then it was called 'getting Rolfed over.' Gradually affection took over, and it was called Rolfing" (Feitas, 1978, p. 18).

STRUCTURAL INTEGRATION: THE APPROACH

Theory

Structural integration is distinct from other forms of structural therapy and the physically oriented psychotherapies in its emphasis on the human connective tissue network (fascia) and, through the altering of the fascia, the achievement of symmetrical balance of the body segments in relation to gravity. While much research can be found on the biochemistry and dysfunction of fascia, there have been few formal attempts on the part of anatomists to chart the path of the fascial sheaths in the human body and little, if any, investigation, to my knowledge, into the mechanical effects of these sheaths upon the shape and alignment of the human frame. It is within this obscure niche that structural integration makes its home. Structural integration views the alignment of the body segments and the support of these segments atop one another in terms of spatial and mechanical principles: If the body segments are out of balanced alignment in the three dimensions of space (the x, y, and z axes), this will cause, through continued usage in gravity, deleterious effects of compression, shear, and rotation that will, over time, take the body further out of alignment, causing further physical stress, and so on.

Structural integration seeks to intervene in this negative spiral through the systematic manipulation of the fascia and movement education of the client to realign the soft tissue that positions the body segments toward an optimal, balanced form. While space does not permit a more extensive discussion of the theory of structural integration, certain global themes can be pointed out.

First, structure determines function; function implies structure. Structural integration views the body as a living kinesiology, a dynamic system of movement. The way a person moves, stands, sits, breathes, and expresses himself or herself indicates the structure of the body, including its freedom and restrictions that allow this pattern of movement. In this way, the structure of the body determines its behavior.

Second, the body is an energy system. The living body can be thought of as an energy system operating within and under the influence of the greater energy system of the earth's gravitational pull. In this view, a living body, as it is subject to the same physical laws as any other material entity, can either experience the accelerating effects of degradation because of misalignment with gravity (the "disorganized" structure) or it can be supported by gravity (an "organized" structure).

Third, with regard to gravity, in describing the proper alignment of the body in space, structural integration uses the example of the "invisible skyhook," an idea probably borrowed by Rolf from the Alexander technique. That is, a client is told to imagine a hook attached to the top of the head that is gently pulling the body straight up toward the sky. While all material objects on the surface of the planet are being pulled directly downward by gravity, when the body is properly aligned and balanced, the negative effects of gravity are lessened and gravity itself can be used as a form of support. That is, a human body can be balanced in the gravity field much like a building or the alignment of the front end of a car so that force flows smoothly through the entire structure rather than encountering shear, drag, friction, compression, and so on.

Fourth, fascia is the "organ of structure." Fascia is defined in *Dorland's Medical Dictionary* (1982) as "the stromous and nonparenchymous tissues of the body." Fascia is essentially a large mass of supporting tissue and integument, including various types of fibers in a ground substance of collagen, that hierarchically invests individual cells, tissues, and the organs of the body. Collagen is a family of specialized molecules that create the extracellular support matrix and makes up 20% of the total protein in the body. Collagen cells are noted for the structural diversity of their various forms: tendons (ropelike structures), skin (woven sheets), the cornea (transparent lenses), and bones (the latticework for mineralization) (Rodnan, Schumacher, & Zvaifler, 1983). Fascia binds the body components together.

It functions as a support mechanism or tissue "scaffolding"; it protects the viscera by cushioning them; it "compartmentalizes" the body by creating the spaces for the various structures; its surfaces are lubricated to aid internal movement. In short, fascia determines human form, shape, and, to a great degree, its quality of movement. This is why it was dubbed by Rolf "the organ of structure" (Feitas, 1978, p. 34).

Procedure

The key to gradually altering the alignment of the major body segments lies in the nature of fascia or, according to Rolf, in its ground substance, collagen.

While fascia is characteristically a tissue of collagen fibers, these must be visualized as embedded in ground substance. For the most part, the latter is an amorphous semi-fluid gel. The collagen fibers are demonstrably slow to change and are a definite chemical entity. Therefore, the speed so clearly apparent in fascial change must be a property of its complex ground substance.... The observable speed of the changes that are induced supports this hypothesis in the light of what we know about the action of colloids and the physical laws governing them. (Rolf, 1977, pp. 41–42)

Woo, Matthews, Akeson, Amiel, and Convery (1975) have shown that chemical changes in the fascial ground substance cause loss of collagen fiber mobility and chronic contracture. One of Rolf's discoveries was that connective tissue, by its biochemical composition, will soften and realign itself when heat or pressure is applied. The heat and pressure, in this case, come from soft-tissue mobilization through the practitioner's fingers, knuckles, palm, forearm, or elbow. The basic procedure is divided into ten sessions, each lasting between sixty and ninety minutes. Prior to the first session, a physical history is usually taken by the practitioner, and the client is photographed while standing clothed only in underwear—both profiles, front, and back—against a grid background. The majority of the work is conducted on a low, padded table.

First Session

During the first hour of work, the practitioner addresses the client's thorax with the intention of slowly and strategically loosening the superficial fascial layer. Much attention is given to the client's breathing pattern and how it can be made fuller and deeper by mobilizing the fascia of the ribs, shoulder joints, and costal arch. As a preliminary foray into the pelvic attachments, the hip joint, the iliotibial tract along the side of the hip, and the hamstrings are also worked on during this session. A small degree of lengthening of the trunk and relaxation of the legs is expected, and clients usually report feeling longer with a noticeable freedom of movement in the pelvis and rib cage (Mixter, 1983). The hour, as will most of the following sessions, concludes with a closing sequence of working on the neck and back, ending with a "pelvic lift." The pelvic-lift procedure is a combination of posterior tilting and pelvic traction with one hand and moderate stabilizing pressure on the abdomen with the other and is similar to the lumbosacral decompression move practiced in osteopathy. It has been experimentally determined that the pelvic lift increases the tone of the subject's parasympathetic nervous system (cardiac vagal tone), with a subsequent return to baseline levels once the manipulative move is completed (Cottingham, Porges, & Lyon, 1988).

Second Session

The second hour stresses working toward balanced fascial movement and toward more horizontal hinge action at the ankle joints. Structural integration practitioners typically view the feet as encompassing the entire anatomy extending below the knees because the musculature of the lower leg controls the action of the feet and ankles and the positioning of the foot arches. Structural integration concludes that releasing the fascial structures of the feet, ankles, and heels creates a better foundation upon which the body may support itself, especially providing better support for the lower back. Clients usually report that the ankle action feels smoother and that their legs feel stronger and more secure (Mixter, 1983).

Third Session

The third hour is devoted to what is referred to by practitioners as the "lateral line" of the body: a line running through either side of the body's thorax including the shoulder girdle, hip, thigh, and lower leg down to the ankle. Special emphasis is paid during this session to the musculature (quadratus lumborum) that bridges the pelvis and lowest ribs of the back. It is theorized that releasing this musculature will result in further improvement in breathing and is another step toward making the pelvis more horizontal (Mixter, 1983).

The first three sessions have addressed the areas of the body thought of in structural integration as being structurally and functionally part of the "sleeve" or the "extrinsic" muscular system of the human body as opposed to its "core" or the "intrinsic" system. The extrinsic-sleeve muscular system includes the larger muscles closer to the body's surface: back, thigh, pectorals, shoulders, gluteal area, and the skin. The core or intrinsic layer is defined as the deeper musculature closer to the central axis of the body: interspinals, adductors, pelvic floor, iliopsoas, diaphragm, and so on, and, by virtue of location, various nerve plexi, the alimentary canal and related organs, the heart, and the genitals. As Kurtz and Prestera (1976) define them, the core is related to one's "being," while the sleeve is devoted to "doing."

Fourth Session

The inside of the leg extending from the ankle to the pelvic floor is the primary territory addressed in the fourth hour. The attempt is made on the part of the

practitioner to more fully differentiate the anterior and posterior fascial compart-
ments of the lower leg and to release the adductor muscles of the inner thighs.
The purpose of this is to begin to create better mechanical communication
through the pelvis to the legs and to increase the support of the pelvic floor. It is
considered by practitioners as being the "first pelvic hour" and the first "core"
hour. Clients often report experiencing a feeling of "lift" through their torsos after
this session.

Fifth Session

The fifth hour is considered a direct continuation of the fourth and deals with
the anterior of the thorax, especially the area of the chest and abdominal muscles.
This is done as preparation for releasing the deep iliopsoas muscles that run along
the lumbar vertebrae from the diaphragm down into the inner hip joint; as such,
they are key hip-flexor muscles. During this session the practitioner also attempts
to educate the client how to consciously contact and activate the psoas muscles
through awareness and movement. The emphasis on the psoas complex is crucial
to structural integration because it was recognized by Rolf as being the only deep
back muscle that connects the thorax to the legs. The "pelvic tilt" or "pelvic rock"
is taught during this session to help the client access the psoas on his or her own
and to deepen the functional connection between the lumbar area and the legs
(Mixter, 1983). The balanced pelvis is a crucial concept in structural integration
because, Rolf notes,

when the pelvis is not balanced, we do not have the upward thrust that creates zero balance,
the sense of weightlessness that can be experienced in the body. When the pelvis is aber-
rated, it does not allow this equipoise, this tranquillity in experience that a balanced pelvis
shows. The combined forces acting on a balanced pelvis are in a moment of inertia near
zero. It is always in dynamic action, but the forces balance out to near zero. (Feitas, 1978,
p. 54)

Sixth Session

The sixth session finds the client lying supine on the table while the practitioner
works from the heel up the center of the back of the leg on either side toward
the deep hip rotators, coccyx, sacrum, and lumbars. Proper foot movement is
emphasized during this session to further align the fascial connection between
legs and pelvis. The deep rotators, coccyx, and sacrum are addressed to free the
sacrum and to create the potential for better alignment of the pelvis with the
lower back. What is often noticed after a well-executed session is that the client's
sacrum responds with the minute movements of breathing. Clients sometimes
report a sense of experiencing "extra" space, and those suffering from chronic low-
back problems regard this session as the turning point of their recovery (Mixter,
1983).

Seventh Session

Now that the body's fascial system has been systematically released everywhere from the neck down, the seventh session is devoted to the neck, head, and face. Once these fascial relationships have been addressed, the client is taught to "lift up through the top of your head" while standing, sitting, and walking. The manipulation, along with the new kinesthetic awareness, tends to bring the client's head and neck backward and up on top of the body, which results in the optimal alignment in the gravitational line with the ear, shoulder, hip, knee, and ankle.

Eighth, Ninth, and Tenth Sessions

The eighth and later sessions mark the "true" application of structural integration because up to this point much of the manipulative effort and strategy, to varying degrees, have been aimed at freeing fascial structures. In the eighth hour the emphasis is almost exclusively on integration. Integration, as understood in structural integration, means directing the client to consciously contact the deeper muscular structures to initiate subtle movements while the practitioner is working. It is also at this point of the three final sessions that the "recipe" becomes rather open ended in terms of individual session procedure and goals. This is because while the general pattern for each of the final sessions does exist, the degree to which it is followed or revised depends upon what the practitioner faces at the moment in the attempt at realizing the goals of the session. In other words, during the final sessions, the recipe is created anew on an individualized basis within the structure and context established by Rolf.

After the tenth session, the work ceases, and it is recommended that the client rest from any more deep-tissue work. It is now a time for rest and further internal integration, as it is theorized that the changes evoked in the body will continue for a definite but variable length of time. Barring the incidence of physical or emotional trauma, it is suggested that the client wait between six and twelve months before further work, and in most cases it is recommended that the client return for an annual "tune-up" session or perhaps work with a structural awareness movement practitioner.

Research Review

In the area of physiological studies, several key experimental investigations must be pointed out. The first was one by Ida Rolf herself in 1962 in which she conducted a series of lab tests on thirty subjects to determine the depth of metabolic change as a result of structural integration. Blood samples were analyzed for blood cholesterol, blood enzymes, redox potential, protein-bound iodine, and various proteins, including albumin-globulin ratio. The results showed a shift in the homeostatic equilibrium of the subjects.

Measurements of peripheral circulation, pulse rate, systolic/diastolic blood pressure, and heartbeat showed consistent changes that she concluded were in the range deemed appropriate for healthy human functioning (Rolf, 1962).

Two other physiological studies of the effects of structural integration were conducted by Hunt (1972) and Hunt, Massey, Weinberg, Bruyere, and Hahn (1977). The first studied the before-and-after electromyograms of subjects who underwent structural integration. Hunt found that the simple movements such as walking, lifting, sitting, and throwing were performed with a shorter period of muscle contracture and with greater energy efficiency after treatment. In the second study, which was more complex, provocative, and controversial, Hunt, Massey, Weinberg, Bruyere, and Hahn (1977) conducted measurements on forty-eight subjects before and after structural integration. Measurements included the State-Trait Anxiety Inventory, electroencephalograph (EEG) recordings, electromyogram recordings, Kirlian photography, and Direct Current (DC) field recordings. Several subjects were further tested during the actual manipulation sessions using DC field recordings, electronic measures at the "chakra" locations, and independent observations by a reputable psychic aura reader. The results found that anxiety levels were significantly lower after structural integration; electrical activity in the right hemisphere of the brain was slightly higher during periods of rest; Kirlian photography showed noticeable changes in the body's energy field; DC voltages were higher; muscular response was significantly higher; and the changes reported by the electronic instruments were independently corroborated by the observations of the aura reader.

Silverman, Rappaport, Hopkins, Ellman, Hubbard, Belleza, Baldwin, Griffin, and Kling (1973) examined the application of structural integration to measure the psychological and physiological changes. Pre-and posttest measurements were conducted on fifteen male subjects and consisted of three electrophysiological tests and two biochemical tests. Results indicated an increased openness and receptivity to stimulation. (As an interesting footnote to this study, the researchers had an independent Rolf practitioner examine the subjects' before-and-after photographs that were arranged in four clusters to judge the degree of change in body posture. The practitioner judged that the cluster having the highest degree of external and internal muscle balance was the same one the researchers determined had realized the most physiological change.)

Most of the research into the psychological effects of structural integration was conducted in the 1970s, and little more has been done since. The majority of studies cited here strongly suggest that structural integration exerts a positive influence on psychological change and function especially in the variables of anxiety, self-awareness, self-esteem, the experience of time, sensory functioning, intimacy, and the acceptance of aggressive feelings.

In a small and uncontrolled study, Davis (1969) found changes in physical structure—measurable lengthening—with concomitant change in behavior and self-perception and sensory functioning. Davis concluded that all subjects experienced an increase in body awareness with specific increases in body confirmation, spatial orientation, and expression of body-related affect.

Using person and scene drawings as her test instrument, Man (1973) compared the drawings produced by individuals being Rolfed to those in a bioenergetics/Gestalt therapy group, a weekend encounter group, and a human relations class. She found that the Rolfed subjects exhibited the least variability in their art productions and speculated that this indicated a greater continuity in body concept.

In a control-group study, Beckett (1975) compared the results of structural integration with psychotherapy. The results indicated greater positive change in self-perception and self-awareness in the structural integration subjects, and the psychotherapeutic benefits realized did not significantly differ from psychotherapy. Beckett qualifies his conclusions, however, by observing that we are comparing a full course of Rolfing, which is typically completed in ten sessions, with a truncated course of psychotherapy, which typically takes longer than ten sessions. It may be that a longer course of psychotherapy would produce more extensive and longer lasting benefits than are typically produced by Rolfing.

Lieber (1975), in a non-control-group study of twenty individuals who had recently undergone structural integration, found that improvement of postural alignment appeared related to positive change in self-esteem, but not in self-concept. Stack (1974), in a control-group study, investigated the possible effect of structural integration on self-concept and general anxiety, but found no measurably significant change. Townsend (1976), in a control-group study, investigated the possible changes that may occur in structural integration. While he found little change in the majority of psychological variables tested, he did find significant increase in the variables of "time competence," "capacity for intimate contact," and "acceptance of aggression."

Long (1977) investigated the changes in two groups of subjects—one undergoing structural integration and the other Gestalt therapy—and a control group. He found no statistical significance in the projective inkblot tests measuring body image or in body chart association tests. While he did find some significant differences in the area of self-concept between the two experimental groups, these may have been "statistical flukes." He did, however, find positive differences in both groups' Draw-a-Person tests as well as positive movement in the Life Effects Questionnaire.

Jenny (1977) measured the before-and-after change in self-esteem in twenty-one structural integration subjects. The results showed significant positive change in five out of eight subscores.

Dickerson (1978), in a control-group study, compared the psychological changes experienced by a group of subjects undergoing structural integration with those participating in a college physical education class. While analysis was exceedingly complicated and subject to interpretation, Dickerson concluded that the data suggest that structural integration did make a difference in the test subjects when compared to the physical education group, but that there was a significant positive difference in the psychological and body-image test results of the structural integration subjects. Of most interest, though, is Dickerson's finding that

long term changes for the Rolfing group on the California Psychological Inventory are more consistent. The Rolfing group maintained or made continued improvement on those CPI scales measuring social maturity, self control, and responsibility. This finding suggests that permanent trait changes may have occurred on those scales that were originally manifest as being deficient prior to the intervention. Further analysis, however, would have to be performed to determine the degree of significance, if any, of this trend. (Dickerson, 1978, p. 79)

Adair-Leland (1980) compared groups of subjects who underwent structural integration, psychotherapy, and hatha yoga. The results failed to show that the structural integration recipients exhibited greater changes in awareness, psychological differentiation, and boundary experience than the yoga and psychotherapy subjects, but the Rolfed subjects had greater positive change in their self-evaluation test results.

Orenstein (1980) conducted a phenomenological study of eight subjects who had undergone structural integration and found that the major experiential themes reported were a new and enriched body awareness, emotional cleansing, mind-body unity, and interpersonal effects. The reported effects were generally positive and suggested marked changes in awareness, ability to cope, positive self-perception, and sense of self.

Current Situation

While still relatively unrecognized by the public at large, structural integration will continue to grow as the spread of the new "alternative" medicine and holistic health movements continues. If it is to become more widely known and accepted, the apparent avenue for it to take is in the area of sports medicine and rehabilitation; the popular fitness press has recently publicized its value and efficacy for the average health and exercise enthusiast (e.g., see Pear, 1993; Steffens, 1989).

The problem of the limited knowledge of structural integration, besides its being ignored by the medical community and insurance industry because of the dearth of empirical studies documenting its physical effects and successes, has been exacerbated by the problems it has experienced as an organization. The Rolf Institute of Structural Integration in Boulder, Colorado, was originally founded by Rolf but became split by a schism about a decade after her death. This organizational split was precipitated by a revisionist effort to reformat Rolf's original theories and perspective and was opposed by many of her original students. According to the latter group, the revisions resulted in an alleged dilution of Rolf's vision and central principles with the incorporation of foreign techniques (e.g., chiropractic and cranial-sacral manipulation) and the introduction of ambiguous philosophy. The issue, while complex, appears from the outside to consist of two essential questions: (1) Who will control the name "Rolfing"? and (2) What will be the fate of Rolf's theory and method? Having either been forced out or ostracized by the Rolf Institute in the battle over these two questions, the core group of Rolf's followers—her handpicked successors—reestablished the original Guild for Structural Integration and are continuing their original commitment to maintaining the purity of Rolf's thought and method. The guild is also located in Boulder, Colorado.

REFERENCES

Adair-Leland, J. F. (1980). *Structural integration and change in body experience.* Unpublished doctoral dissertation, Georgia State University, Atlanta.

Beckett, N. J. (1975). *A study in the psychotherapeutic value of structural integration.* Unpublished doctoral dissertation, California School of Professional Psychology, Los Angeles.

Chernin, D., & Manteuffel, G. (1984). *Health: A holistic approach.* Wheaton, IL: Quest Books.

Cottingham, J., Porges, S. W., & Lyon, T. (1988). Effects of soft tissue mobilization (pelvic lift) on parasympathetic tone in two age groups. *Physical Therapy, 68*(3), 352–356.

Davis, D. W. (1969). *A study of the influence of structural integration upon selected measures of body image in nine subjects.* Unpublished master's thesis, University of California, Los Angeles.

Dickerson, D. A. (1978). *Mind/body unity: An interactional study of the psychological effects of physiological change.* Unpublished doctoral dissertation, California School of Professional Psychology, Berkeley.

Feitas, R. (1978). *Ida Rolf talks about Rolfing and physical reality.* New York: Harper & Row.

Hunt, V. V. (1972). *The neuromuscular effects of structural integration.* Unpublished study prepared for the Guild for Structural Integration, Boulder, CO.

Hunt, V. V., Massey, W., Weinberg, R. S., Bruyere, R., & Hahn, P. (1977). *A study of structural integration from neuromuscular, energy field, and emotional approaches.* Project Report, Rolf Institute of Structural Integration, Boulder, CO.

Jenny, R. H. (1977). *The effects of structural integration processing on self esteem.* Unpublished doctoral dissertation, Fielding Institute, Santa Barbara, CA.

Kurtz, R., & Prestera, H. (1976). *The body reveals.* New York: Harper & Row.

Lieber, R. L. (1975). *Structural integration and change in self-esteem, self-concept, and postural alignment.* Unpublished doctoral dissertation, University of Southern California, Los Angeles.

Long, J. M. (1977). *The body and the art of life maintenance.* Unpublished doctoral dissertation. University of Florida, Gainesville FL.

Man, G. G. (1973). *Art and rolfing: Toward a theory of human change.* Unpublished doctoral dissertation, Union Graduate School, Cincinnati, OH.

Mixter, J. (1983). Rolfing. In C. Lowe & J. Nechas (Eds.), *Whole body healing* (pp. 351–364. Emmaus, PA: Rodale Press.

Orenstein, S. M. (1980). *The rolfing experience: A phenomenological investigation.* Unpublished doctoral dissertations, California School of Professional Psychology, San Diego.

Pear, M. J. (1993, March). All the right moves. *Women's Sports and Fitness, 15*(2), 28–30.

Rodnan, G. P., Schumacher, H. R., & Zvaifler, N. J. (Eds.). (1983). *Primer on the rheumatic diseases* (8th ed.). Atlanta: Arthritis Foundation.

Rolf, I. P. (1962). *Gravity: An unexplored factor in a more human use of human beings.* Boulder, CO: Ida P. Rolf Foundation.

Rolf, I. P. (1977). *Rolfing: The integration of human structures.* New York: Harper & Row.

Silverman, J., Rappaport, M., Hopkins, K. H., Ellman, G., Hubbard, R., Belleza, T., Baldwin, T., Griffin, R., & Kling, R. (1973). Stress, stimulus intensity control, and the structural integration technique. *Confinia Psychiatrica, 16,* 201–219.

Stack, S. L. (1974). *Self-concept changes after structural integration (Rolfing).* Unpublished master's thesis. United States International University, San Diego, CA.

Steffens, D. (1989, January 23). Me and my rolfer. *Us, 3*(94), 64.

Townsend, D. E. (1976). *The effect of body integration on psychological functioning.* Unpublished doctoral dissertation, University of Pittsburgh, Pittsburgh, PA.

Woo, S. L. Y., Matthews, J. V., Akeson, W. H., Amiel, D., & Convery, F. R. (1975). Connective tissue response to immobility. *Arthritis and Rheumatism, 18,* 257–264.

29

Erwin Straus: The Individual, the Senses, and the Beloved Earth

DONALD MOSS

LIFE

Family and Early Years

Erwin Walter Maximilian Straus was born in Frankfurt am Main, Germany, on October 11, 1891, to a wealthy family of Jewish descent. He was the second son of Caesar Straus, a banker and social philanthropist who introduced the idea of housing cooperatives for laboring men into Germany. His mother, Antonie Straus-Negbaur, was a Brooklyn-born woman of German parents and a renowned art collector. Both parents were nominally Protestant, and Erwin Straus identified himself as "Evangelical" (Protestant) at the time of his medical graduation (Straus, 1919; Moss, 1982). Straus's father died when Straus was thirteen.[1]

Erwin Straus attended the time-honored Lessing Gymnasium in Frankfurt. His classical education there included a comprehensive grounding in the learning of Greece and Rome, as well as in literature and the sciences. The gymnasium nurtured Straus's love for Goethe and Shakespeare. He wrote an essay on Hamlet for his Abitur (an examination qualifying him to leave the gymnasium and commence university studies) at Easter time in 1909 (Straus, 1919; Bossong, 1991). Straus returned to the gymnasium in 1971 to speak at a celebration of the school's 450th anniversary and there delivered a second interpretation of Hamlet (Bossong, 1991).

After his Abitur, Straus spent half a year doing practical work in a factory and attended one semester at a technical school (Straus, 1919). In 1910 Straus turned to the study of medicine and philosophy, attending universities throughout Ger-

Erwin Walter Maximilian Straus in his office in Lexington, Kentucky (Photo courtesy of
Simon Silverman Phenomenology Center, Duquesne University).

many, as was the German custom. In the following years he attended the lectures
of the Swiss psychoanalyst Carl Jung in Zurich, as well as those of the leading
figures in the phenomenological movement in philosophy and psychiatry: Edmund Husserl and Adolf Reinach in Göttingen, Carl Stumpf in Berlin, and Max
Scheler, Alexander Pfander, and Moritz Geiger in Munich. He took a special
interest in Scheler's phenomenology with its moral emphasis, and a strong ethical
dimension runs through Straus's published works.

Straus's studies were interrupted in 1914 by five years of military service as an
infantry doctor during World War I, including service at the Polish front. He
was given leave in the winter of 1916–1917 to complete his medical studies, then
returned to the army and was injured late in the war near Armentières in France.

Straus later, while giving an address on education amid the dark days of World
War II, commented that his worldview, like that of many in his prewar generation, reflected the deep-seated optimism of the Enlightenment:

Only those who have known the years before the first World War can fully appreciate the
magnitude of the crisis we are undergoing. During those years most people believed that
in Western civilization man had reached a more or less definitive state of historical development. In accordance with this attitude, the past was interpreted in a peculiar way. We
had heard about wars, about persecutions, about intolerance. . . . But we also had learned
that since 1600, or somewhat earlier, there had been irresistible progress. . . . There was

Erwin Straus with attendees at the Third Lexington Conference on Phenomenology. Attendees include many key figures in American existential and phenomenological psychology (from bottom, left to right, ascending row by row): Erwin Straus, Peter Jones, Amedeo Marrazzi, George Talland, James Edie, George Schrader, Aaron Mason, Herbert Spiegelberg, Richard Zaner, Carl Eisdorfer, Charles Schwartz, William Fischer, Erling Eng, Joseph Parker, Calvin Schrag, Manfred Frings, Amedeo Giorgi, James Beshai, Stuart Spicker, Richard Griffith, and Paul Jossman. (Photo courtesy of Simon Silverman Phenomenology Center, Duquesne University).

general optimism and a feeling of security. And then suddenly that shocking disappointment to optimism and security! Suddenly history with all its good and bad passions was alive again. Suddenly everything which we thought gone forever was here again, and that progressive state which we expected to be the final and lasting one had disappeared. . . . Today the ominous symptoms of still greater changes are showing themselves. All the principles on which the social order of the 19th century were laid are challenged. . . . There is a dissolution of the old world order, but only vague signs of the new one. (Straus, 1941)

Straus's postwar training in neurology and psychiatry brought him to Berlin and the strong influence of Karl Bonhoeffer, a renowned neurologist and father of Straus's friend, the theologian Dietrich Bonhoeffer. He also studied with the prominent neurologists Ludwig Eddinger and Richard Cassirer. Richard Cassirer was a cousin to Straus, as were Ernst Cassirer, the philosopher known for his *Philosophy of Symbolic Forms*, and Bruno and Walter Cassirer, the noted art dealers and publishers.

Years in Berlin (1919–1938)

In the early postwar years in Berlin Straus formed enduring personal friendships with the leading figures of the new movement of "anthropological psychiatry," Victor von Gebsattel, Ludwig Binswanger, and Jürg Zutt. Together they became the "big four" in this new German psychiatry, which interwove phenomenological, existential, and anthropological perspectives. Straus developed the reputation of being the "younger brother" among these older colleagues, but also of being the "one who always had new ideas," because Straus continued to develop new themes in his written work (Spiegelberg, 1972, p. 261). In 1928 Zutt and Straus founded *Der Nervenarzt*, a new psychiatric journal that became the voice for anthropological psychiatry. At this time Straus also developed an important acquaintance with Eugene Minkowski, the French psychiatrist who applied both phenomenology and the philosophy of Henri Bergson to understand "lived time," not objective clock time, but time as the human being lives and experiences it (Minkowski, 1933).

Throughout his early years in psychiatry and neurology, Straus continued to embrace a broad horizon of humanistic pursuits. Straus met regularly with Jürg Zutt to read Greek texts and also joined his cello with the instruments of the physicist Max Planck and the pediatrician Adalbert Czerny to perform chamber music. At one of these chamber music concerts, he met Gertrude Lukaschik, a concert violinist and poet. He married her in 1920, and the two shared a lifetime of music. Together with his new wife and another friend, the pianist Kurt Adler, Straus enjoyed musical weekends visiting von Gebsattel at his new sanitarium at Fürstenberg. The couple also enjoyed traveling south through Germany, across Lake Constance, to visit Binswanger at Kreuzlingen sanitarium in Switzerland. Later Straus recalled the drives to visit Binswanger and the "grim border huts and customs officers" that cropped up at the Swiss border in the "evil Hitler years" (Straus, 1951).

Straus's academic career began in a promising fashion. He was named a Privatdozent in psychiatry at the University of Berlin in 1927 and unofficial extraordinary professor in psychiatry at the Charite Hospital in 1931. In 1933 Hitler and the National Socialists seized power, however, and within two years Straus was forced both to cease teaching and to leave the staff of *Der Nervenarzt* due to his Jewish origins. He continued to practice medicine and participated in a philosophical study group in Berlin with Jürg Zutt, Victor von Gebsattel, the philosopher Jacob Klein, and others, engaging in a kind of Socratic dialogue (Klein, 1977). At this same time he crystallized his viewpoint, and in 1935 he published his most renowned full-length work, *Vom Sinn der Sinne* (English edition, *The Primary World of Senses*).

Emigration and the War Years (1938–1945)

Warned that he was in danger in 1938, Straus paid a large emigration tax of 36,000 German marks for the privilege of fleeing his homeland and emigrating to America. This *Reichsfluchtsteuer* was usually about one-fourth of an individual's property (Bauer, 1982). That year Straus's mother reclaimed her American citizenship, hoping to protect herself and her firstborn son Albert from the Nazis. She also delivered much of her art collection to Herman Goering to obtain protection for the family, but Albert, a photographer, was imprisoned by the Gestapo in 1944 and his health ruined. Straus's mother died in 1942 in Berlin, and Albert survived the war but died in 1950.

Erwin Straus and his wife spent the first eight years after emigration living in hardship at Black Mountain College in North Carolina. Straus taught a kind of "humanistic psychology" and initially shared the artistic and creative enthusiasms of this progressive college. However, he came to view the artistic and educational experimentalism as destructive of traditional culture and was repelled by the schisms and conflicts in the college community. Straus welcomed the opportunity from 1944 through 1946 to conduct intermittent research on obsessive-compulsive disorders at Johns Hopkins in Baltimore, which later formed the basis for his monograph *On Obsession* (1948). There too he obtained his American medical and psychiatric diplomas.

The Post–World War II Period (1946–1975)

In 1946 Straus left Black Mountain for Lexington, Kentucky, to become director of research and education at the Veterans Administration Hospital. Lexington became a second home for Straus. There he gathered a circle of gifted students and colleagues, including such young psychologists as Erling Eng, Constance Fischer, William Fischer, and Richard Griffiths, and commenced to transmit the rich European traditions of anthropological and phenomenological psychiatry and psychology. He established a series of "Lexington Conferences on Phenomenology, Pure and Applied" that served as a catalyst for American interest in phenomenology and existentialism (see Straus, 1964–1974).

With the war over and German reconstruction under way, Straus declined a nomination to accept a chair in psychiatry in Berlin. He chose to remain in his new American home, but restored his relationship with his European friends and colleagues through a series of European visits and lectures in his homeland. Later, he spent a semester as guest professor in Frankfurt in 1953 and a year in Würzburg in 1961.

One of the early postwar journeys, sponsored by a Unitarian medical relief organization, brought an emotional reunion with Straus's onetime teacher and mentor in neurology, Karl Bonhoeffer. Bonhoeffer was in failing health, and his gifted son Dietrich, Straus's onetime friend and contemporary, had been executed by the Nazis for resistance against Hitler. Straus later dedicated his famous essay on the upright posture to Karl Bonhoeffer on the occasion of his eightieth birthday (Straus, 1949/1952). It is the gift and the task of the human being, according to Straus's mature philosophical anthropology, to stand erect, to remain upright in adversity, to confront the current situation face-to-face, and to see beyond the present into the realm of possibility. This theme seems to reflect Straus's personal ethos, as well as his philosophy of human existence.

In the 1960s and 1970s Straus also played a role in encouraging the Department of Psychology at Duquesne University in Pittsburgh to establish an American home for training in phenomenological psychology. He visited Pittsburgh frequently, delivering lectures at Duquesne; two of Straus's students, William Fischer and Constance Fischer, joined the Duquesne faculty. Straus's papers and library are housed in the Simon Silverman Center for Phenomenological Psychology and Philosophy at Duquesne University.

Straus continued to be a prolific writer throughout his almost four decades in the United States. His writings in this period included many new and original contributions—essays and monographs on the phantom limb, the upright posture, the sigh, hallucinations, compulsions, and man's questioning nature—as well as returns to long-familiar themes of his youth. His 1975 essay, for example, "The Monads Have Windows," returned to a theme from the philosopher Gottfried Leibniz that Straus had first picked up in the 1920s: Human beings are separate yet live together in a common world. Human beings are linked by a common access to the spectacle of the shared world. In 1926 Straus had expressed this as follows: "The monads are indeed substantially and essentially separate, but they resemble one another nevertheless, insofar as each mirrors the entire universe, although each from a different vantage point and in different degrees of clarity or confusion" (Straus, 1926, p. 112).

Straus was fascinated by the human gift for seeing and the differences it makes in the texture of human experience. Straus died on May 20, 1975. On his tomb are inscribed the words from Goethe that Straus had used as the title for one of his most famous essays: "Zum sehen geboren, zum schauen bestellt" (born to see, bound to behold).

WORK

Overview of Straus's Publications

In his research and published works, Erwin Straus was an original and creative thinker, in equal parts a philosopher and a clinical observer. In most of Straus's publications he chose as his departure point the familiar phenomena seen in psychiatric and neurological clinics, such as the phantom limb, the hallucination, or the phobias. He then reflected on what must be true of normal human experiencing and of the human individual's normal relationship with his surroundings if such clinical syndromes are to be possible. Pathological phenomena must be understood, according to Straus, as distortions of an already-understood norm (1966).

Straus reversed the nearly universal sequence of theorizing in the psychology of his time. Instead of trying to explain the highest achievements of human beings by concepts borrowed from the study of neurosis and the perversions (as Freud did in trying to understand such luminaries as Leonardo and Moses), Straus sought to deepen his understanding of pathology through phenomenological reflections on examples taken from literature, the arts, or everyday experience. Already in 1926 Straus formulated this approach: "Only the man who carries in himself a virtual image of the intact whole is able to perceive a torso" (1926, p. 123). In this sense, Straus was just as interested in how a human being can originate a scientific theory or view a drama portraying a distant time as he was in how a mentally ill person could hallucinate. Further, if a theory of human perception proposed to explain hallucination, but could not account for the process of scientific discovery, then Straus would judge this perceptual theory to be inadequate (1949/1958). To use one of Straus's favorite examples, when a neuroscientist studies brain processes, two brains are involved, the brain of the experimental subject and the brain of the scientist. Psychological theories must account for both of those brains, for the observed and the observer (1963, 1970).

Straus's publications also returned frequently to a critique of prevailing psychological theory, especially the behavioral stimulus-response model, and Freud's drive theory. Even in his earliest publications, Straus (1930/1982b, 1935/1963) took on these dominant theories in psychology because he believed that both Pavlovian and Freudian models involved fundamental misunderstandings about human experiencing. For Straus this had more than theoretical significance. A brief address he delivered in May 1940 on "Education in a Time of Crisis" illuminates Straus's passion to combat such psychological theories: He pointed out that the moral basis of the Western democracies lies in a dedication to the protection of the independence of the individual. Yet, Straus asks:

What has modern psychology to say about human dignity and freedom? You may open a textbook of psychology and find that the first chapter deals with the question 'What is man . . . ?' The answer is: 'Man is a mass of protoplasm . . . ' This interpretation leaves no room for freedom or dignity, because the reactions of protoplasm demand only mechanical, impersonal schemes, and they can best be controlled by political organizations which do not waste their time with such trifles as dignity. (Straus, 1941)

These remarks anticipated by thirty-one years B. F. Skinner's behavioristic treatise *Beyond Freedom and Dignity*, in which Skinner disavowed freedom and dignity as having no place in a science of human behavior.

The following discussion of Straus's published works will highlight three central themes: the nature of human individuality, the organization of sensory experience, and the holistic biological perspective in Straus's work.

The Problem of Individuality

The themes of an author's youth may be revealing for the passions and concerns of his life. The title of Erwin Straus's Habilitationschrift, his dissertation in neurology, was "Das Problem der Individualität" (The problem of individuality; Straus, 1926). The medical faculty in Berlin criticized this work as excessively philosophical. Straus, however, argued that issues of human individuality permeate all of medicine, and that health and disease are not merely different conditions of physical organisms. For Straus, medicine is an ethical discipline: Each time the physician enters an examining room, he or she encounters the human person as a whole, and this encounter must be informed by an adequate understanding of the human person.

In his 1926 dissertation Straus aligned his work with the widespread new movement affecting the most diverse areas of the sciences and humanities in the first third of the twentieth century, a movement bearing a range of titles: "One speaks of the investigation of structural connections, of Gestalt, of the totality, of the whole, of the person, of the life, and—most comprehensively—of individuality" (Straus, 1926, pp. 27–28).

This dedication to the investigation of totality and individuality involved Straus in a lifelong polemical battle against mechanistic viewpoints and physical realism in the human sciences. Straus's works after this 1926 dissertation circled around the investigation of the nature of human individuality (Binswanger, 1931).

In the 1940 address on education cited earlier, Straus expressed his theory of the individual simply, in terms that are both biological and personal:

As individuals we are born and as individuals we die; as individuals we feel desire, pleasure and pain. As individualities we are marked by some peculiarity, such as the fingerprint; we become individualities in so far as we integrate objective orders and adapt ourselves to them. As individualities we are specimens of a zoological species, and we are restrained to the present in time and space. As individualities we are in a potential relation to the whole of the world, to the past and to the future. (Straus, 1941)

For Straus, the formation of individuality is a process unfolding in time, trans-forming the natural relationship between oneself and the world. Identity is never something happening inside the person (1963/1969). Active engagement with the world is the basis of individuality; the linguistic expressions *I am* and *I do* express not only self, but modes of entering into relationship with the world. Action is personal. It occurs, according to Straus, "within an egocentric environ-ment, it is performed within a temporal horizon open to the future, it is directed toward objects susceptible to change, and it is not triggered by stimuli" (1966, p. 212).

For Straus, the human experience of time is at the core of human individuality (Straus, 1930/1982b; Moss, 1981). The human being is one who becomes or one who "is continuously emergent" (Straus, 1933/1966, p. 217). The human person perceives the future as a horizon to be approached, a horizon of tasks to be completed and destinations to be pursued. This perception of the future invites the individual to view life as an unfolding whole and challenges the person to engage in effortful action to actualize this ever-latent whole. This challenge, for Straus, is the birth of ethical experience. The individual spontaneously perceives what he or she is called to do with his or her life, world, and destiny. This perception of choices and possibilities is an invitation to self-actualization (Straus, 1930/1982b, pp. 128–131).

The once-and-only-once quality of the human life adds seriousness and re-sponsibility to the task of self-actualization. The individual life presents a series of onetime actions and decisions, each of which irreversibly shapes all later actions and events. Time is unforgiving, and one cannot play back the tape. It is primarily through productive activity, or work, that the individual guides the whole of his or her life—its unrealized Gestalt—ever more out of a potential and into an actual being. For Straus, this engagement in life gives objective form to self-expression and lends gravity to human existence. Both neurosis and the modern surrender to mass culture involve evading the central challenges facing each person. Yet the realities of the human work frustrate the individual, because the whole is never fully realized. Each time the individual finishes a task, he or she faces the necessity of a new beginning (Straus, 1930/1982b).

This linkage between ethical experience and the experience of time transforms psychological theories of ethics. For Freud, morality was an external inhibition imposed on human impulses after the fact by civilization. For Straus, on the other hand, "Because ethical behavior is a behavior originally corresponding to the ex-perience of time, it stands just as close to, or just as far from, the biological foundations of the human soul as do sensation and perception" (1930/1982b, p. 130).

The Salvaging of Sensory Experience

For Erwin Straus, the French philosopher René Descartes was a philosophical villain who robbed modern science of the richness of the everyday world of sounds, colors, odors, and textures. Natural science after Descartes tended to view the immediate perceptual world as less valid or real than the objectively measurable world of physical science, the world of molecules, atoms, and subatomic particles. The experiential qualities that make a beloved place so comfortable and familiar are regarded in such scientific accounts as purely subjective, as "secondary qualities," or as mere projections within our brains. Straus (1949/1958) traced this particular understanding of sensations within psychology directly to the physiological research of Johannes Müller and Hermann von Helmholtz in the nineteenth century. Müller wrote in 1837 that a sensation "is not the transmission of a quality or state of external bodies to our consciousness, but the transmission to consciousness of a quality or state of a sensory nerve as induced by external cause, and these qualities differ in the various sensory nerves and are the energies of the senses" (cited by Straus, 1949/1958, p. 144). Throughout his career Straus identified new researchers in psychology and the neurosciences who perpetuated some form of this trend to devalue sensory experience. Pavlov was the object of many of Straus's early critiques. For Pavlov, the world consisted merely of physical processes inside or outside the nervous system (Spiegelberg, 1972, p. 272). Later, Straus criticized Russell Brain's view that "the perceptual world . . . the whole realm of our perceptual experience, is a construct of the percipient's brain" (cited by Straus, 1970, p. 73).

For Erwin Straus, the primary world inhabited by the human being, and about which we have the greatest certainty, is the world of immediate sensory experience. The human being inhabits the earth and is linked to the present place and situation by sympathetic connections. Each of the sensory modalities attunes the person to this same world of places, persons, and objects, but with differences in the mode of contact (1948, pp. 12–13). When the individual *sees*, he or she confronts what is distant, there beyond one's personal boundaries. In *hearing*, the sounds surround and envelop the person. Vision opens the person to objects with shape and color in the surrounding spatial horizon. Sounds unfold primarily in time and have duration and rhythm. A dirty object that is seen lying in the street is distant enough for comfort and not personally disturbing; touching the same filth with one's bare foot brings it into one's personal sphere and arouses disgust (1948, p. 12).

Such sensory dimensions are missed by the theory of isolated sensations processed within the nervous system. In immediate sensory experience, the world presents itself physiognomically; it presents a face for one to enounter. When the individual approaches the world in comfort, health, and vitality, foods beckon, abundance delights one, and beauty enthralls. When one feels secure in one's home or neighborhood, one's senses are attuned perpetually but covertly to familiar sounds, sights, and atmospheres. A sudden unfamiliar noise or an abrupt silence awakens vigilance once again to the surroundings as one seeks reassurance (Straus, 1930/1982b, p. 97). Straus cited a line from Goethe's *Faust* commenting on the individual awakening in the night to find that "Earth—this night too thou art abiding" (*Faust*, part 2, cited by Straus, 1930/1982b, p. 98).

According to Straus, sensory experience is organized around the living, moving human body. The human body is oriented and attuned in each moment to the "action-space" surrounding it. This space is not the isomorphic space of mathematics and physics, in which all dimensions are the same, but rather the human experiential space in which humans seek sustenance, pursue their dreams, and spend their lives. In this human lived space—space as one feels and lives it in daily life—the experiential qualities of high and low, near and far, and light and dark refer back to the human sense organs and to the grasping and locomotive powers of the human body (Straus, 1957/1982a, 1949/1958).

Straus emphasized that we must fully appreciate that humanness involves being mobile within a life-space in which the necessary means of life are unevenly distributed. This basic fact of animal and human life fundamentally shapes both the spatial and the temporal dimensions of the human world:

Sensory experience distinguishes man and animal before all other natural forms. It is the experience of moving creatures. . . . In sensory experiencing, in the I-world relationship, two temporal orders encounter one another and are differentiated: that of my own becoming and that of the world. I experience my Now as a moment in the occurence of the world. (Straus, 1957/1982a, p. 161)

For Straus, these facts of immediate sensory experience have further significance for understanding mental illness. Straus understood many of the problems of psychopathology, of phobias and the obsessive-compulsive, for example, as breakdowns in the normal sympathetic connections binding the human organism to his or her world. The phenomenological foundation of psychopathology lies in this truth: The disturbed individual lives in a strange and different world.

Obsessive patients live in a strange world, basically different from the world familiar to us. If we want to understand children, we have to understand them in their own world. If we want to understand obsessives, we have to understand them in the world peculiar to them. Study of behavior always requires a knowledge of the specific structure of the world in which a species, man or animal, groups or individuals, behave. (1948, pp. 9–10)

This paragraph from Straus's monograph *On Obsession* is the core of the phenomenological approach to abnormal behavior.

Erwin Straus and a Holistic Biology

Straus's descriptions of human and animal sensory experience suggest to us his fundamentally biological orientation. In his Berlin days Straus played a leading role in the new anthropological psychiatry, a movement dedicated to a comprehensive study of the human being, interrogating all of the pathological findings of medicine and psychiatry to elaborate a more adequate understanding of normal human existence. In many of his investigations, Straus labeled his approach as

historiological, emphasizing the importance he gave to the time structure of human experience (1930/1982b, 1933). Later, during his career in the United States,
Straus published a collection of his essays under the title *Phenomenological Psychology: The Selected Papers of Erwin W. Straus* (1966) and ended his preface by
citing and adopting Husserl's famous motto as the guiding principle for his own
work—"back to the things themselves." In summary, we appear to have Straus's
approval when we categorize his work as historiological, anthropological, and
phenomenological. In a broader sense, however, Straus's writings fall better into
the arena of a philosophical and holistic biology.

Straus's identification with phenomenological authors was never complete. In
his monograph *Psychiatry and Philosophy*, Straus criticized Martin Heidegger's
overly abstract characterization of human existence (or Dasein) in Heidegger's
major work, *Being and Time*, and concluded that this viewpoint was inadequate
for use in psychiatry and anthropology: "The analytic of Dasein remains a massive
torso; it lacks any tie with life, nature and lived body . . . in short with the "ani-
malia" that are indispensable for founding an anthropology and a human nosol-
ogy" (Straus, 1963/1969, p. 5). In contrast, Straus chose to label the human being
as a *zoon*, a living bodily creature, emphasizing the human affinity with mother
earth (1975, p. 149). For Straus, the categories of life, death, health, and disease
seemed more adequate to the understanding of human existence than were the
abstract categories of possibility, finiteness, and nothingness (Straus, 1963/1969;
Moss, 1981). Straus especially objected to Heidegger's neuter and impersonal
characterization of Dasein as "it." For Straus, every human being was irreversibly
a he or a she, a thou or an it, both gendered and personal: The individual human
is typically non-whole, not only with regard to temporality and history, but already
through the biologically fundamental difference between the sexes and generations. No man is the man. The new-born baby is a boy or a girl" (Straus, 1963/
1969, p. 11).

Straus's work "Das Problem der Individualität" (The problem of individuality)
(1926) was published in a volume entitled *Die Biologie der Person* (The biology of
the person). This dissertation ends with an assertion that biology and the theory
of the person are converging, that body and mind must not be treated as distinct
(1926, pp. 129–130). The biology Straus advocated was not a reductionistic or
mechanistic biology; rather, it reminds one more of Goethe's theory of colors or
of Henri Bergson's *élan vital*. Nor is Straus's biological viewpoint an expression
of romantic nostalgia; rather, it reflects a passionate commitment to the immediate, experienced reality of human embodiment and the natural world. As he
wrote in *Das Problem der Individualität*, "Even more than biology in general,
medicine—as a special biological discipline—is bound to the world of appearances
in its qualitative fullness" (1926, p. 30).

Straus's early critique of Pavlov reads like a text of cognitive psychology, yet
Straus was not a cognitivist (Straus, 1930/1982b, pp. 49–76; Moss, 1990, 1992).
Both Straus's early cognitive model and the historiological approach of his early
works eventually found their place within a broad biological vision of man, animal,

and world. Straus vehemently combatted any psychological model involving a brain or cogito isolated from the world. For Straus, the structure of the human I-world relationship, and of the animal organism-environment relationship upon which it was founded, can best be understood within a biological framework emphasizing the natural environment, locomotion, sensory experience, and space and time as they are experienced by bodily creatures. In 1967 he emphasized the common biological unfolding of time for animal and human alike:

An organism will remain alive only so long as it is capable of joining issue with an environment in a continuous process of assimilation and dissimilation. To persist, to endure, means to maintain itself against the permanent threat of decay. It means to keep entropy low throughout the whole of life. (1967, p. 765)

Human existential time is not reducible to the biological unfolding of life in the cells of an organism; yet there is a continuity between the animal and human orders that Straus emphasized more poignantly than any other phenomenological author. The paradox of natural continuity within a chain of generations and embeddedness within a natural environment, over against the human experience of standing out in this place and moment, occupied many of Straus's later essays.

Straus's ultimate vision, like the current cognitive theories of Lazarus (1991) and Bandura (1989), is an "interactive emergent" theory of human agency and human individuality. Like other living things, the human individual is an organic "self-sustaining system." Unlike other living systems, the human individual creates plans that direct its own activity. The human is "born" to the primary animal situation (1963/1969), yet is "bound" to transcend it in his upright posture, intellectual-spiritual vision, and philosophical destiny (1963/1965).

In his series of essays on the anthropological significance of the upright posture (1949/1952; 1963/1965), Straus refined his biological perspective, locating the human being's uniqueness in the upright posture of its living body. The human being turns his or her back on the past and faces forward to the future. Straus illustrated the linkage between standing upright, seeing into the distance, and the abstract capacities that distinguish the human being from the animal. The star-filled sky, for example, invites the human being to relate himself or herself, in contemplative detachment, to the surrounding whole (Straus, 1957/1982a).

In Straus's holistic biology, the human being's transcendent vision for distant places and times becomes an emergent property developed in the mammalian ascent from quadruped gait through the lower primate's intermittent biped gait to the constant upright position of the human. Here Straus unified his biological emphasis on the human body and his phenomenological emphasis on the human experiential world with his classical humanistic vision. He found his final validation in the words of Ovid and Goethe: "While other animals look bellywards to earth, he gave to man a lofty countenance, bade him behold the sky and, upright, lift his gaze unto the stars" (Ovid, *Metamorphoses*, 1.84–86, cited by Straus, 1963/1965, p. 659).

To seeing born,
Bound to behold,
To tower sworn,
Me likes the world.
(Goethe, *Faust*, part 2, act 5, cited by Straus, 1963/1965, p. 665)

NOTE

1. The present chapter expands and revises previous discussions of Straus's life and works included in Moss (1981, 1982, 1992). The author is grateful to Amedeo Giorgi and Erling Eng for their assistance in gaining access to Erwin Straus's personal papers and library following the death of Mrs. Straus in 1977, and to John Dowds, Erling Eng, William Fischer, Constance T. Fischer, Lucie Jessner, and Jacob Klein for personal recollections. This chapter draws on the following sources for biographical detail: Bossong (1991), Moss (1981, 1982), and Straus (1919, 1951). The most complete account of Straus's life and work can be found in Bossong (1991).

REFERENCES

The original publication date, if different, appears last in parentheses. Where possible, works are cited in the text by both their original publication date and the date of their English edition (for example, Straus, 1963/1965).

Bandura, A. (1989). Human agency in social cognitive theory. *American Psychologist, 44*(9), 1175–1184.

Bauer, Y. (1982). *A history of the holocaust.* New York: Franklin Watts.

Binswanger, L. (1931). *Geschehnis und Erlebnis, zur gleichnamigen Schrift von Erwin Straus* [Event and experience, concerning the work of the same name by Erwin Straus]. *Monatsschrift für Psychiatrie und Neurologie, 80,* 243–273.

Bossong, F. (1991). *Zu Leben und Werk von Erwin Walter Maximilian Straus (1891–1975).* [Concerning the life and work of Erwin Walter Maximilian Straus]. Würzburg: Königshausen & Neumann.

Klein, J. (1977). Personal communication.

Lazarus, R. (1991). *Emotion and adaptation.* New York: Oxford University Press.

Minkowski, E. (1933). *Le temps vécu: Etudes phénoménologiques et psychopathologiques.* [Lived time: Phenomenological and psychopathological studies]. Paris: D'Artrey.

Moss, D. (1981). Erwin Straus and the problem of individuality. *Human Studies, 4*(1), 49–65.

Moss, D. (1982). Translator's preface. In E. W. Straus, *Man, time, and world* (pp. vii–xvii). Pittsburgh, PA: Duquesne University Press.

Moss, D. (1990, August 14). Erwin Straus, Aaron Beck, and cognitive psychology. In M. Stamenov (Chair), *Experience, consciousness, and meaning.* Symposium at the "Principles of Psychology Congress," William James Foundation, Amsterdam, the Netherlands.

Moss, D. (1992). Cognitive therapy, phenomenology, and the struggle for meaning. *Journal of phenomenological psychology, 23*(1), 87–102.

Spiegelberg, H. (1972). *Phenomenology in psychology and psychiatry.* Evanston, IL: Northwestern University Press.

Straus, E. W. (1919). Zur Pathogenese des chronischen Morphismus [Concerning the pathogenesis of chronic morphinism]. *Monatsschrift für Psychiatrie und Neurologie, 46*, 1–20. (Inaugural dissertation toward completion of the medical doctoral degree at the Freidrich-Wilhelms-University in Berlin)

Straus, E. W. (1926). Das Problem der Individualität. [The problem of individuality]. In T. Burgsch & F. H. Lewy (Eds.), *Die Biologie der Person: Ein Handbuch der allgemeinen und speziellen Konstitutionslehre* (Vol. 1, pp. 25–134). Berlin/Vienna: Urban & Schwarzenberg. [Passages in the present chapter by Donald Moss].

Straus, E. W. (1933). Die Scham als historiologisches Problem. *Schweizer Archiv für Neurologie und Psychiatrie, 31*(2), 1–5.

Straus, E. W. (1935). *Vom Sinn der Sinne* [The sense of the senses]. Berlin: Springer. English edition: Straus, E. (1963). *The primary world of senses.* New York: Free Press of Glencoe.

Straus, E. W. (1941). Education in a time of crisis. *Black Mountain College Bulletin, 7* (no pagination).

Straus, E. W. (1948). *On obsession: A clinical and methodological study.* Nervous and Mental Disease Monographs, Vol. 73. New York: Coolidge Foundation.

Straus, E. W. (1951). Ludwig Binswanger zum 70. Geburtstag [For Ludwig Binswanger on his 70th birthday]. *Der Nervenarzt, 22*, 269–270.

Straus, E. W. (1952). The upright posture. *Psychiatric Quarterly, 26*, 529–561. (1949).

Straus, E. W. (1958). Aesthesiology and hallucinations. In R. May, E. Angel, & H. F. Ellenberger (Eds.), *Existence: A new dimension in psychiatry and psychology* (pp. 139–169). New York: Basic Books. (1949).

Straus, E. W. (1963). Die Verwechslung von Reiz und Objekt, ihr Grund und ihre Folgen. In J. D. Achelis & H. von Ditfurth (Eds.), *Anthropologische und naturwissenschaftliche Grundlagen der Pharmako-Psychiatrie, Starnberger Gesprache, 2*(pp. 4–32). Stuttgart, Germany: G. Thieme.

Straus, E. W. (1965). Born to see, bound to behold. *Tijdschrift voor Philosophie, 27e*(4), 659–688. (1963).

Straus, E. W. (1966). *Phenomenological psychology: The selected papers of Erwin W. Straus.* New York: Basic Books.

Straus, E. W. (1967). An existential approach to time. *Annals of the New York Academy of Sciences, 138*(2), 759–766.

Straus, E. W. (Ed.). (1964–1974). *Lexington Conferences on Pure and Applied Phenomenology, 1–5. Pure and Applied Phenomenology 1–5.* Pittsburgh, PA: Duquesne University Press.

Straus, E. W. (1969). Psychiatry and philosophy. In M. Natanson (Ed.), *Psychiatry and philosophy* (pp. 1–83). New York: Springer-Verlag. (1963).

Straus, E. W. (1970). The sense of the senses. In D. Van de Vate, Jr. (Ed.), *Persons, privacy, and feeling: Essays in the philosophy of mind* (pp. 71–91). Memphis: Memphis State University Press.

Straus, E. W. (1975). The monads have windows. In H. L. van Breda & P. J. Bossert (Eds.), *Phenomenological perspectives: Historical and systematic essays in honor of Herbert Spiegelberg* (pp. 130–150). The Hague: Martinus Nijhoff.

Straus, E. W. (1982a). The Archimedean point. In D. Moss (Trans.), *Man, time, and world: Two contributions to anthropological psychology* (pp. 141–164). Pittsburgh, PA: Duquesne University Press. (1957).

Straus, E. W. (1982b) Event and experience. In D. Moss (Trans.), *Man, time, and world: Two contributions to anthropological psychology* (pp. 1–139). Pittsburgh, PA: Duquesne University Press. (1930).

30

Ken Wilber: Mapping the Evolution of Consciousness

KAISA PUHAKKA

ORIENTATION AND RELATIONSHIP TO HUMANISTIC PSYCHOLOGY

Ken Wilber is a controversial figure among the late-twentieth-century thinkers on culture and consciousness. A leading theorist of the transpersonal movement, he has been compared to Aristotle, Hegel, Nietzsche, and Aurobindo by some of his colleagues, while others find his broad strokes too brash and his all-encompassing views set forth much too boldly. The evolution of consciousness is Wilber's main concern. He finds all of the major sciences, philosophies, and spiritual traditions, both Eastern and Western, relevant to this concern, for they exemplify the process of evolution even as they shed light on it. The light is always partial, however, and how to fit the partial truths together is, for Wilber, the supreme puzzle (1982). A superb synthesizer with an ability to absorb and integrate large amounts of information across various disciplines, he sketches the contours of a panoramic vision of evolution as an unfolding of Spirit through matter, life, and mind.

By "Spirit" Wilber means not the "thing" that evolves but the evolving of all things; not the foundation or stage upon which the evolutionary drama is played but the very drama and the playing. The playing goes on without end, without lower or upper limit. For Wilber, Spirit evolving through prepersonal, personal, and transpersonal manifestations replaces the personal self at the center of development. This amounts to saying that the center is everywhere; interiority is everywhere, even though the human self's access to it may be contextualized and limited at any given time.

Where is evolution headed? Evolution is Spirit's journey toward self-knowledge, says Wilber. Rather than viewing human development as a matter of the self evolving in the direction of increased spirituality, Wilber sees it as Spirit evolving (through us) in the direction of greater self-awareness, greater access to interiority, until at the highest transpersonal levels the gap between "self" and "awareness" altogether disappears, and the interiority/exteriority dichotomy is transcended in a nondual stance that Wilber calls the *superior* viewpoint. Spirit pervades all of physical, biological, and psychological nature, including but reaching beyond the human self. Wilber considers this perspective to include and transcend the person-centered perspective of humanistic psychology.

LIFE AND MAJOR WORKS

Wilber was born in 1948 in Oklahoma City and grew up in Lincoln, Nebraska. His father was an air force officer. As a youth, he was absorbed in the world of natural sciences (biology and chemistry) and mathematics. Referring to his late high-school and early college days, Wilber (1982, p. 58) notes, "My mental youth was an idyll of precision and accuracy, a fortress of the clear and evident." His encounter with the *Tao-te-Ching* changed everything: "It was as if I were being exposed, for the very first time, to an entirely new and drastically different world— a world beyond the sensical, a world outside of science, and therefore a world quite beyond myself." From here on, the investigation of the world beyond the personal self yet accessible to human consciousness became a passion that involved not just Wilber's intellect but his entire being. Beginning in his early twenties and continuing to this day, he has taken up training in various contemplative practices such as Zen and Dzogchen (a form of Tibetan Buddhism) that would enable him to walk the terrain he charts in his writings.

Wilber dropped out of graduate studies in biochemistry to devote himself full-time to the pursuit of his research and writing about consciousness. His first major book, *The Spectrum of Consciousness* (1977), was a synthesis of Western psychological theories and therapies with Eastern spiritual disciplines. From this time onward, Wilber supported himself by his own writings, living outside of institutional affiliations and commitments, free to develop and express his own ideas, free to live a lifestyle of contemplation and writing. To balance mental and spiritual work with embodied living, he at times engaged in manual labor, such as working in gas stations (1982).

Several books and over a hundred journal articles soon appeared. *The Atman Project* (1980) set forth a vastly expanded framework for human development from infancy to adulthood and beyond into transpersonal stages described by diverse contemplative disciplines. *Up from Eden* (1981b) presented a detailed map of the evolution of the human mind and consciousness within this framework. The popular *No Boundary* (1981a), explains Wilber's early ideas in a highly readable style, while some of his more technical works such as *Eye to Eye: The Quest for the New Paradigm* (1990a) discuss the epistemological bases of knowing in the various sciences and how these could be expanded to accommodate the full spectrum of consciousness.

Wilber's ideas, larger than life and expressed through a powerful and often sharply critical writing style, have left few readers neutral or indifferent. Over the years he has engaged in lively debates with people who have taken issue with his controversial ideas, including other prominent theorists in transpersonal psychology (Grof, 1985, 1996; Washburn, 1990, 1995, 1996). Most of these debates were carried on in the pages of journals (May, 1989; Schneider, 1989; Wilber, 1989b, 1990b) and in his most recent books (Wilber, 1995a, 1995b, 1997). Few of his colleagues in transpersonal and consciousness studies have met him in person. To their chagrin, Wilber guards his privacy carefully and rarely makes an appearance in public. He initially accepted invitations to teach, lecture, and give interviews (1987, 1988) but then quickly pulled back from such activity, as he felt thrown off center by the attention and admiration from his audiences. Regarding this experience, Wilber said in a recent interview, "What you get are a lot of people telling you how great you are. Within a short time, you start believing them, and then you're headed for disaster. I simply did not feel competent to appear in public as a teacher" (Schwartz, 1995). Getting Wilber to agree even to an interview is not easy. Yet when he does give his time, he gives generously, and to his small circle of close frends Wilber is known as a devoted friend who can be warm, charming, and funny (Schwartz, 1995).

Wilber's first marriage to his best friend Amy Wagner in 1972 lasted for nine years, after which they parted ways amicably. Two years later Wilber met and married Treya Killam. One week after the wedding, she was diagnosed with breast cancer. The next five years were spent battling a relentless cancer that eventually claimed her life. During those five years Wilber set aside most of his writing and devoted himself full-time to nurturing Treya and, eventually, to helping her to die. *Grace and Grit* (1991), which appeared two years after her death, provides a moving account of the emotional and spiritual struggles and transformations in both Wilber and Treya during those trying years.

The long hiatus in Wilber's writing ended in 1995 with the publication of the first volume of a planned three-volume series, *Sex, Ecology, Spirituality: The Spirit of Evolution* (*SES*) (1995b). This 800-page volume was soon followed by two shorter companion works, *A Guide to Sex, Ecology, Spirituality* (1995a) and *A Brief History of Everything* (1996) A new chapter had just begun in Wilber's writing career. Up to this point, the emphasis had been largely on the upward movement of evolution, but in *SES* the upward movement is balanced by the movement downward: Spirit ascending to higher unities is at the same time Spirit descending to embrace and integrate the manifold of phenomena. By Wilber's own estimation *SES* is his first mature work. It offers an integral vision that encompasses practically everything humans have ever sought to know or be.

The Spectrum of Development

Development, for Wilber, extends from inanimate matter and primitive life forms through the developmental stages of human consciousness to its farthest reaches as manifested by the mystics and sages of various Eastern and Western spiritual traditions. The stages leading to mature adulthood are familiar enough. They have been charted by theorists such as Jean Piaget, Erik Erikson, Lawrence Kohlberg, and various psychoanalysts. Wilber draws especially from Piaget for the unfoldment of the cognitive and mental capacities and integrates these with the dynamic theories of object-relations psychoanalysis (Wilber, Engler, & Brown, 1986). A progressive decrease in narcissism or self-centrism is evident already in the stages leading to mature adulthood. By "narcissism" and "self-centrism" Wilber means normal, developmentally appropriate self-structurations. For example, it is normal for a child in the sensorimotor stage to have her or his self as the center of her or his world, whereas in the formal operational stage self-centrism decreases to the point where the child is capable of empathic understanding of the viewpoint of another person and thus begins to gain wider access to interiority, including that of others.

Wilber identifies four transpersonal stages beyond mature adulthood: psychic, subtle, causal, and ultimate. Through these stages the sense of self or identity becomes more and more flexible and inclusive as self-centrism or narcissism continues to decrease, until at the highest stages of transpersonal development even the subtlest and most inclusive self-structurations are transcended in a sense of identity and connectedness that embraces all.

At each stage things can go wrong, and so there is a spectrum of pathology corresponding to the spectrum of development all the way up to the highest transpersonal stages. Wilber discusses treatment modalities for each pathology and calls attention to the importance of correctly discerning levels of pathology (e.g., prepersonal or transpersonal) so that appropriate treatment can be chosen. For example, he argues that meditation may not be suitable for borderline and other prepersonal pathologies, whereas for an existential depression or "dark night of the soul" that may occur in the lower transpersonal stages meditation may be a successful method of treatment (Wilber, Engler, & Brown, 1986).

The charting of transpersonal development is undoubtedly Wilber's most controversial project. It implies that human development is open ended and that some individuals are "farther along" in development than other people, or that at any given time some people, and perhaps some cultures, have a more encompassing sense of self and a greater capacity for integrating the spectrum of consciousness than others. A number of cultural anthropologists, feminists, and ecophilosophers have criticized Wilber's theory in this regard (Kelly, 1996; Kremer, 1996; Wright, 1996; Zimmerman, 1996). Of course, the idea of development beyond "the average well-adjusted" is not new; it was celebrated in Maslow's notion of the self-actualizer. But in proposing developmental stages beyond self-actualization, Wilber is venturing into ever more rarified realms of human experience where the stakes are set high yet evidence is hard to come by.

Nevertheless, it seems fair to say that Wilber's transpersonal stages have opened up the horizon far beyond anything conceived in Western scientific psychology. This horizon had been there all along, of course, and through the centuries it was explored by the mystics and seers whose anecdotal accounts, couched in religious symbolism and interpretations, only helped to shroud it in impenetrable mystery. More recently, this transcendent horizon was glimpsed by Maslow, and it has been extensively explored by Grof (1975, 1988) and others who are responding to the intensifying search for spiritual meaning among the general population. Unfortunately, for many people this search has amounted to little more than the sampling of weird and fascinating "nonordinary" states of consciousness that, once gone, can leave the person confused and in some cases less stable than before. A clear articulation of the developmental context within which such temporary *states* are converted into stable *traits* may well be Wilber's most valuable contribution to contemporary consciousness research as well as to the increasing numbers of people involved in a spiritual quest (Wilber, 1983, 1995b, Walsh & Vaughan, 1993). For consciousness researchers, Wilber offers a greatly expanded paradigm of scientific inquiry. For those on a spiritual quest, he provides a map for the road.

The Three Eyes of Knowing

The paradigm of consciousness research has been too narrowly modeled after the empirical sciences, argues Wilber. It can be significantly expanded once we realize that the *eye of flesh*, that is, our senses aided by laboratory instruments, is just one of the possible ways in which knowledge is gathered. We also have the *eye of reason* that understands the meaning of text, cultural symbols, and mathematical equations (as well as the meaning of the data the eye of flesh observes). Beyond reason, says Wilber, there is the *eye of contemplation* that intuits directly the nature of reality (and of the meanings deciphered by the eye of reason). Every scientist would agree that the methods of investigation must be appropriate to the phenomenon investigated. For example, the methods of empirical science would not be appropriate for the study of literature or mathematics. The methods appropriate in these disciplines are different, yet in their own way they are just as rigorous as those of empirical researchers and usually require extensive training. The requirement of adequate training and competence is generally accepted for the empirical sciences (eye of flesh) and the hermeneutical sciences (eye of reason). For example, there are elaborate procedures that must be followed in physics in order to observe a subatomic particle. In literary criticism, very different procedures are specified for deconstructing the meaning of a certain text. In each discipline, consensual validation is achieved by a community of individuals competent in the methods of the respective discipline.

We all know that it takes years of training to become a competent physicist or hermeneuticist. But what does it take to become competent in the study of consciousness? Can the eye of contemplation be trained? This question strikes many people as quite foreign, perhaps because the curriculums of our academic institutions do not offer such training. However, methods for such training are available in the various spiritual and religious traditions of the world, such as Hindu yoga, Buddhist meditation, and the contemplative practices of Jewish, Islamic, and Christian mystics. Wilber's point is that an open-minded and rigorous investigation of transpersonal states is possible but usually requires years of training and preparation, not unlike research in the domains of the senses and the mind.

The Pre/Trans Fallacy

Another important concept of Wilber's that helps clear up misunderstandings regarding the transpersonal domain is what he calls the "pre/trans fallacy." This is the failure to distinguish between primitive phenomena of early developmental stages, on the one hand, and insights and experiences that transcend the egoic mode of rational consciousness, on the other. Both types of phenomena are, in their own ways, "nonrational" and "nonegoic," and this is why they can appear similar or even identical. But phenomena of the first type are "prerational" or "preegoic," whereas phenomena of the second type are "transrational" or "transegoic." The pre/trans fallacy can occur in two ways. In the first, "trans" is reduced to "pre." Freud's interpretation of the "oceanic feeling" associated with mystical experience as an irrational, regressive urge to return to the womb is a classic example of such a reduction. In general, the dismissal of all spiritual insights as regressive exemplifies the reductionist form of the pre/trans fallacy. In the second form of the fallacy, "pre" is elevated to "trans." Wilber considers Jung to have been guilty of this elevationist form of the pre/trans fallacy when he failed to clearly differentiate between the prepersonal archetypes of our collective tribal and racial past and the genuinely transpersonal archetypes around which the individuation process unfolds. The elevationist form of the pre/trans fallacy is evident in the various ways in which prerational experience and modes of expression are promoted in the name of higher personal growth.

Wilber's discussion of the pre/trans fallacy may well be one of his most useful practical contributions to the growing numbers of people searching for a spiritual path or engaging in some form of contemplative practice (Schwartz, 1995). Often the spiritual search masks primitive longings rooted in early developmental deprivations (Engler, 1986). On the other hand, sometimes an apparent psychotic break signals a major spiritual breakthrough. An insight into the pre/trans fallacy helps spiritual questers as well as therapists to be more discerning of the nature of the beast they are dealing with.

Holism: Restoring Connectedness in the World

In his more recent writings, Wilber has articulated his philosophy of holism. To be truly holistic, the vision of a whole must include everything, including itself. But more important, it must integrate and connect all that it embraces. So the issue is not holism versus atomism, but fracturedness versus connectedness. Furthermore, the solution cannot be a matter of articulating the best and most holistic position, for this still leaves out the person proposing or accepting the position. Rather, what is required is a transformation of consciousness within the person—within all of us—that shifts the viewpoint from the exterior increasingly to the interior and on to a superior view that is ever more inclusive and connected.

Wilber has sounded a powerful call for us to awaken to the evolutionary process taking place within us, within the universe, not in some distant future but right now (Puhakka, 1995). This evolution is fundamentally open and creative and therefore, at every turn, incomplete and uncertain. We live in systems within systems, contexts within contexts, of indefinitely expanding structures of experiences, meanings, and relationships. These systems are constantly sliding and the contexts shifting, says Wilber. The vision of an open universe unfolding and enfolded upwards and downwards without end effectively removes all bases for certainty and completeness. For many people, the postmodern quicksand world spells despair and a sense of being lost in the ever-shifting contexts that claim power of determination over meaning and values and render human lives pointless and empty. The absolutizing of context is an unfortunate, even if unintended, legacy of much of postmodern thought. Wilber sees the emphasis on context as being appropriate but not going deep enough: We must recognize that the contexts themselves are shifting and evolving, along with everything else. The evolution we are part of excludes nothing, not even the contexts that bound our understanding and awareness. Evolution is the journey of the universe toward self-awareness, now through human consciousness that is becoming increasingly aware of its own contexts.

REFERENCES

Engler, J. (1986). Therapeutic aims in psychotherapy and meditation: Developmental stages in the representation of self. In K. Wilber, J. Engler, & D. Brown (Eds.), *Transformations of consciousness* (pp. 17–51). Boston: Shambhala.

Grof, S. (1975). *Realms of the human unconscious.* New York: Viking Press.

Grof, S. (1985). *Beyond the brain.* Albany: State University of New York Press.

Grof, S. (1988). *The adventure of self-discovery.* Albany: State University of New York Press.

Grof, S. (1996). Ken Wilber's spectrum psychology: Observations from clinical consciousness research. *ReVision, 19*(1), 11–24.

Kelly, S. (1996). Revisioning the mandala of consciousness: A critical appraisal of Wilber's holarchical paradigm. *ReVision, 18*(4), 19–24.

Kremer, J. (1996). The shadow of evolutionary thinking. *ReVision, 19*(1), 41–48.

May, R. (1989). Answers to Ken Wilber and John Rowan. *Journal of Humanistic Psychology*, 29(2), 244–248.

Puhakka, K. (1995). Restoring connectedness in the Kosmos: A healing tale of a deeper order. *Humanistic Psychologist*, 23, 373–391.

Schneider, K. (1989). Infallibility is so damn appealing. *Journal of Humanistic Psychology*, 29(4), 470–481.

Schwartz, T. (1995, May/June). The full spectrum. *Common Boundary*, 34–40.

Walsh, R., & Vaughan, F. (Eds.). (1993). *Paths beyond ego*. Los Angeles: Tarcher.

Washburn, M. (1990). Two patterns of transcendence. *Journal of Humanistic Psychology*, 30(3), 84–112.

Washburn, M. (1995). *The ego and the dynamic ground: A transpersonal theory of human development* (2nd ed., rev.). Albany: State University of New York Press.

Washburn, M. (1996). The pre/trans fallacy reconsidered. *ReVision*, 19(1), 2–10.

Wilber, K. (1977). *The spectrum of consciousness*. Wheaton, IL: Quest.

Wilber, K. (1980). *The Atman project: A transpersonal view of human development*. Wheaton, IL: Quest.

Wilber, K. (1981a). *No boundary*. Boston: Shambhala.

Wilber, K. (1981b). *Up from Eden*. Garden City, NY: Doubleday/Anchor.

Wilber, K. (1982). Odyssey. *Journal of Humanistic Psychology*, 22(1), 57–90.

Wilber, K. (1983). *A sociable God*. New York: New Press.

Wilber, K. (1987, September/October). The pundit of transpersonal psychology: Interview with Catherine Ingram. *Yoga Journal*, pp. 39–49.

Wilber, K. (1988, July/August). Baby boomers, narcissism, and the New Age. *Yoga Journal*, pp. 46–50.

Wilber, K. (1989). God is so damn boring: A response to Kirk Schneider. *Journal of Humanistic Psychology*, 29(4), 457–469.

Wilber, K. (1990a). *Eye to eye: The quest for the new paradigm*. Boston: Shambhala.

Wilber, K. (1990b). Two patterns of transcendence: A reply to Washburn. *Journal of Humanistic Psychology*, 30(3), 113–136.

Wilber, K. (1991). *Grace and grit*. Boston: Shambhala.

Wilber, K. (1995a). *A guide to sex, ecology, spirituality*. Boston: Shambhala.

Wilber, K. (1995b). *Sex, ecology, spirituality: The spirit of evolution*. Boston: Shambhala.

Wilber, K. (1996). *A brief history of everything*. Boston: Shambhala.

Wilber, K. (1997). *The eye of spirit: An integral vision for a world gone slightly mad*. Boston: Shambhala.

Wilber, K., Engler, J., & Brown, D. P. (1986). *Transformations of consciousness: Conventional and contemplative perspectives on development*. Boston: Shambhala.

Wright, P. (1996). Gender issues in Ken Wilber's transpersonal theory. *ReVision*, 18(4), 25–37.

Zimmerman, M. (1996). A transpersonal diagnosis of the ecological crisis. *ReVision*, 18(4), 38–48.

Index

About the Editor and Contributors

CHRISTOPHER AANSTOOS is Professor of Psychology at the State University of West Georgia. He is a fellow of the American Psychological Association and president of its Division of Humanistic Psychology. He is the editor of the journal the *Humanistic Psychologist* and of three books, *The World of the Infant*, *Exploring the Lived World*, and *Studies in Humanistic Psychology*, and has contributed more than seventy publications to a wide variety of books and journals, including four entries in the encyclopedia *Psychology*. He has also served as program chair for several conferences, including "The International Human Science Research Conference" (Carrollton, Georgia, 1984), the "Symposium for Qualitative Research" (Perugia, Italy, 1987), and APA's Division of Theoretical and Philosophical Psychology (San Francisco, 1991). Other research interests include psychosocial, existential, and psychospiritual transformations in life-span development.

TAMARA L. ANDERSON is Director of Clinical Training and Assistant Professor at Rosemead School of Psychology, Biola University, La Mirada, California. Her research interests include women's issues, eating disorders, psychopathology, social and religious systems, and psychological assessment. She provides licensing workshops in the area of child abuse and conducts many continuing-education classes for mental health professionals in the state of California.

MIKE ARONS, Professor of Psychology at the State University of West Georgia, wrote his dissertation at the Sorbonne under Paul Ricoeur, on creativity as an expression of the internal revolution in psychology. As a postdoctoral student, he assisted Abraham Maslow at Brandeis University. Maslow recommended him as chair of the West Georgia Psychology Department, where he helped pioneer one of the first humanistic psychology programs. He boasts over two hundred scholarly writings and projects, has chaired five national and international conferences, and has served as president of APA's Division 32 and the Association for Humanistic Education and on a number of other professional and editorial boards. Current projects include development of alternative "philospiritual" services in psychology; in this interest, he and his class recently initiated a "philocafe" in Carrollton, Georgia. He also inaugurated a new type of cross-cultural educational format, a "Gypsy course," and is working on the planning committee for a Second Saybrook Conference to be held at the University of West Georgia in the spring of 1999.

DANIEL BURSTON is Assistant Professor of Psychology at Duquesne University, Pittsburgh, Pennsylvania. He is the author of two books, *The Wing of Madness: The Life and Work of R. D. Laing* (1996) and *The Legacy of Erich Fromm* (1991).

ALEX CARROLL has worked as a supervisor in group homes serving disadvantaged adolescents for over five years. She is currently teaching English as a second language in Japan and is preparing a series of short stories and a novel for publication. Her research interests include existentialism in nineteenth-century Russian literature, comparative literature, and cross-cultural studies.

J. HAROLD ELLENS is Executive Director Emeritus of the Christian Association for Psychological Studies, Founding Editor and Editor-in-Chief Emeritus of the *Journal of Psychology and Christianity*, and a retired university professor. He previously taught at the Princeton Theological Seminary, Calvin Theological Seminary, Oakland Community College, and Oakland University. He is a retired Presbyterian pastoral theologian and pastor as well as a retired U.S. Army colonel. He is the author of 63 books and over 140 professional journal articles. Currently he conducts a private practice as a licensed psychotherapist and pastoral counselor.

STEEN HALLING is Professor of Psychology at Seattle University. He is the editor of the *International Human Sciences Research Newsletter* and a consulting editor to the *Journal of Phenomenological Psychology*. His research interests include qualitative research methodology, phenomenological psychology, psychopathology, and the phenomenon of forgiveness. He has published over twenty articles and book chapters on these topics, has edited *Existential-Phenomenological Perspectives in Psychology* (1989) with Ronald S. Valle, and has addressed audiences throughout Europe and North America.

ARTHUR HASTINGS studied with Fritz Perls in Gestalt therapy, Milton Erickson in hypnosis, and Tarthang Tulku and Sogyal Rinpoche in Tibetan Buddhist practice. He is currently Professor at the Institute of Transpersonal Psychology in Palo Alto, California. He was the fourth president of the Association for Transpersonal Psychology. He is the author of *With the Tongues of Men and Angels: A Study of Channeling* (1991), coauthor of *Changing Images of Man* (1982), and senior editor of *Health for the Whole Person* (1980).

STANLEY KRIPPNER is Professor of Psychology at Saybrook Institute Graduate School, San Francisco, California. He is a former president of the Association for Humanistic Psychology, the Association for the Study of Dreams, the Parapsychological Association, and two divisions of the American Psychological Association (Humanistic Psychology and Psychological Hypnosis). He is the coauthor of several books with humanistic and existential perspectives: *Personal Mythology, The Mythic Path, Spiritual Dimensions of Healing, Dream Telepathy*, and *Healing States*, and the coeditor of *Broken Images, Broken Selves*.

DONALD MOSS conducts a practice in behavioral medicine and psychotherapy at the Psychological Services Centers in Grand Haven and Muskegon, Michigan. He is the editor of the *Biofeedback Newsmagazine* and consulting editor to the *Journal of Neurotherapy* and the *Journal of Phenomenological Psychology*. He has published over forty articles, book chapters, and reviews on mind-body medicine, existential and phenomenological psychology, and psychotherapy. He has translated two books in psychiatry and education: *Man, Time, and World*, by Erwin Straus (1982), and *Crisis and New Beginning*, by Otto F. Bollnow (1987). Current interests include the anxiety disorders, psychophysiological treatment modalities, and biopsychosocial approaches to primary-care medicine. He is also the current president of a foundation providing voluntary health care services in Falmouth, Jamaica.

KAISA PUHAKKA was born in Finland and holds graduate degrees in philosophy, experimental psychology, and clinical psychology. She is Associate Professor of Psychology at the State University of West Georgia. Her research interests are in Eastern and comparative philosophy, Buddhist meditation, psychotherapy, and transpersonal psychology. She has published over thirty book chapters and articles in these areas and one book, *Knowledge and Reality: A Comparative Study of Quine and Some Buddhist Logicians* (1975).

DON RICE is Professor and Chair of the Department of Psychology, State University of West Georgia, Carrollton, Georgia. He received his B.A. in psychology from Wofford College, his M.A. in clinical psychology from Western Carolina University, and his Ph.D. in psychology from Saybrook Institute. Prior to coming to West Georgia, he taught at Auburn University. In the early 1970s he worked as an assistant to Stanley Krippner at the Maimonides Medical Center in the William C. Menninger Dream Laboratory, Brooklyn, New York. He also completed an internship with the late R. D. Laing at the Philadelphia Association in London. At West Georgia he teaches courses in dreams, psychology of the body, hypnosis, existential psychotherapy, and health psychology. A longtime practitioner of the martial arts, he holds ranks in Shotokan karate, taekwondo, and aikido.

KIRK J. SCHNEIDER collaborated with Rollo May on what was to be May's final publication, *The Psychology of Existence: An Integrative, Clinical Perspective* (1995). Schneider is Director of the Center for Existential Therapy in San Francisco and is on the adjunct faculty at Saybrook Institute in San Francisco. He serves on the Editorial Board of the *Journal of Humanistic Psychology* and is a member at large of Division 32 (Humanistic Psychology) of the American Psychological Association. He has authored over thirty articles on existential psychology, existential-integrative psychotherapy, humanistic psychology, and the psychology of classic horror. His earlier books include *The Paradoxical Self: Toward an Understanding of Our Contradictory Nature* (1990) and *Horror and the Holy: Wisdom-Teachings of the Monster Tale* (1993).

ILENE AVA SERLIN studied with Laura Perls from 1973 to 1978 and then taught at the New York Gestalt Institute. With Laura Perls, she developed a way of working with Gestalt therapy and movement as process. She produced a videotaped interview of Laura Perls in 1988 in which Laura Perls discusses her life and the development of Gestalt therapy. She is a licensed clinical psychologist, a registered dance/movement therapist, and an executive faculty member of Saybrook Institute in San Francisco. She maintains a private practice at Imago: Center for Psychotherapy and the Counseling Arts in San Francisco and Mill Valley, California. Her research interests include the psychology of women, Buddhist meditation and religion, and the use of narrative, myth, and the imagination in psychotherapy.

PAUL SHANE is a graduate student in the clinical studies program at Saybrook Institute and has trained at the Gestalt Institute of Cleveland, Ohio, as well as at the Rolf Institute of Structural Integration in Boulder, Colorado. His interests are in the areas of couples therapy and the history and philosophy of contemporary psychology.

DONALD E. SLOAT conducts a private practice in clinical psychology in Grand Rapids, Michigan. His research interests include personality development, spiritual development, and the relationships among psychology, psychotherapy, and Christianity. In addition to conducting local and national seminars on Christian recovery and shame issues, he has authored twenty-five articles, chapters, and booklets and two books: *The Dangers of Growing Up in a Christian Home* (1986) and *Growing Up Holy and Wholly* (1990).

EUGENE IRVINE TAYLOR, Jr. is a Lecturer in the Department of Psychiatry at Harvard Medical School, a Clinical Associate in Psychology in the Department of Psychiatry at the Massachusetts General Hospital, and Chief Instructor in Aikido at the Harvard Department of Athletics. He is also on the executive faculty at the Saybrook Institute in San Francisco. He has established an international reputation for his scholarship on William James, transpersonal psychology, Asian spirituality, and American spirituality. He has published six books, two monographs, and over seventy book chapters and articles. His books include *William James on Consciousness beyond the Margin* (1996) and, with R. Wozniak, *Pure Experience: The Response to William James* (1996).

HENDRIKA VANDE KEMP is Professor of Psychology at Fuller Theological Seminary in Pasadena, California. She is a fellow of Divisions 2, 24, 26, and 36 of the American Psychological Association and has served as editorial consultant to thirteen professional journals and academic publishers. Her research and teaching interests include family and marital therapy, the relationship between psychology and Christian theology, and the history of psychology. She has published three books and over fifty book chapters, articles, and reviews on these topics. Her newest book, written with B. L. Eurich-Rascoe, is *Femininity and Shame: Women, Men, and Giving Voice to the Feminine.*

FREDERICK J. WERTZ is Professor of Psychology at Fordham University and an independent practitioner of psychotherapy in New York City. He is the editor of the *Journal of Phenomenological Psychology*, a past editor of *Theoretical and Philosophical Psychology*, and a past guest editor of the *Humanistic Psychologist*. He edited *The Humanistic Movement: Recovering the Person in Psychology* (1994) and coedited *Advances in Qualitative Psychology*. He was president of the American Psychological Association's Division of Humanistic Psychology in 1994–1995. He has written on a wide array of subjects: human perception, human development, psychopathology, psychotherapy, criminal victimization, qualitative research methodology, phenomenology, psychoanalysis, and cognitive psychology.

CPSIA information can be obtained at www.ICGtesting.com
Printed in the USA
LVOW01*0042020915

452483LV00008B/44/P